SEP 85

24334A

Patrol Administration

THIRD EDITION

Patrol Administration

Management by Objectives

DONALD T. SHANAHAN

Director
Southwestern Law Enforcement Institute
Southwestern Legal Foundation

ALLYN AND BACON, INC.

Boston • London • Sydney • Toronto

Copyright © 1985, 1978, 1975 by Allyn and Bacon, Inc.,
7 Wells Avenue, Newton, Massachusetts 02159

All rights reserved. No part of the material protected by this
copyright notice may be reproduced or utilized in any form or by
any means, electronic or mechanical, including photocopying,
recording, or by any information storage and retrieval system,
without written permission from the copyright owner.

Library of Congress Cataloging in Publication Data

Shanahan, Donald T., 1932–
  Patrol administration.

  Bibliography: p.
  Includes index.
  1. Police patrol. 2. Police administration.
3. Management by objectives. I. Title.
HV8080.P2S5 1985   363.2′32   84-28447
ISBN 0-205-08384-6

Printed in the United States of America

10 9 8 7 6 5 4 3 2 1 90 89 88 87 86 85

To my mother, Elizabeth, and father, John for their love and guidance

Contents

Introduction

Although this book is entitled *Patrol Administration*, it should be of interest to those involved in all areas of police service. Understanding the principles discussed is important to police managers in every capacity, as well as criminal justice educators and students of police administration and criminal justice. Regional criminal justice academies, state police, and county and municipal police academies will also find the contents useful. In addition, persons responsible for administering an effective civil service system will discover that this text is especially helpful as a resource for promoting police personnel.

Patrol Administration, Third Edition, focuses on the need for a management by objectives approach in this area of law enforcement. The complex policing needs in the United States today call for the development of leaders who can face problems by examining alternatives and by making decisions that are innovative, effective, and systematically implemented.

The elementary objectives of today's patrol administrator are: (1) to protect life and property, (2) to prevent crime, (3) to apprehend criminals, (4) to preserve the peace, and (5) to maintain order. In addition, the patrol administrator must be sensitive to the community's problems in order to help it maintain its stability. A stable community is a prerequisite, since all of the objectives mentioned above must be accomplished within the democratic process. Finally, as leader, the patrol administrator must be able to sustain among subordinates the high degree of motivation necessary for them and the department to achieve the objectives of law enforcement. To effectively accomplish patrol goals, patrol administrators must enhance their ability to conceptualize and must increase their knowledge about the workings of other parts of the police organization, because the operations of these other parts affect patrol success.

The patrol administrator must be sensitive to the needs of the community as well as to its problems. With an understanding of government organization and operations, the patrol administrator must know those persons who are in decision-making positions, and must be able to deal with them effectively and diplomatically while maintaining a neutral political stance. In essence, the patrol administrator needs to be aware of the total environment.

Police administrators should take time each day to review objectives with regard to service, peacekeeping, and crime-related missions, to be able to anticipate trends and the community's police needs. In reviewing objectives, patrol administrators should examine alternative methods in management of human and material resources and procedures, and emphasize the most precious resource: the patrol officer. Today's patrol officer has a questioning attitude toward illogical or irrational orders, so wise patrol leaders will create an atmosphere that allows for free discussion of alternative procedures and will encourage the innovative and creative ideas of the patrol officers. An atmosphere of openness is prereqquisite to the professionalization of a police organization.

The patrol leader must exhibit this same openness toward the community in attempting to understand the viewpoints of both extremists and moderates. Prison riots and community civil disorder point up the need for skillful objectivity and strategic planning. Effective, timely response to these explosive situations is imperative.

The ability to reconcile conflict will be reflected in the stability of the community. The concerns of the community must be uppermost in the mind of the patrol officer. If citizens feel unsafe and are fearful, innovative ways must be found to deal with their concerns. By understanding the total system of government, patrol administrators can gain the proper perspective of their role within that government, and can participate fully in providing leadership for a safe and secure community.

This book points out several areas in the patrol function where job enrichment can be realistically innovated so that talented officers will be motivated to develop within patrol, relating to the other units to increase desired results. With newly developed and innovative programs such as systematic criminal investigation, joint citizen–police committees, and lateral entry into the operational field, along with findings based on scientific experiments, the patrol administrator has an enormous spectrum available for creativity.

Management of human resources is the patrol administrator's most immediate and important function. Since most police departments throughout the country expend 80 to 90 percent of their budget on personnel and anywhere from 50 to 60 percent or more on patrol personnel, there is no doubt where patrol should stand in order of priority. A blend of good management principles, leadership, and understanding of the total patrol function will lead to patrol's effective contribution to police professional status.

The management by objectives approach encompasses the synthesis of scientific management and behavioral science concepts in leadership and the humanistic ideas reflected in participatory management. A good start toward the implementation of these objectives would be the adoption of Standard 8.1 of the National Advisory Commission on Criminal Justice Standards and Goals, *Report on Police*, which follows. A good follow-up would be the adoption of Standard 8.2, *Enhancing the Role of the Patrol Officer.*

STANDARD 8.1
ESTABLISHING THE ROLE OF
THE PATROL OFFICER

Every police chief executive immediately should develop written policy that defines the role of the patrol officer, and should establish operational objectives and priorities that reflect the most effective use of the patrol officer in reducing crime.

1. Every police chief executive should acknowledge that the patrol officer is the agency's primary element for the deliverance of police services and prevention of criminal activity.
2. Every police chief executive should insure maximum efficiency in the deliverance of patrol services by setting out in written policy the objectives and priorities governing these services. This policy:
   a. Should insure that resources are concentrated on fundamental police duties;
   b. Should insure that patrol officers are engaged in tasks that are related to the police function;
   c. Should require immediate response to incidents where there is an immediate threat to the safety of an individual, a crime in progress; or a crime committed and the apprehension of the suspected offender is likely. Urban area response time—from the time a call is dispatched to the arrival at the scene—under normal conditions should not exceed 3 minutes for emergency calls, and 20 minutes for nonemergency calls;
   d. Should emphasize the need for preventive patrol to reduce the opportunity for criminal activity; and
   e. Should provide a procedure for accepting reports of criminal incidents not requiring a field investigation.
3. Every police chief executive should insure that all elements of the agency, especially the patrol and communications elements, know the priority placed upon each request for police service.
4. Every police chief executive should implement a public information program to inform the community of the agency's policies regarding the deliverance of police service. This program should include provisions to involve citizens in crime prevention activities.

Source: National Advisory Commission on Criminal Justice Standards and Goals, *Report on Police* (Washington, D.C.: U.S. Government Printing Office, 1973), p. 191.

If Standard 8.1 is adopted, it would be well to remember that it was written by a staff of personnel and is not a bible but a guide. Each agency must continue to review available research and to modify suggestions to fit the specific police agency.

The revolution in patrol that integrates sound principles, contemporary leadership, intellectual assistance, technological innovation, scientific inquiry, and sincere concern will survive and succeed in our fast-changing society. It is hoped that this edition, which has kept pace with the changing educational needs of the patrol administrator, will help achieve that revolution.

.1.

The MBO of Patrol Administration

Police patrol is the first line of defense for sustaining domestic tranquility. Recently we have heard many voices from many areas telling police how to do their job. Some of these suggestions are realistic and good; others are unrealistic and poor.

If patrol is to be the backbone in a police organization, using more resources than any other unit, then maximum use and effectiveness of the patrol operation are necessary. Citizens should be able to go about their daily activities in a safe and secure manner, and it is to this end that the patrol administrator must work.

To produce this maximum patrol effort, many observers believe that law enforcement must select the best possible candidates, and then train and retrain, drill and drill again, until the patrol operation becomes as sharp as a finely honed blade. This takes good planning. The patrol administrator should take a lesson from Vince Lombardi, who drilled the Green Bay Packers football team until the execution of the play was so smooth it could not be stopped, even when the opposition knew it was coming. This team effort can work for patrol operations.

If the task concept and total-planning process are advanced in recruit school, roll-call training, in-service training, and in the field by the supervisor performing leadership responsibilities in training, the patrol function will be enhanced sufficiently to earn the title "professional." If by doing learning is improved, then the method prescribed above shall allow existing and future patrol administrators to concern themselves with innovation and creativity in managing by objectives.

PATROL HISTORY AND PHILOSOPHICAL ANALYSIS

The oldest form of patrol is the foot beat, yet present-day officers have not had proper instruction on how to use this type of patrol to its maximum

1

effectiveness. It seems that the rhetoric attached to mechanized patrol has resulted in misrepresentation. Instead of viewing all officers as foot-patrol officers with the added mobility of an automobile, citizens tend to believe officers patrol fully in a vehicle and walk only in response to a call for service. Since officers may walk without radios any time they and the dispatcher agree they have the time, and enough cars are available for calls for service, and since an officer with a transceiver may walk any time as long as the radio frequencies are sufficient, I believe the best name for our officers in vehicles is "motorized foot-patrol officers."

An in-depth report on policing from the 1600s to the present day would be inappropriate here. It would be appropriate, however, to give a short account of the events that have had some impact on policing.[1]

The first city in the United States to have a permanent night watch was Boston, Massachusetts, in 1801. This was done by statutes. On March 10, 1807, the first police districts were established.[2]

In England, Sir Robert Peel submitted the Métropolitan Police Bill to Parliament in 1829; this important bill was passed the same year. On September 29, 1829, formal policing began in London when 1,000 men in six divisions were assigned to patrol the city.

As America grew, so did its problems. In 1833 a wealthy philanthropist bequeathed money to the city of Philadelphia to finance a competent police. In the same year, an ordinance was passed to provide for a day force of 24 police officers and 120 night watchmen. Later the force was centralized, and a single head, captain, was appointed by the mayor. However, the ordinance lasted only two years and then was repealed.

New York entered the urban police system in 1844, followed by Cincinnati in 1855. In 1867 the first call boxes were installed, and in 1878 in Washington, D.C. telephones were used in precincts. Cincinnati became the first police department to use the telephone exclusively, and in 1886 replaced its foot-patrol officers with mounted officers in the outlying beats. This seems to be the first example where specific methods of patrol were used for resolving problems of various degrees and complexity.

The first bicycle patrol was apparently initiated in 1897 by the Detroit Police Department. These officers were known as the Scorcher Cops. Their assignment was mostly to apprehend speeding bicycle riders. Detroit also had the first police car, a Model-T Ford with a homemade antenna.

Philosophical Analysis[3]

For our purposes, "philosophy" as used in this text usually refers to a statement, or atmosphere, of why we exist; i.e., a purpose for our existence or a central reason for doing. To give a specific example, the police administrator may indicate, in the philosophy of accountability, that the agency has as its goal to try to measure wherever possible, even though we recognize that the quantitative or qualitative measures of the success of public service organizations are difficult to evaluate. Another way of making the same statement is to indicate that efforts and results relationships are hard to measure; or process and outcome (activities and results) should both be measured, even though exact measures are difficult to make. In essence, the difficulty of measure shall not be the philosophical foundation, but rather the knowledge of difficult measures should insure a practical but honest approach to measuring results. These kinds of leadership statements permeate the personnel operation; i.e., whom shall we promote, and how do we determine who should be promoted? or what measures of patrol productivity are accurate and realistic enough to relate to performance?

Scholars define philosophy as the ultimate rational explanation of things, either by discovery of the reason for their existence or by the systematic study of life and the universe as a whole, to frame a logical and necessary system of general ideas. As we reflect on management by objectives, Raia brings the concept together as follows:

> It is a philosophy which reflects a pro-active rather than a reactive way of managing. It is also a results-oriented philosophy of management, one which emphasizes accomplishments and results. The focus is generally on change and on improving both individual and organizational effectiveness. It is a philosophy which encourages increased participation in the management of the affairs of the organization at all levels . . . Management by objectives is also a process consisting of a series of interdependent and interrelated steps; (1) the formulation of clear, concise statements of objectives; (2) the development of realistic action plans for their attainment; (3) the systematic monitoring and measuring of performance and achievement; and (4) the taking of the corrective actions necessary to achieve the planned results. Finally, management by objectives is a system of management designed to facilitate planning and organizational control, organizing and assigning tasks, problem solving and decision-making, and motivation and self-control, as well as other important management functions and activities. It is also a system which lets some of the things an organization is already doing (perhaps chaotically) be done in a logical and systematic way.[4]

The rational explanation of MBO involves purpose, results, participation, direction, evaluation, and the integration of organizational and human ideals and values. There are several approaches to philosophy—idealism, realism, pragmatism, existentialism, and a mixture of these approaches. For the police agency to be successful in developing a philosophy, which I submit should be through the mixture of approaches, its personnel must be aware of the need to increase their knowledge about the philosophical foundation of MBO, so that accurate and effective results can be accomplished. The patrol leader should be able to distinguish between metaphysics, or the nature of reality; epistemology, or the nature of knowledge; axiology, or the nature of values; and logic, or the science of exact thought.

Why should patrol administrators study philosophy? Because the knowledge they acquire will serve as a foundation for the study of other pertinent topics and will allow for a synthesis of all the academic disciplines involved in effective police leadership roles. Our review of philosophy is miniscule, but it should insure the students an awareness of the importance of philosophical thought.

Leo Daley suggests the following eight values in studying philosophy:

(1) provides a purpose in life, (2) enriches knowledge, (3) fosters desirable intellectual attitudes, (4) satisfies curiosity, (5) permits contact with the greatest minds of civilization, (6) makes life more worthwhile, (7) enhances cultural enrichment, and (8) provides a means of evaluating rapidly changing social events.[5]

The eighth value is tremendously relevant to being able to cope with the environment.

Gibson suggests those problems that every human being faces and that the law enforcement officer must deal with:

1) each person must live with himself, to know, to think, to create, to work, to be, (2) each person must live in his/her universe, protect and explore the environment, and (3) each person must live in a community or society of other persons, competing and cooperating.[6]

Our Constitution is the foundation of our country. Its philosophy, as stated in the Preamble, suggests our purpose for existing:

We the people of the United States, in order to form a more perfect Union, establish justice, insure domestic tranquility, provide for the common defense, promote the general welfare, and secure the blessings of liberty to ourselves and our posterity, do ordain and establish this Constitution for the United States of America.

Preamble
The Constitution of the United States

The patrol administrator must be a scientific generalist, knowing what to expect and how to interpret research findings, but not getting bogged down in the exact measure of everything at all costs. At the same time, the leader, to be effective, must learn the proper mix of data for professional judgment. In addition, cause and effect relationships should be understood. "Because when I light a cigarette, I catch a fish." The lighting of a cigarette has nothing to do with the fish biting. Police usually work from effect to cause. A dead body is an effect. The question is, what or who is the cause?

Teleology involves consideration as to whether there is purpose; i.e., is the world going someplace? Is the department moving in a predetermined direction to achieve specific objectives? For example, the Lincoln, Nebraska Police Department has the following opening paragraphs as a mission statement:

STATEMENT OF MISSION OF THE LINCOLN POLICE DEPARTMENT

It is a cardinal principle of democratic societies that ultimate responsibility for peace, good order and law observance rests with the community of citizens of that society, not with an organized police force.

Although the very complexity of modern societies usually dictates that policing efforts be coordinated and directed by a force of paid professionals, their responsibility is derivative. Their role is to supplement and aid community efforts, not supplant them. And the powers permitted to these police must be carefully defined and limited.

A community which abandons its basic duty to police itself, to a professional police service, will soon find that the police can hope to provide no more than a bare modicum of public order and security and this only through such repressive measures that the basic liberties of a free people are eroded, and the very democracy that the police seek to preserve is endangered. Only if the proper balance is maintained between the basic responsibility of the community and the derivative responsibility of the police can a safe and orderly society be preserved with the least burden on individual rights and freedom.

It is unfortunate, therefore, that the history of urban policing in America in the twentieth century is a consistent record of efforts by the police service to assume a disproportionate share of the responsibility for maintaining social control, and the concurrent abandonment by American communities of their portion of this duty. The result has been an increasing lawlessness which even increasingly repressive measures have been unable to curb. The delicate balance between the traditional roles of the community and the police needs to be restored. Peace keeping must again become a joint police–community effort to stand any reasonable chance for lasting success. In this respect the Lincoln Police benefit from serving a community which is vitally interested in assuring a high level of safety, security and public order, and which is able to assume the responsibility for policing itself. The fundamental mission of the Lincoln Police, therefore, is to provide the leadership and professional support required to sustain and improve the community's efforts and to develop a balanced and cooperative police–community campaign against lawless and disorderly behavior.[7]

Logic, or the science of exact thought, which includes the systematic (an aspect of philosophy helpful to the patrol administrator), is a treatment of the relation of ideas and a study of methods that distinguish valid thinking from fallacious thinking. Simplistically speaking, these methods include:

1. *Induction:* The process of reasoning from a particular to a general conclusion.
2. *Deduction:* The process of reasoning from general principles to particulars included within the scope of that principle.
3. *Syllogism:* A form in which to cast deductive reasoning, comprised of three propositions: (a) the major premise, (b) the minor premise, and (c) the conclusion.
4. *Experimental:* A form of reasoning or problem solving that is largely inductive but sometimes partially deductive as well, which begins with a problem, proceeds to observation of all the data available relating to the problem, moves to the formulation of an hypothesis, and then progresses to tests of this hypothesis to reach a workable solution of the problem.
5. *Dialectic:* A method of reasoning in which the conflict or contrast of ideas is utilized as a means of detecting the truth, comprised of three stages: (a) thesis, (b) antithesis, and (c) synthesis.

Some cautions to be aware of when reasoning are appropriate at this point, as quoted by Dennis Gouran:

1. *Intuition:* Used alone it usually is not sufficient to draw appropriate conclusions. Examine data.
2. *Induction:* Mature and immature thinkers engage in it. Immature thinkers are more likely to jump to conclusions, and should consider extent and quality of information.
3. *Analogy:* Can be helpful in making inferences about a phenomenon, entity, or event on the basis of similarities with other phenomena, entities, and events; but faulty analogy occurs when the things compared are not sufficiently similar to warrant the inference.
4. *Post hoc, ergo propter hoc:* After this, therefore because of this. A fallacy of arguing from mere temporal sequence to cause and effect relationship. That two events are temporarily related does not necessarily imply that one is the cause of the other.
5. *Treating a correlation as a causal relationship:* Closely related to post hoc reasoning is the fallacy of treating a correlation as a causal relationship. Suppose that, after studying the back-

grounds of graduating college students, one discovered that those earning high grade point averages had also earned such grade point averages in college. It would not follow that one's high school GPA determines his college GPA. Both measures would be related, no doubt, to a third factor, namely the individual's level of intelligence.[8]

The fallacy of treating a correlation as a causal relationship frequently appears in the analysis of quantitative data, as Blommers and Lindquist (1960) point out:

No more serious blunder in the interpretation of correlation coefficients can be committed than that of assuming that the correlation between two traits is a measure of the extent to which an individual's status in one trait is caused by his status in the other. It is indefensible, for example, to argue that, because a high correlation exists between measures of reading comprehension and arithmetic problem-solving ability for the individuals in a given group, problem-solving ability is therefore dependent upon reading comprehension or vice versa, that is, that a given student does well in reading because he is a good problem-solver.[9]

Again, Gouran points out:

1. *Perceptual errors:* Beauty is in the eye of the beholder. Observations by the same person can be inconsistent. All police are bad because of a bad experience with one.
2. *Circular reasoning:* The circularity derives from the acceptance of a highly questionable assumption, namely, that anything in print is true. If we could accept such a naive premise, then we would then logically be justified in reaching the conclusion that whatever we read in a case was true. The problem here is not the result of the deductions through reason, but of the following assumption projected into the process.
3. *Non sequitur:* The conclusion does not follow from the premise. A police chief testifies to crime statistics and someone concludes you cannot judge the increase or decrease of crime based on the chief's testimony because of his/her opposition to legalizing marijuana. The problem is that the chief's attitude toward legalizing marijuana is irrelevant to his/her ability to report crime.
4. *Bandwagon:* On matters involving issues for which there are no objective answers, most of us tend to discover a sense of reality and comfort in the judgement of others.[10]

Philosophy should be viewed as a tool to assist the patrol administrator in directing the police organization.

Vollmer Philosophy

August Vollmer was elected town marshal of Berkeley, California in 1905. He later was appointed chief of police when that position replaced the old one of elected marshal. He held the position until 1932. Because of the significance of the philosophy of August Vollmer upon law enforcement, we state it here:

1. The public is entitled to police service as efficient as budget and manpower permit.
2. Courtesy is of paramount importance in all public and private contacts with citizens.
3. Police personnel with the highest intelligence, good education, unquestioned integrity, and with a personal history demonstrating an ability to work in harmony with others are necessary to effectively discharge the police responsibility.
4. Comprehensive basic, advanced, and specialized training on a continuing basis is essential.
5. Broad responsibilities should be assigned to the beat officer.
   a. Crime prevention through effective patrol
   b. Investigation of all offenses
   c. Traffic law enforcement
   d. Juvenile duties
   e. Public relations expert
   f. Report-writer
   g. Thoroughly competent witness
   h. A generalist rather than a specialist
6. Superior supervision of personnel and effective leadership.
7. Good public relations in the broadest sense.
8. Cooperation with press and news media.
9. Exemplary official and personal conduct.
10. Prompt investigation and disposition of personnel complaints.
11. Adherence to the law-enforcement code of ethics.
12. Protection of individual rights while providing for the security of persons and property.[11]

MANAGEMENT BY OBJECTIVES

In Chapter 5, Patrol Planning, we discuss the interrelationship between planning and budgeting in the context of goal achievement, since allocation of resources and budgeting for these resources both directly affect the ability to attain objectives.

Management by objectives (MBO) means defining objectives or goals, allocating resources concurrent with the defined objectives, allowing a complete understanding of the objectives by all members of the department, developing a parallel path between the organization and individuals toward

POLICE CODE OF ETHICS

As a law enforcement officer, my fundamental duty is to serve mankind; to safeguard lives and property; to protect the innocent against deception, the weak against oppression or intimidation, and the peaceful against violence or disorder; and to respect the Constitutional rights of all men to liberty, equality, and justice.

I will keep my private life unsullied as an example to all; maintain courageous calm in the face of danger, scorn, or ridicule; develop self-restraint; and be constantly mindful of the welfare of others. Honest in thought and deed in both my personal and official life, I will be exemplary in obeying the laws of the land and the regulations of my department. Whatever I see or hear of a confidential nature or that is confided to me in my official capacity will be kept ever secret unless revelation is necessary in the performance of my duty.

I will never act officiously or permit personal feelings, prejudices, animosities, or friendships to influence my decisions. With no compromise for crime and with relentless prosecution of criminals, I will enforce the law courteously and appropriately without fear or favor, malice, or ill will, never employing unnecessary force or violence and never accepting gratuities.

I recognize the badge of my office as a symbol of public faith, and I accept it as a public trust to be held so long as I am true to the ethics of police service. I will constantly strive to achieve these objectives and ideals, dedicating myself before God to my chosen profession—law enforcement.

achieving the defined objectives, providing sub-goals for specific components of the organization, establishing short- and long-range goals, designing and implementing programs for achieving the goals, and self-renewal.

Can management by objectives be applied to the police profession? The answers to the questions in the following checklist, designed by Dale D. McConkey to determine the applicability of MBO to nonprofit organizations, indicate that it can.

1. Does the organization have a mission to perform? Is there a valid reason for it to exist?
2. Does management have assets (money, people, plant, and equipment) entrusted to it?
3. Is management accountable to some person or authority for a return on the assets?
4. Can priorities be established for accomplishing the mission?
5. Can the operation be planned?
6. Does management believe it must manage effectively even though the organization is a nonprofit one?

7. Can accountabilities of key personnel be pinpointed?
8. Can the efforts of all key personnel be coordinated into a whole?
9. Can necessary controls and feedback be established?
10. Is it possible to evaluate the performance of key personnel?
11. Is a system of positive and negative rewards possible?
12. Are the main functions of a manager (planning, organizing, directing, etc.) the same regardless of the type of organization?
13. Is management receptive to improved methods of operating?[12]

In order to define the goal of a police agency, it is necessary first to define the role of the agency. The goal cannot be reducing crime if the number-one priority of the role of the police agency is to provide ambulance service, escorts to banks, or towing or wrecker service. The community, government, and police agency must first agree upon the objectives, the role of the police in attaining the objectives, and the amount of resources that are needed. For example, if the community is willing to accept a given level of crime in order to have a two-minute response time to each call for police service, this service should be provided. However, everyone should realize that the priority has been agreed upon by all parties. The police agency should then develop the manpower-workload analysis that provides this service. In most cases the elected officials of the community will communicate their feelings concerning the priorities of service. If the community is apathetic toward gambling and vice, for example, there will be little pressure exerted by the elected officials for strict enforcement of the appropriate laws.

Developing Goals

The police agency should be a partner in developing the goals of the community regarding the police service. It should also act as an extension of the community through the implementation of the policy of the community, as communicated by the legislative and executive branches of local government. When these goals are put in final form, they become the focal point toward which all objectives and sub-goals should lead. One of the most important aspects of leadership in the management by objectives approach is the ability to evaluate, on a continuing basis, all production—to insure it is leading to the total goal of the department. Many times patrol leaders get caught up in the immediacy of the situation and allow resources to be committed into areas that are not concurrent with the defined goals. Monitoring operations that are off on a tangent will prevent misuse of resources.

If the goal and first priority of the police department is to reduce crime, then the patrol force must relate all its actions to attaining that objective. All efforts of the patrol force should be directed toward the prevention of crime. These efforts would include omnipresence, apprehension of offenders and citizen participation in crime-prevention programs.

In the management by objectives approach, the goals of the agency will determine the structure of that agency. It is hoped that police departments around the country will increase their efforts to integrate the traditional hierarchical structures with the management by objectives approach, resulting in a balanced organization that fulfills the needs of both the agency and the officer. This blend may also help produce a new standard of excellence in police service.

Resource Allocation

Goals cannot be simple rhetoric; they must be accompanied by outward signs that can be observed as a commitment to the achievement of stated goals. If the goal "reduce crime (index) by 5 percent this year" is not accompanied by movement of personnel into the critical area necessary to achieve that goal, then commitment is not present. These goals become unreal. Additionally, if support units are not provided with goals to help the operational forces achieve the total goal, there is no commitment. There can be no real goal unless all objectives and programs are designed to achieve the goal. To do this, the proper allocation of resources must be made to each unit so that the objectives and sub-goals, which lead to the accomplishment of the total goals, are achievable.

Understanding Objectives

In order to be understood, the objectives must be realistic and specific. Watch commanders should not be expected to relate to the goal "reduce crime generally." However, they can relate to reducing burglaries by 2 percent in a given section of their areas of responsibility. A sector sergeant and the officers working in the sector can relate to reducing burglaries by one or two in a given period of time. Together, all personnel can analyze the specific problem and coordinate efforts to attain the objectives by using various patrol techniques. This way, the action can be understood by all, implemented, and then coordinated with other units within the department. The reduction of burglary for a given watch, sector, or beat may necessitate the formation of a task force consisting of patrol, criminal investigation, juvenile, crime prevention, and tactical officers. Each member of the task force must understand his or her part in achieving the stated objective. This modular approach may become more and more necessary as the management by objectives approach is increasingly used.

Whatever the objective may be, it should be compatible with fiscal input. The need to view each officer as a precious commodity cannot be forgotten. The objective of reducing burglaries by 2 percent, or whatever, should be viewed from a profit/loss posture. How many officers and how much equipment will it take to accomplish this reduction? What may happen if the commitment is not made? What approach or action will give the correct dividend for the investment made? How much impact will this operation have upon achievement of the total goal? The answers to these questions should be obtained and evaluated before implementation.

Participatory management becomes inherent in the management by objectives approach. Those persons involved in each operation should be consulted for input of alternative solutions. Through this approach, objectives are understood, organizational and individual goals are congruent, objectives are realistic and achievable, coordination between units is easier, and, because of sub-goals, everyone is able to relate. For example, "Officer Smith, your objective for the next month is to reduce burglaries on your beat by 2"; "Officer Doe, because of the complexity of your beat, your objective is to reduce burglaries on your beat by 1"; "Sergeant, your objective for the next month is to reduce burglaries in your sector by 8"; "Lieutenant, your objective for the next month is to reduce burglaries on your watch by 12"; etc.

Specific objectives are also made for criminal investigation, juvenile, and special force officers. Programs are those developed on a real-time basis as they relate to the objectives. Long-range goals (reduce crime) are formulated as a matter of policy, while short-range goals are developed in accordance with priorities, progress of implemented operations, and self-renewal.

Self-Renewal

An integral part of the management by objectives approach is self-renewal. It is necessary to maintain flexibility, so that a change of direction can be implemented when measurements indicate the change will enhance the success factor. All personnel should know where they are going, how they are going to get there, and be able to determine if, in fact, they are going in the right direction. The importance of being able to relate to specific goals is the prelude to self-renewal. That the sector sergeant knows that after three weeks of the month the sector will not achieve the objective if the same method of operation is continued, or if assistance is not obtained, is imperative to self-renewal. It may be necessary, after evaluation, to modify the short-range goals. The modification should not be made, however, unless an in-depth analysis is completed, to include a comparison of similar sectors using criteria compatible to both. Sectors experiencing a large number of burglaries should be making arrests. The reasons why one sector is successful while another sector fails should be reviewed carefully.

It is important to communicate to all officers the information upon which evaluations will be based, how the information is to be used, and over what time period the evaluation will extend. Monitoring experiments is necessary so that renewal of objectives can take place.

Patrol Officer Participation

All personnel must participate and be motivated to implement the plan for achieving the departmental objective. Patrol administrators should urge participation and should motivate all patrol personnel to implement the necessary plans. The approach should be viewed in the context of investment and dividend. Careful analyses of the plans are necessary to insure minimum disruption of the organization's ability to perform the necessary community services. There is some risk in the management by objectives approach, but if patrol and patrol administrators are going to lead law enforcement into the future, reciprocal confidence on the part of all members of patrol is necessary. Patrol officers, possessing an enormous amount of talent ready to be tapped, can contribute creative ideas designed to fulfill themselves and increase the effectiveness of police service. If these patrol officers can show true concern for their communities, it is reasonable to expect the communities to return that concern with respect, support, and participation in the achievement of objectives such as reducing crime. Effective patrol leadership can produce this two-pronged thrust, so necessary to the success of police patrol and a safe, secure community.

Patrol management must not continue in only a responsive mode. Innovation, creativity, willingness to change, and anticipation of future events should prevail in modern patrol administration. There should be no submission to negative thought or pessimism about the future of policing. A goal-oriented philosophy should be emphasized through management by objectives. Results rather than methods should be primary. There should be a blend of excellence in performance of tasks and a mutual understanding of the organizational direction and goals, accompanied by an ability to measure and evaluate the performance of the organizations and individuals. Participatory management; coordination; cooperation; integration of mutual respect; open, up, down, and lateral communication; responsibility-authority-accountability; information retrieval; feedback and follow-up; and internal and external influences are all factors that must be considered when the management by objectives approach is used.

THE INFLUENCES, IDEAS, AND RESULTS

Grady indicates that the success of managers is most influenced by five trainable managerial concepts or approaches, one of which is management by objectives.[13] He states:

> It is also apparent that these influences are inter-dependent and mutually supporting. [Figure 1.1 depicts the concept.]

1. Achievement thinking produces "breakthrough" goals, goals that are beyond those that would normally be expected. They do more than extend past results into the future.
2. MBO produces participation in the objective setting and planning activity. It ultimately results in agreement on the objectives and plans for success and commitment to performance.
3. Feedback is the knowledge of what is happening that insures the implementation of plans that were agreed to under MBO.
4. Positiveness is the effort to recognize success and progress as contrasted to focus on failure. Positiveness supports continuing success and achievement thinking.
5. Philosophy is a statement of beliefs and directions that will be used to determine the direction that plans should take.

> Dramatic change is the final result of success in working to understand and strengthen these influences. Dramatic change is a restatement of the objective of MBO. We're looking for more than past efforts and approaches have produced.

Figure 1.1

MAJOR MANAGERIAL SUCCESS INFLUENCES

THE INFLUENCES	THE "IDEA"	THE RESULT
1. Achievement Thinking	"The Impossible Dream"	Breakthrough Goals
2. M.B.O.	"Let's Shake"	Agreement-Plans
3. Feedback	"Tell Me"	Implementation
4. Positiveness	"Everybody Wants to Be a Star"	Support of Success Achievement Thinking
5. Philosophy	"I Believe"	Continuing Achievement

THE FINAL RESULT ⟩ DRAMATIC CHANGE

IMPLEMENTING MANAGEMENT BY OBJECTIVES

No management by objectives system will work unless the chief and the command personnel support the effort. The amount of interest shown by the top echelon of the department will filter down through the ranks, and response by each level will be greatly affected by the extent of interest. As police management becomes more conscious of the need for flexibility in management structure and style, the importance of the management by objectives approach will be seen. This importance has been recognized by the National Advisory Commission on Criminal Justice Standards and Goals. Its *Report on Corrections* (1973) states:

> As human resources, corrections must make a special effort to integrate various functional specialties into an organization team that holds mutual objectives vis-à-vis the client, not only among its members but also between members and the organization. Accomplishing this organizational climate will require a participatory and nonthreatening leadership style in which employee, offender, and the organization needs are met in a compatible way.[14]

The application to police is obvious. The report also describes sequential steps necessary to achieve the design and implementation of management by objectives:

1. An ongoing system capable of accurately identifying and predicting changes in the environment in which the organization functions.
2. Administrative capability through a management information system to provide data quickly to appropriate organizational members, work groups, or organizational units for their consideration and possible utilization.
3. Clearly established and articulated organizational and individual goals, mutually accepted through a process of continuous interaction between management and workers and between various levels of management. Unilateral imposition of organizational goals on lower echelon participants will not result in an MBO system but another bureaucracy.
4. An ongoing evaluation of the organizational and individual goals in the light of feedback from the system. Such feedback and evaluation may result in the resetting of goals.
5. A properly designed and functioning organizational system for effective and efficient service delivery. In such a system, goal-oriented collaboration and cooperation are organizationally facilitated, and administrative services fully support efforts at goal accomplishment.

6. A managerial and work climate highly conducive to employee motivation and self-actualization toward organizational goal accomplishments. Such a climate should be developed and nurtured through the application of a participative style of management.

7. A properly functioning system for appraising organizational, work group, and individual progress toward goal attainment.[15]

WHERE DO WE GO FROM HERE? MANAGEMENT BY OBJECTIVES

The basic philosophy of this text is that the total talent of each patrol officer (and all other personnel) must be tapped before objectives of police organizations will be accomplished. In order to achieve maximum use of the police organization's manpower, a clear understanding of what is expected from each member of the organization must be established. To manage effectively, it is necessary to minimize surprises and institute anticipatory management (which simply means acting before the fact) rather than crisis management. Consequently, the management by objectives for results process should be implemented for patrol administration. (See Figure 1.2.)

The first phase of this process deals with the philosophy of the police department, its reason for existence, determined by the society served. Each society has values or social principles that are usually expressed through elected officials, particularly the chief executive of the particular community. Therefore, the philosophy of the department considers the department, the community, and the elected officials. It is stated as a foundation upon which goals are built and from which the goals emanate. Each task completed by each member of the department should contribute to the achievement of the major goals of the department and should be performed within the foundation (parameter) stated in the philosophy.

The second phase, defining police program goals, may deal with general statements that are readily acceptable and offer a comfortable distance and range (such as "achieve greatest efficiency," "attain highest quality possible," or "eliminate crime") or with more specific statements (such as "reduce index crime by 5 percent within three years"). Usually a goal will refer to a time span of one year or more in police work and objectives will deal with less than one year. However, the meeting point should be one year. The goal of reducing crime for a specified year is acceptable as one of the goals of a police department.

Phase three deals with performance indicators—events or behavior that show progress is being made. These indicators should answer such questions as: "How long will it take?" "Do we need more manpower?" Per-

Figure 1.2 *Management by objectives for results process*

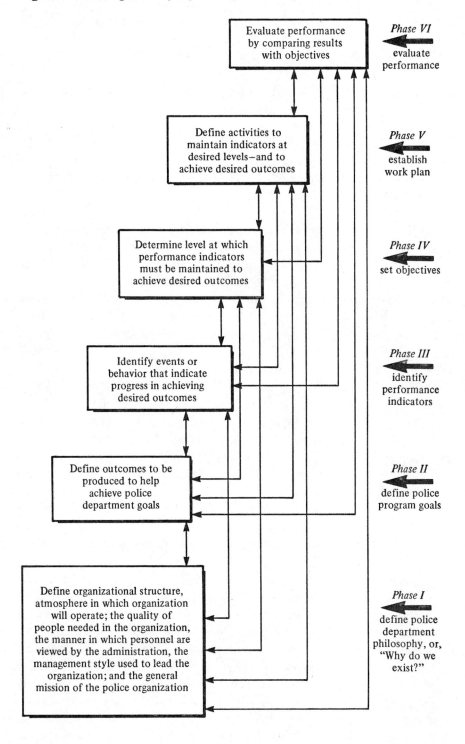

formance indicators should be carefully identified and built into plans of action, standards, and procedures so that inspection and control will help the administration determine what progress is being made. Some of these performance indicators are:

- Absentee reports
- Before and after training scores
- Fleet accident rates
- Quality reporting (preliminary investigation)
- Public satisfaction in calls for service delivery
- Deterrence of crime—victimization surveys
- Reduction of response time

Phase four, setting objectives, should state the minimum level at which the performance indicators must be maintained to achieve the desired outcome. Thus, one way to reduce crime in a police department may be to reduce index crime by 1 percent for the year. This objective setting continues into the sub-objectives of reducing each category of index crime by percent, by unit (Patrol-CID). The next stage of objective setting deals with "feeder-objectives," those specific objectives for the patrol officer. When the patrol officer achieves these feeder-objectives, he or she helps achieve the major goals of the department.

Phase five, establishing a work plan, defines the activities personnel should perform to maintain indicators at the desired levels. The activities could include, among others, reduced response time to emergency calls, 5 percent average per month for the year of new participants in the operation identification program, at least two security surveys (commercial or residential) per month for the year, or an increase in felony arrests by an average of 1 percent for the year.

Phase six, the evaluation phase, has been the most neglected in police work. Evaluation is the process of comparing results with objectives, or determining the amount of success in achieving predetermined objectives—how do we know we did what we said we were going to do?

A records unit can provide an example of how management by objectives can be used throughout a police department. The goal of the department itself may be "providing intelligence or investigation information as a total system" with an objective of "providing retrieval and processing of records information within ten minutes of request." Sub-objectives and feeder-objectives for sections within the records section should provide clear statements of results, so that the achievement of these results assists in accomplishing the objective of the records unit—in turn assisting in achieving the goal of the entire department. The evaluation of the effectiveness of the records manager should be based on performance by comparing results with objectives.

Mali's Five Phases of Managing by Objectives

Paul Mali depicts MBO in the private sector as a five-phase process.[16] Additional steps are incorporated under the five main phases, which are:

1. Finding the objective;
2. Setting the objective;
3. Validating the objective;
4. Implementing the objective; and
5. Controlling and reporting status of the objective.

Phase 1. Finding the objective. The concept of managing by objectives begins with a deliberate and systematic identification of results needed by the organization for survival, growth, improvement, or problem solution. This identification starts with an examination of the organization as it is now constituted. All kinds of analytical situational questions are raised: Where are we? How did we get here? What is our state of affairs? Why are we deficient? What are our opportunities? Trends, projections, and indicators are examined to note situational effects on the organization. The practitioner must give this first phase much time, analysis, and attention, since it is at this stage that drift, aimless tendencies, or incorrect directions are noted, stopped, and redirected.

Results of phase 1: list of attractive and needed potential objectives.

Phase 2. Setting the objective. This setting process involves the management team and its resources through a form of participation until a formal statement of objectives emerges. This statement proposes that a commitment is to be made by an individual, a group, a department, or the entire organization. The formal statement is written, communicated, supported by top management, and interlocked with other groups, and the whole organization is accountable for its implementation. Setting the objectives is a formal process of relating the resources of the organization to the involvement of those expected to deliver the results. It is based on the principle, "If you want to get maximum results from people, get them involved and accountable for these results."

Results of phase 2: formally written statement of objectives.

Phase 3. Validating the objective. This procedure determines the confidence an individual, department, or company may have that an objective can be reached within its stated time. The validation procedure simulates in a "dry run" effects of errors or great difficulties that may emerge. It builds within the objective contingencies to avoid potential errors. The validation procedure assures that resources, facilities, materials, methods, people, and management are ready and willing to reach a desired goal. It is at this point in the overall managing by objectives process that many objectives are discarded as unattainable or unworthy.

Results of phase 3: validated statement of commitment.

Phase 4. Implementing the objective.   Once a validated statement of commitment has been made as a result of phase 3, a motivational system is created to implement completion of the commitment. Setting the objective in phase 2 requires motivators to be built into the objective as an inherent ingredient. Phase 4 develops job plans and activities to begin and carry out action needed for fulfilling the commitment. Phase 2 defines the target; Phase 4 is the implementation strategy for reaching the target.

Results of phase 4: implementation of activities to reach objective.

Phase 5. Controlling and reporting status of objective.   Phase 5 is based on the principle . . . that progress can only be measured in terms of what one is trying to make progress toward. This phase sets up all activities under a schedule in order to measure and report the current status as well as progress toward completing the objective. The controlling and reporting process senses deviations of actual progress from expected progress and reports these deviations for corrective action. The concepts of feedback (measurement of past progress) and feed forward (measurement of expected future progress) give the management team an idea of their present position in relation to where they are going.

Results of phase 5: status reporting schedule toward established targets.

Writing Objectives for Police

If police managers impose objectives on personnel, they will find it very difficult to obtain commitment. If the employee has total autonomy in writing objectives, overzealousness or uncommittedness may result. The synergistic police organization can result when police managers create an atmosphere that develops goal-oriented concepts rather than one that relies heavily on performing tasks.

Writing objectives is difficult. A mutual objectives approach to performance evaluation is also difficult because of the need to develop the proper mix. Reddin identifies a sound objective as one that is measurable, specific, realistic, attainable, and time bounded.[17]

Landon Heffner describes the writing of objectives as follows:

First, it is important to recognize different kinds of objectives. A person who is interested in developing greater skills and capabilities will want to have a good balance of objectives. There are essentially four types of objectives: Routine–objectives that refer to normal work output; Improvement or Problem Solving–these are objectives that involve changing the procedures of an established function; Innovative objectives–representing a substantial change, a truly new approach (the person who is retired on the job never considers this type of objective); and Personal objectives–the setting of personal growth targets that may or may not relate directly to your work. Of these four types of objectives the Routine will be the most common, with the rest varying, depending on your own personal situation.

Second, it is important to know when to write objectives. The answer is simple. Any time you have a task to perform–write an objective. Any time you have a problem to solve–write an objective. Any time you are not satisfied with the results you achieve–write an objective, and any time you are not satisfied with yourself–write an objective.

Third, we must look at how to write an objective. Objectives should be understandable, achievable, challenging, and measurable. In writing objectives it is very helpful to begin by taking complete responsibility . . . "I will," then add the action word that describes what you will do. Specify the result you expect to accomplish, then indicate the date you will achieve this result, and a cost figure, if one can be determined.

When you have written your objective down commit yourself to achieving that objective. If you have a boss, you may want to commit to your boss. You may be surprised to find how much easier it is to get there when you know where you are going.[18]

Morrisey has a detailed set of criteria that he applies to the writing of an objective.

1. It starts with the word "to," followed by an action verb.
2. It specifies a single key result to be accomplished.
3. It specifies a target date for its accomplishment.
4. It specifies maximum cost factors.
5. It is as specific and quantitative (and hence measurable and verifiable) as possible.
6. It specifies only the "what" and "when"; it avoids venturing into the "why" and "how."
7. It relates directly to the accountable manager's roles and missions and to higher-level roles, missions, and objectives.
8. It is readily understandable by those who will be contributing to its attainment.
9. It is realistic and attainable, but still represents a significant challenge.
10. It provides maximum payoff on the required investment in time and resources, as compared with other objectives being considered.
11. It is consistent with the resources available or anticipated.

12. It avoids or minimizes dual accountability for achievement when joint effort is required.
13. It is consistent with basic company and organizational policies and practices.
14. It is willingly agreed to by both superior and subordinate, without undue pressure or coercion.
15. It is recorded in writing, with a copy kept and periodically referred to by both superior and subordinate.
16. It is communicated not only in writing, but also in face-to-face discussions between the accountable manager and those subordinates who will be contributing to its attainment.[19]

Personal Objectives

The structure of any organization should be devised in such a way that each element or level of the structure contributes to the total effort. The same process is used when an individual attempts to analyze where he or she is, where he or she wants to go, and the effort necessary to get there. In a police department where a college degree is a prerequisite for advancing to the position of captain, it is obvious that a lieutenant who wants to advance should obtain a degree. Some of the sub-objectives and feeder-objectives for this person would be course work, money, and time expended as part of the effort, which the lieutenant would balance against the position of captain. If the lieutenant uses a work breakdown structure to illustrate and so understand the total effort, he or she may decide it is not worth it. The lieutenant may also decide on an alternative course of action if the objective set is not valid for a variety of reasons.

Suppose a certain lieutenant has passed a written examination for promotion and has completed the stage of the oral interview board (oral examination), or has completed the assessment center part of the procedure; but on the final list of candidates for promotion he finds he has not placed high because of a low score in one part. His critique of the poorly performed stage indicates a weakness on his part in the areas of leadership, flexibility, tolerance and sensitivity to other viewpoints, and communication skills. If his major objective is to become a captain, then his first level of support would be to build a model of the person he should be in order to place first on the promotion list. The model would include the total competencies an individual needs in order to become a captain and would identify the weak areas that this lieutenant would have to overcome. The next stage would be to identify the resources available for learning the competencies. Finally, he would have to develop his strategy for making use of the resources, including time, money, and risk factor. Table 1.1 identifies the type of learnings the lieutenant may lack and the type of resources available, to help him improve his competency so that he may be more capable of achieving his objective.

Table 1.1

Type of Learnings	Type of Resources
Knowledge	Readings; lectures; discussion with other leaders.
Insight and Understanding	Analysis of own experience; experimentation; feedback from group members.
Attitudes or Feelings	Trying out new attitudes in role playing; permissive discussion; counseling.
Skills	Workshops; case problem exercises; practice in real groups.

Source: Reproduced by permission of Leadership Resources, Inc., 1750 Pennsylvania Avenue, Northwest, Washington, D.C. 20006.

A REALISTIC MODEL OF MANAGEMENT BY OBJECTIVES IN THE POLICE DEPARTMENT

As the first priority for a police agency's goals, I would suggest the crime prevention aspect. The following is an unrefined design for a police agency, which outlines the philosophy or organizational purpose, goals, objectives, means, and measures of effectiveness.[20]

STATEMENT OF ORGANIZATIONAL PURPOSE

The Police Department exists for the purpose of maintaining social order within prescribed ethical and constitutional limits. As an agency of municipal government, the Department will abide by sound principles of administration to carry out its mission in as effective and efficient a manner as possible. Full cooperation and coordination with other governmental and private agencies providing services within the City will be maintained.

Initiate Programs Aimed at the Prevention of Crime

A top priority for the Department in the performance of its mission is the prevention of criminal behavior. This includes the more traditional, if largely neglected, specific crime prevention programs in such areas as burglary and auto theft, as well as programs aimed at fundamental physical and social causative factors. Crime prevention programs will stress the role and responsibilities of the individual citizen in cooperating with the police to promote community security.

Respond to Calls for Service that Relate to Suspected Criminal Activity

Since a great many of the causative factors of crime are beyond the scope of effective police intervention or control, and since they are not being dealt with adequately by other institutions in society, it is apparent that considerable effort will still have to be devoted to such line operations as detection, apprehension, and detention of suspected offenders.

Respond to Community Service Calls Involving Minor Code Violations as well as Noncriminal Matters

A substantial majority of the calls for service to which the police respond involve incidents that are either noncriminal in nature or so minor that no arrests are made. The police department as an agency of the municipal government is the appropriate vehicle through which these services can be provided. Attention will be given to follow-up, as well as initial response, in those noncriminal calls for service requiring it, so that needless repetition will be avoided.

Provide Emergency Services in Relation to Accidents, Illnesses, Civil Disorders, and Disasters

The police department is open on a twenty-four-hour basis, with sufficient mobility to deliver quick response. Its purpose will be to supply trained personnel capable of providing emergency services, to preserve the life and personal safety of all persons, protect the community from criminal and irresponsible disruption, and provide for social order in times of disaster.

Seek Efficient and Effective Administration while Providing for the Career Needs of Departmental Personnel

It is the responsibility of the organization to balance rational administration with the needs of employee self-fulfillment in order to maximize Departmental efficiency and effectiveness. It is only in this manner that the goals of the Department can be meaningfully pursued and the community properly served.

Goals

The following are the goals proposed for the police department.

1. Provide for crime prevention programs involving all available resources.
2. Provide for positive measures against established criminal activities.
3. Provide for the expeditious and prudent apprehension of suspected offenders.
4. Provide thorough and appropriate police-related investigation.
5. Provide for emergency services that relate to the protection and preservation of life and property.
6. Provide for social order during times of unusual occurrences.
7. Provide such services that contribute to the preservation of community health, safety, and general public assistance.
8. Provide for effective coordination between agencies related to the criminal justice process.
9. Provide for effective and efficient departmental administration and for the career needs of departmental personnel.

The establishment of departmental goals is a step in the right direction, but this is not enough. Quantitative objectives must be established to define the means (or program to be used) of achieving the objectives and to set the standard to be used to measure the results. This activity should be mandatory for each public agency. The efficiency and effectiveness of a

---

GOALS, OBJECTIVES, MEANS, AND MEASUREMENTS

Goal #1—Provide for Crime Prevention Programs Involving All Available Resources

Objective: Reduce residential burglaries by _____ during FY 19__ - 19__ over previous fiscal years.

Means: Implement Operation Identification in _____ homes in the community by the beginning of FY 19__ through homeowners' groups, Chamber of Commerce, community programs, and other civic organizations.

Measures: Measure the effectiveness of Operation Identification by the reduction of home burglaries in general and the rate of burglaries among homes participating in the program.

Recovery rate of property stolen from Operation Identification homes.

Means: Participate with city planners in reviewing residential building codes to make recommendations regarding minimum standards for locks, windows, and other security devices. This is the responsibility of the Planning and Research Section.

Measures: Evaluate the burglary rate in statistical reporting areas that represent the housing developments incorporating the new security standards.

Means: Coordinate with school officials to identify potential truants and control truancy. Community Programs Technician.

Measures: A reduction in daytime burglaries.

Objective: Reduce commercial burglaries by ———— during FY 19— – 19—.

Means: Develop a program for merchants identifying common factors leading to community commercial burglaries and techniques available to combat those factors. Use Community Programs Technician and PST Trainee for this program.

Prepare and gather supplementary brochures and visual aides for use in presentations to business groups.

Provide trained PSTs to tour business establishments and make recommendations regarding burglary prevention techniques.

Provide follow-up checks with commercial representatives to determine what preventive actions have been taken by those businesses previously inspected.

Measures: Rate of decrease in burglaries committed at businesses adopting recommended crime prevention measures and at businesses that did not follow recommendations.

Significant percent of those businesses receiving a prevention inspection that actually implement recommended crime prevention measures.

Objective: Reduce the number of repeated disturbances of the peace calls during the calendar year of 19—.

Means: Implement a thirty-hour crisis intervention program for all patrol personnel between February 1 and May 31, 19—.

Develop a referral system of area agencies or individuals that provide various public services. This system is to be used in crisis intervention referrals by all members of the department.

Implement crisis intervention as a patrol function by June 1, 19—.

Develop a follow-up procedure on referred cases with the PST IV Referral Technician assigned to the Community Relations Section.

Measures: A statistically significant decrease in repeat disturbance of the peace calls between June 1, 19___ and December 31, 19___ as compared to similar previous time periods.

Record the number of referrals and follow-ups made during the same reporting period.

Goal #2—Provide for Positive Measures against Established Criminal Activities

Objective: Increase burglary arrests by _____ over a sixty-day period.

Means: Organize special enforcement units to stake out high burglary areas identified on the basis of statistical data and police intelligence.

Coordinate all burglary reports with all other forms of police intelligence (FI cards, suspicious circumstance reports, etc.) to develop comprehensive burglary dossiers to be provided to SEU (Special Enforcement Unit) and other operations personnel.

Provide for extensive interviews of all burglar arrestees by SEU personnel, to develop data on MOs, location of stolen property, identification of additional suspect, etc.

Measures: Increase of burglars arrested over sixty-day period as compared to previous time periods.

Objective: Increase the percent of stolen property recovered by _____ over a sixty-day period.

Means: Use a Special Enforcement Unit to provide surveillance on known fences, pawnshops, and flea markets.

Use Investigative Technicians to compile comprehensive lists of stolen property emphasizing those items readily identifiable (i.e., serial or ID number, complete descriptions, uniqueness of items, etc.) for dissemination to SEU.

Provide extensive interviews of all suspected thieves arrested by SEU personnel.

Use Investigative Technicians to provide follow-up on all thefts emphasizing accurate property descriptions.

Measures: Increase of recovered stolen property over sixty-day period as compared to previous time periods.

Similar strike of surveillance teams can be used to attack any similar high-frequency crime (e.g., auto-boost, bike thefts, street drug sales and use).

The specific kind of special enforcement should depend upon an analysis of criminal statistics. This data should be fed into a Management Information System on a daily basis and analyzed monthly. The results of this analysis should determine the offensive actions of the Department.

Goal #3—Provide for the Expeditious and Prudent Apprehension of Suspected Offenders

Objective: Decrease the incidence of "resisting arrest" by —————— in FY 19__ – 19__ and 19__ – 19__.

Means: Implement a twenty-five-hour training course through squad meetings (one half hour twice a week) to run between January 1 and June 30, 19__. Course material to include practical training in laws, methods, and techniques of arrest. (Methods would include training in planning arrests, timing arrests, etc.)

Implement an ongoing physical fitness/self-defense training program to be attended by all Operations field personnel.

Implement a training course concerning the psychology of arrest and the principles of persuasive speaking to run concurrently with the practical training course described above.

Measures: Percent decrease in charges of "resisting arrest."

Decrease in officer injuries in the commission of an arrest.

Decrease in citizen complaints evolving from arrests.

Objective: Bring about 20 percent increase in arrests regarding valid "in progress" crimes. Comparison periods to be FY 19__ – 19__ with FY 19__ – 19__.

Means: Develop a system of strategic manpower deployment based upon intelligence data and MIS data aimed at providing personnel in high crime areas.

Develop systems of closing avenues of escape by response techniques established by a special study force and included in written form and squad room training. Systems to be enforced by responsible unit or responding supervisor.

Analyze information-gathering techniques used by desk personnel and data dispatch procedures to seek improved means, through training, of dispatching personnel to crime scenes.

Measures: Decrease in response time to crime scenes due to improved manpower deployment, SEU activity, response techniques, and data dispatch procedures.

Increase of at-the-scene arrests.

Increase of on-view arrests.

Goal #4—Provide Thorough and Appropriate Police-Related Investigations

Objective: Significantly increase (1 percent to 5 percent, etc.) the development of investigative leads resulting in arrest or probable identification of suspects through use of criminal intelligence files.

Means: Develop and implement a total system capable of effectively gathering, collating, storing, and disseminating criminal intelligence by July 1, 19___.

Establish an intelligence unit under the Investigative Coordinator using Investigative Technicians having data systems training. Theirs will be the responsibility of developing a prototype intelligence system. Assistance will be afforded through an advisory task force comprised of a representative cross-section of departmental personnel.

Establish through the above-named groups a report technique to be used by field personnel in preparing intelligence reports.

Implement briefing-debriefing meetings between shift personnel with an intelligence monitor to record pertinent data.

Establish an intelligence file system that will make total intelligence packages (suspect histories, acquaintances, vehicles, MOs, cross-references, etc.) readily available to police personnel.

Contact neighboring communities and agencies to tap their intelligence about crime for inclusion in departmental files and reports.

Measures: Increase in clearance rates resulting from use of criminal intelligence files during FY 19___ – 19___ as compared to FY 19___ – 19___ and FY 19___ – 19___.

Objective: Significantly improve investigative cost effectiveness by decreasing the ratio of investigative hours expended to cases cleared.

Means: Establish criterion for determining case expenditures that will provide for the greatest degree of successful case dispositions and manpower utilization. Investigative standards to be implemented by July 1, 19___.

Analyze case variables to determine those elements conducive to a successful investigation.

Develop minimum standards for case investigations including the level of investigatable elements available, working caseload, time allotted in relation to investigatable elements, etc.

Implement levels of investigation using Investigators, special unit personnel, and nonsworn Investigative Technicians.

Measures: Decrease in manhours expended on noninvestigatable cases.

Increase in cases cleared in ratio to intelligence manpower expended.

Goal #5—Provide for Emergency Services that Relate to the Protection and Preservation of Life and Property

Objective: Increase employees' capability in first-aid and safety activities.

Means: Develop and implement a twenty-six-hour first aid and safety course to be presented in fifty-two consecutive one-half hour sessions annually beginning the week of July 1, 19___. Components of this course will include:

- Utilization of City swim lagoon and City lifeguard to instruct departmental patrol personnel in life-saving and water safety.
- Utilization of PG&E safety personnel to instruct departmental patrol personnel in electrical safety.
- Utilization of departmental accredited instructors to provide refresher first aid, applicable to field unit use (i.e., choking, bleeding, respiration, shock).
- Utilization of fire department personnel to instruct in rescue techniques.

Measures: Pre-instruction and post-instruction exams to ascertain the percent increase in knowledge and ability gained through the training program.

Objective: Decrease by a statistically significant degree the response time to emergency calls while decreasing in the same manner personnel injuries and property damage sustained as a result of emergency responses. Comparison to be FY 19___ – 19___ with previous years.

Means: Develop and implement by April 1, 19___, a sixteen-hour driver training program designed to provide qualifications for all sworn personnel by July 1, 19___. The program will use departmental instructors certified by the California Highway Patrol Driver Instructor six-week course.

Deploy shift personnel in a strategic manner based on statistical data while continuously reviewing with personnel the most direct routes to various city locations.

Train Information Technicians in data gathering and radio procedures to direct field personnel using the most complete location available (i.e., the Lexington Garden Apartments, east complex, southeast side).

Measures: Decreased response time (statistically significant).

Reduced incidence of personnel injury and property damage because of emergency responses (statistically significant).

Goal #6—Provide for Social Order during Times of Unusual Occurrences

Objective: Increase the level of departmental readiness to respond to the scenes of unusual occurrences.

Means: Develop and maintain a local emergency activation program that will have deployed all available personnel within a two-hour period at proper locations, equipped and *informed* as to their responsibilities in the operation. All personnel will know the purpose and procedure of this program.

Squad room training sessions reviewing personnel emergency action, reporting stations, and equipment check-off list.

A field exercise simulating the call-up and deployment to specified locations and the performance of specific duties.

Operational guidelines and directives updated at least once annually and disseminated to all personnel involved.

Measures: The time required to call out and deploy fully equipped personnel to a simulated disaster area.

Written tests concerning assembly points, code designations, equipment location, identification procedures for equipment release, and individual's role and responsibility within the operation.

Objective: Increase departmental capability for controlling mass disorder threatening life and property.

Means: Organize and actively train an unusual occurrence force expert in crowd control, rescue techniques, and the suppression of a planned and prolonged armed attack.

Coordinate with adjoining law enforcement agencies and emergency forces (i.e., fire, ambulance) to establish unusual occurrence procedures and responsibilities.

Prepare advanced procedures for making and processing mass arrests consulting with the court system to determine areas of special concern.

Determine equipment responsibilities and provide all necessary means for the personnel to meet these responsibilities.

Measures: Degree of readiness of unusual occurrence force as determined through testing and drills.

Percent of necessary equipment available.

Increased understanding among all personnel on procedures to be followed regarding personnel deployment, supervision, individual responsibilities, and equipment issue.

Understanding determined through testing and drills.

Goal #7—Provide Such Services That Contribute to the Preservation of Community Health, Safety, and General Public Assistance

Objective: Increase formal action taken on abandoned property over FY 19___ – 19___ compared to FY 19___ – 19___.

Means: Assignment of Police Service Technicians to seeking out and reporting parties responsible for the abandonment of property such as automobiles and refrigerators.

Measures: Decreased incidence of abandoned property. Increase in reports.

Objective: Correct all hazardous conditions in public streets.

Means: Assign responsibility to Police Service Technicians to spot and immediately report any hazardous condition and its exact location for corrective action by the appropriate city department.

Measure: Percent increase in hazardous conditions corrected.

Objective: Increase student awareness in traffic and personal safety.

Means: Develop a city-wide school safety program appropriate to the various grade levels for presentation by September 1, 19___.

Use Police Service Technicians and Police Officers in presenting programs to all city schoolchildren.

Use outside firms and sources for equipment, materials, expertise, and instructors for presenting specific areas of safety to students.

Measures: Passing test scores on all material presented to insure retention of important points within the program and to allow certification.

Goal #8—Provide for Effective Coordination between Agencies Related to the Criminal Justice System

Objective: Increase communications between the court system and the police department.

Means: Creation of a Court Liaison Officer whose primary responsibility is the coordination of data and relations between the court system and the police department. (The court system includes the judges, and staff, District Attorney's office, Public Defender's office and Marshal's office.)

Development of in-house training on the court system for police personnel with sessions involving court system personnel.

Exchange work program allowing members of the court system and police department to accompany one another in the course of their work day.

Measures: Before and after substantive examinations designed to measure increases in understanding of court systems operation.

Objective: Increase in "intelligence" exchange between local offices of the criminal justice system and the police department.

Means: Representative meetings between staff and line personnel of the various segments of the criminal justice system to ascertain specific intelligence needs. This program will be coordinated by an Investigative Coordinator, Investigation Unit.

Development of specific report techniques, data gathering systems, reproduction and routing proceures that will generate the required intelligence for appropriate dissemination.

Goal #9—Provide for Effective and Efficient Departmental Administration and for the Career Needs of Departmental Personnel

Objective: Review and refinement of departmental goals and objectives.

Means: Establish a task force representative of departmental structure to analyze existing goals and evaluate the validity and progress of objectives. It would be the responsibility of this force to insure departmental understanding of all goals and objectives pursued by this organization.

Measures: Test personnel understanding of departmental goals and objectives.

Increased personnel involvement in the goal/objective establishment process.

Objective: The equitable and meaningful performance evaluation of all departmental personnel.

Means: A task force representative of the department to analyze current personnel evaluation processes and propose alternatives. It would be the representative's responsibility to ensure that evaluation measures would accurately reflect the worker's performance and provide real meaning to the worker as well as to the needs of the department.

Personal communications to all persons evaluated and to all persons evaluating setting forth in straightforward terms the intent, means, and standards used in the evaluation process.

Continual involvement by all levels of departmental personnel in study and revision of personnel evaluation procedures.

Measures: Increased standardization of personnel evaluations.

Increased common understanding of the evaluation process by all levels of departmental personnel.

Increased training programs based upon meaningful personnel evaluations.

---

police agency should be determined for the evaluation of the agency's performance against a measurable set of standards. Standards such as "protect life and property" or "provide law and order" are not good enough.

SOME THOUGHTS CONCERNING THE EFFECTIVENESS OF MBO: AN ANALYSIS

Managing by objectives is not a perfect management concept. Consequently, it is appropriate to think about some of its liabilities as well as its assets, to insure an objective perspective. Any management technique, for that matter, will be affected by people who have different values, attitudes, performance capabilities, frames of reference, and intellectual integrity.

Problems

1. Confusing immediate problems requiring immediate solutions with longer-term objectives, simply because of a desire to include all things into a policing by objectives philosophy.[21]

Comment

Each police agency should identify practical constraints for policing by objectives to insure flexibility.

2. Many MBO programs stumble because they are extended too far down the organizational structure.[22]

Comment

There is nothing wrong with MBO going down the structure, as long as each level of the police hierarchy relates the objectives realistically to the specific contribution they are able to make. Each level should learn from the process and in time will become accustomed to setting practical objectives. The essence of MBO is direction setting.

3. Often objectives are not attained because individuals have less control over their own results than they expected.[23]

Comment

The reason why implementing MBO takes several years is that time becomes a teacher. Nothing is lost, as long as all employees are moving in the same direction based on the philosophy and goals of the organization.

4. Often an MBO program is implemented in a vacuum with no regard for the organization's basic environmental climates.[24]

Comment

The reason why MBO is implemented by integrating the principle of planning, MBO, and managing change is to determine the total environment that controls the appropriate schedule of MBO implementation.

5. Often a company (department) becomes so engrossed in its MBO program that it neglects to recognize or develop opportunities that did not exist when its objectives were set.[25]

Comment

A critical ingredient of MBO is to remove personality from performance measurement and deal with creativity and results. MBO in a police agency enhances opportunity identification.

6. Executing an MBO program often takes more time than originally contemplated and makes retaining a fluid position more cumbersome.[26]

Comment

The most critical factor of patrol leadership is the ability to maintain fluidity. It is no more difficult to maintain fluid positions in an MBO program than it is in ordinary police operations, when performed by an effective leader.

7. Many times there is a mistaken assumption that an MBO program guarantees creative involvement at lower levels.[27]

Comment

The level of sophistication of a policy agency, the participation climate, and individual competence determine the amount of creativity at all levels of any organization.

THE FUTURE, POLICING BY OBJECTIVES, AND THE THIRD-WAVE SOCIETY

The Social Development Corporation has been involved with policing by objectives (PBO) for quite some time. Recently they published a handbook for improving police management, *Policing by Objectives*. The handbook reinforces, by in-depth analysis of MBO-practicing police agencies, the concept I believed to be relevant many years ago.

The following benefits to the police organization were identified by the MBO-practicing police organizations. These benefits vary, based on skills and commitment of agency personnel and program implementation; therefore they should be thought of as potential, rather than automatic:

1. *Coordination of effort:* Because it is a systematic process which involves all levels of an organization in working toward common purposes, PBO ensures that efforts are coordinated. Within the broad framework of departmental mission and goals, individual units can plan their activities, confident that other units are planning their work for the same purposes.

2. *Results-oriented planning:* PBO enhances departmental decision-making because it is results oriented. Various courses of action can be compared for cost and results, and a decision made as to which alternative is most appropriate for the department. Also, decision-making is improved because the stated goals of the department serve as terms of reference for the decision-makers. The policy makers, in effect, set clear priorities for the department, and, as a result, unit or individual functions are performed with less confusion over which activities are more important to the department.

3. *Improved communication:* By involving people of all levels in the design and operation of the PBO program, both vertical and horizontal communications are improved, because PBO crosses organizational lines and ranks and forces communication to make the program succeed. If the department has a particular crime prevention objective, then it is likely that patrol might design a plan of action which includes a security program; but, to make it work, training will be required for certain personnel. It then follows that the training unit, in designing its programs, would include the necessary security training. Thus, units and personnel are encouraged to cooperate to achieve a particular objective.

4. *Development of managers:* The organization benefits from the development of managers through PBO. By making people responsible for results, and by giving them the authority to carry out their responsibilities, personnel develop or improve their management skills. Thus, instead of supervising or controlling patrol operations, patrol commanders and their personnel examine their problems and resources, plan solutions, and monitor progress.

5. *Clearer picture of department:* Because the PBO department has examined its problems, stated its goals, developed objectives and appropriate plans of action, and had documented this process, the workings of the department and its ability to achieve are more realistically presented. The department is able to state its needs and describe its limitations more clearly. This clear picture of department capabilities can help improve public relations. The public will see that the department knows what it is about and will not harbor any false hopes about what the department can achieve with its resources.

6. *Better organization.* PBO is a rational process of planning, executing, and reviewing. Therefore the work of the organization can be more orderly and less haphazard than that of an agency that does not actually review its problems, resources, and results. In fact, some departments, rather than develop a comprehensive PBO program, use the principles of the approach to organize their work and solve problems.

There is a commonly held belief that police work is simply too random for a particular agency to plan its work. How does one predict a bank robbery or a heavy snowstorm? PBO can still be used by police, and, in fact, its use will help police respond better to the unpredictable. PBO can help a department gain some control over its future.

Obviously PBO will not control acts of God or felons, but it will help an agency control everything within its power. Data can be analyzed and used to predict the general shape of things to come. Plans can be devised in advance of particular events, whether natural or criminal, and thus, enable the department to be prepared. By drawing on the experience of its personnel and remaining flexible, PBO can help a department, if not predict its future, at least prepare for various possibilities.

7. *Improved staffing.* Departmental organization and staffing can be improved by PBO. Because of its results orientation, police managers examine their organization in terms of what it accomplishes rather than the activities it performs. For example, sworn police officers may be assigned to issue parking tickets. In an analysis of resources the manager of the department may recognize that the cost of sworn personnel issuing parking tickets exceeds the results achieved by that activity. Alternatives should then be considered. Another example is the radar squad which each year issues more speeding tickets. An analysis of the results might indicate that accidents continue to rise even though a decrease of accidents was the reason for the squad's existence. Thus, it may be necessary to identify high-accident areas and station the squad at those locations. If that fails then possibly the radar squad concept is not appropriate and ought to be abandoned. PBO does help the police manager make the best use of resources, because results determine whether and where the department's limited resources are invested.

8. *Improved responsiveness.* The ability of a department to respond to future circumstances can be improved by PBO. Because PBO is future oriented, projections of work based on historical records are made. The allocation of resources is planned in relation to what work is anticipated. Because priorities are known in advance, and unit and individual responsibilities are clear, a department can respond quickly and decisively.

9. *Better attitude toward change.* Because of its future orientation, PBO can engender in a department a more positive attitude toward change. A department that has used PBO becomes used to the process of change and recognizes change as an integral part of the PBO program.

Benefits to the Individual

Below are some of the numerous benefits PBO can bring to the individual manager and his or her subordinates.

1. *Job-related performance evaluation.* One of the most significant benefits of PBO to the individual is that evaluation is based upon results and not appearance. With PBO, jobs are generally clearly defined and expectations are mutually agreed to by both line personnel and managers. The benefit of this particular exchange to the manager is that, because the job, the milestones, and the nature of the evaluation are understood in advance, the manager does not devote energy to controlling the employee but rather to operations and programs. It would then follow that PBO provides more time for management by reducing the need for close supervision.

2. *Greater involvement by all ranks.* In PBO the individual officer benefits from having considerable say in what a particular job will be. Having in hand the overall purposes of the department, the police officer (manager or subordinate) can recommend a design for the job which will suit the organization best.

3. *Improved morale.* Officer morale can be high in a PBO department, because job requirements are clearly defined and often mutually agreed upon. There is no confusion between manager and subordinate as to what is required of the subordinate or, for that matter, of the manager. Studies have shown that where employees do not know what is expected of them, their sense of security suffers, and they tend to become overly cautious in their performance. This often results in poor performance and rapid turnover of personnel. PBO can develop a circumstance in which personnel clearly understand what results are expected of them and that they will be evaluated on those results. Where this is the case, performance and morale are high.

4. *Individual skill development enhanced.* Individual skill development is enhanced by PBO. Because PBO is a rigorous planning, execution, and review process, the personnel involved in the program will acquire or improve their management skills. Their sense of growing and developing in their jobs will contribute to their sense of well being. People who come to a job expecting to participate in it but who are relegated to a monotonous routine, about which their opinion is never sought, are bound to become dissatisfied. PBO gives police personnel and managers an opportunity to develop and learn.

5. *Reduction of unpleasant surprises:* Because PBO is a comprehensive and systematic planning process, many future contingencies can be anticipated and allowances made for them. PBO's future orientation requires the manager to plan for the future and lay out strategies that minimize disruptions. The assessment functions of PBO also help identify problems, drains on resources, and alternative courses of action that can reduce the number of surprises that may confront a manager.

6. *Satisfied employees:* Job satisfaction is implicit in many of the benefits described above. The aggregate effect of job freedom, evaluation by results achieved, personal development, job clarity, and self-supervision is that police officers feel positive about themselves and their job.[28]

Third-Wave Society

Alvin Toffler, author of *Future Shock*, has a philosophy about the way we
view ourselves. He sets forth his thoughts in his book entitled *The Third
Wave*. The book explores the economy, personality of the future, changing
values, the post-nuclear family, technology, and politics. The patrol administrator reading this volume should anticipate the historical awareness necessary to synthesize the information in order to apply it to today's
and tomorrow's police administration. One specific change Toffler identifies as important is the willingness of police to strike.

Mr. Toffler says "Today we are viewing the impact of the third tidal
wave of change in history (the first was launched by the agricultural revolution and the second by the industrial revolution). The third wave is creating
a new civilization in our midst with its own jobs, life-style, work ethics,
sexual attitudes, concepts of life, its own economic structures and political
mindsets. This third wave civilization is challenging the power elites in
both capitalist and socialist societies."[29]

Sir Robert Peel worked very hard to have his tenets of reform accepted. You could hardly argue with their basic objectives even today.
However, society is more complex, and the earth grows smaller. Some
thoughts on the changes in society that change police administration are
appropriate, since the police organization is also in transition in the mix
of leaders now administering the police agencies of our country.

Toffler exposed the idea of the transient society in America in *Future
Shock*. Darrow seems to agree with Toffler.[30] He expounded upon the
idea, which seems to be important for the patrol manager to understand.
In using philosophy as a foundation, remember that one's perspective is
an essential problem in communication; i.e., where you are imparts how
you see things. Industrial society has influenced the value systems of many
of us, and a cadre of commonly held beliefs are under attack. The fundamental beliefs we have had include the growth and productivity factors, the
belief in a market economy, and the strong results we should be able to
attain through the application of science and technology.

The attack on these fundamental beliefs seems to address three questions: (1) Why is it that everything seems to be falling apart around us?
(2) Why is everything becoming so complicated? (3) Why is it that nothing
works out?

The first question: *Why is it that everything seems to be falling apart
around us?* This question deals with a fragmentation of values. In the past
it seems we had a normal curve regarding values (Figure 1.3), where a
portion of our populace were allergic to work, another portion were
workaholics, but the major portion persevered; and from this group the
leaders of our country were chosen. However, recent history indicates that

Figure 1.3 *Traditional values*

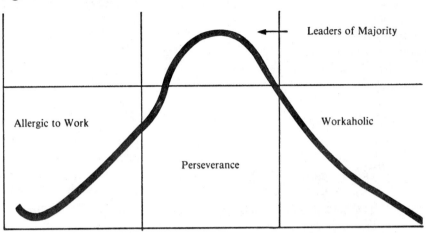

our values have become diffused or fragmented where we have no clear-cut majority, and the appearance of conflict has permeated society. The conflict brings with it an increase in the difficulty of communicating, because of where we are in this conflicting society. Finally, determining leadership becomes a problem because values are distributed (Figure 1.4).

The second question: *Why is everything becoming so complicated?* In reflecting upon this question, one must look to science and technology, their numbers and advancement. When things were simple, we did not speak of the criminal justice "system," we did not view the decisions made by the police administrator as affecting the courts, and so forth. However, systems do interact with other systems and within a system, and today a change in one system is felt by nearly all the systems. The replacement of the horse by the gasoline engine brought about great change in economic,

Figure 1.4 *Fragmented values*

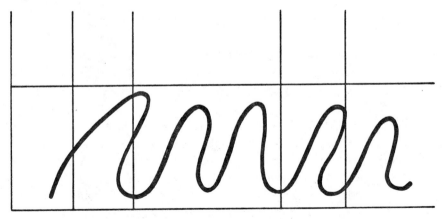

Figure 1.5 *System interaction*

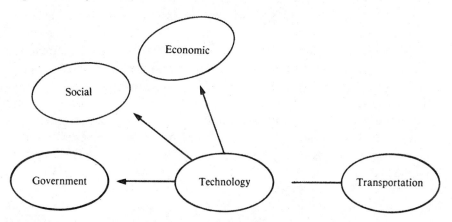

governmental, and social systems (Figure 1.5). Because of this interaction, there is also a change in values, which again causes problems in communications. The increase in number and advancement in technology brings with it a loss of public confidence in making big changes. We place a premium on incrementalism because the results are more certain. We see ten-year plans developed in two-year modules or modular planning.

In Figure 1.6, if we are at point A and the most desirable place to be is point C, but the only way to get there is by implementing radical change at point A, it is likely we will continue along the incremental path toward point B, even though it is the wrong way. This is for no other reason

Figure 1.6 *Planning philosophy*

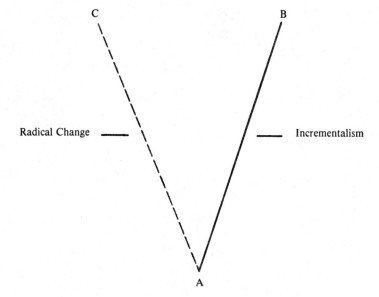

than that it is predictable and can be measured. Furthermore, we can say how great it is compared to what was before, even though what was before was lousy.

The third question: *Why is it that nothing works out?* This question deals with the nature of humankind. If human beings conceive of the ideal and do not reflect on their limitations, if they think in terms of perfectionism and cannot attain it, then things will not work out. Patrol leaders must make decisions within their environment, but should try to make the most effective decision . . . increase knowledge, skills, and abilities. All good has some bad attached to it, and all bad has some good flowing from it (Figure 1.7).

This concept is related to the way systems interrelate, in that the bad causes some good which then causes some more bad. This develops a sense of frustration because the program you had hoped to be meaningful causes other effects, and even in-depth planning cannot cover all potential consequences.

The responses to these questions are broadening purpose and defining goals and objectives in more realistic terms; rather than trying to be all things to all people, which is unattainable. If things seem to be falling apart because of a diffusion of societal values; if things seem to be more complicated because of greater size and complexity associated with advanced technologies; and if things do not seem to work out because our human limitations cause us to fail to reach the ideal, then we can only respond

Figure 1.7 *Systems interrelation*

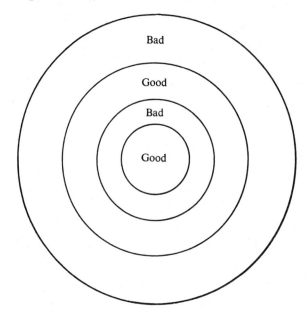

in one of three ways: (1) "Oh, things will work out, they always do"; (2) "To hell with it, I don't care"; or (3) "We have to work harder and smarter to get things done." The patrol leader can only select the third response.

To be more specific, Cohen relates the philosophy of today by addressing leadership styles in the New York City Police Department.[31] He identifies tradition-oriented and reform-oriented police commanders as well as several important events which have taken place in the past two decades and which have had considerable impact on traditional police systems. One is nationalism, the revolt against colonialism and the emergence of independent nation-states in Africa and Asia. Racial inequality and discrimination are addressed on a national scale. "For the first time in the history of their nation, race relations became inextricably intertwined with

Figure 1.8 *The police organization as an operating network.*

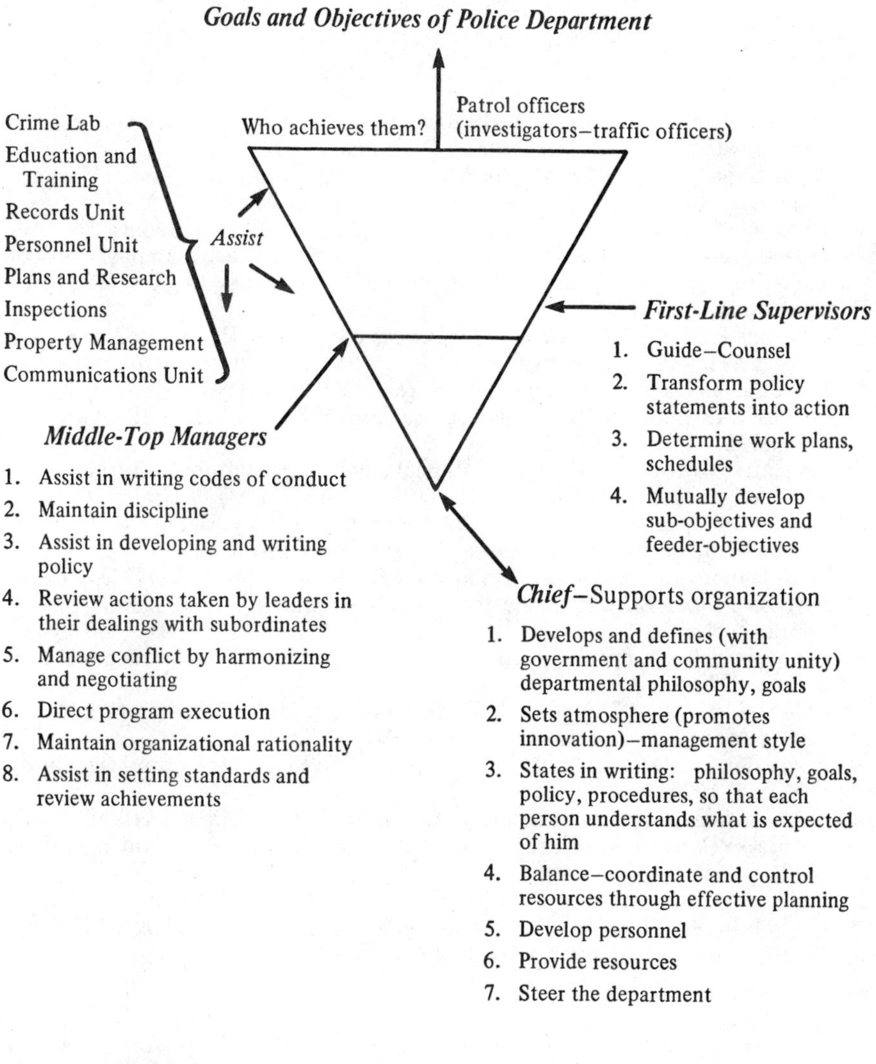

Goals and Objectives of Police Department

Who achieves them?

Patrol officers (investigators—traffic officers)

Crime Lab
Education and Training
Records Unit
Personnel Unit
Plans and Research
Inspections
Property Management
Communications Unit

Assist

First-Line Supervisors

1. Guide—Counsel
2. Transform policy statements into action
3. Determine work plans, schedules
4. Mutually develop sub-objectives and feeder-objectives

Middle-Top Managers

1. Assist in writing codes of conduct
2. Maintain discipline
3. Assist in developing and writing policy
4. Review actions taken by leaders in their dealings with subordinates
5. Manage conflict by harmonizing and negotiating
6. Direct program execution
7. Maintain organizational rationality
8. Assist in setting standards and review achievements

Chief—Supports organization

1. Develops and defines (with government and community unity) departmental philosophy, goals
2. Sets atmosphere (promotes innovation)—management style
3. States in writing: philosophy, goals, policy, procedures, so that each person understands what is expected of him
4. Balance—coordinate and control resources through effective planning
5. Develop personnel
6. Provide resources
7. Steer the department

American foreign policy."[32] Cohen suggests that the civil disorders that followed these events are the second part of the reason for the change in philosophy.[33]

Policing must develop a body of knowledge, a flexible management style, and vision in its leadership so that crisis management becomes a thing of the past. "As a society," writes Robert Heilbroner, "we move into a future on the grand dynamic of history."[34] The criminal justice system cannot afford to disregard this sage observation. It cannot afford to continue to operate through authority and tradition while society around it becomes more humanitarian, egalitarian, empirical, utilitarian, pragmatic, scientific, professional, and automated.[35]

The proper implementation of a management by objectives approach to patrol administration will aid police managers in meeting the challenge of the future.[36]

NOTES

1. William J. Bopp and Donald T. Schultz, *A Short History of American Law Enforcement* (Springfield, Ill.: Charles C Thomas, 1972).
2. Roger Lane, *Policing the City, Boston 1822–1825* (Cambridge, Mass.: Harvard University Press, 1967), p. 11.
3. Condensed from an unpublished paper, "Philosophy Applied to the Administration of Criminal Justice," by Professor B. Edward Campbell, School of Justice Administration, University of Louisville, Louisville, Ky., 1980, with permission.
4. Anthony P. Raia, *Managing by Objectives* (Glenview, Ill.: Scott, Foresman, 1974), pp. 11–12.
5. Leo Charles Daley, *Philosophy* (New York: Monarch Press, 1925), p. 3.
6. C. Gibson Raymond, unpublished lecture, University of Indiana, Bloomington, Ind., 1976.
7. Reprinted with permission of the Lincoln Police Department, Lincoln, Neb.
8. Abridged and adapted from pp. 104–108 in *The Process of Group Decision-Making* by Dennis S. Gouran. Copyright © 1974 by Dennis S. Gouran. Reprinted by permission of Harper & Row, Publishers, Inc.
9. Paul Blommers and E. F. Lindquist, *Elementary Statistical Methods in Psychology and Education* (Boston: Houghton Mifflin, 1960), p. 405.
10. Gouran, op. cit.
11. Bopp and Schultz, op. cit., p. 88. Reprinted by permission from the publisher, Charles C Thomas.
12. Dale D. McConkey, "Applying MBO to Non-Profit Organizations," *S.A.M. Advanced Management Journal* (January 1973): 12.
13. E. Daniel Grady, *M.B.O. for the Not for Profit Enterprise* (San Jose, Calif.: Lansford, 1975), p. 3.
14. National Advisory Commission on Criminal Justice Standards and Goals, *Report on Corrections* (Washington, D.C.: U. S. Government Printing Office, 1973), p. 449.
15. Ibid., p. 446.
16. Paul Mali, *Managing by Objectives* (New York: John Wiley & Sons, 1972), pp. 12–14. Reprinted by permission of John Wiley & Sons, Inc.

17. W. J. Reddin, *Effective Management by Objectives* (New York: McGraw-Hill, 1971), p. 19.
18. Landon Heffner, *Policing by Objectives*, Vol. 1 (Hartford, Conn.: Social Development Corporation, 1976).
19. George L. Morrisey, *Management by Objectives and Results* (Reading, Mass.: Addison-Wesley, 1970), p. 62.
20. *Use of Manpower in a City Police Force* (Bethesda, Md.: Social Development Corporation, 1973), pp. 18–31.
21. Charles H. Ford, *MBO: An Idea Whose Time Has Gone*, Bloomington, Ind.: Business Horizons, 1979). Condensed in *AMA Management Digest* (May 1980): 4.
22. Ibid., p. 5.
23. Ibid.
24. Ibid.
25. Ibid., p. 6.
26. Ibid.
27. Ibid., p. 7.
28. V. A. Lubans and J. M. Edgar, *Policing by Objectives: A Handbook for Improving Police Management* (Hartford, Conn.: Social Development Corporation, 1979), pp. 12–15.
29. Alvin Toffler, *The Third Wave* (New York: William Morrow, 1980), jacket.
30. R. Morton Darrow, condensed from an unpublished paper, "A Philosophy of Today," School of Police Administration, University of Louisville, Louisville, Ky., 1978, with permission.
31. Bernard Cohen, "Leadership Styles of Commanders in the New York City Police Department" *Journal of Police Science and Administration* (1980): 128. International Association of Chiefs of Police, Gaithersburg, Md.
32. Norman R. Yetman and C. Hoy Steele, *Majority and Minority, The Dynamics of Racial and Ethnic Relations* (Boston: Allyn and Bacon, 1975), p. 551.
33. Cohen, op. cit., p. 128.
34. Robert L. Heilbroner, *The Future as History* (New York: Harper and Brothers, 1960), p. 16.
35. Project Star, *The Impact of Social Trends on Crime and Criminal Justice* (1976), p. 347. California Commission on Peace Officers Standards and Training, Law Enforcement Assistance Administration, Anderson-Davis, Cincinnati, Ohio.
36. For further discussion, see Peter Drucker, "What Results Should You Expect? A User's Guide to MBO," *Public Administration Review* (January/February 1976).

•2•

Leadership Behavior and Work Motivation

The aim of leadership is to accomplish a desired mission by motivating the behavior of subordinates. There can be no leadership if there is no one to lead. Results are related to the performance of the total team. In understanding the leadership role, it is first necessary for the leader to evaluate carefully the basic needs of the people to be led. Second, the leader must determine what leadership style he or she will use to attain the desired behavior from personnel. Third, the leader must create an atmosphere in which members of the organization feel significantly involved to express their true feeling regarding any situation. In any leadership situation, it is necessary for adjustments to be made on the part of the leader and the personnel being led.

The common denominator among all effective leadership is stating the desired objective and then simply doing all the things necesssary to accomplish it. The steps between the statement and the accomplishment include analysis, evaluation, application, and implementation.

THE NATURE OF MANAGERIAL LEADERSHIP

Leaders are born, leaders are developed, leadership is abstract, power is in the position, power is in the person, leaders have certain traits, leaders behave in a certain way, and leadership is a process of influencing through standards of excellence. By their very nature, leaders and leadership must translate the abstract by the use of insight into present results, and act upon this situation.

The fact is that leadership is an art which fits the knowledgeable individual in an organization, is analyzed by the individual, and produces the predetermined results of that organization.

CONTINGENCY THEORY

The most self-conscious people in the world are its leaders. They may also be the most anxious and insecure. As men of action, leaders face risks and uncertainty, and often display remarkable courage in shouldering grave responsibility. But beneath their fortitude there often lies an agonizing sense of doubt and a need to justify themselves.[1]

What will tomorrow's leaders be like? They will not be characterized by a list of "personality traits" or by some specific "leadership style"; they will emerge from among those who best understand and are able to lead a society that will insist on:

- An increasing emphasis on the quality of life rather than on the quantity of goods produced or owned
- Moving away from independence toward a concept of interdependence among individual institutions and nations
- Living in harmony with nature rather than working to conquer it through technology
- A trend away from the concept of competition toward a concept of cooperation
- De-emphasis on technological efficiency in favor of social justice and equity as primary social goals
- Self-development of an organization's individual members instead of the dictates of organizational convenience
- Participatory management rather than dogmatism and authoritarianism
- Reinstallation of the work ethic—not as an unavoidable and unpleasant duty but rather as a principal means of self-fulfillment
- Recognition of leisure as a meaningful activity in its own right

This list underscores the need for nontraditional leaders for the future. Surprisingly, though, these leaders will also need to possess and advocate "traditional" values that are seemingly out of vogue at the moment:

- Incorruptible personal integrity
- Respect for the property of others—this returning value will be coupled to an increasing quality of life in a world of declining quality
- Reassumption of and social stress on individual responsibility versus "let the government or someone else do it"
- The desire to develop a clean and orderly society—a demand born of three factors: desire for a higher quality for life; a decrease in the availability of material goods (quantity of life); and social pressures brought about by the increasing number of people on earth.[2]

LEADERSHIP CONTINGENCY APPROACH

Fred E. Fiedler has been wrestling with a theory of leadership for over twenty years.[3] Using the performance of work groups as his criterion,

Fiedler suggests that three variables are significant for leadership effec-tiveness: leader–member relations, task structure, and position power.

Leader–member relations are the most important factor, since the manager the group accepts, trusts, and likes does not have to pull rank in order to get things done. Yet it is not the only necessary ingredient, for the well-liked leader may not act any more wisely than one who is dis-liked. Task structure means the degree to which a given task can be pro-grammed or done by workers. Clearly, the more a job can be so structured, the more power the manager has, regardless of his or her leader–member relations or position power. The least important variable is position power – the degree to which a position itself enables the leader to get the group to comply with and accept his or her direction. It is of least significance because it is related more to reward and punishment power than to genuine influence.

These three factors interact with the leader's knowledge of the group, familiarity with the task at hand, the homogeneity of the group, and similar particulars to define the favorableness of the situation. This is the degree to which the situation enables the manager to exert influence and control over the group process. It signifies the number of elements that the leader has going for him. To speak in terms of extremes, the ideal situation is that in which a well-liked manager who has great position power deals with a structured task and leads a homogeneous group that he knows well and that accepts him. The bleakest situation is that in which a disliked manager who has weak position power tries to lead a heterogeneous group in the performance of a vague or ill-defined task.

Fiedler has come up with certain conclusions that go against the ac-cepted stereotypes. Both directive, managing, task-oriented managers and human relations-oriented, nondirective managers are successful under cer-tain conditions. Also, in both very favorable and very unfavorable situa-tions, the controlling, managing, directive leadership style seems to work best.

Moreover, both highly accepted and highly rejected leaders perform best if they are controlling and directive. Apparently the highly accepted manager can be forceful because he or she is accepted, whereas the rejected manager must be forceful because he has no alternative – if he tries to be nondirective, the group may abandon the task entirely. This agrees with the finding that structuring can be increased with impunity if considera-tion is high, but that lowering structure does no good if consideration is low. Finally, leaders who are in the intermediate range, being neither ac-cepted nor rejected markedly by the group, perform best if they are per-missive and nondirective.

One of the greatest virtues of Fiedler's findings is that they avoid a polarizing either-or model. His theory provides for a range in leadership behavior, varying according to the practical situation the manager faces. It also allows for a change of behavior as the favorableness of the situation changes. It therefore circumvents the pitfall of rigidity, of adherence to a given approach regardless of the pragmatic circumstances of a particular group or task. Thus as Fielder notes, the head of a research team might adopt a consultative and participative approach at the outset for the simple reason that no one really knows for certain how to proceed. Once a given plan and appropriate strategies have been decided upon, however, the leader might become rather firm and forceful, as far as any major deviation from the plan is concerned.

Organizationally, too, Fiedler's theory has much in its favor, for any firm has certain options open to it, as he points out. It can attempt to alter the personality of the manager, an estimable but generally fruitless task. It can train its managers in the various leadership styles, a worthy but time-consuming chore that promises no sure results. It can seek to place managers in situations that are best suited to their natural leadership attitudes and behavior, a realistic procedure but hardly universally applicable. Then again, it can change the manager's position power, making it more or less strong; it can alter the task structure, making it more or less programmed; it can modify the leader–member relations, making a group more cohesive. This three-pronged approach, according to Fiedler, is more realistic than any of the others.[4]

My earlier statement about leadership being an art is emphasized by Fulmer when he uses a table (Table 2.1) to show theories of human effectiveness applied to the process of learning to lead, wherein he states,

> Could it be that our wisest approach is to see all the theories at once, and at the same time, draw some consensus theory of our own, which remains most useful to us as long as it remains unwritten.[5]

LEADERSHIP: QUALITY, TYPES, AND STYLES

The most important quality of the patrol leader is his ability to set an example in creativity, innovation, and flexibility. He must be willing to learn (knowledge is power), be susceptible to new ideas, and be ready to take that extra step in achieving his goal. Other attributes include an understanding of group dynamics, motivational theory, fiscal management, and open-agency concepts. Sincerity and enthusiasm, intelligence, experience, goal-orientation, courage, integrity, and ability to communicate and teach (know your direction, believe in what you are doing, and then communicate these directions clearly and unequivocally, with tact and diplomacy) are

Table 2.1   *Theories of Human Effectiveness*

	System 1	System 2	System 3	System 4
Rensis Likert	(Exploitive-Authoritative)	(Benevolent Authoritative)	(Consultative)	(Participative Group)
Douglas McGregor	Theory X Reductive	Traditional	Theory Y Developmental	
Warren Bennis	Bureaucracy Authoritarian, Restrictive Management Structure		Democracy Goal-Oriented, Adaptive Management Structure	
Robert Blake	1,1 Neutrality and Indecision	1,9 9,1 Unbalanced Concern for People or Production	5,5 Compromise Middle of the Road	9,9 Integration of Resources
Chris Argyris	Autocratic Relationships Conflict and Conformity	Manipulative Relationship	Authentic Relationships Interpersonal Competence	
Abraham H. Maslow	Lower-Need Fixation Halted Growth		Self-actualization (Eupsychia) Realized Potential	
Frederick Herzberg	Meaningless Work Hygiene Seeking		Meaningful Work Motivation Seeking	
Erich Fromm	Escape from Freedom Conformity, Manipulation, Destructiveness		Freedom Spontaneous and Responsible Behavior	
Texas Instr. (Myers)	Authority Orientation, Interpersonal Conflict, Meaningless Goals, Restrictive Systems		Goal Orientation Interpersonal Competence Meaningful Goals Helpful Systems	
Keith Davis	Autocratic	Custodial (Maintenance)	Supportive (Motivational)	Collegial
Alvin Zander	Authoritarian	Democratic	Laissez-faire	
Malcolm Shaw	Controlling Communicator	Relinquishing	Withdrawn	Developmental
Tom Harris	I'm O.K. and You're Not O.K.	I'm Not O.K. and You're O.K.	I'm Not O.K. and You're Not O.K.	I'm O.K. and You're O.K.

Source: Reprinted with permission of Macmillan Publishing Co., Inc. from *The New Management* by Robert M. Fulmer. Copyright © 1974, Robert M. Fulmer.

all valuable leadership qualities. Individual feelings regarding the difficulty of the task cannot be considered, since effective decisions are often those that seem the most difficult. Good judgment, humility, empathy, dependability, perseverance, decisiveness (quick mind accompanied by analytical process), and realism affect total leadership ability. In addition, a good leader gets along well with other people.

Each patrol leader must determine which of these qualities he possesses and then maximize them to the fullest. Most police officers can remember more than one supervisor who impressed them greatly. All of these effective leaders did not possess the same leadership qualities. One supervisor may be enthusiastic and intelligent, set a good example, be decisive and understanding, and pave the way with his sincerity. Another may be quiet, patient, intelligent, fair, receptive, and experienced. Yet both are capable of leadership. The idea is to be true to yourself—recognize the individual qualities in your makeup, use and expand your talents to their limits. The ability to lead may be something everyone thinks he or she possesses, but if it is not developed at the right time it may slip out of reach.

If we stipulate that all decisions must be made for the good of the department, then it must be assumed that decisions will always take into consideration the human element. The effective leader is a leader at all time. The effective leader will correct the commission of a poorly executed task whether or not it is being done within his own area of authority. The effective leader feels that any decision that affects the department affects him as an individual, and he will do whatever is necessary to make that decision a positive one. He/she chooses to keep his/her outlook broad and to work effectively for the welfare of the organization as a whole, leading his unit in attaining the objective that relates to the objectives of the total organization. This is nothing wrong with setting personal or professional goals so long as they coincide with the overall goals of the organization. It is only wrong when personal goals conflict with the goals of the organization and are valued over those goals. This fact must be explained to subordinates, or the result will be confusion, conflict, and disintegration of the department. In a sense, a good leader will be his brother's keeper and will demonstrate concern about all those units within the department that need help. The geometric axiom that the whole is equal to the sum of its parts applies. Consequently, each unit in the department must contribute its share in moving the total organization forward.

Laurence Peter states in *The Peter Principle*: "In a hierarchy, every employee needs to rise to his level of incompetence."[7] The incompetent individual in a position of authority, as Peter describes him, enlarges upon little things that are of little or no significance to the organization. He has reached his level of incompetence and, in most police agencies, he will not be demoted, but left alone or moved horizontally to a position of lesser importance. Such a situation frustrates the younger, more capable leaders.

It has been said that there is no real power in our urban society, there is only movement by inertia, and our leaders can only slightly change the direction of the movement. Those who disagree with this say that there is an arithmetic of politics; if you can identify the right numbers and then add those numbers together, the sum is power.

Stated earlier was the belief that knowledge is power; but, in addition to knowledge, there must be the ability to involve others, to motivate them in the performance of their duties, to be dynamic, and to make things happen. You know who you are, you know where you fit in the organization, you know where you want to go, you are willing to work hard to get where you want to go, and you know how you are going to get to that goal. The total of all of these is power; they include all the necessary attributes for goal achievement.

Making things happen involves change. Change should be approached in the proper manner, with an awareness of policy, rules, regulations, organizational ability to change, and especially the human aspect of change. A realization that not too much can be done alone is important. In fact, there are strict limitations on what can be accomplished by any individual acting alone in any organization. Since others are needed, it is imperative to have understanding among the unit leaders within a department. It is not necessary to know the communication commander's job better than he or she does if one is patrol commander. It is necessary for each leader to have a good knowledge of what the other positions involve and to know the abilities of the leaders of all other units and the relationship among all units. It is beneficial simply to enjoy a cup of coffee with the leaders of other units. These informal meetings allow for honest expression, and real knowledge and information on both sides is given and absorbed. Under these conditions, the human element takes priority and the positive results from these occasions are tremendous. There is no room in a police agency for personal animosity if effective leadership and a desire to move the department forward exist. Police leaders cannot afford personal quarrels with other police leaders within the organization; cooperation is necessary. Decisions made by the leaders in a department must be made not for personal gain but for the good of the department. Do not take cooperation for granted. Hard work builds good will and in the long run pays off.

It is necessary to understand how to use the postion of leadership in a positive way. Schein brings the concept of self-actualization into better focus for us in a discussion of man and his relationship to Maslow's hierarchy of needs.

> The kinds of assumptions which are implied about the nature of man can be stated as follows:
>
> a. Man's motives fall into classes which are arranged in a hierarchy:
> (1) simple needs for survival, safety, and security; (2) social and

affiliative needs; (3) ego-satisfaction and self-esteem needs; (4) need for autonomy and independence; and (5) self-actualization needs in the sense of maximum use of all his resources. As the lower-level needs are satisfied, they release some of the higher-level motives. Even the lowliest untalented man seeks self-actualization, a sense of meaning and accomplishment in his work, if his other needs are more or less fulfilled.

b. Man seeks to be mature on the job and capable of being so. This means the exercise of a certain amount of autonomy and independence, the adoption of a long-range time perspective, the development of special capacities and skills, and greater flexibility in adapting to circumstances.

c. Man is primarily self-motivated and self-controlled; externally imposed incentives and controls are likely to threaten the person and reduce him to a less mature adjustment.

d. There is no inherent conflict between self-actualization and more effective organizational performance. If given a chance man will voluntarily integrate his own goals with those of the organization.[8]

The personnel of the patrol force should be viewed from a new perspective. Leadership demands the ability of setting the goals of each employee and the organization to make them coincide. If the leader knows and understands the hierarchy of needs and is himself self- actualizing, he can ccontribute better to the accomplishment of self-actualization for those who are subordinate to him.

Types of Leadership

Flexibility plays an important part in leadership today. Leaders must know the difference between autocratic leadership, democratic leadership, and laissez-faire leadership and when to use each. One type of leadership will not work in all situations.

The *autocrat* usually makes a decision without allowing the group to participate. He or she is extremely authoritarian and makes everyone aware of who is the leader and who is the follower. The autocrat does not want his position of supervision to be questioned and so usually leads through fear, which makes him a driver. He is arbitrary to a fault, but he does well in times of emergency. When there is a need for decisiveness, there is no time for participation; time is of the essence. The autocratic leader will shine under such circumstances. However, there is no flexibility to change, it is difficult to get the best results when his type of leadership is used over a long period of time.

The *democratic leader* allows those persons who work with him to participate in the decision-making process. He or she understands that their ideas and suggestions are a key to greater motivation and commitment to the decision. This type of leader does not need to be arbitrary or use extreme authoritativeness. He believes that when people are allowed to help decide issues concerning themselves and how they will be affected, they will become involved in seeing that the job gets done. The democratic leader is people oriented. He realizes that it is the little things that count. Take a sergeant, for example, who supervises a squad and does some of the following: (1) asks an officer about his sick child; (2) knows when an officer needs extra time off and plans the work schedule to meet all responsibilities and still give the officer the time; (3) schedule officers' holidays where it really means something to each; i.e., Martin Luther King's birthday, St. Patrick's Day, July 4th, Christmas, and Yom Kippur. These, often thought of as minor elements, can make a big difference to the individual when she or he feels they indicate that the sergeant really cares. The results of this style of leadership are usually goal achievement, improved performance, higher motivation, and a step closer to total self-actualization for the sergeant's team.

The *laissez-faire leader* usually does not fulfill the needs of his subordinates. He pays little or no attention to what is going on and is directly opposite from the autocratic leader. He feels insecure in most areas, which is why he exercises little leadership. In other words, he does not know, so he tells his employees to do what they think is right. It is true that flexibility in leadership allows subordinates to think for themselves in order to test their abilities. Laissez-faire leadership is therefore appropriate at times, as long as the concept is explained to employees. For example, a patrol commander allows a group of patrol officers—some agents (college graduates) and some experienced investigators—to work on a team-policing project. They are advised that there will be mimimum supervision; the team will be expected to obtain conclusions from the project. This approach allows each member to participate completely. Laissez-faire leadership is appropriate for this specific situation. The leader should be very careful in selecting the team participants.

Styles of Leadership

In *The Leader Looks at Styles of Leadership* Warren H. Schmidt points out the five most typical styles, ranging from highly leader-centered to highly group-entered.

> When you are the recognized leader of a group, you have certain prerogatives and power. How you use these powers will affect both the productivity of the group and the freedom of the subordinates or

group members. As you, the leader, use less of your authority and power, the group members gain greater freedom in making decisions; as you use more of your power, the group freedom declines.

Telling. The leader identifies a problem, considers alternative solutions, chooses one of them, and then tells his followers what they are to do. He may or may not consider what he believes the group members will think or feel about the decision, but they clearly do not participate directly in the decision-making. Coercion may or may not be used or implied.

Persuading. The leader, as before, makes the decision without consulting his group. However, instead of simply announcing his decision, he tries to persuade group members to accept it. He describes how his decision fits both the interests of the organization and the interests of the group members.

Consulting. The leader here gives the group members a chance to influence the decision from the beginning. He presents a problem and relevant background information, then asks the members for their ideas on how to solve it. He may give his tentative solution for their reaction. In effect, the group is asked to increase the number of alternative actions to be considered. The leader then selects the solution he regards as most promising.

Joining. The leader here participates in the discussion as "just another member"—and agrees in advance to carry out whatever decision the group makes. The only limits placed on the group are those given to the leader by his supervisors. (Many research and development teams make decisions this way.)

Delegating. The leader defines a problem and the boundaries within which it must be solved. Then he turns it over to the group to work out a solution that makes sense to the implementers. He agrees to support their solution as long as it fits within the boundaries.[9]

Telling, persuading, consulting, joining, and delegating make up a continuum. The leader's position on the continuum changes as the situation changes. Personal value systems developed over the years from home life, church, school, social and economic conditions, and total learning experience will affect his or her choice of style. These values influence individual perspectives with relation to others and the job. If experience has shown aggressiveness is rewarding, attempts to obtain rewards through aggressive behavior will be made. Know thyself; attain self-actualization; be aware of similar and conflicting values from the organization, society, and other institutions in the community that may affect your ability and the ability of your subordinates to perform. A result of this awareness will be confidence in oneself as a leader. The level of confidence given each subordinate will be determined on an individual basis after the performance of tasks and an evaluation of the quality of work.

It was once said that there is nothing wrong with an egomaniac as a leader so long as he knows it and the rest of his staff or subordinates also know it. However, there is a problem when the subordinates know it and the leader doesn't. The important aspect is understanding. The same applies when the leader selects his style of leadership, whatever it may be. All should understand what type is being used. The dictator-type of leader usually has a problem with delegation in that this type usually overestimates his own ability or underestimates the ability of his subordinates. In this case, he usually surrounds himself with yes-men, and the leader who surrounds himself with yes-men "is like a pilot flying blind, with instruments that tell him only what they believe he wants to see instead of their true reading. Moreover, that sort of dictator drives all strong, independent, original minds out of the organization and silences all critical discussions of his policies so that when the crash comes, there is usually no alternative policy that anyone has been formulating, and no leaders of any quality there to take over command."[10]

"When Henry Ford took over all the decision-making of his company and set spies on the managers to try and catch them making decisions on their own, he was ensuring that the crash when it came would be cataclysmic; indeed it is believed it was fifteen years before the firm showed a profit again."[11] Absolute dictatorship carries within it the seeds of its own destruction; it cannot survive for long.

The position on the continuum is not important. What is important is to know where one is in relationship to the situation at hand. Flexibility and objectivity enhance the leadership potential.

MACRO AND MICRO FACTORS OF LEADERSHIP

We addressed the macro-leadership concept in the preceding chapter when we discussed the philosophy, goals, objectives, and sub-objectives of the different levels of police hierarchy. If we were to relate this to discipline, we would find the present process used is permeated by the "due-process" approach to discipline, rather than allowing anarchy or "all knowing" chiefs of police. In the transition of leadership in American policing, the macro-leadership apparently most viable is to use the "apppropriate" style for the "situation," analyzing all pertinent data. Macro deals with the prevailing fabric of a society. The literature on leadership in this country is based on self-reliance and teamwork, not necessarily exclusive of each other, but at the same time not necessarily integrating the two concepts. You know some people are brilliant, they can plan, are analytical, can write, speak, recommend courses of action, and at the same time are terrible potential leaders. These are the kinds of people who should stay in a plush room and have the problem slid under the door so they can slide the solution out under the door; but never ever let these people influence other people; their human relations skills are atrocious.

This leads us into the micro-factor of leadership. These factors are involved in the truths, qualities, styles, and values of the leader. When related to the change process, we are dealing with information, skills, behavior, and attitude. When dealing with the literature, we consider, the Jackass Fallacy, Strength Management, Machiavelli, Guerilla Management, Idiosyncratic, to name a few. Many times, in all the literature, we are discussing the same principles, based upon thought or research, only using a different vocabulary.

THE LEADER AS A MOTIVATOR

The leader as a motivator is just the same as the parent, having what makes him/herself tick and finding out what is important to the ones he or she is attempting to motivate. Most of us do things because there is something in it for us. Even to the point of giving to the poor. What's in it for us may be that we are acknowledged as being charitable, we gain fame, we satsify our ego, or we are anonymous but with the good feeling that we have helped and, in the eyes of the Almighty, are viewed with favor. It is difficult to exactly identify scientifically why people are motivated. Some say power, others say greed, or money, or reward, or knowledge, or truth, or stature, or . . . .

In one view of motivation, Vroom[12] identified the following as determinants for job satisfaction:

Determinants For Job Satisfaction

Determinant	Factors Involved
Supervision.	Satisfaction with the leadership. Consideration from superiors. Interaction with leaders. Employee-centered supervision. Participation in decision making. Ability to influence job conditions. Degree of autonomy. Amount of recognition.
Work Group.	Attractiveness of the group. Ability to satisfy worker needs. Small and cohesive rather than large groups.

Positive interaction among members.
Acceptance and liking by the group.
Interdependence of group and
   individual goals.

Job Content.

Job level and status.
Job enlargement, job enrichment, and
   job rotation.
Control over work methods.
Control over work pace.
Use of skills and abilities.
Success in work performance.
Responsibility.

Wages.

Relative standing rather than the
   absolute wage level.

Promotion Opportunities.

Fair competition for advancement;
   may have a negative effect on the
   fearful or unambitious.

Hours of work.

Shift work may have negative
   consequences depending on use of
   leisure time, family reactions, and
   so forth.

Vroom continues the discussion with an expectancy theory using the formula:

$$\text{Motivation} = \Sigma \text{ Valance} \times \text{Expectancy}^{13}$$

Why do people behave the way they do? What motivates them? Are there values or ethics of a high moral standard which cause them to do what they say they will do? Is the respect for human dignity equal to the precepts of our Constitution? To understand why people behave the way they do, you need to understand the internal frame of reference that is the individual's subjective world. The changing world of experience is factual phenomena integrated with the perception of people. Perception is a complex process. Kast and Rosenzweig put it this way:

Perception, Cognition, Motivation

(1) The effect of various events on behavior depends on how they are perceived by the individual. Similarly, if behavior results after a period which allows thinking or problem solving, personal attitudes play an important part in fashioning the specific response. Value systems are affected significantly by total past experience and current situations.[14]

Influences on Behavior in a Work Environment

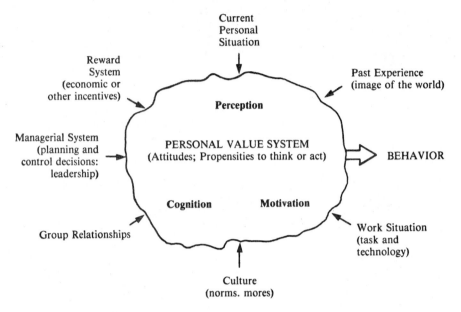

Source: Fremont E. Kast and James E. Rosenzweig, 2nd ed., *Organization and Management: A Systems Approach.* (New York: McGraw-Hill, 1974), p. 251.

Perception: Perception is the means by which stimuli affect an individual; through perception an individual selectively notices different aspects of the environment. Whether or not certain aspects of the environment are noticed depends on both the nature of the stimuli and the individual's previous experiences.

Cognition: Cognition involves the process of knowing, which includes perceiving or awareness, reasoning, and judgment or decision-making. The term implies a deliberate process of acquiring knowledge, and is associated with rationality. Like perception, cognition is affected by an individual's environment, needs and desires, and past experiences.

Motivation: Motivation is "what prompts a person to act in a certain way or at least develop a propensity for specific behavior. This urge to action can be touched off by an external stimulus, or it can be internally generated in individual thought processes."[15]

Some other versions of motivation are: Porter and Lawler's:[16] direction of behavior, effort, and perspective; Kurt Lewin's:[17] B = f (P,E): behavior is a function of (f) both person (P) and environment (E); and Martin Evans's,[18] Robert House's,[19] and Terrence Mitchell's:[20] Path-Goal; i.e., leader's effectiveness depends on leader's impact on performance, satisfaction, and clear goals for attainment regarding subordinates.

Sayles joins motivation with commitment in his discussion of leadership and suggests three components:

1. The potential payoff perceived by subordinates for improved performance;
2. The degree of acceptance and security perceived by subordinates;
3. The effective "management" of interaction patterns.

Sayles continues in the discussion and addresses the theory of motivation by stating,

> There are many links in the chain and, for employees to be motivated, they must all appear credible. The leaders must do more than offer a reward for a job well done. The links of the extended chain must be satisfied. Employees must believe:
>
> 1. They have the capacity (based on past experience and self-confidence) to improve performance,
> 2. The improved performance will not be excessively costly in terms of energy, friendships, or other personal sacrifices including future obligations and commitments (i.e., what will be expected "next time 'round"),
> 3. This improved performance will result in demonstrably good "results," i.e., something others can measure, assess, or perceive — some significant difference from the situation before,
> 4. The result will be appraised as commendatory, as a positive contribution,
> 5. The result will be rewarded,
> 6 The reward will be perceived as equitable by the subordinate.[21]

Meaning of Equity

Equity has its own body of theory, which is a distraction for us here. But, for the sake of explanation, it is worth noting that one of the most-used conceptions of perception of equity is as follows:

Subordinates view rewards as equitable when:

$$\frac{\textit{Rewards received by them}}{\text{Their inputs (effort, previous training, skill level, personal characteristics)}} = \frac{\textit{rewards received by others}}{\text{others' inputs}}$$

Thus, the more experience and status the individuals have, the greater must be their perceived reward to be considered equitable. Equity is always relative, not an absolute—rewards are compared with what relevant others are receiving.[22]

Employees at all levels from vice-president (Chief, Deputy-Chief) on down want a considerate, understanding, and appreciative boss.[23] In developing the conceptual skills necessary to be an effective patrol leader, it is necessary to view the agency from your present position and know how your decisions affect others. In addition, you cannot become angry because your supervisor acts like a dictator if you turn around and act the same way to your subordinates. If a certain behavior does not motivate you, then you must be sensitive to your own behavior and ask yourself if it does not motivate your subordinates.

The Carlson Model

Carlson, a Harvard social psychologist, after reviewing a host of studies of social relationships, concluded that there are primarily two basic dimensions to all human intercourse. That is, most things we say or do to each other can be located in one of four quadrants created by these two dimensions:

1. Dominance—Submissiveness
2. Affection—Hostility

Thus nearly all give-and-take between people reduces itself to some combination of these two basic dimensions.[24]

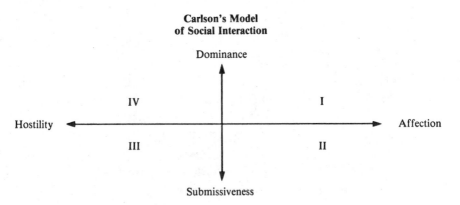

Carlson's Model
of Social Interaction

Using Carlson's model (and referring to the diagram), it would be reasonable to predict the following subordinate reactions, given the range of supervisory behavior described:

Quadrant	Leaders' Actions	Subordinates' Reactions
I	1. Dominance (modest support, but no trace of hostility)	Respect and trust
	2. Substantial supportiveness	Affection
II	3. Supportiveness and some dependence	Helpfulness
	4. Submissiveness	Arrogance
III	5. Distrust	Wariness, rejection
	6. Punishment	Wariness, rejection
IV	7. Aggressiveness; over hostility	Fear and resistance
	8. Boastfulness, exploitation; usually great awareness of status	Inferiority, distrust

Clearly leaders are risking the wholesomeness and the stability of the relationship when they move out of Quadrant I. To be sure, in Quadrant II there may be a subordinate reaction of helpfulness, in response to the dependency expressed by the supervisors, but this can easily shift to arrogance should the supervisors appear too dependent, too submissive. Quadrants III and IV provoke fear and hostility, an abiding sense of insecurity. (Those impressed with transaction analysis may note the similarity between Quadrant I and the adult role; Quadrants II and III and the happy and angry child, respectively; and Quadrant IV and the severe parent.)[25]

Nothing motivates me more than for someone to say to me, "What do you think?"

In conclusion, James Owens offers a list for managers to use in enhancing motivation of officers.

1. Provide clear, specific, and reasonable job goals.
2. Explain the reasons for, and the importance of, every job and assignment.
3. Provide the opportunity for people to discuss and participate in plans and decisions affecting them.
4. Encourage a friendly, social group atmosphere.
5. Help people develop a high degree of personal and professional pride in their work.
6. Find ways to enlarge and enrich jobs so that the work is more interesting to employees.

7. Rotate jobs and change assignments in order to relieve boredom.
8 Praise people for work well done.
9. Demonstrate sincere personal interest in, and respect for, the group.
10. Provide opportunities for training and career growth.
11. Provide special assignments to challenge workers, help them grow, and make their jobs more interesting.[26]

COMMUNICATION AND DELEGATION

It may seem strange at first to combine the abilities to communicate and to delegate as one topic for discussion. However, real delegation must be communicated in a real way. Believing you possess responsibility and authority is different from truly possessing responsibility and authority. What is intended to be communicated may in fact not be what is communicated. For example, let's take this remark: "I give you the responsibility and authority to accomplish the mission." If the person (delegate) to whom this was said (1) does not have specific duties assigned, (2) must clear all actions with the supervisor, (3) cannot use resources as seen fit to accomplish the mission, and (4) cannot make commitments on the part of the organization, then the communication is ineffective and meaningless. Without communication there can be no leaders in law enforcement. Without delegation, maximum efficiency and economy will not be accomplished by the organization.

Communication

The term *communication* comes from the Latin word *"communis"* or common. In essence, when people communicate they are attempting to share a commonness with another party or group, to share information, or an attitude.[27]

Briefly defined, communication is the art of transmitting information from one person to another. People who speak to each other do not always communicate in the strict sense of the term, nor do they always convey the intended message, even when the listener is attentive. For a variety of reasons, messages are sent and not received, or they are sent and misunderstood.

It is important that every citizen be capable of communicating properly; the art of communication is so critical to policemen that their whole professional world depends on it. Police officers are, first and foremost, communicators.[28]

Communication has to transfer ideas, and at the same time insure an understanding on the part of the recipient that results in feedback from the recipient to the sender. Because of the volume of people in their command, patrol administrators must possess the ability to communicate well. Objectives of the organization must reach the patrol officer in language understood, and the feedback from patrol officers must reach the patrol administrator. In between there are levels of command and supervision that have the potential to interfere with the downward and upward communication. Horizontal communication is emphasized in organizational relationships. For true feedback, the distortion must be minimized or eliminated completely.

Three things are important to the communicator: (1) What do I intend to communicate? (2) How am I going to communicate? and (3) To whom am I communicating? Communicating is a management activity. It is a process by which a manager takes action, and it is a basic police management problem. There are many forms of communication: talking, writing, sound, signal, gesture, time, color, and space, the latter being the silent language. There is a saying in police organization concerning those who talk about accomplishing the mission and those who accomplish it; i.e., "Action speaks louder than words." One of the first things a patrol leader learns about handling riots and demonstrations is never to bluff. If a particular course of action is stated, he must be able to carry it out or he will lose face (which in this case can mean the same as losing the ability to communicate, because there is a loss of credibility).

These actions could be called the language of behavior. If a sergeant says to a patrol officer in a gruff voice, "Don't bother me now," he more than likely will not be bothered at all, now or in the future. This turn-off could easily be avoided by the sergeant if he maintained an awareness about his ability to communicate.

As a part of leadership, the patrol commander takes time to know his officers. Included in the knowledge is the fact that each has to be communicated to in a different way. For example, some officers enjoy nicknames but others become indignant at their use.

The use of positive or negative approaches must be comprehended by the leader. Behavior (gesture communication) can be the same, but at two different times and two different locations, the message is different. If the lieutenant at roll call criticizes the actions of an officer, he or she may be doing so as an example to the others. However, to the one being criticized, the example has lost all meaning, and the embarrassment has become the message. Therefore, the lieutenant should communicate privately.

The story is told about an American scholar who was sent to Japan to teach American history to Japanese university professors. He had taught the course for some time, but since he did not speak Japanese, he wasn't sure whether they understood his lectures. He therefore asked for an interpreter. The interpreter advised him that the class was only understanding 50 percent of what was going on. The American was discouraged and upset, but what he didn't know was that he had inadvertently insulted the group by requesting an interpreter. In Japan a sign of an educated person is the ability to speak English. The Japanese professors felt that the American had caused them to lose face, because he had implied that they were uneducated when he requested the interpreter. The delegation of questioning to the interpreter in order to determine effective communication was improper. Communication was not successful.

The patrol commander must learn how to act, must know when to communicate personally and when in writing, and must develop a sensitivity to the timing of his or her communications. Timing can affect the whole communication process.

The author has been a member of oral boards for promotion in various places around the country. One aspect of communication has been pointed out as common to each of these experiences. All candidates view the length of the oral test as having a bearing on how well they did in this stage of the promotional process.

Americans working for companies in foreign countries must learn a new meaning of time when dealing with officials of these countries. When asked to wait five, ten, thirty, or even forty-five minutes to keep an appointment, the Americans become insulted, not realizing that the wait is really just the beginning of the process. In Latin America, for example, business and pleasure are combined and some people take an hour to do what Americans would do in five minutes.

There are four components of the communication process: (1) the originator of the message, the person who begins the process of communicating; (2) the message (gestures, pictures, words, etc.); (3) the person to whom the message is directed (sometimes called the decoder, since it is that person who must decode the message to be able to understand it); (4) the response to the message, or the action taken by the recipient of the message after decoding. If these four are properly related, the result is good communication.

There are various formal and informal organizations within any large organization. Among these are the formal and the informal communication systems. In police agencies the informal system of communication, or grapevine, must be recognized so that it can be used for the benefit of the department. The patrol administrator can have a tremendous effect on the informal communication system if he or she approaches the question properly. In a department that has roll-call training, the second week on a topic is usually used as time for discussion. If the patrol administrator reviews the topic and thinks about a relationship between the topic and a current item of interest in the department, he can make a roll-call into a real "rap session" between himself and all subordinates. The patrol administrator must be aware of the fact that all personnel can recognize sincerity. Additionally, all items of interest discussed at these formal/informal sessions will be considered important. Follow-up on the part of the patrol leader is vital to the success of this type of approach to the informal communication network.

The police leader should (1) recognize that an informal communication system exists in the department; (2) understand that it exists because all members of the department want to know what is going on and feel important if they can expand upon information to their peers, thus projecting an image of "I'm in the know"; (3) develop credibility that will insure factual feedback; (4) identify personnel and methods for joining the communication system or cooperating in an effort to make communications effective.

If the patrol administrator wishes to act as a change agent, he or she can use his or her ability to communicate at the informal session. For example, the chief would like to attempt a change in procedure for the department and wants to get a feeling for acceptance. The patrol administrator can use the roll-call session as a sounding board to get feedback for the potential procedure. The project may be presented in a formal way, but an informal approach is used for effective communication.

There is a need to communicate by whatever means is most effective at the time. The patrol administrator must communicate in an authoritative manner for one situation; in a democratic or laissez-faire manner in another; and, in the third way, allowing for freer uninhibited expression, in still another. He or she must have his finger on the pulse of the situation with regard to each situation to be effective.

The formal communication system of the department consists of general orders, special orders, directives, memoranda, reports, rules and regulations, and standard operating procedures. This system is necessary, especially in the larger police departments. The patrol commander must decide for himself when the formal, formal/informal, or informal system is the proper approach to communicate. A good sense of organization and understanding the goals of a good written directive system will help alleviate the bureaucratic red tape that prevents many organizations from moving forward. The salvation of police organizations will be the effectiveness of horizontal coordination, cooperation, and communication between the leaders of detectives, patrol, traffic, records, training, and communication. Formal communication should be reviewed and evaluated to insure that it succeeds in its primary purpose, the dissemination of information. Formal communication should not inhibit free thought. Many chiefs complain about hallway conferences, especially when they take place after a formal conference. At this point the leader should review the manner in which communication is taking place.

Another way of evaluating effective communication is through feedback. The communicator should observe and inspect the recipients' oral behavior and actions. The delegation of responsibility and authority also carries with it accountability, so the patrol commander must communicate, delegate, and follow up for accountability and evaluation of the communication process. This evaluation determines his or her ability as the initiator of the communication as well as whether or not the message was received as intended. Tone of voice and facial expression can completely change the meaning of a message. Thus, the acceptance of the delegation is influenced by these factors.

Most people cannot learn anything while talking. To learn one must be able to listen effectively. A police leader should learn to be a good listener. Effective listening is necessary for the leader-subordinate relationship because it embodies respect. Some call it empathy. Whatever the word, the point is that each person wants to be heard and have his or her viewpoints considered. To identify with the other person increases one's understanding of what the other person is trying to say. Police leaders should remember that they were once patrol officers.

Rank also has a great impact on the validity of statements in police work. In most cases, the message given by a captain will be accepted more by patrol officers than one by a sergeant (if not, the captain is in trouble). The same credibility is attributed to the "expert" from the outside who may come into the department as a consultant. Personnel will listen more to what this expert says than to a person within the department, even though the qualifications and credentials may be exactly the same. Thus, there is all the more reason for the patrol administrator to be a good listener and attain the credibility necessary to be an effective leader.

The following sayings, heard for many years in police organizations, are just as valid today: (1) Don't assume your men know, tell them; (2) Don't assume you know how your men feel, ask them; (3) Don't assume your men understand, clarify for them; (4) Insure feedback by acting out the two-way communication principle.

Effective listening. The ability to listen is a basic communication skill. It involves self-discipline and a willingness to put oneself in the other person's place. So many times managers are so involved with issuing orders about situations that they do not consider the human aspect of listening. Talking *at* someone does not consider the feelings of the individual, and usually no real listening takes place. Each of us has certain values, attitudes, and beliefs that can be challenged by the other person. If the communication leads to negative interaction, emotional reaction takes over, resulting in ineffective communication. A good approach for all police managers to use is the questioning technique. If you can really listen, you can insure effective receipt of a message by asking: What do you mean by that statement? Is this the critical point you have been trying to put across? Have you satisfactorily defined the problem? What is the objective you are trying to achieve? Many times the most interesting people are those who are good listeners.

Barriers to effective communication. Two factors that complicate the process even more are the sender's skill as a communicator and the receiver's ability to translate the message. Intelligence is not the only consideration. Many apparently intelligent people have difficulty communicating with one another. Frequently difficulties stem from differences in training and experience. How many technical people, for example, have been able to convey adequately to a layperson what they do on the job? The frame of reference is simply too foreign for the nontechnically oriented person to understand, except in a very vague way.

Communication theorists also call our attention to the effects of "noise" and "filtering." Noise in this case means any distraction that tends to divert the receiver's attention from the message. This may be one's preoccupation with one's own thoughts at the moment, or the temporary distraction of an external stimulus. In either case, the message is blotted out or distorted by the interruption.

Filtering, as the word implies, is the technique of selective interpretation of the message according to the receiver's experience. This "experience

Figure 2.1 *The blocking of a message that occurs when sender and receiver are "mismatched"*

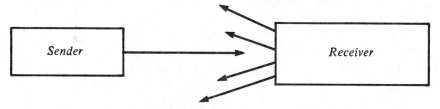

Causes of mismatch of sender and receiver

1. Lack of common background
2. Lack of interest
3. Serious difference in viewpoint
4. The "generation gap"

Figure 2.2 *Both noise and the receiver's unique-experience filter adversely affect communication*

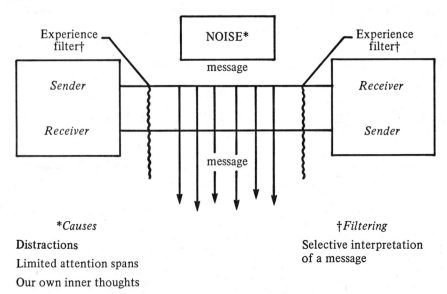

<table>
<tr><td>*Causes</td><td>†Filtering</td></tr>
</table>

*Causes	†Filtering
Distractions	Selective interpretation of a message
Limited attention spans	
Our own inner thoughts	

filter" is composed of prejudices, preconceptions, and the normal human tendency to make instant judgments about the significance of any message. Its influence on our ability to interpret a given message is obviously a complex product of what that message means to us personally; in short, how it affects our own well-being.

The experience filter subtly tunes our emotions in and prevents a purely rational interpretation of the message. Depending on our experience with the questioner and our state of mind on any given day, we can react in a variety of ways to the same question. For example, the boss's query, "When will you have that report finished?" can be accepted as a simple request for a time estimate or as unbearable harassment. There are at least half a dozen possible reactions, depending on the individual experiences of the two and on their relationship with each other.[29]

Today's patrol administrator cannot ignore factors that might cause intended messages to be distorted. The volume of critical situations alone demands accurate information. The department as a whole must inform its managers, who in turn must inform its middle management, to allow for discussion and dissemination of accurate feedback, explanation of decision (the why), and improved decision-making. If the chief of a police department signs a general order implementing a procedure, only to find out one week later that an employee organization is submitting a grievance because no one asked the people affected by the procedure what impact it would have (and the impact is quite negative), then the person(s) responsible for ineffective communication and insensitivity should be taken to task. The art of talking to each other is a basis for human dignity and mutual respect.

In conclusion, the following techniques should be used to achieve communications skills at the management level:

1. Focus on a person's behavior, not on the person himself or herself.
2. Focus on observations rather than on inferences.
3. Focus on specific situations rather than on abstractions.
4. Give feedback as soon after the event in question as possible.
5. Share information instead of giving advice.
6. Focus on alternatives rather than on the "right way."
7. Give only the amount of information the receiver can handle (people normally can handle 7 ± 2 bits of information). If these bits are linked together, they are perceived as only *one* bit. Such linking makes it possible for the individual to handle more data.
8. Discuss *events* rather than *why* events happened (at least initially).
9. Focus on the present and future, not on the past.
10. Make communication a two-way process.
11. Establish a rapport; *both* manager and employee should be willing to listen and understand.
12. Let those involved know the purpose of the communication—in advance. This will give the receiver a chance to arrive with certain ideas to contribute and will lessen fear of "what may happen."
13. Use "I" language; take personal responsibility for the message.
14. Focus on a continuum of ideas (not "either/or" extremes); accept alternatives.
15. Focus on behavior and events that can be changed; avoid matters that neither manager nor employee can do anything about.
16. Ask the receiver to paraphrase the ideas you hope to have conveyed in your communication (to ensure that your message has been properly understood).[30]

Delegation

In today's police organization, it is impossible for a police chief to carry out personally all the responsibilities assigned to his department. In fact, the reason goals are stated and the organization exists is to help the chief fulfill his responsibilities. In order to do this properly, the chief must delegate, and he must communicate the delegation clearly and concisely. There must be real delegation, not merely a sense of delegation, and the chief should not be afraid to put it in writing, when practicable, and assign responsibility and accountability. The chief in effect is saying: (1) Here is the goal; (2) I am assigning you the responsibility to achieve that goal; (3) I am providing you the resources, manpower, and material to achieve the goal; (4) I am delegating you the authority to achieve that goal; and (5) I hold you accountable for achieving that goal. There is, of course, a limiting point when the chief must stop giving authority. Decisions concerning this limited authority should be well thought out in order to have complete understanding between the communicator and the listener.

When the chief gives the patrol administrator the message described above, he should then make sure that the patrol administrator is knowledgeable about delegation and knows how to use it. It is not easy to delegate properly. It takes strength, courage, foresight, and good leadership. A failure to delegate properly contributes to the total failure of the police department. The patrol administrator cannot be insecure or afraid, unwilling to admit limitations (this aspect has no bearing on ability to perform a task), so enthralled by his own importance that he feels the department depends only on him; or an individual who must have all the answers. When Franklin D. Roosevelt died and Harry S. Truman replaced him as president, there was some concern over President Truman's ability; yet President Truman made one of the most significant decisions of World War II.

The patrol administrator should follow the golden rule of administration: the primary responsibility is developing people. Leadership should be provided to insure the continuance of operations, even when the leader is not present. The team concept should prevail in all areas of the organization.

In the past it usually took months before new officers were recognized by veterans. In many cases information and good training were obtained by observation only. This is not a proper attitude and shows insecurity and lack of confidence. It is hoped that patrol administration of the present and future will provide an attitude of sharing all information and knowledge in order to provide improved service to the citizens of the community. In the case of the officer in the field, a more competent and informed officer will be of greater assistance in times of emergency than one who is less informed. Increased use of field training officers (given compensation) is recommended as a way of providing enlightened officers in volume. Recognition of the impact that veteran officers have on new officers is essential to the total well-being of the patrol force.

The patrol administrator needs courage to delegate, because of the danger of potential mistakes. An important part of delegation is to give direction and then monitor the subordinate in order to evaluate his or her ability to perform under stress. Commanders must be allowed to learn and develop and to benefit from their mistakes. The department as a whole will benefit in the long run. The patrol administrator should not be afraid to select a delegate, as long as the basis of selection is ability.

Delegating means sharing responsibility. The patrol administrator should be aware of the ability of the person to whom he is delegating so there is no great mismatch. Knowledge of the delegated task is important in order to make the match work. This knowledge enables the delegator to delegate all or only part of the task according to the individual. The patrol administrator should neither try to do everything himself, nor delegate without following up. Without follow-up, the job may never be accomplished. If the whole task is delegated, then a clear, concise statement indicating this is in order. If part of the task is delegated, an equally concise statement should be communicated regarding what is and what is not delegated.

The patrol administrator must remember that he can delegate everything except ultimate responsibility; he is responsible for everything performed or not performed by the personnel who work for him. This statement places the principle of delegation in its proper perspective. Delegation will bring out strength, weakness, and character, not only in the one doing the delegating, but also in the selected delegate. Careful selection is necessary. Some subordinates do not want the responsibility and this should be considered.

In traditional terms, according to Louis Brownslow in a lecture given over thirty years ago, there are some things that cannot and should not be delegated, although advice and aid can be solicited.[31] Functions that cannot be totally shoved off to subordinates include: (1) the fiscal functions, (2) the personnel functions (measuring the people to be placed into command tasks), and (3) the planning function. The third function should, however, be done by all personnel at every level.

Authority is necessary for the delegate. Usually he or she will need the authority for planning, supervising, performing routine tasks, organizing in his or her area, coordinating, and delegating to subordinates.

To sum up regarding delegation:

1. Delegate to the most capable subordinate.
2. Delegate similar tasks and activities to one subordinate.
3. Support the delegate in the use of discretion regarding the authority he or she possesses.
4. Define clearly and concisely the limits of delegated authority.
5. Remember responsibility/authority/accountability.
6. Establish and define expected results.
7. Communicate to insure understanding of what is expected and what criteria will be used to evaluate the performance of the delegate.

According to William H. Newman and Charles E. Summer, Jr., in *The Process of Management*, there are three inescapable features of delegating. These are especially true for the contemporary patrol administrator involved in implementing management priorities that have been used by business. Every time a manager (police captain) delegates work to a subordinate (police lieutenant), he performs three actions:

(1) He assigns duties; that is, the man who is delegating indicates what work the subordinate must do. (2) He grants authority. Along with permission to proceed with the assigned work, he will probably transfer to the subordinate certain rights, such as the right to spend money, to divert the work of people, to use raw materials, to represent the company (department) to outsiders, or to take other steps necessary to fulfill the new duties. (3) He creates an obligation. In accepting an assignment, a subordinate takes on an obligation to his boss to complete the job.[32]

By recognizing that no delegation is complete without a clear understanding of duties, authority, and obligation, an administrator can often save himself a good deal of trouble. These attributes of delegation are like a three-legged stool: each depends on the other to support the whole, and no two can stand without the third. The understanding is communication. Patrol commanders should delegate authority, commensurate with responsibility, and then hold the delegate accountable.

DECISION-MAKING AND AUTHORITY

Decisions made by all levels of authority in police work should be made with the decision-maker knowing full well that the decision may be subjected to Monday-morning quarterbacking. For the patrol officer on the beat, it will be the courts reviewing, possibly for months, his or her decision to make an arrest. For the sergeant or lieutenant, it may be the press and specific segments of the community regarding a decision that resulted in personal injury to a citizen. For example, a patrol officer is assigned the task of executing a warrant on an individual for assault. The officer calls for assistance from his or her partner and begins the process. When the named individual finds out the police are at the door, he becomes excited and climbs the fire escape to the roof. Superiors are called to the scene and a decision has to be made. Should the arrest for assault be made under the existing conditions, or should the officer retreat and execute the warrant under less stressful conditions? Would the pressure of the arrest cause a loss of life? The supervisors are under the gun and can feel fairly sure their decision will receive critical review.

The captain or commanding officer and a command staff officer must decide on a recommendation for disciplinary action concerning a patrol officer. These command officers must realize that all decisions must be made for the betterment of the department. In reaching a decision, many facts must be analyzed. In most cases decisions must be based on the specific merits of the situation. Each level of authority must make decisions, and the knowledge of what it takes to make effective decisions is a tremendously important aspect of patrol administration.

Decision-making is the essence of management. Problem definition is the first step in effective decision-making. Decisiveness will be exercised according to the amount of authority possessed by the persons making the decision, timeliness of the situation, and the person(s) or group(s) affected. The numerous times a patrolman uses discretion—the use of judgment followed by a decision—have been recognized. In police agencies especially, there must be an acknowledgement of the decision-making authority granted to each area affected by the decisions. Then there can be clear policies concerning the amount of authority possessed by each in decision-making. If supervisors and administrators must delegate and in so doing relinquish authority to the delegates, it is imperative that agreement is reached and understood on how much authority has been granted. Additionally, American society must clearly define how much authority it wishes to give to respective police agencies.

These points are clearly identified in the report "Standards Relating to the Urban Police Function," prepared by the American Bar Association and published in the May 1973 issue of *The Police Chief.* The following excerpts from these standards are reported here because it is the patrol administrator, the patrol supervisor, and officers who implement policy and make the decisions relating to these standards. These standards should be reviewed and studied in depth by students of patrol administration. They relate directly to the use of manpower and other resources available to the patrol administrator in attaining the objective.

Because the patrol administrator is so intensely involved with the performance aspect of the police agency, he must know the consequences of his decision at each stage. Questions concerning how the decision will affect the community, government, criminal justice system, the department as an organization, his officers, and himself should be considered. To do this he must know the interrelationships between each person or group. It should be recognized that one's personal experience, morals, family, and values will affect his ability to make decisions. If things are "right" at home, it is more likely decisions will be made after clear thought and analysis of the situation. If things are not right at home, the personal complications are carried to work. Thus a patrol officer may take the wrong position when backing up a partner on a burglary or a robbery call. The sergeant assigns the wrong officer to a beat car and then becomes sarcastic when he or she questions the assignment. The lieutenant conducts a raid on a gambling operation and moves too fast or too slowly, resulting in the loss of the evidence. The patrol commander fails to communicate clearly,

STANDARDS RELATING TO THE URBAN POLICE FUNCTION, AMERICAN BAR ASSOCIATION

2.5 Role of the local chief executive. In general terms, the chief executive of a governmental subdivision should be recognized as having the ultimate responsibility for his police department and, in conjunction with his police administrator and the municipal legislative body, should formulate lawful policy relating to the nature of the police function, the objectives and priorities of the police in carrying out this function, and the relationship of these objectives and priorities to general municipal strategies. This will require that a chief executive, along with assuming new responsibilities for formulating overall directions for police services, must also:

1. insulate the police department from inappropriate pressures including such pressures from his own office;
2. insulate the police department from pressures to deal with matters in an unlawful or unconstitutional manner; and
3. insulate the police administrator from inappropriate interference with the internal administration of his department.

Part III. Methods and Authority Available to the Police for Fulfilling the Tasks Given Them

3.1 Alternative methods used by police. The process of investigation, arrest, and prosecution, commonly viewed as an end in itself, should be recognized as but one of the methods used by police in performing their overall function, even though it is the most important method of dealing with serious criminal activity. Among other methods police use are, for example, the process of informal resolution of conflict, referral, and warning. The alternative methods used by police should be recognized as important and warranting improvement in number and effectiveness; and the police should be given the necessary authority to use them under circumstances in which it is desirable to do so.

3.2 Avoiding overreliance upon the criminal law. The assumption that the use of an arrest and the criminal process is the primary or even the exclusive method available to police should be recognized as causing unnecessary distortion of both the criminal law and the system of criminal justice.

3.3 Need for clarified, properly limited authority to use methods other than the criminal justice system. There should be clarification of the authority of police to use methods other than arrest and prosecution to deal with the variety of behavioral and social problems which they confront. This should include careful consideration of the need for and problems created by providing police with recognized and properly limited authority and protection while operating thereunder:

1. to deal with interferences with the democratic process. Although it is assumed that police have a duty to protect free speech and the right of dissent, their authority to do so is unclear, particularly because of the questionable constitutionality of many statutes, such as the disorderly conduct statutes, upon which police have relied in the past.

2. to deal with self-destructive conduct such as that engaged in by persons who are helpless by reason of mental illness or persons who are incapacitated by alcohol or drugs. Such authority as exists is too often dependent upon criminal laws which commonly afford an inadequate basis to deal effectively and humanely with self-destructive behavior;

3. to engage in the resolution of conflict such as that which occurs so frequently between husband and wife or neighbor and neighbor in the highly populated sections of the large city, without reliance upon criminal assault or disorderly conduct statutes;

4. to take appropriate action to prevent disorder such as by ordering crowds to disperse where there is adequate reason to believe that such action is required to prevent disorder and to deal properly and effectively with disorder when it occurs; and

5. to require potential victims of crime to take preventive action such as by a legal requirement that building owners follow a burglary-prevention program similar to common fire-prevention programs.

3.4 Legislative concern for feasibility of criminal sanction.   Within the field of Criminal Justice Administration legislatures should, prior to defining conduct as criminal, carefully consider whether adequate authority and resources exist for police to enforce the prohibition by methods which the community is willing to tolerate and support. Criminal codes should be reevaluated to determine whether these are adequate ways of enforcing the prohibition. If not, noncriminal solutions to all or a portion of the problem should be considered.

Part IV. Law Enforcement Policy-Making

4.1 Exercise of discretion by police.   The nature of the responsibilities currently placed upon the police requires that the police exercise a great deal of discretion. This is a situation that has long existed, but is not always recognized.

4.2 Need for structure and control.   Since individual police officers may make important decisions affecting police operations without direction, with limited accountability, and without any uniformity within a department, police discretion should be structured and controlled.

4.3 Administrative rule-making.   Police discretion can best be structured and controlled through the process of administrative rule-making by police agencies. Police administrators should, therefore, give the highest priority to the formulation of administrative rules governing the exercise of discretion, particularly in the areas of selective enforcement, investigative techniques, and enforcement methods.

4.4 Contribution by legislatures and courts.   To stimulate the development of appropriate administrative guidance and control over police discretion, legislatures and courts should actively encourage police administrative rule-making.

  a. Legislatures can meet this need by delegating administrative rule-making responsibility to the police by statute.
  b. Courts can stimulate administrative development in several ways including the following.

  i.   Properly developed and published police-administrative policies should be sustained unless demonstrated to be unconstitutional, arbitrary, or otherwise outside the authority of the police;
  ii. To stimulate timely and adequate administrative policy-making, a determination by a court of a violation of an administrative policy should not be a basis for excluding evidence in a criminal case unless the violation of administrative policy is of constitutional dimensions or is otherwise so serious as to call for the exercise of the superintending authority of the court. A violation per se should not result in civil liability; and
  iii. Where it appears to the court that an individual officer has acted in violation of administrative policy or that an administrative policy is unconstitutional, arbitrary, or otherwise outside the authority of the police, the court should arrange for the police administrator to be informed of this fact, in order to facilitate fulfillment by the police administrator of his responsibility in such circumstances to reexamine the relevant policy or

policies and to review methods of training, communication of policy, and supervision and control.

4.5 Method of policy-making. In its development of procedures to openly formulate, implement, and reevaluate police policy as necessary, each jurisdiction should be conscious of the need to effectively consult a representative cross-section of citizens in this process.

Part V. Control over Police Authority

5.4 Need for accountability. Since a principal function of police is the safeguarding of democratic processes, if police fail to conform their conduct to the requirements of law, they subvert the democratic process and frustrate the achievement of a principal police function. It is for this reason that high priority must be given for ensuring that the police are made fully accountable to their police administrator and to the public for their actions.[33]

causing a misunderstanding of an order and an employee grievance. For effective decision-making, personal contentment is necessary.

Because most decisions cause change, especially internally, it is important for the patrol administrator to know his officers. For example, implementation of a manpower distribution plan on the 15th of the month as opposed to the 22nd (the date for change of shift) could result in rejection of the plan. When personnel are informed of pending decisions and feedback is obtained, timing becomes an asset for the patrol commander. The officers of the unit are more likely to accept the decisions if they are involved. They also will agree to the reporting of information necessary to evaluate the decision.

The management by objectives approach for patrol administration can only be accomplished when periodic evaluation of the goal is performed. If the approach taken to implement the program is found to need modification because the patrol commander made an error in judgment, then admitting the error, explaining the how and why of the error, and taking corrective action will result in respect for the commander. In this way, responsibility for decisions, right or wrong, is demonstrated. The example will do more in helping the patrol commander gain support for implementing the program than a hundred pages of explanation on why the department needs the change. Knowledge of his officers—knowledge that they will make mistakes and need help in correcting their judgments—gives the commander the empathy necessary to lead.

Knowledge by the officers that the patrol commander does not make decisions sitting in an ivory tower, that he does make mistakes, does take corrective action, is willing to change, does go to the core of the problem to obtain facts, and is willing to listen with objectivity to suggestions made by the people affected helps identify him as a leader. With this attitude, decision-making and authority will settle at the right level, just as water seeks its own level. Decisions that should be made by patrol officers should not be made by sergeants, and decisions that should be made by lieutenants should not have to be made by captains. The management by objectives approach for the patrol administrator should result in improved decision-making at all levels. Knowledge of the personnel will keep him or her keenly aware of the appropriate level of decision-making authority in order to maintain a proper balance.

Decisions affecting the department are discussed in more detail in Chapter 4, "Organization for Patrol." The patrol administrator must have knowledge of the other units within the department, because his decisions have a domino effect. The action taken by the patrol unit will result in movement by communication, records, criminal investigator, fiscal, and so forth. Therefore, the consequences of the decisions should be anticipated. What may appear to be a good decision for patrol today may result in disaster for planning and research tomorrow.

Criminal Justice System

In demonstrations of riots or any other situations when large groups of people gather, the patrol commander is usually in charge. Decisions made under these circumstances affect other facets of the criminal justice system, especially if they involve arrests. The patrol administrator must have knowledge of the system, its abilities, liabilities, and capabilities. The courts, prosecutors, and parole, probation, and correction aspects directly concern the police. Whatever impact his plan has on these partners should be considered, and effective communication should be developed between the components of the system.

Government

The patrol administrator should be aware of politics, internal pressures, special interest groups, political organizations, and the overall impact of these on the police department. Exposure to the political scene and a study of federal, state, and local government are necessary to make effective decisions. The political questions of conservative vs. liberal, radicalism, new left, extreme right, etc., must be placed in proper context in order to make effective decisions relative to each. The police commander should know the confines of each elected official. Committee assignments and voting blocs should be documented. Government votes on operating budgets, and government is made up of individuals. The patrol administrator's decisions that affect these individuals are very important, requiring excellent judgment.

The Community

Of all the influences that affect the decision-making of the patrol administrator, none should be more important than the influence of the citizen served. The police commander must learn to develop the sensitivity necessary to act before the fact in all areas where public interest is concerned. In order to do this, feedback from all aspects of the community must be considered: business community, schools, churches, community organizations, charitable organizations, elected officials (who have a direct line to their constituents), and the press. The enlightened patrol administrator will be aware of the many ways to ascertain information that are helpful in making decisions affecting the community. The authority vested in him by the community willingly for democratic government should be guarded well.

Western philosophy on problem solving is that one must act or do something in order to solve problems. A decision must be made to do something: don't just stand there, do something. However, the Oriental philosophy, which is directly opposite to this, says that sometimes the best decision is to do nothing and in time the problem will solve itself. When used selectively, this philosophy can be most effective. One danger should be considered. If the decision is made to do nothing concerning a problem, this decision should be communicated to the officers so that the accusation of indecision is negated. The decision to do nothing is a decision in itself and should be conveyed to all concerned as a decision.

No man is an island: the patrol administrator must be aware of all influences when making a decision. The more knowledgeable he is about the aforementioned forces, the more effective his decision. If the patrol administrator considers a proper definition of the problem, gathers and analyzes the facts, and considers solutions, alternative solutions, and consequences to each objectively, the right decision is more likely to be selected. Patrol administrators should realize the need to work as long and as hard as necessary to implement the programs. Only after evaluation and reaffirmation of the goals can a rest be taken, and then only long enough to catch a breath.

LEADERS AS TRAINERS

The leader who realizes responsibility to subordinates in the area of training is in effect actively participating with the police chief in the primary mission of the administration, developing people. One of the many by-products of career development upon promotion is that the newly promoted supervisor will relate his or her previous area of expertise to the new area of responsibility, and will enlighten the present subordinates to improve their overall ability.

Many times a patrol officer does not take action in a particular situation because he or she fears making a mistake. The young patrol officer may also be afraid to call the supervisor for help because the response may be, "Don't they teach you anything at the academy?" Although change is upon us, and our education and training centers have improved police training tremendously, the young patrol officer is at first still apprehensive. If training is good in the beginning and confidence is built by the repetition of doing, the officer begins his or her career in a much better position.

There is a need to continue training of officers in the field. One method is roll-call training. Second is the personal training given by the individual supervisor. Third is formal in-service training. In some areas, the training program uses the matrix system in that line commanders conduct portions (leadership and supervision) of the in-service program. If the leader of the line operation teaches it, he must practice what he preaches.

In most departments today some type of roll-call training is conducted. The International Association of Chiefs of Police has over two hundred topics available for use at roll-call training. In the majority of cases, one officer or supervisor attending the roll-call training session has been involved, in an in-depth capacity, in the area being discussed. The order implementing the roll-call training program should include the following:

> All persons responsible for conducting the roll-call training program shall be especially aware of personnel possessing expertise in the area being discussed. These individuals should be used whenever their talents will enhance the presentation of information and knowledge.

The second part of the training mentioned is the one-to-one relationship between leaders and their subordinates. The leader must keep in mind his responsibility to point out the individual officer's respective areas of improvement as well as to feed back to the administrator information necessary to formulate in-service training for the department as a whole. It is one thing to correct the individual deficiency of a particular officer and something quite different to pinpoint a training need for an entire department.

Figure 2.3 *Criminal Justice Center, Sam Houston State University, Huntsville, Texas*

A good example of a training program focus would be the importance of protecting the crime scene. Many times supervisors are more guilty than anyone else of curiosity, which may result in the destruction of good evidence at crime scenes. It is important to feed back this type of information to command and training personnel for inclusion in the in-service program.

Another area that underlines the importance of personnel training is the interaction of officers with citizens. Reviewing reports and statistics that may indicate a total review of personnel procedures relative to a need for in-service training is also necessary. Arrests, bodily harm during arrest, rock- and bottle-throwing incidents, damage to police vehicles and other police equipment, injured officers, insensitivity, and complaints should be analyzed by patrol administrators to glean information indicating topics to be included in total in-service training.

Vertical and horizontal communication are important in designing training programs. The patrol administrator should solicit information from all levels of authority on areas where training might improve the operation of the department. Any and all ideas on how the training shall be conducted (methods and personnel) are also valuable. Upon receipt of the information, communication between the patrol administrator and the director of education and training will help solidify a meaningful in-service training program. The immediate supervisor is better qualified to suggest training needs because of his close observation of officers' performances of a variety of tasks. Participation by all levels in selecting the topics will enhance the value of material presented at in-service training. If the in-service program is looked upon as a wheel, with all participants (patrol officers, sergeants, lieutenants, commanders, and staff) as the spokes, then a true team effort is procured and the total product is improved.

The Learning Process

In order to instruct anyone, it is necessary to understand the learning process. Experience has shown that the majority of line supervisors at every level have neglected the training aspect of leadership. This does not mean that no individual training has been given at all, but rather that this aspect of the leadership responsibility has been relegated to a low place on the list of responsibilities. It is possible that setting a good example has been viewed as fulfilling this particular need. In many cases this is sufficient, but reviewing the fundamentals is always good procedure. Again, the ability to communicate is valuable, as a part of the teaching and understanding of the learning process and its relationship to the student. The following definitions concerning learning and instruction are excerpted from *Techniques for Police Instruction*, by John C. Klotter, dean of the School of Police Administration, University of Louisville.[34]

Learning is defined as:

> ... the process of acquiring new knowledge, skills, techniques, and appreciation which will enable the individual to do something that he could not do before.[35]

If we analyze this definition, it becomes obvious that learning anything new is an active process. When the sergeant observes a patrol officer making an arrest and points out to the officer several points that may endanger his or her life if repeated in another arrest situation, the new knowledge, technique, and appreciation of this instruction are active.

Instruction is defined as:

> ... all of the instructor activities that contribute toward leading, guiding, directing, and controlling the thoughts and actions of the students as they learn.[36]

This definition is synonymous with advice given a newly promoted sergeant. "You are now a first-list supervisor and you are responsible for guiding, counseling, directing, and controlling your men. You're responsible for everything they do or do not do." The first-line supervisor must be keenly aware of the many ways he can influence his men in the instructor-student relationship. First, learn by doing; second, use the five senses as the tools of learning; third, explain and then demonstrate when possible; and fourth, let the student do it again to insure that the information the sergeant has tried to impart has been assimilated by the patrol officer.

Klotter describes the following types of learning:

Knowledge. Where the student is helped to understand and retain facts, procedures, principles, and information. If the primary objective of the instructor is to teach knowledge, the approach will be different than it would be if the primary purpose were to teach skills.

Skills. The act or a series of acts which are performed instinctively without the conscious effort of thinking. Skills are not truly learned until they become almost instinctive, and they will not become instinctive unless there is much practice. Some examples of skills that are taught in police training are: driving the vehicles, operating weapons, and self-defense.

Techniques. Techniques are a way of thinking and acting based upon knowledge and often upon skills as well. Techniques are developed by applying knowledge and skills and cannot be developed adequately until there has been much practice.

Appreciation. Usually defined in terms of attitudes, ideals, interests, habits, likes, and dislikes. Attitude usually determines the effectiveness of efforts.[37]

He also defines certain principles of learning:

Motivation. Since learning is an active process, the student must be motivated to learn for himself. The instructor must, therefore, create a desire to learn.

Purpose. Learning is much more rapid and effective when it is purposeful. An individual rapidly acquires skills, knowledge, techniques, and appreciation when these achievements are necessary in order to attain the realization of some purpose.

Adjustment. When the student learns either skills, knowledge, or techniques, he, to a certain extent, must make an adjustment.

Activity. This is simply learning by doing.

Association. The student associates new material with past learning. The instructor must be careful in communicating with students so the interpretation of the message is correct.

Realism. Is the material presented realistic from the standpoint of application? Is the material functional? Is the material realistic as far as the level of the student is concerned?

Incidental Learning.   Incidental learning refers to the learning which occurs while the learner is doing something else. Such things as habits, attitudes, and character tactics are learned almost exclusively through this process of incidental learning. In some instances these outcomes are most important or as important as the information and skills being taught. These habits, interests, attitudes, and appreciations may be either favorable or unfavorable, depending upon the instructor. Often the student develops the same attitude toward a subject as that exhibited by the supervisor. Therefore, if the instructor takes a lackadaisical attitude toward the instruction, there is little chance that the student will consider it seriously. On the other hand, if the instructor demonstrates sincerity and enthusiasm the men will feel the same way toward the material being presented. There is no better way to develop appreciation than by example. When we consider that much of our learning is through this process, it is impossible to place too much stress on this principle of learning. The instructor teaches "the whole student, not just the subject matter."[38]

A good leader will keep in mind these basics as well as his specific role as a trainer. In the management by objectives approach, his goals will be the achievement in his men and women of motivation, proper attitudes, and good habits. A valid goal for the supervisor would be to have his officers feel, "I know where our patrol leader is going and I'll follow him."

DISCIPLINE, A MANAGEMENT RESOURCE

Discipline is a function of command. It is a resource of management the good leader can use as a way to attain his objectives. Discipline can be used in a positive way so that the patrol leader and his officers develop and achieve goals together. One definition of discipline is that it is training or experience that corrects, molds, strengthens, or perfects. Such discipline allows for a professionally oriented superior police agency.

Bernard Baruch once said that "our freedom is the freedom of self-discipline." Self-control or self-restraint to the patrol administrator should equal power. Power means the ability to influence people, and one of the best ways to influence people is through the example of self-discipline. The patrol administrator who presents an attitude of cooperation and helpfulness to his officers so that they can improve and be promoted through positive discipline decreases the need for negative discipline. Negative discipline is necessary; police departments must have certain operating rules and regulations. But if the patrol commander exerts enough self-discipline to motivate the individuals working for him to exhibit their own self-discipline, he can develop officers who want to follow the rules, do the right thing, and earn more freedom. These officers will need less control and supervision, and the atmosphere will be one of positive discipline.

No one wants to be the bad guy, and one way to avoid it is to create positive discipline. However, realistically speaking, there will be times when negative discipline must be applied. At such times, basic ingredients of leadership, firmness, and fairness must be exhibited to overcome the unpleasant aspects of these situations. The patrol administrator, when meting out this type of discipline, should always be sensitive to the overall consequences of the decision. In today's complex field of police personnel management, the patrol leader cannot make decisions concerning discipline in a vacuum. With potential employee organizations, court trials, and injunctions facing each decision, the patrol leader should concentrate on making the decision in a fair and ethical manner, considering all alternatives. When conflict is involved, the decision must be made for the overall best interests of the department. Decisions made yesterday concerning a given matter may not be the same today regarding the same matter because of our changing society.

Documentation

Documentation regarding discipline is related to performance evaluation in that any significant information, both positive and negative, must be included. It is virtually impossible to commit to memory all incidents concerning each man or woman. It is also difficult to be objective and unemotional at all times. Written documents are subject to inspection and therefore create a feeling of fairness. When documentation is done in a professional manner, the department and the individual benefit. It is a sad state of affairs when a patrol officer attempting to obtain a promotion is knocked down in the efficiency category for poor performance when he or she was never told by the sergeant about his or her weakness and the steps available for improvement.

Many departments today use the daily activity form for compiling information concerning work performance. Patrol officers are required to account for their time during a tour of duty. Additionally, sector sergeants and watch commanders can use the activity reports to provide information concerning supervisory performance and productivity. If at all possible, one activity report should be used throughout the operating forces wherever an officer is assigned (patrol, traffic, detectives, etc.). Review of the activity reports by the immediate supervisor is proper.

Following are some activities that should be included in the activity report. The information suggested is not all inclusive and would necessarily be modified depending on the size of the department, resources available, and its specific needs.

Name of officer(s)	Calls for service
Vehicle number	Inspection:
Day, month, year	Security
Watch, sector, beat	Building
Odometer reading:	Field interviews
Start	Foot patrol
Finish	Accidents investigated
Total miles	Hazardous moving violations:
Vehicle condition:	Number issued
Start	Felony arrests
Finish	Misdemeanor arrests
Equipment condition:	Narcotic arrests
Start	Follow-up investigations
Finish	Unavailable for service (court)

Supervisor Information:
Field reports reviewed
Preliminary investigations observed
Case preparation supervised
Administrative duties
Personal contacts

To be meaningful, the information for activity reports must be compiled, key-punched, and entered into a computer. The information concerning each patrol officer can be provided to the sergeant in printout form on a monthly basis. This information will point out trends, indicate areas of performance that need a close inspection by the supervisor, and produce periodic summaries of significant activity accomplishment for supervisory and command review. After the supervisor reviews the report, comments concerning the officer's performance, good and bad alike, can be written on the activity report for later retrieval. These comments, if transferred into computer language, can be forwarded to the officer's supervisor along with information concerning the activity.

With this type of documentation the supervisor can provide both the leadership discipline and the correction discipline necessary for which he is responsible. Additionally, the printout will help the supervisor make recommendations regarding the training needs, work assignment, and career development and promotional potential of each individual. Most of all, this documentation causes supervision to communicate up, down, and laterally. The activity report is a good way to teach all personnel the value of documentation. As a patrol officer is promoted to sergeant, or lieutenant, he or she observes the use of documentation by his or her supervisor; this effective method is highlighted all through the officer's career.

Each level of patrol authority should possess some method of documentation on a consistent, continuing basis. Middle management has the activity reports for specific performance identification, and command has the use of the log that places emphasis on due dates and inspection. A supervisor has a responsibility to each officer to indicate objectively how and when the officer can improve performance. Some form of documentation used in each police department will enhance the potential for using positive discipline.

Using Discipline

Patrol leaders who use positive discipline make it easier for everyone. This kind of attitude and the proper documentation will result in negative discipline being used sparingly, but effectively. Officers usually will not care as much if the supervisor does not believe in the goals of the department. Some police officials say, "You show me a sloppy, careless patrolman and I'll show you an uncaring sergeant." Experience has shown that no one wants to be a nonentity. If a man is made to feel that he doesn't belong, he will perform accordingly. Therefore, a supervisor must let his officers know that he is concerned with each one. It is most important for each supervisor to provide the necessary discipline, to maintain momentum along the road toward attaining the objective, and also to bring back into the fold anyone who strays. When officers do stray, they need to know that a supervisor is sure to be there, and just as sure, some form of corrective action will take place. The supervisor must know the individual officer and determine the best approach to take to bring about improved performance in the future.

Step one. In most cases, the first step for a supervisor in patrol to take in order to attain this improved performance is the consultation. The supervisor should talk pleasantly to the officer, attempting to find out why he or she is not performing adequately. After determining why, the supervisor should offer ways in which the officer might adjust his or her attitude or work routine to improve the patrol effort. Counseling the officer on how to identify potential police hazards and suggested response to these anticipated problems could be one area of concern. Relating the environment to a crime problem and teaching the officer how to react to each situation on his beat could be another. If the proper attitude and approach are taken by the supervisor so that the sincerity of his caring is projected, it is more than likely that this guidance and counseling will be sufficient to correct any deficiency the patrol officer may have.

In reality, a police patrol officer is the epitome of individualism the majority of the time. Only when he becomes a part of a squad during demonstrations or civil disorders does he give up this tremendous responsibility for discretionary judgment. Even the most active patrol sergeant will observe his patrol officers only during part of their tours of duty. Furthermore, as mentioned in the discussion of delegation, the sergeant must allow patrol officers to use discretion to improve their ability to make decisions even though mistakes will occur. In addition, patrol officers are involved with unsavory characters on a daily basis, and this increases temptation and opportunity for neglecting their duty. However, officers are in public view almost constantly where their activities are observed by the community. The expectation of the citizens of the community that police officers be above reproach cannot be denied. All of these factors point out the need for supervision to guide and counsel the patrol officers regularly in order to maintain performance standards.

Step two.   The second step of discipline, which is usually a formalization of the first, is for the supervisor to talk to the officer in a more formal atmosphere and simply "tell it like it is." The officer should be told what she or he is and isn't doing. The sergeant or supervisor should remain calm so the officer will listen not to the supervisor's emotion, but to the message. The supervisor should think about how he is going to communicate in this setting so he does not become the catalyst that results in the officer's becoming more deficient, requiring further negative discipline. This critical analysis of the officer's performance should be all business and should conclude with an explanation of any possible consequences of the inadequate behavior. After the officer is dismissed from the interview, the supervisor should document the proceeding.

Such an explanation amounts to a warning. The supervisor clearly states his refusal to accept careless, below-standard police performance. Officers should be told of impending line inspections in the area of deficiency on an irregular basis. The inspection should be overt. After the inspection the supervisor should contact the patrol officer and let him know where he stands—if he is making progress. At the first sign of "no progress" the supervisor should enter the next stage.

Step three.   The third step should be formal documentation. At this point, guidance, counseling, and warning have not sufficed. Again the officer should be interviewed and the positive and negative aspects of his work performance evaluated objectively. At the end of this meeting, the supervisor should hand the officer a letter addressed to the personnel officer via the chain of command. The letter summarizes the action taken by the supervisor from the beginning and should also contain the results of action to be taken if the deficiency continues. Everything at this point is formal and is entered into the personnel file of the officer.

Step four. The last step is the actual recommendation of punishment. Each department varies according to the organizational form and the amount of authority relative to discipline vested in the sergeants, lieutenants, captains, etc. It should be recognized that certain individuals will respond only to proactive disciplinary action. Whatever the action, dismissal (this is usually the prerogative of the chief), suspension, loss of days off, or loss of vacation days, the punishment should fit the crime. How great was the deficiency? Was the deficient action willful or an honest mistake? Was the act due to laziness or sloppiness? How long has the offender been in service? What is his past record? Is there a reason for the action? Actually, by this point the supervisor has gone to extreme lengths to determine the why of the performance. For example, there are times when an officer just doesn't have it, and the kind thing to do, after all levels and a variety of supervisors have tried to effect improvement, is to dismiss the man from the force. These situations involve a waste of time of many good men and women, but keeping the individual on the force wastes his or her time and prevents another more qualified person from entering the force.

The Leader and Discipline

The good leader must determine when and what type of leadership he or she will use in a given situation. In the case of planning, there is room for participatory management. The same theory applies to discipline. The good leader will use the complete range of discipline at the right time, the right place, and for the particular individual, taking all information into consideration. The good leader in patrol will not pass the buck ("Lieutenant, I brought this man to you because . . . .") or be afraid to use any type of discipline necessary. Nor will the good leader be insecure regarding his authority so that he becomes the obnoxious, unbearable supervisor who penalizes someone for any and all infractions. The effective leader will use the leadership or positive discipline in such a way that negative discipline will be needed only sparingly. However, everyone should be made aware of the certainty of discipline where appropriate. This is similar to the traditional deterrence of crime: the swiftness and sureness of arrest, conviction, and corrective action. The ineffective use of discipline in a police department, especially in patrol, will cause a complete breakdown in morale, indicating failure of the patrol commander to maintain internal esprit de corps.

In attempting to have the punishment fit the crime, it is important to look at the character of the offense as opposed to the results of the error. This character of the offense should also be included in the deficiencies when no bad results occur. This points up the theory of placing limited authority to discipline in the hands of the first-line supervisor. When a police department is organized in a manner where the first-line supervisor has the authority to grant vacation, extra days off, holidays, and disciplinary actions within certain guidelines, it has the ability to be an effective department. It is the sergeant who spends most time with the level of execution who in turn really achieves the objectives. The men should look to the sergeant for direction in striving to perform in an excellent manner. When the sergeant has the power to influence, he has true power, and with the proper usage he will mold and motivate his officers to achieve the goal. When a sergeant has to seek approval for his every move relative to these factors, he has no real authority or powers, and therefore his ability to influence is decreased. Consequently, his ability to produce is decreased. The sergeant having a true position becomes the key supervisor. Many departments organized in this way have moved forward in effective policing in today's society.

Action becomes necessary as soon as possible after the deficiency occurs. Discipline at the time of the offense achieves more than later correction of the deficiency. Correct timing is necessary to make discipline effective. Discipline must be firm, fair, consistent, and uniform. Although each man should be judged individually, there must not be radical differences in punishment throughout the department for similar offenses.

As confidence in a law enforcement agency increases, so will the reports of complaints by citizens concerning police action. Some of the complaints will be substantiated and result in disciplinary action; others will be unfounded or false. In either case, the police must welcome the complaints and provide a vehicle for resolution of the complaints. This should be initiated by the department. An image of openness and willingness to rid the department of undesirables will result, in the long run, in a better department. However, discipline should be meted out to an officer found guilty of an infraction (discourtesy, neglect, etc.) on the basis not of results or the importance of the person who made the complaints, but of the character of the infraction. The men of the department must be able to realize that the investigators of the complaints and decisions made from these investigations will be fair, impartial, and objective and will not tolerate false accusations without action being taken against those persons responsible. This can be done only where law permits.

Everyone likes to be recognized and given a pat on the back when something worthwhile is accomplished. The use of the commendation is good positive discipline. The use of praise for an individual in public should be saved for those performances that are truly outstanding. The use of praise too often reduces its effectiveness, but in private, if a man or woman earns it, the supervisor should praise accordingly.

The patrol leader disciplines himself first and then motivates others to do the same. The patrol administrator's decisions should be based not on popularity but on doing what is right.

PERSONAL ATTENTION, INSPECTION, AND CONTROL

In the management by objectives approach to patrol administration, the police leader in patrol should consider as part of his goal: (1) making the staff-inspection unit useless with regard to patrol, and (2) acting before the fact in achieving the two added responsibilities stated in the introduction to this book: maintaining community stability and enhancing internal esprit de corps. Certain situations call for the intervention of the patrol administrator. After determining that a situation should have his personal attention, the patrol administrator must decide to what degree he should become involved. Certain factors are important. First, citizens have a tendency to rate credibility and capability to perform certain tasks directly to rank. Second, the higher the rank, the more resources the individual controls and therefore, the broader the scope of intervention. Third, the timing of the personal attention may indicate a lack of confidence in subordinates to resolve problems.

The patrol administrator must stay alert and aware of specific situations that might enlarge into large issues internally and externally. He must continue to be sensitive to such situations, watching actions and reactions. He can gain understanding by observing and analyzing lower-level decisions and can give positive suggestions on a timely basis. He should evaluate the effects of his suggestions objectively and finally step in if personal attention seems necessary.

The patrol administrator's ability to apply this principle of personal attention to inspection and control will improve as the other qualities of leadership develop. When the patrol administrator knows the individual patrol commanders, ascertains the ability of each to perform under stress, evaluates the method of problem solving used by each, critically analyzes the use of resources (manpower and equipment), and documents faithfully and on a continuing basis, he will have reached a point where the principle will show a positive approach to management by objectives.

The suggestions of the administrator, if used properly, will cause line inspections to permeate the entire patrol force, and this in time will prevent problems from arising and instill the planning process at the patrol officer level. If the patrol officer uses the principles of planning in his daily operations, it is more probable that his objectives will be accomplished. It follows that if the patrol administrator develops the personal goals of his leader, and these goals parallel the goals of the organization, it is more likely that the objectives of the department will be achieved.

Personal attention, inspections, and control contribute directly to effective use of resources. Management is defined as getting the most with the least. A stipulation has been made generally in law enforcement that no great increase in resources is forthcoming. Apparently this is true, and the improvement of law enforcement will come instead through the innovation and creativity of those involved within the system and the help of scientists, educators, and other professionals. The management by objectives approach is designed to obtain maximum utilization of resources.

The first step in planning is to recognize needs. Inspection should be one of the processes through which this first step is accomplished. The inspection can be either before or after the fact. There are cases where it will be impossible for inspection to recognize the need before the fact, but inspection should make this a goal.

Inspection, when related to agencies outside law enforcement, indicates quality control. Through inspection and control, law enforcement intends to produce superior service to the community. Inspection and control therefore become synonymous with the planning and directing responsibilities of the administrator. Normally, patrol is the largest unit and therefore has the greatest operating budget. For example, a review of a recent survey would reveal the following:

City A – Total budget	$40,627,268.00
Salary budget	$37,142,703.00
% of total budget	91.4%
City B – Total budget	$21,025,220.00
Salary budget	$20,277,970.00
% of total budget	96.4%
City C – Total budget	$17,320,856.00
Salary budget	$15,764,801.00
% of total budget	91%

Other departments allocated 67.9%, 86.5%, and 91.5% of the budget for salary. The patrol administrator must reflect upon the responsibility of administering the proportion of the budget applied to the police force. In doing so, the need to apply the personal-attention principle to inspections and management by objectives becomes obvious.

This method of inspection as a supervisory tool is good as long as the positive aspects are emphasized. The follow-up then becomes a reality in that those responsible for performing the tasks believe inspection will take place at each level, thereby increasing the probability of successful completion of the tasks and achievement of the goals.

Some of the objectives of the inspection process are to: improve teamwork; increase production; provide superior service; anticipate future problems; resolve community and internal problems; improve maintenance regarding building, equipment, records; and achieve quality control.

Inspection

There are two kinds of inspection: staff and line, or authoritative. The larger police departments of the country operate with a staff-inspections unit; the smaller departments cannot afford the luxury. In the case of the latter, the need for quality line inspection is emphasized.

Staff inspections. *Staff inspections* are those performed by personnel having no direct control over the persons or things being inspected. Larger departments have a staff inspector who is usually equal in rank to those in charge of operations the inspector must inspect. Officers assigned to these units usually possess a high degree of loyalty, integrity, strength of character, technical skills, working knowledge of the department, forcefulness, initiative, tact, diplomacy, objectivity, and courage. The staff unit should project an image of openness, uniformity, willingness to define training needs, and cooperation with operating units for the purpose of promoting efficiency and economy for the entire department.

Line inspections. *Line inspections* are those made by the patrol supervisor responsible for the patrol operation. It is essential that inspections show the results of procedures used, to determine the need for modifications and provide accountability and justification.

To the patrol administrator, inspection means responsibility for performance by each level between the patrol officer and himself. The administrator cannot inspect each call for service, written report, or the criminal conditions of each beat, but he can and should develop a continuing inspection process in order to get a realistic accounting of each level of authority and provide personal attention where appropriate. The following checklist will assist in accomplishing this mission. It is not all-inclusive but will give some insight regarding the personal-attention principles and the amount of time and effort needed for application.

- Do you personally use the concept of anticipation?
- Do you consider in advance? Think through in advance?

- Do you ask the questions, Who am I? Where am I going? and, How do I intend to get there?
- Is my time organized to the point where appropriate reflection is given to the answers?
- What is the total Part I crime for my area of responsibility?
- What is the total Part I crime by category?
- What is the projected Part I crime for my area on a daily, weekly, monthly, quarterly, semi-annual, and annual basis? What is the comparison between last year and the present year by time?
- What does analysis reveal as the average total Part I crime for each month on a daily basis?
- Regarding the crime rate, what is the violent crime total (murder, rape, robbery, aggravated assault), and what is the property crime total (burglary, larceny over $50, and auto theft)?
- Do your subordinates complete assignments on dates as requested (due dates)?
- What inspections have been made lately?
  1. Roll call
  2. Revolver
  3. Foot patrol
  4. Filing systems
  5. Activity reports
  6. Arrests in high-crime areas
  7. Mileage (This is done to prevent passing of mileage from one shift to another and also to have total mileage for a shift compatible with the beat configuration. In other words, if an officer has a beat size of two city blocks by three city blocks and recorded fifty miles of driving during his tour of duty, he would have made few critical observations. There may be exceptions; however, on an average, the size of the beat should be compatible with the crime problems and the miles of driving. Obviously, outlying beats of larger size would require more mileage during the tour of duty in order to give proper coverage.)
- Are there any areas where constant presence would resolve the crime problems? For example, if a busy intersection has a purse-snatch problem, the application of police officers at all times would alleviate the problem. Intelligent use of manpower could produce the result without disrupting the total patrol sector. Determining the time of day and day of week is necessary, and allowing the team concept between beats is helpful.
- If this approach is used, have you evaluated the effectiveness, and if successful, have you discontinued the assignment after it has served the purpose?

- Do you set the proper example in dress? Attitudes?
- Does your positive attitude permeate your areas of responsibility?
- Have you complimented anyone lately for outstanding performance?
- Do you set priorities?
- Do you inspect as you insist patrol officers patrol, in an irregular overt posture?
- Do you insist upon primary and secondary missions where appropriate? In other words, if the patrol administrator must assign manpower to a given situation but the amount of time does not constitute a full day's assignment, are these resources utilized in a secondary assignment?
- Have you evaluated your position on the ladder of administrative principles?
    1. Do you plan, organize, etc.?
    2. Do you "get the job done"?
    3. Do you document?
- Are you creative and innovative? What have you done that is creative or innovative?
- Do you solicit imagination and creativity, or do you say, "Don't bother me with that hare-brained idea"?
- Are you sensitive to potential internal conflicts between:
    1. Patrol officers
    2. Patrol officers and supervisors
    3. Supervisors and commanders
    4. Internal units
- Do you understand manpower allocation and distribution?
- Do you communicate?

Line commanders, especially patrol leaders, should appreciate the formal inspection unit, if one exists. The unit is an extra set of eyes and ears that assists the patrol administrator to act before the fact. Proper attitude and lateral communication will make the inspection process more acceptable and productive. Despite the pressure of other duties, the practice of using a log to indicate inspection time will be beneficial in the long run to the total operation. The analysis of crime and a review of what crime information from analysis is reaching the patrol officers through reports and pin maps will reveal answers to:

1. Are crime maps maintained on a current basis?
2. Are the maps and information accessible to the patrol officer?

3. Do supervisors insure reviews of current crime information by patrol officers? If not, why not?
4. Is manpower distribution timely?
5. Are subordinate commanders making personal inspections?
6. Are support units producing appropriate and meaningful information at a rate that is useful for operational commanders?
7. Is lateral communication taking place? If not, why not?
8. Have the personnel responsible for achieving each objective been supplied with the proper amount of resources?
9. Did the person most involved in a problem have an opportunity to express his or her ideas as to how it might be solved?
10. Is coordination taking place between operating units (patrol-detective-juvenile-special operation) to avoid duplication and wasted efforts?
11. Can any other resource possessed by the department be used to solve problems?

The patrol administrator can help himself by using written material. As stated earlier, the internal analysis of crime will help in accomplishing "reduction of crime" and "maintaining internal esprit de corps." The other goal, community stabilization, can be assisted by reading books on police administration, formal education, and a general awareness of what is taking place around the country. This information will come from other law enforcement agencies, intelligence reports, national newspapers, magazines, television, and radio. Additionally, the patrol administrator should become familiar with reports by federal regulatory and administrative agencies such as HUD and HEW,[39] which can give an insight into potential pressure and influence that may come to bear on the patrol force. A look at welfare-rights organization, availability of employment, and educational institutions reveals the extent of police involvement and the preparation necessary to meet these problems properly.

In order to be prepared to satisfy the community stability aspect of leadership, the patrol administrator must stay tuned to local radio and television and review the local newspapers. It is necessary to develop personal rapport with community leaders for mutual trust and credibility. The way to act before the fact is to be in a position that leads citizens to bring forth their problems out of confidence and trust. Small police problems then stay small and do not become city-wide or community-wide issues. It is easy to solve the small problem; it becomes much more difficult if the problem enlarges and affects many people. The awareness of what is going on in the community and the ability to relate this to anticipated police problems are essential for effective patrol administration.

Control

Control should be viewed as a means of maintaining a certain quality or standard of performance of which the force can be proud. The patrol administrator should use control as a method of helping all personnel produce a quality product. Control should also insure that minimum deviation from standards is the order of the day. The administrator should communicate to all personnel that this positive use of control is for the benefit of the total patrol force. Quality performance reduces the need for negative discipline and enhances each individual patrol officer's chances of promotion. Repetition of quality routine activity makes goal achievement easy. When the patrol administrator assures personal attention appropriate to the rank and/or condition of the situation, standards of excellence should prevail in the majority of police actions taken by patrol personnel. There is a direct relationship among the patrol administrator, his personal attention, the inspection and control process, and the number of times personnel of the unit are commended or disciplined. When the proper follow-up is done by first-line supervision, middle management, and command patrol leaders, the need for discipline is reduced.

When police departments issue written policy command and supervisory personnel understand it and see to it that the level of execution understands it, then the department can move forward with common goals. Each level will be able to withstand most pressures from within and without the department. The policy and control process will help insulate the patrol leader from these unwarranted pressures and reduce temptation to enhance personal prestige. This same attitude also will help the police agency to get the team effort in achieving the goals. If personal gain is put aside, then the goals of each member of the department will be the same as those of the department. This is, in effect, a simple definition of administration. As in a field reporting system, the first administrative control is located at the sergeant or first-line supervisor level. A high degree of performance at this point reduces the need for other levels to inspect. The first-line supervisor should seek to make personal attention, inspection, and control on the part of the patrol commanders unnecessary. Quality police performance for the community can be improved by this process.

The standards of excellence should relate to all facets of police activity. If police leaders allow illegal searches of persons and vehicles or similar actions, patrol officers will use these methods to achieve the goal when pressures are placed upon them to reduce crime or stop vice. It is most urgent, then, that patrol commanders inspect and control through personal attention in order to accomplish the mission and at the same time insure propriety of action in the methods used to achieve the goal. The end does not justify the means. The objective should be obtained by means of leadership, proven patrol techniques, experimentation and innovation in patrol, and the use of police ability and intelligence against the potential criminal. Effective communication, leadership, and motivation will instill in patrol personnel a desire to perform in a superior manner. Inspection and control then becomes a matter of pride. Everyone wants work inspected when a good job has been done. Preparation for inspections through education and training is necessary to fulfill the role of fully participating in the policy-making decisions of the department. The personal attention, inspection, and control process will help immeasurably to attain full knowledge of what exists within the patrol force and create effective relationships with other units.

The patrol administrator who quotes relevant statistics, forecasts trends from historical data in a selective and logical manner, states grassroots examples concerning the problem at hand, and suggests simple yet effective solutions to problems with consequences considered knows what real responsibility and authority is all about. Government officials will seek his advice, members of his command will gladly follow him and ask his directions, patrol effectiveness will be superior, other leaders within the organization will cooperate and coordinate in an improved manner, the potential for reaching the objective will improve, and professionalism will have been achieved.

USE OF RESOURCES

Since police agencies are not in the business of producing a product for profit in the traditional sense, it is not as easy to evaluate their resources in terms of profit and loss. The law enforcement product of service and order maintenance is mainly intangible and therefore difficult to measure. However, this in no way means that the manager of a police agency should not administer as if he were actually producing a measurable product. Police leaders must use the total resources of the department as if they were their very own and insist that all others in the department do the same. Each citizen pays tax dollars that are used to purchase the resources of a police agency; therefore, they are all investors. It is difficult to place a priority on any one resource in a police department. However, a review of each of the resource categories (manpower, material, equipment, supplies, electricity, and fuel) in terms of cost would list manpower first, since the majority of the police budget is made up of salary for police personnel. Patrol administrators should consequently be keenly aware of using human resources as the number-one priority. This use should not be to the detriment of the other resources, but the patrol officer should be regarded as the most precious commodity possessed.

Law enforcement and the function of patrol can be compared to business and industry, since the principles of administration can be applied to both. The big difference, which must be completely understood, is that policing aims to provide service–law enforcement and order maintenance–not to make a profit. The police department's existence results from the failure of certain segments of our society to live up to a fundamental rule of human relations: to respect the rights, property, and lives of our fellow human beings. Personal relations in our society involve the most complex and controversial of all human endeavors, and it is with this area that police work generally, and patrol specifically, are concerned. Patrol must mediate, counsel, and perform a repressive function in a permissive society and do it effectively and efficiently. Traditionally, police work has set a priority on law enforcement. Today, the priority has been challenged. James Q. Wilson points out this challenge in "Dilemmas of Police Administration" when he writes:

> The dilemmas of police administration arise out of the difficulty confronting a chief who seeks policies which can guide his men in performing the order-maintenance function and a technique which will prove efficacious in serving the law-enforcement function. The conflict over how the police should behave in order-maintenance cases results from differing expectations as to the appropriate level of public or private order and differing judgments over what constitutes a just resolution of a given dispute. In a homogeneous community, where widely shared norms define both the meaning of order and the standards of justice (who is equal to whom and in what sense), the police role is comparatively simple. But where the community, usually because of differences of class or race, has no common normative framework, the police have no reliable guides to action and efforts to devise such guides will either be half-hearted or a source of important public controversy. The conflict that arises over the performance of the law-enforcement function, on the other hand, arises out of the lack of any technique by which crime can be reduced significantly and without incurring high costs in terms of other values–privacy, freedom, and so forth. The dispute about the law-enforcement function is, unlike the dispute over order maintenance, not over ends but over means.[40]

More recently, the same topic has arisen for consideration by the American Bar Association in stating standards relating to the urban police function. See pp. 76–79. The patrol administrator must have full knowledge of the goals for the department in order to use the resources placed in his care to their fullest extent.

Manpower

In managing the human resources of the patrol unit by objectives, the patrol administrator must realize that the departmental goal can only be achieved through this resource. There is an interdependent responsibility between subordinates and superiors to achieve the goal. William Bopp, in *Police Personnel Management*, includes among the supervisory tasks "the creation of a working environment conducive to productivity."[41] The patrol administrator has all levels of authority between himself and the level of execution as an extension of himself, and he should set the stage for efficiency and economy in management. Demonstrated success in human relations among top management should result in similar success throughout the patrol force. Similar actions regarding other resources should also produce positive results.

The management by objectives approach suggested in this book (and expressed to a certain extent on the Patrol Planning Council) accentuates the exploration of untapped talent in all members of the patrol unit. Talent overlooked because of lack of opportunity, nonsolicitation, insecurity of supervision, or lack of communication is talent wasted.

In *The Human Organization* Rensis Likert identifies a Table of Organization and Performance Characteristics of Different Management Systems. The table indicates an organization variable and reports the relationship between the variable and four classes of systems. Likert asked several hundred managers to indicate the most productive system with which they were familiar. The vast majority chose system 4, described as follows:

1. The direction of information is down, up, and with peers.
2. A substantial amount of teamwork exists throughout the organization.
3. Decision-making is widely done throughout the organization.
4. Decision-makers are well aware of problems.
5. Subordinates are fully involved in all decisions related to their work.
6. Except in emergencies, goals are usually established by means of group participation.[42]

Likert then proceeds to examine the effect on performance of three basic concepts of system 4 management: (1) the manager's use of the principle of supportive relationships; (2) the manager's use of group decision-making and of group supervision; and (3) the manager's high performance goals for the organization.

The principle of supportive relationships is stated as follows:

The leadership and other processes of the organization must be such as to ensure a maximum probability that in all interactions and all relationships within the organization, each member, in light of his background, values, desires, and expectations, builds and maintains his sense of personal worth and importance.[43]

This interdependent responsibility and supportive relationship equally involve the patrol supervisor and all subordinates. When a sergeant can understand the way one of his squad members reacts to a certain situation and takes the time to guide and counsel, then interaction, support, and communication have taken place. The squad member's actions in the next situation receive praise for an outstanding achievement from the sergeant. In a situation where food arrives for the squad after it had been clearing up a large disorder for an extended period of time, the sergeant may take his place at the end of the line. Each action of support indicates that the sergeant cares for his officers. The sergeant shows how important his patrol officers are. Proper implementation of the principle of supportive relationships will contribute to the achievement of the goal, through increased productivity.

The second concept, of group decision-making and group methods of supervision, involves interaction between supervisors and subordinates and assuring subordinates at each level. The Patrol Planning Council may essentially fulfill these requirements. The council is not a committee where the patrol administrator can say the group made the decision, but an effective force of using manpower resources and tapping talent in a very real sense.

The third concept, high performance aspiration throughout the organization, deals with performance goals. It involves pride in the uniform and the department. This concept evolves from the needs and desires of the members of the organization and the integration of these needs and desires with those of the shareholders, customers, suppliers, and others who have an interest in the enterprise.

In applying the concept it is necessary to set objectives. Each member of the patrol unit must set objectives concurrently with the supervisor. Additionally, the goals of the police department must integrate the goals of government, other agencies, criminal justice systems, and, most importantly, the citizens of the community. The American Bar Association's "Standards Relating to the Urban Police Function" recommended setting goals and priorities in a way that will achieve the goal of the particular locality.

Practically speaking, the patrol leader, no matter what rank, must implement the concepts. No one officer from a squad or platoon or district should be allowed to disrupt the smooth operation of the team. Abuse of sick leave, reporting late for work, leaving an assigned task or beat unnecessarily without consideration of the goal, not answering calls promptly, failing to back up other officers when appropriate, unacceptable appearance, and obnoxious attitudes are all areas about which supervision must inquire and take action in order to avoid a reduction of effectiveness and a spread of negative attitude.

The supervisor must understand totally the relationship between resources and money. The money belongs to the taxpayers, and they have a right to expect efficiency and economy in its use. It is estimated that the cost of one two-man patrol car operated around the clock is $100,000 a year, or more. The first place the supervisor must realize this enormous responsibility is the allocation and distribution of the patrol force. The second is the supervisor's application of leadership. A sector sergeant in a large police department who supervises a squad of fourteen men and women may have a budget of approximately $250,000 a year. The supervisor must realize the effect of lost man-days, lost man-hours, etc., on the expectations of the taxpayers. The management by objectives approach is offered for patrol so that managers in police work can assimilate their responsibilities with total expenditures and realize a profit—a high degree of excellence in performance. For example, crime analysis reveals Saturday evening as the highest crime time of the week. The supervisor who allows his patrol officers extra days off on Saturdays is not using resources advantageously. The crimes occurring due to less coverage cost the citizen time, money, and possible personal injury.

The concept of using leadership to create efficient use of manpower is basic and should not be forgotten. Consistency should exist in the application of this type of leadership. Credibility can only be developed when a fair application of principles is maintained constantly. There should be no waste of manpower. The patrol administrator's use of proper planning, education, training, procedures, personal attention, inspection, and control can eliminate or reduce poor use of resources.

To conclude this discussion of efficient manpower use, several paragraphs from *Police Personnel Management* by William J. Bopp are presented for review. He stresses the need to find the best position for each individual officer according to his or her talent. The Los Angeles County Sheriff's Department Career Development Program has been successful in achieving this objective, thereby increasing the value of the manpower resource. Important by-products—disseminating information, paralleling individual and organizational goals—have also resulted.

In 1971 the Los Angeles County Sheriff's Department began what is now considered a model career development program. The program is automated and administered by the Department's Career Development Bureau. According to agency literature, the impact of this computerized system is manifold: (1) rapid retrieval of personnel information, (2) 24-hour response to emergency personnel inquiries, (3) manpower survey capabilities, (4) comparative capabilities for evaluating departmental strengths and weaknesses, (5) accurate accounting of manpower movement, and (6) prompt, updating capabilities.

This system offers a complete index of individual training accomplishments, experience, education, special talents, personal goals, and collateral information essential to career planning, internal movement, specialization, and promotion. The initial input of information was gained from a detailed questionnaire completed by all sworn employees. Due to the comprehensive nature of the instrument, a two-week period was allowed for its completion. Each completed questionnaire represented a career profile. The forms were then collected and the data was coded and computerized.

As new employees are inducted into the department, they are required to complete the career questionnaire. In-service personnel must update their profiles on a yearly basis. Incidental updating may be accomplished more frequently when a major status change occurs, such as the achievement of a college degree. In addition to the personnel data, the system contains information on manpower levels in specialized units, projected vacancy factors, and skills, experience, and education currently desired by each unit. Deputies considering transfers to specialized components have at their disposal computer-furnished information which allows them to prepare for assignments in anticipation of the department's growth, manpower turnover, and so forth.

An important adjunct to the Los Angeles County Career Development Plan is the career counseling program. Career counseling is a joint venture undertaken by line supervisors and a group of full-time counselors. The functional objectives of the program are (1) to furnish deputies with career information pertinent to their situation, (2) to gather data from employees regarding personal goals, (3) to encourage officers to enter high-need areas, and (4) to assist officers with personal problems by referring them to appropriate sources of help.

In summary, Los Angeles County Sheriff's Department Career Development Program has the following broad objectives: (1) to effectively utilize the agency's human resources; (2) to provide a system for identifying and fulfilling organizational and individual needs; (3) to improve the effectiveness of selection, placement, development, promotion, and retention of personnel; (4) to assist personnel in assessing and developing their individual abilities; (5) to achieve a more effective match between the man and the job; (6) to improve morale; (7) to decrease the rate of manpower turnover for reasons of job dissatisfaction; (8) to develop personnel at all levels of the department; and (9) to provide counseling for mobility, development, orientation (to the police academy), retirement, and personal problems.

Few police departments will be able to implement as sophisticated and as far reaching a career development program as the Los Angeles County Sheriff's Department, which is a rather large agency.

But, despite the limitations of size, budget, and technology, most size-able law enforcement agencies can implement a modified version of the plan, for the concept is sound. The extent to which a department can embark on such a program is directly dependent on the resources it can muster. The Los Angeles plan has been able to harness technology for a humanistic end which still serves the organizational requirements of a metropolitan police agency. It is an encouraging sign.[44]

Material, Equipment, Supplies, Electricity, and Fuel

Other resources that receive less of the budget than manpower, but must be adequately cared for in order to allow the department to operate effectively, are such things as vehicles, shotguns, buildings, radios, and revolvers.

Years of experiences with vehicle accidents reveal the following:

1. Most patrol force accidents occur while officers are on routine patrol, other than responding to other officers in trouble.
2. The more serious accidents occur while officers are responding to emergency or perceived emergency situations.
3. Driver attitude is very important in preventing accidents.
4. Many departments provide in-depth training in the use of firearms, but accept a driver's license as evidence that an officer is capable of driving a police vehicle.
5. Patrol officers are not instructed of appropriate policy for driving police vehicles, as they are, say, for using their service revolvers.
6. First-line supervisors have the most important role to play in developing patrol officers into good defensive drivers.
7. Attention to driving habits must be given on a continuing basis (whenever bad habits are observed) rather than only when accidents occur.
8. If preventable accidents occur, individual attention must be given to correcting the deficiency that contributed to the accident.
9. Education and training should be continuous in (a) recruiting, (b) correcting for errant drivers, (c) restrengthening. It will have the greatest impact on solving the vehicular accident problem in terms of lost resources, including manpower.

This list is not all-inclusive but points out some basic areas to be considered when the patrol leader attempts to improve the use of resources.

Other methods of improving resource effectiveness involve the formal inspection process connected to roll call and inspection prior to the start of a watch. Implementation of a proper roll call can result in great savings regarding equipment. Additionally, watch commanders can set examples of efficiency by providing a meaningful roll-call procedure. Information given at roll call should be relevant to the officers attending; obsolete or ambiguous information should be eliminated or the commander will seem unprepared. A review of available information before roll call will reveal what information is already possessed by members of the watch. This information should be repeated only in exceptional cases. Procedures regarding the collection of data for the oncoming watch should be written out. This data would include hot-sheets, crime maps, special attention, etc. Officers who have been on regular vacation or sick leave should be required to update their information.

Inspection should be made by the watch commanders daily at roll call and should include uniform and personal equipment. After roll call has been completed, sergeants should accompany officers to their respective relief posts. If a vehicle is involved, inspection of it should be made for damage, cleanliness, operating condition, and any equipment carried. If any abnormalities are present, reports of specifics should be made. If the vehicle is unsafe to operate it should be grounded. Minor problems due to careless inspection can result in serious consequences (e.g., oil levels directly affect the engine operation). Improper care will also affect the performance of the officer's service revolver. One must consider the effect of equipment failure in a life-or-death situation. The result will be proper care of equipment.

The saving of money by proper attitude and knowledge in the area of resources is exemplified by the case of an officer assigned to the research and development unit. He found that one police department had been operating under a procedure in which the patrol wagon was required to make three individual trips in order to complete the arrest process when a male and female were arrested together. First, the male and female were taken from the point of arrest to a district station, at which time arrest forms were completed. Second, the female was taken to the women's detention facility, where identification forms and processes were completed. Third, these arrest forms were then returned to the district station. In reviewing the process, the officer realized that by first taking the woman to the women's detention facility, one trip could be eliminated. The saving in manpower and fuel when multiplied by the number of arrests made under these circumstances was tremendous. All members of the patrol force should consider similar ways of economizing.

PARTICIPATORY MANAGEMENT AND MOTIVATION

Likert's concept of group decision making was discussed earlier in the chapter. This concept will be expanded upon in this section on participatory management and motivation. Although the group has been defined as the basic structural unit of an enterprise, any group is made up of individuals. In any organization goals are achieved through congruence of individuals and the organization. The patrol administrator should be able to determine not only the type of leadership he will use at any given time, but also the amount of participation in managing and the amount of job enrichment (self-actualization) that is desired. Participation is a positive factor and valuable managing device.

The group is made up of individuals who jointly contribute their specialized services, coordinated in a manner to achieve the enterprise's purpose. The concepts of specialization, the purpose of the enterprise, and coordination are involved.

The services that individuals contribute to groups are always specialized services: i.e., they differ one from the other. The bases for this differentiation are (1) the place where work is done, (2) the times at which work is done, (3) the persons with whom work is done, (4) the things upon which work is done, or (5) the method or process by which work is done.[45] These bases for differentiation correlate to the patrol force as follows:

1. High-crime versus low-crime areas; patrol versus booking.
2. The evening shift (which usually contains more crime and calls for service) versus the night watch or day shift.
3. Individual officers, who possess different values, backgrounds, goals, etc.
4. and 5. The selected method of patrol: foot, auto (one-man, two-man), plainclothes, burglary, K-9, etc.

Each officer is related in a special way to each consideration, and the patrol leader must identify his officers in this way.

The second concept concerns the purpose of the department.

The members of the group must accept an enterprising purpose; i.e., they must be contributing their specialized services toward the attainment of an end which is specified for them. The purpose or end of the group is its *raison d'être*. This purpose must change from time to time, but the purpose at any time is always the formal objective of all members of the group. However, this enterprising purpose need not coincide with the needs which induce each individual to contribute his services to the group. (This is why the patrol leader has to develop differing management tools to motivate the individual.) A football player may recognize the purpose of his team to be the defeat of an opponent; at the same time his personal reason for belonging to the team may have little to do with such defeat. In other words, enterprise purpose and individual purpose may not coincide.[46]

Some patrol officers are working in the police department only to have a job. Others are working to gain experience. (These members are those who have higher education degrees and are using the position as a stepping-stone.) Some are dedicated to law enforcement and look upon the position as a career. The patrol leader should recognize these personal reasons and insure that, whatever they are, leadership is provided to enable each to coordinate his or her goals and objectives with those of the department.

Since specialized services are being contributed by individuals for the attainment of the enterprise purpose, it is essential that the services be coordinated if the purpose is to be attained. "Coordination . . . is the orderly arrangement of group effort to provide unit of action in the pursuit of a common purpose."[47] The specialized services must be so combined that harmony and balance will be achieved. Coordination involves bringing into common action, combining in harmonious action.[48] The patrol administrator is responsible for initiating the essential team effort and the managers (captains, lieutenants, sergeants) are responsible for carrying out this coordination.

Participation Management

Nowhere in administrative work is coordination more important than when determining how far the patrol officer will continue with his or her preliminary investigation, what offenses will be involved, and the responsibility for follow-up. At these times the administrator is concerned with whether or not to specialize. One view is that specialization occurs whenever patrol fails to achieve its primary responsibility of prevention. Others say that specialized investigators are best used in follow-up work, and therefore their presence at the crime scene is indicated only when a crime is of unusual importance, involving considerable injury or property loss.

The patrol officer must determine whether or not investigators are in fact needed at a particular scene. This involves participation in management, with the use of discretion and coordination for achievement of goals. Patrol, detectives, youth, research and development, and records should meet to discuss and participate in a decision. For example, should robberies committed by juveniles be followed up by youth, detectives, or patrol units?

These discussions usually result from an increase in workload of the detective unit. The active participation of captains, lieutenants, sergeants, and patrol officers is necessary since the decision directly affects their responsibilities and their individual and collective workloads. Each unit has to make similar inquiries and then report to the committee. The results of this method are coordination between units and participation in management.

Participatory management in patrol should include participation by command officers, middle management, and the level of execution (major, captain, lieutenant, sergeant, and patrol officer). If a sergeant is participating with a lieutenant, the sergeant is then the subordinate. If the sergeant is participating with a patrol officer, the sergeant is then the superior. This linking system carries up and down the chain of command. However, patrol administrators must also be aware of the input that employee organizations have on the participatory process. Their cooperation should be solicited when using participatory management as a managing device.

In general terms, all members of the patrol force participate in the reduction of crime. They also participate in the rewards—a proclamation of a superior performance by government, a complimentary cartoon in the newspaper, recognition from business and industry, professionalism, etc. This means that members of the patrol force should be allowed to make decisions with management in areas where they are directly affected. Persons involved in the decisions that affect them will be more inclined to accept and effect the necessary change, achieve the goal, and be enriched through real authority (as opposed to a sense of authority).

As Alvin Toffler defined it in *Future Shock*, "Change is the process by which the future invades our lives."[49] Law enforcement must control the rate and direction of change in relationship to the criminal justice system, government, and other agencies. Law enforcement must be able to articulate and communicate desires, wishes, and goals. In order to do this, law enforcement must educate itself in the ways necessary to control the rate and direction of change. It is necessary to become open and intelligently expressive of sensitivities and frustrations.

> The roots of police failure are buried deeply in the failures of society, and every day these roots are deepening and strengthening their hold. If the state of police is not changed, if police continue to be exploited in their weakness, then they may one day turn, and the nightmare of a police state will be upon us. Already large segments of our population—among them those whose protection should be the policeman's most cherished task—instinctively turn their heads in retreat at the sight of a police car. They have come to believe that in the eyes of the police, their very existence is a sin. Others look upon the police as so incompetent, so stupid, and so corrupt that they

are no better than the criminals with whom they deal. To them, the police problem is something far beneath them, that is manifested only in the ghettos and poverty areas of this country, and that is beneath their notice. The policeman is not insensitive to these attitudes. They merely compound his frustration and his misery and accelerate the cycle of his degradation, driving him ever more deeply into the "closed fraternity."[50]

All talent within the patrol force must be tapped. Participatory management and job-enrichment methods are only managing devices. Planning, innovation, finding alternative solutions to problems, and effective decision-making should become routine. Communication and dissemination of information to all concerned are necessary before any participatory management can take place.

Job enrichment and personal development are enhanced when officers are allowed to express their ideas and thoughts about a subject before any decision is made. For example,

> *Question:* Officer, what would be the best type of patrol for this beat?
>
> *Answer:* Well, Sir, the burglars appear to be working in pairs, using an auto, so from my observation and working the beat for two years, I would recommend one man on foot, and one man in a car on the perimeter.
>
> *Question:* Should they be in uniform or plainclothes?
>
> *Answer:* The offenses appear to be committed by professionals so I think we should try to apprehend them in a way which would also prevent future offenses, therefore plainclothes.
>
> *Decision:* Approved.

In essence, the leader is not sharing authority, but rather allowing participation. Carey has explained this clearly: "Action initiated by the responsible head to bring his subordinates into the picture on matters of mutual concern is not a sharing of prerogatives of authority, rather it is an extension of the opportunity of participation in the development of points of view and the assembly of facts upon which decisions are made."[51]

Included in the question of manpower distribution in the example above are decisions concerning the size of sectors (worked by sergeants), size of beats (worked by patrol officers), and the configuration of both. These decisions in turn directly affect span of control and the determination of whether any motorized-patrol beat or foot-patrol beat should be one- or two-man.

Participation and a feeling of belonging can best be initiated if each level is involved in planning from the beginning. Therefore, when workloads are established from computer printouts and displayed over the existing patrol configuration, it is time to communicate, disseminate, and call for participation. As the operation proceeds, patrol captains have an opportunity to express their needs and set goals and priorities for their areas of responsibility. Additional input concerning the best approach for achieving goals is available. Lieutenants offer suggestions concerning watches, sergeants concerning sectors, and patrol officers concerning beats. The result is agreement on goals, priorities, methods, and an enhancement of internal esprit de corps.

Continuing with our example, the International Association of Chiefs of Police distributes a case study titled "Manpower Allocation and Distribution" that discusses making a decision on the assignment of one or two officers to a beat. Factors to consider are:

1. The number of situations in which more than one person is arrested at one time.
2. The number of arrests involving resistance.
3. The number of arrests involving the possession of weapons (the foregoing bears a direct relationship to the frequency of disturbances, assaults, and acts of violence).
4. The frequency of calls for service.
5. Nature of area, street design, degree of congestion, etc.
6. Natural boundaries that might interfere with assistance from other police units.[52]

After careful analysis and workload study, the watch commanders and sector sergeants make recommendations covering the size and configuration of sectors. The patrol officers working the individual beats are then consulted regarding those beats that should be manned by two officers, considering the factors mentioned above. The patrol officers can point out areas of concern that are not identified when dealing with statistics alone. Each neighborhood has its own personality and attitude. The patrol officers have intimate knowledge of, and relationships with, these neighborhoods, and their input is significant. The concept of cooperation and participation takes into consideration the complex and changing needs of our patrol personnel. People-oriented leaders, using the several styles of leadership appropriately, can develop the patrol function into an offensive technique easily capable of accomplishing the mission. When participatory management and motivation combine, an atmosphere of innovation and creativity prevails.

THE LEADER AND INDIVIDUAL PERFORMANCE

The evaluation of performance throughout the United States has traditionally been treated in one of three ways. First, no attempt at performance evaluation has been made. Second, performance evaluation has been accomplished through a haphazard process. Third, an honest attempt has been made to evaluate personnel based on realistic factors.

Various errors have been made in the past, e.g., citing the number of arrests or number of traffic citations issued as a major criterion in evaluating the performance of an officer. An officer spends the majority of his or her time on noncriminal activities, and performance of these activities must become more important in the total evaluation. Also, there has been a lack of training of those supervisors designated as raters. The question of integrity in rating by supervisors is related more to their lack of knowledge of the process than to a deliberate intent to invalidate it. Prejudice and subjectivity are human characteristics, however, and they should be considered when designing the form to be used for the department. All factors that affect the total performance of officers and supervisors should be included as part of an honest, effective performance evaluation. In fact, standards of excellence must be stated and rating based on merit is essential if police work is to continue on the road toward professionalism.

Every employee has the right to be told honestly and objectively his or her level of performance. The immediate supervisor (in patrol, the sergeant, lieutenant, or captain) is the most appropriate person for this task. When the performance rating has a bearing on an officer's position on the promotion list, it is obvious how important this evaluation becomes. Performance evaluation, promotional potential, and personal fulfillment are directly related. We all would like to improve our performance, know that our jobs are vital to the success of the organization or mission, be recognized for our efforts, and know that we are performing our tasks accurately and professionally. Standards of excellence for the different positions and just what constitutes satisfactory or outstanding performance as related to these positions should be clearly stated for everyone to understand. Additionally, the patrol administrator should realize that the chief sets the standards formally, and rightly so, but each level of authority also sets standards by applying degrees of compliance to the formal standard. Sergeants implement their level of performance when they give an officer an outstanding rating for accomplishing 75 percent of the formal standard needed for that rank.

Patrol administrators would do well to insure that sergeants and lieutenants have an opportunity to express their opinions and ideas relative to standards. The standards should be realistic, measurable as much as possible, relevant, attainable, surpassable, based on above average productivity, accepted by superior and subordinates, and uniformly examined.

Effective performance evaluation has numerous advantages. It:

1. Aids in assigning appropriate tasks.
2. Identifies strengths and weaknesses.
3. Provides information for career development.
4. Isolates specific attitudes and traits.
5. Assists in identifying potential supervisors.
6. Insures that line commanders take a personal interest in subordinates.
7. Improves ability to solve departmental and work problems.
8. Provides feedback for training purposes.
9. Assists in salary decisions.
10. Serves as a check-and-balance system in the recruitment-and-selection process.
11. Fulfills personal need of employees to know their level of performance.
12. Improves transfer procedure (the transfer of a man or woman without proper evaluation of specifics and identification of abilities, liabilities, and communication not only causes dissatisfaction for that person, but also disrupts the units from which and to which he or she is transferred).

A recent study indicated approximately 3,200 individual tasks are performed by the police. To have written standards for this amount of tasks is illogical. But, just as the patrol administrator must learn to lead according to the existing conditions in his community and department, so should the standard of performance as related to the individual tasks on a priority basis be implemented according to position and existing conditions.

Training and Forms

The greatest asset of a supervisor is his or her ability to develop people. Whether or not the supervisor is aware of it, he or she is continually appraising each officer. If a department is to overcome to any degree the pitfalls of human beings in rating other human beings, honest effort must be made to evaluate personnel on a formal basis. In order to do this, it is necessary to develop the proper form for the respective police agency.

Irving B. Wicker, Jr., has suggested a five-step approach in developing the appropriate forms:

1. Determine the goals and purposes of the form.
2. Select and define, in depth, those traits to be evaluated.
3. Determine the degrees of differentiation between "poor" and "outstanding" performance.
4. Explicitly define those degrees (i.e., "unacceptable," "fail," "average," and so forth).
5. Assign weights for each degree, where appropriate.[53]

Once the appropriate form has been decided upon, explanation of departmental policy regarding the use of the form is necessary. This should be presented in the form of a general order or its equivalent, stating who shall be evaluated and by whom; how the evaluation shall be performed and at what time intervals; what specific responsibilities are placed upon the sergeant, lieutenant, captain, etc.; what shall be done with the results of the evaluation; and where the final place of filing shall be located.

Supervisors must be trained both as raters and as teachers, for the improvement of the officer, using information gained through the evaluation, is most important. Realistically, supervisors cannot be expected to be professional teachers, but they can train officers using the basic principles of teaching. One description of these basic principles calls for: (1) explaining the task to the officer, (2) demonstrating how the job is to be done, (3) observing the officer do the job, (4) evaluating his or her performance. Another way of putting it is to (1) prepare the learner, (2) present the operation, (3) try out performance, and (4) follow up.[54] Whatever the case, the supervisor should plan for the training session. He must be sure he has the proper equipment (form, pen, flashlight, etc.) to perform the task exactly as he wants it done; try to make the training interesting (a sergeant could tell a story of his experience relating to the same task); make the situation as valid and realistic as possible by explaining and illustrating when possible; question the officer as appropriate; indicate potential pitfalls; allow the officer to perform the task fully and do it as many times as necessary until satisfied he knows how to do it; have him relax, and advise him that help is available at any time; and evaluate and redirect instruction as appropriate.

It is essential for the rater to be trained in rating employees. Obstacle and objective awareness are necessary in order to make the performance evaluation meaningful and successful. The patrol administrator has a responsibility to insure that all supervisors under his command have been fully trained. He must maintain lateral communication with the administration of other units within the department to satisfy his leadership role relating to standard application of the performance evaluation policy. If there is one complaint a patrol commander is sure to receive when discussing performance evaluation, it is, "How do you expect us to rate our men objectively when the supervisors of (X) unit give their men top efficiency?" There is no excuse for this practice. All leaders must make sure they make objective evaluations.

The first-line supervisor/sergeant is especially important in training raters. It is necessary to have formal classroom training wherein problems discussion and resolution and consensus may take place concerning the tentative procedure. One major problem coming out of the training session may concern the collection of data necessary to rate officers. The recommendation made in the section about officers' activity reports is applicable. Productivity rates can be determined from these reports and key-punched for input into the computer. Printouts should be supplied at least monthly to the respective supervisor to assist primarily in performance evaluation, even though other decisions regarding workload analysis and manpower deployment can be made from the same printout. Sergeants, who usually have a larger span of control, especially need this type and style of information.

Pitfalls

There are several pitfalls that should be discussed by the supervisor during the training session so all raters will be on the same track when they evaluate their subordinates. The better supervisor will make the better rater. The less effective supervisor will carry the same traits into performance evaluation as he demonstrates in his daily leadership.

Acting as the good guy will destroy an evaluation system. The grapevine of a police department is such that the abuse of an objective rating system by one unit will spread throughout the department and cause a decline in the overall value of the system. You do not help a man by rating him outstanding if in effect he is average in a specific category. None of us deserves "outstanding" in each category just because we are human, consequently imperfect. Another pitfall is directly opposite the good-guy approach. The supervisor just cannot be bothered with justifying any ratings of outstanding or unsatisfactory. Therefore, he places all of his officers in the three columns of satisfactory, average, or above average.

A third pitfall is what is known as the "halo"—the rater tends to evaluate in terms of a general impression rather than on the basis of specific traits.[55] Another pitfall is the misuse of authority. When the sergeant uses the performance evaluation as an ax to chop off the head of a subordinate, he is showing leadership by fear, which is totally unacceptable. Objectivity, honesty, and sincerity must be projected by the supervisor, or the mutual trust necessary for valid evaluation is lost.

A common pitfall is the inability of supervision to agree on the value of the categories. What is outstanding to one supervisor may be poor to another. The classroom training given at the beginning of implementation of a rating system is the place for the necessary clarification to occur.

Next, let's consider the pitfall of prejudice. It is easy for any of us to imprint in our minds certain images of people who may be different than we are. Our value judgments are influenced by our church, family, education, and environment. An honest effort must be made on the part of each rater to attempt objectively and sincerely to keep out any opinion based on prejudice. Close to this is the pitfall of subjectivity. This error can be carried to the extreme. For example, when a sergeant plays golf and one of his patrolmen is a good golfer, they become a twosome on the course. At work they have similar temperaments and get along with each other well. The natural tendency for the sergeant is to carry his feelings into the total evaluation and then give an incorrect performance rating. Additionally, when this occurs, the sergeant is leaving himself wide open for the charge of favoritism, which can affect morale in a very negative manner. Patrol commanders should be alert to review carefully any evaluation made by sergeants giving the appearance of possible favoritism.

The pitfall of recency occurs when too much weight is placed on an employee's behavior immediately prior to a rating deadline. Most evaluations are intended to cover a specific time frame, such as six months or a year. If a supervisor does not keep comprehensive notes on a subordinate's activities throughout the evaluation period, there will probably be an inclination to overemphasize the most easily recalled behavior, which is usually the most recent behavior.

All of these pitfalls can be overcome if personnel are made aware of them and take the appropriate steps to alleviate those ingredients that cause them.

Implementing Performance Evaluation

To implement the program of performance evaluation by general order, the following steps should be carried out.

1. Publish standards for all to understand. They should be realistic, with controls included for review and possible change. Also include a policy statement outlining the fact that the superior of a rating officer cannot cause the rating officer to change any evaluation mark.
2. Select and explain the performance evaluation form (using participatory management).
3. Provide instructions for completing the form.

4. Provide training (formal, roll call, individual as needed) for rated officers, rating officers, and reviewing officers.
5. Indicate the types of reports (i.e., quarterly, semi-annual, etc.) and whom they affect (i.e., probationary patrol officers, patrol officers, sergeants, lieutenants, newly promoted personnel, etc.).
6. State the time periods for submission of each type of report.
7. Indicate the responsibilities of the rating officer (the supervisor to whom a rated officer reports, usually the immediate supervisor). These responsibilities include: review of planning the interview; avoidance of pitfalls; achievement of departmental objectives; accountability for completion of tasks; understanding discipline; data collection and demonstration; meeting completion dates for performance evaluation submission; consultation, guidance, and counseling techniques; following instructions on completing the form, which should be signed by the rated officer indicating the fact that the evaluation procedure was carried out.
8. Indicate the responsibilities of the rated officer to accept the rating or to disagree with it and state the reason for the disagreement.
9. Indicate the responsibility of the review officer (officer next in the chain of command above the rating officer) to review all performance evaluations within his authority, comment positively or negatively as necessary, and insure proper submission of reports by time, date, and location.
10. Advise each level of authority above those mentioned of the possibility, responsibility, and authority to comment as appropriate where an evaluation indicates less-than-satisfactory performance (recommended retraining, discipline, etc.).
11. Provide for evaluation to be kept in central location, preferably the individual's personnel file.
12. Maintain confidentiality as necessary.
13. Allow for controls that will insure some type of action with regard to officers receiving unsatisfactory evaluations.
14. Include a procedure outlining the importance of the system, the recourse available for an officer who feels he or she has been rated unfairly, and the necessary response by the rating and reviewing officers.

Rating Methods

No police department should be satisfied with using one rating method without reviewing other methods for possible improvement. Most methods have both advantages and disadvantages, and the method selected should be tailored to fit your department. Whatever method is used, be sure to explain it fully.

Lazy method.   The supervisor who relies on the lazy method rates his men and women on the basis of his memory and certain obvious characteristics that he likes or dislikes. He does not collect or document any data on which to base his judgments. Some supervisors are able to use this method, and they may do a good job with it, but experience has indicated a greater potential for misjudging. The core of rating becomes a value judgment. Patrol supervisors should always have some form of documentation available on which to rely when making these all-important judgments.

Ranking.   With the ranking method, the supervisor selects an individual in his squad and places him or her in a position of rank from lowest to highest based on overall performance. He is comparing each of his officers with the other, sometimes using several sub-factors. The problem arises when Sergeant A's squad is compared with Sergeant B's squad. The lowest-ranking officer in A squad may be better than the highest-ranking officer in B squad.

Paired comparison.   The supervisor using the paired comparison method compares the performance of each activity by each officer on his squad with that of every other officer with the placement first to last. The final position is determined by the number of times an officer was judged to be better than all the others. A disadvantage of this method is that the younger patrol officers usually place lowest because of inexperience and may become discouraged.

Proportion method.   The proportion method presupposes that, in any group of officers, a small proportion of them will score in the upper 10 percent, another small percentage will score in the lower 10 percent, and the majority score somewhere in between. This is similar to a professor's grading on a curve. For example, if a patrol administrator had fifty men and women under his command, five would fall in the upper scale, five would fall in the lower scale, and the other forty would be at both sides of the center and the center itself.

Numerical method.   In the numerical method, the supervisor places an officer on a scale from low to high using a number of factors; i.e., judgment, leadership, quality of work, etc. This method is easily prepared and

Judgment

poor	1	2	3	4	5	6	7	8	9	10	*outstanding*

easy to use. However, be sure to place an exact value on each number and describe the factors involved.

Word method. The word method is similar to the numerical method, except that the implication of the position on the scale is given. For example, in evaluating judgment with the word method the supervisor would indicate if the judgment used by the officer was poor – needs help continuously, or good – needs help occasionally, or outstanding – makes judgment on his own and needs very little guidance.

Factor check-off method. A checklist type of evaluation form is used in the factor check-off method. The factors are listed horizontally and the value judgments vertically. For example, in patrol, the supervisor would see "quality of work," "initiative," "knowledge," "personal appearance" in the horizontal column and check the box matching his or her judgment on the vertical column, from choices such as "not satisfactory," "improvement needed," " average," "above average," " meets standards," "excellent," " exceeds standards," or "outstanding." Instructions usually accompany the form and provide discussion of each section and block. A disadvantage of this method, as well as the numerical and word methods, is the potential for needing many different forms because of the specificity involved.

Narrative form. The narrative method is not suggested for larger departments because of the difficulty of controlling quality of evaluation. Smaller departments may use this method to great advantage because the supervisor will be able to go into great detail discussing each person working for him. The supervisor must be able to communicate well in writing. In a sense, this method forces him to learn how.

Critical-incident method. The critical-incident method asks the supervisor to document any extraordinarily good or bad performances of the essential duties during the rating period. Patrol administrators must define those areas that are essential rather than routine duties. The handling of these essential areas is specifically documented. For example, a patrol administrator using this method to evaluate a patrol commander would look for (1) ability to communicate: Does the commander know how to talk, and does he know how to adapt the language and content of his talk depending on the audience? This task includes the ability to analyze his audience; or (2) action at the scene of a barricaded person: Can the commander maintain control (fire discipline)? Does he direct (lead) and not do? He may be in the front line directing supervision and officers but he is not actually doing the specific tasks. There are many more specific essentials. In each case, the patrol administrator documents performance, and at evaluation time, the discussion involves the incident and the associated leadership qualities necessary to accomplish the objectives of the position in the essential areas.

Forced-choice method. The forced-choice method uses psychological scale and test construction. It must be designed for each individual department. The supervisor is asked to select two items from a group of four descriptive items. One item selected should be the most characteristic of the person and one item should be least characteristic.

Most	*Least*	
_____	_____	Temperamental
_____	_____	Everyone likes him or her
_____	_____	Autocratic
_____	_____	Low-key but effective leader

The supervisor doing the rating usually must select from a set of approximately forty; this number varies depending on the department. Some of the sets include statements that apply to the ratee totally and others do not apply at all. This method attempts to reduce any prejudices on the part of the rater. It is best used when attempting to make an exact evaluation of the officers. The system is expensive, much exploration is needed, and completing the form takes a lot of time. Also, supervisors sometimes feel these tests cannot be trusted because of the fact that they do not know the relative weight of their selection in the set.

The Mutual Objectives Approach to Performance Evaluation[56]

The general principles which have been discussed can be applied to almost any system of appraising performance which the manager may be required to use. It does seem logical to me, however, to include the best available logical extension of these principles which are at the same time consistent with the management by objectives approach to patrol administration. The mutual objectives method is versatile. Even if the organization suggests some other rating form, the mutual objectives approach has great value as the underlying base. Ratings and other types of judgments can always be made after this procedure has been followed. Here are the basic steps:

I. *Set mutual performance objectives.*
   A. Call in subordinate before start of evaluation period.
   B. Determine as clearly as possible the job responsibilities.
   C. Determine specific performance objectives for next period.
   D. Two conferences may be necessary:
      - First discuss task of setting objectives.
      - Think over a couple of days, return with suggestions and set final objectives.
   E. Put in writing in explicit form.

II. *Plan strategy for reaching objectives.*
   A. Mutually discuss possible strategies.
   B. Help subordinate to think productively about methods for reaching his or her goals.
   C. Eliminate unproductive methods.
   D. Probability of improvement increased.
   E. Demonstrate to subordinate that the superior is on his side helping him to succeed.

III. *Agree on indicators of performance.*
   A. Determine together what evidence will be used as the basis for evaluation.
   B. Reduces misunderstanding about standards.
   C. Both think about specific evidence to be gathered.
   D. Recognition of sensitive areas in advance (subjective-opinion).

IV. *Review performance at end of appraisal period.*
   A. Discuss performance in light of objectives.

V. *Go through steps I through III for next appraisal period.* This would usually be done as the concluding part of the performance-review discussion suggested in step IV. But if time is not available during that session, another one should follow soon. Figure 2.4 gives an illustration of how this mutual objectives method might work .

Basic to the success of this method is a relationship of integrity between the supervisor and employee. In particular, the employee should feel that the supervisor is genuinely trying to help him or her grow and develop. If this process is carried out in a punitive atmosphere in which the motivation of the supervisor appears to be to nail the subordinate to the wall with specific commitments, the method is likely to have serious

Figure 2.4 *Mutual objectives for appraisal*

Name: John Mason   *Department:* Patrol
Period: January 1 – June 30, 19—

Job duties	Specific objectives	Strategies	Performance indexes
Respond to calls for service Etc.	Protect life and property Reduce crime Etc.	"Directed preventive patrol" Use of informants Etc.	"Time to respond" Reduction in Pt. I crimes Etc.

Name: John Mason   *Department:* Patrol
Period: January 1 – June 30, 19—

Job duties	Specific objectives	Strategies	Performance indexes
Preventive patrol Etc.	Safeguard liberty Assist community Etc.	Telltales A.D.T. Alarms Security surveys Etc.	Relations with community Complaints Verified commendation Civility Quality and quantity of work Etc.

Source: Paul A. Albrecht, *Discussing and Improving an Employee's Performance.* Reprinted by permission of the Industrial Relations Center/The University of Chicago. Copyright 1964 by the Industrial Relations Center/The University of Chicago.

undesirable side effects. Too close supervision by the superior and too much rigid detailed planning are hazards to avoid.

Despite these disadvantages, the mutual objectives approach is an exciting and promising one. It embodies many of the principles of effective appraisal discussed earlier. The objectives of the appraisal are clearly in mind. The emphasis is on performance rather than on traits. The careful use of words and the avoidance of vague abstractions are encouraged by outlining the objectives in writing in advance and by setting up "operational indexes" of performance to be used in appraising progress. By focusing on specific and detailed objectives and performance, many of the first-impression, halo, and stereotyped-judgment biases are reduced.

Results-Oriented Performance Evaluation[57]

Several police agencies are working with performance standards, performance indicators, and results-oriented performance. The Kansas City,

Missouri Police Department has experimented with results-oriented performance evaluation as a supervisory training and development tool for managing and coordinating work results. Through the setting of work standards and performance objectives, officers receive not only proper guidelines but also a sense of self-esteem and worth. This program communicates performance expectation, performance standards, and performance results. It is designed to achieve the following objectives:

1. To communicate organization and professional law enforcement standards to subordinates;
2. To communicate supervisory expectations;
3. To measure the productivity and contributions of subordinates; and
4. To identify performance deficiencies and needs.

The evaluation instrument has four sections—police work standards, job assignments, performance traits, and evaluation summary.

Police Work Standards

1. Attendance: sick days, injury days, absent days, late days, disciplinary days, etc.
2. Care of equipment and clothing: vehicle and equipment, cleanliness, upkeep, damage, clean clothing and leather, etc.
3. Physical traits: weight, hygiene, etc.
4. Miscellaneous: general order manual, report manual, etc.

Job Assignments

1. Crime prevention: building checks, surveys, car checks.
2. Community relations: citizen complaints, commendations.
3. Enforcement: response time, felony arrests, etc.
4. Miscellaneous: disciplinary actions, citations, etc.

Performance Traits

1. Attitude: toward department, supervisor, assignments.
2. Teamwork: with department, supervisors, peers.
3. Initiative: self-initiated activites, crime investigations, improvement suggestions, crime prevention.
4. Professional objectives: educational improvement, promotional interests.
5. Miscellaneous: community relations skills, handling arrests.

Evaluation Summary

Evaluation of the grades received by the officer in the three previous sections.

At this stage, this approach begins with a conference between the rater and the ratee in which the categories used to measure performance, the way each category is measured, and the percentage gained or lost rate for each category are explained. In essence, the rater and ratee clearly understand the performance evaluation procedure.

Behaviorally Anchored Rating Scale

Individual performance should add to the achievement of organizational goals. Policing must make some assumptions about goals, since they are difficult to define. In the measurement of quantity and quality of performance, data must be valid and reliable, and must indicate success. Data collected from people are going to have some subjective input, and we should attempt to minimize it. We can count numbers of arrests, tickets issued, etc., but we must also strive for quality of performance. The symbolic nature of policing, the identification of standards, the difficulty of measuring street sense, calmness, the use of force, deterrence, and crisis intervention (e.g., is one officer better than another if he/she doesn't make an arrest in a family dispute), all add to the difficulty of measuring quality. Each agency sets an atmosphere indicating which role is most important—law enforcement, service, or peace keeping—and rewards accordingly.

The beginning of performance evaluation was political; the spoils system, if you will, where the boss rewarded for loyalty. This was totally subjective and may only have resulted in doing the wrong thing better. Next was task-oriented evaluation, which dealt with standard methods of measuring each task in the bureaucracy. Lately we see the scientific: behaviorally oriented evaluation which involves reliability, validity, and professional management, and which looks for results and for behavior that is improving performance through feedback that modifies behavior.

The Dade County Florida Department of Public Safety uses the following information to explain the use of behavior performance appraisal.

An aspect of performance appraisal that deserves special mention is what has come to be called the *content issue*. The content issue centers on the focus of performance appraisal: should subordinates be appraised in terms of personal traits or job behaviors? Traits are those things that many managers look for in an employee, but that often are hard to define. Examples commonly used in performance appraisal are traits such as loyalty, commitment, and judgment. In contrast, behaviors in performance appraisal deal with how an incumbent goes about accomplishing his or her job; for example, an officer's behavior in a particular domestic disturbance situation. However strong the respective arguments may be, their resolution must be based on the relative utility of the two approaches for personnel decision-making purposes.

The purpose of performance counseling is to help the employee improve on his or her current job and therefore increase the likelihood that he or she will advance in the organization. Problems in performance counseling most often arise because of disagreement between a supervisor and his or her subordinate on what constitutes adequate or good performance. The problem may be defined as the "yeah, but" phenomenon; that is, a supervisor tells his subordinate that he needs to improve such-and-such aspect of his job and the subordinate says, "yeah, but . . . " Traits such as *judgment, appearance,* and *initiative,* which are commonly appraised on police jobs, are particularly vulnerable to the "yeah, but" phenomenon. Part of the reason is that those kinds of complex traits, however important, are often ambiguous, difficult to appraise, and therefore too difficult to discuss with subordinates.

Nonetheless, things such as *judgment* are important to job success; even a superficial understanding of many police jobs suggests that a good deal of judgment is involved. The point, however, is that terms such as "judgment" are always subject to various definitions and interpretations. To the extent that differences in the meaning of a trait exist between a supervisor and his subordinate, the effectiveness of employee counseling is jeopardized. Failure to share the meaning of what is being appraised may cast the supervisor in the role of judge, rather than observer of job performance. As a result, the supervisor may be less receptive to the appraisal process and to his responsibility to provide performance feedback to his subordinates. The net result is that both the supervisor and the subordinate may become defensive and may miss the opportunity to improve job performance. It seems that the primary recommendation for trait approaches to performance appraisal comes from tradition: "We've always done it that way." That doesn't seem to add up to a very strong reason to continue their use, especially when something better is available.

In contrast to trait-oriented performance appraisal is behavior-oriented performance appraisal. This form is like the one we will use for road patrol officers. The primary distinction between the two is that the former focuses on the person in the job, while the latter deals with the job, which happens to be occupied by a person; the emphasis is on job behavior standards and not on the employee. For example, consider the following descriptions:

Officer "A" is first at the scene of a homicide where several people are milling about. The officer calls for assistance and asks the crowd to step back.

or

Officer "B" is the first at the scene of a homicide where several people are milling about. The officer calls for assistance and stands by the victim while the crowd mills about, waiting for a superior officer to arrive on the scene.

The results seem obvious; Officer "A" has protected the scene from contamination, removal of evidence, etc., while Officer "B" allowed the scene to be contaminated. Several points about performance can also be illustrated by this situation. Specifically, while one supervisor might conclude that Officer "A" showed good initiative, another supervisor might conclude that he showed good judgment, or both good judgment and initiative, depending on how they define these traits. What the supervisors would agree on, however, is that Officer "A" handled the situation better than Officer "B." Moreover, the subordinates involved probably would also agree on what is good procedure versus what is bad procedure in the situation described. All of them, supervisors and subordinates, would be reaching a conclusion on the basis of observable job behavior, not on some abstract and separate notions of what particular traits mean.

When the focus is on job behavior itself, issues such as the meanings of traits become irrelevant. What is relevant is how the subordinate handles the job situations he or she encounters. (In a police department, it is poorly handled situations that cause trouble, not traits.) Both supervisors and subordinates can understand job behavior, thereby increasing the likelihood of agreement and decreasing the likelihood of conflict. Agreement and lack of conflict benefit performance counseling in at least two ways.

First, the subordinate is not as likely to perceive the counseling interview as a personal attack; the emphasis is on the job rather than on his or her personal characteristics. As a result a subordinate may be less defensive and more likely to perceive the interview as in his best interest. He may thus try to improve his performance within his present job and thereby enhance his chances for advancement within the organization.

The second contribution of a behavioral orientation to the performance counseling process derives directly from its inherent specificity. One of its most important aspects is that it answers the question, "How do I improve my job?" Behavior-oriented performance appraisal identifies, in behavioral terms, specific levels of success within a dimension (e.g., report writing) of job performance. As a result of this specificity, the supervisor is cast in the role of performance observer and reporter rather than judge. As such he is in a better position to substantiate his ratings in job-related terms that are understandable to both the employee and himself. In addition, the supervisor can point out the specific behaviors that the employee must manifest in order to show improved performance on his or her job.

Specificity of behavioral rating scales also bears directly on the identification of job training needs, another major result of the performance appraisal process. It is likely that some of the behaviors required to demonstrate improved performance on a given job will not be part of the subordinate's behavioral repertoire and so will provide little assistance in such situations. Therefore, he or she must first be made aware of their content and their impact on job performance. Behavioral performance appraisal, because of its job-centeredness, can be useful not only for identifying training needs but for setting specific learning objectives as well.[58]

Section 1607–E.E.O.C. Guidelines for Employment Selection Procedures

Legal guidelines that require job-related performance evaluation. The work behaviors or other criteria of employee adequacy, which the valid test is intended to predict or identify, must be fully described; in addition, in the case of rating techniques, the appraisal form(s) must be included as part of the validation evidence. Such criteria may include measures other than actual work proficiency, such as training time, supervisory ratings, regularity of attendance, and tenure. Whatever criteria are used, they must represent major or critical work behaviors as revealed by careful job analyses. Job analysis is required for validation purposes.

Job analysis takes two forms: (1) task analysis, or the results of the behavior of the job incumbent; and (2) worker analysis, which concentrates on the actual behavior patterns of the job incumbent. Job analysis should be systematic and comprehensive; should identify duties for satisfactory job performance; should define job elements; should set forth knowledge, skills, abilities, and other worker characteristics that are required for successful job performance; and should be on record for use when the basis of a test or selection procedure is legally challenged.

For information purposes, there are several validation processes: rational validation, content validation, construct validation, differential validation, concurrent validation, and criterion validation.

Criterion-related validity is the method most preferred by the E.E.O.C. for establishing the soundness of a test, since this method is the most susceptible to empirical and quantifiable measurement. The guidelines provide:

For the purpose of satisfying the requirements of this part, empirical evidence in support of a test's validity must be based on studies employing generally accepted procedures for determining criterion-related validity .... Evidence of content or construct validity ... may also be appropriate where criterion-related validity is not feasible. However, the evidence for content or construct validity should be accompanied by sufficient information from job analyses to demonstrate the relevance of the content (in the case of job knowledge or proficiency tests) or the construct (in the case of trait measures). Evidence of content validity alone may be acceptable for well-developed tests that consist of suitable samples of the essential knowledge, skills or behaviors composing the job in question. The types of knowledge, skills or behaviors contemplated here do not include those which can be acquired in a brief orientation to the job.[59]

Criterion-related validation requires a great deal of statistical input and is designed to measure the relationship between scores achieved on a test and later job performance. It is, in fact, the best method for predicting job performance. Procedures used to establish criterion-related validation involve statistical correlation between scores achieved on entrance tests and the measurements of job performance.

Certain information may be helpful for personnel decisions and should be collected, including: background information, interview test results, job description, systematically quantifying pertinent data, and standard of performance or quality expected.

Part 1607.1–E.E.O.C. Guidelines

It has also become clear that, in many instances, tests are used as the basis for employment decisions when there is no evidence of their validity as predictors of employee job performance. Where such evidence in support of presumed relationships between test performance and job behavior is lacking, the possibility of discrimination in the application of test results must be recognized. A test lacking demonstrated validity (i.e., having no known significant relationship to job behavior), and yielding lower scores for classes protected by Title VII, may result in the rejection of many who have necessary qualifications for successful work performance.

Part 1607.4–E.E.O.C. Guidelines

Evidence of a test's validity should consist of empirical data demonstrating that the test is predictive of, or significantly correlated with, important elements of work behavior that comprise or are relevant to the job or jobs for which candidates are being evaluated.

The Future of Performance Appraisal

Frank Landy addresses the future of performance appraisal very adequately when he states:

> A performance appraisal system must not only satisfy a department's personnel, but must also bear the weight of supporting decisions which may be scrutinized in the course of court cases of alleged discrimination. Further, the identification of performance quality is necessary for motivational programs of personnel and personal development. This last use highlights the future of performance appraisal systems. Patrol officers, becoming more aware of the complexities of their roles, realize that they perform in overlapping roles requiring different skills at different times. The maintenance of these skills and the development of new ones require feedback of the most sophisticated sort rather than global ratings of effectiveness. Almost all of the current theories of work motivation depend on an accurate and discriminating assessment of various aspects of work performance. For example, a Management By Objectives (MBO) program depends on the identification of individual strengths and weaknesses; it also depends on the identification of changes in these levels over time. A well constructed performance measurement system can provide such data. An improved performance appraisal system may fulfill the traditional goals of research and administrative decision-making, and an improved system can make a unique contribution in the form of providing the information necessary for the implementation of motivational programs.[60]

SELECTING AND PROMOTING "THE PATROL LEADER"

The patrol force of any police department will stagnate if the leaders are inefficient and ineffective. The success of the patrol force will ultimately be a result of leaders who are goal oriented and who use the management of objectives approach. In order to develop appropriate leadership, objective ratings of potential leaders should be included in the process of promotion within a police agency. There are excellent patrol officers and investigators who are crackerjacks in their field; however, it would be disastrous to promote them because as leaders they would fail. There are other excellent patrol officers who should be promoted because of demonstrated ability to lead, but they cannot convey their ability in writing, or they get uptight before an oral board.

Probably the most critical selection decision occurs at the first level of supervision; success here directly and obviously affects the daily operations of the agency. There should be little doubt that police agencies in general do not consistently identify capable supervisors. Unfortunately, once that first promotional level is attained, subsequent promotion often appears as the lesser of perceived evils—demotion or continued ineptitude.

The well-worn admonition that the best police officers do not necessarily make the best supervisors is occasionally ignored, resulting in damage to both the individual and the department. Since most police administrators patiently follow the traditional career ladder, it seems that many more have achieved leadership positions despite the system rather than because of it.

The quest for objectivity in the preparation and grading of testing instruments has led to an emphasis on written exams that permit only one correct answer, at least in theory, on subject matter deemed important to the position. The greater the competition for comparatively few promotional positions, the greater the emphasis on written exam results. Hence, the selection agency may focus on assuring a "good" distribution of test scores rather than on relating test items to actual job requirements.

Recognizing that not all police supervisory and management skills are evaluated well through written exams alone, police managers place greater weight on oral interviews as the rank aspired to increases. But apprehension about oral interviews exists, ranging from questions of structured versus unstructured interviews to participation of citizens versus "professional." As with written exams, the inherent limitations of the process (in the sense of evaluating actual job behaviors) are often glossed over.[61]

Whom shall we promote? Ten-thousandth of a percentage point separates in strict rank order a large number of candidates; but some move to the top of a competitive list simply by component weightings (e.g., veterans' preference) that may give certain questionable factors unintended influence. There is a great need for police agencies to determine reliability and validity for their individual promotional programs. Job analysis and behavioral analysis for the position open should be identified so that, for the person selected, excellent performance will result. The managerial skills, knowledge, and ability tailormade to the agency should be measured so that the most qualified fill the roles of organizational leadership.

Byham and Wettengel compare three methods of promotion, as follows:[62]

Assessment Center	*Panel Interviews*	*Paper & Pencil Tests*
Built around dimensions carefully defined through job analysis, and all dimensions are systematically covered.	While dimensions from research may be used, more often no list is used or an inadequate list is used. No real attempt to cover all of the dimensions is made in the interview due to the usual lack of structure.	Tests may be selected by job analysis, but tests only attempt to predict certain of the dimensions. For example, tests are poor at determining interpersonal dimensions.

Assessment Center	*Panel Interviews*	*Paper and Pencil Tests*
Dimensions are agreed upon by management before use. This creates an acceptance and understanding of them.	Usually not the case.	Usually not the case.
The involvement of higher-level managers in the selection of assessment center dimensions, and as assessors allows them to make effective use of assessment center reports and to believe in the results because they understand the system.	Membership of higher-level managers on interview panels often increases their distrust of the Panel Interview process as they feel it is unreliable. Thus they discount the results.	Unless a specific cut-off score is used as in Civil Service Examinations, the users of the test results seldom know how to integrate the test results with other performance data.
Multiple exercises are used. The participant can be observed in different situations: group and non-group; small and large group exercises that require preparation and those that do not; exercises where the participant is a subordinate, peer, supervisor; exercises requiring oral, written and other skills.	Single exercise.	Tests may be slightly different depending on tests used but all generally emphasized written and cognitive skills.
Uses multiple judgments (3 to 6 assessors) which increase accuracy and decrease bias.	Uses multiple judgments.	Quantitative score. Use of score may be judgmental.
Trained observers are used.	Participants in panel interviews are seldom trained and seldom have adequate time to plan the interview.	
Assessors usually do not know participants.	Interviewers usually do not know participants.	
Assessors are several levels above participants and thoroughly know the target-level job.	Interviewers are several levels above participants and thoroughly know the target-level job.	

Assessment Center	Panel Interviews	Paper & Pencil Tests
Real behaviors observed.	What a participant says he would do or has done is determined. Follow-up of important areas possible.	Participants often say what they think will get a high score in nonability tests.
Formal method of recording observations used.	Usually no formal method of recording observations of behavior or insights.	Formal method of collecting data used.
Large amount of data on participant obtained.	Small amount.	Small amount.
Procedure delays final decision until all information about participants is obtained.	Research indicates that interviewers quickly jump to a decision, and their subsequent questions are often an attempt to reinforce the first decision.	Highly quantitative.
Highly structured program producing quantitative results.	Low in structure. Low in quantitative results.	Highly quantitative.
Validities usually around 4 to 5.	Little known about validity.	Seldom above 3.
Technique flexible to various jobs.	Technique flexible to various jobs.	Less flexible because content validation for supervisory and managerial jobs is more difficult to achieve.
Relatively easy to establish content validity (job-relatedness).	Difficult to establish content validity (job-relatedness).	Difficult to establish content validity (job-relatedness).
Criterion-related validity research should be conducted.	Criterion-related validity research should be conducted.	Criterion-related validity research should be conducted.
Produces insights into development needs that can be beneficial whether or not the participant is promoted.	Not usually the case.	Not usually the case.
Process is understandable to participants; they see it as a fair means of evaluating all areas of management potential.	Participant evaluation of fairness depends on interviewers. Most interviewees feel interview covers only a portion of important management skills.	Often misunderstood, biases carried over from negative school experiences.

As you can see, criterion-related validity needs to be conducted in all three methods. Promotional programs should be fair on their face and fair in fact. One major concern of administrators is the integrity of the system, no matter which is used.

There is another process known as the "structured oral," or, as the author has renamed the program (developed for the Dallas/Fort Worth Airport Department of Public Safety), the "structured assessment promotional process." In this situation, the first phase is the submission of a resume and written statement of what the promotion of the individual to lieutenant will do for the agency. The second phase is a take-home exam consisting of ten medium-level-of-difficulty questions, with responses being weighed by defined dimensions of management. The next phase is a take-home exam of ten questions of higher-level difficulty, with responses being weighed by defined dimensions of management, with footnotes and bibliography required. The last phase is a panel interview; however, each member of the panel must submit the question and answer expected in advance, so that each member knows what is expected and what dimension of management is being measured. This process attempts to do what the assessment center does, except it is not as costly.

The assessment center is the latest process being used by many police agencies to select future leaders. This process is dynamic and uses a "standardized evaluation of a person's capabilities and behavior habits compiled and based upon an experience involving multiple inputs."[63] According to most reports, the modern process was begun by the Germans in World War II, followed by the U.S. Office of Strategic Services. Their use was followed by Harvard Professor Henry Murray, and then American Telephone and Telegraph research director, Douglas Ray. Police agencies are now using the assessment center.

The police agency assessment center usually requires that the following process be completed: establish the objective for the assessment; select the target position (Field Sergeant); define the dimension to be assessed (there are behavioral dimensions which include self-control, written/oral communication skills, leadership skills, flexibility, mental dexterity, and analytical skills; planning and organizing dimensions; and decision-making dimensions—these are not all inclusive; select exercises designed to elicit the appropriate dimension (in-basket group discussion, etc.); train assessors; present the program; give feedback to participants; and evaluate.

Brown[64] seems to give an excellent account of the positive factors and problems and limitations of assessment centers.

An Overview of Positive Factors

1. ACs provide a broad-based approach to the evaluation of personnel.

2. ACs match the individual to the job.
3. ACs appear to meet EEOC standards more so than the traditional means of paper and pencil tests and/or panel interviews.
4. ACs serve as a training tool.
5. Candidates feel it is a fairer process for promotional determination.
6. It is as valid or more valid than any other currently used technique.
7. ACs serve to select managers of the future.

Problems and Limitations of Assessment Centers

1. ACs are expensive to operate.
2. Those not selected to attend will feel rejected.
3. ACs produce a great amount of anxiety.
4. ACs tend to identify and promote the organizational man.
5. ACs tend not to forecast managers of the future (concurrent validity, not predictive validity).
6. People would rather be judged on real-life experience, not simulated.
7. There has not been enough research to determine validity.

The assessment center is not a panacea, but, for those who are responsible for selecting future leaders, the process is understandable, logical, and tremendously susceptible to the appropriate validity.

THE PATROL MANAGER AND LABOR RELATIONS

The new patrol officer enters police work hoping to rise on merit. New management and personnel techniques have impressed him with the belief that promotion will come his way as he demonstrates his ability and intelligence. There is now so much material available to him on police administration, patrol operation, planning, criminal investigation, etc., that he may even be more informed than the veteran officer. When such informed college graduates with degrees in police administration gain experience, it is probable that these young officers will ask why orders are given and insist upon being involved in change and decision-making. When enlightened leadership does not allow participation to a degree compatible with achieving the objectives of the organization and the individual, the new patrol officers seek alliance with organized labor in order to have a say about their salary, wages, conditions of work, and policy. The new patrol officer has the intelligence to have something to say. If not allowed to say it, he or she will find another way, usually through the employees' organizations. These organizations include: (1) the National Police Union, (2) the International Conference of Police Association, (3) the Fraternal Order of Police, (4) the State Research Association, (5) state employee clubs, (6) police officers' clubs, (7) the Police Officers' Association, (8) local fraternities, and (9) benevolent associations. The young patrol officer of today has seen victory by one or more of these organizations in the area of salary, overtime, civilian review boards, etc., and finds them enticing.

These organizations have used the courts, civil suits, and executive action to resolve problems to their satisfaction. They have also demonstrated muscle in the political arena. Police departments are different for the young officer of today. Patrol commanders need to reflect on the needs, views, and values of this new patrol officer in order to manage by objectives properly. If being a police officer is complex and diverse, being a patrol commander is more so. Patrol officers of today will only sit by for so long to allow police leadership to do what they believe should be done. If the leadership fails, the result is internal conflict, external conflict (established authority), and community instability; none of which contributes to a professional image.

Does this sound like militancy? If it does, then we must ask, as William J. Bopp does in his book *The Police Rebellion*, "Why did the police become militant in the first place?" Officer Dick MacEachern, president of the Boston Police Patrolman's Association (BPPA), offers one view:

> We are sick of being thrown to the dogs. Our militancy started when everyone else's became accepted. Everyone began clamoring for their rights and, all of a sudden, the cop was left holding the satchel. The city police administration, they all began yielding to pressure groups. But who ends up the loser? The bad guy? It's the cop who's trying to represent the public and government the best he can and then finding the government isn't sure of itself. So they back step and we get the heat. . . . Militancy [of the police] just had to come. There's nothing wrong with the word. What it means is that you're not sitting on your dead ass.[65]

Former Detroit Police Commissioner Ray Girardin echoes MacEachern's sentiments:

> Police these days have been on the defensive and are fighting back and they're going to the man who speaks their language. . . . They feel they are handcuffed.[66]

What this means is that the officer has a view and would like the right of having that view at least considered. Patrol has the largest number of officers and the greatest likelihood of potential internal conflict.

Patrol administrators, beware, because you are leading officers who will not accept "Do it because I told you to." Conflict resolution or managing conflict should be an intricate part of the patrol administrator's education. Today, managing conflict is as difficult as managing change and has to be understood as well, to keep disrupting forces from destroying the department. Patrol leaders must be aware of what a healthy, viable patrol force consists of. It should definitely not be made up of a group of yes-men. When disagreement exists but is open, forthright, honest, and based upon true conviction on the part of the speaker, it must be respected and considered as an intricate part of effective decision-making. Disagreement should not be considered negativism or radicalism. As a patrol administrator, you would do well always to ask the opinion of your most outspoken patrol commander who has different viewpoints from yourself. Your goals should be the same; the method is different. When you consider all opinions (alternatives), you will be closer to the most effective decision. Sergeant, if you work a sector, a squad of men, and you lead them with, "Do it because I told you to," the only brain you are using is your own. It is upsetting when you can't solve a particular problem relating to crime, community, etc. Would you like some help? Would you care for some innovative approaches? Change your style! Include your young intelligent patrol officers.

The 1980s

The following thoughts are condensed from an article by Richard M. Ayres and are intended to create a laboratory of analysis for instructors and students.

- Will Congress apply the NLRA to the public sector?
- What changes will take place, if any, if Congress does apply NLRA?
- Should police have the right to strike? What are the consequences?
- Collective bargaining legislation is necessary and is here to stay.
- A national police union will be formed. What are the consequences?
- Because of the complexity of public sector bargaining, conflict is actual.
- Taxpayer revolt, inflation, tight budgets will increase frustration of participants.
- Increased police strikes will result in police–citizen isolation/alienation.
- Improved strike preparation by government officials will decrease number of strikes.
- Research can identify correlations in police-strike–crime/disorder activity.
- Police strikes must include violence.

- Most police salaries will be determined by public referendum.
- Police perceptions are "We are not appreciated."
- Police values have changed resulting in "Police Job" rather than career, commitment, dedication.
- Increased education for some officers has caused and will continue to cause a conflict.
- Management effectiveness has not improved enough to avoid job alienation.
- The 1960s have come to be known as the age of the dissident.
- The 1970s as the age of the litigant.
- The 1980s will be the age of employee confrontation.
- There is very little the police administrator can do to change the course of the "police employee organization" evolution.[67]

The importance of the patrol officer and his role has been recognized by the National Advisory Commission on Criminal Justice Standards and Goals. The recommendations in Standard 8.2 of its *Report on Police* are presented here for objective discussion.

STANDARD 8.2 ENHANCING THE ROLE OF THE POLICE OFFICER

Every local government and police chief executive, recognizing that the patrol function is the most important element of the police agency, immediately should adopt policies that attract and retain highly qualified personnel in the patrol force.

1. Every local government should expand its classification and pay system to provide greater advancement opportunities within the patrol ranks. The system should provide:

   a. Multiple pay grades within the basic rank;
   b. Opportunity for advancement within the basic rank to permit equality between patrol officers and investigators;
   c. Parity in top salary step between patrol officers and non-supervisory officers assigned to other operational functions;
   d. Proficiency pay for personnel who have demonstrated expertise in specific field activities that contribute to more efficient police service.

2. Every police chief executive should seek continually to enhance the role of the patrol officer by providing status and recognition from the agency and encouraging similar status and recognition from the community. The police chief executive should:

a. Provide distinctive insignia indicating demonstrated expertise in specific field activities;
b. Insure that all elements within the agency provide maximum assistance and cooperation to the patrol officer;
c. Implement a community information program emphasizing the importance of the patrol officer in the life of the community and encouraging community cooperation in providing police service;
d. Provide comprehensive initial and in-service training thoroughly to equip the patrol officer for his role;
e. Insure that field supervisory personnel possess the knowledge and skills necessary to guide the patrol officer;
f. Implement procedures to provide agency-wide recognition of patrol officers who have consistently performed in an efficient and commendable manner;
g. Encourage suggestions on changes in policies, procedures, and other matters that affect the delivery of police services and reduction of crime;
h. Provide deployment flexibility to facilitate various approaches to individual community crime problems;
i. Adopt policies and procedures that allow the patrol officer to conduct the complete investigation of crimes which do not require extensive follow-up investigation, and allow them to close the investigation of those crimes; and
j. Insure that promotional oral examination boards recognize that patrol work provides valuable experience for men seeking promotion to supervisory positions.[68]

A CONCLUDING THOUGHT: PATROL PERSONNEL

Previous discussion has pointed out the wide choice of management styles available to patrol administrators of today. The selection of the right style as it relates to the forces working on the individual leader, the group, the environment, and the new patrol officer is now more critical to success than at any time in the past. What it takes to motivate the new better-educated and more skillful patrol officer is different from what it took to motivate his forerunner.

Each patrol manager should study the patrol officers he manages closely before deciding which leadership style to use. Consideration should be given to the officers' response to authoritarianism, to permissive environments, and to methods of motivation, as well as to their thoughts on money versus career advancement. You cannot lead today if your knowledge about leadership is ten years old. Today's professional patrol manager uses management as a resource, and treats the patrol officer with respect and dignity, using an approach that recognizes knowledge, skill, aptitude, and expectations. This approach is based on an environment where the patrol leader and patrol officer work toward mutual objectives, using their combined talents to solve problems and achieve results. It is an approach of power through people rather than power over people. However, some officers may feel more secure with authoritarian or paternalistic approaches. Consequently, the patrol leader must be flexible in his style of leadership because of situation, environment, and technology, almost to the point where he develops, as Alvin Toffler called it in *Future Shock*, an "ad-hocracy style." Whatever style is selected, however, it should be the one most appropriate to achievement of the objective.

The new patrol officer wants to be consulted in the decision-making process, especially when his future is affected. This desire has great merit because it signifies commitment to objective achievement by the officer, who is a potential source of innovation and creativity. In addition, it shows dedication and loyalty to the police discipline on the part of the new patrol officer. This loyalty must be integrated with loyalty to the specific organization.

The social trend of egalitarianism, as addressed in Project Star, has not excluded the police. Changes in the economic, social, political, and technological environment have caused the new patrol officer to seek a sharing of power. If managerial elitism does not decrease to allow him a share, the power will be taken – by militant police unions. The new patrol officer wants to be rewarded monetarily, through appropriate praise and recognition, and with results achievement. He wants to be criticized, but constructively and justifiably, by a patrol leader who behaves as a leader, demonstrating ability, skills, and knowledge. Most of all, the new patrol officer wants his talents tapped and a chance to demonstrate his knowledge, ability, and aspirations.

NOTES

1. Abraham Zaleznik, *Human Dilemmas of Leadership* (New York: Harper & Row, 1963), p. 1.
2. Ross Lawrence Goble, "Leadership for a Society in Transition," in *Management for the Future*, Lewis Benton, Ed. (New York: McGraw-Hill, 1980), pp. 135–137.
3. Fred E. Fiedler, *A Theory of Leadership Effectiveness* (New York: McGraw-Hill, 1967).
4. James J. Cribbin, *Leadership Skills for Executives* (New York: American Management Association, Extension Institute, 1977), pp. 28–29.
5. Robert M. Fulmer, *The New Management*, 2d ed. (New York: Macmillin, 1978), p. 329.
6. Ibid., p. 328.

7. Laurence J. Peter, *The Peter Principle* (New York: Wm. Morrow, 1969).
8. Edgar H. Schein, *Organizational Psychology* (Englewood Cliffs, N.J.: Prentice-Hall, 1965), pp. 56–57.
9. These materials are from the monograph *The Leader Looks at Styles of Leadership*, by Dr. Warren H. Schmidt, which is a part of the Looking-Into-Leadership series published and copyrighted by Leadership Resources, Inc., 1750 Pennsylvania Avenue, N.W., Washington, D.C. 20006. They are reproduced here by special written permission of the publisher.
10. Anthony Jay, *Management and Machiavelli* (New York: Holt, Rinehart & Winston, 1971), p. 139.
11. Peter Drucker, *The Practice of Management* (New York: Harper & Row, 1954), chap. 10.
12. See Victor H. Vroom, *Work and Motivation* (New York: John Wiley & Sons, 1964), pp. 105–159.
13. Ibid.
14. Fremont E. Kast and James E. Rosenzweig, *Organization and Management: A Systems Approach*, 2d ed. (New York: McGraw-Hill, 1974), p. 251.
15. Ibid., p. 254.
16. Lyman W. Porter and Edward E. Lawler III, *Managerial Attitudes and Performance* (Homewood, Ill.: Richard D. Irwin, 1968).
17. Kurt Lewin, *Field Theory and Social Science* (New York: Harper & Row, 1951).
18. Martin G. Evans, "The Effects of Supervisory Behavior on the Path–Goal Relationship," *Organization Behavior and Human Performance* 5 (1970).
19. Robert J. House, "A Path–Goal Theory of Leader Effectiveness," *Administrative Science Quarterly* 16 (1971).
20. Robert J. House and Terrence R. Mitchell, "Path–Goal Theory of Leadership," in *Organization Behavior and Industrial Psychology*, Kenneth N. Wexley and Gary A. Yul, eds. (New York: Oxford University Press, 1975), pp 177–186.
21. Leonard R. Sayles, *Leadership: What Effective Managers Really Do and How They Do It.* (New York: McGraw-Hill, 1979), p. 58.
22. Ibid., p. 59.
23. See Fritz Roethlisberger, "The Elusive Phenomena," Harvard Business School, Division of Research, Boston, Mass., 1977.
24. Robert Carlson, *Interaction Concepts in Personality* (Chicago: Aldine, 1969).
25. Sayles, op. cit., pp. 62–63.
26. James Owens, *The Effective Manager* (Washington, D.C.: Management Education, Ltd., 1977), p. 32.
27. Wilbur Schramm, ed., "How Communication Works," in *The Process and Effects of Mass Communication* (Urbana, Ill.: University of Illinois Press, 1954), p. 3.
28. William J. Bopp, *Police Personnel Administration* (Boston: Holbrook Press, 1974).
29. Roger M. D'Aprix, *How's That Again* (Homewood, Ill.: Dow Jones-Irwin, 1969), pp. 10–11.
30. Grant E. Mayberry, *First Line Management* (New York: American Management Association, 1979), p. 37.
31. Louis Brownslow, "The Administration Process" (lecture to the graduate school of the U.S. Department of Agriculture, February 1939).
32. William H. Newman and Charles E. Summer, Jr., *The Process of Management: Concepts, Behavior and Practice* (Englewood Cliffs, N.J.: Prentice-Hall, 1969), p. 60.
33. American Bar Association, "Standards Relating to the Urban Police Function," *The Police Chief* (May 1973): 60. Reprinted by permission of the American Bar Association.
34. John C. Klotter, *Techniques for Police Instruction* (Springfield, Ill.: Charles C Thomas, 1971). Reprinted by permission.

35. Ibid.
36. Ibid.
37. Ibid.
38. Ibid.
39. See James S. Kakalik and Sorrel Wildhorn, *Aid to Decision-Making in Patrol* (report prepared for the Department of Housing and Urban Development by the Rand Corporation), for an example of available information that may influence patrol.
40. James Q. Wilson, "Dilemmas of Police Administration," *Police Administration Review* 28 (September/October 1968): 412.
41. Bopp, op. cit., pp. 80–81.
42. Rensis Likert, *The Human Organization* (New York: McGraw-Hill, 1967), pp. 3–11.
43. Ibid.
44. Bopp, op. cit., pp. 94–96. Reprinted by permission.
45. Chester I. Barnard, *The Functions of the Executive* (Cambridge, Mass.: Harvard University Press, 1939), p. 128.
46. Robert Tannenbaum, Irving R. Weschler, and Fred Massarik, *Leadership and Organization, A Behavioral Science Approach* (New York: McGraw-Hill, 1961).
47. James D. Mooney and Alan C. Reiley, *The Principles of Organization* (New York: Harper and Brothers, 1939), p. 5.
48. Henry C. Metcalf and L. Urwich, eds., *Dynamic Administration and the Collected Papers of Mary Follett* (New York: Harper and Brothers, 1940), p. 71.
49. Alvin Toffler, *Future Shock* (New York: Bantam Books, 1971), p. 20.
50. James F. Ahern, *Police in Trouble* (New York: Hawthorn Books, 1972), pp. 248–249.
51. H. H. Carey, "Consultative Supervision and Management," *Personnel* 18, no. 5 (1971): 283.
52. Copyright 1966 by IACP, Inc. Material based upon survey conducted by Field Operations Division.
53. Irving B. Wicker, Jr., "Training Law Enforcement Officers to Rate," *Police* (June 1972): 47–48.
54. Thomas Riley, *Teaching an Employee to Do a New Job* (Chicago: Industrial Relations Center, University of Chicago, 1964).
55. E. L. Thorndyke, "A Constant Error in Psychological Ratings," *Journal of Applied Psychology* 4 (1920): 25–29.
56. Paul A. Albrecht, *Discussing and Improving an Employee's Performance*, pp. 24–26. Reprinted by permission of the Industrial Relations Center/The University of Chicago. Copyright 1964 by the Industrial Relations Center/The University of Chicago.
57. Material from Kansas City Police Department. Reprinted with permission.
58. Metropolitan Dade County Department of Public Safety, Performance Appraisal, Dade County, Florida, 1978, used with permission.
59. Equal Employment Opportunity Guidelines, Section 1607.5(a). Department of Labor, Washington, D.C., 1978.
60. Frank Landy, *Performance Appraisal in Police Departments* (Washington, D.C.: The Police Foundation, 1977), p. 13.
61. Roger Reinke, *Selection through Assessment Centers* (Washington, D.C.: The Police Foundation, 1977), p. 9.
62. William C. Byham and Carl Wettengel, "Table of Comparison of Assessment Center Method of Promotion with Panel Interview and Paper and Pencil Tests," *Public Personnel Management* (September–October 1974): 45–53.
63. Third International Congress on the Assessment Center Method, *Standards and Ethical Considerations for Assessment Center Operations* (Quebec, Can., May 1975), p. 2.

64. Gary Brown, "What You Always Wanted to Know about Assessment Centers but Were Afraid to Ask," *The Police Chief* (June 1978). International Association of Chiefs of Police, Gaithersburg, Md.

65. *The Boston Globe*, 15 June 1969, p. 8.

66. Ibid., 15 December 1968, p. 88.

67. Richard M. Ayres, "Police Labor Relations in the 1980's, Conflict or Cooperation," *The Police Chief* (December 1979): 62–64. International Association of Chiefs of Police, Gaithersburg, Md.

68. National Advisory Commission on Criminal Justice Standards and Goals, *Report on Police* (Washington, D.C.: U.S. Government Printing Office, 1973), p. 195.

.3.

The Social Psychology of Patrol Administration

GOVERNMENT AS A SOCIAL ORGANIZATION

American society, like any other society, wants tranquility so that citizens can continue the business of living. The trichotomy of law enforcement, services, and peace keeping, along with all the sub-objectives of these three tasks, is the essence of tranquility for these citizens. Most people would rather live under a government not especially to their liking rather than a state of anarchy in which citizens cannot go about the business of living. This does not mean that revolution will not take place in societies that have been pushed to the brink, but rather indicates a resistance to prolonged uncertainty of some kind of order. How we think is how we act in our environment.

Daniel Glaser provides us with some insight about our society regarding crime:[1]

> The types of predation subject to criminal penalty will continue to increase as victims gain more government backing against those who injure their persons, properties, or civil rights. This trend will not reflect the polarization of our society by the class conflict that Marxists predict, but rather the cross-cutting of interest-group alignments in our pluralistic democracy. Yet the inclusion process will expand state protection for the poor and the weak who are in large groups of voters, and will reduce the ability of the wealthy and powerful to victimize them. Simultaneously, the generalization of values will foster more tolerance of deviant conduct that does not injure others and that the criminal-justice system cannot effectively prohibit,

145

although such a trend may occasionally be reversed by puritanical backlash. The causes of crime vary with the offense, the offender, and the circumstances, so crime prevention by eliminating causes is a complex problem. Yet the victimizations that most disturb people—murders, muggings, breakins, and purse snatchings—are committed disproportionally by adolescents. Such predations can be diminished if we reduce the age segregation in our society, guarantee employment, augment motivation in education, and eliminate discrimination against minorities. Radical criminologists insist that such goals will be attained only when the working class creates a socialist revolution, and probably not by our election process. On the other hand, conservatives either denigrate these goals or question their feasibility. This book has argued that these goals—law enforcement, service, peace keeping, community tranquility—can be achieved within our political and economic system, and that our society is moving toward them.

The full-service police agency that tries to provide all things to all people has difficulty because of the norm measurement of increase/decrease of crime. Police officers are used by the lower socioeconomic groups of citizens the way others refer to their doctors or ministers. Presently, police agencies are screening calls for service simply because of expense. These agencies involved with screening usually go through a public education process before implementation.

The order maintenance responsibility, which seems to contain the other two (service and law enforcement), is the crux of the tranquility discussed earlier. The social control function of the police, persuasive or coercive, is within the control of government. The control through policy, the political process, direction of the policy, is complex because of our pluralistic, democratic society. Professional police administrators want to provide the police tasks necessary to maintain a tranquil community, however, walking the maze of conflict is difficult. Figure 3.1 depicts the conflict potential for the police administrator just because of the position in the community. What about which laws to enforce, to what degree, and to which groups? What about the whole issue of discretion? How do you give credibility to the social services function of the police? Why aren't the social service agencies available twenty-four hours a day, seven days a week, 365 days a year, as the police are available? Whenever other professionals need the police for a situation, the police are there, and usually this is for a control function. However, the police do not have reciprocity.

Thus, it is as an agent of control that the policeman participates in a divided labor with social workers, doctors, clergymen, lawyers and teachers in maintaining social integration. The problems he faces appear to be a failure of integration within the integrative system, so that he cannot mobilize the other agents when he needs them.[2]

Figure 3.1 *Conflict by position*

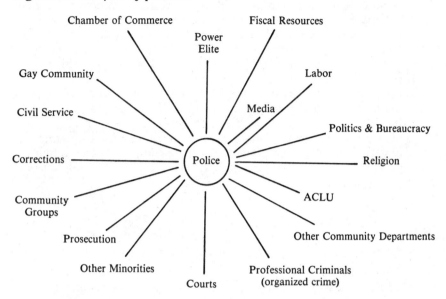

Who controls and has the power to hold the police accountable for performance? Government! The first question for the patrol leader is, how can he or she become politically astute, i.e., who has the power? What group? What individual? How is government organized? Who forms coalitions? Who is the chairperson of the finance committee? Can preferential treatment be read into past policy statements and requests for implementation? Is there anyone who can force the police department to selectively enforce a given law? The answers to these questions are an important arsenal of knowledge necessary for the patrol leader to be politically astute.

To begin, human beings are quite different when they are alone versus when living in an organization. External politics affect the organization and internal politics affect the individual within the organization. The police agency is open and vulnerable and, to be effective, should not allow others to manipulate it for individual or group gains.

Rapp and Patitucci conclude:

- Most economic, social, and physical problems within a community can be solved best at the local level, yet most local governments do not have the capacity to use available resources in a manner that will produce the desired results.
- The conditions that affect the ability of local-government officials to get things done are most often unique to the specific community; general prescriptions about how to solve urban problems and improve the performance of all local governments are not generally applicable.

- Although local-government officials can learn much from their private sector counterparts, a local government cannot be managed exactly as a private business is managed.
- Many individuals, working within and outside a local government, affect its performance; these individuals and the institutions they represent must be considered and involved in taking actions to improve performance.
- There are no quick solutions or easy answers to the challenge of making local governments work better. It is a long-term undertaking that must recognize the interplay between political and bureaucratic forces, between citizen demands and financial realities, between management responsibilities and employee rights, and between local prerogatives and state and national priorities.[3]

As a social organization, government performance must be related to changes in community conditions. Police organizations must do the same; however, the police may not always have accurate knowledge of the client or of consumer preferences. The results achieved by the police organization must in some way be matched with the conditions preferred by the citizens of the given community. Citizen surveys are one avenue, with the results of the survey being used as data to analyze, so that performance indicators and success can be measured. The police organization is a resource-dependent organization and, because of this situation, must be aware of the potential to be manipulated. Therefore, it is essential for the patrol leader to have a systematic view of the input and output process to synthesize the components and sub-components (activities), in order to match the performance of patrol with one of the ultimate conditions of a community desired by its citizens . . . safety and security (Figure 3.2).

Also, police administrators deal with people, organizations, environment, and technology as priorities. In doing so, the administrator must understand the social control output as making society more predictable, which organizations are designed to do, i.e., reduce uncertainty. Society needs laws, but the limits of law are not the statutes, but the capacity to enforce these laws.

Government must also be involved with the society by determining the scope of the police function not confined to protecting life and property and enforcing the law. Various neat but commodious classification schemes have been suggested to cover the range of police activities.[4] None of these schemes does justice to the richness of police work. Here is a nearly exhaustive list of police functions, specifying at least one country where each is performed:

(1) protecting life and property (U.S.); (2) enforcing the criminal law (Britain); (3) investigating criminal offenses (France); (4) patrolling

Figure 3.2 *The relationship of performance to the achievement of desired community conditions*

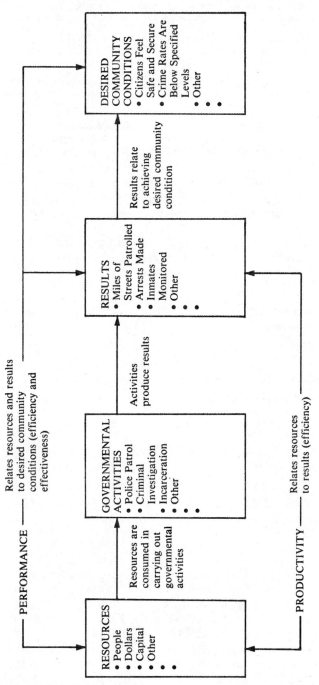

Source: Reprinted by permission of Westview Press from Brian W. Rapp and Frank M. Patitucci, *Managing Local Government for Improved Performance.* Copyright © 1977 by Westview Press, Boulder, Colorado.

public places (Germany); (5) advising about crime prevention (Canada); (6) conducting prosecutions (Britain); (7) sentencing for minor offenses (Germany); (8) maintaining order and decorum in public places by directing, interrupting, and warning (U.S.); (9) guarding persons and facilities (France); (10) regulating traffic (Norway); (11) controlling crowds (Germany); (12) regulating and suppressing vice (U.S.); (13) counseling juveniles (Netherlands); (14) gathering information about political and social life (France); (15) monitoring elections (Italy); (16) conducting counter-espionage (France); (17) issuing ordinances (Germany); (18) inspecting premises (Germany); (19) issuing permits and licenses (Britain); (20) serving summonses (Norway); (21) supervising jails (Norway); (22) impounding animals and lost property (Britain); (23) advising members of the public and referring them to other agencies (Scotland); (24) caring for the incapacitated (U.S.); (25) promoting community crime-prevention activities (Scotland); and (26) participating in policy councils of government (France).

While no police organization does all these things, many do most of them. And bewildering as the variety is, the list ignores housekeeping functions required to maintain the organization.[5]

Bayley continues by stating, "Police are defined largely by what they do but never by how they are organized and rarely by how they are controlled."[6] Thus, he gives the following definition: "Police are a group authorized in the name of territorial communities to utilize force within the community to handle whatever needs doing. This formulation ties police to government in its most common contemporary form, namely, with a territorial mandate."[7]

Within this relationship of government and the police, using the historical perspective, Bayley discusses the studies of what police do with regard to the three different measures of the nature of activity. He explains that assignments are what the police say they are undertaking, occasions are the situations police encounter when they are mobilized, and outcomes are the actions police take in any situation. He concludes with the following:

So many explanations have been put forward to explain the nature of police work because different measures have been used. One would not expect the same factors to account for variations in all of them. At the same time, these measures of police work are not wholly independent of one another. They are interrelated in two ways. First, changes in one affect changes in the others. For example, assignments influence the kinds of occasions that come to the attention of the police. Similarly, the kind of event brought to the police shapes what the police can do. Second, independent factors affecting one measure of the police function may affect others. For example, public opinion about the need to enforce certain laws influences both formal

Figure 3.3 *Bayley's measures of police work*

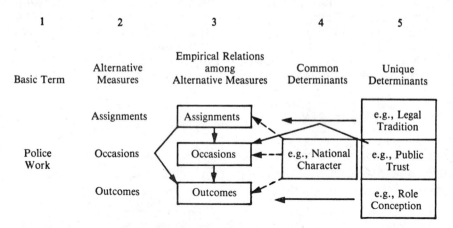

Source: Reprinted from David H. Bayley, "Police Function, Structure, and Control in Western Europe and North America: Comparative and Historical Studies," in *Crime and Justice: An Annual Review of Research*, ed. Norval Morris and Michael Tonry, 1979, The University of Chicago Press. Reprinted with permission.

assignments and outcomes. National traditions may affect what the people bring to the police as well as what the police do.

The conceptual and empirical points that have been made about the three measures of police work are illustrated in Figure 3.3. The relation between column 1 and column 2 is definitional. "Assignments," "occasions," and "outcomes" are distinguishable meanings of "police work." The relations shown among the boxes in column 3 are empirical, as are the relations between columns 3, 4, and 5. Separating common from unique determinants helps to organize the wealth of hypotheses suggested to account for differences in "police work." Legal tradition, for instance, probably impinges only on assignments; public trust only on occasions. But reactive or proactive instigation may affect both occasions and outcomes, while national character influences assignments, occasions, and outcomes.[8]

Bayley has at least partially demonstrated some of the complexities and conflict included in the performance of the police function. In a democratic society, the patrol leader should focus on the analysis of the agency in relationship to the function to develop professional performance. To emphasize the complexity of patrol leadership, Rumbaut and Bittner put forth what may be considered a challenge to the development of the necessary skills, knowledge, and ability to meet the challenge:

> The problems of policing are not simply problems of finding "efficient" and "effective" means; they are problems of ends, of competing social values, interests, and priorities, the resolution of which raises fundamental moral and political issues to be decided by an informed

citizenry, not only scientific or technical issues to be decided by experts and technocrats. Hence, the most hopeful prospect for substantive police reform is the influence an informed public can exert on the direction of change in police agencies. Such a prospect is at best uncertain. Meanwhile the present dominance of technocratic values and interests in police reform will likely continue to be achieved at the expense of democratic values and interests.[9]

PATROL POLICY AND SOCIETY

Policies for administering patrol have been, should have been, and are under scrutiny, to produce the best patrol product available for each police agency. Naturally, police discretion and use of deadly force will continue to be of interest on a long-term basis because of their serious nature. However, as the patrol leader well knows, police must work every day, and any transitional period must be met with what is available. Consequently, concerns of long standing are one thing, community-approved policies for daily use are another. Two reports have addressed the policy issue:

> The police in the United States exercise considerable discretion. Police discretion is paradoxical. It appears to flout legal commands, yet it is necessary because of limited police resources, the ambiguity and breadth of criminal statutes, the informal expectations of legislatures, and the often conflicting demands of the public. . . . The existence of police discretion has often been denied by police administrators and its legitimacy withheld by legislators, but it can no longer be ignored. The police are professional decision-makers who exercise discretion. . . . [10]

> Given the range of responsibilities which the police have, they cannot be held to a system of decision-making which involves no risk-taking—anymore than can psychiatrists in deciding whether to release a person who has attempted suicide or parole board members in voting upon the release of an inmate. The formulation of police policy and its articulation to the public would, over a period of time, begin to educate the public into recognizing that the police must not only exercise discretion, but must assume a risk in doing so. Prior statements which "put the community on notice" with regard to police functioning in various areas would afford some relief from the current dilemma in which, in the absence of such police formulations, the police are both subject to ridicule for not exercising discretion and subject to condemnation for making such judgments when they do not work out.[11]

The policing needs of the community should be met with due consideration of all factors involved. Some of the inherent factors include: responsibilities, arrest procedures, use of civilians and paraprofessionals, assignment, auxiliary police, response time, screening calls, costs of police service, diversion, and relation with the community.

Figure 3.4 *Service-call decision-flow process*[12]

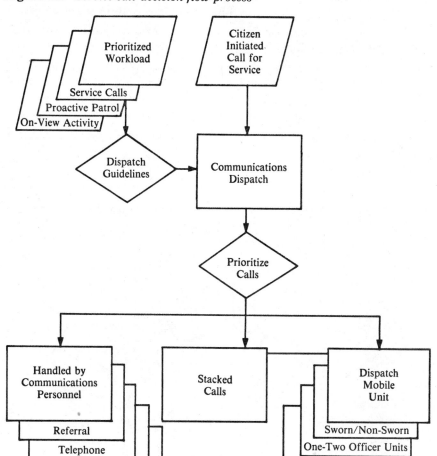

Managing Patrol Operations addresses the issue as (1) reducing workload to provide more patrol time, (2) offering the public information about the reality of policing, and (3) attempting tried and proven and innovative programs.[13] Figure 3.4 shows how screening and prioritizing calls can assist in making policing more efficient and effective.

FACTORS IMPACTING PATROL PERFORMANCE

Patrol is the police organization's social control. The leaders wish to be free from interference by government, but this is not likely. Even autonomy, as we have seen, is not a panacea; therefore, accountability must prevail. What accountability? In our society, the pressures will continue, re accountability; but there should be an understanding between police and citizens of what it means. This also has to be balanced in the political arena. Elected officials have a responsibility to question police policy. This should be done in a way that maintains legitimacy while minimizing any taint of political interference. The common understanding of the police function provides an arena for objective critical review of policy conflicts. One way of viewing the interrelated web of forces that affect the ability of public officials to use available resources to get things done (i.e., performance) is through Figure 3.5.

Figure 3.5 *Twelve factors affecting the performance of a local government*

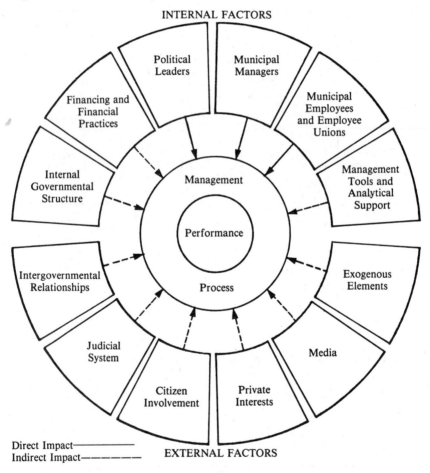

Source: Reprinted by permission of Westview Press from *Managing Local Government for Improved Performance* by Brian Rapp and Frank Patitucci. Copyright © 1977 by Westview Press, Boulder, Colorado.

The patrol leader checklist for internal factors:

- Understand the city charter (county, state) and administrative regulations affecting relationships between and among governmental agencies, and know the extent of authority the police have in this relationship;
- Be intimately aware of the financial practice of government, e.g., which agency receives how much money and why, and what can I do to insure that the police agency is receiving the maximum financial assistance within realistic constraints of government;
- Who are the political leaders, why were they elected, what should my relationship be with each, are there any techniques I can use to effectively present my views designed to honestly impress each political leader?
- Have I increased my education to better communicate with municipal managers who usually have been schooled in public administration (holding advanced degrees)?
- Am I capable of maintaining appropriate relationships with employees, union and non-union, to obtain commitment to excellent performance?
- Have I developed my analytical skills?
- Do I know where and what kinds of information to collect and how to analyze that information so I can provide answers to questions of government?
- Am I aware of responsibilities given to other agencies of government (especially social services) by law, which will assist us in viewing citizen service systematically? (This will provide for the agency best equipped to handle a specific task to do so.)
- Does patrol policy provide for citizen involvement?
- Are specific strategies designed to achieve citizen cooperation; i.e., educational programs to help citizens protect themselves, security surveys, operation identification, neighborhood crime watch, appropriate ordinances to improve security, and citizen patrols?
- Have I developed the ability to transmit information to the media on a timely basis?
- Do I encourage police personnel to write and speak effectively for the department?
- Have I provided literature for search and research of contemporary topics?
- Are my commanders capable of anticipating problems involving civic associations, business associations, etc., and are they able to present points of view on current issues?
- Am I aware of my total environment, i.e., geography, demography, socioeconomic indicators, and social trends?

The point is, history and social literature assist us in awareness so that problems or potential problems can be anticipated.

As a patrol leader, I am aware of recent civil disorders and prison riots. Consequently, history, being aware of who is involved and some of the extreme responses concerning disruption, could identify particular information for analysis. Regarding this statement, the following literature would be relevant.

A number of events aided the disaffection of youth and the growth of radicalism.[14] Skolnick has suggested that eight events were particularly important.

> One was the nonviolent southern civil rights movement. Considerable disillusionment followed upon the brutal treatment of civil rights workers and blacks who were only attempting to exercise their rights as citizens. A second event was the war on poverty, which promised much and delivered very little. Third were the events at Berkeley which cast university administrators in a new light and reshaped the image of the actual functions of the university in the society. The university and its administrators were seen to reflect the same corruption that pervaded the larger society.
>
> Fourth, the escalation of the Vietnam War and the attendant credibility gap regarding governmental policies were blatantly counter to the will of the people which supposedly was sovereign. Fifth, the involvement of the universities with the Vietnam War and with the military establishment in general clearly destroyed the claim of academic neutrality and corroborated the belief in academic corruption.
>
> The draft was the sixth factor. Student deferments were restricted, and many students faced the possibility of being called to participate in a war which they believed was immoral. Moreover, the draft was perceived as violating basic rights of individualism and voluntarism. A seventh factor was the continuing inability of the government to resolve problems of race, poverty, and urban decline. Finally, the eighth factor was confrontation with police on campus. Police violence radicalized a number of students who had been either moderate or uncommitted.[15]

What Mr. Skolnick determined may or may not be believed by police, but what is important is that the patrol leader is aware that some people potentially perceive this information to be accurate. Thus, contingency responses can be formulated proactively.

Rapp and Patitucci classify the twelve factors another way:[16]

People-related Factors
- Political leaders
- Municipal managers
- Municipal employees and their unions

Management Systems
- Management tools and analytical assistance
- Financing and financial practices

Structure
- Internal government structure
- Intergovernmental relationships
- Judicial system

Interest Groups
- Private interests
- Media
- Citizen involvement

Other
- Exogenous elements

Here factors are placed into five categories according to the nature of each factor. In this classification, the term *people-related factors* describes the decision-makers who have a major impact on the performance of local government. *Management systems* is a classification for the tools used by these actors in carrying out their responsibilities. *Structure* and *interest groups* refer to structural, political, legal, and human constraints on the ways in which governmental actors use available tools to achieve performance.

MANAGEMENT COP CULTURE, STREET COP CULTURE

Are street officers social workers? Are police officers understanding, sensitive, tough, courageous? Do police officers prevent crime as well as apprehend criminals? What stage of moral development have police officers and police managers reached? Or are the stages of moral development situational? Figure 3.6 shows stages of moral development and corresponding

Figure 3.6 *Kohlberg's stages of moral development applied to human communities*

Stage	Model
SOCIETIES BASED UPON PRINCIPLES	
6. Universal Truths	The "Knowledge Society"–Self-fulfilling individuals; Self-adjusting conflict resolution
5. Jeffersonian Ideals	Social Contract–Administrative legalism; Meritocracy–Negotiated conflict resolution
SOCIETIES BASED UPON CONVENTION	
4. Law and Order	Complex, heterogeneous societies
3. Peer Pressure	Consensus communities
SURVIVAL-DRIVEN SOCIETIES	
2. Market Place	Interactive tribes (Pragmatic reciprocity)
1. Authoritarian–Fear of Punishment	Tribalism (Pecking order)
0. Pre-Social	Instinctive–Survival of the fittest–"Law" of the jungle

Source: L. Kohlberg, "Stages and Sequences: The Cognitive Development Approach to Socialization," in D. A. Goslin, ed., *Handbook of Socialization Theory and Research* (N.Y.: Rand McNally, 1969).

models of societies based upon principles, convention, and survival. The police are intimately involved with all of these societies at the same time, no matter where they are working, on the street or in the office.

Using the stages of moral development and the corresponding societal models as a frame of reference, the patrol leader learns by means of specific responses to the following social and values issues, as applied to his or her agency, community, and neighborhood (beat):

- Our citizens are concerned more with quality of life than with the accumulation of material items.
- Our citizens want to participate in decisions affecting their lives.
- Cooperation is more important to the majority of the citizens of the community than are conflict and competition.
- Acting out life is more important than watching movies or TV.
- People want challenges to their creative abilities.
- Technology causes as many problems as it does benefits to humankind.
- People prefer a clean environment to one providing many jobs.
- Our country would be better off if children were educated to find inner satisfaction rather than to be a success and make a lot of money.
- Economic growth makes people want to acquire more possessions rather than enjoy non-material experiences.
- It is more important to teach people to live with basic essentials rather than reach higher standards of living.
- It is more important to learn to appreciate human values as opposed to material values.

As students discuss these issues, they should remember that human dignity prevails, and that each individual is of value, even police officers—especially police officers.

Ianni and Ianni have found two competing, and sometimes conflicting, cultures emerging and functioning in a police agency.[17]

A conception of the "good old days" is the organizing ethos for "Street Cop Culture," which organizes individual officers and precinct social networks into a social system. This nostalgic sense of what the old days were like in the department may or may not be an accurate interpretation of the past, but it represents the way street cops believe the department should be today. It is the values of this culture, operationalized in a series of maxims guiding behavior, that form the group reference for precinct-level officers. Interviews and behavioral analysis in the precincts indicate that a number of social and political forces have weakened this "good-old-days" culture, so that the organic structure of the department is disintegrating. These forces have contributed to the development of a new head-quarters-level "Management Cop Culture," so that what was once a family is now a factory. This new Management Cop Culture is bureaucratically juxtaposed to the precinct-level Street Cop Culture. Unlike other bureaucratic systems, in which the upper echelon of the hierarchy is recruited from socioeconomic and educational levels different from the lower ranks, managers at all levels in the department began as cops. There is no lateral entry. Not only the values, say the cops, but also the real loyalties of the bosses are not to the officers but to the social and political networks that make up the Management Cop Culture. While there is some uneasy accommodation between these two cultures, they are increasingly in conflict, and this conflict serves to isolate the precinct level from the headquarters level. The result is disaffection, strong stress reaction, increasing attrition, and growing problems with integrity. This in turn reinforces the resistance of the Street Cop Culture to attempts by headquarters managers to produce organizational change. Instead, the social organization of the precinct becomes the major reference structure for the officers.

Both cultures share the mission goals of the organization, to combat crime and to insure a safe and secure city. Where the two cultures differ is in how they define these general goals and in how they answer the more concrete question of how such goals can be achieved. The Street Cop Culture sees local response as more important than preplanned and "packaged" solutions to problems that may or may not come up in the day-to-day work of policing. The street cop's standard for performance is in the concept of the "professional" cop. In this context, professionalism refers to on-the-job experience and a street sense that permits the street cop to recognize people and situations that are "dirty" and that require police intervention. While planning is not eschewed, it is this reactive "gut-level" ability to recognize, identify, and respond in the field, rather than the internalization of some standardized set of procedures, that characterizes "good police work." Decision-making thus takes place on a personal and immediate basis. Relationships among officers are structured in such a way that they are mutually supportive, and their common interests bind them into a cohesive brotherhood which personalizes task performance as well as social relationships. Command relationships, therefore, are formed in the same way, and the individual's loyalty to his or her working peers and immediate supervisors is part of the same social bond that incorporates the individual and his or her organizational unit into larger organizational structures.

Management Cop Culture is concerned with the problem of crime on a system-wide or city-wide rather than local level. It is not that management cops are unconcerned with crime at the local level, but rather that their sense of territoriality encompasses all of the city; and so they are placed in the position of having to allocate resources throughout the system, based upon some set of priorities. These priorities must be weighed and established within a set of political, social, and economic constraints and must be justifiable within each of these contexts, as well as within the policing context. Law enforcement is not the immediate day-to-day planned, well-designed, and efficiently implemented program in which the individual officer and the unit that is his or her reference group are impersonal variables to be considered.

One of the many organizational theories that has been influential in the development of management concepts, maintains that decisions are made on either valuative or factual premises. Given values and information, individuals will more likely reach decisions based on values. Whether he or she is in the Street Cop or the Management Cop Culture, the individual's identification with groups or task units focuses decision-making on particular goals and behaviors. His group identification requires that he select only such alternatives nominally open to him that will also fit with the behaviors he expects from other members of his group. In addition, however, there are organization-wide values which are meant to influence decisions. The congruency of group (by which we mean precinct-level) and organization (by which we mean departmental) influences is especially pertinent in looking at precinct-level versus headquarters-level influences on behavior. While either may influence the individual through his or her set of values or information, our observations convinced us that at this point in time it is the precinct-level or Street Cop Culture values that determine the day-to-day activity of policing. Since these values underwrite and inform the social organization of the precinct, they act as a determinant for the behavior, and even for the unconscious dispositions and attitudes, of its members.

Officers are graduated from recruit school with certain attitudes, which may or may not coincide with the atmosphere of the present street officers. Therefore, to survive, the new officers must endure change quietly and with a great amount of analysis concerning how he or she will behave. The new officers in essence have to learn this culture and integrate the roles of the formal and informal organization into a mode of conduct. Each supervisor or commander expects officers to behave in a certain way, and many times just to get along he or she has to relate to each (Figure 3.7).

Figure 3.7 displays the relationships among the various structures and processes which arm the social organization of the precinct. The two cultures—Management Cop Culture and Street Cop Culture—interact in the precinct through the four structures. The Authority Power Structure is activated only from the Management Cop Culture to the Street Cop Culture and is the channel through which policy directives and procedures flow downward. The Peer Group Structure and the Socialization Structure do not connect the two cultures, since each socializes its membership to a different set of values or ethos. The Class Group Structure is the avenue through which the two cultures communicate informally. The processes

Figure 3.7 *The social organization of the precinct*

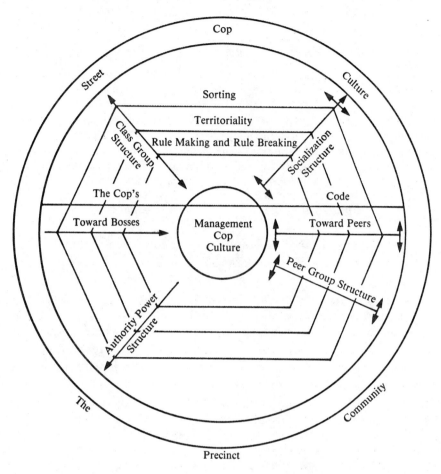

of Sorting, Territoriality, and Rule Making and Rule Breaking operation-alize the social action within each of the four structures, and in doing so adjust each to the local precinct environment. Each process is expressed in the form of behavioral expectations or "rules," which set the limits of acceptable behavior and which are expressed in the Cop's Code. Since the Peer Group Structure and the Socialization Structure do not interrelate the Street Cop Culture with the Management Cop Culture, the processes are culture specific in these two structures. As a result, the Cop's Code is subdivided into one set of maxims that tells the officer how to behave toward and with peers and another set which tells him or her how to behave toward and with management or peers.

The last chapter on "Change" addresses the issues discussed here and highly recommends "participation, real participation, in planning change from the beginning, from the street officer."

Also impacting the culture of the officer is the impact of the community on the officer's perspective. This is summed up by Wilson and Reiss:

> Plunging the police into a political arena in which the most emotional and provincial concerns set the tone for decision-making is not likely to ease the problem of recruiting and holding able men for the force.[18]

> A major concern of the patrolman arises from the inconsistent expectations and contrary authorities that now define his task—his superiors, "politicians," the public, all provide him with various and conflicting definitions of his function, usually (it seems to him) by criticism after the fact. Subordinating him to community councils that regularly and variously debate his role is not likely to increase his sense of confidence or the attractiveness of a police career.[19]

The research by Ianni and Ianni appears to voice questions critical to the changing nature of policing in the United States. The situation as it is presented identifies an emergent problem of management versus street officers and the deteriorating effects of such conflict. However, the generalizability of the research is of concern in the areas of size of agency, centralized or decentralized organizational design, management practices, implementation strategies of any solution to a similarly found problem, standards of measurement, and the amount of effective planning which takes place in the agency from top to bottom. Most important, the patrol leader should examine the department to determine if the two cultures exist and, if so, should analyze appropriately and develop solutions to any situation detrimental to effective performance.

PATROL MANAGEMENT AND STRESS

Perhaps the most important single quality of the leader is empathy. I believe respect for the dignity of men and women and willingness to listen and to be sensitive and considerate of others, no matter what status or position they occupy, reduces resistance and enhances cooperation. However, analysis and understanding come from knowledge of how people perceive and of what kinds of things affect stress, so patrol leaders can decide when and how to intervene. Thoreau once said, "It takes two to speak the truth, one to speak, and another to hear." The leader must listen, observe, and remember that behavior is affected by environment. When you receive a message that the chief wants to see you, how do you feel? (What did I do wrong?) So when you send for someone, wouldn't it be nice to also give the agenda or partial agenda? Answer the question, "Who am I," because your self-concept affects your "construct system," and an individual's previous experience influences his or her perception of a situation, which in turn influences his or her behavior. Buchanan[20] explains "construct system" this way: Our picture of reality (and thus what we respond to) is influenced by our previous experiences. As a result of our efforts to make sense of, and to integrate, the things we encounter, we each develop certain enduring, systematic points of view. These points of view may be called "construct systems." In our continuous attempts to satisfy our needs with least cost to us, we organize, or "construct," our experiences in ways that give them qualities such as value and consistency. This construct system forms the basis of our expectations, our beliefs regarding "what causes what," our assumptions, and our goals. Thus success in one situation determines to some extent our expectations for success in future ones. For instance, being rejected by one college (or, more accurately, feeling that one has been rejected) influences a student's approach to another college. And, since all of us have had different and unique experiences which we have integrated in our own unique fashion, each of us has a highly individualistic point of view. To each of us, therefore, any situation, and any possible course of action, looks different from the way it does to any other person. At the same time, we each tend to see various situations in a predictable manner—there is consistency in our points of view. We tend to be optimistic or pessimistic in outlook, to be dependent or independent of others, and so forth.

It is also true, however, that the part of a person's construct system that guides his behavior in a specific situation—what he responds to and how he sees it—is influenced by his immediately prior experience, or his "set." We can see how this operates by considering the accompanying pictures A, B, and C. If you look first at picture B and then at C, you are

A   **B**   **C**

likely to see both as old women. But if you look first at picture A, you will see C as a young woman. How you see C is influenced by what you saw in (your perception of) the previously viewed picture.

The fact that one's perception is influenced by one's previous experience is particularly important to the leader. It points up the need to anticipate that the leader's own view of a situation will be influenced by his construct system and by his "set." (An obvious example of the effect of "set" is the way a person sees a situation differently if he or she is a leader than if he or she is simply a group member with no special responsibility.) This phenomenal perception also underscores the importance of finding out what the other person sees, by inquiring about, and by listening to, what he or she says. It is hazardous first to assume that he or she sees it as the leader does and then to criticize the individual for not seeing it in the same way. By being aware of differences in perception, leaders can check both views against the facts, thus taking advantage of an opportunity to modify behavior–the other person's or their own–by changing one basis of it– the perception of the facts.

It is imperative that patrol managers become aware of avoidance/coping mechanisms regarding stress. This information includes psychological and physiological data. Tables 3.1 and 3.2 indicates stress sources and stress symptoms.[21]

Stratton places major stressors into four categories:

1. Stressors external to the organization such as attitude of public and frustration of the criminal justice system.
2. Stressors internal to the organization such as poor pay and poor training and supervision.
3. Stressors inherent to police work such as shift work, role conflict, fear and danger, startle situations, and consequences of actions.
4. Stressors due to the individual such as marriage responsibilities, lack of self-confidence, and life style.[23]

Axelberd and Valle relate nutrition and sedentary tasks to stress.

In recent years, our society is becoming more aware of the direct relationships between the foods we eat and our physical and emotional state. In a society that emphasizes efficiency and convenience, it is easy to sacrifice good eating habits. We fall into the habit of eating foods that are easiest and quickest to obtain, a combination that rarely results in a well-balanced, nutritional diet.

Police officers, because of time constraints, unusual working hours, and the unavailability of restaurants that serve nutritionally balanced meals, are particularly susceptible to the development of poor eating habits. In addition, police officers are especially prone to obesity due to the surprisingly sedentary nature of their job. Studies conducted by physicians and nutritionists, along with statistics from various health insurance companies, have shown a positive correlation between poor nutritional habits and degenerative disease, ulcers, hypertension, and backaches.[24]

Table 3.1 *Summary of Stress Sources Identified in a Review of 134 Student Papers Submitted to the FBI Behavioral Science Unit*

Marital considerations	25
Excessive work loads (promotion, change in assignment)	17
Shooting Post-Syndrome	14
Ineffective management (vague rules and regulations)	12
Peer pressure (necessity to conform)	10
Financial problems	7
Failure (worries about competency or ability)	5
Minority (self-evaluation)	5
External (problems before entering police work)	4
Death of friend or family member	4
Shooting (officer shot)	3
Fear	2
Unfavorable public contact	2
Shift work	1
Demotion	1

Table 3.2 *Compilation of the Symptoms of Stress as Mentioned in the FBI Papers*

Alcoholism or significant change in consumption	39
Increased aggression (toward public/other officers)	22
Physical illness or symptoms (ulcers, cardiovascular, rash, nervousness, excessive sick days, psychosomatic)	17
Paranoid	12
Suicidal – outward expression	11
Depression	10
Withdrawn from other officers – no contact	7
Visible nervousness – shaking	7
Sexual problems	5
Decrease in physical appearance	5
Antagonistic toward fellow employees	5
Workaholic	4
Arrogance	4
Express disenchantment	4
Religious fanaticism	2
Accident prone	1
Non-support of family	1
Irrational behavior	1

Kroes and Gould list some major stressors in policing.

SOME MAJOR STRESSORS IN POLICING[22]

Stressors Shared with Other Occupations

Administration	(1) Administrative policy concerning work assignments, procedures, and personal conduct, and (2) Lack of administrative backing and support, including the relationship and rapport between patrolmen and their administrators.
Job Conflict	Situations in which officers are caught between discrepant expectations.
Second Job	Holding down an additional part-time job.
Inactivity	Physical and/or mental work underload or idleness.
Shift Work	Having to work hours other than the normal work schedule.
Inadequate Resources	Lack of the proper materials, equipment, etc., necessary to carry out one's job.
Organizational Territory	Working in an alien environment.
Job Overload	Having too much work to do in a given time, or having work to do that which is too difficult to perform, given one's skill level.
Responsibility for People	Having excessive responsibility for the lives and welfare of others.
Inequities in Pay or Job Status	Being underpaid and under-recognized for one's work, compared to other occupations.

Police Specific Stressors

Courts	Court rulings, procedures, leniency, and treatment of police officers.
Negative Public Image	Unfavorable attitudes held by citizens toward police officers.
Racial Situation	Confrontations between police officers and minority group members.
Line of Duty/Crisis Situations	Duty situations which either pose as a threat to the police officer or may overwhelm him emotionally.

In addition, it is clear that inadequate nutrition leads to loss of concentration, leading to longer working hours and greater inefficiency—all of which viciously contribute to more stress, which leads to greater wear and tear causing more inefficient behaviors.

Selye lists some stress-related outcomes:[25]

- high blood pressure
- kidney diseases
- allergic diseases
- nervous diseases
- digestive diseases
- diseases of the heart and of the blood vessels
- inflammation of skin and eyes
- sexual problems
- cancer

Two major factors contributing to stress and disease are inadequate eating habits and lack of proper physical exercise. A third factor concerns the overuse of stimulating chemicals such as caffeine, nicotine, and thenine.

All of the above activities (not eating properly, then not exercising properly, and then overusing stimulants) are related. The first two lead to the third, and they form a debilitating syndrome.

What kind of stress for what kind of officer is developed over what period of time for the following: felony arrests (personal and property); traffic arrests and citations; clearance rate/part one offenses; dispatch time/ running time/response time; conviction rate; citizen attitudes and complaints; district attorney quality control of cases; reported/victimization crime; accidents; enforcement and arrest index; fleet (police auto) accidents; absence rate; attrition rate; miles driven; cost per unit; productivity; riots; criminal justice system; input and output; and many more? There are also stressors for the manager included in the above. Kroes suggests three methods to reduce stress: (1) identify stressor, (2) prepare officer to handle stress through education and training, and (3) provide stressed officers with help from others.[26]

Eisenberg identified sources of psychological stress in six categories addressing the internal organization, external factors, and the officers themselves.[27] The first is intraorganizational practices and characteristics, which include poor supervision, lack of career development opportunities, inadequate reward system, offensive policy, excessive paper work, and poor equipment. The second is interorganizational practices and characteristics including jurisdictional isolationism and absence of career growth opportunities. The third category is the criminal justice system practices and characteristics—ineffectiveness of the correction sub-system, unfavorable court decisions, misunderstood judicial procedures, inefficient courtroom management, and preoccupation with street crime. The fourth category is public practices and characteristics including distorted press accounts of police incidents, unfavorable minority attitudes, unfavorable majority attitudes, derogatory remarks by neighbors and others, adverse local government decisions, and ineffectiveness of referral agencies. The fifth category is police work itself, such as role conflict, adverse work scheduling, fear and danger, sense of uselessness, absence of closure, people pain, the "startle" (quick response needed at any time), consequences of actions taken by the police officers, and the effects of years of longevity in the department due to the fact that the officers' work and reputation are cumulative. The sixth category, the police officer himself/herself, which includes self-competence, fear, nonconformity, ethnic minority officers, and female officers in relation to primarily male departments. Eisenberg addressed stress mainly as it affects police officers.

Family-related problems, such as not seeing their children enough, poor social planning, and worried spouses are also concerns of patrol managers. The Kansas City, Missouri Police Department has a program, "The Marriage Partner Program," which was developed as a response to four premises:

1. An officer cannot function adequately at work if he faces chronic stress at home.
2. Every officer at some point in his career will find himself in a period of excessive stress which could adversely affect his career and family life.
3. Wives of police officers can be trained to see early warning signals of their husband's periods of excessive stress and can learn techniques of reducing the consequent patterns of irrational behavior before job performance becomes affected.
4. Wives often feel alienated from their husband's careers; and as a result, develop strong antagonisms toward the police department, which further aggravates the marriage relationship.[28]

Family communication is important, as exhibited by the department psychologist. The Dallas, Texas Police Department and the Los Angeles Sheriffs Department have psychological counseling programs designed to avoid the last-ditch "cry for help" when it may be too late to assist officers and their families.

The stress reduction program of the Quincy, Illinois Police Department includes the following steps: (1) improve quality of department supervison of all officers, (2) develop career ladder with detailed job achievement steps, salaries, training requirements, and experience requirements that will afford each officer an equal opportunity to advance according to motivation and capability, (3) develop an incentive system to enable each employee within the department to receive both tangible and social (recognition) rewards according to their merit, motivation, and performance, (4) review departmental policies prior to implementation for modification of appropriateness, (5) reduce the amount of time and effort expended by officers in completing and filing reports on paper, and (6) find all other areas of stress to develop programs to eliminate or reduce stress levels.[29]

Patrol managers should increase their awareness of stressors both for their officers and for themselves. Managers are fallible and subject to the stressors of the manager's complex life, both at work and at home. Anxiety and frustration are always a part of the patrol manager's life because of the nature of the job. Each of us wants psychological stability and self-actualization. Threatening situations become stressful; therefore, the coping mechanism is critical. Failure to cope properly can result in false perceptions, failure to reason objectively, dysfunction, confused cognitive processes, and potential physical illness.

Sometimes these situations bring conflict, and managers must deal with the situation from within. The managers want to be liked by the officers, yet they want good performance, to be promoted, and to be looked upon by the chief as a good manager. Sometimes the choice or decision to be made is one of the lesser of two evils, but the decision must be made . . . conflict. The decisions of management, especially performance evaluation and discipline, cause conflict, because you may want to be promoted but you dislike the above tasks. You the manager must cope or adjust. Do not adjust by becoming aggressive against people, or by withdrawing or deceiving yourself. Maintain your self-worth, and deal with situations from your adult ego state, using facts, not emotions, yet realizing what emotions are involved. In other words, answer the question, "Why do I feel the way I do?" To repeat, know yourself, your principles, your value systems, and where you are going–direction.

THE PATROL MANAGER'S PSYCHOLOGICAL ENVIRONMENT: TRANSACTIONAL ANALYSIS

> The life which is unexamined is not worth living
> —Plato, *Apology*

In examining life, the approach is important. Transactional analysis is simple, and is presented in layman's terms. For the patrol manager, it is essential to know how to stay in the adult ego state to survive and progress. The founder of transactional analysis, Dr. Eric Berne, knew the importance of the simplicity of language. The patrol manager, by tasks or by on-the-job training, is highly trained in observing behavior. The next step is to know how to respond to other people's behavior. In other words, analyze the transactions of people. Berne believed that by doing this at a particular time, it would be consistent with past influence, including prenatal and parental, and what might follow. Transactional analysis is common to all people regardless of culture or background. Therefore, transactional analysis helps one to understand human behavior and its alternatives (hopefully for the better), is simple in language, and is based on observation.

Life positions ("I'm O.K., You're O.K."; 'I'm O.K., You're Not O.K.") seem to be determined by the stroking that a person receives. Stroking comes from the human physical contact infants receive from birth. Transactional analysis suggests that adult people too need stroking. We all need to be "acknowledged" as being someone. Complaints about police officers, which are investigated by internal affairs, usually are concerns of citizens regarding strokes. Most of us, when we complain about service, are saying we were not stroked. An infant knows what behavior will result in strokes (rewards). After the reward, reinforcement takes place, as does continued positive behavior. However, when there is a lack of stroking, there may be negative behavior, which results in negative strokes. Negative strokes are better than no strokes at all, because you are then recognized and are not considered a nonentity. Berne states, "All people have in differing degrees three ego states, parent, adult, and child. Although we cannot directly observe these ego states, we can observe behavior and from this infer which of the three ego states is operating at that moment."[30]

The parent ego state is a result of the kind of conditioning people have received from their parents, teachers, or other influential figures since

Figure 3.8 *Parent, adult, child ego states*

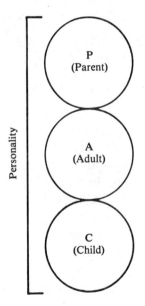

childhood. The patrol manager acts as a *critical* parent when he/she exhibits dogma and opinions, and as a *nurturing* parent when he/she exhibits sympathy or praise. The parent ego state is evaluative and you hear, "You Should, Shouldn't."

The adult ego state behavior is rational decision-making or problem analysis. It does not contain emotion, prejudice, or subjective statements. The adult deals in the reality of the world and examines alternatives, probabilities, and values before behaving.

The child ego state is behavior based on emotions. This state uses impulses and attitudes learned from child experiences. When a parent ego state addresses a child ego state, the manner in which the person adapted to parental authority will determine his or her response. Lynch explains the three parts of the child ego state as follows:[31]

> The *natural child* is the part that is very young, impulsive, untrained, and expressive. When his needs are met, the manager responds out of the child state with affection. Angry rebellion at having his needs frustrated is also a reaction of the child state in police managers.
>
> The *little professor* refers to the unschooled wisdom that we observe in children. It is the part of the child ego state that is able to influence the motivations and feelings of other people. It is through this aspect of the child ego state that the infant figures things out — when to cry, when to be quiet, and how to manipulate his or her parents. This aspect can be indicative of a highly creative mind, even though many of the child ego state creations might be impractical if not developed by the adult ego state. The police manager's capacity to create and fantasize is directly related to the degree to which he is able to permit the little professor in himself to work.
>
> The third aspect of the child ego state is the *adapted child.* This is the part of the child ego state that exhibits modifications of the natural child's inclinations. These adaptations of natural impulses occur in response to parental training and demands from significant authority figures. When the manager complies, procrastinates, acts like a bully, withdraws, or in other ways behaves as he did in response to the demands of his parents, he is acting from his adapted child state.
>
> Each of the ego states is important to the manager's being effective in daily interactions with others. Effective decision-making requires that the police manager be able to process data through the adult state without undue influence from the child and parent ego states. However, in order to have fun, he must be able to indulge in his child ego state. To give support to others or to exercise control of situations, he must be able to rely on his parent ego state. Good adjustment comes when he is able to use the ego state that is appropriate to the situation.
>
> The police manager can diagnose ego states in himself and others by observing the visible and audible characteristics of the person. (See Figure 3.9.)

Figure 3.9 *Clues to ego states*

	Parent Ego State	Adult Ego State	Child Ego State
Voice Tones	Condescending, putting down, criticizing or abusing	Matter-of-fact	Full of feeling, high-pitched, whining voice
Words Used	Everyone knows that . . . You should never . . . You should always . . . I can't understand why in the world you would ever . . . I'll put a stop to that once and for all . . . If I were you . . . Stupid . . . naughty . . . ridiculous . . . shocking . . . poor thing . . . good girl . . . good boy	How . . . What . . . When . . . Why . . . Who . . . Probable . . . In what way . . . I think . . . I seem . . . It is my opinion	I'm mad at you . . . Wow, terrific! (or any words that have a high feeling level) . . . I wish . . . I want . . . I dunno . . . I guess . . . Bigger . . . Better . . . Best
Postures	Puffed-up with pride, super-correct, very proper	Attentive, eye-to-eye contact, listening and looking for maximum data, continual action	Slouching, playful, beaten down, burdened, self-conscious
Facial Expressions	Frowning, worried or disapproving looks, chin jutted out, furrowed brow, pursed lips	Alert eyes, maximum attention given	Exicted, surprised, downcast eyes, quivering lip or chin, moist eyes, rolling eyes
Body Gestures	Hands on hips, pointing finger in accusation, arms folded across chest, patting on head, deep sigh	Leaning forward in chair toward other person, moving closer to hear and see better	Spontaneous activity, wringing hands, pacing, withdrawing into corner or moving away from laughter, raising hand for permission, shrugging shoulders

Life Positions

There are basic assumptions that people make about themselves, others, and the environment. The patrol leader makes assumptions about his or her organization, peers, supervisor, job, subordinates, and government and about his or her own expectations and the expectations of the others mentioned above. Behavior of managers results from the interaction of style and expectation.[32] Life positions are usually more permanent than ego states. Hersey and Blanchard explain:

> The positions are learned as a result of reinforcements received throughout life for expressions of need and responses to expressed needs. These assumptions are described in terms of "okayness." Thus, it is stated that individuals assume that they are either OK or *not* OK, or as people they do or do not possess value or worth. Further, that other individuals are OK or *not* OK. There are four positions that result from these possibilities; neither party has value (I'm not OK, you're not OK); you have but I do not have value (I'm not OK, you're OK); I have value but you do not (I'm OK, you're not OK) and we both have value (I'm OK, you're OK). People with each of these life positions could be described as follows:
>
> *"I'm not OK, you're not OK"* people tend to feel bad about themselves and see the whole world as miserable. People with this life position tend to give up. They don't trust other people and have no confidence in themselves.
>
> People with a *"I'm not OK, you're OK"* life position often feel that others are generally more competent than they are and generally have fewer problems. They tend to think that they always get "the short end of the stick."
>
> People who feel *"I'm OK, you're not OK"* tend to supervise others closely because they think no one can be trusted to do things as well as they can. They are often dominated by their critical parent.
>
> *"I'm OK, you're OK"* is suggested as the ideal life position. People with these feelings tend to have positive outlooks on life. They seem to be happy acitve people who succeed. They make use of their happy child and nuturing parent, while seldom using their destructive child or critical parent.[33]

Structural Analysis (Transactions)

Structural analysis is an analysis of the personality, or the process of identifying which ego states are involved in a given transaction. The beginning ego state makes a statement (stimulus); there is an ego state which accepts the statement; then, either the same or a different ego state responds; finally, the original ego state accepts the response in the same or a different ego state. We all vary in our behavior; accordingly, our ego states vary when we speak or when we respond when spoken to. Sometimes ego states get mixed, because a person may enhance one and hide another, or one may be blocked. This occurs, for example, when a chief is serious and never smiles, so that the parent is blocking out the child. At the same time, all processing is done through the adult. Figure 3.10 shows a *complementary* transaction.

In a complementary transaction, response to the stimulus should be the expected or predictable one. There are several complementary trans-

Figure 3.10   *Complementary transaction*

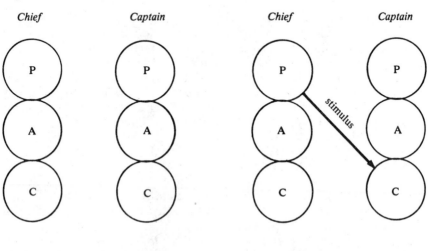

Chief of Police
Captain of Patrol

Parent to Child
Chief: "Captain, I want
your budget in by Nov. 1."

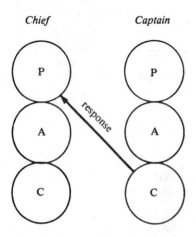

Child to Parent
Captain: "Yes, Chief, I'll
have it done on time."

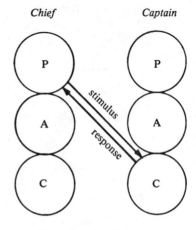

"Complete Complementary
Transaction"

actions: parent to parent—parent to parent; child to adult—adult to child, etc. Continual open communication exists in a complementary transaction. This does not mean, however, that the content is open, or that factual data are being communicated. *Crossed* transactions are explained by Lynch as follows:[34]

> In some transactions with others, the manager may immediately be aware that something has happened to disrupt the relationship. For example, after an initial exchange, he and the subordinate may stand glaring at each other, turn their backs on each other, change the topic abruptly, or show puzzlement at what has just occurred. These behaviors suggest that the transaction has resulted in a disruption of communication. In most instances, the manager initiating the transaction has received a response that was inconsistent with his expectations. Such transactions are referred to as *crossed transactions*. A crossed transaction occurs any time the person initiating the transaction receives a response that is perceived as inappropriate or unexpected. As an example:
>
> *Capt.:* Have you spoken to the chief about the court schedule? (adult to adult)
>
> *Lt.:* No, and I'm not about to. He can go jump in the lake. (child to parent)

In the example above, the captain is communicating from his adult state, expecting a reasonable adult reply. The lieutenant, however, responds out of his child ego state in an angry, rebellious manner. The lieutenant's reponse is directed to the parent in the captain. The subsequent conversation will largely be determined by the response the captain makes. He may chose to stay in the adult ego state and explore what accounts for the feelings the lieutenant has toward the chief. If he moves to his parent ego state, he may either berate the lieutenant for his poor attitude or be sympathetic. In either case, the crossed transaction results in a change in the level of communication between the individuals.

Ulterior Transactions

Ulterior transactions are on two levels, the social level and the psychological level. The spoken social level masks the unspoken psychological level. Staff/Command conferences conducted in a "show-and-tell" atmosphere are ulterior transactions. In this setting the chief usually gives instructions or states opinions about policy in a way that says one thing (social) but means another (psychological). Commanders usually find out quickly about

Figure 3.11 *Crossed transaction*

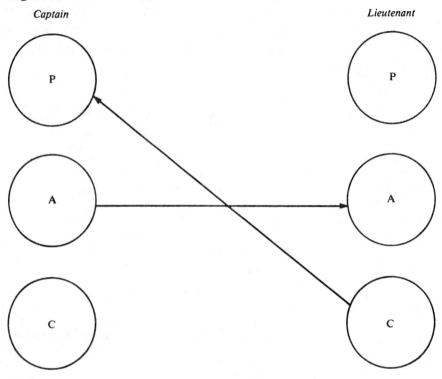

these, since the first time they give criticism they believe to be constructive and asked for (a social response for the adult ego state), they are responded to from the parent to the child, "You better do your homework."
Figure 3.12 illustrates the ulterior transaction.

Social Level Chief	A–A: I like the deadly force policy distributed to you this morning. What do you think?
Command Officer	A–A: There is one aspect which I would modify about warning shots.
Psychological Level Chief	P–C: I have done a good job of research on the subject and this is the finished product, a deadly force policy for the department.
Command Officer	C–P: "Looks good!"

Thus we observe the ulterior transaction on a social and a psychological level, which tends to block open, honest communication. These
transactions often lead to gamesmanship, which, when psychological, leads
to negative feelings. Is this good for the organization?

Figure 3.12 *Two-level ulterior transaction social and psychological level*

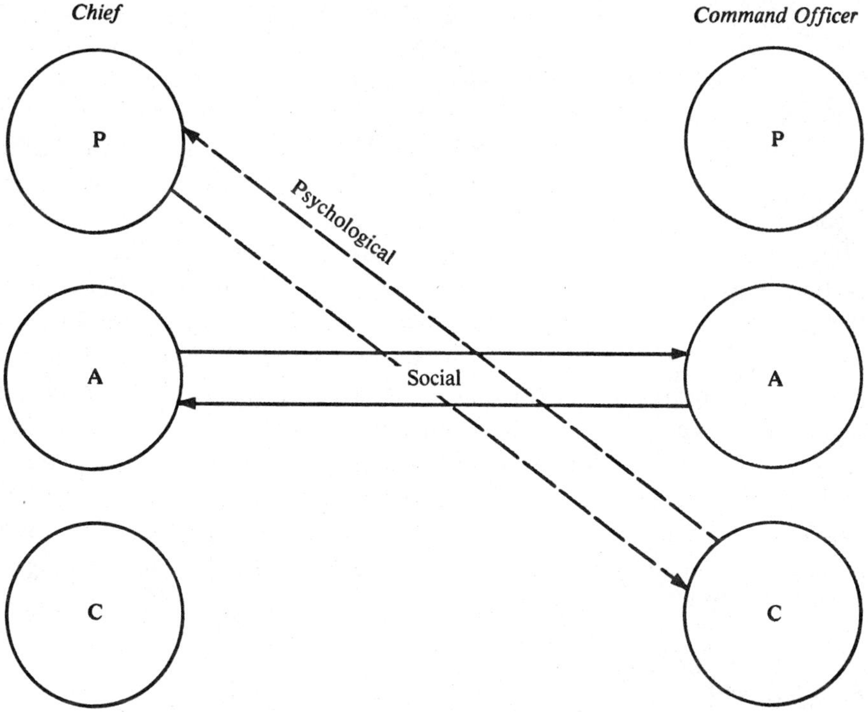

Time Structuring

Strokes, positive or negative, are better than no strokes at all. Usually strokes follow each other in a series. In transactional analysis, there are five ways that people transact or do not transact in the use of time. *Withdrawal,* or the avoidance of strokes, occurs when people decide not to interact, or when one person does not respond to a statement made by another person. Withdrawal can be planned or, at the other extreme, engagement in fantasies. Withdrawal should not be long term, and each person should recognize when it is being used in order to stay effective. *Rituals* provide some stroking, usually a complementary transaction such as a "hello." More strokes are involved when the rituals are extended; for example, when a respected chief visits the department. A third way to structure time is through *pastimes.* The International Association of Chiefs of Police provides a setting for pastimes. Chiefs and command officers visit and relate to other similar agencies and talk about computers and budgets and sometimes tell war stories. The next time structure is *activity,* or work. Cleaning a shotgun, completing a staff study, or writing a general order is work. Activities are usually adult, and the strokes are positive if the atmosphere provided by the leader is adult and gives people a chance to feel "O.K." *Games* are a more complex way of structuring time, and are used by people to receive or give negative feelings. One game is "If it weren't for you, I could." This game is repeated and usually has a person blaming someone else for his or her own inadequacy. Persons playing this game rationalize their behavior and feel "O.K." Another game is "Yes, but." Here the person gives one reason after another why he or she cannot accomplish a certain task. For example, a sergeant says, "I sure would like to make captain but I can't find time to study." A captain responds, "Why don't you give up some of your golf time?" The sergeant says, "I would, but I need the exercise." The captain replies, "Then why don't you get up an hour earlier and use that time to study. That would add up to many hours of study over a period of time, wouldn't it?" The sergeant replies, "Yes, but I can't seem to concentrate when I awake." No matter what you offer, the response is "Yes, but," so the payoff is bad feelings all around. Other games include: "Ain't it awful," "Let's you and him fight," "Kick me," "Now I've got you, you s.o.b. (NIGYYSOB)," "Gee, you're a wonderful professor," "See what you made me do," "Blemish," "Corner," "Stupid," "I'm only trying to help," and "What would you do without me."

A Synthesis

Situational leadership theory (the type of leadership used depends on the situation) and transactional analysis have been integrated and explained by Hersey and Blanchard.[35]

> The three ego states in T.A. are parent, adult, and child. Individuals whose behavior is being evoked from their child ego state can be either a destructive child or a happy child. The destructive child seems to be associated with maturity M1, and therefore, the leadership style that is necessary with that child ego state is S1. Low "strokes" are appropriate because too much socioemotional support along with the high structure may be viewed as permissiveness and support for their destructive behavior. If you are interacting with a happy child, movement is toward maturity M2, and thus the style that seems to be most effective is S2. Now there is a need for more two-way communication, socioemotional support, and facilitating behavior along with the structure.
>   Individuals whose behavior is being evoked from their parent ego state can be either a nurturing parent or critical parent. The nurturing parent seems to be associated with M2, and, therefore, the leadership style that is necessary with that parent ego state, as illustrated in Figure 3.13.

Any role defining or structuring has to be done in a supportive way. Too much task behavior without corresponding relationship behavior might

Figure 3.13 *Relationship between situational leadership theory and ego states and life positions associated with Transactional Analysis (T.A.)*

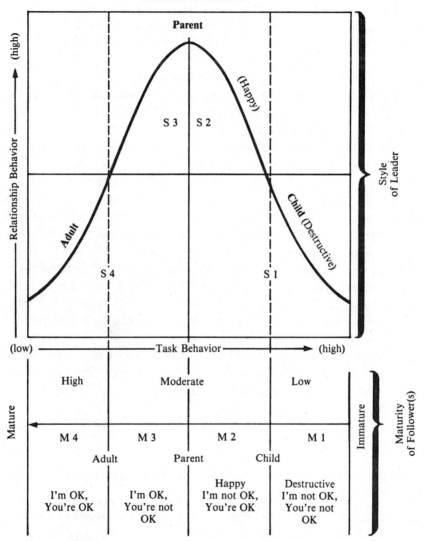

suggest to nurturing parents that the person trying to influence them does not care for them, and this might move their ego state more toward a critical parent. That form of parent ego state tends to be associated with maturity level M3, because a style S3 tends to work best when trying to work with a critical parent ego state. If leaders use a high task style with critical parents, it just tends to evoke more critical parent "tapes," and soon these leaders may find themselves in a win–lose, parent/parent-power struggle. To work with individuals with a critical parent, leaders first must try to develop a good personal relationship with them, before they are able to use effectively either of the high task styles (S1 and S2).

In working with people whose behavior is being evoked from their adult ego state, leaders can use an S4 style and leave them alone. These people are already thinking in rational, problem-solving ways and, provided they have the competence to do their jobs, tend to prefer to be left alone.

As illustrated in Figure 3.13, individuals with an "I'm not O.K., you're not O.K." life position tend to be associated with maturity level M1 and thus need high direction and close supervison. People who feel "I'm not O.K., you're O.K." are related to maturity level M2 and thus need both direction and socioemotional support. They will appreciate direction from leaders because they think these people are "O.K.," but they also need high relationship behavior to help increase their "O.K." feelings about themselves. People who feel "I'm O.K., you're not O.K." tend to be associated with maturity level M3. (Remember we are talking about normal people with this ego state and not "mentally disturbed" people, whom psychiatrists like Berne would be referring to in their discussions of T.A.) These individuals feel "O.K." about themselves and tend to require high relationship behavior from others before feeling "O.K." about them. People with life positions of "I'm O.K., you're O.K." seem to relate to maturity level M4, because they can be given responsibility and can be left alone and still feel good about themselves and other people.

Transactional analysis should be used as a tool by patrol managers if they are to be more effective in their leadership roles. By understanding what makes people do what they do, and feel the way they do, we can act and improve the police profession.

NOTES

1. Daniel Glaser, *Crime in Our Changing Society* (New York: Holt, Rinehart and Winston, 1978), p. 481.
2. Elaine Cumming, Ian Cumming, and Laura Edell, "Policeman as Philosopher, Guide and Friend," *Social Problems* 12, no. 3 (1965). Published by Society for the Study of Social Problems.
3. Brian W. Rapp and Frank M. Patitucci, *Managing Local Government for Improved Performance* (Boulder, Colo.: Westview Press, 1977), p. xviii.
4. American Bar Association, "Standards Relating to the Urban Police Function," *The Police Chief* (May 1973); President's Commission on Law Enforcement and Administration of Justice, *The Challenge of Crime in a Free Society* (Washington, D.C.: U.S. Government Printing Office, 1967), chap. 4; John A. Webster, *The Realities of Police Work* (Dubuque, Iowa: Kendall/Hunt, 1973), pp. 13–14; James Q. Wilson, *Varieties of Police Behavior* (Cambridge, Mass.: Harvard University Press, 1968), p. 18; and David H. Bayley, "The Police and Political Development in Europe," in *The Formation of National States in Europe,* Charles Tolly, ed. (Princeton, N.J.: Princeton University Press, 1975).
5. David H. Bayley, "Police Function, Structure, and Control in Western Europe

and North America: Comparative and Historical Studies," in *Crime and Justice, An Annual Review of Research,* Norval Morris and Michael Tonry, eds. (Chicago, Ill.: The University of Chicago Press, 1979) pp. 111–116. Reprinted by permission of the University of Chicago Press.

6. Ibid., p. 113.
7. Ibid.
8. Ibid., pp. 122, 123.
9. Ruben G. Rumbaut and Egon Bittner, "Changing Conceptions of the Police Role: A Sociological Review," in *Crime and Justice, An Annual Review of Research,* Norval Morris and Michael Tonry, eds. (Chicago, Ill.: The University of Chicago Press, 1979), p. 284.
10. National Advisory Commission on Criminal Justice Standards and Goals, *Report on Police* (Washington, D.C.: U.S. Government Printing Office, 1973), p. 22.
11. President's Commission on Law Enforcement and Administration of Justice, *The Police* (Washington, D.C.: U.S. Government Printing Office, 1967), p. 20.
12. Donald F. Cawley, H. Jerome Miron, Fred Newton, and Victor Strecher, University Research Corporation, *Managing Patrol Operations* (Washington, D.C.: Law Enforcement Assistance Administration, 1977), p. 73.
13. William G. Gay, et al., *Improving Patrol Productivity,* Vol. I (Washington, D.C.: National Institute of Law Enforcement and Criminal Justice, 1977), p. 86.
14. Robert H. Lauer, *Perspectives on Social Change* (Boston: Allyn and Bacon, 1977), p. 269.
15. Jerome H. Skolnick, *The Politics of Protest* (New York: Ballantine Books, 1969), pp. 100–105.
16. Rapp and Patitucci, op. cit., pp. 25–26.
17. Elizabeth Reuss Ianni and Francis A. J. Ianni, *Street Cops vs. Management Cops; The Social Organization of the Police Precinct* (Washington, D.C.: The Institute for Social Analysis, The National Institute of Law Enforcement and Criminal Justice, Law Enforcement Assistance Administration, U.S. Dept. of Justice, 1975), pp. vi, 104, 105.
18. James Q. Wilson, *Thinking about Crime* (New York: Basic Books, 1975), p. 119.
19. Albert J. Reiss, *The Police and the Public* (New Haven, Conn.: Yale University Press, 1971), p. 77; and James Q. Wilson, *Varieties of Police Behavior* (Cambridge, Mass.: Harvard University Press, 1968), pp. 288–290.
20. Paul C. Buchanan, *Individual Motivation, Looking into Leadership* (Fairfax, Va.: Executive Library, Leadership Resources, Inc., 1972), pp. 6–7.
21. Charles A. Gruber, "The Relationship of Stress to the Practice of Police Work," *The Police Chief* (1980). International Association of Chiefs of Police, Gaithersburg, Md. Review of police students' papers submitted to the Behavior Science Unit of the F.B.I. Academy during the 1978 spring session.
22. William Kroes and Sam Gould, "Job Stress in Policemen: An Empirical Study," *Police Stress* 1, no. 2 (1974).
23. John Stratton, "Police Stress: An Overview," *The Police Chief* (1976). International Association of Chiefs of Police, Gaithersburg, Md.
24. M. Axelberd and Jose Valle, "South Florida's Approach to Police Stress Management," *Police Stress* 1, no. 2 (1981): 13–14.
25. H. Selye, *The Stress of Life* (New York: McGraw-Hill, 1956).
26. W. Kroes, *Society's Victim–The Policeman: An Analysis of Job Stress in Policing* (Springfield, Ill.: Charles C Thomas, 1971).
27. T. Eisenberg, "Labor Management Relations and Psychological Stress–View from the Bottom," *The Police Chief* (1975): 54–58. International Associations of Chiefs of Police, Gaithersburg, Md., p. 40.
28. Also see James W. Sterling, "Changes in Role Concepts of Police Officers," *The Police Chief* (1972). International Association of Chiefs of Police, Gaithersburg, Md.; and *The Police Chief* (February 1980): 28.

29. Gruber, op. cit., pp. 68–69.
30. Eric Berne, *Principles of Group Treatment* (New York: Oxford University Press, 1964), p. 281.
31. Ronald G. Lynch, *The Police Manager* (Boston: Allyn and Bacon, 1978), pp. 266–268.
32. Jacob W. Getzels and Egon G. Guda, "Social Behavior and the Administration Process," *The School Review* LXV, no. 4 (winter 1957): 15–16.
33. Paul Hersey and Kenneth H. Blanchard, *Management of Organizational Behavior: Utilizing Human Resources*, 3rd ed., © 1977, pp. 78–79. Reprinted by permission of Prentice-Hall, Inc., Englewood Cliffs, N.J.
34. Lynch, op. cit., pp. 272–273.
35. Hersey and Blanchard, op. cit., pp. 312–314.

4

Organization for Patrol

The patrol force of a police agency is traditionally structured as a hierarchy. But organizing human beings together in a way that produces maximum effectiveness for the organization is a rather complex problem, and job satisfaction for the individual cannot be reached if the rigidity of the traditional structure is maintained.

ORGANIZATIONAL THEORY

In the chapter on leadership we discussed motivation as a leadership responsibility. In connection with the concept, the study of organizational theory is addressed to assist the patrol manager to synthesize the theory and practice. Police organizations are administered by the underlying premises of theory, and officers are affected by the structure and situations of organizational life. In searching for the most effective means to lead the patrol function, this chapter attempts to provide the theoretical base and lend more utility to it for the patrol leader. The accompanying chronology of classics of organizational theory should provide students with resources to increase their knowledge and understanding of organizational theory and to relate the concepts to the reality of today and tomorrow.

SYSTEMS OF ORGANIZATION

Organizational theory and leadership motivation are needed to develop an actualized police agency. This means that a combination of the following theories must be applied to the task at hand: (1) classical (Luther Gulick); (2) bureaucratic (Max Weber); (3) scientific (Frederick Taylor); (4) informal (Hawthorne Studies); (5) systems (Daniel Katz and Robert L.

Of the Division of Labour (1776)
—*Adam Smith*

The Principles of Scientific Management (1916)
—*Frederick Winslow Taylor*

General Principles of Management (1919)
—*Henri Fayol*

Bureaucracy (1922)
—*Max Weber*

The Giving of Orders (1926)
—*Mary Parker Follett*

Notes on the Theory of Organization (1937)
—*Luther Gulick*

The Proverbs of Administration (1946)
—*Herbert Simon*

The Scalar Principle (1947)
—*James D. Mooney*

Foundations of the Theory of Organization (1948)
—*Philip Selznick*

Suggestions for a Sociological Approach to the Theory of Organizations (1956)
—*Talcott Parsons*

General Systems Theory—The Skeleton of Science (1956)
—*Kenneth E. Boulding*

Parkinson's Law or the Rising Pyramid (1957)
—*C. Northcote Parkinson*

Cosmopolitans and Locals (1957)
—*Alvin W. Gouldner*

Management and Technology (1958)
—*Joan Woodward*

Theories of Bureaucracy
—*James G. March and Herbert A. Simon*

Two Approaches to Organizational Analysis: A Critique and a Suggestion (1960)
—*Amitai Etzioni*

Organization Theory: An Overview and an Appraisal (1961)
—*William G. Scott*

Mechanistic and Organic Systems (1961)
—*Tom Burns and G. M. Stalker*

The Principle of Supportive Relationships (1961)
—*Rensis Likert*

Dramaturgy (1961)
—*Victor A. Thompson*

The Concept of Formal Organization (1962)
—*Peter M. Blau and W. Richard Scott*

Patterns of Organizational Accommodation: Upward-Mobiles, Indifferents and Ambivalents (1962)
—*Robert Presthus*

Democracy is Inevitable (1964)
—*Philip E. Slater and Warren G. Bennis*

Organization Theory and Political Theory (1964)
—*Herbert Kaufman*

The Causal Texture of Organizational Environments (1965)
—*F. E. Emery and E. L. Trist*

Organizations and the System Concept (1966)
—*Daniel Katz and Robert L. Kahn*

Organizations in Action (1967)
—*James D. Thompson*

Organizational Choice: Product vs. Function (1968)
—*Arthur H. Walker and Jay W. Lorsch*

Organizational-Environment Interface (1969)
—*Paul R. Lawrence and Jay W. Lorsch*

The Peter Principle (1969)
—*Laurence J. Peter and Raymond Hull*

The Short and Glorious History of Organizational Theory (1973)
—*Charles Perrow*

The Craftsman, the Jungle Fighter, the Company Man, and the Gamesman (1976)
—*Michael Maccoby*

Source: Jay M. Shafritz and Philip H. Whitbeck, eds., *Classics of Organizational Theory* (Oak Park, Ill.: Moore Publishing Co., Inc., 1978), pp. vi., vii. Reprinted with permission.

Kahn);[1] and (6) leadership (personal identity coupled with dynamic enthusiasm and dedication resolving the questions Who am I? Where am I going? and How do I intend to get there?). In addition, behavioral science concepts should be applied: for example, (1) Rensis Likert's "Linking Pin" and "System 4"; (2) McGregor's "Theory X and Theory Y"; (3) John J. Moore's and Jay W. Lorsch's "Beyond Theory Y"; (4) Chris Argyris's "Mix Model"; (5) Robert Blake's and Jane Mouton's "Managerial Grid"; (6) David McClelland's "Achievement Motivation"; (7) Abraham Maslow's "Needs Hierarchy"; and (8) Frederick Herzberg's "Two Factor."[2]

Leaders in patrol should seek the appropriate formula. No one combination can be applied to all police departments. In order to find the tailor-made approach for an individual department, managers at all levels should be exposed to the various concepts. The challenge facing patrol is tremendous, and the management by objectives approach should be used as a base from which to meet this challenge. This will allow for flexibility in organization and organizational concepts so the patrol force can change as the mission changes. Using management by objectives, the leaders can prepare valid evaluations regarding the accomplishment of the objectives, i.e., define role expectations. MBO allows patrol officers and leaders an opportunity to determine where they stand regarding individual performance. They can devise sub-goals from the overall goals set for the patrol force (desire, opportunity, vulnerability of victim, physical facilities, neighborhoods). The leaders can determine the amount of resources available to accomplish goals and sub-goals; allocate and distribute manpower for maximum utilization; identify training and education needs, deficiencies, and attributes; enhance internal cooperation through the use of goal-achievement versus goal-failure standards; increase the opportunity for total involvement by all personnel in goal-oriented philosophies; specialize only as needed; and use program, project manager, ad hoc organization, and task-force concepts as appropriate to achieve goals.

THE MISSION

The patrol force must be flexible in order to accomplish the mission, whatever the priorities may be regarding that mission. Scholars in the field of patrol administration have stated on several occasions that a police department is number one (if police agencies were rated) if it is number one in the community served. With regard to the norm, a discussion of four views regarding the establishment of mission priority is informative. (See Table 4.1 on traditional and proposed goals.)

View One

The usual mission as stated by August Vollmer, J. Edgar Hoover, and Bruce Smith places priority on law enforcement:

1. Protection of life and property, which includes the prevention of criminality;
2. Reduction or suppression of crime;
3. Apprehension of offenders;
4. Recovery of property;
5. Preservation of the peace through order maintenance; and
6. Regulation of trr ffic, and performance of miscellaneous calls for service.

These are valid objectives and the order of priorities seems difficult to contest. However, when we look at the amount of time officers spend achiev-

Table 4.1 *Police Goals*

Traditional	Proposed
• Protection of life and property, which includes the prevention of criminality	• Safeguard freedom
	• Protect constitutional rights of citizens
• Reduction or suppression of crime	• Promote respect for law and justice
• Apprehension of offenders	• Preserve democratic processes
• Recovery of property	• Develop reputation for fairness, civility, and integrity
• Preserve peace	• Win respect of citizens
• Regulation of traffic, and performance of miscellaneous calls for service	• Use reasonable amount of force
	• Preserve life and property
	• Prevent crime; reduce opportunity
	• Enforce laws
	• Detect, apprehend, and detain suspicious offenders
	• Promote and preserve community stability
	• Resolve individual conflict

Source: Neil C. Chamelin, Vernon B. Fox, and Paul M. Whisenand, *Introduction to Criminal Justice* (Englewood Cliffs: Prentice-Hall, 1975), p. 68.

ing the mission as stated, we realize that the majority of the time is spent maintaining order and performing miscellaneous services.

View Two

A second view, proposed by James Q. Wilson, is that:

> First, the police should recognize clearly that order maintenance is their central function—central both in the demand that it makes on time and resources and the opportunities afforded that it makes in the lives of the citizens.
> Hunting criminals both occupies less time (at least for the patrolman) and provides fewer chances for decisive action. How well disputes are settled may depend crucially on how competent, knowledgeable, and sensitive the police are; how fast the crime rate mounts is much less determined on the level or nature of police activity.[3]

It has been estimated that the order maintenance and service functions account for approximately 70 percent of the total police-patrol tasks. At times the percentage has gone as low as 60 percent and as high as 78 percent. This average is determined by the clientele of the community. If the community is a "bedroom community," the percentage is even higher in the areas of miscellaneous calls for service and order maintenance. If the community has a high-density population and high crime, the miscellaneous calls for service decrease proportionately with the increase in crime. When the viewpoint is analyzed by the professor and the student of patrol administration, the following aspects should be considered:

1. What proportion of training in police academies across the nation is devoted to the performance of order maintenance and miscellaneous services?
2. What proportion of training is devoted to the mechanics of police work?
3. Is the impression received from the percentage realistic in that the remaining 30 percent may be the crucial performance area? James Sterling makes the analogy between this time and the time of the surgeon. Surgeons spend most of their time diagnosing the problem and carrying out preoperative and postoperative responsibilities, yet the crucial time is the time spent in the operating room performing the operation.[4]
4. What do police leaders place most confidence on when the time comes for performance and promotional evaluation: arrests? lower crime rates? courtesy? community relations? charges of misconduct?
5. Is it valid to say that the only officer who causes controversy is the one who works: for example, makes arrests, has increased citizen contacts (field interrogation reports), does not patrol as though he or she were wearing blinders?
6. How then is the best way to reduce the crime rate: deployment? social advancement? increased science and technology? increased help in the prosecution, courts, and correctional field? Have the police advanced too far? Should the police wait for the rest of the administration of justice system to catch up? Should there be more administrative trials rather than more criminal trials? Should the legislature reduce the number of criminal laws? Should the police begin training and education so that they can become capable of responding to white-collar crime (embezzlement, security, theft, large-scale fraud, etc.)?
7. What consideration will legislatures across the country give to the recent action by government? Should the number of criminal laws be reduced?

The *cluster approach* is one method being used in response to the first three aspects mentioned above.

Cluster approach to professional police training. The Regional Training Academy at Independence, Missouri, which is the primary police training facility for the five-county metropolitan Kansas City area, has adopted a type of professional training called the cluster approach. This new concept was developed under former Kansas City Police Chief Clarence M. Kelley.

This approach deviates from the traditional method of training police officers. Generally police training has concentrated upon teaching the proper techniques and procedures relating to the police function, with only a few hours relating to police–citizen relations. The cluster approach emphasizes the human relations aspect of the police function. It is introduced at the beginning of the training course. This approach hits at the heart of the 70 to 80 percent of the time officers spend dealing with people, rather than the 20 to 30 percent of the time when the mechanics of policing is necessary.

The Regional Training Academy concentrates the first 136 hours of training in the area of humanities and social science. The instructors for these humanities and social science courses come from outside the academy staff. Professors from the University of Missouri, Rockhurst College, Penn Valley Community College, and Central Missouri State University, including a human relations specialist and psychologist, are among the staff members.

Courses given in the first cluster include philosophy of the Constitution, sociology, criminology, psychology of personal adjustment, applied psychology, social psychology, juvenile delinquency, police ethics, liabilities of the police uniform, off-duty conduct, abnormal psychology, intergroup conflict and prejudices, history of police, stress negotiation, police discretion, and social problems. In addition to those courses directly aimed at the officer's role in dealing with people, the curriculum contains more than eighty other courses in both classroom and practical instruction. The Regional Academy includes as part of its practical instruction courses in persuasive speaking, vocabulary building, and speed reading.

Another course taught is propriety. This course is similar to a course taught to military officers at the Wentworth Military Academy and Junior College in Lexington, Missouri. Practical instruction is used in a four-week-long situational-location training. At this time entrant officers leave the classroom environment completely and move into the Regional Academy's mock police station. From here they are dispatched in specially marked Academy police cars to locations throughout the city of Independence. At these locations, which include businesses, intersections, taverns, residences, schools, and banks, officers encounter the types of calls they will face when they become full-fledged police officers. Mock situations are created in the most realistic manner possible, and an instructor is assigned to each location as an evaluator. At the end of the situation a critique is made of the entrant officer's performance, and further specific training is given as appropriate. In order to understand how the other person feels, each officer is subjected to both chemical mace and tear gas in order to feel the effects of these nonlethal weapons on the individual, so that his or her decisions regarding these weapons will be knowledgeable.

Only time will tell how successful this program and approach will be. However, innovations of this type and the training of our new officers in law enforcement are most refreshing, and more creative approaches should be forthcoming throughout the law enforcement community. Research in the field of training and many other aspects of law enforcement is necessary. The Regional Training Academy should be commended on its attempt to use all the resources within the community to produce an improved product from training academies. The recognition of the need to train and educate officers in the area of human relations, because this involves what officers actually do the majority of their time on duty, has arrived.

View Three

The third view of the mission, where the priorities specified include all of those presented, is a joint statement by elected officials, the community, and the police department. The International Association of Chiefs of Police and a special committee created by the IACP worked with the American Bar Association to develop the ABA "Standards Relating to the Urban Police Function." The following excerpts express what I believe are necessary objectives and priorities.

(2.2) MAJOR CURRENT RESPONSIBILITIES OF POLICE

In assessing appropriate objectives and priorities for police service, local communities should initially recognize that most police agencies are currently given responsibility, by design or default:

  (i)   to identify criminal offenders and criminal activity and, where appropriate, to apprehend offenders and participate in subsequent court proceedings;

  (ii) to reduce the opportunities for the commission of some crimes through preventive patrol and other measures;

  (iii) to aid individuals who are in danger of physical harm;

  (iv) to protect constitutional guarantees;

(v)   to facilitate the movement of people and vehicles;

(vi)   to assist those who cannot care for themselves;

(vii)   to resolve conflict;

(viii)   to identify problems that are potentially serious law-enforcement or governmental problems;

(ix)   to create and maintain a feeling of security in the community;

(x)   to promote and preserve civil order; and

(xi)   to provide other services on an emergency basis.

(2.3) NEED FOR LOCAL OBJECTIVES AND PRIORITIES

While the scope and objectives of the exercise of the government's police power are properly determined in the first instance by state and local legislative bodies within the limits fixed by the Constitution and by court decisions, it should be recognized there is considerable latitude remaining with local government to develop an overall direction for police services. Within these limits, each local jurisdiction should decide upon objectives and priorities. Decisions regarding police resources, police personnel needs, police organizations, and relations with other government agencies should then be made in a way which will best achieve the objectives and priorities of the particular locality.

(2.4) GENERAL CRITERIA FOR OBJECTIVES AND PRIORITIES

In formulating an overall direction for police services and in selecting appropriate objectives and priorities for the police, communities should be guided by certain principles that should be inherent in a democratic society:

(i)   The highest duties of government, and therefore the police, are to safeguard freedom, to preserve life and property, to protect the constitutional rights of citizens and maintain respect for the rule of law by proper enforcement thereof, and thereby, to preserve democratic processes;

(ii)   Implicit within this duty, the police have the responsibility for maintaining that degree of public order which is consistent with freedom and which is essential if our urban and diverse society is to be maintained.

(iii)   In implementing their varied responsibilities, police must provide maximum opportunity for achieving desired social change by freely available, lawful, and orderly means, and;

(iv)   In order to maximize the use of the special authority and ability

> of the police, it is appropriate for government, in developing objectives and problem priorities for police services, to give emphasis to those social and behavioral problems which may require the use of force or the use of special investigative abilities which the police possess. Given the awesome authority of the police to use force and the priority that must be given to preserving life, however, government should firmly establish the principle that the police should be restricted to using the amount of force reasonably necessary in responding to any situation.[5]

The patrol administrator would be in a much better position to walk that tightrope between personal liberty and community security if these standards were followed. One can see why patrol administrators and their organizations must maintain flexibility in order to change as the mission changes and to achieve the objective.

View Four

Another set of priorities for criminal justice in the United States was expressed on August 9, 1973 when then President Nixon signed a bill authorizing $3.2 billion for assistance of local and state law enforcement agencies over the next three years. On that day, a commission of state and local officials, after a two-year study, presented a "Master Plan" designed to reduce crime and improve criminal justice during the next decade. Since 1968 LEAA has channeled $2.5 billion into local police work. The Master Plan against crime was detailed in a 318-page report drawn up by a twenty-two-member committee made up to study the problem, financed by a $1.5 million federal grant. A major recommendation—and one that has caused the most controversy—was for prohibition of handguns. The commission urged that, no later than January 1, 1983, each state should take the following actions:

> Private possession of handguns should be prohibited for all persons other than law-enforcement and military personnel. Manufacture and sale of handguns should be terminated. Existing handguns should be acquired by states. Handguns held by private citizens as collectors' items should be modified and rendered inoperative.

Between 1946 and 1981 more than 40 million handguns were manufactured in the United States or imported from other countries. (Source: FBI

Uniform Crime Reports, 1981.) "Nowhere in the world," the study added, "is the private ownership of handguns on a per capita basis as high as in the United States. Nowhere among the industrial nations of the world is the criminal homicide rate as high as in the United States."

The committee set as its goal the reduction of crimes of violence, murder, rape, aggravated assault, and robbery. Such crimes, the study said, "threaten the very existence of the humane and civilized society." It proposed four priorities for reducing crimes:

1. Prevent juvenile delinquency,
2. Improve delivery of social services,
3. Reduce delays in the criminal justice process, and
4. Secure more citizen participation in the criminal justice system.

In the section on decriminalization the commission recommended that the states remove from the list of crimes such offenses as vagrancy, drunkenness, and minor traffic violations. It also urged states to reevaluate their laws on gambling, marijuana use and possession for use, pornography, prostitution, and sexual acts between consenting adults in private. Such reevaluation should determine if current laws best serve the interests of the state and the needs of the public. The criminal justice system, the study said, is ill-equipped to deal with these offenses. These crimes place an unwelcome and heavy burden on law enforcement resources throughout the nation. And the laws regulating these offenses are open to abuse and to increasing constitutional challenge.

Valid Evaluation

Once the objectives, or the mission, have been selected, the structure of the organization can be designed to achieve these objectives. When the community states that the priorities should be (1) law enforcement, (2) response to calls for service, and (3) order maintenance, then the resources of the department can be formulated to achieve these objectives in this particular order of priority. The priorities can be turned upside-down, and the distribution of the resources can be changed likewise.

The patrol forces will be given the primary responsibility for attaining the objective, and each individual within the patrol function can be evaluated according to how well he or she contributes to attaining the goals according to the priorities. The patrol administrator can then place emphasis appropriately and evaluate each level of authority to the patrol officer.

Role Expectation

Each patrol officer should report to his tour of duty knowing exactly what role he is to play relating to the mission and the approach he should take. James Q. Wilson, in *Varieties of Police Behavior*,[6] indicates three styles of police organization: legalistic, nightwatchman, and service.

The author believes that most police departments today use a combination of two of the three styles mentioned. No matter what style or combination of styles used, the officer going on patrol should be aware of what is expected of him and his role in the community. Should he be aloof or friendly? Should he view violations as black or white with no gray? Should he respond to human needs with officious retorts, or be the caretaker of the less fortunate? Should he take $2 from his own pocket and buy food for a mother and children until the welfare check arrives, or should he call the Welfare Department and notify them of the immediate need? How should he respond to the merchants on his beat? How should he respond to elected officials? How do the clientele he serves expect him to respond?

The answers to these questions may not be easy, but a clear as possible picture should be painted for the patrol officer concerning his role and its relationship to the community. The need for flexibility in a role is important not only for the patrol officer but for the patrol leader as well. The human situations facing the patrol force on a daily basis do not remain static. The solutions to these must change to meet each one as presented.

In meeting these different situations, it is important for an officer to know that his actions are approved and support for his decisions will be forthcoming from police officials if necessary. The policy manual published by the Los Angeles, California Police Department in the January 1973 issue of *Police Chief* is a tremendous step forward in providing officers and supervisors alike with the realistic objectives and guidelines necessary to meet these situations.

Sub-Goals

When the goals of the patrol force are stated (e.g., reduce crime, respond to calls for service within three minutes), each patrol commander, supervisor, and officer has a chance to contribute to the objective. Patrol commanders distribute manpower as needed, watch commanders present clear pictures of problems and recommend solutions, sector sergeants spur officers on in a way that enhances team effort, and individual officers plan their tours of duty to obtain maximum use of resources in attaining the objective. In order to attain goals, planning is important.

The combination of the use of the planning process by patrol officers to the fullest and participatory management is an untapped resource for patrol forces around the country. If the planning process were really used by all patrol officers, it could result in the reduction of one crime per year for each officer. This statement is based upon years of experience, observation, and practical application by many patrol commanders.

The inspection procedure of recognizing a need, which is the first step in planning, can work to enhance an officer's capability to achieve goals. A sector sergeant working a squad of officers in today's patrol force would improve his potential for achieving goals if he were to instruct those officers in total planning. This is especially true in a smaller department, where it is so important for each officer to contribute all of his or her talent in order to achieve the goals, since the patrol officer is responsible for delivering the total police service.

Available Resources

When realistic goals have been identified for the patrol organization, patrol commanders look to the ready manpower and equipment to determine if they have enough. In most cases, there are never enough resources. The management by objectives approach analyzes beats, sectors, watches, units, and divisions to determine if assigned resources are used properly in attempting to reach the goal. The responsible commander has built-in accountability; therefore, he uses live inspection (as discussed in Chapter 2) to determine if all resources are being used properly. Tours of duty that match crime by time of day and day of week become centers of attention when failure to achieve a decrease in crime is the issue. Failure of beat officers to recognize the neighborhood problem that ultimately develops into a violent confrontation causing loss of manpower, complaints against police, lower public image, etc., cries out as a failure on the part of the administrator to communicate, lead, act before the fact, and use sensitivity. The failure to use these human resources greatly reduces the chance of goal achievement. (The allocation and distribution of manpower for maximum use will be discussed in a later chapter.)

Identification of Education and Training
Needs, Deficiencies, and Attributes

One patrol precinct or one patrol watch of a department is doing well in the reduction of crime. Another is doing well in community involvement. Still another is achieving sub-goal number 3, which is to increase merchant's installation of alarm systems and other security devices that make their businesses more difficult to burglarize (crime prevention).

The goal of each precinct or watch, however, was to achieve all three objectives, and each failed in at least one. A review of not only what is wrong regarding each failure, but also what is right in connection with the areas where the goals have been achieved, is necessary. Reduction in crime for one may have occurred because arrest and case presentation are carefully done so that convictions are higher, thus reducing the chance of a particular individual committing multiple offenses. Another watch may have an officer who, through education, is able to communicate and sell ideas to merchants. These revelations provide good feedback and can be used in helping patrol operations achieve sub-goals and major goals. Methods that work well are expanded, deficiencies are corrected, and cooperation and mutual desires are solidified.

Internal Cooperation

A patrol commander complains that it took a record section ten minutes to supply one of his officers with auto-theft information. The communications dispatcher describes how he tried for five minutes to raise the patrol officer on the air to assign him a call for service. These complaints will not disrupt the force if commanding officers remain objective and understanding. But if emotions and subjectivity creep in, compartmentalization and inefficiency occur. The management by objectives approach helps prevent this sort of activity and reveals the reasons for not achieving goals. The opinions of officers, supervisors, and commanders of units not involved will be relegated to a backseat. The patrol force must be served by other line or service units, or else we deal only in rhetoric when we allude to patrol being the backbone or patrol delivering the primary function and all other units existing to support patrol. However, it is a much smoother organization when failure to meet standards on the part of a unit is indicated by controls, rather than by the commanders of patrol voicing dissatisfaction with existing operational administrative and logistical support. The management by objectives approach is much more realistic when it comes to identifying responsibility, authority, and accountability.

Total Involvement and Goal-Oriented Philosophy in Specialization

The need to specialize arises out of the failure of patrol to produce the total police product. When patrol doesn't prevent the crime, then someone must try to apprehend the person responsible for committing the crime. If patrol can perform its task in a satisfactory manner, there is no need to specialize. Today, however, it is all but impossible to avoid specialization.

The management by objectives approach to patrol administration holds the patrol officer accountable for everything that occurs on his or her beat. This responsibility, accompanied by authority, allows the officer to make decisions at the level of execution, and also gives the patrol officer a chance to be self-actualizing, or to have a feeling of being fulfilled in the performance of his or her daily tasks. At the same time, the patrol commander who is held responsible for crime increases and decreases has control over the investigation aspect of crime. The patrol commander has the opportunity to observe which officers really have the aptitude for investigation. These aptitudes can be defined in depth and assignments can be made by category of crime (arson, robbery, homicide) as deemed appropriate by the patrol commander. Specialization in larger departments may be necessary in the case of vice, narcotics, auto theft, bad checks, and homicide. However, the majority of police departments in the country can be organized by the objectives approach, thereby improving the chance for all personnel to be involved in goals and/or sub-goals related to their position in the organization.

The St. Louis Police Department has used a concept of calls-for-service patrol cars and preventive patrol cars. The sub-goals for each group are different. All cars are under the watch commander who directs the watch in accomplishing the major goal.

In effect, the management by objectives approach attempts to hold each patrol officer, supervisor, and commander totally responsible for his or her own area of responsibility, provides resources to achieve the stated goals, allows for discretion, and documents for accountability. Doesn't this make each of these officers a police chief in his or her own right. Won't each of them become involved in the philosophy of achieving goals? MBO should enhance the success of the patrol operation and reduce the need for specialization. Patrol officers should not be report takers, responders, or mere protectors of crime scenes, but totally involved members of police work using all their talents to the fullest. It is necessary to look upon the patrol officer as completely capable of response, analysis, and investigation of any situation requiring police action. Continued selection, education, and training of capable men and women will produce the type of patrol officer that is good for policing and our country.

Students of patrol administration must be aware of police organizations as they exist today in order to change the structure as the need arises. Additionally, the principles of organization that apply must be understood so that decisions affecting the patrol function do not disrupt the department as a whole. A later chapter discusses the importance that the patrol force must attach to the team-policing concept presently and in the future.

ORGANIZATION OF COMMAND

Chain of Command

Lines of authority and channels of communication are necessary in order to have action at one point transmitted to other points within the organization. Any functioning organization uses this fundamental principle of the chain of command. Authority may flow only downward, but communication flows up, down, and laterally. Lateral communication is very important in the organization. (It is emphasized in the section on organizational divisional relationships.) This principle is very close to the principle of unity of command. When a patrol administrator communicates or directs an order to anyone below the level of his immediate subordinate, he relieves that immediate subordinate of any responsibility or accountability regarding the order. This is intolerable and disrupts the organization. Additionally, the lower-level subordinate who receives the order doesn't really know to whom he should then report. Should he report back to his immediate supervisor, or should he bypass him and go directly to the supervisor who issued the order? There may be exceptions, such as when the middle supervisor is on vacation or medical leave, but in these cases the subordinate who receives the order has the responsibility to inform his immediate supervisor of such incidents upon his return to duty. The aspect of supervision where the superior is responsible for everything a subordinate does or does not do is highlighted. Patrol leaders who issue orders to subordinates not immediately below them should show the courtesy of advising recipients that the order has been given in the absence of the patrol leader's immediate subordinates. Respect and courtesy are two-way streets: respect begets respect.

Unity of Command

Unity of command means that only one supervisor has command of each squad or unit within the patrol organization. Conversely, each subordinate reports to only one supervisor. As a patrol administrator you report to the chief or deputy chief of operations, and your deputies as commanders report only to you.

As stated above, if these reports or orders bypass the proper individuals, then the chain of command is broken and officers do not know to whom they report. Confusion will take over. A man or woman is frustrated when he or she says, "The captain tells me to do one thing, the lieutenant tells me to do another thing, and the sergeant tells me to do something else. I don't know who to listen to."

In certain situations the supervisor must give orders to officers who are not under his command routinely. If a bank holdup occurs and pursuit takes place, a patrol sergeant may have to issue orders to detectives in order to have a successful conclusion of the incident. Or, the detective sergeant would be remiss in his duties if he did not take action where he found a patrol officer committing a violation of departmental rules. These situations are exceptional and should not be carried over into normal operations.

2 exceptions [in emergency / reputation of dept. is at stake

[Span of Control]

there is a definite # of subordinates that can be effectly supervised by 1 boss. and this # shouldn't be exceeded.

Span of control is based on the capability of one person to direct, control, and coordinate the talents of a number of people in attaining the objective. Individual ability, time and place, and the nature of the task to be performed are all involved. A patrol administrator who attempts to have too large a span of control is usually overestimating his own ability or underestimating the ability of his subordinates, in whom he may lack confidence. *time, distance, effect span of control*

Some administrators indicate that the ideal span of control is one to four, others say one to six, while still others say one to thirty is reasonable. Flexibility in span of control is necessary for patrol operations simply because time and area have such an impact. An excellent sergeant may be able to supervise twenty officers in an urban area because of the small size of the beats. Yet their number would be impossible as soon as he removed these beats to a suburban area where the beat size would be multiplied by five. In a patrol force where the interrelations are simple, a patrol sergeant may supervise fifteen officers, but if other factors are included (e.g., economic, community stability, political pressure) the number must be reduced. The patrol administrator must consider all factors before arriving at the decision that is best for his force and his department.

Span of management. The patrol administrator of a progressive police department where commanders are of a high caliber, well-educated, and knowledgeable about administrative practices can increase his span of management. He must be careful to insure that the commanders have reached a stage of sophisticated development concomitant with the increased responsibility and authority necessary for the broadest span of management.

Responsibility, Authority, and Accountability

Responsibility, authority, and accountability in organization were discussed in depth in Chapter 2. To simply restate these principles, however, when a supervisor delegates a responsibility to a subordinate he must also delegate the commensurate authority. Additionally, the superior must follow up to insure the completion of the assignment and should hold the subordinate accountable for completion. The subordinate has an obligation to use the authority properly and should expect to be held accountable for its use. Patrol administrators must delegate authority to the appropriate level and should give only enough authority to be sufficient to accomplish the mission. If delegation is used optimally, the patrol commander can use the extra time for innovation and creativity.

Assignment of Tasks

Even though the patrol administrator is responsible for the entire patrol force, the assignment of the tasks of patrol cannot be accomplished by him alone. The chief of police holds him responsible for achieving the objectives of patrol. However, the administrator assigns the accomplishment of certain tasks within patrol to members of his command. These commanders in turn assign partial responsibility for the task to the immediate supervisors and so on, to the level of execution. Thus, each member of the force is assigned a responsibility for performing specific tasks.

The patrol officer's retort to this may be, "If I am being held responsible for performing a certain task, I would like to be clear on what the task is." This is certainly reasonable, and an explanation should be given by the supervisor to the subordinate when the assignment is made. The definition of the task should (1) not be too rigid, (2) not be too broad, (3) allow for personal initiative, (4) consider duplication of effort, and (5) provide an avenue for honest expression of opinion by the subordinate.

Work Plan

To plan work so that the maximum effectiveness of each worker is attained is a must for any organization. In the management by objectives approach to patrol administration, planning is a sine qua non in obtaining positive results.

Planning how work is to be divided includes separation by (1) function, (2) area, and (3) time. Figure 4.1 provides an example of planning using these three methods of organization.

Other aspects to be considered in planning separation are clientele, purpose, and level of authority. In planning the work by clientele, consideration would be given to stolen-car rings, narcotic addicts and peddlers, prostitution, juvenile offenders, etc. (In this case, clientele means the people grouped together by crime.) When grouping according to clientele, the police leaders must be fully knowledgeable about specialization, its advantages and disadvantages (see below). Questions concerning the importance

Figure 4.1 *Organization by function, area, and time*

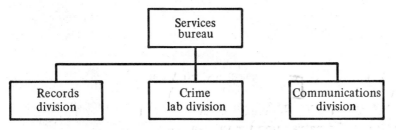

1. *ORGANIZATION BY FUNCTION*

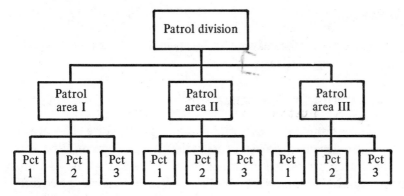

2. *ORGANIZATION BY AREA*

    PATROL AREA = Each area responsible for 1/3 of community.
    PRECINCT   = Each precinct responsible for 1/9 of community.

3. *ORGANIZATION BY TIME*

Patrol Chief

Watch Commander	Watch Commander	Watch Commander
Watch I, 8 AM–4 PM	Watch II, 4 PM–12 PM	Watch III, 12 PM–8 AM

Each watch commander responsible for patrol function for entire community for eight-hour period.

and value of the particular work assignments, the demands of the situation (which may require sniper teams, riot-control units, etc.), the amount of disruption to the total organization, degree of sophistication in development of individual personnel, and proportional needs should be analyzed and planned for in depth. When planning by purpose, we refer to traffic control or public relations activities. Again, the need must be considered. If the purpose of traffic is to increase the enforcement index, then fragmenting the task would cause inefficiency. When organizing by purpose, do not be afraid to combine tasks to achieve the goal that is the purpose of the organization.

Specialization

The need for specialization should be based upon investment and dividend: How much return will this investment pay in terms of reduced burglary or robbery, and to what extent? What will be the effect upon the area from which the patrol officer was taken? The decision should be planned for and analyzed very carefully. The advantages—specific responsibility is placed, proficiency in performance is accomplished, public support for the specialty is more easily obtained, special interests may develop additional resources —all should be weighed against disadvantages—increased complexity of the organization; compartmentalization; increased duplication, especially in records; a decrease in general interest of the specialized field; and the tendency for officers to refer citizens to the special unit for anything concerning the area of specialization.

Centralization and Decentralization

The FBI has offices around the country. Consequently, because of geographical necessity, the decentralization of operations is imperative. Where an area and population are mixed in size and density as in the case of a municipal police agency, the decision of decentralization becomes more difficult. Should all patrol officers report to the headquarters' facility and then to the beat, or should they report to the precinct and then to the beat? This question must be answered by each specific department. The patrol administrator has to consider how much time it takes to travel to each beat, the need for two roll-call sessions for each shift or watch, availability of resources, and the amount of room necessary to operate in each manner.

The advantages of a centralized command are improved control, direction, and coordination. Also, communication is made easier since command officers can contact all officers in the central facility. The major disadvantage of centralization is the potential for all orders to come from the chief. This stifles the initiative of commanders and prevents the development of individual talent.

The advantages of decentralization are that personnel assignments are made closer to the actual beats, which makes shift changes easier; training is more effective because of the smaller number of officers; supervision of personnel within the district is more effective; and officers have the chance to develop. The disadvantages of decentralization are that it is difficult for the chief to direct, control, and coordinate the department; the ability to communicate decreases; negative competition between district commanders may develop (crime reports may be manipulated); and costs increase.

The patrol administrator of the future must be able to manage complex organizations, and to handle conflict, change, and his own personal adaptive mechanisms to keep up with our increasingly complex society. To do this, he must know who he is, where he is going, and how he intends to get there.

PATROL ORGANIZATION OPERATIONAL NUMBERING SYSTEM

Patrol commanders and field supervisors should be able to identify the approximate location of any police vehicle and police personnel merely by

Figure 4.2 *Chart of organization, large department*

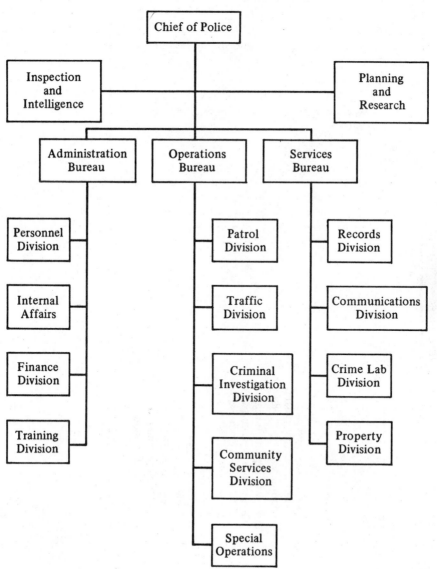

Table 4.2 *Table of Organization, Large Department*

	Chief	Asst. Chief	Major	Capt.	Lieut.	Sgt.	Patrol Officers	Police Women	Civ.	Total
Chief of Police	1									1
Inspection & Intelligence			1		1	3	9		2	16
Planning & Research			1		2	3	6		20	32
Operations Bureau		1								3
Patrol Division			1	5	25	150	1500	10	50	1741
Traffic Division			1	2	10	25	150		10	198
Criminal Investigation			1	3	15	30	175	10	20	254
Community Services			1	2	5	15	30	5	10	68
Administration Bureau		1								3
Personnel Division			1		2	5	10	1	10	29
Finance Division			1		1	2			20	24
Internal Affairs			1		2	6	12	2	10	33
Training Divison			1		2	8	5	1	5	22
Services Bureau		1								3
Communication Division			1		4	12	50		50	117
Crime Lab Division			1		2	5			25	33
Records Division			1		2	7	20		30	60
Property Division			1		2	3	20		20	46
TOTALS	1	3	14	12	75	274	1987	29	288	2683

Table 4.3 *Table of Organization, Medium-Sized Department*

	Chief	Capt.	Lieut.	10	Patrol Officers	Civilian	Total
Chief of Police	1						1
Planning and Inspection			1	2	4	10	17
Uniform Division		1	5	10	65	5	86
Criminal Investigation		1	4	8	24	5	42
Administrative Services		1	3	4	8	3	19
Technical Services		1	2	4	12	50	69
TOTAL	1	4	15	28	113	73	234

161 SWORN
73 CIVILIAN

Table 4.4 *District or Precinct Table of Organization, Large Department— Decentralized Command*

	Capt.	Lt.	Sgt.	Ptlm.	Ptlwm.	Civ.
DISTRICT COMMANDER	1					
Executive Officer		1				
Desk Officers			3	7		
Civilian Clerks						10
SUBTOTAL	(1)	(1)	(3)	(7)		(10)
TACTICAL COMMANDER		1				
Sector Sergeants			1			
Sector Patrolmen				14		
Tactical Sergeants			1			
Tactical Patrolmen				14		
Detective Unit			1	2	2	
SUBTOTAL		(1)	(3)	(30)	(2)	
WATCH COMMANDER		3	9			
Sector Sergeants						
Sector Patrolmen				126		
SUBTOTAL		(3)	(9)	(126)		
TOTAL	1	5	15	163	2	10

GRAND TOTAL = 196

Figure 4.3 *Chart of organization, medium-sized department*

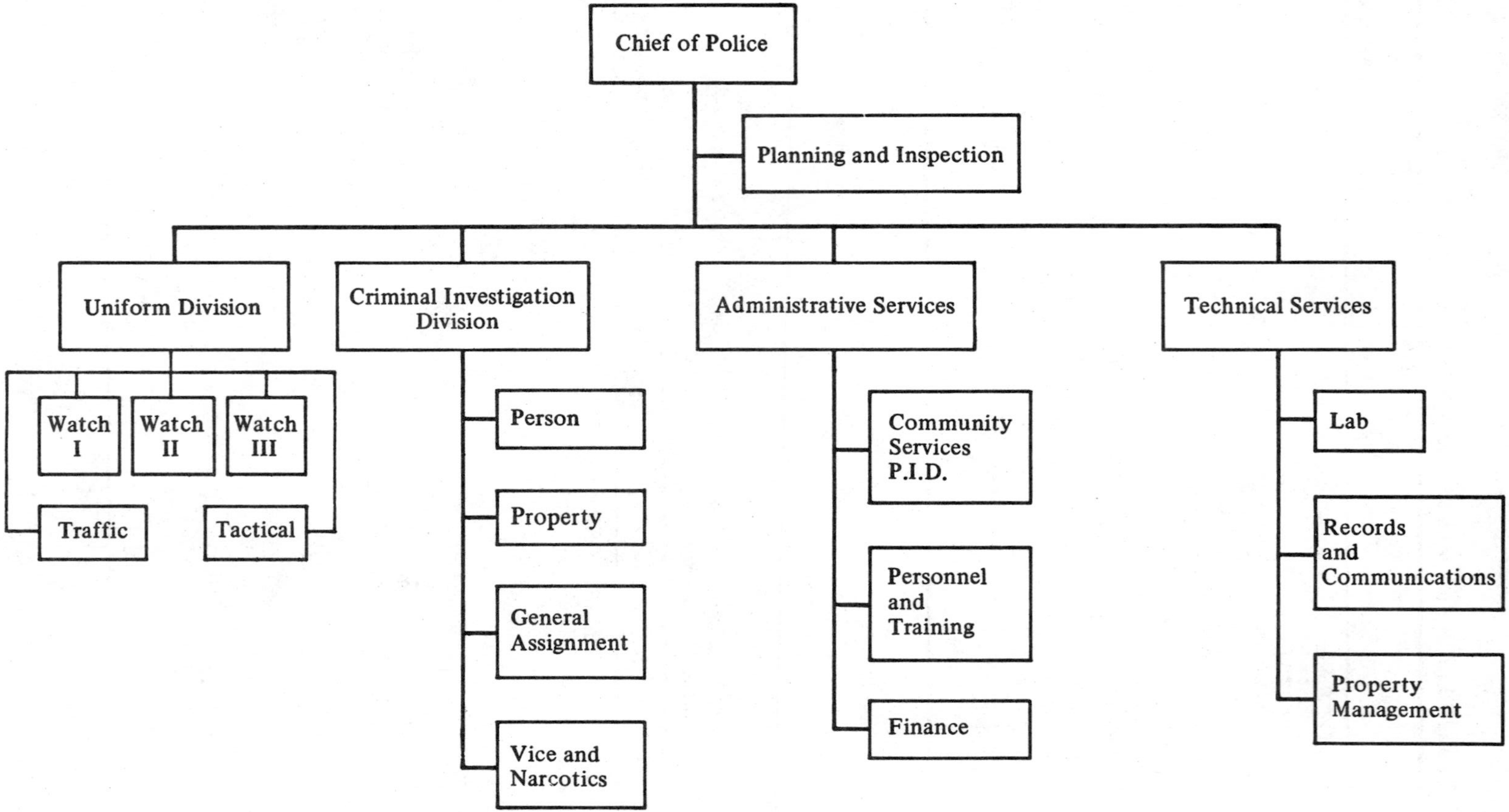

Figure 4.4 *District or precinct chart of organization, large department–decentralized command*

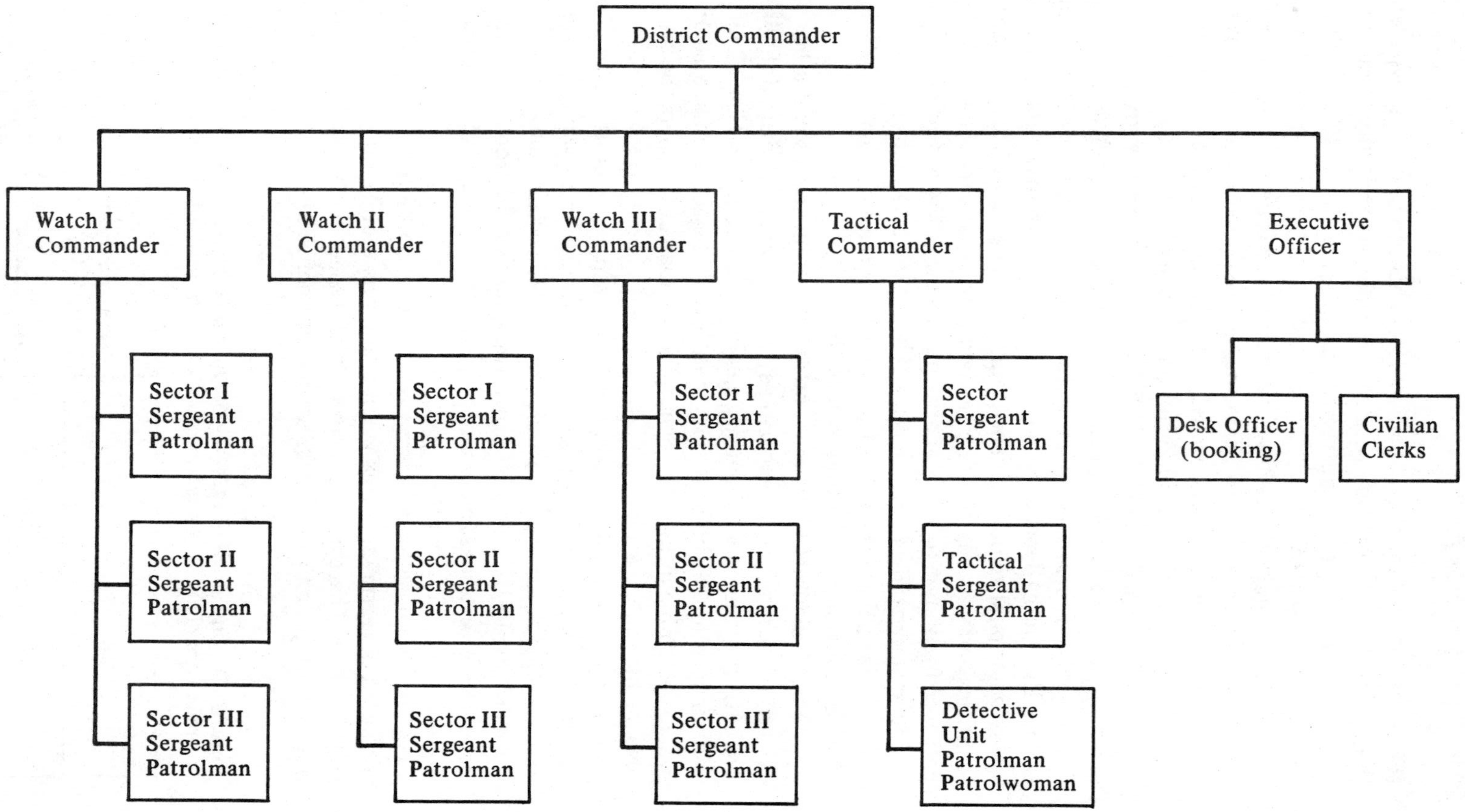

District Commander

Executive Officer
- Desk Officer (booking)
- Civilian Clerks

Watch I Commander
- Sector I Sergeant Patrolman
- Sector II Sergeant Patrolman
- Sector III Sergeant Patrolman

Watch II Commander
- Sector I Sergeant Patrolman
- Sector II Sergeant Patrolman
- Sector III Sergeant Patrolman

Watch III Commander
- Sector I Sergeant Patrolman
- Sector II Sergeant Patrolman
- Sector III Sergeant Patrolman

Tactical Commander
- Sector Sergeant Patrolman
- Tactical Sergeant Patrolman
- Detective Unit Patrolman Patrolwoman

the call number of the individual vehicle. This can be done at least within the area in which a beat car is assigned specific responsibility. Additionally, supervisors may also be identified so that responsibility at each level can be applied as is necessary.

Smaller departments having a centralized organization (one central police facility where all patrol personnel are assigned) do not have too much difficulty in identifying the individual beat car, the assigned location of the beat car, and even the name of the officer assigned the particular beat because of the small number of vehicles assigned to any given shift. For example, if ten or twenty vehicles are assigned to a shift, numbering officers from ten to twenty or ten to thirty with fixed beat assignments is simple. Even if the department uses a manpower resource-allocation system where additional vehicles and beats are added for eight-hour overlaps, the identification is easily made. Paramount in importance is the ability of patrol commanders to know at any given time of the day or night where, and how many, officers are on duty. Also, when situations require supervisory personnel, it is beneficial to be able to contact the appropriate supervisor responsible for the area concerned.

Patrol administration must be careful to insure that all other units exist to support patrol. Numbering systems must be instituted that allow the patrol commander to identify easily the number and type of vehicles and the location of the beat. The identification system must also enable him to determine if the vehicle contains one man or two men, the sergeant responsible for the sector or shift, and the lieutenant responsible for the zone or shift. Figure 4.5 is an example of shift I in a patrol force divided by shift and sector.[7] The next shift, shift II (0800–1600) would change only slightly and the same type of assignment would occur. However, when the third shift (shift III, 1600–2400) arrived, there would probably be an additional sector or at least more manpower added to the patrol functions. Figure 4.6 shows an example of shift III.

The real need for a systematic and practical numbering system for the small department arises when situations require all personnel to be called to duty. There may be an overlap of responsibilities and call numbers must reflect an accurate identification of personnel. The larger, decentralized

Figure 4.5 *City X–Shift I (2400–0800). In this example, cars 11 and 21 could be two-man cars. This is possible because of the number of cars and officers.*

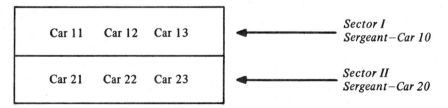

Figure 4.6 *City X–Shift III (1600–2400). The numbers from one to nine would be used for the chief of police or other officials throughout the department. The size of this department would be between seventy-five and one hundred.*

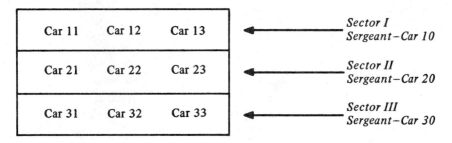

department faces this difficulty daily, not merely when riot squads or tactical squads are called to respond in large numbers. Manpower accountability is essential to the successful solution of emergency situations. Therefore, a smooth transition must take place when a department builds from the routine application of personnel to the amount necessary to quell a serious problem. Planning is most important, and a key to this type of planning is having the normal system compatible with that used in unusual situations.

If a large department were decentralized, and the normal numbering system allowed for the accomplishment of those goals previously stated, it might be set up in this way: City Y has nine districts: 1, 2, 3, 4, 5, 6, 7, 8, and 9. Each district is commanded by a captain. The call number for the captains (commanders) are 100, 200, 300, etc. Every vehicle with a call number beginning with the first digit of the captain's number is located within his district. Figure 4.7 shows the city divided into districts. Each district commander has a given number of lieutenants, sergeants, and patrol officers under his command. These personnel are identified by individual and location. Each patrol force would apply the numbering principle within its department.

The commanding officer of each district has three shift commanders and an administrative and operations lieutenant. No matter which shift is presently working, the shift commander of each district has the same last two numerals. Therefore, to identify the shift- (watch-) commander on duty in the second district, the leader would call for car 201. If he wanted his contemporary in district IX, he would call for car 901; in district V, 501. An operation lieutenant (or crime-control lieutenant) in district VIII has call number 802; in district VI, 602. The administrative lieutenant of each of the districts is assigned call number (03), which means district IV administrative lieutenant is identified as 403.

Figure 4.8 shows how the system works in the sectors. If a patrol commander wishes to contact the sergeant responsible for sector 1 in district

Figure 4.7 *City Y–The number of the district identifies the location within the city.*

District I	District II	District III
District IV	District V	District VI
District VII	District VIII	District IX

District I	=	Northwest	=	Captain (100)
II	=	North	=	Captain (200)
III	=	Northeast	=	Captain (300)
IV	=	West	=	Captain (400)
V	=	Central	=	Captain (500)
VI	=	East	=	Captain (600)
VII	=	Southwest	=	Captain (700)
VIII	=	South	=	Captain (800)
IX	=	Southeast	=	Captain (900)

I, he requests car 110. The supervising sergeant of sector 1 in district IX has call number 910; call number 630 belongs to the supervising sergeant of sector 3 in district VI.

The next part of the system identifies the individual beat cars within the sector and district. This is somewhat difficult in terms of exact location because of the differences in configuration of sectors by district and geographic influence. However, with the same principle, identification by location can be achieved to suit the purpose for which the system is intended.

Figure 4.8 *City Y*

District I	District II	District III
Sector I Sgt. -110 Sector II Sgt. -120 Sector III Sgt. -130		
District IV	District V	District VI
District VII	District VIII	District IX

Figure 4.9 *City Y*

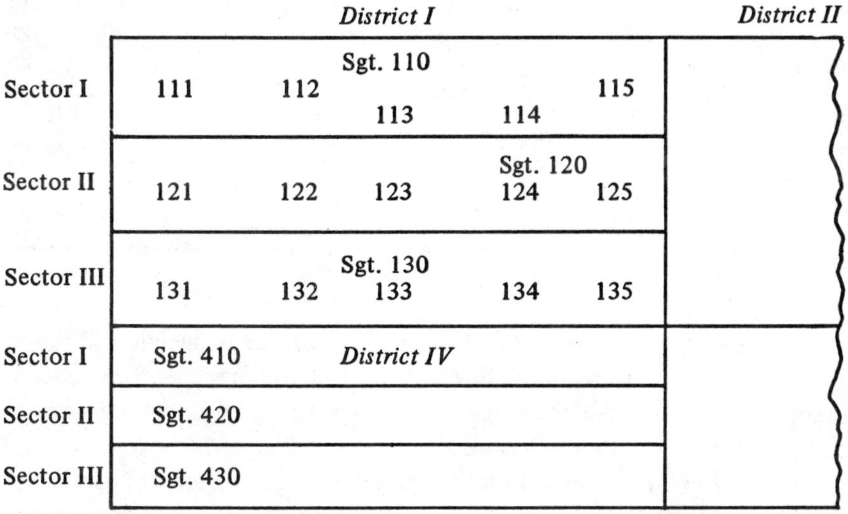

	District I					District II
Sector I	111	112	Sgt. 110 113	114	115	
Sector II	121	122	123	Sgt. 120 124	125	
Sector III	131	132	Sgt. 130 133	134	135	
Sector I	Sgt. 410	*District IV*				
Sector II	Sgt. 420					
Sector III	Sgt. 430					

Figure 4.9 shows that district I, northwest section of City Y, can be identified by location down to the beat car. Car 111 can be identified as the first car in sector 1, district I. Departments using two-man and one-man cars in patrol may want to identify the first car in the sector as a two-man car. Other departments may want to identify the first car as one equipped to transport prisoners. In any case, as long as consistency in numbering is maintained, identification is simple.

A practical application of the principle might be used in the following situation. The time is midnight. An annual dance that has never been unruly in the past is taking place in district V. As the dance ends and the youths leave the school, several altercations take place and a small riot breaks out. Rocks and bottles are being hurled at patrol cars and officers. Destruction of the school begins. You, the patrol commander, estimate a need for twenty men to assist you in abating the situation. You would not call for the needed manpower from one area and leave it unprotected. If the department policy were that all first cars in each sector are two-man cars, it would be a simple decision of calling 611, 621, 811, 821, 411, 421, 211, 221, 511, and 521. This request is for manpower near the location and does not deplete any one of the other districts unnecessarily. Beat cars adjacent to the positions of the responding cars would simply cover the areas vacated.

A numbering system that identifies units from all parts of the department is easily developed in planning for serious emergencies. In the patrol force this involves simply following the same principle for the team concept. A department receives information that a demonstration soon to take

Table 4.5 *District Manpower*

District I	1 sergeant	9 patrol officers	call number 1510, -11, -12
District II	"	"	1520, -21, -22
District III	"	"	1530, -31, -32
District IV	"	"	1540, -41, -42
District V	"	"	1550, -51, -52
District VI	"	"	1560, -61, -62
District VII	"	"	1570, -71, -72
District VII	"	"	1580, -81, -82
District IX	"	"	1590, -91, -92

place has the potential for developing into violence. A decision is made that one hundred officers should be readily available to respond as needed. If manpower were to be drawn from the districts, the numbering system and manpower could be developed as shown in Table 4.5.

Leadership would have to be provided in order to control and coordinate this amount of personnel. This numbering also follows the routine. The leadership could be provided by the commanding officer of the district in which the demonstration is taking place. The prefix "15" identifies the team as being in a special condition, the third number identifies the district from which the team has come, and the last digit identifies each car in the team. Numbers 1510, -20, -30, etc., would identify the team supervisors.

There are many variations of numbering systems, such as number and letter combinations (one adam one, one adam two). The system used by the police agency should meet the needs of the particular department. It is recommended that the system be designed in a manner that enhances the efficiency and effectiveness of the patrol force.

FORMAL AND INFORMAL ORGANIZATION

When two or more people decide to coordinate their effort and action, possess the ability to communicate in order to achieve this coordination, and agree that there is a common goal which they will give up a certain amount of individuality to attain, a formal organization exists. The amount of effort and individual dedication each individual is willing to contribute will determine the success of the particular organization.

The patrol administrator must set the example of total commitment. Each goal set must be realistic, attainable, and analyzed for maximum approach so that he can lead the patrol force in accomplishing it.

The formal organization in the patrol force extends vertically from the chief of patrol to the patrol officer and laterally from the watch commander on the number-one shift in district A to the watch commander on the number-two shift in district A, from one leader of middle management a different division or unit to another, and so forth. What is essential for the formal organization is that it be able to accomplish the mission. The patrol administrator must realize that the organization should remain flexible. Priorities change. Therefore, when a new mission is stated, the organization should be developed in a way to best accomplish the new goal. This flexibility is the secret of the patrol administrator of the future. As the police leader develops his ability to communicate, change in mission and organization is resolved much more easily because the patrol force becomes one in understanding and reacting.

Formal organizations are grouped by time, geography, service, function, and process. Jobs are well defined. Responsibility, authority, and accountability are assigned and tasks are specified. Organizational charts and tables of organization are drawn and relationships among the different units through systematic policies and goals are stated.

As the organization grows, so do the complexities of the communication process and interpersonal relationships. These complexities grow at a far greater rate than does the actual number of employees. The enlightened patrol administrator is aware that formal organizations must create informal organizations so that sincere communication can take place among all members. Respect for the individual is important. No matter what rank, the individual must be respected as an important component of the organization and a partner in accomplishing the mission, not regarded as a number or a machine or impersonal object. Patrol leaders should remember they were patrol officers at one time and realize the importance of personal choice and participation in decision-making on matters that affect the individual.

Informal organizations in police work, such as bowling teams, pistol teams, and softball teams, are not unlike those of any other formal organization. (All formal organizations have some types of informal organizations.) The effective patrol leader realizes his people have certain attitudes and behavior patterns that usually show up in a grouping of people who have similar likes and dislikes. For example, there are some police officers who are fine softball pitchers and exert a great deal of influence over other policemen at work just because of their sport skill. This influence can be used to enhance the goals of the organization. Police sergeants and lieutenants who are coaches of the softball team or pistol team may have influence over police officers formally and informally. The informal leaders may rise out of the group naturally or may be part of the formal organizational leadership as well as the informal. In both cases, there is freedom of expression and association. The patrol leader should have a finger on the pulse of these groups in order to maintain a common purpose of mission between his leadership and the leadership of the informal organization. Patrol officers complain about the same things and usually desire a common reward and goal. Patrol officers, sergeants, etc., have their own method of communicating and will react uniformly to a threatening situation.

For example, a patrol sergeant tells his squad they are not making enough arrests (although the amount is related only to statistics, not to quality and reduction of crime). The informal leaders suggest to the squad that they patrol with blinders on. They do not look from side to side but merely drive a police vehicle or walk down the street without observing. The squad of officers makes arrests only when there is no alternative. Consequently, the number of arrests is reduced to almost nothing. The sergeant is in trouble and has to communicate with the informal leaders to save face. The enlightened sergeant would have discussed the arrest situation before making the statement. The recognition of the informal leader and the positive use of his position will reduce conflict in the goals of the organization and the individuals within it.

Patrol leaders must allow patrol officers to feel that they are an integral part of the organization and are considered as such when decisions are made about goals and methods to be used in achieving these objectives. When procedures are written and implemented, open, honest communication between managers and employees will produce the necessary information to determine the effectiveness of the procedure. If change is necessary, the formal/informal communication will result in a smooth transition from one procedure to another.

There is nothing more healthy than for the chief of patrol to be in an operational room with majors, captains, lieutenants, sergeants, and patrol officers discussing honestly the whys and wherefores of specific approaches to reducing crime. The uninhibited statement of a patrol officer indicating the need for an increase in arrest of narcotic addicts in a given area as the best way to reduce dwelling burglaries, showing facts and figures justifying his statement, is music to the ears of a patrol leader. A sergeant who argues his case for two foot beats in a given area as the best patrol technique to reduce robbery, tells how he will provide the coverage without additional manpower, and states what the percentage reduction will be after implementation is a thinking, planning sergeant. Healthy dialogue, objective thought, and mutual respect help coordinate the informal and formal organizations. Participatory management of this type does not take much time and will reward the patrol leader more than sufficiently for whatever efforts he makes.

The informal organization develops because of, and responds to, conditions or needs. The patrol administrator should be ever alert so he may assist the development in a manner conducive to achieving the objectives of the patrol force. Giving support, warmth, empathy, trust, respect, and confidence to the developing informal organization displays the kind of leadership that will bring together the objectives of the informal and formal organizations.

ORGANIZATIONAL ATMOSPHERE

The patrol administrator is responsible for setting the tone of the patrol force. Management by objectives must reach the level of execution in a realistic manner and atmosphere. Most of us have been in situations where the "atmosphere was so thick, you couldn't cut it with a knife" and have felt uncomfortable. There are many types of environments within which an officer must work. Some of the environmental forces can be controlled by the patrol officer and some cannot. Patrol commanders can control a certain number of these forces and the impact they have on their subordinates. The forces that affect the behavior of patrol officers most are their immediate supervisors. If an officer understands the sub-goals of his or her unit or squad and is supported by his or her supervisor in the quest of achieving these sub-goals, he or she will be encouraged to move forward. Anxieties and frustrations come from not knowing exactly what the goals of the organization are and what the role played by each member in helping to achieve these stated goals is to be.

An atmosphere of confusion created by a weak leader who is unable to set priorities, cannot determine when a job is well done, makes inadequate and unintelligent use of resources, and shows indecisiveness will result in a stagnant patrol force. Patrol officers will perform according to the relationships, interaction, and conflict forces that surround them. Usually, occupation socialization takes place first in which the majority of friends and supporters are other police officers. Next, the relationships between the officer and his or her customers, peers, and supervisors affect the officer's behavior. The conflict comes when there is a question in the officer's mind as to how he should present himself to various other people or groups. For example, judges and attorneys may expect an impartial and aloof approach in the courtroom, while the officer's friends, family, clergyman, and citizens in general expect a more friendly approach. Since the patrol officer is the actual performer in attaining the objectives, the patrol commander must set an atmosphere in which the negative influences over which he has control are reduced to a minimum and have minimal impact on the officer.

An atmosphere that creates a total feeling of belonging in each member of the patrol force is the responsibility of the patrol administrator. He must be careful to avoid thinking that because he directed ten subordinates to carry out his philosophy of using their command authority to support the level of execution in reaching goals, it will automatically be done. The patrol administrator must follow up to insure that his patrol force is permeated with an atmosphere in which there is: (1) freedom of thought; (2) support for open objective statements by anyone wishing to move the department forward; (3) acceptance of officers' decisions even though they may sometimes result in mistakes; (4) a view of disagreement as a positive and healthy force in the organization; (5) openness to positive change; and (6) authority – in the proper perspective, as it relates to the security of the individual and his or her relationship to others, whether they be peers, supervisors, or subordinates.

Change for the sake of change is unacceptable. Destructive criticism should be eliminated. However, disagreement should not be construed as a negative reaction if it is accompanied by justification. If the patrol administrator welcomes feedback and sets the atmosphere for honest and sincere thought by members of the patrol force, he or she will go a long way toward making participatory management, conflict management, and change management realities. An atmosphere that makes all personnel feel comfortable even when discipline is meted out has to be open and above board. An atmosphere in which the leaders appear as supporters of the personnel doing the job tends to increase performance quality. Support here means reducing red tape, providing appropriate information, enhancing relations with other divisions or units that provide a service to patrol, and causing an increased team effort to achieve organizational goals. Decisiveness; analysis; consensus; communication with newspaper personnel, government, and other facets of the criminal justice system; and alleviation of any aspects of the environment that might reduce the officer's ability to achieve the objectives are important. If support such as this can be granted a patrol officer, he can dedicate his total tour of duty to those patrol tasks that he is most capable of handling.

The patrol administrator who exudes confidence, knowledge, respect, and enthusiasm sets an atmosphere of harmony. He transmits this to the patrol officers and will make them enthusiastic about their jobs. The patrol administrator who exudes incompetence, insecurity, and indecisiveness, and who resorts to authority because of his inability to direct, will transmit an atmosphere of anxiety and frustration that results in a dulled patrol force. The student of patrol should recognize these personality traits not only in the administrator, but also in each member of the patrol force. Individuals make up the organization – individuals have personalities, organizations have atmosphere.

ORGANIZATIONAL RELATIONSHIPS

Police officers who have been educated to hold leadership positions realize how much career development is necessary for effective leadership. Until the time is reached when most leaders in patrol have had the opportunity to experience career development, they must get this experience using their own time and effort.

The more enlightened patrol administrator has a sensitivity to the needs, purpose, desires, and goals of all the other divisions within a police organization. Since the patrol administrator initiates procedures, he or she must know the effect upon the other units within the organization. Good judgment is an important aspect of leadership. The more knowledge the patrol administrator has about the other units within a police organization, the more capable he or she is of making good judgments. In addition, the leadership necessary for his own patrol force requires that he know when to initiate communications to leaders of other divisions that require change. For example, an officer who indicates to the communications division that he or she is in the rear of a given address and is stopping a car bearing a certain license tag with several occupants needs to know the status of the auto (stolen or not) and the person to whom that auto is registered. The officer's performance and procedure will be affected by the length of time it takes for him to receive this information from the communications unit. The patrol leader should be aware of the approximate length of time taken to give the requested information to the patrol officer. If this appropriate support is not effective and efficient—if the response time is too long—it is the patrol leader's responsibility to initiate the action necessary to correct a situation that may endanger his personnel.

INTELLIGENCE AND INSPECTIONS

Intelligence Section

Patrol administrators must have proper intelligence, with the main ingredients being quality of intelligence and accuracy. Since intelligence has a direct effect on his manpower deployment, the patrol administrator should be aware of the procedures and tactics and techniques used by the intelligence division to gather information. He should also be able to ask valid questions, which in turn will help him to make judgments about the number of officers he will commit to specific situations. If his intelligence is accurate and the need indicates the deployment of ten officers in reserve status, then the intelligence unit not only has done its job with regard to gathering intelligence, but also has effected the positive use of manpower. If an intelligence unit is responsible for protecting important persons who enter the community, then the quality of planning that is done by the intelligence unit will directly affect the deployment of manpower by the patrol division. In this case the traffic division would also be affected, because of the route and publicity given the visit of important persons.

The patrol administrator, therefore, relies heavily on the input from the intelligence section since it determines (1) the number of officers necessary to accomplish the mission, (2) the method of deployment, (3) the effect on the daily operations of the department, (4) the effect on crime, (5) the assignment of responsibility, and (6) the extent to which this adjustment would disrupt the plans of the entire patrol force—i.e., each patrol supervisor is making his own plans so he needs to know ahead of time if a change is being contemplated so that he can adjust his planning accordingly.

Inspections Unit

The inspections unit of a police department is naturally the eyes and ears of the chief of police. However, since most inspections include the patrol force, the patrol administrator should be aware of the purpose of inspections and the techniques used by the inspections unit. This awareness could reduce the possibility of duplication in any follow-up situation. The need for feedback from the patrol officers and their immediate supervisors to the patrol administrator concerning the subjectivity/objectivity of the inspections unit within a police organization is most important.

The ability to get the job done in an inspections unit requires that diplomacy be in the forefront of the qualities possessed by personnel assigned to that particular unit. Tact is necessary whenever any type of criticism is involved. Since no one enjoys being criticized, diplomacy in communicating need for improvement is primary. Members of the patrol force who need to have methods of improvement related to them must be put in a position to accept these suggestions positively. Improvements will be made and hostility will be avoided when diplomatic officers are assigned to the inspection unit. Even though the members of the inspections unit do the inspecting, they are part of the total team of a police organization and need to be projected as such. It is important to understand that the human desire for recognition and reward is a strong personal thing and that commendation as well as criticism is therefore appropriate.

The patrol administrator is more likely to act before the fact if the inspections unit can provide an in-depth study of deficiencies that may have been missed during the patrol administrator's own personal inspection in his areas of responsibility. Sincere cooperation between the patrol administrator and inspections unit is desirable because of its bearing on the accomplishment of the total mission. Confidentiality is necessary. If officers know that they can trust an inspector they will be more open in telling about procedures that need improvement and suggesting controls that might resolve problems.

It is the patrol administrator's responsibility to insure that the officers of his command understand the nature of inspection, the need for inspection, the appropriate attitude toward the inspections unit, the results to be obtained from good inspections, and the help that inspections can give individual officers in everyday patrol. If all of the units within a police department exist to support the patrol function, then it is very important for the patrol administrator to understand the maximum use of the inspection process. He must believe in it and must have the belief permeated throughout the patrol force. Personal inspection by the patrol administrator can enhance the support and value of the inspections unit. The inspection unit will assist after line inspections have indicated a need for possible city-wide inspections of the same problem found in a given area.

The relationship principle applies to Intelligence, Records, Communication, Property, Budgeting, and Research and Planning. Positive relationships with all other units assist the patrol administrator immeasurably.

EMPLOYEE ORGANIZATIONS

Organizations formed for the benefit of police officers have existed for many years. The Fraternal Order of Police (FOP) was founded in 1915 and has national membership of over 200,000 active and associate members. FOP, the International Conference of Police Association (ICPA), and the National Police Union (NPU) are all involved in economic, social, and political activity related to police. There are also local organizations, such as police benevolent associations, police clubs, and police officers' associations. Additionally, there are state organizations, like the Police Officers Research Association of California (PORAC).

The patrol administrator must be aware of each employee organization that exists within his force and understand its objectives, motives, techniques, and structure in order to work in harmony with it for the good of the department. Police chiefs will naturally develop policy regarding management and labor relations. However, most problems that develop in a police agency have their roots in the patrol force. This is because of the environment in which the patrol officer must work. The patrol officer must stand on the front line of the demonstrations, work round the clock in all kinds of weather, and be subject to a change in days off or hours worked because of a crime increase or parades or athletic contests. The patrol officer is the one who usually becomes the object of police-brutality charges and is involved in the critical confrontation of riot and arrest. Other units within a department are also answerable to issues of disagreement, but not to the extent the patrol force is.

The patrol administrator and patrol commander must recognize the key roles they play in using good leadership to avoid unnecessary friction between management and employee organizations. When incidents of crime, potentially violent confrontations, or any other situations requiring a buildup in manpower occur, it is incumbent upon patrol leaders to use their personnel wisely. They must consider amount of manpower, hours of need, support resources, and any other facts that have a bearing on the situation and an impact on the individual patrol officers. Today's patrol officers are educated and intelligent and question the procedures used in solving problems. They will not hesitate to offer suggestions concerning different approaches to solving problems that would improve their lot. Officers will continue to join together in their fight against negative influences on police departments. This is obvious in the case of the fight against civilian review boards, where employee organizations have spent a great deal of money in defending their institution and implementation. Patrol leaders must not be the catalyst in the formation of employee organizations because of their unenlightened leadership. Where employee organizations exist, management should work in harmony with them, retaining management prerogatives, to move the police department forward.

Some forward-thinking chiefs of police have formed advisory committees within the different units of their police departments to try to resolve minor complaints at the lowest level of supervision and command. The basic purpose of this type of committee is to resolve the minor problems that are specifically related to that unit. Members usually consist of elected police officers who represent each rank in the unit. Meetings are held on a regular basis. The chairman of the committee is the highest-ranking officer of the unit. For example, in a patrol precinct with a captain as a commanding officer, he would be the chairman. This is natural, because he is the one who has final say in resolving minor problems occurring within his precinct or command. Also on the committee would be a lieutenant, sergeant, and three patrol officers, one from each watch or shift. If the precinct contained detectives and civilian personnel, then one each of these would be elected to the committee. Given the proper atmosphere, this type of participation and feedback ensures that small problems remain small and are resolved easily.

Patrol administrators would do well to initiate and/or follow up on this type of employee relations in an effort to act before the fact (in effect, using the management by objectives approach in achieving goals).

There are times when the complaints of employees cannot be resolved in this manner. Some of these complaints will be planned by existing employee organizations in an attempt to test the strength of particular chiefs and command officers, including patrol commanders. A calm, friendly, firm demeanor is required when dealing with these situations. To reiterate, understanding the motives, methods, and structures of those with whom one is dealing is essential, and knowledge of departmental rules, regulations, policies, and procedures always helps in communicating the proper message at the right time. The patrol leader should not allow himself to be placed in a position from which he has no exit. Absolute statements should only be made when there is no possibility of a change in policy, rules, laws, etc. The leader should remember that most employee representatives have become adept in the art of negotiation, compromise, bargaining, and intellectual volleyball in areas of self-improvement and collective advantages for the brotherhood. The goal is to move the department forward as a team, while at the same time providing an area of influence for management and employees that will best achieve that goal. One of the better ways to do this is through a written grievance procedure.

Grievance Procedure

Every employee wants to feel that he or she is a part of the department, just as every citizen wants to feel that he or she is a part of the country and possesses certain rights and privileges. When one feels that one's rights and/or privileges have been violated, in his or her mind, redress is in order. If satisfaction is not forthcoming to the individual, rational approaches become less palatable, and frustration, negativism, and disruption become the order of the day. There is danger not only from the loss of the individual's contribution, but also from the effect that this alleged or real mistreatment has on other employees. Personnel of the same status tend to identify with each other, especially when one seems to have been treated unfairly. When the mistreatment affects a group of personnel, the danger of disruption is expanded proportionately. Some police chiefs, to silence officers whom they consider troublesome because they have spoken out on certain conditions they believed to be unfair, transfer the officers repeatedly. The chief who uses this method has been described as being the best friend an employee organization ever had: each new assignment allowed the officers to attract more men and women into the employee organization.

Grievance procedures for a police department should be in writing and published as a general order. In the case of a police agency where an official agreement is signed with a police officer association, the grievance procedure should be a part of the agreement. The following guidelines should assist the leader in writing general orders about grievance procedures:

1. Define the grievance: Grievance means the claimed unjust treatment, violation, misinterpretation, or inequitable application of any of the provisions of the agreement or rules, regulations, and procedures covering working conditions applicable to the employees of the department.

2. Outline the grievance procedure.
3. Encourage informal resolution of the grievance.
4. Prompt resolution and action are desirable.
5. Grievances may be presented to the supervisor with or without the representation of employee organization.
6. A friendly atmosphere may enhance the early resolution of the grievance.
7. A review of the grievance between the officer and the representative of the employee organization may take place before it is presented to the immediate supervisor.
8. If settlement is not forthcoming, the grievance is then presented in writing. The statement should contain:
   a. nature of the grievance,
   b. date of matter, and
   c. supervisor's reply stating facts he took into account in answering the grievance.
9. The reply should be made within a given period of time (five calendar days, ten working days, etc.).
10. Acceptance or rejection of the answer is made in writing by the grievant.

The procedure is followed up the chain of command until it reaches the chief. There may be variations of the procedure when dealing with specifics, but having a basic procedure to allow individuals to voice their grievances and to provide for redress is the important factor. Patrol administration involves leadership with understanding, empathy, fairness, firmness, and an open patrol force to insure harmony with employees, employee organizations, employee organization representatives, and the management of personnel. Police unions are here now and will expand into police agencies across the country. It is essential that police leaders learn the art of negotiating.

NOTES

1. A more comprehensive description of these concepts may be found in: (1) Luther Gulick, "Notes on the Theory of Organization," in Luther Gulick and Lyndall, eds., *Papers on the Science of Administration* (New York: Institute of Public Administration, 1937), pp. 1–45; (2) Max Weber's writings on bureaucracy in H. H. Gerth and C. Wright Mills, trans., *From Max Weber: Essays in Sociology* (New York: Oxford University Press, 1946); (3) Frederick W. Taylor, *Scientific Management* (New York: Harper & Row, 1947); (4) F. J. Roethlisberger and W. J. Dickson, *Management and the Worker* (Cambridge, Mass.: Harvard University Press, 1939); and (5) Daniel Katz and Robert L. Kahn, *The Social Psychology of Organization* (New York: John Wiley & Sons, 1966) and Stanley

Young, *Management: A Systems Approach* (Glenview, Ill.: Scott, Foresman, 1967).

2. (1) Rensis Likert, *New Patterns of Management* (New York: McGraw-Hill, 1961) and *The Human Organization* (New York: McGraw-Hill, 1967); (2) Douglas McGregor, *The Human Side of Enterprise* (New York: McGraw-Hill, 1960); (3) John J. Morse and Jay W. Lorsch, "Beyond Theory Y," *Harvard Business Review* 48 (May 1970): 61–68; (4) Chris Argyris, *Management and Organizational Development* (New York: McGraw-Hill, 1971); (5) Robert R. Blake and Jane S. Mouton, "Corporate Excellence through Grid Organization Development" (Gulf Publishing Co., 1968); (6) David C. McClelland and D. G. Winter, *Motivating Economic Achievement* (New York: The Free Press, 1969); (7) Abraham Maslow, *Eupsychian Management* (Homewood, Ill.: Irwin, 1965); (8) Frederick W. Herzberg, *Work and the Nature of Man* (Cleveland: World, 1966).

3. James Q. Wilson, "Dilemmas of Police Administration," *Public Administration Review* 29 (September/October 1968): 402.

4. James Sterling, "Police Community Relations: From Them and Us to You and Me" (speech delivered to the International Association of Chiefs of Police, National Institute of Police Training and Community Functioning, Miami Beach, Florida, 31 October 1971).

5. American Bar Association, "Standards Relating to the Urban Police Function," *The Police Chief* (May 1973). Reprinted by permission of the American Bar Association.

6. James Q. Wilson, *Varieties of Police Behavior: The Management of Law and Order in Eight Communities* (New York: Atheneum, 1970).

7. The examples use only a small span of control for the purposes of explanation.

5

Patrol Planning

Planning may be defined in several ways: outlining a course of action to achieve an objective, developing a method of procedure, or arranging parts to facilitate the achievement of the defined objective. Whatever definition you may use, do not forget that planning has a direct effect on crisis-oriented leadership. To put it another way, move hindsight up to foresight and minimize second guessing or Monday-morning quarterbacking.

SOME THOUGHTS ABOUT THE PLANNER

In the discussion of change, we realize the inputs of management by objectives and planning. Comprehensive planners for criminal justice are no different in the knowledge skills and abilities they need to effectively perform the planning function than are police planners and leaders. Gibbons, Yospe, Thimm, and Blake describe the various roles and functions of the planner:[1]

1. *Analyst-Synthesizer*
   The planner frequently analyzes nonquantified information inputs into the planning process, and when technical expertise is not available he or she is left with the task of analyzing data produced by the various justice agencies. Related to this task is often the important function of synthesizing the information and data inputs for presentation to advisory and policy groups, criminal justice agencies, community groups, and the public media.
2. *Communicator*
   The planner must be a communicator *par excellence,* developing formal and informal communication patterns with key actors among the political, community, advisory, and policy boards; with criminal justice agencies; and with community groups and the public media. Group and interpersonal communication skills are essential ingredients to the planner's ability to play the "linking" role in the complex planning process.

3. *Leader-Persuader-Motivator*

Inevitably, at various points in the planning process, the planner must exercise a clear leadership role in his or her relationships with individuals and groups. In fact, the planner is often looked to by individuals and groups to provide direction and motivation. Not infrequently a planner's leadership will take the form of persuasion to move individuals and groups from noncommitment and "drift" to a specific focus and decision.

4. *Advocate*

Planning by definition is a change process. The planner as advocate is a legitimate role when facts and circumstances warrant his or her expressions and when his or her knowledge extends beyond that of individuals and groups. Stated another way, advocacy is compatible with the role of the professional planner defined as an individual who is not value-free and whose role is more than that of technical expert and executive secretary.

5. *Innovator-Strategist*

The planner frequently combines functions of innovator and strategist to deal with the multitude of substantive planning issues as well as the range of value conflicts inherent in the planning process. In his or her professional capacity, the planner is viewed as an "idea" person who also has an experientially based knowledge of how best to manage planning problems.

6. *Negotiator-Mediator*

At any point in the planning process, the planner may have to assume the role of negotiator or mediator. The fact that the planner is viewed by participating individuals and groups as having a certain "neutrality" in conflict situations makes one or another of these roles appropriate in given circumstances.

7. *Administrator-Implementer*

Depending on his or her position in an organizational arrangement, a planner may have to fulfill the role of agency, bureau, or unit administrator. Thus it is imperative that a planner have knowledge of administrative processes, since planning efforts reach into agency policymaking and operations. The implementing role may be less well defined but may well encompass involvement in details of plan implementation as well as implemetation strategies.

Shanahan and Whisenand list the following as attributes of a good planner:[2]

- values the good plan/planning process over building his/her own values in the plan;
- recognizes that his/her own values will inevitably creep into the plan;
- knows his/her own values;
- can tolerate (at the very least) a highly ambiguous environment;
- can function with minimal formal power;
- is patient;

- recognizes that power to the planner springs from the authority of competence, a handle on the funding, and the possession of more accurate and comprehensive data than anyone else in the system;
- recognizes that grant administration (operations) drives out planning;
- does not attempt to impose a planning structure upon others, especially one that might result in frustration, time/effort slippage and lack of creativity; and
- is humble.

We could add to the list, evaluation, since planning, implementation, and evaluative (PIE) are all part of planning. Evaluation means should we keep it; change it; throw it away? Did it do what it was supposed to; if not, why not; what do we do now?

Administrators must make decisions based on the planning process. Anyone assigned as a planner should understand administration as it applies to their agency. The chief should realize when outside help may be needed, based on his or her understanding of the capabilities of in-house personnel. Outside assistance is usually independent and objective, and knows how to research problems from a broad base of experience. On the other hand, in-house planners must know the community and the department, must be able to collect and analyze data with ease, must relate to all relevant individuals and organizations, and are held accountable for recommended plans. Planners, therefore, should study organizational behavior to form conclusions from empirical data and to strengthen the skills to diagnose and prescribe.

Manheim goes on to project thoughts about the police planner and the necessary skills, knowledge, and abilities in the larger context of social planning. An effective planner in a government agency is one who learns the available ways for escaping the apparatus of coercion and achieving opportunities for spontaneous initiative.[3]

The function of the social planner in any social system is to effectively conceptualize the parameters of needed social change, through analysis of the entire context of the social problem in question. Manheim's concept of "principal media" is particularly useful in explaining the function of planning. Specifically, Manheim suggests that effective characterization of a particular social problem requires an understanding of the interdependence of a particular event and the manifold factors that really cause it. (In this sense, principia media denote those interrelationships.) Thus, planning involves problem definition and the ability to think in advance about the consequences of any action taken to ameliorate the problem. In this sense, social planning is rational creative thinking directed toward reconstruction of society, through conceptualization of the entire environment in which a particular social problem exists.[4]

The planner in a government agency must distinguish between *political* thinking and *planned* thinking. As Manheim states: "All political thinking automatically formulates its fundamental terms ad hoc according to the special circumstances of the time."[5] In contrast, planning is a disciplined way of looking at the future. As such, the planning process is guided by a value system toward the identification of specific alternative actions and their consequences.

The entire process requires the careful investigation of a social problem in its entire social context. Thus, research into the social and economic causes of crime assists the planner in identifying the most effective direction for program development. By exploring the environment in which crime occurs (i.e., the community), the planner is able to develop a conceptual base for goal-setting and decision-making. This conceptual base for planning gives structure and direction to criminal justice problem-solving efforts and transforms the current ad hoc activities of the planning agency into a coherent set of activities which provide feedback to the planning process.

THE COMPLEXITIES OF POLICE PLANNING

As we discussed in the first chapter, incremental planning appears to be the most realistic, because of the planner's inability to perceive a projected state of affairs. Others have made similar statements. Banfield explains that this is because of (1) our inability to predict the future beyond a few years; (2) our inability to discover goals on which all can agree; (3) the decentralized character of the political system; and (4) the lack of knowledge or effective means to achieve ends.[6] Friedmann says, "Comprehensive planning is incompatible with the narrow intent involved in the competition for power and influence characteristic of any political system."[7] Braybrooke and Lindblom point to the deficiencies in the knowledge necessary for problem solving in the planning arena, including absence of comprehensive information, the costliness of complex analyses, and the diverse forms that policy problems take.[8]

THE PERFECT PLAN

The use of this heading is emphasized because there is probably no perfect plan.

The police planner and administrator can review the amount of research necessary for planning a program and weigh the costs against

Figure 5.1 *General Planning Process Model*

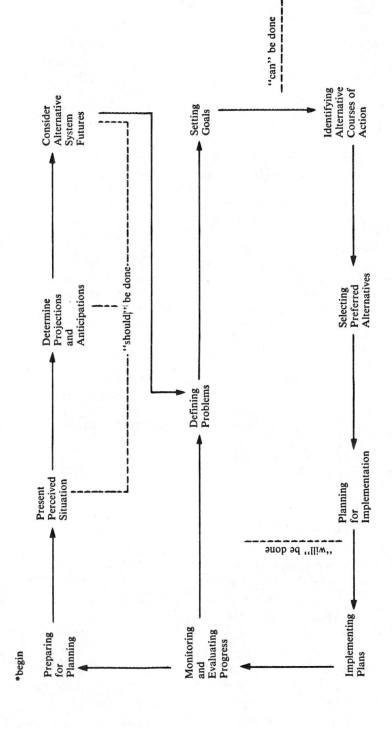

incremental planning, can review master plans providing guidance for years against what the agency is capable of doing, or can plan as effectively as possible within the organizational, governmental, and social environment. Figure 5.1 shows an important consideration: i.e. "should" be done, "can" be done, and "will" be done. I submit—plan, plan intelligently, plan realistically, but plan.

WASHINGTON—A report on the abortive attempt to rescue the American hostages in Iran, prepared for the ranking Republican member of the Senate Armed Services Committee, revealed Thursday that "major errors" were made in the planning and execution of the operation.

Important factors in the failure, the report said, were inadequate training and maintenance, poor contingency planning and intelligence, and "fragmentation of command responsibility."

The report, which was prepared by the committee staff for Sen. John Tower, R–Texas, said the Pentagon possessed "a plan, but charged unexpected contingencies," such as bad weather, the collision at the refueling site, and the unexpected appearance in the desert of a busload of Iranians.

On the maintenance of the helicopters used, the report said: "It is clear that the particular unique demands of the mission were clear to the mechanics and that special measures were taken to assure parts availability."

But it concluded: "It is clear that as a planning matter, no special maintenance concept or serious thought was given to somehow elevating the probabilities of success from a maintenance point of view."

On the intelligence aspects of the mission, the report said: "There was no common understanding of the electronic warfare threat—the danger of being intercepted, jammed, or detected by radars."

DALLAS MORNING NEWS, JUNE 6, 1980

FUNDAMENTALS OF PLANNING

Traditional police planning has been based on what has worked before. However, many of the past statements concerning preventive patrol, standards, performance criteria, clarification of the police role, goals and objectives, or community expectations, to name a few, are no longer valid.

Another problem with the planning process in police agencies stems from the line–staff relationship. Conflict between these two groups has resulted from unclear lines of authority, unrealistic recommendations by staff planning officers, lack of effective communication between line and staff officers, confusion over program responsibility, contradictory follow-up information regarding progress of implemented plans, lack of understanding of each other's roles, resistance to change, and a lack of clarity about the respective positions and their relationships to the organization as a whole and its goals. In other words, line and staff officers should know what is expected of them, how each contributes to achieving the objectives of the organization, and how cooperation between line and staff enhances objective achievement.

One of the obstacles to improved relations in the past, which to some extent exists today, has been the lack of qualified planners working in the police agencies of our country. It is time for police departments to either hire a planner and researcher or cultivate capable in-house personnel to perform this highly important task.

At this point, it would be appropriate to refresh our memory on the concept of the "scientific method," the formal step-by-step approach scientists use in solving any problem. Before scientists embark on an experiment or study, they go through the following procedure:

- They decide the particular hypothesis or theory they wish to test.
- They precisely formulate all of the definitions, criteria, and categories they will use during the test.
- They ensure that the instrument used to measure the results is reliable and appropriate to the task.
- They take steps to eliminate any bias that might affect the outcome.
- Finally, the scientists must be certain they have sufficient resources and personnel to collect complete and accurate data.

A patrol administrator must realize that, in order to bring about results that justify his position, planning must be done in a calculated, methodical, analytical, and realistic manner. Progressive police agencies have been shown the way by knowledgeable chiefs to systematic means of determining what is to be accomplished and the route that should be taken to achieve the objectives.

When a police agency has been instilled with the value of good planning, the results are obvious:

1. Decrease in complaints against officers;
2. Innovative ideas from all levels;
3. Increased apprehension rates;
4. Decrease in Index Crime;
5. Increased community stability;
6. Improved relationships with government at all levels;
7. Better coordination within the criminal justice system;

8. Accolades from all regarding the manner in which the department responds to demonstrations, disorders, parades, athletic contests, barricaded persons, hostage situations, assassinations, ambush, and other situations.

Patrol especially must act before the fact, or else events of the future, which could have been anticipated, will be left to chance. If a person goes shopping without planning a list of what to buy, usually he or she will forget some articles, requiring another trip to the store. The same theory applies when we (1) begin a detailed investigation, (2) begin patrolling a beat, (3) assign work to men and women as supervisors, (4) develop alternatives to resolve a crime problem, (5) allocate and distribute manpower, (6) write orders or procedures, and (7) plan tactical operations or administrate a department, division, etc.

In most police agencies today resources are limited. Therefore, each member of the agency must contribute to the fullest in order to accomplish the mission. One contribution in particular, which requires few if any material resources, is for each member to develop the ability to do his or her own planning. Patrol leaders should be familiar with completing staff work, writing general orders (or at least the first draft), and communicating ideas and opinions for culmination of reports. Even though the formal planning unit (if one exists) will assist all other writers in planning, if necessary, this most basic management function should be done by all parts of the police organization. It is recommended that the planning process become a part of and be taught to recruit and in-service training officers. The results this effort would have on the total police operation would surely be beneficial.

Why Plan?

1. *Plan to achieve objectives, to help clarify and implement policy by defining the immediate objective or purpose.* Specify when any plan will be implemented. Where is the best place to start the implementations? What will be the cost of the implementation of the plan? These questions are important and should be considered. In identifying our plans, we should stress the fact that they are reasonable and attainable. Obstacles must be considered and priorities set. Primary and secondary missions and goals must be developed in order to include realistic approaches. The plans must be consistent with the policy and organizational objectives.

2. *Plan to put ideas to work.* Creativity and imagination are most important parts of the planning process. In an organization where individuals in key positions are limited only by their own imagination, they usually develop specific abilities and contribute to the accomplishment of

the total goal of the organization. Timing is most important when we speak of planning. If ideas are to be put to work, there must be an awareness of the proper time to implement.

3. *Plan to make things happen.* If the chief of police gives an assignment to a patrol administrator and expects it to be done in two weeks, the administrator's first task is to outline his plan of action. He must ask himself questions such as What has to be done? Who will do it? How will it be done? When is the best time to do it? Where should he start? Will it be necessary to make a schedule? What equipment will be needed? Materials? How much money will it cost? How much manpower should be included? The answers to these questions are essential if the deadline is to be met.

4. *Plan to be prepared to act before the fact.* By acting before the fact through proper planning, crisis management is avoided. To act before the fact, assign activities to people according to their skills, knowledge, motivation, and interests. This points up the need for administrators to be able to recognize talents of individuals that can be used in a projected course of action. Projecting a course of action includes deciding, looking ahead, thinking through, assembling, and evaluating.

5. *Plan to cope with change.* In coping with the change that is taking place in law enforcement, it is necessary to adjust and adapt. Individual abilities should be developed to entertain constructive criticism; knowledge of when people are criticizing constructively is important. Proper planning and explanation while proceeding will dissolve some of the problems that cause difficulty in adapting and adjusting. Disagreement with ideas is not inherently negative. However, review and analysis are necessary to justify positions.

6. *Plan to maintain control.* It is said that power is having the ability to make things move a specific way. It is highly improbable and almost impossible for things to go your way in terms of power if you do not plan, outline your steps, and approach the movement in an analytical way. When considering change, remember that power really means controlling the rate and direction of change. Making organizations capable of changing is most important and is directly related to proper planning.

Principles of Planning

1. *Take time to plan.* Take time to think. Everyone should allot a certain amount of time each day just to sit back and think. This basic requirement of planning is fundamental, yet it is forgotten by many administrators. In taking time to think about plans, areas of disagreement should be considered and alternatives developed.

2. *Planning should be top-down and bottom-up.* In an organization everyone should plan. Managers plan management, policymakers plan policy, middle management plans implementation, patrol officers plan operational activity.

3. *Involve and communicate with those concerned.* The involvement and communication must occur at the beginning of any planning to be effective. Change in the implementation of plans has a much better chance of succeeding when the persons affected by the change are involved in the initial planning stages. Consider line and staff relationships and the possibility of the domino effect taking place. Change in one unit in an organization usually affects other units within that organization. By involving people you enhance participatory management and the democratic philosophy of managing by objectives.

4. *Plans should be flexible and dynamic.* Plans should include preparations for adjustments by having alternative courses of action. Lazy planning should not be accepted.

5. *Evaluate and revise.* As in staff studies, the initiating staff officer must follow up on the procedure, plan, etc., to determine its effectiveness. After the documentation and evaluation, revision should take place to obtain the best possible results and determine new objectives. No plan can be complete without evaluation, revision, and documentation.

Steps in the Planning Process

1. *The first step in planning is recognition of the need for the plan.* Apparent needs must be verified by investigation and analysis. Police should be alert to discover common events that may impose unusual burdens upon them. The following are some of the needs that should be recognized when planning.

(a) *There is a need for good intelligence.* The patrol force must have quality intelligence, because this affects manpower planning, a most valuable asset, and in some cases can be a matter of life and death. Intelligence will provide the administrator with information related to what areas have the potential for several incidents occurring at the same time, the possibility of false calls, suspicious calls, the number of marked cars and unmarked cars, uniformed officers and plainclothes officers. Good intelligence can help him determine the need to provide a new system of responding in dangerous situations, the number of officers to assign to an individual police unit, the amount of communications equipment necessary for a given area, and the type of back-up tactics that should be available.

(b) *There is a need for good inspection, both line and staff.* Inspection should be closely related to the planning aspect of patrol administration because inspection can point out the deficiencies and the need for adjustment and planning to overcome these deficiencies. Good line and staff inspections are very positive and should produce an end product enhancing the professional attitude and performance of the department, especially the patrol function.

(c) *There is a need for liaison between police and government.* The ability to utilize resources of local government through recognition of needs and the knowledge of where these agencies within local government can contribute to crime reduction is of tremendous value. There is a need for liaison between police and community groups. There is also a need for liaison between police and activists in the community. If a dialogue can be developed with persons who are demonstrating and who sincerely believe in what they are doing, and an understanding of how they wish to accomplish their purpose is developed, the plan that results can involve a tremendous saving in manpower. The need for understanding and mutual cooperation between police and the business community is also very important. The recognition of the need for planning (e.g., for the downtown business section during the Christmas holidays) can result in great respect for the police agency. Good planning will use manpower effectively. Increased patrol coverage in the business area at peak shopping periods improves the feeling of safety for citizens. This type of planning increases support for the law-enforcement agency. The need for mutual planning by the police and school authorities has become obvious in recent years.

Recognizing the need for a planned liaison between the police and other law enforcement agencies is imperative. During the riots of 1968 in many areas, the need for metropolitan assistance was obvious, yet not many plans of that type were in force. By communicating problems facing metropolitan areas, the need for plans that will enhance the total contribution to law enforcement within a given area will be recognized. Maintaining liaison between the police officers and courts can affect time wasted in court while cases are postponed or delayed. Cases that were lost through poor prosecution or improper testimony can be analyzed critically. Specific training can be provided to upgrade the capabilities of officers to give testimony compatible with proper presentation and prosecution. Liaison between the police and correctional officials should result in plans being written for response by local police agencies to jails, penitentiaries, and prisons throughout the country. Patrol administrators would do well to consider close communication with prison officials in order to develop appropriate plans for combating any potential riot situations in the prison system.

(d) *There is a need to recognize warning signals.* When incidents occur, a critique of the response should be undertaken to determine if there is a need for adjustment. There are several warning signals that should alert patrol administrators to the need for possible adjustment in existing plans or for the initiation of a plan where one does not exist. Some of these signals are: (1) injury to officer, (2) injury to innocent person, (3) escape of a prisoner, and (4) loss of property in police custody.

To enable him to act before the fact, the administrator should seek out early warning signals through analysis of factual data, analysis of existing plans after somewhat successful operations, planning and inspecting, and reviewing the many valid ideas received from the level of execution and first-line supervisors that may either improve the operation or prevent actions that might adversely affect the operation.

Plans should be filed so that effective review can take place and plans updated. Review and proper filing can save many hours of unnecessary research.

2. *The second step in planning is statement of the objective.* An accurate definition of the problem is necessary before the objectives can be stated. Problem definition involves time and effort but once it is done, the objective can be stated very clearly. The final statement should incorporate in general terms the answer to how to achieve the objective. For example, when the objective is to apprehend the criminal: "He may be apprehended by increased patrol or selected coverages of potential victims." Many times the best answer is not known until data has been collected.

3. *The third step in planning is the gathering and analyzing of relevant data.* In order to provide an estimate of the situation on which to base his decisions, the patrol administrator must gather and analyze data about the situation. Operational plans are affected greatly by the analysis of relevant data. The type of data, the course of the collection, and the tabulation analyses will vary according to the purpose of the plan. In most cases the question of what, where, when, who, how, and why must be answered. The answer to these questions must also be related to the basic problem and its solution.

The voluminous information needed for an all-inclusive reorganization plan may be found in Appendix A of *Police Planning* by O. W. Wilson. It may be helpful to list here as an example the basic data Wilson found necessary in creating a reorganization of the patrol division.

    a. Personnel strength arranged by shifts and assignments.
    b. Basis used in the establishment of shift hours.
    c. Basis used in organization of motorized beats.
    d. Basis used in the organization of foot beats.
    e. Number of shifts.
    f. Number of beats on each shift covered by one-man patrol cars and by two-man patrol cars.
    g. Number of foot beats on each shift.
    h. Average daily number of motorized patrolmen on actual patrol on each shift during the past six months.

    i. Average daily number of foot patrolmen on actual patrol on each shift during past six months.

    j. Duties of patrolmen (distinguish between foot and motorized if there is a difference) in:
- the enforcement of traffic regulations
- the enforcement of vice regulations
- the supervision of juveniles
- the investigation of crimes
- the search of crime scenes for physical evidence
- the investigation of traffic accidents
- the checking of the security of commercial establishments
- the inspection of taverns, bars, dance halls, and other licensed recreational establishments

    k. How many minutes before the beginning of their shift are they required to report for duty?

    l. Do any patrolmen report on or off duty from call boxes without reporting at headquarters?

    m. Are evidence technicians, equipped and trained to search crime and accident scenes for physical evidence, assigned to the patrol division? to other divisions?[9]

In this stage of the process there are factors to consider that affect problem identification and problem analysis: incomplete thinking and poor execution during planning and organizing steps; failure to integrate the data collection program; not determining how much and what kind of data to collect; not enough time, not enough money or people, and a failure to distinguish between inductive and deductive reasoning. Do not make decisions on the solution to a problem and then work back to the problem.

    4. *The details of the plan must be developed.* Organization of personnel and equipment must be considered, procedures must be outlined, orders must be drafted, and schedules must be completed. For example, if large numbers of men and women are to be grouped together to meet a particular situation, include in the plan a schedule indicating when the eight-hour tour of duty is up, so that officers can be properly relieved. Continuation past the eight-hour tour of duty would entail a cost that should be considered in the plan. If plans are developed so that most men and women are working at critical times, a reduction in manpower and costs can be achieved. These details should be included in any plan.

    5. *Agreement and disagreement with the plan must be solicited.* Whenever possible, the plan should be drawn up in enough time to allow the information to be disseminated to the personnel involved so that any objections can be resolved. By considering the objections, the leader may develop a better plan. Concurrences and nonconcurrences to the plan should be reviewed, and wherever necessary the answer to the nonconcurrences should be made so that the chief can make his decision based on pros and cons of any question. This increases the chance of the plan being accepted

by the chief. If modifications are suggested with concurrences from the staffing process, the modifications should be considered and included if they improve the total concept of the plan.

Before submitting the final recommendation to the chief, the patrol leader should insure that the developed plan is current. Plans written for response to correctional facilities especially need to be updated since there are different problems occurring today from those a year ago.

Consideration of outside factors that may influence the plan is important. If the cooperation of other community agencies is necessary for the success of the plan, the patrol administrator must take the initiative to solicit this cooperation, by presenting an intelligent, factual background of the reasons for the plan.

The planner must participate in a staff capacity during implementation. In most cases of patrol planning, depending on the type of plan, the officer or supervisor responsible for planning should be on the scene. Wherever the initiator of the plan is located within the organization, he or she is responsible for the implementation of the particular plan.

6. *The last step includes the revision or modification of the implemented plan wherever necessary.* This step is needed so that the initiator of the plan can document, monitor, and evaluate the implementation of the plan. The initiator may suggest change after a short period of time, or an extended period. The initiator should also be willing to admit the plan has been less than successful in reaching the objective.

Crisis management can become a thing of the past for the patrol administrator, but only if intelligent planning is incorporated into the daily routine of the particular department.

Weighing Alternative Plans

"Planning is fundamentally choosing, and a planning problem arises only when an alternative course of action is discovered."[10] There is hardly any decision made by patrol administrators that does not have an alternative, yet these administrators accept recommendations from subordinates that are incomplete and do not include alternatives. The tendency to select the first solution to a problem, or to develop only one course of action for an anticipated problem (when some planning has been done), is what the author calls *lazy planning*.

To avoid lazy planning, the modern administrator must be aware of certain facts. (1) The way things were done years ago is not necessarily the proper or most productive way; innovation is often more important than tradition. (2) Planning is almost never a waste of time; it usually results in saving time. (3) The administrator must consider the effects of his or her decision on people both in and out of the department, in an effort to choose the course of action most suitable for all. (4) The fact that a solution is proposed by the formal planning unit does not mean it is the best answer. The unit may not have even considered any alternatives.

THE FORMAL PLANNING UNIT

Since most police departments around the country are small and are limited in manpower and resources, the need for a formal planning unit must be analyzed very carefully. The administrator must weigh the investment versus the dividend. If the planning concept can be truly communicated to all personnel (especially supervisors), then the need for a formal planning unit will decrease. The first step in planning is recognition of need. The department with proper orientation already has the personnel needed to accomplish the first step. A suggestion box can be used to elicit suggestions from all officers. In most cases, the administrator of a small department realizes that each officer is a precious commodity and must be utilized to his fullest. The decision to combine the planning and inspection function into one unit with the minimal assignment of specialized officers may be appropriate. In taking this route, the need for training as many officers as possible in understanding the amount of effort necessary for each member of the force to contribute to the planning and inspection function should be realized.

In larger departments (200 people or more), there is little question about the need for a formal planning unit. Manpower allocation and distribution become so important on a broader scale that in-depth workload analysis must be part of the planning process.

The formal planning unit should attempt to project an image of assistance to the operating units. One way to project such an image could be through the introduction of a new reporting system into a police department. All affected personnel should be introduced to the new method, the reason for the new system explained, and the results expected clearly stated. In other words, the planning unit should demonstrate to operating personnel that the introduction of the new reporting system was planned and that the who, what, when, where, how, and why were answered. Additionally, members of the unit should be on hand around the clock to assist the operating unit in a smooth transition. This also will enhance the planning unit's acceptance by the department.

Solicitation of the affected units to participate in the planning of new procedures, revised rules and regulations, computer formats, information retrieval, activity sheets, evaluation reports, and personnel action memos will cause the principle of participatory management to permeate all units coming into contact with the planning unit. When people are consulted with regard to operations that they must carry out, the knowledge that they participated in the decision will make any change more acceptable and cause the implementation to be a smooth and coordinated effort. For a police organization to function properly, all steps should be taken to avoid crisis management. This can only be done through planning.

PROJECT PLANNING
(PATROL PLANNING COUNCIL)

The patrol planning council is an innovation designed to include participation of all ranks in the operation of the patrol function, through the use of completed staff work as an individual planning tool, problem-solving conferences, and brainstorming (applied imagination techniques) conferences to resolve planning problems.

The council should only be created through a serious selection process. Members included in the council are patrol officers, sergeants, lieutenants, captains, and majors, along with the patrol administrator. (The makeup depends upon the size of the organization.) Members should be solicited in a practical way, placing emphasis on voluntary participation, serious review and evaluation of the program, freedom of expression, constructive criticism, and practical application. All members should be willing to accept the assignment of completed staff studies as appropriate and any part of the other types of conferences.

The goal of the planning council is to carry out the function of patrol in the most professional, efficient, and effective manner possible. Democratic leadership involving participatory management in the problem-resolution area is essential. The patrol administrator should be prepared to act as chairman of the conference and must be knowledgeable in order to insure a consensus resolution to the problem. Additionally, the patrol administrator should attempt to have every supervisor under his command aware of the planning process through the completed staff work, problem-solving conference, and brainstorming procedure. The techniques applied are not those of command alone, but can be used at every level of supervision within the department.

Usually staff studies are assigned to an individual or a group of individuals when the time limit is not a critical factor. For example, if an analysis of a particular crime problem necessitates one month's investigation in order to develop valid data, the staff study method could be used.

If a problem has existed for some time but has erupted in the patrol unit recently, then the problem-solving conference should be used. An example could be fleet safety: The problem of accidents has existed in the unit and its efficiency has not equaled the national average with regard to fleet safety, but in the past two days the unit has experienced an unacceptable number of accidents while on routine patrol. The patrol administrator wants an answer as soon as possible, but wants the problem well thought out; therefore, he invites the appropriate members to participate in a problem-solving conference.

If the problem has not previously existed, or has not presented itself before, and there is a need for immediate resolution, the brainstorming session can be utilized. For example, the taking of hostages during a holdup calls for a new response procedure and time is of the essence.

When the patrol administrator includes all levels of patrol as a part of the operation of the patrol function, the unit develops its ability to be capable of change. The strategy and techniques of change are used in that the persons affected by the change are involved in the planning and implementation of that particular change. The patrol administrator thus becomes a change agent or an initiator of change, hopefully to the benefit of the total department.

This concept is reinforced by the New Haven, Connecticut Police Department. In a discussion of the department's "Directed Deterrent Patrol" program, which is described as an innovative method of preventive patrol, the planning team is described as follows:

> Perhaps the key to the success of the project lies in the formation of a permanent planning team. The team shares the responsibility for the project construction, operation, and day-to-day monitoring.
>
> The operational planning team incorporates civilian and sworn personnel from several divisions of the department organization. There are six full-time members. Each member has a specific function in the operation of the program. The capability of the department to maintain a planning staff to continuously identify target crimes, collect and analyze data is of major importance in developing and institutionalizing new patrol procedures.[11]

INTERNAL/EXTERNAL POLITICAL PLANNING

The word "political" is used in this book, in several places, to mean characterized by shrewdness; tactfully and skillfully contained; sagacious in devising or promoting a policy." This is exactly what you, the patrol administrator, must have in mind with regard to the internal planning process. All members of the department are on the same team, but each is a different personality. Each of the commanders of the staff and other line operations controls the support necessary for you to accomplish the mission. The art of lateral communications includes being artful in address and procedure. Planning the method or procedure you are going to use to communicate is as important as the content of the message. You cannot be lazy, you cannot assume that everyone knows or should know your message, and you cannot deliberately embarrass anyone if you wish to be successful in gaining internal cooperation and support. There is no substitute for sincerity when attempting to promote a policy change or procedure that will benefit the patrol force. In most cases the lateral communication will be one of either pointing out an error by a member of the support unit or initiating a procedure that will take the burden of a task from the patrol officer. In the past the task usually was given to the patrol officer, since no one would speak up in his or her behalf. Now, however, the task may very well be performed more efficiently by the support unit.

In the case of an error by a member of the support unit, the responsibility of the patrol leader to point out nonsupport (intentional or unintentional) is as basic and important as any other characteristic of leadership. After the identification of the error, the approach taken to correct it becomes the most important. Additionally, after the correction is made and a disposition agreed upon, the patrol leader is remiss if he does not report to the person identifying the problem and advise him or her of what action was taken. This type of support enhances the credibility of the leadership of the patrol commander.

The latter situation, communicating a new task procedure, makes the patrol leader an initiator of change. Therefore, he must consider all aspects of the situation and the steps for implementing change before making the initial approach. The basic steps of the planning process should be known. With this completed, he can approach the leader of the support unit with the best method available, showing the expected results for the good of the department as a whole. The leader should avoid giving the impression of wanting a procedure changed just to enhance one's own unit in the eyes of the chief. Honesty of intent must accompany the approach, or cooperation between units will not be forthcoming. Nothing can replace mutual respect and understanding among patrol and all other units in the department. It is incumbent upon each to make decisions for the good of the department, even at the risk of personal losses or temporary divisional disruptions.

The patrol administrator will develop a reputation of fairness, objectivity, and honesty through demonstrated activity. Situations will arise when the patrol force is guilty of errors. It is at this time that cooperation in the future will be decided. Constructive criticism and corrective action must be taken as well as given. The corrective action taken must be fed back to the commander of the support division to complete the cycle.

One patrol commander reports that while attending roll call one day, one of the officers was complaining bitterly about the dispatcher in the communications unit. The officer's complaint was valid, but he misunderstood the reasons for the delay of necessary information. The patrol commander allowed the officer to spend one tour of duty with the dispatcher at his desk. When the patrol officer found out about the responsibilities and amount of work involved in efficient dispatching, his outlook changed, and he became a better officer for it. Futhermore, the officer informed his peers, other patrol officers, of the dispatching operations and a better team effort resulted.

The internal political planning process is meant to be straightforward, because all members are on the same team. But the approach of one member to another has to be planned if optimum results are to be achieved. The goals of the department must be the goals of each member of the force, but especially of the leaders of different units and divisions, since they are expected to have a more complete understanding of the total operation and its interacting parts.

External Political Planning

Keeping politics out of the police department is a valid goal when it means avoiding interference in administering a professional organization, or when it means decrying an administration that promotes personnel because of political influence, compromises ethics, and is intimidated by political pressure. *External political planning* for the patrol administrator means responding to the needs of the duly elected officials of the community in which he serves. The response to the elected officials does not mean that the patrol administrator will play partisan politics, since the response shall be to all local and state elected officials, regardless of party. The goal of the patrol administrator is to respond to the needs of the people of his jurisdiction. By utilizing the elected officials as true representatives of their constitutents, the patrol administrator can swiftly resolve problems before the fact. If this is not possible, then immediate reaction after the fact may extinguish a potentially explosive issue within the community. Either way, good communication is necessary.

The art of planning as a politician by the patrol administrator thus means using diplomacy, being tactful and clever, initiating action to reduce chances of explosive issues, and opening lines of communication with elected officials. Planning courses of action to achieve objectives then becomes all-inclusive, since the community and the department participate in whatever procedure is selected.

An example of this association between the elected official and the patrol commander might be as follows: Each patrol commander is responsible for knowing what areas of his command are represented by which official, both local and state. (There is no need to include federal officials in this type of political planning, although responsiveness to federally elected officials is not lessened.) Using a map of the command, he outlines the federal, state, and local boundaries as appropriate. He then initiates communication with each representative located within the boundaries. A mutually beneficial common ground can be established, always keeping in mind the goal of better service to the citizen, and a procedure for contact set up. This procedure should allow for a twenty-four-hour-a-day contact, which means the availability of each must be considered. Private telephone contact should be established. The trust and confidence necessary for success would then be initiated. Honest communication is very important, and complete understanding of the enormity of the many problems to be discussed must be solidified.

The theory behind this type of planning is that these two important people, having common community interests, are working in harmony in order to act before the fact. No problem will be solved easily if allowed to fester and grow. A concentrated and cooperative effort on the part of the elected officials and the patrol commander lessens the opportunity for misunderstanding, misuse and underutilization of resources, and false rumor. The intelligent pooling of authority, communication, information, contacts, and knowledge of the area should help prevent disharmony between the police and the community.

The support of the elected officials is a starting place for gaining support of the total community. Patrol administrators should be aware of what community support means to the patrol operation. Without it, the patrol commander can accomplish very little; with it, he can accomplish much.

STANDARD OPERATING PROCEDURES

Contrary to all that may have been said, written, or expected of police officers, they are human, do make mistakes, and are imperfect. Consequently, a structure of organization in policing exists today whereby most of the decisions made by the officer, or at least the more important decisions, are reviewed and evaluated by supervisors.

Policy may be defined as the general direction of an organization under which the personnel must operate. If contains principles that guide the actual work of the department. Usually policy is stated in general terms and is used to attain objectives. In effect, it provides guidelines upon which procedures, rules, and individual actions may be based, leaving room for individual interpretation, directions, and initiative. We must have policy in order to have innovation and creativity.

Rules, on the other hand, tell subordinates exactly what to do in a prescribed situation. All organizations must have rules, with the essential feature of flexibility. Coordination and complete compliance are necessary in certain situations. Whenever the development of a plan reveals the need for training, standard operating procedures, or rules and regulations, the department should set down in writing and disseminate information that will help officers save time and react professionally as appropriate.

Standard operating procedures are a must. Without them, there would be no team effort, and achievement of the objectives of the patrol operation would be unlikely. Not long ago an officer who worked in an evidence technicians unit stated that no matter how much experience he had, he would still use the procedure as written, step by step, to insure uniformity of performance. He added, "I don't care what anyone says about me going by the book, I know I won't ever perform differently and I won't leave anything undone." Naturally if the officer had to testify in court, he could use the same procedure and overcome any defense objection. Additionally, if officers read the *Miranda* warning from a card issued by the department, they will not have to worry about giving the suspect his or her rights as prescribed by the Supreme Court. Procedures on conducting line-ups, booking prisoners, etc., must be standard in order to comply with the law in certain cases, and to produce satisfactory performance by all divisions throughout the police department.

All patrol leaders should participate in recognizing areas where standard operating procedures would improve the department or prevent an officer from being injured. The range of help that is possible is wide and varied. Therefore, alert and aware patrol administrators must attempt to infuse the patrol division with the planning concept. A sergeant, while watching one of his officers testify in a lower court, observed that the officer was standing alongside the defendant with his weapon on the side closest to the defendant. With just a flip of the small leather strap, the weapon could have been in the defendant's possession. Result, standard operating procedures: all officers (when testifying) will stand on the side and slightly to the rear of prisoners with their gun side away from the prisoner.

Sloppy or careless police work should never be acceptable. However, standard detailed plans or procedures should not be implemented for picayune tasks, as they might reduce innovation and initiative.

WRITTEN DIRECTIVES

The chief who puts his policy into *written directives* provides the department with sound direction and projects himself as a leader who wants good communication and dissemination of information. Written directives include all general orders, special orders, personnel orders, and memoranda.

Directives are used to clarify the purposes and objectives of the department and of subordinate elements within it so that all activity is conducted toward a single purpose.

Types of Written Directives

General orders are written directives that pertain to the permanent policy and procedures for the definite future of the police department. Examples of proper subjects of general orders are:

1. Institution of permanent procedures, rules, and policies, and manuals related thereto;
2. Permanent changes in organization;
3. Installation of permanent programs that affect more than one unit subordinate to the issuing authority; e.g., citizen complaint, internal affairs procedure, etc;
4. Permanent personnel policies and procedures including recruiting, hiring, training, and promotion policies, but not including changes of status, such as transfers and promotions; and
5. Use of public facilities and equipment.

Those directives affecting a specific unit, a specific event, or circumstance of a temporary or self-canceling nature or involving only specific segments of activities are called *special orders*. Examples of proper subjects of special orders are:

1. The assignment of individual duties at public gatherings or parades;
2. Seasonal change of uniforms;
3. Annual budget preparation and special instructions for this year completed; and
4. Assignment of police vehicles.

Personnel orders cover changes in position, transfers, promotions, etc. They include:

1. The appointment of new personnel;
2. The assignment or transfer of members from one unit to another;
3. Promotions;
4. Commendations;
5. Suspension and dismissal; and
6. Resignation or retirement.

Written information not warranting a formal order can be conveyed through *memoranda*. They are used to direct any segment or all of the department personnel in specific situations or to inform them of coming events. Examples of proper subjects of memoranda are:

1. Date, time, and place of "Police Week";
2. Available schooling; and
3. Court decisions and opinions by the legal officer.

Authority for Written Directives

General orders are usually issued by the chief of police. Special orders are usually issued by the chief or with his approval. For example, a patrol commander desiring to issue a directive affecting units other than his own would have to forward the directive to the chief for approval. In many cases the directives are staffed (gaining concurrences and nonconcurrences from appropriate personnel) before being issed at the direction of the chief. Personnel orders are prepared by the personnel officer and issued at the direction of the chief. Memoranda may be issued by any level of command at the direction of the chief. It is most important for all members, especially at the supervisory level, to understand the authority for issuing orders. Unity of command can be broken and confusing if the system is nebulous or assurance of understanding is not completed.

General Considerations

Consideration should be given to the distribution of each type of order. Deciding who receives a copy of an order is important in improving efficiency and economy. For example, a copy of an order affecting an individual patrol officer should be sent to that officer. A second copy of the personnel order should be sent to the patrol officer's commander, to keep him or her informed.

Other considerations concerning standard operating procedures that the patrol administrator should completely understand are preparation, indexing, general format, cancellations, and amendments. Experience has shown that orders and procedures that are read and clearly understood will benefit the total department.

Patrol commanders should be aware of what it takes to prepare standard operating procedures. An example concerns the U.S. Supreme Court decision that a suspect be advised of his or her constitutional rights of representation by counsel at any lineup in which he or she is made to appear. Procedures for implementing the ruling must be developed to insure standard operation with respect to compliance of the mandate.

The first step in planning is recognition of need. This need becomes rather obvious from the decisions in *United States* v. *Wade, Gilbert* v. *California,* and *Stovall* v. *Denno* [reported in *U.S. Law Week* (June 1967), p. 4597]. The objective is to prepare appropriate instructions and information necessary for understanding and executing courses of action to be taken when persons are to be placed in lineups, and to insure proper dissemination in the form of a standard operating procedure. Data must be gathered relevant to the objective. It should include information on: (1) legal questions, (2) persons represented by counsel, (3) persons not represented by counsel, (4) indigent persons, (5) emergency lineups, (6) waiver of right to presence of counsel, (7) responsibility for conducting the lineup, and (8) preparation of appropriate forms to implement waiver of right to counsel.

The next step is to answer the who, what, when, where, why and how with the collected data. The procedure or final draft, as it is commonly called, is then written so staffing can take place. In this example, staffing with the following persons would be beneficial: (1) attorney general of the state; (2) district or state's attorney; (3) chief judge of the circuit court; (4) chief judge of district or local court (if the names of the judges do not apply to your area, it would mean those judges who would rule or judge the admissibility of the procedure used by your department for conducting lineups); (5) legal advisor (if applicable); (6) public defender (if applicable); (7) local bar association; (8) all operational commanders, because of the importance and effect the procedure would have on the outcome of criminal cases; (9) especially the operational commanders directly responsible for conduct of lineups; and (10) any unit that may be affected by the procedure.

The resulting procedure should be practical, feasible, and easily understood and should include any information that might be helpful for implementation. For example, in *Schmerber* v. *California* (348 U.S. 757, 772–779), the court held that compelling a suspect to submit to a withdrawal of a sample of blood for analysis for alcoholic content and the admission into evidence of the analysis report did not abridge the privilege against self-incrimination. [*Holt* v. *United States* (218 U.S. 245) case supports the *Schmerber* decision.] In this case a question arose as to whether a blouse belonged to a defendant. A witness testified at the trial that the defendant had put on the blouse and that it had fit. The defendant argued that the admission of testimony was erroneous because compelling him to put on the blouse was a violation of privilege against self-incrimination. The court rejected the claim as an extravagant extension of the Fifth Amendment. The Fifth Amendment privilege offers no immunity from fingerprinting, photographing, measurement, appearance in court, or a requirement that the accused stand up or make a gesture. In other words, these things do not abridge the privilege against self-incrimination. This information supports and explains that part of the procedure that advises the force: It is not a violation of the Fifth Amendment privilege against self-incrimination to require a suspect to participate in a lineup. The suspect who refuses to do so may be required to do so as long as counsel is present. The in-depth example is given to point out the type of effort needed when completing staff work for standard operating procedures. (Note: a review of all orders that may need to be amended or rescinded must take place to avoid any conflict.)

TACTICAL PLANNING

Tactical Planning concerns specific circumstances at designated places. When the patrol leader can anticipate these problems, he can develop the best solution. Tactical planning for disasters; for strikes, especially if your department faces picketing on a regular basis; for major crimes such as bank robberies; and for prison riots. (Also see Chapter 7, Special Operations.)

Tactical plans are flexible in that they are developed to meet certain needs but they can be adjusted at any time. The flexibility can be developed optimally if the basic tactical plan is a good one. The basic plan should be well thought out to achieve a smooth, coordinated performance at the time of implementation. Standards of excellence in planning result in tactical task forces operating with precision and efficiency.

Emergency Planning

Consider a hold-up or robbery in progress at the main bank in your town, which would be a major crime. The use of force or fear is present, and it is safe to assume the perpetrator is dangerous. As any good officer, no matter what rank, would do, you assess the situation and decide what course of action you are going to follow. Take a position out of the line of sight and the line of fire. Put something–the building, police vehicle, or door–between you and the suspect. Determine if there is a need to consider potential victims of injury or danger, and decide if medical aid should be on the way. The next step is a quick review of action for confrontation. Remember, sloppy or careless police procedure has cost officers their lives. Be careful to avoid any surprise tactics that will not give you complete command of the situation. Partial success at this point could lead to injury to others or yourself. In addition, you may serve as a catalyst to the suspect's actions; he may harm someone or take a hostage.

If your assessment reveals no danger to others and the suspect is not aware of your presence, you should remain outside and select the most advantageous position to secure the premises and await the arrival of assisting units. In this case, time is on your side. You should attempt to have the superior position so that when the suspect comes outside, you are in command. Waiting outside and keeping the suspect unaware of your presence make it less likely that hostages will be taken or injuries will occur.

If the suspect has fled before your arrival, then those parts of the preliminary investigation that have not taken place should be completed. The responsibilty for completing the preliminary investigation depends on department policy for this procedure. If patrol or criminal investigators are responsible, and to what extent, is determined by the chief; however, the command officers should have input. The following definition of preliminary investigation should improve the tactical planning for major crimes:

1. Proceed to the scene with safety and dispatch. Emphasis should be placed on safety, since there is no help whatsoever if you do not arrive.
2. Aid the injured if required.
3. Determine what crime has been committed, if any. This is most important because many officers are awaiting information to help them determine their approach to the suspect, if encountered.
4. Arrest the perpetrator if possible.
5. As soon as you can, advise the dispatcher of a discription of the suspect(s) and method and direction of escape.
6. Protect the crime scene and cause the proper collection of evidence.
7. Locate witnesses and get identification and all other information concerning the victim, suspect, and incident.
8. Write your report clearly and accurately, remembering that you may need the information to testify in court and that other people have to read your report. Reproduce this incident as closely as possible. Usually at this point the investigator continues the investigation.

The management by objectives concept emphasizes to the patrol administrator the need to accomplish the mission no matter what the situation. Plans that have been written and are available to meet anticipated emergencies best fulfill that need. No matter who—night commander, inspectors, duty officers, and/or a platoon commander—is in charge after the regular working day, each should be responsible for knowing how to implement such plans.

An example of a tactical plan is a riot or civil disorder plan. The type of information required for this plan includes:

1. Coordination with outside agencies, such as:
   a. Fire department
   b. Health department
   c. Transit and traffic
   d. American Red Cross
   e. Public worker
   f. Medical examiner
   g. Medical society
   h. Civil defense and disaster
   i. Local, state, and federal authorities

2. Internal Information:
   a. Call-up system
   b. Location of necessary equipment (including emergency equipment)
   c. Communication
   d. Command and supervising assignments
   e. Instruction on effective implementation
   f. Feeding and housing of personnel
   g. Arrest and detention procedures (emergency)
   h. Security of buildings
   i. Staging areas
   j. Transportation

The list could go on and on. However, the important aspect is to learn the relationship between good planning and achieving the objective in emergency situations.

Events Planning

Planning for special events differs from emergency planning in that good intelligence and communication are a matter of cooperation between the police and the person(s) responsible for producing the event. Rapport should be developed between the officials and police, and meetings should be held where issues can be discussed. The importance of these meetings cannot be overemphasized, because it is at these meetings prior to the event that police manpower becomes the patrol administrator's primary concern. The patrol commander realizes his primary function and should contribute to the fullest as a participating member of the committee. However, he should always be thinking about using resources of other agencies to achieve the objective without using a police officer (e.g., in many cases the use of equipment to block off street access can serve just as well as a police officer). The other question to be considered regarding the use of police manpower is the policy of the department concerning the use of police versus private security for situations that require security, but which are privately run and profit-making. Some departments allow officers to work at these events, but the organization must pay the officer. Other departments do not allow officers to moonlight, and in these instances, the organization must hire private security. Some departments will supply officers for events only where police authority is required, and the private organization must pay for the officers' time. The decision becomes a matter of priorities, manpower, and other resources.

If all or part of the responsibility falls on the police, they should be interested in the following information:

1. Type of event:
   - Political rally
   - Athletic contest
   - Local holiday celebration
   - July 4th parade
   - Kentucky Derby
   - Rose Bowl
   - Rock 'n' roll dance
2. Location:
   - Football or baseball stadium
   - Exposition hall
   - Civic center
   - Parade route
3. Time:
   - Date(s)
   - Time beginning
   - Approximate duration
   - Time ending
   - Time of unusual features
     (You may need to change deployment of personnel from place to place as special features occur.)
4. Approximate number of people attending
5. Parking facilities:
   - VIP
   - Press
   - Picture mobile command vehicle (if used)
6. Communications:
   - Call numbers: decision must be made to use regularly assigned call number or special call numbers used for special events.
   - Pre-positioned telephone lines should be checked to insure means for private conversation.

7. Traffic control:
   - Vehicle
   - Pedestrian
   - Perimeter of event
   - Normal flow for other areas
8. Government agencies:
   - Fire department (ambulance)
   - Water department
   - Public works
9. Other agencies:
   - Telephone company
   - Gas and electric company
   - First aid (Who is available?)
10. Restricted areas:
    - Unauthorized persons
    - Unauthorized vehicles
11. Arrest considerations:
    - Holding area for prisoners
    - Transportation of prisoners
    - Destination of prisoners (The location may be different from normal location.)
    - Central location where press and relatives are notified of arrests

Each event has certain aspects that call for adjustments in the plan, even to the point that actions change while the event is taking place. Yearly events usually have certain basic problems that will allow the use of a master plan that can be implemented routinely. Usually there are areas where improvements can be made. This is brought out when a critique of the operation for strengths and weaknesses is completed.

Most police departments have responsibility for at least a few yearly events. The principles of planning for those events apply no matter how large the crowd or what type of event. The Sugar Bowl and Mardi Gras are held each year in New Orleans, and plans must be prepared in order to provide protection of life and property and a safe, smooth flow of vehicular and pedestrian traffic. The Kentucky Derby in Louisville, Kentucky and the Preakness in Baltimore, Maryland each involves parades— yearly events for which appropriate planning must take place. In both cases, no permit is needed for the horse race, but the parade that precedes the race must have a permit. Information must be obtained about the time and location, anticipated size of the crowd, parking, medical aid, etc. From this, information and instructions can be disseminated to the appropriate personnel of the police agency.

Approval of Tactical Plans

Approval of the plans is determined by the number of divisions or units involved that may have to commit manpower. For example, if members of patrol, traffic, and criminal investigation units are assigned responsibilities, approval for implementation of the plan must come from the commander of the operation bureau or his equal, depending on the size of the department and title. In the case of the Kentucky Derby, officers from all bureaus are involved; therefore, approval must come from the chief. Coordination by the commanders of the respective units may be necessary, or the formation of a committee with individual responsibility assigned for producing a final plan may suffice.

Sample Plan

The plan for the Kentucky Derby could be written as follows (*Note:* This does not reveal actual plan used by the Louisville Division of Police.):

TWENTY-FIRST ANNUAL KENTUCKY DERBY PARADE AND RACE

Location:	Churchill Downs Race Track
Date and Time:	Appropriate police coverage shall begin at 0900 hours and continue until completion of the event and the securing of the detail, which will be approximately 1900 hours.
Purpose:	The purpose of the police detail is to:

1. Provide for the smooth flow of vehicle and pedestrian traffic;
2. Protect parked vehicles from vandalism and theft;
3. Provide assistance where necessary with adequate patrol coverage, including receipt of complaints. (This can be done by having one or more well-known locations at the racetrack.); and
4. Have a reserve force available that could be used to alleviate potential disruptions.

Attendance:	Parade Route—100,000 people Race—80,000 people

Parking:	Official parking Public parking Reserved parking Prohibited parking Buses, taxicabs Emergency vehicles (This information would aid in coordination and flow of traffic.)
Barricades and/or Signs:	Locations should be selected to save manpower but achieve the objective.
Responsibility:	Name of ranking officer in command Name(s) of assisting officers and area of responsibility
Required Action:	*Traffic unit* should:

* Indicate the number of supervisors and officers
* Make assignment (traffic control, etc.)
* Determine location of assignments
* Set up reporting time (adjusted to need)

If assignment changes by time and location, a chart showing the changes should be made available.

Similar instructions would be given by each unit—e.g., patrol, criminal investigation, special operations (plainclothes pickpocket squad).

Appropriate uniforms and equipment necessary should be part of plan.

General Information: General information that would be of importance to all personnel would be placed here, such as:

1. Location of command post
2. Telephone number of command post
3. Location of medical facilities
4. Fire apparatus available, location and phone number
5. Lost person and property disposition
6. General prohibited areas
7. Locations in need of frequent inspections. Lavatories would be one location where vending-machine robbing and pickpocketing could take place.
8. Maps of the areas showing the parade route
9. Charts showing individual officers and exact location of assignment

Alternate plans and routes should be developed depending on conditions, weather, intelligence, and police hazards.

PLANNING CAREER ROTATION

Over the years the police recruit has been accepted into the club with some reluctance. Once the recruit proved himself, it was all right to talk to him. The credibility factor may have been part of it, but not all of the acceptance came from the officer's proving himself. Some of the reluctance came from the insecurities of older officers who thought that these new officers might do a little too much work or have just a little edge in education and intelligence—thus, "Don't tell them anything, let them learn the same way we did." Thankfully, most department personnel have abandoned this attitude. The prevailing thought today is that the sooner the new officer can learn, the more assistance he will be when the going gets rough. As the new officer develops, certain skills will surface and should be recognized. At the same time, deficiencies should also be noted so corrective action can be taken promptly for the benefit of all.

Attitude and behavior make or break any police agency. Attitudes of the patrol officer and patrol administrator are of prime importance, because the first line of defense is also the first view of the department by most of the citizens of the community. If police work generally, and patrol work specifically, is to become a profession, then the work of patrol must be viewed as such, and the criteria included in the making of a professional must be attained in order to earn the term. James Ahern in his book *Police in Trouble* states, "The policeman's task, as it is now performed, is by definition the kind of work that is performed in our society by professionals."[12]

James Q. Wilson, former director of the Joint Center for Urban Studies at M.I.T. and Harvard University, writes:

> Occupations whose members exercise, as do the police, wide discretion alone and with respect to matters of the greatest importance are typically "professionals"—the medical profession, for example. The right to handle emergency situations, to be privy to "guilty information," and to make decisions involving questions of life and death or honor and dishonor is usually, as with a doctor or a priest, conferred by an organized profession. The profession certifies that the member

has acquired by education certain information, and by apprenticeship certain arts and skills, that render him competent to perform these functions and that he is willing to subject himself to the code of ethics and sense of duty of his colleagues (or, in the case of a priest, to the laws and punishments of God). Failure to perform his duties properly will, if detected, be dealt with by professional sanctions—primarily, loss of respect. Members of professions tend to govern themselves through collegial bodies, to restrict the authority of their nominal superiors, to take seriously the reputation among fellow professionals, and to encourage some of their kind to devote themselves to adding systematically to the knowledge of the profession through writing and research. The police are not in any of these senses professionals. They acquire most of their knowledge and skill on the job, not in separate academies; they are emphatically subject to the authority of their superiors; they have no serious professional society, only a union-like bargaining agent; and they do not produce, in systematic written form, new knowledge about their craft.

In sum, the order-maintenance function of the patrolman defines his role and that role, which is unlike that of any other occupation, can be described as one in which *subprofessionals, working alone, exercise wide discretion in matters of utmost importance (life and death, honor and dishonor) in an environment that is apprehensive and perhaps hostile.*[13]

We are not and cannot be all things to all people. The performance of all tasks now assigned to police as a professional matter, using the traditional methods, is quite impossible. The total resources of government should be employed; e.g., the police should not specialize in crisis intervention for family trouble calls, but should call upon the expertise of the governmental social agency to follow up on these family counseling problems. Police should be trained to handle the initial contact of family cases using the generalist concepts and provide a procedure that allows for follow-up by the social agency. The police role should be defined and then performed professionally. The patrol administrator must work to this end. Words are fine, theories are good, but it is at the actual implementation phase where the critical issues are won or lost relative to professionalism. A beginning, based on the President's Crime Commission *Task Force Report: Police* (1967), is the police-agent program. The police-agent program attempts to develop career rotation for those officers possessing the education and potential for expertise in selected areas of police work.

Table 5.1 shows how officers can be monitored during their career. At some point, promotion is attained or the appropriate career niche is located to allow for parallel goals between the individual and the organization.

Table 5.1 *Career Rotation for Police Agents*

Agent	Date of Appointment	Date of Completion of Entrance-Level Training	First Assignment	Time in Assignment	Second Assignment	Time in Assignment	Third Assignment
Adam	1–1–70	5–1–70	Patrol–foot High Crime	6 months	Patrol Research	6 months	Personnel Recruitment
Thomas							
Charles							
Peter							
Edward							
Frank							
George							
Harry							
Ivan							
John							

Responsibility for Career Rotation

There are two areas of responsibility for career development; one lies with the individual officer, and the other with the department.

Individual officer. The U.S. Marine Corps has a motto of always being ready. The officer who desires career development should always be ready if he wishes to take advantage of opportunity. Responsible administrators always try to select the best man for the job. Education, background, initiative, and participation and activities in law-enforcement organizations that enhance professionalism are all criteria used in deciding whom to select. The officer who has the answers (because he has studied the appropriate material, or because he has gone to school), who can intelligently communicate, and who demonstrates the ability to produce in his present position, is likely to be the one selected for new challenges, new horizons, and career development. All of these qualifications can be achieved by the individual officer.

The officer should be specific in identifying his personal objective, and should delineate a strategy for reaching it. The following Career Launching Checklist may help:

1. Do I know the things I do best?
2. Have I found some things I like to do very much?
3. Do I work better by myself or with other people? What sorts of other people?
4. Do I know what talents I do not have?
5. Do I know the things I very much dislike doing?
6. Have I gotten professional advice on the fields of work I ought to consider for myself?
7. Does my education prepare me for these fields, or do I need further education or specialization courses or some sort of internship before making a full-fledged beginning?
8. How hard am I willing to work physically and mentally? Can I work long hours?
9. What are my work habits? Short bursts of very intense effort? Or a steady pace?
10. Have I talked with people doing jobs I think I might or should be interested in so that I have first-hand information on what they do, how they do it, and what a typical day is like for them?[14]

The department. The department and the patrol administrator have a primary responsibility to develop people, the most precious resource. The patrol administrator must be aware of the talent existing within his command.

> When recruits are properly selected they bring to the job considerable native ability but little knowledge or experience to police work. In a short time, they must be prepared to operate alone on the streets under a variety of conditions that call for knowledge of laws and ordinances, legal procedures, police practices, and human relations. As they progress, they must not only acquire more of the same kind of knowledge but also should develop some specialized understanding of investigative techniques and scientific crime detection. This will enable them to conduct initial or preliminary investigations and to preserve vital evidence for a specialist who will assist them on difficult cases.[15]

Initial training with a recruit begins at the police academy or education and training center. After this it is the responsibility of the supervisor, middle management, and the patrol administrator, at least in the area of the patrol function, to develop the individual talents and abilities of the officers working with him.

Lateral Entry

If law enforcement is to be truly professional, then some form of lateral entry in all phases (operations, administration, and services) must be implemented. Law enforcement should spell out its desires to the legislature and the community in order to gain understanding and decrease the possibility of law prohibiting the implementation of lateral entry. There are additional concerns regarding lateral entry within the police community.

First, the men and women in the field who have started at the bottom feel that it is unfair if the promotions go to people from the outside. The career officers of the individual deparments think their years of hard work in that department should be rewarded by promotions from within. Second, there is a fear that the most-qualified officers of the smaller departments would move to the larger departments where there would be higher pay and improved fringe benefits. This fear can be rejected because the local communities will learn to appreciate the need for qualified personnel. The community will demand professional police officers and be willing to pay the appropriate wages to recruit and retrain this caliber of personnel. Quality is not commensurate with size. Additionally, there would be a decrease in the disparity between wages paid in the smaller departments as a result of this type of lateral entry. Third, lateral entry requires at least statewide uniform job classification and requirements. These are being developed today in the field of law enforcement in many states. Minimum standards set by state training commissions certainly are congruent with the idea of having job classifications, job requirements and qualifications, and minimum standards on training written at the state level. This is certainly a first step in preparing to have lateral entry and transfer within a state and between states.

In addition to the fact that professionalization will not come until law enforcement has lateral entry on a broad scale, several other observations should be considered. An intimate view of a department where lateral entry has been experienced has shown lateral entry can work and enhances the department as a whole. The New York City and San Francisco Departments are involved in exchanging officers of equal rank within their departments. These officers are gaining experience, knowledge, and exposure in those individual departments and have both learned and contributed to the department to which they have been assigned. The concept of lateral entry creates incentive for personnel to pursue education, to expand the thought process, and to make themselves more capable in order to be promoted or gain reward within their own levels of supervision. The competition that would develop among all members of the law enforcement community and outside the law enforcement community would be a positive one.

The National Advisory Commission on Criminal Justice Standards and Goals summarizes the concept in their *Report on Police,* Standard 17.4, "Administration of Promotion and Advancement," which states:

> Every police chief executive, by assuming administrative control of the promotion and advancement system, should insure that only the best-qualified personnel are promoted or advanced to positions of greater authority and responsibility in higher pay grades and ranks. Agencies that have not developed competent personnel to assume positions of higher authority should seek qualified personnel from outside the agency rather than promote or advance personnel who are not ready to assume positions of greater responsibility.
>
> 1. The police chief executive should oversee all phases of his agency's promotion and advancement system including the testing of personnel and the appointing of personnel to positions of greater responsibility. The police chief executive should make use of the services of a central personnel agency when that personnel agency is competent to develop and administer tests and is responsive to the needs of the police agency.
> 2. The police chief executive should consider recruiting personnel for lateral entry at any level from outside the agency when it is necessary to do so in order to obtain the services of an individual who is qualified for a position or assignment.[16]

Although studies have shown that an increase in pay, future potential, living conditions, challenge, and loss of seniority are obstacles to lateral entry and transfer, it appears that the pension factor itself is really the major obstacle to transferring an officer from one department to another throughout the country. However, the studies also reveal that if existing obstacles to the lateral transfer were removed there would be a surge by members of the law enforcement community to develop new skills and capabilities that would cause them to be considered for promotions.[17]

The Teachers' Insurance and Annuity Association operates a central retirement fund that teachers throughout the country may join. This may not be the exact answer to the obstacle of pension rights and funds; however, it shows that there are models which may assist in solving problems.

After lateral entry. Probably the major problem regarding lateral entry is the question of credibility after someone enters a department. Individuals both in an out of the law enforcement community may be hired by a given police organization. The background and credentials possessed by the individuals may be outstanding and relevant to the positions for which they were hired. However, the background and credentials are not a panacea to obtaining credibility. Developing trust and confidence, having meaningful relationships, and projecting sincere dedication will enhance credibility and acceptance by the other members of the department.

Credibility can be developed in different ways. One way is for the lateral entrant to be put in a position especially in the field, where decisions must be made. The person who without hesitation makes his or her decision projects an image of someone who knows what is going on and has good judgment. Second, credibility can be achieved by an individual who is analytical, who is a good planner, who is goal oriented, and who demonstrates these talents by giving support to the operational units. When this person is a staff officer responsible for contributing to the total goal of the department, he can support his claim for credibility by action. The projection of a feeling of sincere desire to contribute, even to the smallest detail, in any way possible, will be felt by other members of the department and help gain that much-needed respect.

Other individual qualities that will develop credibility for persons selected for lateral entry within a department are similar to the qualities of any good leader: firmness, fairness, empathy, dependability, and enthusiasm. The road to acceptance is not easy. Developing credibility is not easy, and the knowledge of how, when, and where to project those qualities that will accumulate trust, confidence, and credibility for the individual is most important. Persons entering other departments through lateral entry would do well to analyze the what, when, where, how, and why while searching for the right methods to demonstrate individual abilities.

FIVE-YEAR PLANS

All plans are only as good as the department's ability to implement them. Most police departments around the country have not and do not concern themselves with five-year plans for a variety of reasons. Those departments that do know the painstaking effort that goes into producing a report that outlines the goals and approaches for the next five years. With experimentation taking place throughout the country in all facets of the criminal justice system, but especially in law enforcement, five-year plans will become more prevalent.

We need only look at regional criminal justice planning to realize the necessity of multi-year and annual planning. A review of the importance of regional criminal justice planning points up many factors that are basic to planning, but also points out to the patrol administrator the need for developing a broad, comprehensive outlook on his position as related to state and local government; county government; city and county managers; Model Cities; OEO programs; manpower development and training; Health and Human Services; Highway Safety Act; and the Juvenile Delinquency Prevention and Control Act. As an example of the interrelationship between government agencies and the patrol administrator, the Department of Housing and Urban Development had a report prepared by the Rand Corporation entitled *Guide to Decision-Making in Police Patrol.*

Regional criminal justice planning begins by identifying problems, priorities, alternatives, and goals. The patrol administrator must understand his position relative to these goals and determine what resources are necessary for him to become an active participant (even if it is through his chief) in problem resolutions, innovations, and attainment of the objectives. Planning, budgets, and statistical analyses are next on the agenda. From here, organization must take place, and money, personnel, and material must be distributed. The planning agency advises that 40 percent of all resources shall go to local centers of government. Developing plans, setting goals and sub-goals, and collecting data relative to crime in the inner city, suburban, and rural area will involve patrol administration, no matter what size department, or whether the agency is a state, county, or a municipal police organization.

The understanding and skill of the patrol commander becomes tremendously important when the allocation of funds is based on costs, risks, benefits, feasibility, and political and community factors. The patrol administrator must be able to cope with the relationships between all other persons involved and himself.

Finally, regional criminal justice planning uses documentation, evaluation, and multi-year (in many cases five-year) and annual plans to go forward. Implementation is not easy. Potential obstacles must be considered, especially the difficulty of planning at a regional level and implementing at a local level.

The questions Who are we? Where are we going? and How are we going to get there? strike the very heart of five-year planning. A discussion of the review of considerations and steps involved in the development of such a plan by an actual municipal police department will be helpful here.

The Dallas Five-Year Plan

The Dallas Police Department issued its five-year plan in March 1973. Chief Frank Dyson wrote the foreword presented here. The points to dwell upon are reflections on past and future, effective police service, efficiency, human development and growth, partnership with government and community, personal commitment, and administrative expertise.

> In seeking to develop a comprehensive plan to guide the activities for the Dallas Police Department in the next five years, it has been critically necessary to dwell in depth on what this Department is all about—its reason for being, its role in the community, the mistakes of the past, and hopes for the future. This plan is an initial step into our future and its ramifications are many. First, the community will receive the direct benefits of increased excellence in the rendering of effective police service. Second, the city government will realize economy of the highest order through police capability of weighing its operations in terms of cost/effectiveness. Third, each of the personnel of the Department will be able to realize his own maximum potential in terms of personal advancement in an enhanced career path, to perform as a total policeman on the front line of the attack on crime, and to achieve recognition as a community professional in the true sense.
>
> The Dallas Police Department, in close partnership with the community and the city government, is now ready to bring implementation of a new era. We will proceed with that necessary degree of caution inherent in applying change and innovation. Research, experimentation, evaluation, and planning must precede action. A total commitment to optimum police effectiveness on a massive scale as outlined in this plan must be carefully implemented.
>
> I am personally committed to the future of this Department and believe that, through close cooperation and a unity of effort, we will set trail-blazing precedents which will truly be turning points in law-enforcement history.
>
> To all of you reading this report, I would like to add two important words of caution: First, the report and its summary should be read and quoted in context. The plan is an integrated and interrelated effort and undue emphasis placed on any single item could be both misleading and detrimental to the global effort. Second, a plan for change

is only as good as the mechanisms it provides for feedback of information and adjustment based upon incremental results. The plan should not be considered as ultimate and unchangeable. It can and will be adjusted to meet needs which are identified as we progress. [Signed] Frank Dyson.[18]

Generally, the Dallas Police Department began with an operational concept and listed major features. The specifics are important mostly because they deal with those features in the area of patrol across our nation that will earn for policing total acceptance from the citizens. The plan includes the following (note these are partial descriptions of the major features):

1. Decentralization of police service.
2. Development of generalist/specialist police officer, who will perform all general functions of the line officer plus develop a specialty expertise to provide a total range of required services (photography, investigation, drug abuse).
3. Operations of generalist/specialist officer in team-policing.
4. Development of resources-tracking and information-delivery system to provide predictive resource allocation.

The next section sets department goals, such as:

Goal I: Crime reduced to five (5) index offenses per 1,000 population.

Goal III: Ninety percent of all Dallas homes and businesses enrolled in computer-identification system.

Goal V: Traffic injuries at 300 per 100,000 population.

Goal VIII: Zero loss of personnel due to lack of career opportunity.

Acceptable progress toward each goal is then spelled out in a series of posture statements. This is done in order to determine where the department is at any given time and also to revise acceptable goal gradients.

The next consideration is to be realistic and review the limitations or constraints that the department will face. Included among the restrictive features are competition from industry for qualified personnel, pension systems that make lateral entry prohibitive, timing, and attitudes, both within and without the department—specifically, the role of the police as viewed by the other facets of the criminal justice system and government agencies.

Strategies

There is no way to implement a five-year plan unless there is developed a strategy or technique that considers change and the most advantageous method to accomplish the change. Change can and will usually affect other government agencies, the community, and the criminal justice system. Two strategies that should be included are information and participation. Disclosing to other parties what you are doing and allowing them to participate in decisions affecting them will definitely enhance the ability of the department to succeed. Patrol administrators should be intimately involved in communicating the changes to these other agencies.

Concept Development

Most programs cannot be implemented in their entirety and result in complete success. It is therefore necessary to experiment in order to work out the bugs. Limited implementation with a pilot project calling for a total operation on a limited basis, or limited operation on a total basis, is helpful; e.g., decentralize one whole precinct, or implement team-policing throughout the department. In either case, the experimentation and in-depth demonstration should provide the information necessary to decide, at critical stages, if adjustments are necessary.

Human Resources

Where can private funds help most in the development of law enforcement? They can help most by developing people in law enforcement, because without good people, all the science and technology are useless. The human relations of law enforcement necessitate the development of human resources first and foremost. The five-year plan in Dallas shows ways to develop these resources. Increased rewards at the patrol-officer level are a must for law enforcement if professionalism is to be a reality. Horizontal growth at the patrol-officer level is essential.

The police agency striving for a high level of service delivery that satisfactorily meets the community's needs, but on a cost-effective basis, must develop a capacity to systematize human resource planning. If taxpayer dollars are to be spent wisely, i.e., to provide an adequate service return, the agency must be able to do the following:

1. Determine quantitative objectives that serve to direct the efforts of all members of the police agency;
2. Isolate and identify those specific human resource skills and requirements throughout the organization that are necessary to achieve those objectives;

3. Create and build a capacity for continuous analysis of community needs and the level of skill or expertise required by the police dedicated to serving those needs;

4. Conduct continuous review of all personnel policies and practices in order to make necessary modifications that will lead to optimal use of police resources on a cost-effective basis; and

5. Build a data collection capability in terms of human resources so that effective forecasting, planning, and evaluation of personnel needs can occur.

Middle-management overload is a major problem when a vertical career path is the only achievement potential. Under such a reward system, personal advancement tends to take expertise away from the street and builds unrealistic layers of supervison. Figure 5.2 shows how this middle-management layer may be redistributed during a five-year plan by the availability of both vertical and horizontal career paths with appropriate monetary and career awards. Figure 5.3 reflects the combined vertical and horizontal career-path structure that will permit:

1. Monetary and status rewards along horizontal paths; personal growth and incentive to remain in field services.

2. Utilization of noncommissioned personnel at a lower pay scale to perform more routine functions.

3. Lateral entry at any level of organization with no threat since individual growth opportunity minimizes competition for vertical growth.

The plan identifies specific action to support the development of such an organizational structure and man it properly. These efforts are generally concerned with three ideas:

1. Know what the job is.
   a. Job requirements identification
   b. Role definition
   c. Task and function analyses
   d. Improved training programs
2. Know and select the right person for the job.
   a. Selection-system improvements
   b. Continuous selection-criteria validation
   c. Continued emphasis on minority recruitment
   d. Continued experimentation with women in police service
   e. Lateral entry opportunity development
   f. Human resources tracking and forecasting development

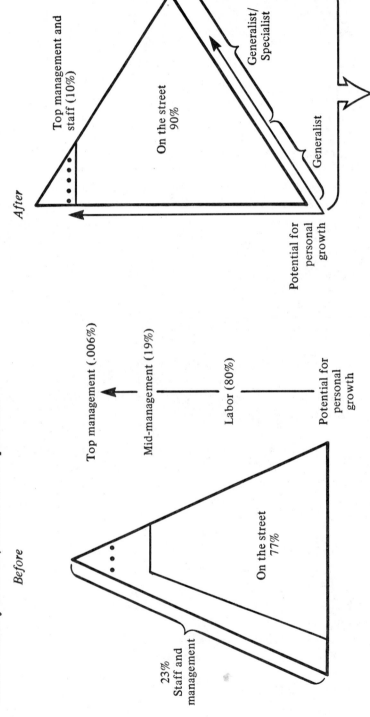

Figure 5.2 *Concept of redistribution of police personnel*
Source: Courtesy of Dallas, Texas Police Department.

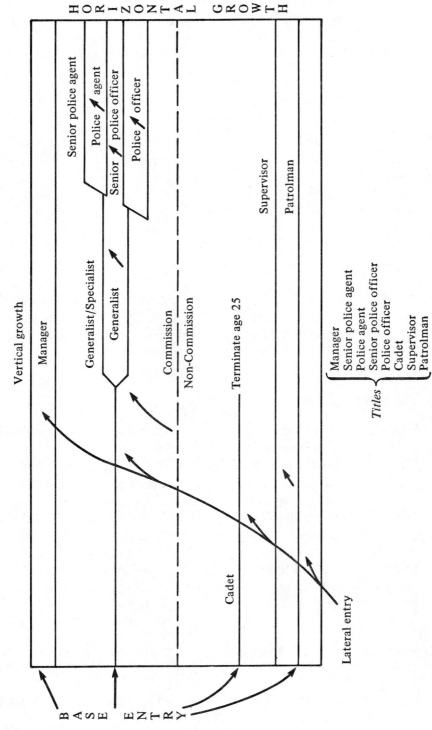

Figure 5.3 *Proposed organizational structure.*
Source: Courtesy of Dallas, Texas Police Department.

3. Retain the right person in the job.
    a. Current human-resources assessment
    b. Transitional assignment plan
    c. Career-path development—vertical/horizontal
    d. Positive disciplinary system implementation

Systems Resources

In this day and age technology must be provided for the department in the form of computers and information-delivery systems. The hardware and software necessary to supply the data for decision-making relative to performance, efficiency, costs, and effectiveness must also be included in order to evaluate.

Support

It is well known that the communication center of police agencies is the heart of the operation. Proper support by staff in the areas of planning and budgeting and providing a physical facility to carry on the program is as important to law enforcement as logistics is to the army.

Summary of Five-Year Plans

Five-year plans will have a tremendous impact on law enforcement. The answers to where we are, where we are going, and how we intend to get there can only be obtained by this type of planning. Departments that develop the in-house ability or outside assistance to accomplish this planning will be more prepared to cope with the future. Patrol administrators around the country should not be afraid to communicate with each other in order to be helpful. Knowledge of operational concepts, department goals, objectives, constraints, management plans, operational plans, support plans, manpower, equipment, and facility resources along with master-programs understanding are available and waiting for interested and dedicated police commanders.

PLANNING FOR MAXIMUM EFFECTIVENESS

Patrol planning for maximum effectiveness by the administrator simply means that by setting a good example of planning for his unit, the patrol administrator can permeate his own unit with this principle of administration and also affect all other units within the department. Each level of authority, from himself to the level of execution, will then have the proper direction and specific guidance to accomplish the patrol mission.

Planning in the Patrol Unit

The patrol administrator views the total picture of increases and decreases in crime rates, community stability, and internal esprit de corps. It is his responsibility to develop as well the ability to view the component parts of the picture, because it looks different to the patrol officer, sergeant, lieutenant, and captain. Any problem, the resolution of the problem, and the planning of that resolution require the patrol administrator to consider manpower (his most valuable resource) and equipment. In order to achieve maximum effectiveness, it will be necessary to analyze the problem in terms of time of day, day of week, location of occurrence, and the specific crime (robbery, burglary, auto theft) or incident. Assignment of personnel and equipment will be determined by the size of the problem. In the case of school disruptions or rock and roll dances and similar operational problems, the patrol commander can gain some help from intelligence, both overt and covert.

No leader should ever be afraid to ask the patrol officer on the beat to give his or her impressions in order to help the department. This advice should also apply to each level of supervision. Many times the supervisor mistakenly believes that because of his time on the job he automatically knows more about the situation, but anytime a leader sits in an ivory tower and tries to plan operational action, failure is likely to result. Nothing is more important for the patrol administrator than to keep in contact with every level of authority under his command. When the patrol commander makes his decisions concerning the implementation of an operational plan of action, he should consider all personnel input and empirical data relevant to the problem. This helps pinpoint potential problems. The result is maximum effectiveness, because only the amount of manpower and equipment necessary to achieve the objective is used.

It is possible for this type of planning to be done by all personnel in patrol, which should result in little wasted time and effort. For example, if a patrol sergeant is working a sector containing eight beats and a problem of robbery arises on one beat at a location adjacent to a second beat, good planning could result in almost constant coverage of that particular location without disrupting the total sector (see Figure 5.4). If the sergeant and the men and women of his sector plan properly, by analyzing the

Figure 5.4 *Robbery, Sector #1, Watch 4-12*

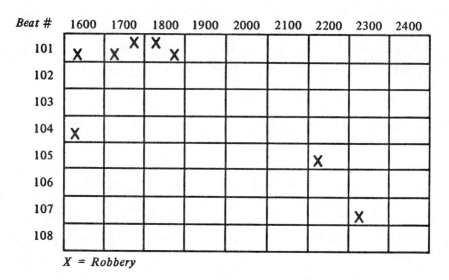

X = Robbery

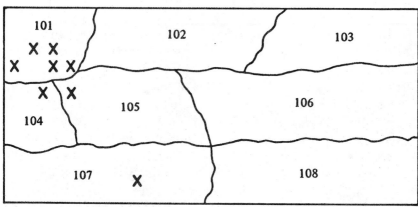

Robbery by location — Pin map

	Sun	Mon	Tues	Wed	Thurs	Fri	Sat
101					X X	X X X	
102							
103							
104							
105							
106							
107							
108							

robberies by beat, by time of day, by location, and by day of week, together they can develop an irregular schedule where cars number 102, 104, and 105 can assist car 101 in inspecting the police hazard. As the figures indicate, the problem exists on Thursday and Friday between 1600 hours and 1800 hours. This does not mean there should not be a plan for the other days of the week, but by being selective in the patrol procedure, the sergeant and his officers can obtain maximum results from within their own sector of operation.

This type of planning does not mean assistance will not be needed if the problem continues or enlarges, but it does mean that the teams of men and women have contributed their best efforts in attempting to resolve the problem without additional resources. The enlightened patrol commander would be aware of the problem and knowledgeable about the plans and efforts of the sergeant and his officers. Consequently, he would be ready to assign the additional resources to resolve the problem at the appropriate time.

Communication among all levels is important because of timing and in order to ensure that no area of the community receives less service and protection than required. The principle here is the same as in civil disorders: do not call all of your forces to the location of the disruption because you may leave an area unprotected, thereby causing greater losses in that unprotected area. Emphasis is placed on communication, team effort, and total planning.

Patrol Planning and Other Units

The next phase of this operational planning has to do with the effect of patrol planning for maximum effectiveness on other units within the department, outside of patrol. The goal of this type of planning is to resolve problems without duplicating effort and to utilize the expertise of all units involved.

Facts indicate that narcotics addicts must commit crime in order to support their habit. To what percent this group has contributed to the crime problem is immeasurable at this time, but we can safely say it is substantial. Crime reports have also borne out the fact that young people are involved in more crime now than at any time since the beginning of records. This leads to the realization that cooperation, coordination, and good planning are essential among units of the police organization if specific crime problems are to be resolved.

Let's, for example, take a situation in which a given area of the community is plagued with dwelling burglaries. Analysis of the crime reports of this area reveals the approximate time of day, day of week, modus operandi, and all other information relevant to the crimes. First, it is a problem for patrol since this is the first line of defense. Second, it is a problem for the investigation section since the follow-up of felonies will most likely be made by the investigator. Third, the youth division will be concerned with the problem. And fourth, for a total effort, members of the narcotics unit would be included. To plan for maximum effectiveness in this case, the following procedure is recommended:

1. Chart the burglaries on a pin map. The problem of dwelling burglaries can be plotted over a period of weeks. A comparison can be made by the week to determine the trend by locations. In analyzing burglaries it is difficult to place the time of occurrence specifically because of the hours that people are away from home. Preliminary investigations will help, but in-depth follow-up will be necessary to close the gap when trying to determine the exact hour the crime took place. More than likely, selective enforcement will be necessary to combat dwelling burglaries. Most departments change shifts at 0800, 1600, and 2400 hours or 0700, 1500, and 2300 hours; in departments where permanent shifts exist, the time of shift change is more than likely the same. The burglary problem will not coincide with these shift changes; therefore, selective enforcement is necessary for time of occurrence.

2. Determine by the hours, as close as possible, when the burglaries are being committed.

3. Glean from the reports of the burglaries as much information as possible about the incidents (method of entry, exit, items taken, etc.).

4. Prepare a presentation to disseminate the information to all concerned.

5. Contact the commanders of other units you believe can assist in resolving the problem.

6. Request a meeting to include the patrol, criminal investigation, youth, and narcotics units as participants.

7. Explain the problem and request suggestions on the plan of attack.

8. Remember, patrol is the primary unit of prevention, so the patrol commander should first inform the citizens of the area where the burglaries are occurring and implement a program of awareness and involvement from the community. Inviting representatives from the community to the police district to show them exactly what is occurring in the area where they live is a good start. Sincerity and openness on the part of the patrol commander in presenting the problem is a positive factor.

9. Prepare a team plan utilizing the expertise of each unit, avoiding duplication of effort.

This kind of planning and cooperation among units is essential in any progressive policy agency. When the individuals involved in achieving the objective are involved in the planning and told the reason why they are doing something, success is more likely to occur. It is grass-roots participatory management.

In the category of auto theft, because of the mobility it may be necessary for the crime analysis unit to keep a pin map for the entire city. This is especially necessary in departments that are decentralized, because the location of theft may be in one district and the location of recovery in another. In departments that are centralized, one pin map charting the location stolen and location recovered is all that would be needed, since all officers report to the same location for roll call. In either case the same procedure for pinning the map would be used, the difference being that in larger departments, which are decentralized, the crime analysis unit would be responsible for advising the different districts of related offenses.

Figure 5.5 shows the information that would be revealed by a stolen-auto pin map. The letter X indicates the location where the auto was stolen. The letter Y indicates where the auto was recovered. On a pin map, each letter would be indicated by a different color pin. Additionally, the date can be put on top of the pin. From this it can be determined if most thefts were on weekends, for example, which may indicate joy-riding. The next step is to use a rubber band to connect the location stolen and the location recovered. The rubber bands may show a pattern; i.e., the autos are being stolen in different parts of the city but abandoned in the same area. If this is the situation, selective and effective enforcement can take place at the location of recovery and probable routes between the theft and recovery.

A good reporting system, based on integrity under Uniform Crime Reporting, is a must for a law enforcement agency to be effective in planning and resolving crime problems. Reporting systems that contain procedures for daily readouts of crime during the previous twenty-four hours; posting of the crimes by time of day, day of week, and location on pin maps; and controls that insure the dissemination of this information to patrol officers by patrol supervisors are excellent. Second, when the crime patterns are plotted so that comparisons can be made, supervisors are able to judge the success or failure of the patrol officers, the method of partol being used, and whether or not assistance is needed. Computer printouts will substitute for pin maps wherever this technology is available.

To achieve the objectives in patrol, it is necessary to get the information to the person most responsible for achieving these objectives, the patrol officer. A pin map maintained in a current status, which is easily acces-

Figure 5.5 *Representation of a stolen-auto pin map*

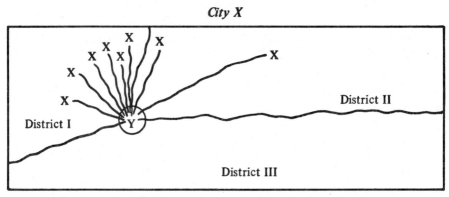

X = Location of stolen auto
Y = Location of recovered stolen auto

sible and presented clearly, is a valuable tool and a good way to allow all levels to participate in the common goal of crime prevention and apprehension.

Each member involved in the patrol function should have an interest in the product. When responsibility, authority, and accountability are present, then interest will follow. When a patrol officer is held accountable for the beat and the procedure is available to show his or her production (this means all aspects of policing, not just arrests), he and all levels know they are part of the organization.

Results

The results of good planning will be apparent when that administration accomplishes the objectives or goals. Planning, directing, and controlling are in the forefront, with organizing, coordinating, staffing, reporting, and budgeting rounding out the responsibilities of the patrol administrator. The patrol administrator is a department head, and as such, he takes the resources supplied by the chief of police and utilizes these resources in a way that produces a superior product of service for the community. The police chief uses planning to implement policy, define policy specifically, state the purpose and objectives of the policy, and set forth the procedures that he believes best to achieve the objective. The patrol administrator must have input into the policy, have his input considered, and, after approval, accept the decision and make every effort to implement the policy as if it were his own. Patrol is the largest division in the police department and also has the greatest potential for disgruntled employees;

therefore, an affirmative action image by the patrol administrator will help greatly in providing a well-coordinated organization. Moving out into the field, speaking at roll calls, explaining policy, and showing the total patrol operation how planning and preparation result in an efficient implementation of a program are all part of a good patrol administration.

When management plans properly, then it can be expected that this good planning will be of value for everyone in the department. If the chief comes in to work in the morning and growls at the assistant, this impression will be passed on to the other subordinates. The same holds true with planning. If the chief and patrol administrator plan properly, captains, lieutenants, sergeants, and patrol officers will plan accordingly. The result will be anticipation of future events and the development of methods to resolve these events to the advantage of the department.

BUDGETING: A PLAN OF ACTION

It has been said that a budget is nothing more than a plan of action, usually for the coming year. Budgeting is a good example of the tremendous results that may be accomplished from good planning. The Planning Programming Budgeting System points out planning and budgeting relationships. A budget can be defined as "a plan for the coordination of resources and expenditures."

A budget calendar shows suggested budget preparation on a calendar year basis. (See Table 5.2.) Planning and preparation are obviously essential to the program. The chief administrator, department heads, and finance officers are involved in the final decision, but the patrol administrator must submit the preliminary information concerning his needs and should be prepared to appear before governmental bodies to justify requests. The anticipation of critical questioning and probable responses is a must for the enlightened patrol administrator. He must communicate effectively and present himself as an aware and knowledgeable leader.

There are numerous types of budgets used today, including the line-item budget, the performance budget, and the program. After a brief description of these kinds of budget, the discussion will concentrate on the Planning Programming Budgeting System.

Line-Item Budget

A line-item budget emphasizes input (money in) by organizational units and amounts allocated to an object of expenditure within the unit. It is the simplest system of accounts.

Table 5.2 *Suggested Police Department Budget Preparation Calendar Fiscal-Year Basis*

What Should Be Done	By Whom	On These Dates
Issue budget instructions and applicable forms	City Administrator	November 1
Prepare and issue budget message, with instructions and applicable forms, to unit commanders	Chief of Police	November 15
Develop unit budgets with appropriate justification and forward recommended budgets to planning and research unit	Unit Commanders	February 1
Review of unit budget	Planning and Research Staff with Unit Commanders	March 1
Consolidation of unit budget for presentation to chief of police	Planning and Research Unit	March 15
Review of consolidated recommended budget	Chief of Police, Planning and Research Staff, and Unit Commanders	March 30
Department approval of budget	Chief of Police	April 15
Recommended budget forwarded to city administrator	Chief of Police	April 20
Administrative review of recommended budget	City Administrator and Chief of Police	April 30
Revised budget approval	City Administrator	May 5
Budget document forwarded to city council	City Administrator	May 10
Review of budget	Budget Officer of City Council	May 20
Presentation to council	City Administrator and Chief of Police	June 1
Reported back to city administrator	City Council	June 5
Review and resubmission to city council	City Administrator and Chief of Police	June 10
Final action on police budget	City Council	June 20

Schedule is for a large department requiring eight months to develop and process the budget and gain administrative and council approval for it. Other major departments may be on different schedules as a matter of convenience for the administrator and council.
Source: National Advisory Commission on Criminal Justice Standards and Goals, *Report on Police* (Washington, D.C.: U.S. Government Printing Office, 1973).

Line-Item Budget Example
Police Department (Organizational Unit)

Salary (object of expenditure)	$183,000	Auto–Buy	4,000
Printing and office supplies	3,000	Auto repair and Maintenance	3,600
Uniforms	6,000	Building repair and maintenance	500
Photo supplies	450	Radio	1,250
Gas and oil	7,000	Rent	600
Heat	600	Insurance	1,800
Miscellaneous	2,500	Training	6,000
Protection equipment	1,800		
Auto–Rent	1,560	TOTAL	$223,660

Performance Budget

A performance budget is difficult to apply to many police activities. The major emphasis is on input (money in) compared to output (what additional performance will be achieved). This application is not difficult to use in some areas, as shown in the example, but becomes more difficult in areas of crime-related activities; e.g., what do you expect from the addition of one patrol officer to a department?

Performance Budget Example
Transportation

One position is provided at the Central Garage to meet work load resulting from maintenance requirements on electric starters, now standard equipment on motorcycles.

   1 Auto Electrician
      Salary
         General $ 5,468.

One position is added to the First Division Garage where the ratio of vehicles to maintenance personnel is so high as to require constant relief from the Central Garage.

   1 Mechanical Helper
      Salary
         General $ 4,284.

Increasing use of automobiles and motorcycles results in an annual increase in fleet mileage of approximately 1,000,000 miles. This increase is followed by the need for additional petroleum.

     Expense $18,797.

Program Budget

A program budget focuses attention on programs of work and the cost of these programs. The full cost of a program is reflected in dollars and therefore allows for broad cost planning.

Program Budget Example

		Cost
Administration		
Salaries	$ 18,118	
Salaries–overtime	10,000	
Contractual services	3,453	
Materials and supplies	4,100	$ 35,671
Detective bureau		
Salaries (new: one detective)	126,821	
Contractual services	800	
Materials and supplies	156	
One listening device	2,000	
Two desks	288	
Two chairs	142	$130,207
Youth bureau		
Salaries	40,982	
New typewriter	360	$ 41,342
Accident investigation and traffic control		
Salaries	202,835	
Salaries–overtime for serving warrants	3,000	
Contractual services	750	
Materials and supplies	5,750	
Two Stephenson radar units	1,400	$213,735
School traffic protection		
Salaries and wages	44,620	
Contractual services	60	
Materials and supplies	395	
Safety patrol picnic	500	$ 45,575

Planning Programming Budget System (PPBS)

PPBS is a combination of the other three types of budgets into a systematic approach of using budgeting as a decision-making tool. PPBS focuses on fundamental objectives and identifies costs and benefits of major alternative courses of action. In PPBS there is some interchangeable vocabulary.

For example, an "objective" may also be a goal, sub-goal, ultimate objective, program objective, or sub-objective.

Since the impact of budgeting in the organization is so important and the PPBS is management by objectives, the process is shown here briefly to indicate the proper planning process. The patrol administrator must have a working knowledge of the budget process. In most police departments today, the line-item budget still is used. However, as police departments and local governments learn the advantage of the PPBS, more and more agencies will use the management by objectives approach in their management planning. Justification, which is the essential word in budgeting, will be integrated with the objective. It must be understood that evaluation and progress measurement need continued study in order to become more meaningful.

Objectives.[19] The central term of the PPBS structure. A police agency must develop explicit objectives to make possible a genuine agency-wide understanding and a common approach toward their achievement. These objectives should provide specific grounds on which to base the answers to three key questions:

1. What services must be provided (primary and secondary services)?
2. What group is each service intended to satisfy (juvenile, traffic, etc.)?
3. What specific need or goal of the group is the service intended to satisfy?

If this process is correctly applied, the objectives developed consistent with the answers to the questions should become standards for the agency.

Programs. A program is a package of each and every one of the agency's efforts to accomplish a particular objective or a like group of objectives. If the objective were to reduce crimes against persons within a given area, the program would be composed of all agency activities and expenditures put to that purpose. In a PPBS system there are no recognized objectives except those that can be identified with a program specifically designed to fulfill them.

Program alternatives. Means other possible programs besides those already decided upon. This, therefore, creates a comparison of two or more programs (i.e., two or more possible approaches) toward fulfilling the same objective.

Output. In a police agency an output should have all of the following properties:

1. It is a service.
2. It is produced by the police agency or under the agency's guidance and authority.
3. It is the result of a particular program.
4. It is the sort of service that can be appropriately singled out as an indicator of the program results. It must be a program end-product, and an important one.
5. It is considered by the agency as satisfying an explicit objective or related set of objectives.

In order to be considered an output, the good or service produced must satisfy an explicit objective and must be an indicator of program results.

Progress measurement. What does PPBS regard as progress in a given program?

1. The output that had been planned has materialized.
2. The output distribution that had been intended has been completed.

An affirmative answer would be demonstrated by fulfillment of the program. Therefore, progress measurement could be:

1. How closely does the production progress match planned progress?
2. How well is the output distribution proceeding as compared with the distribution plan?

Input. The total quantity of manpower, facilities, equipment, and materials applied to the program is the program input.

Alternative ways to do a given job. Takes the program as given and raises possibilities for changing the mix of inputs and thereby redirecting the program. Alternative ways to do a given job involve operational matters, not policy questions.

1. The timing of the service, or
2. The quantity or quality of the item or service being produced, or
3. The unit or total cost of the service.

Systems analysis.   A group of techniques attached to a way of approaching problems. From the standpoint of an individual police agency, two PPBS areas may be especially adaptable to benefit-cost techniques.

1. The posing and evaluation of program alternatives; i.e., determining the benefit-cost advantage, if any, of shifting to different output and/or distribution patterns so as to satisfy objectives better.
2. The measurement of progress in a given program; i.e., determining the benefit-cost advantage (if any) of changing the input mixed so as to produce and/or distribute the output more efficiently.

Narrative.   PPBS is an administrative tool that emphasizes a systems approach to management by determining the objectives of the agency and then developing programs to achieve those objectives. In order to attain its objectives, an agency must develop a program or several programs of activities designed to achieve the desired objectives. A key to the PPBS approach to management is developing program alternatives. This allows for the consideration of programs besides the obvious or those already decided upon, and thereby allows a comparison of two or more programs or methods to achieve the objective.

In order to apply a PPBS to a police agency, one must redesign the agency according to the objectives of the agency as opposed to the more traditional organization by function. For the purpose of this segment we will define as objectives of a police agency:

- Primary Objective—The control of crime.
- Objectives—Prevention of crime.
             Detection of crime.
             Apprehension of criminals.

Therefore, in management by objectives, the objectives are used to determine both the functional and hierarchical structure or organization of the department.

In traditional organization by function, the development of the agency starts with the opening units and uses these units as a hierarchical and functional means of operation. This type of agency is built from the bottom up. Functions such as patrol and traffic are grouped in a hierarchical classification; i.e., line, by like or similar activities rather than by the ability to achieve a common objective (see Figure 5.6.)

In a PPBS of management by objectives the agency is built from the objectives down. The primary objective and sub-objectives are determined

Figure 5.6 *Traditional organization by function.* (These charts are not intended to represent complete organizational structures.)

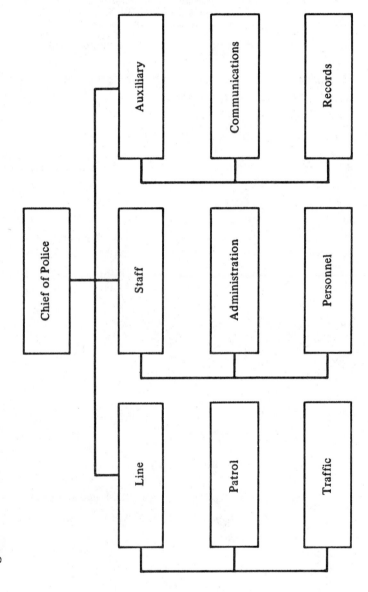

and the structure of the organization is built from the objective down (see Figure 5.7).

Just as management by the PPBS demands specific objectives, specific objectives should be demanded of the system. What is the specific focus of the PPBS? The aim is to specify the objectives of spending programs and then to minimize the cost of achieving these objectives or to determine whether costs exceed benefits. By the (1) specification of objectives, (2) investigation of alternative means of achieving the objectives, (3) minimization of the costs or comparison of costs and benefits, and (4) systematic use of analysis, the police administrator should maximize the return to the citizens of tax dollars spent.

Systems information. Although it does not seem consistent with the PPBS requirement of determining objectives and then structuring programs to meet these objectives, several formats are available for applying PPBS to police agencies. The format should meet the needs of the individual department and should be selected on that basis.

Szanton's Detailed Police Program Structure[20]

1. *Control and Reduction of Crime Program*
   a. Prevention/Suppression
      (1) General Purpose Patrol
      (2) Special Purpose Patrol (by type of offense)
      (3) Intelligence
      (4) Community Relations
   b. Investigation/Apprehension
      (1) Crimes Involving Major Risk of Personal Injury
         (a) Murder
         (b) Assault
         (c) Rape
         (d) Armed Robbery
         (e) Burglary–Homes
         (f) Arson
         (g) Etc.
      (2) Crimes Not Involving Major Risk of Personal Injury
         (a) Theft
         (b) Unarmed Robbery
         (c) Auto Theft
         (d) Burglary–Commercial
         (e) Fraud
         (f) Forgery
         (g) Etc.
      (3) Vice
         (a) Narcotics
         (b) Prostitution
         (c) Gambling
         (d) Etc.

(continued)

Figure 5.7 *Organization by objectives*

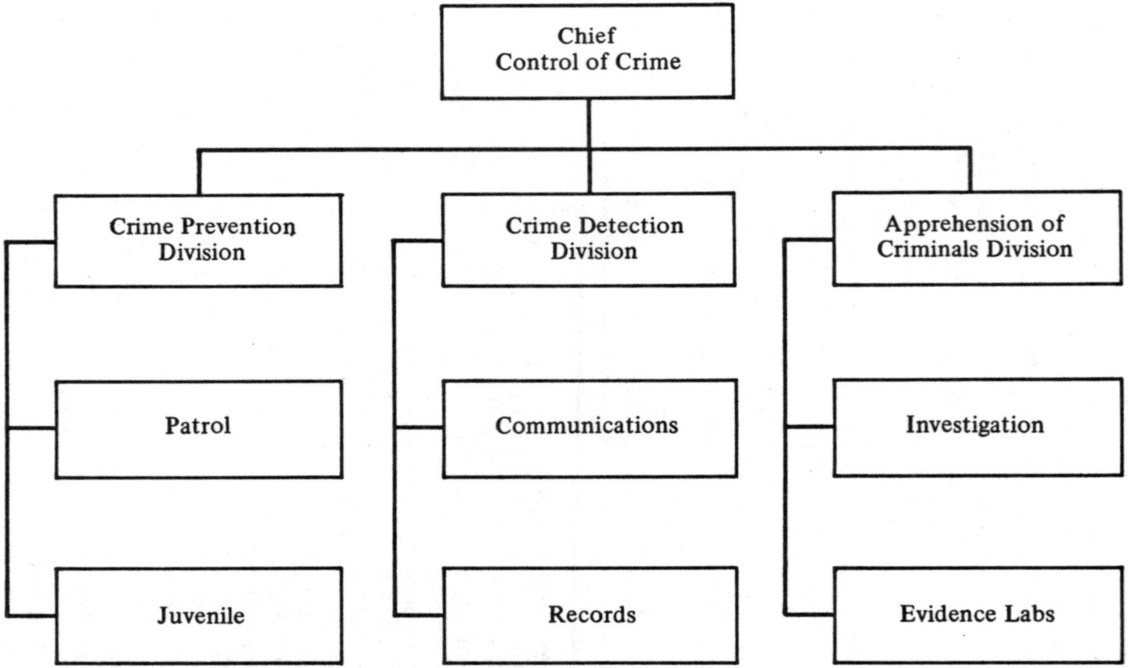

Figure 5.8 *Plan for the development of a PPBS in a police agency*

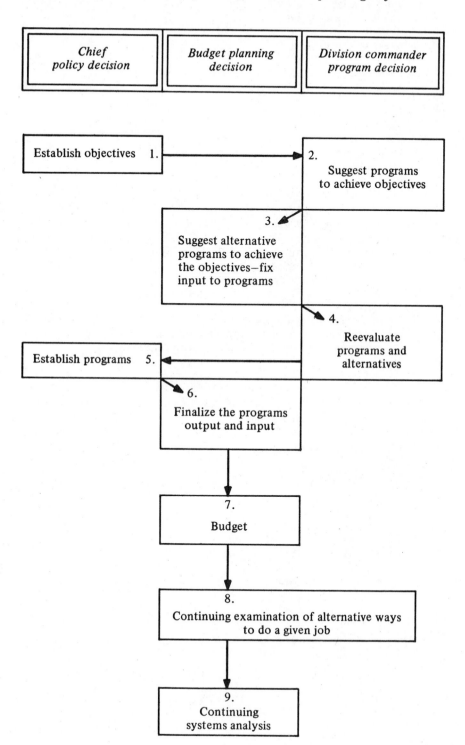

    c. Prosecution
       (1) Interrogation
       (2) Preparation for Trial
       (3) Trial
    d. Recovery of Property
       (1) Autos
       (2) Other Personal Property
       (3) Commercial Property
    e. General Support
       (1) Communications
       (2) Records and Data Processing
       (3) Technical Services
          (a) Fingerprint
          (b) Ballistics
          (c) Polygraph
          (d) Laboratory Analysis

2. *Movement and Control of Traffic Program*
    a. Traffic Movement
       (1) Direction of Traffic
       (2) Enforcement of Traffic-oriented Parking Rules
       (3) Emergency Road Services
       (4) Weather Emergency Procedures
       (5) Identification and Reporting of Congestion Points
    b. Traffic Safety
       (1) Enforcement of Regulations
          (a) Patrol/Apprehension of Moving Violations
          (b) Enforcement of Safety-oriented Parking Rules
       (2) Driving Training
       (3) Educational Programs
       (4) Vehicle Inspections
    c. Accident Investigation

3. *Maintenance of Public Order Program*
    a. Public Events
       (1) Sporting Events
       (2) Public Ceremonies
          (a) Parades and Receptions
          (b) Public Meetings
          (c) Cornerstones, etc.
    b. Minor Disturbances
       (1) Private Quarrels
       (2) Parties
       (3) Drunkenness
       (4) Derelicts
       (5) Miscellaneous Nuisances
    c. Civil Disorder
       (1) Prevention
       (2) Suppression

4. *Provision of Public Services Program*
    a. Emergency Services
       (1) Fire
       (2) Medical
       (3) Power Failure
       (4) Flood
       (5) Civil Defense
       (6) Miscellaneous

  b. Missing Persons
  c. Lost Property
  d. Miscellaneous

5. *Administration and Support Program*

  a. Direction and Control
     (1) Direction
     (2) Planning and Development
     (3) Internal Inspection and Review
  b. Training and Personnel
     (1) Recruitment
     (2) Training
        (a) Basic
        (b) Advanced
     (3) Testing, Evaluation, Promotion
  c. Public Relations
  d. Supporting Services
     (1) Records (noncrime) and Data Processing
     (2) Communications
     (3) Budget
     (4) Property

Riggs Simplified Police Structure

---

1. *Control of Criminal Behavior*

  a. Vice (liquor, narcotics, prostitution, gambling)
  b. Rackets (larceny, loan sharking, organized crime)
  c. Crime against Property
  d. Crimes of Violence to Persons
     (1) For profit
     (2) Not-for-profit
  e. Youth or Juvenile Crime

2. *Public Services Activities* (primarily noncriminal)

  a. Emergency Medical Services
  b. Security in Public Buildings (city hall, courts, etc.)
  c. Traffic
     (1) Safety
     (2) Movement of Goods and Services
  d. Crowd Control (i.e., crowds at public events, athletic contests, etc.)
  e. Inspection and Licenses
  f. Control and Support (a residual category for administrative and staff units)

Figure 5.9 *Sample budget.* (This is not intended to represent a complete budget, but rather to demonstrate the PPBS application to a police agency.)

Program	
Administration and support	$ 515,776.00
Apprehension of criminals	857,915.00
Crime prevention	240,473.00
TOTAL FISCAL BUDGET	$1,614,164.00

CRITIQUE

All good planners invite critique. Just as the problem-solving conference method has a provision to consider consequences of acceptable solutions, so the participants are told to look beyond the solution, so does the patrol administrator have to look beyond the plan. For example, if a plan is developed for response to a large disturbance at an all-girls' high school and policewomen are available, the police commander must consider carefully his decision of using men with training or policewomen without training. The use of men may bring a charge of police brutality, which must be anticipated. The use of policewomen may not be as efficient (if they are not trained), but the consequences of using policewomen would be, if not positive, at least more acceptable.

The decision to use canine teams in crowd control is one where the consequences are critical. More than likely another approach would be taken because of the potential results.

One of the best methods of anticipating possible solutions to problems before the fact is a regular evaluation of plans and procedures. Continuous critiques, especially after using a particular plan for special events or unusual critical confrontations, keep the total patrol force updated.

After the riots of 1968 following the death of Dr. Martin Luther King, the Justice Department requested the International Association of Chiefs of Police to develop after-action reports. These reports were to document and evaluate procedures used in coping with civil disorder. Additionally, there was a need to critique the level of cooperation among federal, state, and local government; federal, state, and local law enforcement; and adjacent local law enforcement agencies. The review would show how police had cooperated with each other in identifying problems and the solutions used to resolve these problems. Problems in most cases were too big for the smaller police departments and mutual aid was necessary for survival. As each of the reports was reviewed, similarities in the responses became evident.

Prior events and the disorders themselves made it obvious that social change was upon us. The need to adjust and cope by evaluating and re-evaluating procedures used in response to civil disorders was of prime importance. History now shows that the change was met, efficiency was increased, and the challenge to law enforcement was accomplished. The author has spent many hours reviewing plans regarding disorders, demonstrations, and events and respectfully submits the great value of critique: There always seems to be some way to improve a plan or procedure.

Recent events in Miami, Florida, have reemphasized the need for effective planning.

Table 5.3 *Program—Apprehension of Criminals*

Objective	Programs	Output	Input	
To apprehend violators of the law.	*Response* To respond to emergencies within 3 minutes & nonemergencies within 10 minutes of receipt of call 90% of the time	Calls for service Observations 45% of Patrol Div.	4 lts., 8 sgts., 63 off., 26 vehs., 6 offices	$556,315
		100% of Dispatchers	4 Dispatch, 1 office	47,100
			1 sgt., 3 off., 1 veh., 1 office	32,600
	Investigation and Arrest To increase the rate of arrest by 8%	Crime scene inv. Scientific inv. Field interpretations 50% of S.E.D.	1 lt., 1 sgt., 3 off., 1 mechanic, 1 veh.,	
		20% Helicopter	2 copters	43,760
	Vice & Narco To increase the rate of arrest by 10%	Bar checks Surveillance of organized crime activities 40% Detective Bureau 70% of Narco Detail	2 sgts., 9 off., 9 off., 10 vehs.	90,100
	Investigation and Prosecution To increase the number of solved cases by 8%	Follow up inv. Custody of evidence Court witness 30% I.D. Section	1 sgt., 3 off., 1 veh., 2 offices	46,480
		20% Training	1 I.D. tech. 2 off., 1 photo tech, 1 chrk, 4 chemists, 4 offices, 1 veh.	29,600
			1 sgt., 1 officer, 1 office	11,960
			Total Program Cost	$857,915.00

Source: Tables 5.3 through 5.5 are from an unpublished paper by Lee Burt Hawkins, Eastern Kentucky University, 1974.

Table 5.4 *Program—Planning, Control, and Administration*

Objective	Programs	Output		Input	
To maintain a modern, well-managed, and progressive police agency	*Planning & Control*	Planning & Research	75% of Admin. Div.	1 chief, 1 sec., 1 veh., 2 offices	$29,325
	To plan for future needs of the agency	Budget Control	20% Vice & Intelligence	1 lt., 3 off., 1 sec., 3 offices	14,345
		Statistical Analysis	90% Admin. Commander		
		Training	100% Personnel	1 capt., 1 sec., 1 veh.	31,310
		Administrative Reports	95% Planning & Research	1 veh., 2 offices	15,950
	To control spending	Personnel Records	20% Training	1 officer, 1 office	14,976
		Maintain Buildings	100% Payroll	1 officer, 1 office	7,660
			95% Uniform Commander	1 sgt., 1 office	8,400
	Department Administration	Office Administration	Commander	1 clrk., 1 office	
	To coordinate the activities of the various units of the Department.	Payroll Processing	5% Patrol	1 capt., ½ sec., 2 offices, 28 vehs.	62,035
		Inspectional Process	5% Traffic	1 lt., 2 sgts., 11 off.	
		Records Checker	5% Helicopter	2 clrks, 1 parking control, 3 offices, 12 veh.	13,175
		Improve Efficiency	100% Investigation Commander		
	To provide general support for the various units of the Department.	Processing Paperwork	100% Service Commander	1 capt., 2 clrks., 2 offices, 1 veh.	44,000
		Inventory & Storage of Equipment and Supplies	5% Property	1 capt., 1 service off. ½ sec., 3 offices, 1 veh.	44,200
			100% Records	2 prop. clrks., 2 off. 1 lt., 2 clrks.-supvrs.,	10,400
			100% Maintenance	12 clrks, 4 offices	160,600
			100% Cadets	1 jntr., 2 mech., 2 veh.	32,500
				11 P/T cadets	26,900
				Total Program Cost	$515,776.00

Table 5.5 *Program—Crime Prevention and Deterrence*

Objective	Programs	Output	Input	
To prevent violations of the law through communication with the citizenry and to deter violations of the law through aggressive police activities	*Crime Prevention:* To reduce the incidence of Part I and Part II crimes by 8%	Community Relations Talks & Presentations Films Brochures Youth Activities	25% Administrative Div. 20% Vice/Intelligence 5% Planning/ Research 20% Training 100% Public Relations	1 chief, 1 sec., 1 veh., 2 offices 1 lt., 3 off., 1 sec., 3 officers, 1 veh. 1 off., 1 office 1 off., 1 office	$ 9,875 15,341 798 20,275
	Crime Deterrence: To increase the omnipresence of police by increasing the time an officer is available by 10%	Uniformed Patrol Helicopter Patrol Traffic Patrol	5% of Patrol Div. 10% of Traffic Scetion 65% of Helicopter	4 lts., 8 sgts., 63 off., 26 vehs., 6 offices 1 lt., 3 sgts., 11 off., 3 clrks., 11 vehs. 1 lt., 1 sgt., 3 off., 1 mechanic, 1 veh., 2 copters	63,044 24,670 106,470
			Total Program Cost		$240,473

NOTES

1. Don C. Gibbons, Joseph L. Thimm, Florence Yospe, and Gerald F. Blake, Jr., *Criminal Justice: An Introduction,* © 1977, pp. 149–150. Reprinted by permission of Prentice-Hall, Inc., Englewood Cliffs, N.J.
2. Donald T. Shanahan and Paul Whisenand, *The Dimensions of Criminal Justice Planning* (Boston: Allyn and Bacon, 1980), p. 449.
3. Karl Manheim, *Man and Society in an Age of Reconstruction* (New York: Harcourt, Brace, 1949), p. 160.
4. Ibid., pp. 168–170.
5. Ibid., p. 9.
6. Edward C. Banfield, "The Use and Limitations of Metropolitan Planning in Massachusetts" (paper presented at the Fifth Working Conference on Metropolitan Area Planning and Regional Development, Joint Center for Urban Studies, Metropolitan Area Planning Council, June 1965), pp. 12–14. See also Banfield, "Ends and Means in Planning," *UNESCO International Social Science Journal* 11 (1959): 365–368.
7. John Friedmann, "Introduction: The Study and Practice of Planning," *UNESCO International Social Science Journal* 11 (1959): 336. However, he does not counsel us to abandon the planning goal. See Friedmann, *Retracking America.*
8. David Braybrooke and Charles Lindblom, *A Strategy of Decision* (New York: The Free Press, 1963), chaps. 2, 3.
9. O. W. Wilson, *Police Planning* (Springfield, Ill.: Charles C Thomas, 1968).
10. Billy E. Goetz, *Management and Control* (New York: McGraw-Hill, 1949).
11. "Directed Deterrent Patrol, an Innovative Method of Preventive Patrol," New Haven Department of Police Service, New Haven, Conn., 1979.
12. James Ahern, *Police in Trouble* (New York: Hawthorn Books, 1972), p. 176.
13. James Q. Wilson, *Varieties of Police Behavior* (New York: Atheneum, 1970), pp. 29–30. Wilson cites Michael Banton, *The Policeman in the Community* (New York: Basic Books, 1965), pp. 105–110 as the source for this analysis of the professional role.
14. Marion S. Kellog, *Career Management* (New York: American Management Association, 1971) p. 31.
15. The President's Crime Commission on Law Enforcement and Administration of Justice, Task Force Report, "Police" (1967), p. 137.
16. National Advisory Commission on Criminal Justice Standards and Goals *Report on Police* (Washington, D.C.: U.S. Government Printing Office, 1973), p. 437.
17. "Portable Police Pensions, Improving Inter-Agency Transfers" (New York: College of Insurance, 1971).
18. Presented through courtesy of Dallas, Texas Police Department, Glen King, Chief of Police.
19. The following material on PPBS comes from Samuel M. Greenhouse, "The Planning Programming Budgeting System: Rationale Language and Idea-Relationship," *Public Administration Review* (December 1966).
20. Ibid.

Patrol Techniq

Patrol Tech...

296

opening an...
know wh...
Additio...
Be so...
kno...
sa...

The choice of patrol techniques to be used by the patrol officer is basic in most cases, but the importance attached to that choice has been underestimated. The achievement of the total objective of the patrol force depends upon selecting the proper technique for the specific situation. Foot patrol for community relations, motorized for mobility, and canine for special events and suspect search are just a few. When officers at the level of execution are able to select one of several patrol techniques based on existing conditions, objectives are more readily attained. This chapter discusses the several techniques available.

FOOT PATROL

It has been said that foot patrol is the most expensive method or type of patrol. However, a more realistic approach is that the application of foot patrol should be measured by the net income, so to speak, that this type produces for a given location and clientele. Police departments should institute in-depth studies to determine the training needed for foot patrol. The patrol administrator who attempts to achieve the objective should not limit himself to an analysis of the expense of each type of patrol alone but include an analysis of the expense as related to the accomplishments made by a given selection or method of patrol.

If one had gone through a police academy years ago when foot patrol was the predominant method used by the police department, instructions would probably have been given as follows:

> Know the people on your beat, their occupations, and their habits; know personally night watchmen, janitors, and all other persons who may be working at unusual hours of the day and night; acquaint yourself with operators of taverns, poolrooms, and clubs and all laws relating to the proper conduct of such establishments; know the

closing hours of all business establishments on your beat; re your call boxes and your fire alarm boxes are located. hally, know the same information about the adjoining beats. intimately involved with the residents of your beat that ledge of when they are away on vacation and advice about the eguards they should take to insure the protection of their property an be given freely and accepted sincerely. Know not only those proven law-abiding residents, but also those of questionable character. Be alert for any vice activities being conducted on your beat or post. First-aid training is necessary to save lives and decrease the possibility of serious injury—and you just may have to deliver babies. Make yourself familiar with all locations of important buildings, city, state, and federal, within your area. Exercise great vigilance in your inspection process of police hazards. (Note: a *police hazard* is defined as any event that requires police action or, better yet, any situation that may induce an incident calling for some police action.) Note all removal of residents and all new additions to your beat. Be vigilant to prevent fires. Make every effort to curb juvenile delinquency. Carry out any plan necessary or that you are capable of with regard to crime prevention. Maintain a night reference book containing records of the name, address, and telephone number of the owners of all business establishments on your beat. Know the location of all safes on your beat and encourage the owner to keep the inside of the building well lighted and especially to have a light burning over the safe, to prevent crime. Be aware of any pawnshops or secondhand dealers or junk dealers where the disposal of stolen goods could take place. Be suspicious by nature and inquisitive at all times with regard to persons or vehicles that appear to be out of place. Build up your sources of information and note any person whom you could call upon to help in case of emergency. Patrol constantly and intelligently. Keep a case book where all arrests are noted for information that you may need at a later date. Original notes should be kept meticulously so that you would be able to testify in court in a knowledgeable and intelligent manner. In summary, you must attain the objectives by winning the confidence and respect of the public. You can do this by performing your duties in an efficient, honest, and businesslike manner, by projecting yourself as an exemplary member of the community, and by setting an example both on and off duty.

While this last task still remains a very important part of the duties of the patrol officer, we have seen changes made in patrol. Task forces, tactical, team policing, have all involved the patrol function. It has been estimated that 70 to 80 percent of the officer's time today is spent on noncriminal activity. This increases the need for closer contact with people living in the area of an officer's beat.

In most departments today there are enough transceivers for each officer to have one provided for his or her particular beat, especially is he or she is working a one-officer car. This constant communication increases the types of patrol available for the patrol administrator and for assignment to a given area or situation. In areas of high concentration, such as downtown areas where policing today has a tremendous investment, a foot officer is most appropriate, especially if he has a walkie-talkie. Most cities have, or are in the process of developing, their inner-city areas to the point where the tax base will be increased. Proper patrol techniques are an integral part of the total process of rejuvenation of these business districts. The foot officer has not become obsolete, and foot patrol is an effective type of patrol for progressive law enforcement agencies if proper analysis accompanies its use.

Walking the Beat

Generally, the only regularity of patrol is its irregularity. Specifically, the officer must know his beat intimately and be prepared for anything. Since the foot beat is not as large as a motorized foot beat, he must develop constant patrol, yet be able to give the impression that it will be difficult for anyone to know exactly where he is at any given time. The intelligent patrol officer knows the patrol hazards (persons, property, places, and situations) and anticipates the consequence of his actions with regard to these hazards.

When walking a beat, an officer can place himself in hypothetical situations to determine the best way of handling each given situation. This approach in evaluation will help him to develop alternate solutions to problems. He can do this on each shift, using holdups on the day shift and 4–12 shift, burglaries on the 12–8, and auto theft on the 4–12 and 12–8 shifts. This preparation of response to the given situations develops the thought process so that reaction is speedy yet intelligent, avoiding jumping to conclusions. It will increase the patrol officer's confidence in knowing what to do in a given situation.

The foot patrol officer knows the "how" of walking his beat. He has had explained to him and understands how to set priorities when determining which hazards need more attention than others. This is related to shift. The day shift emphasizes omnipresence, while the night shift has the advantage of darkness. The officer should use darkness as a tool; i.e., on day shift you walk by the curb, on night shift you walk next to the buildings. At night, whenever you get to the corner of a building, stop and look around the corner before you proceed. The officer surveys his beat to determine which business establishments have silent alarms, which have audible alarms, and which have no alarm at all. It is important for him to know by what means these different alarms will be set off. This knowledge enhances his ability to decide correctly how he will approach the establishment when he believes a burglar to be inside. He will also be able to advise assisting officers of any pitfalls in their approach to the building. By doing a survey of the building and studying the alarm systems, he will learn the possible escape routes from the building, which will improve the search technique.

Priorities.   When a determination is made regarding which premises do have alarms and which do not, priorities can be set to inspect premises according to needs. If a building has an alarm system, the officer should have procedures available on how to inspect the building to determine whether or not anyone may be inside. Premises not having alarm systems are a greater potential hazard than those that do. In developing a plan of action on how to patrol a beat, it is necessary to set priorities so that the places more in need of inspection are inspected more than those which are not. This does not mean that some premises will not be inspected; it allows for more effective patrol. This priority system is just part of the total thought process necessary for a foot officer, so that he obtains an intimate knowledge of his beat. The day-shift officer knows that when walking by business establishments he will observe certain things; if these things are different, he will become suspicious and inspect further. An officer can develop a nonverbal communication system between the community and himself. For instance, while walking his beat the officer passes a grocery store, knowing that at a given time of the day he should see a certain person operating the business. This person usually gives a routine signal, which means everything is in order. If the officer sees or notices anything different or unusual, this indicates that things are not running normally and should cause him to inquire further.

Inspection procedures and telltales.   The only regularity of patrol is its irregularity, and we must expand this concept to the actual technique used when inspecting premises. Do not try up each door the same as the one before. This results in routinizing, which is the greatest evil to patrol. Whenever checking a door for entry, use the flashlight to look for fresh pry marks around the complete door, but most importantly, around the hinges, doorknob, and locks. Pry marks might also be made by a saw; burglars may attempt to force their way into the building by sawing the bolts or locks holding the door. In any such case, it is important that you do not enter the building yourself. Call for assistance and use proper building-search techniques. However, by using the described survey method and attaining an intimate knowledge of the respective premises on your beat, you can improve your building-search technique.

The word "telltale" is most familiar in the eastern United States, but the procedure is used in many police departments around the country, under a different name. It means that in inspecting premises, a piece of tape or string of cotton is placed across entrances and exits to buildings and doorways to allow for a more efficient inspection the next time. The officer can use matchbook covers, match sticks, toothpicks, or any such item that can be placed anywhere that would indicate that the area being inspected has been disturbed.

Some supervisors have used this technique in order to inspect officers. Sergeants have told officers that they will place telltales to indicate whether or not officers have inspected certain premises and have inspected them properly. It is a valid method so long as it is used overtly. There are other ways to handle officers who do not perform; the advantage gained in resolving a problem with one officer is not worth the effect a covert operation may have on the other officers within a supervisor's area of responsibility.

Observation

Observation is one of the advantages of foot patrol. It is necessary that the foot patrol officer enhance any tools available to him and this includes observation. In improving this ability, he should first know what to look for in any given area. For example, travel depots have baggage stolen by con artists. The officer, therefore, should look for this type of person and crime. Hospitals have rapists and purse snatchers; therefore, he should look for persons who may commit those crimes. Business areas have commercial burglars; residential areas have dwelling burglars, purse snatchers, etc. The officer must become instinctively familiar with this type of potential for crime.

The basic rule in observation is to look for differences. The officer should note any unusual dress (a person just does not belong), unusual mannerisms, or ways of doing things that do not appear to be normal. The officer should give special attention to those who pay too much attention to him or who try to avoid his glances and to those who are loitering for no reason. He should make special note of those who have no apparent destination. The officer should look up and down, not only horizontally, while patrolling, because there may be lookouts in unfamiliar places, observing his actions while a partner is committing a crime.

Total observation is the use of all senses while patrolling your beat. It does not necessarily mean that you have to see it to know that a crime has been committed in your presence. If you are standing on a corner and glass breaks behind you, you may turn and see someone running from the smashed store window with some item. It is your hearing that has alerted you to the crime committed.

In developing observation, the officer should increase his objectivity so that when viewing something, he sees the whole, not just what he would expect or like to view or part of the whole. It is necessary to understand that each of us views things from individual perception. In police academies there is usually a very simple demonstration of observation. The instructor, while teaching the class, has one of his secretaries or associates come into the room and hand him a piece of paper. They discuss the paper for a minute or so in front of the class. After the assistant leaves, the instructor asks each member of the class to describe the person as he saw him. There will be many different descriptions. When an officer is actively participating in patrol, he will find this same situation whenever he attempts to get descriptions from different people who observed the same incident. For instance, in a bank robbery he would have different descriptions from the teller, the manager, and from the person outside who saw the subjects running away.

Factors of attention.   There are several factors that should be considered in the observation process. For instance, the factor of size: when someone is unusually tall or unusually short, attention is drawn to him. Or a person is walking normally, but as soon as he sees the officer, the person begins to run. At this point, the officer should be ready to observe. Other factors involved are those of shape, repetition, interest, sound or noise, or the striking quality, organic condition, of an individual. The ability to understand what has been observed in analyzing and viewing these factors is most important.

The ability to observe properly depends on mental capacity, clearness and quickness of mind, the amount of observation the mind can absorb, educational background, previous experience, and occupational background. Other factors affecting information received from citizens, when officers obtain descriptions of persons who have committed crime or when citizens have been the victims of crime, include the citizen's vocabulary and ability to relate an actual observation to the police. The amount of time between the incident and the time it is being reported is also important. Additionally, if people have had similar incidents happen to them in the past, they will be better informed and better able to give accurate descriptions. The emotional state and age of the person who makes the observation are other factors. Younger people, especially males around the age of thirteen, usually give the best descriptions.

Prosecution.   It is important for the patrol officer to realize that the observation made and descriptions given at the time of the occurrence must be available at a later date if prosecution takes place. Inaccuracy of fact will bear heavily on the credibility of testimony given in court. Poor use of words, poor expressions, and exaggerations all tend to discredit the witness.

Experience has shown that most police officers have good control of all their senses, have the power and ability to concentrate when duty is at hand, are able to form a clear and accurate picture of what they see, and are able to look beyond the initial observation to what else will be affected by their ability to observe properly and accurately. However, training repetition is necessary if proficiency is to last.

Pointers on description and observation.   Describing another person or event is difficult. Common mistakes in describing events stem from similarity of different events, bad lighting, emotional conditions, suggestions from others, and time lapses. When they are attempting to obtain descriptions, officers should use and explain to people, "portrait parle" and stress the importance of physical features in the descriptions of individuals. Officers should realize that the head is divided into three parts: the hairline to eyebrows, the eyebrows to the bottom of the nose, and the bottom of the nose to the chin. These three areas should always be considered individually when obtaining descriptions to transmit to other officers for possible apprehension.

Other pointers on observation and description include:

1. Observation is complete and accurate awareness of surroundings.
2. Officers should make notes of observations. Specifically, they should answer who, what, where, how, and why.
3. Factors significant in causing errors concerning an observed event are:
   a. false perception
   b. false interpretation
   c. memory
   d. time lapse between incident and recall
4. The most important element of any personal description is any outstanding or distinguishing peculiarity or characteristic.
5. The eye-level method is the best method for estimating a person's height. (International chart: 5′6″ and under = *small;* 5′6″ to 5′10″ = *medium;* and 5′10″ and over = *tall.*)
6. *Visible scars or marks* are those visible when the individual is fully dressed.
7. Where the time for observation is short and there is an absence of outstanding features, concentrate on the ear and nose.
8. The form of the nose is observed in profile:
   a. depth of the root
   b. general form of the line of the nose
   c. the slope of base
9. Since the ear is the part of the body with a minimum of variation

in form, it is acknowledged to be the most important factor of the identification of the whole face. The ear is composed of a series of ridges and hollows of which it is accepted to describe only the ridges. (Terms: *helix, lobe, tragus, antitragus,* and *folds.*)

10. Description of hair is valuable: color (light or dark brown, black, dyed, etc.), straight or curly, clean or dirty, position of part.
11. All descriptions should be complete.

In summary, observation consists of really seeing what is viewed, developing the ability to tell what was seen, and training ourselves to insure accuracy.

Hazard Factors

Most important to the foot patrol officer is the ability to recognize those factors that create hazards. His doing so is a definite asset in preventing crime or the possibility of crime. Eliminating the opportunity for successful completion of a crime (that is, desire and opportunity) becomes a direct challenge to the foot patrol officer.

Conspicuous and Inconspicuous Patrol

Good patrolling means going through all areas regardless of conditions, in all kinds of weather, day or night. (Patrol comes from the French word "patroluiler," which means going through mud puddles.) Remember that criminals choose the time to work and they choose their time when they think you are not doing your job. As a good patrol or selected foot-patrol officer, you have a choice to patrol conspicuously or inconspicuously.

In the conspicuous patrol you are attempting to decrease crime by removing any opportunity for the successful completion of crime. This patrol allows the public and the criminal to know you are on the job, in the belief that omnipresence discourages any thief, whether amateur or professional, from committing a crime by increasing the risk. Conspicuous patrol promotes good public relations, even though it obligates the officer to the public in that they will see you and more likely seek your help. In patrolling conspicuously you must be very alert to avoid any routine patrol.

Inconspicuous patrolling means that type of patrol activity that attracts little attention: walking close to buildings, dropping in alcoves, walking up and down alleys, walking through parking lots and out-of-the-way places. This is part of the apprehension-prevention concept. That is, if a professional is working on a beat it is probable that no amount of preven-

tion will deter him; the officer must concentrate on i
in order to apprehend the offender, thereby preventing

The best possible patrol would be a combination of
and inconspicuous patrol. For successful patrolling, one o.
is to avoid developing any set habits whatsoever. Do no
place each day; do not talk to the same residents at the
day; if coffee is needed when beginning a shift, drink th ____ at a different place and purchase your coffee from a different location each tour of duty. The foot patrol officer is still the most important segment of policing, responsible for information and regarded as the eyes and ears of the department.

Disadvantages of Foot Patrol

One disadvantage of the past has been alleviated with the availability of the walkie-talkie. Foot officers are available for calls for service, though on a limited basis in the areas where they are patrolling. Another disadvantage is the lack of mobility, in that it often requires much time and energy to answer a call for service, since the officer must travel on foot. Consequently, it is most important that a foot officer or a selected foot officer plan his patrol strategy wisely and that physical fitness programs be an integral part of the patrol program.

[handwritten annotations:] ① Selective foot Patrol ② Use of walki talki inhances foot Patrol ③

Advantages of foot Patrol
① observation is inhances
② easier for premises inspection
③ develop informent
④ develop better knowledge of area
⑤ eyes & ears of dept.
⑥ better police community relations

FOOT PATROL RESEARCH[1]

Recent research in patrol was conducted as a part of the safe and clean neighborhood program in the state of New Jersey. The program provided funds for the foot patrol officer to stabilize and upgrade neighborhoods in thirty cities in New Jersey. The planning and evaluation began in 1976 and all participants agreed on an evaluation design in 1977; the evaluation ended in 1978.

Preliminary statements in the conclusion of the research indicate that typically foot patrol has been rejected as antiquated by agencies and irrelevant to contemporary policing. In most cities it is a "tack-on" supplement program and not integrated into overall patrol strategies. A New Jersey chief of police who approved foot patrol became convinced of foot patrol value as a part of total patrol strategy, but always qualified "if we can still respond to calls."

The new city of study is Newark, New Jersey. The city is typically urban with most of the common urban ills and generally accepted solutions to city problems.

foot officers involved are mostly white, walk in pairs, and are
than their colleagues in cars. They walk foot patrol usually because
they are bored in cars, they like to meet people, and the regular hours (five
days a week) are attractive. The primary concern of the officers walking
in the business and residential districts are the merchants and residents
using the streets and the services of the merchants.

The researchers used a less conservative approach in their analysis;
e.g., individual-respondent mean scores were used in statistical analysis.
The reasons for using this approach, "the less conservative model of
analysis," are:

1. There is a definite pattern in the findings.
2. The consistency persists despite conflict between the police union
   and the city.
3. It confirms the impression from early qualitative analysis that
   foot patrol is recognized and has beneficial results. These impressions were gained interviewing chiefs, city officials, merchants,
   and other relevant persons and walking foot patrol in many New
   Jersey cities as well as London and Birmingham, England;
   Glascow, Scotland; and Sydney and Melbourne, Australia.
4. This effect is powerful because it reflects the activities of police
   officers who, for the most part, are untrained in foot patrol practices, who often do not want to be on foot patrol, who are not well
   integrated into the patrol force, and who are on the foot beat one
   shift per day. Given the modest strength of the stimulus, the consistency of the findings is impressive. (This point can be cut both
   ways. It can be used to argue that stimulus was so slight that
   choosing the less conservative analysis was inappropriate. Given
   1, 2, and 3 above, the evaluators chose to believe the former
   interpretation.)

Summary of Findings

1. The first major finding, significant regardless of analytical approach used, was that residents were aware of levels of foot patrol.
2. Generally, crime levels, as measured by the victimization survey
   and reported crime (to the extent that reported crime measures
   it), are not affected for residents or commercial respondents at
   a significant level. There seem to be no strong trends in the data.
3. In measures dealing with citizens' perception of crime, a different
   pattern emerges. Consistently, residents in beats where foot
   patrol was added see the severity of crime problems diminishing
   in their neighborhoods at levels greater than the other two areas.

Street disorders, serious crime, drug usage, vandalism, victimization of the elderly, and auto theft all are perceived to be less of a problem. The greatest decreases occur in perceptions about street disorders, victimization of the elderly, and auto theft, all of which are street crimes potentially controllable by foot officers. Commercial respondents report a different pattern. When statistical significance is found (street disorder, drugs, teenage loitering, prostitutes, auto theft, rape, and shoplifting), the trend is that the perceived severity of the problem is greatest in the "added" beats (with the exception of auto theft) and least in the "dropped" beats.

4. In looking at the perceived safety of the neighborhood for residents, a pattern similar to that for perceived severity of crime problems emerges. Of the six times statistical significance is found, five favor the "added" beats.

5. A similar pattern emerges in responses to questions about what protective measures residents and merchants take to avoid crime. In three cases—crime avoidance efforts during the day, a composite of crime avoidance efforts, and non-weapon protection against theft—residents of the beats that added foot patrol indicated a greater reduction in the use of protective measures than persons in the other two conditions. No items of significance appeared in the analysis of the commercial respondents' responses.

6. The final attitudinal dimension is the evaluation of police services by resident and commercial respondents. For residents, statistical significance is obtained in all twelve measures; more positive or less negative responses occur in the areas that added foot beats in ten of the twelve measures. Of these ten, two of the questions deal with police services generally and the rest deal with the residents' evaluation of motor patrol services. The overwhelming impression is that positive attitudes gained from foot patrol generalize to other patrol services, an important finding in inner city urban areas, where both citizens and police protest police–citizen alienation.

Thus, the general impression is that, while foot patrol does not have a significant effect on crime, it does affect citizens' fear of crime, the protective measures they take to avoid crime, and the perceived safety of their neighborhoods in consistent and systematic ways. In general, when foot patrol is added, citizens' fear of typical street crimes seems to go down and generalized feelings of personal safety go up.

Finally, foot patrol officers surveyed in New Jersey generally seem to have higher levels of job satisfaction, a more benign

view of citizens, and a more community-oriented view of policing than their colleagues on motor patrol.

On Cost Analysis

The argument on cost analysis is summed up: as more and more police
officers conduct the same activities, the benefit derived from those activities
begins to diminish, so that even if the initial productivity of a motor patrol
officer is ten times that of a foot officer (a questionable assumption, given
the research on preventive patrol and rapid response to calls for service),
a point is reached at which the benefits accrued from a foot officer are
greater than those accrued from the addition of the motor officer. If it can
be shown that there are definite benefits from foot patrol—and the
evaluators believe that that has been demonstrated—and if those benefits
are of value to police agencies and communities, they can be attained at
relatively nominal cost, given the expense and known lack of effectiveness
of motor patrol.

Reviewing, then, this study has found that foot patrol significantly
affects citizens' feelings of safety and fear, as well as their evaluation of
police services. The argument has been that foot patrol attains these goals
under the most difficult of urban circumstances and for people who are
relatively weak and vulnerable.

The goals have been achieved despite the lack of training for foot
patrol officers; the low status of foot patrol as an assignment; the lack of
integration of foot patrol into overall patrol strategy; and the patrolling
of beats for only one shift, five days per week.

We do not suggest that these findings warrant a wholesale return
to foot patrol. There are many cities and areas within cities where the
physical distances between residences and businesses are so great that it
would be unreasonable to expect foot patrol to have a great effect. Further, the empirical literature regarding police strategies is beginning to
suggest a variety of strategies that might have effect, depending upon the
nature of the community problem, the available resources, the mix of
strategies available, etc. But it is an oversimplification to say that foot
patrol is too expensive or that it is simply a public relations technique.
In fact, there are powerful suggestions in this study that foot patrol may
well be an important ingredient in any mix of police strategies that attempt to deal with current problems in congested areas of large cities. If
we are concerned about the problems of the management of the interactions of strangers in cities, foot patrol can be an important factor. It will
not solve all of the community needs. But for those citizens who live, work,
and conduct business in the hearts of our cities and who are threatened

and made fearful by the conduct of strnagers, it offers promise of fear reduction and, by so doing, improvement in the quality of urban life. But it may offer promise of even more.

Conclusion

The program demonstrated value to urban residents who are in great need of it. If the goal of the Safe and Clean Neighborhoods Act was to increase the feelings of safety for citizens using the streets, it has attained that goal. The data here does not show that the program has reduced crime, but there are reasons to believe that if foot patrol were properly integrated into a total police strategy, the potential for doing so exists.

Recommendation. We believe foot patrol could be strengthened in the following ways:

1. Raise the status of foot patrol officers to equal that of other units. The rationale behind this recommendation is that if foot officers are to make their maximum contributions to a complete patrol strategy, their work must be seen as being at least as important as motor patrol. If it is, there are indications that many officers would be drawn to foot patrol both because of inherent characteristics of the work and the potential for regular assignments. As it is, motor patrol still tends to be a magnet which draws many good officers out of foot patrol. If foot patrol is considered important and rewarding, the resulting potential for continuity of assignments can further the officers' familiarity with residents and merchants, and citizens generally. This in turn will enhance all the benefits of foot patrol and provide the best opportunity to test foot patrol's potential to deal with crime.
2. Increase the use of foot officers to respond to calls for service. Research into police response to calls for service indicates that rapid response rarely is warranted. Citizens properly handled by telephone are comfortable with predicted delays. The use of foot officers to respond to all but those rare calls when speedy response is justified will increase the familiarity of the officer with the citizen and vice versa. In addition to having important consequences for citizens' attitudes, the use of foot officers responding to calls for service in their beats can increase their stock of information about citizens, crimes, and victims. This has a crime reduction potential.
3. Provide specific training for foot patrol reflecting its functions.

Although not codified, we believe that knowledge and skill exist about foot patrol that could be systematically taught to officers, both pre- and in-service. Foot patrol is not a slow version of motor patrol but has distinct goals and methods. Our review of existing literature suggests that, though there is relatively little valuable literature regarding foot patrol, materials (perhaps especially case materials) could be developed which could be useful for teaching.

4. Attempt to find ways to use the information foot officers get about criminal activities and individual criminal events as a result of their closeness to a neighborhood. There is research suggesting that effective information gathering and processing has the greatest potential of all current police strategies to increase police effectiveness in dealing with crime. Foot patrol officers have a unique potential to gather information and place it in context. If this information is to be of strategic use, police agencies have to learn both to reward its organization and distribution and to process it effectively.

5. Emphasize closer integration of officers into neighborhood activities. This is not be confused with recommendations that officers move into communities or become public service officers. It suggests, instead, that officers could become neighborhood consultants regarding crime and public order issues. This will require training and flexibility of hours but may have great anti-crime value.

6. Increase the flexibility of hours so that officers are in beats at times of highest street activity and when residents most want to use the streets. This might require data-gathering and analysis by the foot officer, but such activities could bring the officers into closer relations with citizens.

MOTORIZED FOOT PATROL

Motorized foot patrol should be, and is, the most prevalent form of patrol in the United States today. Motorized foot patrol combines the advantages of foot patrol (observation, sources of information, eyes and ears of the department, citizen contact, community relations) with the mobility necessary to alleviate the disadvantages of foot patrol.

Motorized foot patrol calls for a complete team effort between the dispatcher and the motorized foot patrol officer. Each motorized foot patrol officer is furnished with a portable radio so that he maintains constant communications with the dispatcher. Several procedures are available today in the use of the walkie-talkie: e.g., changing batteries after each tour of duty or having portable rechargers in the vehicles themselves. Officers working the motorized foot patrol method must be made aware of the proper manner of carrying these walkie-talkies. On what side shall it be carried, opposite the revolver or on the same side? Will the safety lanyard be carried parallel to the body or across the body? How shall it be worn during periods of inclement weather? At different seasons? They must also be concerned with inspection of the condition and procedure for care and use of this equipment.

If the officer decides to patrol on foot, he must consider several things in parking his vehicle. He must answer two basic questions about the parking location: (1) At what place will the vehicle pay most dividends in omnipresence and prevention? (2) What is my plan for walking so as not to be too far away from the vehicle in case of needed mobility? If the car is not available to be used effectively in the apprehension of an offender, the advantage gained by the motorized foot officer is lost. The officer must also be sure to lock the car and close the windows to prevent anyone from firebombing, stealing, or damaging the vehicle.

To have efficient motorized foot patrol officers, it is necessary that a manpower allocation and distribution study precede the assignment of motorized foot patrol beats. Beat layouts must be compatible to the motorized foot patrol concept of responding to calls for service so that the officers can perform this foot patrol facet of their total patrol responsibility.

The combining of motorized patrol with foot patrol should in no way represent any fault finding with the type of motorized patrol that has been prevalent in law enforcement for the past few years. Instead, it is a meaningful advancement of both systems of patrol brought about through the development and general use of the personal radio. Consider the equation in Figure 6.1.

This equation conveys the fact that originally we had a beat car, either one- or two-man, with a radio. Now the radio has been removed from the vehicle, but in its place the officers have been given personal radios

Figure 6.1 *Beat car to foot-motorized unit*

A. 1 — 2 man beat car $\left(-\left(\begin{array}{c} \text{car} \\ \text{radio} \end{array} \right) + \left(\begin{array}{c} \text{personal} \\ \text{radio} \end{array} \right) \right)$ 1 — 2 man foot motorized unit

B. 1 — 1 man beat car $\left(-\left(\begin{array}{c} \text{car} \\ \text{radio} \end{array} \right) + \left(\begin{array}{c} \text{personal} \\ \text{radio} \end{array} \right) \right)$ 1 — 1 man foot motorized unit (portable) that they can take with them wherever they go. They still have the traditional capability to patrol their assigned beat in an irregular pattern while in their vehicle, but now they can also park and lock vehicle, notify the communications center, and continue their patrol on foot. After completing their objectives through walking the beat, they return to the vehicle, notify the communications center, and once again become motorized unit. At any time while they walk they can be ordered back into their vehicle by the communication center. The communication channel for this motorized foot patrol has not been altered (see Figure 6.2).

Selective patrol operations are indispensible and will continue to be the backbone of the police service. Patrol officers are responsible for the performance of all primary police tasks. To be efficient in his duties a patrol officer must use all the tools available. The squad car created increased mobility and contained the communications equipment vital in maintaining the lifeline of the officer on the street. Now the squad car serves as transportation around the beat and can be used for quick arrival at the

Figure 6.2 *Foot/motorized-patrol communications channel*

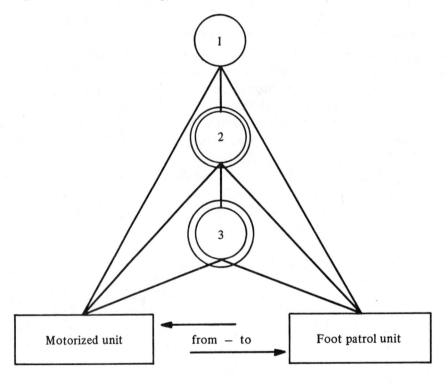

1. Communications center
2. Field lieutenant
3. Patrol/Tactical sergeant

scene of a crime, disturbance, etc., when needed. While on foot, through individual contacts with citizens, the officer can fulfill his patrol objectives and gain the positive community support necessary to achieve the total goals of the department.[2]

SELECTIVE FOOT PATROL

Selective foot patrol involves the discreet selection of a given area of a community where foot patrol at certain times would produce patrol objectives more than any other type of patrol. Selective, or limited, foot patrol is used because twenty-four-hour foot patrol would not produce wanted results any more effectively than, say, selected foot patrol for an eight-hour watch and thus would waste manpower.

Selective foot patrol combines the old with the new. Computer printouts regarding manpower allocation and distribution and the appropriate method of patrol can be used to determine whether selective foot patrol or twenty-four-hour patrol would be most effective. Selective foot patrol uses all the quality know-how, judgments, duties, and responsibilities of the regular foot patrol.

It is also concerned with community stability. We have often seen an officer lose contact with persons or residents of the area within which he is working because of mechanized patrol. In some cases, alienation and hostility develop to the point that he is considered an occupation force. Clearly written procedures and professional police training can decrease this type of confrontation and conflict between the patrol officer and the community. The increase in mechanized patrol was accompanied by confrontation, especially in the urban area, so the use of innovation–selective foot patrol–should help solve this particular problem.

Selective foot patrol affects both crime and community stability.

Crime

In solving the crime problem, the first step is to use historical crime data to determine that the given area is not too large for effective foot patrol and is temporally distributed so that an eight-hour shift of foot patrol officers can be effectively implemented. In some cases a sixteen-hour broken shift may be necessary to solve the several categories of crime occurring in a given area at different locations and times. Each area (outline of that area could be in the shape of a straight-away, cross, T-shape, X) to be covered by the foot patrol officer must be designed so that it is within his means to do the job for which he has been assigned.

Second, the administrator must isolate and analyze each particular situation and determine the best method of patrol to decrease the particular crime prevailing on the beat. Thus, the patrol administrator must analyze, evaluate, and act "before the fact."

Third, after choosing the best method of patrol, the administrator must then select the appropriate officer to perform that method of patrol for a given category of crime. For example, in the purse snatch category of robbery we would look to our younger officers who have the running ability to apprehend any subject perpetrating such a crime and who possess the alertness and aggressiveness to maintain constant vigilance on a given area. The patrol leader must advise the officer of the total situation and then evaluate, document, and inform the officer of the effect his patrol has had on that given area and that given category of crime.

In effect, the area of selective foot patrol for crime problems contains within it the total application of patrol administration. We see planning, selection, training, informing, leadership, documentation, analysis, evaluation, and flexibility. Allowing the officer to be part of the initial planning of the selective foot beat will enhance the possibility of success. The selection of the area by using the historical data for a given eight-hour period must be done on a need basis. All the principles of organization must be taken into consideration; e.g., span of control and unity of command.

Community Stability

The other main purpose for using a selected foot-patrol beat is to maintain community stability within a given area. Experience tells us that in certain cases police officers can be catalysts to riots and explosive situations. This can develop from an officer's mishandling of a family problem or a fight or a disorderly drunk person on the street, and it can occur anytime from the evening hours to the morning hours when most bars close.

An indication that the leader in patrol must take special interest in a given area comes from the occurrence of crime there and the realization that community stability in a given area is poor because police officers are being assaulted and beaten and have to call for officer assistance each time they make an arrest. Selective foot patrol is one of the methods to combat this type of activity against officers in urban areas. The police leader must continually be aware of these types of activities and maintain a feeling of the pulse of the respective communities within his area of responsibility so that he may determine the degree to which this hostility has extended and know when selected foot patrol would be the best method to alleviate the condition.

Community relations units may render assistance to patrol in given areas by identifying potential problems (poor police attitude, no recrea-

tion facilities, etc.). However, it is the immedia[t]
leaders of the command structure who are resp[...]
community's stability, not the community re[...]
relations units should be used to suppleme[...]
tions person—the beat officer—in solving [...]
the proper officer to walk a foot beat is [...]
available for solving community relati[...]

An example is a street intersection w[...]
cupied by a bar, a grocery store, a cleaning estab[...]
dromat. This intersection had problems throughout the eve[...]
into the early morning. Arrests had been made in the area and ea[...]
officers made arrests, rocks and bottles were thrown, police vehicles were
damaged, officers were injured, and the community in general was shaken.
The identification of the obvious problems and the analysis of the in-depth
problems indicated a need for a concentrated effort by a selected police officer with the ability to deal with this type of a situation. The officer chosen
in effect was given a staff study to do while working his beat. After months
of working this beat, the officer realized that the majority of the community
was in support of the police officers working in that area. However, a very
few of the younger males were attempting to exercise leadership over a
larger group of young people in the area and found that by showing this
type of contempt for the law-enforcement officers, leadership would come
their way. Selected foot beats were initiated for eight-hour periods, from
6:00 P.M. until 2:00 A.M. The result, a reduction in criminal activity, was
almost instantaneous. While this particular officer was working, no other
incidents such as had been experienced in the past with relation to community stability and assaults on officers or explosive incidents occurred.

Selective foot patrol, especially with constant communications
available, has a definite place in law enforcement today. It is difficult to
envision any period in the future when selected foot patrol would not be
one of the best possible solutions to a given problem. Technically, the officer must know how to patrol on foot, be able to relate to crime problems,
know the importance of community relations, and have a feeling of belonging both to the police organization and to the community that he is serving. If these qualities exist, the selective foot patrol beat will be a success.
Beneficial results will prevail in police agencies where patrol leaders have
developed the expertise to use selective foot patrol properly.

2 MAN Cars Advantages:
① on the hand consultation
② More observant
③ safer
④ greater deterrence
⑤ help keep alert

MOTORIZED PATROL

Advantages

The effectiveness of motorized patrol cannot be denied. To accomplish the
three basic missions of a patrol officer: (1) prevent crime and disorder, (2)

① used in conjunction with Foot Patrol
② greater response time
③ increase apprehension of felons
④ Provides protection
⑤ Transportation
⑥ greater mobility
⑦ Cheaper than foot Ptl.
⑧ Less fatigue
⑨ More conspicuous
⑩ more available for Calls for svc.
⑪ Safer

and (3) provide a superior product of service to the commu-
ty's society the auto is sine qua non.

ention of Crime and Disorder

The auto allows an officer to respond rapidly to any incident, and, since apprehension is directly related to response time, the auto increases the opportunity for apprehending the criminal. Less fatigue on the part of the officer in driving as opposed to other types of patrol allows him to be more alert, especially at the end of his tour of duty. The auto easily handles the prevention aspect of patrol, since an irregular driving pattern allows different approaches. Double-back, concentric, stationary, and zig-zag patterns are all part of the unpredictable patrolling of a beat. The quadrant style of cutting off escape routes is available only to auto patrol. There is no way to do an effective manpower-workload analysis and implementation if auto patrol is not one of the choices of patrol methods. In the outlying section of urban areas, the beat sizes are legitimately large enough so that the only way each citizen is provided his fair share of police protection and service is by the use of auto patrol. Omnipresence, conspicuous patrolling, and reducing opportunity for successful completion of crime are all important parts of crime prevention. The auto is instantly involved.

Disorders, whether large or small, can be controlled most effectively if the ability to respond with sufficient force (people) is available at all times to the patrol commander. If it's an athletic event that erupts; a rock concert that ends in a highly emotional state, sending thousands of youths into the streets at the same time in a frenzied condition; or a spontaneous incident, such as an arrest on the street of a drunken couple at the time the bars are closing, the auto patrol provides the tool to meet the time and force factor. Additionally, where an officer needs assistance, just the fact that vehicles are on the way with sirens, lights, or both activated may reduce the probability of serious injury to an officer.

Two factors are significant when dealing with auto patrol. One is the need to control response to the many different situations by number of cars and approach of cars. The other is the need to emphasize proper driving techniques, especially when patrolling routinely (most police accidents occur on routine patrol) to insure an adequate fleet safety record. The importance of supervision in patrol is highlighted when attempting to resolve these two problems. It seems that when officers have certain calls (robbery in progress, assist an officer), all hell breaks loose inside them. The adrenalin begins to work and they become the only persons on the road. Good supervision is tantamount to a good fleet safety record.

If the officer is provided with proper information, he will be able to place himself in a position to prevent a recurrence of the same crime by developing a strategy for patrol. If an officer recognizes police hazards, he will realize the hazard of a bus-transfer corner, for instance. Intersections where people must transfer from one public conveyance to another are locations where purse-snatching can be prevented. An officer who is aware will position himself at that location at critical times in order to prevent any such incident. From this point he can proceed to the next location on his beat where his presence gives him the opportunity to receive maximum dividends for his investment of time as a preventive action. Combining instinct, knowledge, awareness, planning, and information with the officer, auto, and communication creates a real tool for prevention.

Let's add to this three types of crime prevention cited by the International Association of Chiefs of Police.[3] The first method is the use of mechanical devices: safes, locks, burglar alarms, bullet-proof glass, light, leaded or barred windows. The second is controlling conditions through athletic clubs, recreation centers, dispersing gangs, and returning juveniles to their homes. The third is juvenile counseling. When the thought process is put to use by each officer in the crime prevention area, resources are provided, and proper training is available, there will result an all-purpose officer with enough challenge for an immersion into the patrol function and the potential for improvement in innovation and creativity in the patrol force.

Law Enforcement

The mobility given an officer by the auto will also enhance the inspection of persons, places, and things that might be termed violations and will thus lead to an improved ability to enforce the laws of the community. Weather is not a deterrent to the use of the auto. The auto permits the patrol function to be accomplished constantly. In performing the law enforcement tasks of arrest, search and seizure, field interview and investigation, the auto can carry that equipment necessary for these tasks.

Service

Any incident that affects any one of our citizens becomes at the time of occurrence an all-encompassing situation when related to the interaction between the citizen involved and the police department. Statistically speaking, more than two-thirds of the police calls for service are of the non-criminal nature. In effect, policing has become primarily a service agency.

There is really nothing to equal the feeling a citizen gets when a call for police service is made and in a matter of minutes an officer arrives to provide intelligent service. Giving prompt service and knowing what to do after arriving are equal partners in response to calls for service. We may reduce response time by adjusting the formula in manpower-distribution studies, but it will be to no avail if after the officer arrives he does not complete the request knowledgeably and sincerely.

For any department to give service to the best of its ability, a distribution of the patrol force according to need, by time and place, should be the policy followed. The use of all types of patrol and reduction of response time to call for service are basic ingredients for consideration when reaching a decision on proper beat layout. The proper layout has a large impact on a department's ability to respond to calls for service effectively.

One-Officer Car

Very few police departments can afford to assign two officers to every beat car. Even in the past, when most of the officers in a police department were walking beats, the patrol leader had to decide where and when officers would walk alone or in pairs. A foot officer walking alone must know where the closest call-box is located and possess the equipment to signal a partner for assistance (whistle, flashlight, baton). Each officer, in any type of patrol, should develop for himself the best method to obtain assistance by the quickest means available. Developing rapport with the citizens on the beat is of primary importance, since many times it is a matter of self-preservation.

In deciding upon the use of the one-officer car, patrol administrators should consider police hazards, calls for service, seriousness of crime, amount of criminal activity by time and place, arrests, access to the individual officers by other officers (this factor considers the routes that would be taken by assisting officers in case of emergency; it is more relevant in outlying areas), assaults on police officers, and incidents where weapons have been used. (These same factors apply also in determining the beats where two-officer cars should operate.)

Advantages of one-officer car.   There are numerous advantages to one-officer cars. First, the cost of providing two-officer cars to every beat is not always feasible. The use of one-officer patrol would reduce costs. Second, the area covered by patrol can be double that handled by two-officer cars. Third, the ability to respond to a citizen's call for service would be increased. Many calls can be handled by one person. Instead of having two officers out of service as would be the case with a two-officer car, the second person

would be available for additional calls. Fourth, the one-officer car operation enhances the team concept. Each of the officers assigned a one-officer
car beat within a sector of patrol is like a player on a team. If one officer
makes an error, it might make him unavailable to assist his fellow officers,
so he automatically becomes more aware of the position he plays on the
team. This makes for an improved total operation. Fifth, one officer alone
knows he must perform using his own ability primarily. This makes him
more observant, more aware, and more alert regarding his surroundings.
He or she is not distracted by the conversation of a partner. He operates
more intelligently and objectively since he does not have to prove himself
to another officer. It is easier to evaluate the officer operating a one-officer
car, and it is easier to place responsibility, authority, and accountability.
This placing of responsibility, authority, and accountability is a motivating
factor for individual performance.

Officers in Britain, some observers have said, must be more courteous
because they do not have the assortment of weapons that American officers
have. This may not be totally true, but one point is very significant. The
British police must develop courtesy and the ability to go that extra step
because of the lack of weapons, and also the British culture is affected by
gentlemanliness. This does not mean less masculine, but the British police
officer does not resort to authority quite so fast as his American counter-
part. On the other hand, the American police officer has developed from
the concept of self-reliance and masculinity and has consequently resorted
to his authority quicker. The one-officer car is compatible with increased
courtesy. Finally, the use of more cars on the street via the one-officer car
system gives the impression of police being everywhere and decreases the
sense of fear in the community.

Objections to the one-officer car. The first objection usually raised is
that officers are safer when they work in pairs. The Uniform Crime Reports of the Federal Bureau of Investigation show that more officers are
assaulted while operating the one-man car than the two-man car.[4] Additionally, with one-man cars officers are more likely not to take chances
or perform carelessly. The two-man vehicle operation does lead to the officers' being slightly more reckless.

There is another theory that the officer in a one-man car will not perform aggressive patrol. The theory is rejected because of years of experience
walking a beat alone without any communication. The independent officer
and his intelligent use of procedures and cunning will prevail in the
art of aggressive patrol. Two officers in a car will not necessarily insure
aggressive patrol; in fact, it may only insure more recklessness and
unproductiveness.

Another objection to the one-man car is that the officer cannot drive a car and observe at the same time. However, no studies have shown that when there are two men in the car observation is increased or improved. The one-man-car operation demands that the officer be more observant rather than less.

In the final analysis, the selection of the one-officer or the two-officer car needs study and review. The patrol administrator must necessarily take into consideration the safety of the officer.

Success of the one-officer car. For the one-officer operation to be successful, standard operating procedures should be written and published. Procedures should be applied locally, but certain principles can be applied to all one-officer car operations. (1) Team effort between dispatcher and officer is essential. The officer must let the dispatcher know what he is doing (e.g., when stopping a vehicle, inform the dispatcher of the tag number and the location of the stop). The dispatcher should attempt to give the one-officer car officer as much information as possible about an assignment. (2) The one-officer patrol car officer should know the beat and for the most part stay within the boundaries, understand the part played by the dispatcher regarding his or her own safety, and respond only "in the direction of" rather than necessarily "to" a call given to the officer on an adjoining beat. He should stay within his own beat, ready to strike, always alert, and at the most appropriate location.

The administrator also must consider the supporting services necessary to sustain the increase of vehicles to provide one-officer car service. Only after conducting a manpower-workload analysis and evaluating resources can the final decision be made. If he or she makes this on a need basis, the administrator can feel confident of a proper decision.

Two-Officer Car

There is justification for two-officer vehicles. Factors to consider have been stated previously under the one-officer car operation. The patrol administrator should not be limited to the use of two-officer cars when the situation indicates a need for more officers. Intelligence gathering becomes a significant factor under certain conditions relative to assignment of manpower to a particular beat.

For example, a patrol commander may receive information that after a demonstration, one of his officers will be surprised and attacked, and if he resists too much, he might even be killed. Assessment of the information is so very important because from the intelligence gathered, a decision must be made on manpower assignment. If the intelligence is accurate and the time can be pinpointed, it is not too difficult to make effective decisions. If the approximate time of the predicted attack is not available, then the decision becomes more difficult. Factors to be considered in this situation involve manpower available and manpower flexibility. Should the patrol leader supply two officers to the beat involved? Should he supply two officers to each adjacent beat? Should a supervisor ride with the beat officer involved? What additional equipment should they carry, if any? If a shotgun is selected, should it be carried openly? Questions such as these must be answered by the patrol administrator. The best answer is a decision based upon need, conditions, and, most important, the safety of all officers concerned. The ability to be flexible, an asset developed by the patrol administrator, should provide any resource necessary to resolve the problem. The solution may be a three-officer car for a given period of time. The administrator should be willing to make this decision.

Evaluating the Effectiveness of One-Officer Versus Two-Officer Patrol Units[5]

The issue of one- versus two-officer patrol units has been a subject of debate among police researchers for over twenty years. While many decry the postulated merits of one-officer patrol, recent surveys indicate that an increasing number of U.S. metropolitan police departments are adopting this staffing strategy. Despite this major change in manpower allocation, the effect such a change would have on police patrol has not been widely researched. Most statements made on the subject have been speculative. It is now known what the implications of using one- versus two-officer patrol units are, let alone which of the two methods of patrol should be adopted under different circumstances.

Issues and Performance Measures

The pros and cons of each staffing strategy, as debated in the literature, are remarkably consistent. Briefly the arguments are as follows:

> For a given manpower level, the use of one-officer units enables the fielding of twice the number of patrol cars as the use of two-officer units. This doubling of units allows for an increase in (1) police visibility; (2) time spent on preventive patrol, hence increasing the probability of detecting a crime in progress; (3) average area covered by patrol. It also allows for a decrease in response time. To achieve this same level of patrol by using two-officer units would involve doubling the number of patrol officers, a very expensive proposition.

Alternatively, for a given cost constraint, more units may be fielded using one-officer, as opposed to two-officer, staffing, again allowing for improved patrol performance. Thus the use of one-officer patrol units provides a more efficient, cost-effective service system than could be realized thorough the use of two-officer units.

On the other hand, two-officer cars are preferred to one-officer units for reasons of safety. The presence of a second officer provides built-in cover for the first officer. Two-officer units do not take as long to service calls as one-officer units due to the additional manpower available on the scene. One two-officer unit is less expensive than two one-officer units, and since many calls cannot be handled by single one-officer units, the cost of servicing such calls is higher for one-officer staffing than for two-officer staffing. Thus, the use of two-officer patrol units provides a safer and better quality service than the use of one-officer units.

It is interesting to note the type of reasoning that is being employed in these arguments. For example, the arguments in favor of one-officer patrol are products of "linear" thinking: "It is obvious that patrol coverage can be twice as intensive with 2 one-man cars as it can be with 1 two-man car" (Chicago Police Department, 1963: 213). As will be shown later, situations arise where patrol "intensity" due to two one-officer cars may be less than twice, twice, or greater than twice that of one two-officer car.

From the arguments stated above, one may elicit relevant performance measures by which to evaluate the effectiveness of one- versus two-officer units. Those measures chosen for comparative analysis include:

1. expected area covered by patrol;
2. response time from the nearest vehicle to a randomly occurring incident;
3. expected frequency of patrol;
4. visibility of patrol;
5. probability of intercepting a randomly occurring crime in progress;
6. probability of officer injury;
7. comparative costs.

Kaplan goes on to discuss probabilistic models which are constructed to compare the two staffing strategies, including in some instances numerical examples using actual experimental data from the study: Patrol staffing in San Diego: One- or two-officer units which illustrate the models used. Kaplan continues his discussion, addressing each measure chosen from comparative analysis; i.e., coverage, response time, patrol frequency, visibility, crime interception, officer injury, and costs. The mathematical equations used are too voluminous for our purposes, and the interested student is referred to the journal article for a closer look at the discussion.

This article began with a discussion of the postulated advantages of one- versus two-officer patrol. Relevant performance measures were elicited from this discussion, and models were constructed to formalize expectations about the levels of these performance measures under the two staffing strategies. The results include:

1. Doubling the number of available units in a beat increases the expected area covered by less than twice.
2. Increases in coverage gained by a switch to two one-officer units per beat are most significant when:
   i.   beat sizes are large,
   ii. travel speeds are low,
   iii. coverage is defined for low travel times.
3. Given that units are free, the reduction in expected travel time due to a switch to two one-officer units is only around 28 percent.
4. If one-officer and two-officer units have equal service times, and allowing for the possibility of busy units, the reduction in expected travel time due to a switch to two one-officer units does not exceed 40 percent.
5. Response delays are less frequent with many "slow" servers (one-officer units) than with few "fast" servers (two-officer units). Hence, the reduction in response times (including queuing delay) due to a switch to one-officer staffing may be quite large.
6. If one-officer and two-officer units have equal service times, then a switch to two one-officer units per beat will increase patrol frequency by at least 100 percent. If one- and two-officer units have different service times, patrol frequency is likely to increase by more than 100 percent, though it may increase by less than 100 percent.
7. Percentage increases in absolute visibility are the same as percentage increases in patrol frequency. Noticeable increases in police visibility are only likely to set in after some initial, "critical" level of one-unit patrol has been reached.
8. The increase in the probability of intercepting a randomly occurring crime in progress due to a switch to two one-officer units per beat may be less than, equal to, or greater than 100 percent, depending on the fraction of time units are out of service.
9. The magnitudes of interception probabilities are small.
10. Increases in interception probabilities due to the adoption of one-officer-per-unit staffing are most significant for beats with heavy workloads.
11. In San Diego, the probability of officer-specific injury is roughly the same for one- and two-officer staffing.
12. The additional cost due to switching from one two-officer unit per beat to two one-officer units per beat is the cost of maintaining a second vehicle, which in San Diego is $2.51/hour/unit.
13. Equal-cost alternatives favor maximum use of one-officer units. In San Diego, 1.84N one-officer units may be fielded for the same cost as N two-officer units.

The conclusion by Kaplan:

- Research was not meant to be exhaustive.
- One important item is the need for backup support when using one-officer vehicles. Both the frequency of backup requests and the logistics of backup assignments may be investigated analytically.
- The patrol frequency and crime interception models may be improved by relaxing the uniformity assumptions: patrol may be spatially distributed according to a coverage function, and crime may take on a spatial as well as temporal distribution.
- Investigate the distinction between interception and apprehension. Kaplan notes that there is no attempt to distinguish between apprehension and interception; equivalently, the tacit assumption being made if Pr (apprehension $\times$ interception) = 1.0.
- For officer safety, more examination of injury statistics from different cities are required.
- Assessment of on-scene performance of one- versus two-officer units is required.

Hopefully, we will be able to develop standards of performance.

FOOT AND AUTO COMBINATION: A TEAM APPROACH

There are two combinations of patrol games that can be played: one by the two-man car; the other, by a one-man car with a foot beat included. For the former, the manpower-workload study has indicated a beat should be a two-man car operation. Other statistics indicate a need for increased preventive patrol of a given location within this two-man beat. One way to accomplish this preventive patrol would be to make two one-man cars out of this one two-man car while maintaining the essential features of the two-man car concept. Intelligent and informed officers will resist the change from a two-man car to a one-man car or even two one-man cars if it is done arbitrarily and without explanation. Patrol administrators should therefore handle this patrol decision using participatory management. Benefits may accrue that might not be possible ordinarily. Including personnel in the decision-making process is most important when attempting to implement change. In this case, if the officers involved are consulted and the procedure is explained and if ample time is provided for them to offer suggestions, agreement should be reached to give it a try. The commander must emphasize the fact that, whatever the outcome, he will be responsible for any negative accusations that might be made by the citizens. (A potential exists for reduced response by both cars.) The entire procedure involves these steps:

1. A concentrated area needing more preventive patrol within a two-man beat.
2. The objective of the procedure is stated to the officers and supervisors involved.
3. The call numbers of the new two one-man cars are determined; e.g., 911 and 911A (this procedure is the only one involving this type of call number, which distinguishes the method being used).
4. The supervisor and officers review together the areas and category of crime [*robbery* (purse snatching, etc.), *burglary* (commercial-dwelling)] by time of day, day of week, and location.
5. The administrator determines ahead of time the way the area will be patrolled—either random saturation or each officer shall allot a given time for coverage of the area.
6. In no case will either officer respond to a call for service without the other.
7. If for any reason (lunch, personal) one officer is out of service, so is the other.
8. If an on-view situation occurs, the officer observing will call the other before taking action. (The second car will not have anything delaying response and in most cases will not be more than a few streets away.)
9. The leader sets up a procedure for a careful analysis of crime prior to, during, and after the use of the combination-team effort.
10. The leader assures the officers that the deployment is temporary and is being attempted to resolve a specific problem. After the problem has been resolved, the traditional two-man car will be reinstated. This is necessary and will be accepted. Officers realize the reasons why cars are two man. They will accept this procedure knowing it is being done for a reason and on a need basis. If trust and credibility are not included, the innovation will fail.
11. The supervisor advises the communications personnel of the procedure and describes to the dispatcher his important role in accomplishing the objective.
12. The supervisor documents and commends as appropriate all concerned after the goal has been reached.

A similar team effort is employed between the one-man car operation and the foot officer. Coverage of a given area where many incidents of crime occur can be done by time and location. When prevention has not worked, a game of apprehension can be implemented. An officer working a foot beat can make himself obvious at one end of the beat. The perpetrator at the other end, thinking he is clear to commit his crime, does not realize the one-man car officer has taken a position of surveillance (and possibly has received help from his supervisor who would cover an escape route). As a result, the perpetrator is caught in the act of committing the crime.

A game of inspection of police hazards between the foot officer and the one-man car officer can be played by having each responsible for one part of an hour. For example, the car officer will be responsible from the hour to quarter past and from the half-hour to quarter of the hour. The foot officer would be responsible for a given location from quarter past to the half-hour and from quarter of the hour to the hour. This rotation can be changed anytime they agree, by the day or during the watch. In this example, whatever time an offense occurred, the officer responsible would have to justify why it occurred and why he didn't make the arrest.

TWENTY-FOUR-HOUR PATROL

The leader in using twenty-four-hour patrol was the Indianapolis, Indiana Police Department, which began using it in September 1969. Since then, many police departments across the country have developed the twenty-four-hour patrol operation. The success or failure of their plans depends on several categories that are common to all of the programs but must be evaluated by each department on an individual basis. If omnipresence is believed to be the leading factor to decreasing crime, one would presume that twenty-four-hour patrol has to be a good procedure. However, other considerations, such as cost, risk, accidents, crime, and the actual relationship of crime to the omnipresence approach, must be reviewed before a conclusion can be drawn.

The initial planning for twenty-four-hour patrol includes budgeting, specification, and maintenance. Local government must be willing to expend, in some cases, a sizeable amount of money to initiate this type of patrol. The Indianapolis program necessitated a budget increase of more than $400,000, which moved the fleet from 110 vehicles to 455 vehicles. Average annual increases in vehicle replacement, prevention maintenance, repair costs, and insurance premiums also must be considered. As with all programs, the effectiveness of such a plan must be measurable. Therefore, standard criteria and measuring devices must be set up prior to implementation to insure proper and accurate evaluation. The administrator should be able to state honestly the amount of success or failure of a program and recommend either continuing because of the amount of success or discontinuing because of failure. If the plan has not failed completely, but has not paid off to a worthwhile extent, the department should state so frankly and take the appropriate action.

Internal Orders

Prior to implementing such a plan, it is necessary to put in writing orders covering the "who," "when," and "where" concerning the use of police department vehicles. Will all personnel be issued a marked vehicle? If not, who, and what rank? Those personnel who are issued a marked patrol vehicle for full-time use must have clear and concise responsibilities spelled out. The Indianapolis, Indiana Police Department states the following responsibilities:

> The department purchases the vehicle, provides all preventive maintenance, gasoline, repairs (mechanical and body), and pays for insurance coverage. Field lieutenants, sergeants, and patrolmen are usually the first to be issued personal marked patrol vehicles. They are solicited to use their patrol vehicle while off duty, but when doing so, must maintain radio contact at all times so as to be available for emergencies which may occur in their immediate vicinity. Individual officers are responsible for cleanliness of their vehicle, inside and outside, must change their own flat tires when off duty, and are responsible for washing their own car.[6]

Areas of Analysis for Evaluation

If the goal of the plan is to reduce crime, it is necessary to determine which crimes are related to this type of patrol. Preventive patrol is usually most successful with potentially suppressible crimes such as burglary, robbery, auto theft, and larceny. Therefore, an evaluation relative to these specific crimes would be most meaningful.

In addition to achieving the goal of reducing crime, omnipresence patrolling provides these byproducts: added man-hours on patrol, increased patrolling, availability of officers for mobilization under emergency conditions, and response to calls for service while in off-duty status. These are very difficult to evaluate. Other areas regarding extra patrol that can be measured are: (1) travel for preventive maintenance, repairs, etc. while off duty; (2) patrol time picked up at change of shift; and (3) additional patrol time for each officer reporting for work and returning home.

Accidents and Citations

The categories of increased or decreased fleet and citizen accidents and increased issuance of citations are important to any program involving greater use of marked patrol vehicles. Very few patrol administrators are satisfied about the number of accidents involving their police vehicles. More accidents occur while on routine patrol than in response to emergency, and the twenty-four-hour patrol plan increases the use of police vehicles in routine patrol or nonemergency conditions. Therefore, a very important consideration for the administrator is the possibility of more fleet accidents. When relating the twenty-four-hour patrol program to the total picture, if citizen accidents can be decreased, the program will show a saving for the citizen in terms of loss of money, loss of time from work, repair bills, hospital costs, insurance premiums, and most of all, possible saving of lives. The category of citations is relative and must be equated to enforcement index and decrease of accidents.

Prince George's County, Maryland, police officers using their patrol cars during off-duty hours made 1,438 arrests in the first year of the experimental project, according to a report released recently. The report, considered the most complete ever attempted by any police jurisdiction on an off-duty patrol car use program, said 139 of the arrests were for serious crimes, 354 for misdemeanors, and 900 for traffic.

The county instituted the project in the hope of reducing crime by having more cars on the streets at all hours of the day and night. The 365 police officers—about two-thirds of the force—who participated in the program were permitted to take their patrol cars home and use them off-duty hours for shopping, running errands, and even dates. All told, they investigated 12,799 incidents, 7,355 of them responses to situations observed by the off-duty policemen themselves.

Other advantages resulting from the program included increased contact between policemen and citizens, quicker response to calls by off-duty personnel returning to duty for emergencies, and increased morale.

Decision

Whether or not to use twenty-four-hour patrol is a decision to be made after considering many factors. Comparisons of similar advantages and restrictions among departments are most helpful, but in the final analysis, each department must be its own judge regarding implementation of the program. Experimentation in one area or one shift or one district or one division may help decide on the proper course of action.

The Indianapolis Police Department, the members of the department, the city, and the government officials should feel great satisfaction in their attempt to produce better methods of police service. The following is a conclusion drawn from a study of the twenty-four-hour patrol plan of the Indianapolis Police Department by Raymond A. Walton, Jr.

This study has attempted to analyze the Indianapolis Police Department's Fleet Plan. To arrive at a conclusion on a cost vs. savings basis, as many areas as possible have been translated into dollar values. Table 6.1 gives the findings.

. . . the result of this study is that the citizens of Indianapolis have thus far saved about $1.3 million on the Indianapolis Police Department Fleet Plan.

Further, it is recommended that any police department considering conversion to a Fleet Plan should include in this conversion a pre-established method of collecting data for periodic analysis of the plan's effectiveness. In this way a department can either justify the continuation of a Fleet Plan or make necessary changes in the plan which keep it an on-going and effective program.[7]

OFFICER SAFETY AND SURVIVAL

No discussion of patrol and the use of one-man vs. two-man patrol can be concluded without reviewing what has happened in the past relative to the safety of police officers. The patrol administrator must never forget the time when he was a patrolman. He must always be aware of what was most important to him then. Providing the patrol officer with the knowledge that his leaders have painstakingly researched the criteria involved in deciding on the selection of the type of patrol has high priority.

Table 6.1

Costs		
Initial cost		$ 650,000
Minus the 255 cars which would have been purchased under the old Plan in 1969, 1970, 1971		−$ 510,000
	Net Cost	$ 140,000
Increase in Preventive Maintenance/Repairs		$ 317,000
Increase in cost of insurance coverage		$ 52,000
Savings		
Car Washes		$ 7,000
Decrease in Visible Crimes		$ 500,000
Decrease in Citizens' Accidents		$ 700,000
Increased Man-hours of Patrol Time		$ 635,000
Total Costs		$ 509,000
Total Savings		$1,842,000
	Difference	$1,333,000

Source: Raymond A. Walton, Jr., *Study of Twenty-Four-Hour Patrol* (Indianapolis: Indianapolis Police Department). Reprinted by permission.

The fact that their safety has been considered stands out in the minds of patrol officers.

Officer Deaths

A review of the history of officers killed in the police field reveals significant facts of which the administrator should be aware. These facts indicate areas of concern for the patrol administrator, especially when the need for increased training is shown. If by emphasizing a particular police technique an officer's life may be saved, the emphasis placed is more than worth the effort involved in review of statistics and the appropriate follow-up to reduce fatalities. If most officers are killed when attempting to take a person into custody, then the inspection process by line commanders of proper arrest techniques should be first priority.

Figure 6.3 gives a regional breakdown for law enforcement officers killed 1970–1979.

Figure 6.3 *Law enforcement officers killed 1970–1979*

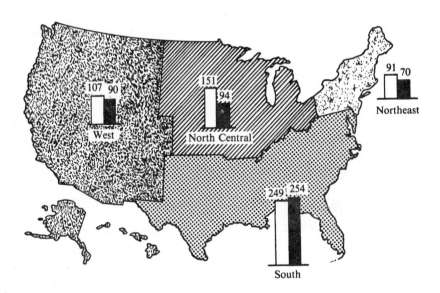

Total, All Regions
1970-1974 ☐ 611 KILLED
1975-1979 ■ 532 KILLED

13 24
*Puerto Rico
U.S. Virgin Islands
Guam
Foreign

Source: Federal Bureau of Investigation, *Uniform Crime Reports, 1979* (Washington, D.C.: U.S. Government Printing Office, 1979), p. 308.

Law Enforcement Officers Killed[8]

In 1979, 106 local, county, state, and federal law enforcement officers were feloniously killed as compared to 93 in 1978. During the 10-year period, 1970–1979, 1,143 officers were slain. It should be noted that the collection of statistics regarding officers killed in the line of duty was expanded in 1971 to include United States' territories (Puerto Rico, the Virgin Islands, and Guam). Also, the gathering of data on slain federal officers was begun in 1972. Therefore, 10-year data on officers killed include figures for United States' territories since 1971 and federal officers since 1972.

Year	Number of Victim Officers
1970	100
1971	129
1972	116
1973	134
1974	132
1975	129
1976	111
1977	93
1978	93
1979	106
Total	1,143

Geographic Locations

As in previous years, more officers (49) were slain in 1979 in the country's most populous region, the south, than in any other. Twenty-three officers were killed in the western states, 16 in the north central states, 13 in the northeastern states, 3 in Puerto Rico, and 2 in Guam. The accompanying chart shows the number of law enforcement officers killed in the geographic regions during each of two successive 5-year periods, 1970–1974, and 1975–1979. Information on officers feloniously killed in 1979 by geographic division and population group is presented in the following table.

Of the 106 officers slain during 1979, 101 were from 87 different local, county, state, and federal law enforcement agencies in 30 states. As indicated above, the remaining 5 were from Puerto Rico and Guam. Among the states, California, with 10 officers slain, lost more officers in line-of-duty deaths than any other. The state of Texas followed with 8 officers killed.

Circumstances Surrounding Deaths

During the year, 19 officers were slain by persons engaged in the commission of a robbery or during the pursuit of robbery suspects, and 7 lost their lives at the scene of burglaries or while pursuing burglary suspects. Twenty-one officers were killed while attempting arrests for crimes other than robbery or burglary.

Amush situations accounted for 11 officers' deaths in 1979. Seventeen officers were slain responding to disturbance calls (family quarrels, man-with-gun calls, bar fights, etc.) and 15 were killed while enforcing traffic laws. Nine officers lost their lives while investigating suspicious persons or circumstances, 4 while handling mentally deranged persons, and 3 while engaged in the handling, transporting, or custody of prisoners.

Types of Assignment

Seventy-one of the officers slain in 1979 were on patrol duty, and of those, 68 were assigned to vehicles and 3 were on foot patrol. The perils inherent in patrol duties are substantiated by the fact that, in recent years, officers assigned in this capacity have consistently been the most frequent victims of the police killer. The patrol officer is often placed in dangerous situations and must react to circumstances as they occur without the benefit of detailed information or planning. He is repeatedly in contact with suspicious or dangerous individuals, each of whom could constitute a threat to his personal safety.

What is most important to the patrol administrator is the fact that most officers are killed while attempting other arrests. The arrest reports in the *Uniform Crime Reports* of 1979 provide information pertaining to the number of officers injured or killed because of improper techniques of arrest. The patrol commander should perform an analysis of his patrol command similar to that done by the FBI to compare it to the national trend. Additionally, whatever conclusions are drawn from the analysis of the facts can be disseminated throughout the field, listing areas of special concern for each situation and officer. An awareness of the potential for injury or death by activity is most beneficial to the officer.

It has been suggested that policing would become more professional by following the methods used by Vince Lombardi of the Green Bay Packers. This point is exemplified in reviewing these statistics on the arrest techniques and situations in which law enforcement officers were killed. Refining the officer's task and the procedures used in attempting to accomplish his mission is most important. Expertise in methods of patrol and arrest techniques can contribute to a decrease in the number of officers killed. Officers' lives may be taken in an ambush because this type of an operation cannot be prevented. However, detailed analysis and review of actual incidents could make officers aware of the atmosphere conducive to possible ambush and would provide some training. Better preparation should result in a decrease in the number of officers killed in the line of duty.

The 1979 FBI *Uniform Crime Reports* give the hours of the day law enforcement officers were killed. Of a total of 1,143 officers killed nationally, 488 were killed between the hours of 9:00 P.M. and 3:00 A.M. This means that almost one-half of all the officers killed in the nation were killed during that six-hour span. An analysis of this information can be disseminated to officers in the field. That, in conjunction with the analysis of information pertaining to the activity, would reveal to the officers that they should be more careful between those hours and when performing those tasks that have a greater degree of possibility for their injury or death. Figure 6.4 is a 1970–1979 analysis of situations.

Assaults on Officers

Another table of the 1979 *Uniform Crime Reports* shows the type of assignment of officers assaulted on the job. Forty-eight percent were in one-officer vehicles, 32 percent were in two-officer vehicles, 6 percent were on detective or special assignment, and 14 percent were on other assignments. Of all assaults on police, the vehicle patrol officer was the victim in 80 percent of the cases.[9]

Officer Survival[10]

In attempting to provide all officers of the department with a preventive role regarding officer death, the officer survival program of the California Specialized Training Institute and the Los Angeles Police Department performs an analysis of officer deaths and develops identifiable learning points. They used the following information in one of their programs for 1979.

1. On a national scale, the felonious killings of law enforcement personnel have steadily declined since 1973. Although this is an encouraging trend, an examination of the 1978 California peace officer murder statistics revealed an increase, exceeding this state's annual averages over the same period (eleven average, 1973–1977).
2. In 1978, no significant patterns were established for the day of the week or the month of the year of officer murders as California police officers were slain every day of the week and in eight of the twelve months of the year. Traditionally, state and national statistics covering law enforcement officer murders reveal that the majority of police officers are killed during the "hours of

Figure 6.4 *Situations in which law enforcement officers were killed 1970–1979*

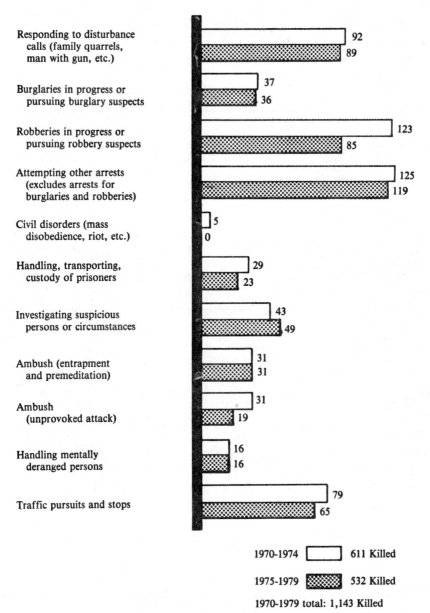

Source: Federal Bureau of Investigation, *Uniform Crime Reports, 1979* (Washington, D.C.: U.S. Government Printing Office, 1979) p. 338.

darkness." The 1978 "hours of darkness," from 1800 to 0600 hours, accounted for ten deaths which represented 83 percent of the California peace officers murdered in 1978. Officers must remain cautious as no day of the week, month of the year, or time of the day renders them invulnerable.

3. The size of the agency and the area policed—urban versus rural—did not grant the officers immunity from a death situation. During 1978, small, medium, and large California police agencies, as well as urban and rural areas, were affected.

4. With 66 percent, or eight of the twelve California police officers murdered in the presence of a partner, a responding unit, or additional members of an arrest team, a concerted effort must be directed toward the examination of tactical situations involving multiple personnel. Although "safety in numbers" seems a logical theory and remains to be advocated at all costs, police personnel must address the issues that create a false sense of security and relaxation among officers. They need to identify the physical and verbal teamwork tactics that are not being properly utilized to reduce the lethal threat of a tactical field situation.

5. Patrol duties within a law enforcement organization remain the most hazardous assignment. The fact that field officers are the most frequent targets for the police killer substantiates the perils of police patrol; however, officers employed in other capacities may be confronted with equally tense and dangerous circumstances. This was evident in the 1978 murders of a Detective and Detective Sergeant while serving search and arrest warrants. In-service training must continue at all levels, with an additional emphasis toward those units involved in the apprehension and service of arrest and search warrants.

6. An analysis of the ages and length of police experience among the twelve officers murdered in 1978 demonstrates that the older and more experienced officers constitute the majority of the deaths. The issues of complacency, routine, and the attitude that experience and tenure remove an officer from danger are still prevalent. Training programs must be developed to combat the attitudinal changes that accompany increased age and time on the job and realistically develop training situations that will maintain an officer's safety perspectives.

7. Physical fitness must always remain a highly sought commodity in the field of police officer safety. In nine of the twelve 1978 death incidents, a suspect younger than the officer was responsible for his demise. It is worth considering that the older officer's physical condition, as well as the general tendency to feel less threatened by a young or female suspect, might increase the threat of injury or death.

8. During field duties, law enforcement personnel have frequent contact with suspicious and dangerous individuals who constitute a threat to the officer's personal safety. The police officer is an aggressive individual who actively represses crime. He constantly places himself in situations where he must deal with an

individual's unknown background and determine quickly and accurately the person's involvement in a criminal act. The aggressiveness required in police work must be tempered with sound decision making and solid tactics, as eight of the twelve slain officers were killed during officer-initiated activities.

9. A peace officer cannot relax in any pedestrian or vehicular situation, as highlighted by the deaths of six officers in 1978, two during pedestrian approaches and four during vehicle pullovers.
10. The concept that an officer shall be aware of an individual's hands remains obvious, as handguns were utilized to murder 83 percent, or ten of the twelve slain peace officers.
11. During 1978, five of the twelve officers, or 42 percent, were murdered with their own or their partner's service weapon. Training programs must concentrate on weapon retention and protection of the officer's danger zone.

It is our hope that the identification of the above issues will enhance the safety of all law enforcement personnel through training information and the practice of awareness.

CANINE TEAMS

The use of dogs as a method of supporting the patrol officer has been accepted by enlightened police administrators. Some police departments have canine units with their special operations or tactical divisions, and some departments use dogs on a need basis. The use of canine teams on patrol depends on the need and evaluation by the patrol administrator as to the dividends received from applying such patrol to a given area or situation. Police dogs are used in preventive patrol, crowd control, security of buildings, building searches, trailing escaped convicts, detecting crimes, and locating marijuana, explosives, and missing persons.

Many police departments in the United States use canine teams. Some of these are Baltimore, Maryland; Washington, D.C.; St. Louis, Missouri; Jefferson County, Kentucky; Philadelphia, Pennsylvania; Miami, Florida; and Chicago, Illinois.

Some departments, such as Los Angeles, California, lease dogs to provide security for selected facilities. Additionally, some departments have assigned a limited number of canine teams on a permanent basis to special units, such as the Scientific Investigation Unit, for the purpose of detecting marijuana and explosives.

Breeds

Several types of dogs are used in police work around the world: German shepherds, bloodhounds, Labradors, and Doberman pinschers. More departments use the German shepherd than any other type of police dog. The State of Georgia has used bloodhounds for years, for the sole purpose of apprehending escaped convicts. However, the German shepherd is accepted by police trainers throughout the world as the best all-purpose dog at present available for training. Experiments at the larger training establishments during the last twenty years have shown that no other breed surpasses, and rarely equals, the German shepherd for police-dog duties.

The preference of police trainers for these dogs does not by any means exclude the use of other breeds. An individual dog of a breed not favored as a whole is frequently trained up to the working standard required of a police dog. Among these are the Doberman, Rottweiler, boxer, Airedale, and the Labrador retriever. The latter are used both as normal patrol dogs and for security at the royal residences. Since 1965 four Labradors have been trained in the United States to detect concealed drugs and have been most successful in finding drugs hidden in sealed tins, plastic containers and bags, drawers, and cupboards, and in other places. The London Metropolitan Police Force uses more Labradors than any other breed except German shepherds.

Duties

Dogs normally patrol for at least seven hours a day, working early, late, or night shifts. Another hour a day is allowed for feeding, grooming, and exercising. A dog's real value is to serve as a deterrent and to detect crime, rather than only in emergencies. The way dogs are used necessarily depends on the area to be policed: whether it is urban or rural. In the former, dogs are used to patrol near vulnerable premises; in rural areas, they are used to patrol near a strategic point to which they can be quickly conveyed. In recent years this system has been extended and greater use is now made of groups of dogs and handlers on special patrols to combat a particular policing problem. Where unit policing schemes (a group of police officers is responsible for policing an area instead of individual officers patrolling fixed beats) are in operation, the dog and handler teams have been added to these units and are available to work with the unit wherever they will be of most use. The issue of personal radios to officers has meant a more efficient use of police dogs, and the increased use of wireless-equipped vans to patrol and transport dogs and handlers has added to their operational efficiency. Dogs can be conveyed quickly to the scenes of crimes, to places where rowdyism is likely, or to any place where there is need for their services. "In addition to patrolling, searching, chasing, and tracking criminals, dogs are used for recovering stolen property which has been abandoned and for finding missing persons. The scope of properly trained and handled police dogs is likely to be extended with further experience based on continuing experiments in new methods of deployment."[11]

In a recent publication, O'Block, Doeran, and True[12] concluded that canines are a positive, cost-effective means for crime control in eight functional areas: (1) as a psychological deterrent; (2) to search buildings or areas; (3) to defend their handler against attack; (4) to track down criminals or lost persons; (5) to control unruly crowds and gatherings; (6) to detect marijuana and narcotics; (7) to detect hidden explosives; and (8) for general patrol.

In conclusion, the use of the canine team should depend upon the need of the protected locality. Positive and negative aspects should be considered, and the decision based on the best method of patrol for the solution of the problem and the attainment of the objective.

HELICOPTER PATROL

The Los Angeles County Sheriff's Office in 1955 joined the New York City Police Department in using helicopters directed primarily at water patrol and rural inaccessible areas. The border patrol, state highway patrols, and state police use aircraft helicopters for traffic enforcement, athletic events, parades, and disturbances.

Project "Sky-Knight" was the code name for a project that was to determine if the concept of using helicopters for routine police patrol was feasible. This was a joint venture between the Los Angeles County Sheriff's Department, the Aircraft Division, Hughes Tool Company, and the Law Enforcement Assistance Administration. The location of the project was Lakewood, California, which had experienced a crime increase between 1961 and 1965 of 42 percent.[13]

Helicopter patrol was applied in a mesh effect, combining alternatively east to west, and north to south patterns, with particular attention given to high-hazards major offense areas. The period of patrol was 10:00 A.M. to 6:00 P.M. and 6:00 P.M. to 2:00 A.M. The first year's results showed a decrease of major crimes by 8 percent.[14]

To evaluate the concept further, Los Angeles County Sheriff Pitchess removed two patrol cars from each of two shifts, day and evening, for a four-month period. The audited cost of helicopter patrol was $65,333. Savings through deletion of two ground units was $42,265. The quantity of work did not decrease, arrests were 63 percent higher in the test months, and the number of cases handled was 32 percent higher.[15]

Many other police agencies throughout the country are now using helicopters for routine patrol. It is, in fact, one of the reliable methods of patrol that police administrators and patrol administrators have to deal with specific problems and situations. The selection of this type of patrol for a given type of situation necessarily means planning and analyzing to insure maximum return on your investment.

The Kansas City, Missouri Police Department and the Baltimore, Maryland Police Department are two of many that are applying helicopter patrol to specific crime areas, responding to calls for service in minimum time and, all in all, gaining the many byproducts of service for their communities through helicopter patrol. There are many similarities between departments that use helicopter patrol in the areas of selection, training, patrol assignments, and use of accessories.

Preacquisition Planning and Justification

As in any other major purchase for a police department, planning is most important in order to effect a smooth operation. The Kansas City Police Department identified its work, prior to the purchase of helicopter, as Project 67, after the operational demonstration during the International Association of Chiefs of Police Convention in 1969 at Kansas City, Missouri. The pilots, helicopters, and logistics were provided by the Aircraft Division of Hughes Tool Company. The project lasted ten days. Response to calls for service was the number one priority. The final project report contains reference to innumerable incidents where the provided service was of great value. The crime category of the robbery and burglary were the specific targets. The time of day and area of city where these crimes were prevalent were established. A comparison of five days of October 19–23 without the helicopter to the five days of October 26–30 with the use of the helicopter was made. There was a 21 percent decrease in these crime categories with the use of the helicopter. Project 67 did not encompass the totality of acquisition planning and justification. For example, the city's 316.8 square miles can be patrolled by helicopter crew three times while the automobile accomplishes the same feat once. The airborne crews' observation capabilities are ten to one over ground patrol.[16]

All parts of the planning process must be developed into a helicopter program.

Selection and Training

Officers applying to be helicopter pilots in the Kansas City Police Department must have fifteen years of service remaining with the department, at least five years of experience, excellent general physical conditions, and vision of 20/100 correctable to at least 20/20, with the ability to distinguish color signals red, green, and white. The Baltimore Department selects an individual who has already shown an ability to fly helicopters and usually has hundreds of hours of flight time. (For example, one of the first helicopter pilots had approximately 2,700 hours flight time, mostly in combat.) In this case, the individual hired will then proceed on through the police training academy and after graduation is assigned to the helicopter unit. During the academy training, experience in patrol is gained by the future pilot in order to help him relate to the ground forces in a more knowledgeable way when he begins piloting a helicopter on his regular assignments. Officers selected must pass the Federal Aviation Administration physical examination given by an FAA-approved flight surgeon. Selected personnel are then placed in temporary trainee status until a private pilot's license is obtained. Training for the pilots comes under the Federal Aviation Agency Requirements.

Observation officers are selected from within the patrol unit by a fair and equitable procedure. Assignment is for sixty days, during which time an officer must demonstrate the ability to complete the observation officers' training course. Initial training includes: (1) flight orientation of one hour; (2) visual acuity testing and training for three hours; (3) geography, high-rise obstacles, contact points, safety corridors, etc., for one hour; (4) preventive helicopter maintenance for one hour; (5) accessories-equipment training for one hour; (6) communications training for thirty minutes; and (7) specialized report writing for thirty minutes.

Communication and Equipment

The helicopter patrol is usually equipped with two radios. One is the regular police communications-system radio that has the ability to communicate with all patrol areas as well as a city-wide band. This allows the helicopter patrol to communicate to a ground unit no matter where the helicopter is assigned just by switching to the respective patrol area. The city-wide frequency usually is used for operations during emergency conditions and automatically makes the helicopter available for riots, demonstrations, etc. The second radio affords the helicopter communication with the airport and other aircraft. The helicopter should also have a loudspeaker system, a siren, and illumination capability. Depending on operational requirements, armor and stretcher-bearing equipment (hoist) may be necessary. For example, there may be a fire in a hotel with people trapped on high floors. The helicopter could rescue many individuals with the hoist and stretcher-bearing capability.

Patterns of Patrol

The first pattern of patrol, mentioned earlier, was the mesh pattern where the helicopter patrol was north and south and then east and west. The mesh pattern can be used for a specific type of patrol as well as a specific type of search. The second type of search is similar to a concentric circle search. The pilot flies to the place of occurrence of the crime and then makes a 360° turn. From there he enlarges the perimeter in a systematic search pattern. The limits of the circle searched are determined by the information available concerning the suspects and potential route and method of escape. Every conceivable type of search is available from the helicopter. In some instances, information from the ground forces will guide the movement of the helicopter and the method to be used for the particular search. Two points should be made: (1) safety first, and (2) the more slowly the pilot makes the flight, the better the search. Additionally, if two helicopters are used for the search, coordination is imperative.

Riot, rescue, and flood operation. If the helicopter is used for civil disorder, flood, or rescue operations, two pilots should be assigned. The helicopter should have dual controls as a precaution against crash if one pilot is injured or incapacitated.

Landing sites. Landing sites should be preselected and approved. Dissemination of these sites to the appropriate personnel will improve the total operation.

Patrol Procedures

Analysis of crime by time of day and day of week and location as is done in manpower distribution must also be done for effective helicopter patrol. The primary and secondary functions must be identified, i.e., response to calls for service, crime deterrence, preventive patrol, and apprehension. The evaluation criteria and the procedure to be used for evaluation must be stated. Additionally, how to obtain maximum use of helicopter patrol as it relates to each goal, how to use the natural advantages of the helicopter effectively, and the best way to coordinate the ground forces with the helicopter should be considered.

Response calls. The following list of calls is not all-inclusive, but it does cover most situations where the helicopter will become involved. In most cases the helicopter will give assistance to the patrol forces in: arrests, car checks, pedestrian checks, building checks, area illumination, business-building roof inspection, recovery of stolen cars, prowler calls, robbery calls, car chases, detection of fires, aerial surveillances, and traffic control.

Once the patrol pattern is decided, a decision must be made as to when and under what conditions the helicopter patrol will leave the control zone and respond to one of the calls for service. In most cases, this decision is made by command, generally allowing for emergency conditions, in which cases the observer usually makes the decision.

Air–Ground Coordination

If a type of helicopter patrol is used that necessitates coordination between the helicopter and tactical ground units (Figure 6.5), several considerations should be resolved: (1) Will the helicopter and the tactical response team work in the same area? (2) If the helicopter and the tactical response teams do work in the same area, will they both give coverage in the same subarea at the same time or at different times? If they do not work the same area at the same time, will it be necessary to cover that area with another tactical team, or will it go uncovered during the time the helicopter is away from the control area? All personnel involved must be briefed so

Figure 6.5 *Helicopter patrol in control areas with tactical ground support*

City X

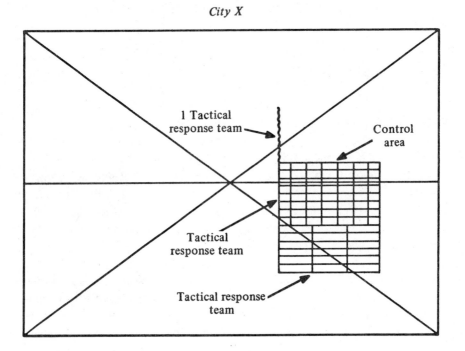

that the decisions can be understood by everyone and the maximum utilization of each unit will take place.

Where helicopter patrol is used without tactical and ground support (Figure 6.6), then the officers working the control areas as a matter of daily routine must be notified. Middle management, research and development (Crime Analysis Units), and helicopter command should meet to determine time of day, day of week, location of crime, and potential patterns of helicopter patrol. If prevention is primary, then the helicopter must patrol, by order of priority and crime hazard, the area where crime has been prevalent. For example, if robbery and burglary are primary concerns, then the location and time of the crimes must be recorded and the patrol patterns of the helicopter must be such that it patrols that area at the times indicated. The ground officers must know of the pattern in order to coordinate their efforts as a total team.

In many police departments, the call numbers of the beat cars are placed on the vehicles in a way so that the helicopter observer could advise car 10A to go north one block and west two blocks to intercept suspects who may have just committed a crime. Without such identification and communication, the effort will be less than sufficient.

Figure 6.6 *Helicopter patrol in control areas without tactical ground support*

City X

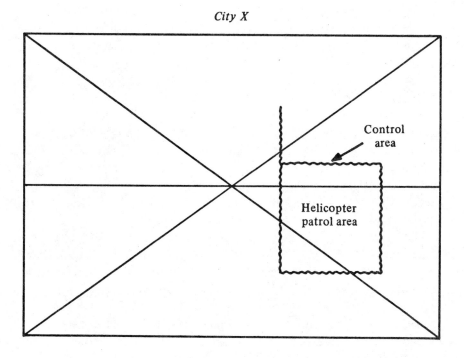

Assistance from personnel manning the helicopter. There may come a time when it will be necessary for the observer of the helicopter to become the assisting officer. For example, in the case of a one-man car operation the observer can act as the back-up car. If such assistance seems indicated, the pilot, because of safety factors, has discretion concerning the decision to land. If the decision is made to land and assist, the pilot must insure that the aircraft is secure. Only in the case of imminent physical danger to one of the other officers should the pilot leave the aircraft. This is not likely since the helicopter will usually be working in conjunction with several ground units, especially in municipal law-enforcement agencies. If the situation occurs in rural areas, then the procedure stated above should be followed. Operation of the helicopter when responding to all types of calls and the procedure to be used should be in writing.

Advantages of the Helicopter Patrol

The major advantage of the helicopter patrol is that officers can observe incidents and situations from the air much more quickly than on the ground and therefore are able to respond in minimum time. Officers in the air have a much broader view of an area than ground units. Because of this view, they are able to direct ground units and increase the possibility of successfully completing the mission. In unusual conditions, the helicopter patrol is able to see possible attackers that the ground officers may not see and thus increase the safety of the ground units. The helicopter is also more effective than other types of patrol in the following situations, among others.

Business/community relationships. Several police departments around the country have set up code numbers for identifying various vehicles. For example, in one department, the trucks belonging to a wholesale liquor business that is subject to hijacking have letter and number combinations that are easy to spot from the air. Additionally, the color of the truck is added to the code combination to improve identification. Any business having trucks that have a high probability of being hijacked is invited to join the program.

The helicopter is a tremendous asset in times of surveillance of professional criminals who may be nervous or difficult to follow and spot. Planning with the ground units is essential, since the ground units wish to be unobserved, and the need for coordination is obvious.

Snipers, ambush, barricaded persons. With the increase of incidents involving snipers, ambush, and barricaded persons over the last few years, the helicopter has proved to be a tremendous and valuable tool. The situation that occurred in New Orleans where persons went to the roof of a hotel and were sniping has shown the value of the helicopter patrol. This incident, I am sure, has shown other departments throughout the country the need for aerial photographs that can be taken by the helicopter patrol. This act of planning may save the lives of many persons in the future.

Missing persons. Missing persons, especially children, have been located more quickly than ordinarily possible by using the helicopter. The noise made by the engines and loudspeaker system of the helicopters are effective in this procedure. Most parents should identify the police helicopter as an extension of the officer on the beat so they can develop the proper relationships among children, the police, and the police helicopter.

Crowd control. Experience has shown the use of the helicopter for crowd control to be of great value. Being able to direct ground units and having a total picture of athletic events, parades, demonstrations, or mini-riots provides assistance in the following areas: (1) saves manpower; (2) utilizes each squad and patrolman to the maximum; (3) improves traffic flow; (4) increases accuracy of crowd estimates; (5) improves decision making; (6) allows for immediate intelligent planning; (7) allows observation of splinter groups who may break off from the main group of disruptors and cause trouble (the helicopter officer can relay this information to ground forces who are then able to move in immediately and prevent disruptions and personal and property damage); (8) allows constant surveillance of previously identified leaders who have disrupted groups and who may have slipped ground surveillance; (9) gives the chief of the department immediate, accurate coverage of the situation at the command and control center within the headquarters buildings not only for his own information, but also for the other selected and appointed officials of government as appropriate.

Evaluation of Helicopter Patrol

As stated earlier, comparisons were made in crime rates in the Lakewood and Kansas City Projects that indicated a decrease in crime because of the use of helicopters. It necessarily follows that an additional study must be done to evaluate the crime rates of adjacent communities to see if the crime was displaced to other areas or if it was in fact reduced overall. The in-depth analysis of such studies is very difficult in terms of the many variables involved. When any new type of patrol is implemented, a study of the effects on the area involved should involve a comparison with areas that are similar but without experimental patrols.

An analysis of the Lakewood and Kansas City Projects was done by Dr. Michael D. Maltz, program manager of mobility systems for the Center of Criminal Justice Operations and Management of the National Institute of Law Enforcement and Criminal Justice, LEAA, Washington, D.C. The accompanying two examples (Figure 6.7) show how the helicopters are presently evaluated and how Dr. Maltz believes they should be evaluated. The first example is typical of the accounting found in most police departments' annual reports. It gives the reader an idea of the effectiveness of a helicopter in countering robberies, but only a vague idea. It does not show how the effectiveness is related to the actions of a helicopter or the rest of the department. The second example is a more thorough evaluation of the role of the helicopter. First, the evaluation is based on the total number of calls for service that indicated robbery in progress, not on the number of cases in which the final classification of the incident was robbery. The report found:

> Most police resource allocation studies are based on the statistics of final classification of calls for service. To show why this is misleading, consider the following hypothetical example: A robbery alarm goes off in a liquor store and a police car rushes to the scene. The owner of the store comes out and apologizes to the policeman saying it must have been a false alarm, or it must have been tripped by accident. "But while you are here, could you take care of this drunk that's setting on my door step and bothering my customers?" Such a call is logged as drunk and disorderly in terms of final classification, yet the resource one police-patrol unit was allocated on the basis of robbery call.[17]

Additionally, Dr. Maltz said, with all the present emphasis on reducing police-response time, it is difficult to find any police department that collects statistics with a view to determining usefulness of reduced response time. It would seem to be a fairly simple matter to assign a special code to the in-progress or other emergency calls and calculate the response time and other measures for those calls separately from the nonemergency calls. This type of data is crucial in assessing the value of air-mobility projects.

Dr. Maltz also points out that a comprehensive evaluation of a police air-mobility program was prepared by the Los Angeles Police Department for the 1970 annual report of the helicopter section. Although Dr. Maltz's report and the annual report were prepared independently, many of the evaluations are similar. Both reports conclude that not only is the proposed type of evaluation useful, but also it can be implemented practically by a police department. The point is that evaluations of any program are an important part of a total process. There is a need for continued evaluations and innovations in the law enforcement areas relating to helicopter

Figure 6.7 *Two examples of helicopter evaluations*

1. *Present* (As it might appear in a police department's annual report):

   In 1970, the police helicopters were instrumental in effecting three arrests of robbery suspects. This is a 50 percent increase over 1969.

2. *Proposed:*

Dispositions of 146 "Robbery in Progress" Calls

	Success, e.g., arrest	No success	False Calls	
Helicopter used	3	17	24	Success rate using helicopter: $\frac{3}{20} = 15\%$
Helicopter not used	6	44	51	Success rate not using helicopter: $\frac{6}{50} = 12\%$

Helicopter not used because:

Not scheduled to fly at that time	21
Unscheduled maintenance	10
On another assignment	8
Pilot not available	4
Other	7
	50

Helicopter used unsuccessfully because

Unable to locate suspects	8
Long time delay in getting to site	5
Other	4
	17

Source: Michael D. Maltz, "Evaluation of Police Air Mobility Program," *Police Chief* (April 1971). Reprinted by permission.

patrol. The use of the helicopter patrol as a positive tool cannot be questioned. However, the effective use of it is something that needs time and study and experimentation—something of which law enforcement needs more.

BICYCLE PATROL

Bicycle patrol will continue to be a selected method of patrol. In managing by objectives, the means to achieve the end goal should always be a game of "anything goes" when applying specific patrol methods to crime problems. Whatever works best for preventing crime by category and area shall be the selected method. The patrol administrator need only have a willingness to innovate and to participate intimately in solving problems by other than traditional ways.

European countries have used bicycles as a method of patrolling for years. Baltimore, Maryland used bicycles as far back as 1915 when sixteen officers patrolled the northern areas of the city. Bicycles were used during World War II by the British. In some oceanfront resorts, bicycles are used for patrolling the boardwalks in the late evening and early morning hours when fewer people are walking.

Bicycle patrol was initiated in the Baltimore, Maryland Police Department by the author when he was chief of patrol.[18] The philosophy of using what works best in selecting the proper patrol for a given problem was applied. One of the police districts was experiencing an increase in residential burglaries. Preventive and apprehensive patrol had not been successful using the conventional auto patrol, and foot patrol would not give the officer enough mobility to respond in time to increase the possibility of apprehension. Additionally, the alleys in the rear of the homes were too narrow for the patrol car. Since bicycle patrol contains ingredients of all the advantages of foot patrol plus mobility, it was selected as the method of patrol for decreasing the crime.

Several aspects of the selection process came into focus, including: maintenance, size of the beat, number of hours, training and equipment, storage, and changing shifts.

Maintenance

In writing the specification for the purchase of the bicycles, the maintenance aspect should be included. As in the auto patrol, some of the minor repairs, such as fixing flats, and adjusting a bolt or nut, may be taken care of with a small repair kit. The major repairs should be done by an expert, and this should be so stated in the contract.

Beat Size

The size of the beat had to be determined so as to obtain maximum effectiveness. After analyzing the crime by time of day, day of week, etc., it was decided that a six-block straight-away beat would produce the best results. The officers were to work the front and rear of both sides of the street. The size was small enough for concentrated patrol and large enough for diversion to reduce boredom.

Number of Hours

Analysis of the time of occurrence of the index crimes indicated a need for patrol from approximately 9:00 A.M. until midnight. It was therefore decided to have two shifts, one officer to work from 8:00 A.M. to 4:00 P.M., and his relief officer to work from 4:00 P.M. to midnight. The days selected were Monday to Friday, since very few burglaries were occurring on Saturday and Sunday when most people were home from work.

Training and Equipment

After discussing the training aspect of learning how to ride the particular bicycle with the experts, it was decided that approximately two and one-half to three days would be needed for the first two officers. This was necessary so that the original officers could then train any additional officers who might be selected at a later date. Questions such as: How do you patrol when being chased by dogs? How far is the nearest gas station? are important. Training in the beginning will alleviate many problems later on.

The regular equipment of a foot officer must be carried during patrol on bicycles. The baton, citation book, flashlight, and whistle are basic. In addition to the regular equipment, the officer must have a warning bell, chain and lock, tire repair kit for minor repairs, clips to hold the baton and flashlight, basket, leather folder to hold reports, and any other material that might be necessary for a particular locale.

Storage of Bicycles

It was thought that a problem might exist as to where the officer could store his bicycle when he decided to go on foot patrol. Experience showed that both the business establishments and residents of the area are most happy to have the officer leave his locked bicycle in their stores or homes, and this was not a problem during the experiment.

Changing Shifts

How the officers would attend roll call and proceed to their beats had to be considered. If the distance is acceptable, the officer can ride the bicycle to and from the beat. If the distance is too far, the bicycle can be transported to and from the beat by car, station wagon, or cruising patrol wagon. This is not a serious problem and can be overcome easily.

Evaluation

Total evaluation of the project is not yet complete, but continuance of selected bicycle patrol in Baltimore suggests at least a measure of success. A decline in burglaries and an overwhelming enthusiasm on the part of the residents in the area indicate a need to consider other areas that might profit by such patrol.

A byproduct of the experiment was its tremendous value to community relations. Youth in the neighborhood are recognized by the officers. One officer has the kids waiting for him at school break. Another officer stated, "I've got one group of youngsters who follow me around on my rounds; I call them my posse." Another officer was heard to say, "I've been told that this is the first time in years that residents have invited officers into their homes for food and drink."

The bicycle patrol, with communications from the walkie-talkie available, has many assets when used properly. It appears to be one of the methods of policing and is here to stay, usually on a selected basis. This method of patrol is as applicable to urban policing as it is to rural or resort areas. It all depends on the imagination of the patrol administrator.

SCOOTERS

Scooters have been and are being used in various ways throughout the country. Cities such as Detroit and Washington have used scooter patrol as a replacement for foot patrol. The use of scooters in an area suitable to this type of patrol has several advantages. The scooter increases the officer's ability to move around his beat more frequently. The loss of observation from scooter patrol is minimal, and the mobility provided for apprehension far outweighs any loss. One department revealed that an officer assigned to a Vespa scooter in a business area surrounded by high-rise public housing was able to chase a young purse-snatcher up and down curbs, along sidewalks, and in alleys and areaways and finally apprehend.

Cushman scooters, which have roofs, are excellent for patrolling the high-density area of the business districts. They protect the officers dur-

Figure 6.8 *Scooter patrol for supervisors*
Source: Courtesy *Spring 3100,* New York City Police Department.

ing inclement weather, allowing continuous service of parking citations (until police officers can be relieved of this task).

An area of concern is the speed with which scooters should be operated. The primary objective for police is mobility at safe speed. Officers should be carefully trained in this aspect of scooter patrol.

Areas of Patrol

Scooters are useful in patrolling park and recreation areas, where the shortest distance from the present position of the officer to the location where he may be needed is across the grass and field of the park. This added dimension may be quite advantageous during periods of high use of the park facilities.

The selection of scooters as the method of patrol should be made very carefully. An analysis of the total situation in the area where scooters are assigned is necessary. The administrator should consider size of beat, crime, citizen relation, mobility, flexibility, price, and upkeep. If the application is made in an urban setting, efforts must be made to minimize the possibility of theft of the scooter. Some scooters are small enough to be picked up easily by two men and carried away. In selecting an area for use, this disadvantage should be considered.

Crowd Control

One of the less-publicized features of the scooter patrol is its use in crowd control. One officer, trained properly, can control and influence many people. With techniques similar to those used by horse-patrol officers, people can be made to move in the direction desired by approaching from the front and directly at a group, or approaching from the side in a sort of layer effect to move people back from a given point. When officers on scooter are in a squad or team, there is a forceful result with maximum safety for the officer. This method is very successful in dispersing crowds with minimum contact between the officer and persons in the crowd.

MARINE PATROL

The need for marine patrol units will obviously be determined by the amount of water area requiring police services. Most ports in the United States have some type of marine unit—New York, Baltimore, New Orleans, and San Francisco are just a few. There are also inland police departments that provide water patrol; for example, Jefferson County, Kentucky patrols areas of the Ohio River.

The type of boat for marine patrol depends upon the duties and responsibilities of the particular police department. The New York Police Department uses a launch; the Dade County, Florida Department of Public Safety uses a speedboat. The size of the patrol boat will also determine the equipment carried, from the minimum amount to numerous weapons and rescue material. Equipment may include deep-sea diving or scuba-diving equipment, as some departments have divers assigned to the marine unit.

The Dade County, Florida Department of Public Safety lists the following responsibilities for their marine patrol unit:

1. Enforce state laws and county ordinances.
2. Promote water safety and conduct safety inspections.
3. Perform routine patrol.
4. Assist United States Coast Guard and other law enforcement agencies.
5. Remove navigational hazards.
6. Tow disabled craft as practicable.

Figure 6.9 *Dade County, Florida Department of Public Safety removing hazard to navigation*

Source: Photo courtesy Dade County, Florida Department of Public Safety.

Figure 6.10 *Dade County, Florida Department of Public Safety towing a disabled fishing boat*

Source: Photo courtesy Dade County, Florida Department of Public Safety.

Marine patrol units perform routine patrol as needed. During inclement weather the patrol craft remains berthed but is available for any emergency that might arise. The U.S. Coast Guard is responsible for enforcing federal law as it pertains to vessels, harbors, and waterfront facilities. When state or local laws are violated, the responsibility belongs to the local police department. Such a situation occurred in the Baltimore, Maryland harbor in 1972 when the captain of a ship anchored in the harbor was assaulted by a member of the crew, and there was a potential for other violence erupting. The Baltimore City Police Department was required to take the necessary action. In March 1972 the U.S. Coast Guard called on the Dade County, Florida marine patrol unit to take action in a case of destruction of private property. Even though jurisdiction responsibilities are separate, experience has revealed that cooperative efforts and assistance between the U.S. Coast Guard and local police department units always exist.

HORSE PATROL

Ask any patrol commander who had a potential riot evolving and has exhausted his manpower in numerous assignments if horse patrol has any value in police work, and the answer will be a resounding yes. Many veteran officers argue that the value of horse patrol for crowd and traffic control alone compensates for the investment allocated to the mounted unit. However, patrol administrators cannot make decisions without considering all the facts.

Usually, the officers assigned to horse patrol in a police agency (federal, state, or local) have a high degree of camaraderie. Their personal appearance and the appearance of the animals are well above the standards set for the department as a whole. The men assigned to the horse-patrol unit are required to work more hours since they must arrive early and stay late to take care of the horse and equipment.

Horse patrol is in limited use throughout the country. Areas with difficult access routes are conducive to horse patrol. However, helicopter and other types of air patrol are quickly replacing the horse.

Advantages

Because of the size of the horse (the average horse used in patrol weighs approximately 1,100 pounds and stands fifteen to sixteen hands high, or sixty-three inches at the intersection of the neck and shoulders), people are inclined to respect them and their riders. This factor is most important in crowd control.

Because the officer on horseback is above the crowd, he is able to observe traffic problems others would miss. This ability to pinpoint congestion increases his impact on the safe and smooth flow of traffic.

Urban police departments have used horse patrols in parks, waterfronts, and beaches quite effectively. Patrolling large parks on foot is obviously impractical, and it is difficult to travel in an auto on surfaces other than the paved arteries. The horse can move from one point to another in a straight line, thereby reducing response time. Additionally, if the horse-patrol officer is equipped with a walkie-talkie for constant communication, his total patrol technique is improved.

Disadvantages

There are disadvantages as well in horse patrol. The horse and the officer require special equipment, and the officer's uniform (especially the trousers) wears out quickly. It is necessary to have costly special housing for the horses. Stables, hostlers (people to tend the horses and stables), and food are extra items required of a mounted section. The odor and cleanliness factor can cause health problems. Training must be provided for the horse, officer, and the horse and officer together. The total process tends to result in permanency in assignment of officers.

Conclusions

During the May Day 1972 demonstrations in Washington, D.C., hundreds of scooters were used by officers in crowd control situations. The author observed skilled officers manipulate crowds of people rather effectively. They were excellent in performance. This demonstration takes some of the edge off the argument that horses are invaluable in crowd control.

Each police department must determine for itself the need of mounted patrol. It is clear that budget restrictions will demand justification based on cost/effectiveness. The limited activity of horse patrol will be considered by most elected officials. If horse-patrol tasks do not increase in number and effectiveness, economic restrictions will phase them out.

INNOVATIVE PATROL[19]

The Innovative Patrol Operations is a project which replaces random patrol with a system which guides the movement of patrol units with written instruction based on an analysis of crime and workload data. The unique features of the program are that it uses the entire patrol force, not a specialized unit, and emphasis is on the deterrent effect of the patrol officer.

The emphasis in bringing about this innovation in policing has been to foster the participation of department members from all levels in the planning of the project. We have stressed the importance of building the capacity for planning of each individual police department in order to make them self sufficient in bringing about future change. Even though the major thrust is designed for small and medium size police departments, the concept may be applicable to any police department, regardless of size.

Rationale

The steady increase in the nation's crime rate, overburdening demand for services by the public, and the economy crisis are all factors which have served to emphasize the need to increase the productivity of the police. Police departments of small and medium size have often been preoccupied with day-to-day problems and have devoted little or no time to well-designed planning. While police departments have developed some abilities in managerial and financial planning, very few have been able to build their capacity for operational planning. Indeed, most lack the basic tools necessary to engage in operational planning.

This project examines several facets of manpower resource utilization by police departments. Several opportunities for improvement have been identified, including systems of manpower allocation, deployment, and the methodologies and strategies of patrol operations. The project is funded through a grant approved by the Connecticut Planning Committee on Criminal Administration (CPCCA) and awarded to the South Central Criminal Justice Supervisory Board (SCCJSB), a regional criminal justice planning unit.

The impetus for the creation of the project category came from many sources, two of which were certainly major driving forces. As the economic crisis continues to affect the functioning of our municipal governments, the need to bring to an optimal level the utilization of presently existing police department resources becomes imperative. The inability of local government to expend more capital (and in many cases the reduction of financial support of police services) moves us into a new era in which police organizations must explore all avenues toward maximizing the productivity of resources they now possess.

Traditional police procedures have in recent years been drawn under close examination to determine their effectiveness and begin the exploration for alternatives. The police department of Kansas City, Missouri has completed a landmark experiment designed to test the traditional beliefs held of the patrol function. The effect of random patrol on several areas, particularly the reduction of crime, has not been shown to be significant. The mandate of the study is clear: we must continue to scrutinize the methods and purposes of police patrol and develop alternatives which prove more effective.

With these directions in mind, the process of the project needed definition. SCCJSB staff members, Touche Ross Consultants, and the police personnel who comprised the project advisory board joined together to formulate this definition. The sections which follow this introduction detail the steps in the process, but essentially the emphasis has been on establishing a collaborative working relationship with police personnel and stressing the involvement and participation of all members of the department. The project began in two towns and has developed a core of essential elements which are transferable to many departments of small and medium size.

Process

The process of improvement in police operations is one in which police personnel are intricately involved. The development of the capacity of police personnel to conduct effective operational planning is the most desired result.

Formation of the Planning Team

The preliminary step, one which often serves to set the tone of the change process in the project, is the creation of a project planning team. The participation of a wide range of individuals from within the organization was encouraged. Participation in the change effort by all elements in a police department leads to a greater commitment to and responsibility for the direction of the project.

The planning group includes supervisory and field personnel from the patrol division, as well as administration and specialized units representation. In short, the team consists of representatives from all parts of the organization which the innovation would affect.

For example, with the initiation of the project in the Milford Police Department, the Superintendent organized his team to include the following personnel: Inspector of Operations, Inspector of Administration, Captain of Patrol, Captain of Detectives, Lieutenant in charge of Records Division, Crime Prevention Officer, Police Union President, and he appointed a patrolman as Crime Statistics Analyst.

Patrol Operations

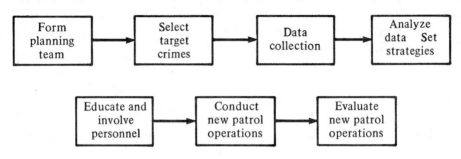

Workload Distribution

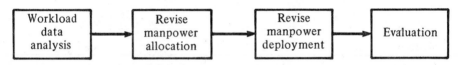

The group membership does not remain stagnant; other personnel are included with the core group in decision-making meetings on a rotating basis.

The most desirable result is building the capacity of department personnel to engage in continuous operational planning and to make them self-sufficient in bringing about change.

Target Crime Selection

One major focus of the project is the formulation of patrol strategies which will affect the rate of certain suppressible crimes. These crimes, i.e., residential and commercial burglaries, auto theft, and armed robberies, are assumed susceptible to the influence of the presence of a policeman and it is these crimes which have been selected by participating police departments. The selection of these target crimes is influenced by a department's perception of the concerns of the community for safety and law enforcement. Smaller communities may have different concerns than larger cities.

Some towns have chosen vandalism, bicycle theft, and traffic accidents as crimes for analysis while others were concerned about armed robbery, auto theft, and commercial burglaries. Most departments in the project began with a selection of a few categories and have added others as the project progressed. Once the selection of crimes is complete, it is necessary to choose the elements which would prove most practical in the development of patrol strategies. These elements would vary by crime type, but might be, i.e., time of day, day of week, victim (person, type of building, type of auto, etc.), point and method of entry, known suspects' description, and other similar classifications. The elements chosen were judged useful in the determination of patrol strategies.

Crime Data Collection

The selection of target crime categories and their elements leads immediately into the initiation of the data collection function. The task of data collection is a continuous effort in providing the planning team with accurate and timely crime specific information. There is both process and product in this effort.

Data collection is done manually and/or with the aid of an automated system. The South Central region police departments are fortunate to have the services of CIRRS (Case Incidental Regional Reporting System), from which a variety of information can easily be retrieved. Manual data collection consists of reading case reports as timely as possible and extracting crime element information, structuring it in a usable form. It is important that data collection keep pace with the needs for this information by the planning team.

Each department had to determine who within their ranks would have the responsibility for this function. In South Central departments, a variety of solutions were found, i.e., Hamden's Police Planner has this responsibility, Milford has appointed a patrolman as Crime Statistics Analyst, and North Haven has divided the function among several sworn and civilian department personnel.

The products of data collection are usable informational and planning tools. A "profile" of each crime is composed from the data which gives an aggregate picture of the elements in that crime. A crime "trend" report is compiled which gives an accurate representation of year-to-year and month-to-month variations in the level of crime. Simultaneously, a large-scale map is maintained (using an acetate-overlay technique) which displays the incidence of crime by location and time of occurrence (various colored adhesive signal dots are used to achieve this). The maps are a vital tool in patrol planning and also serve an informational function for all departments. These products: profiles, crime trends, and maps, are made available to all police personnel in the department and serve the planning team in strategy formulation sessions.

Data Analysis and Strategy Setting

The planning team meets regularly to assess current data. They first use the crime trends to identify crimes which show heavy increases and which pose an immediate challenge for action. Crime data sheets and profiles supply information about crime patterns in time of day, modus operandi, and other factors. Crime maps are used by the group to pinpoint locations and times of occurrence. The planning team reviews the data and decides which crimes to focus their efforts on, decides which locations to concentrate on and the time for selected patrol action to take place.

The primary step in strategy setting is the development of a patrol operations methodology which best reflects a crime deterrence philosophy. This methodology is in essence the overall plan of action to be enacted by patrol. One such method, used extensively by several project participants, is called Directed Deterrent Patrol. Briefly, this method directs patrol units to certain locations at specific times to create a highly visible presence. Other methodologies might also be developed, such as split-force concept, or team policing operation.

The planning team, having determined its methodology, then develops the mechanisms which comprise the specific details and techniques of the operation. Among these details would be role responsibilities, communications procedures and logistical considerations. The planning team also prepares for the implementation of the planned acitons. Implementation is a critical stage in the project. In East Haven, for example, Chief Joseph Pascarella determined that before the new program was to be implemented, it was important to have each of the three patrol squads meet to discuss the plans, gain a clear understanding of the program, and be encouraged to actively participate in the shaping of the future direction of the program. All South Central towns began their new operations initially on one shift in order to field test and adjust the new systems. The monitoring and evaluation of the newly implemented patrol operations is carried on diligently by the planning team. These tasks include on-site observations of field operations, maintenance of statistics on the operation which reflect its level of functioning, and close attention to patrolman feedback on the new program.

Figure 6.11

MILFORD POLICE DEPARTMENT
Superintendent William Bull
Innovative Patrol Operations

Crime Analysis Summary

Crime	Period
Commercial Burglary	*July, August, Sept.*

Time:

Day:

Monday	19 Offenses	Saturday	19 Offenses	*Month:*	July	48
Tuesday	19 Offenses	Sunday	19 Offenses		Aug.	37
Wednesday	11 Offenses	Weekend	2		Sept.	35
Thursday	16 Offenses	Unknown	2			
Friday	19 Offenses					

Target:
   46 were small businesses, 18 were restaurants, 5 large stores, 7 industrial, 14 offices, 14 schools, 2 country clubs, 12 gas stations, 1 motel, 2 public buildings

Entry point:
   25 rear door, 27 side door, 19 rear window, 25 side window, 6 vent, 7 front door, 4 front window, 3 roof, 3 wall, 6 unknown, 1 basement window

Property taken:
   66 money, 11 office equipment, 2 large appliances, 6 small appliances, 7 T.V., stereos, radios, 7 tools, 3 machinery, 5 liquor, 2 cigarettes, 2 jewelry, 6 nothing taken, 19 other than mentioned

Suspects:
   There were 19 W.M. suspects, 12 W.M. between 14 to 18 years, 6 between 19 to 23 years, 117 unknown

Major areas:
   From Seemans Lane to Greens End, New Haven Ave. from Buckingham Ave. to Lindy St., Post Rd. from W. River St. to Forest Rd. to include the Holiday Inn, Gardenway Nursery, Munson St.

   There were 16 entries between 2400 and 0200, 7 between 0200 and 0400, 4 between 0800 and 1000, 3 between 1600 and 1800, 1 between 1800 and 2000, 1 between 2000 and 2200, 3 between 2200 and 2400, and 11 unknown times, 71 in addition to the above between 2400 and 0800, 1 between 1600 and 2400. 19 entries were on Mondays, 19 on Tuesdays, 10 on Wednesdays, 16 on Thursdays, 19 on Fridays, 19 on Saturdays, 19 on Sundays, 2 on weekends, and 2 at unknown times.

Note:　The above figures include attempts.

Source: Reprinted by permission of the Connecticut Planning Committee on Criminal Administration.

Products of the Project – Directed Deterrent Patrol

Few police departments give their patrol officers any guidance or direction, in a consistent manner, in their daily patrolling activities. This condition exists primarily because an accurate picture of when, where and how crime is happening is not maintained and integrated into patrol operations planning. Officers on patrol, when not handling a complaint, are ordinarily free to roam within an assigned territory even though some areas within this territory, and elsewhere in the town, have a higher probability of crime occurrence. Traditional apprehension oriented police personnel now have begun to recognize the important function which patrol serves in the deterrence of crime.

The need for a more crime deterrent responsive patrol system was readily recognized by participating project departments. The major methodology utilized to date by South Central departments is Directed Deterrent Patrol. The concept was originally developed by the New Haven Department of Police Service and later modified by the South Central police departments. This system takes many forms because patrol operations of dissimilar size towns vary, but has as its core the replacement of a random patrol operation with one which directs patrol units to target areas at specific times on the basis of current crime data assessment.

In contrast to the traditional system, a patrolman would have detailed written instructions guiding his activities during part or all of his free patrol time. Prior to the implementation of a new patrol system it was necessary to educate all department personnel in the roles each of them would have in the operation. Continuous efforts have been made in some departments to inform and involve all departmental personnel in the process of the project. Supervisory personnel, patrolmen, and dispatchers all had new and unfamiliar responsibilities to fulfill. Supervisors, for example, had to be well informed about the new procedures in order to assist their men. They also knew exactly when and where their men were to be and what they should be doing.

Directed Deterrent Patrol guides a patrol unit into an area where his presence will be a deterrent to crime.

Hamden.   In one such patrol in Hamden, the objective is to reduce the opportunity for commercial burglaries. During late night hours, a patrol unit is dispatched to the target area. The officer has written instructions which define his target area, suggest strategies (such as parking his vehicle and walking around the backs and sides of buildings and checking entry points), and describe the suspect set. While he is engaged in this patrol he is not called to handle any complaints unless they are emergencies. Guidelines and procedures have been established which determine the situations in which the patrolman can abort his assignment. During all shifts, all patrol units have specific "concentration" instructions which direct them into areas of their assigned territories in which they maintain highly visible patrol until they receive an assigned complaint. Upon

Figure 6.12 *North Haven patrol officer directed patrol instruction sheet*

North Haven Police Department
Directed Deterrent Patrol $\dfrac{Code}{D\text{-}15}$

Objective: Reduce the occurrence of traffic accidents on Washington Avenue between Clintonville Road and Blakeslee Avenue from 4:00 P.M. to 6:00 P.M.

General Instructions:

Observe traffic, assist traffic when necessary, make apprehensions for motor vehicle violations

Activity #:	Location:	Activity:
1	Washington Avenue & Clintonville Road	Park for ½ hr. in the entrance driveway of St. Barnabus Church on Washington Ave. 4:00 P.M.–4:30 P.M.
2	Ferro Lane & Washington Avenue	Park in North driveway of old Radz service station for 15 minutes. If necessary leave car and assist traffic entering Washington Avenue from Lincoln Street and McDonald's. 4:30 P.M.–4:45 P.M.
3	Franklin Street & Washington Avenue	Park in exit driveway of Thrifty's close to north curb for ½ hour. Leave car for part of the time to stand on corner of Franklin Street to assist with traffic. If necessary eliminate traffic problems. 4:45 P.M.–5:15 P.M.
4	George Street & Washington Avenue	Park in driveway of Citgo on the extreme north side close to curb for 15 minutes. Observe traffic violations at the light at shopping center. 5:15 P.M.–5:30 P.M.
5	Blakeslee Avenue Washington Avenue	Park for 15 minutes in south exit driveway of Burger Chef restaurant for traffic observations. 5:30 P.M.–5:45 P.M.
6	Washington Avenue from Clintonville Road to Blakeslee Avenue	Patrol area for 15 minutes; if needed station yourself at any one of the traffic posts.

Written by: _____ *Time of run:* 2 hrs. *Approved for field use:* _____

Source: Reprinted by permission of the Connecticut Planning Committee on Criminal Administration.

completion of handling the complaint they would return to the target area and continue their patrol.

Branford.   In Branford, a directed patrol intended to reduce the occurrence of traffic accidents uses a different method. In this case, the officer dispatches himself during a short specified time period and remains highly visible in a target area. He may park his vehicle in a conspicuous location, slow down traffic by pacing his speed (and thus affecting theirs), and might issue summonses to careless drivers. For the short period which this assignment takes he is not assigned any other tasks.

North Haven. In North Haven, during the Halloween season, several directed patrols were initiated in order to reduce vandalism. In this method, patrolmen were not informed in advance of when the patrol was to commence. The dispatcher would radio a code which would be matched by the patrolman to one of several instruction sheets in his Directed Patrol operations notebook. The sheet would state location and outline his actions in exacting detail. Where he was to park, in which direction he was to walk, and in which direction he was to drive were all prescribed by the instruction sheet.

East Haven. East Haven has implemented a system which fully directs the free patrol time of a police officer. As often as possible, at least every few days, the squad which is preparing to work a shift assesses the crime data and plans deployment strategy for the number of patrol units working. Written instructions detail the patrol unit's movements by one-half to one-hour time periods and coordinates this movement with other units in the field. When a patrolman is assigned a complaint, he handles it and returns to the schedule of movement. Another approach used has been to split the force using some units to handle all calls while the remainder closely follows the directed instruction sheet.

Milford. In Milford, a deterrent patrol to reduce armed robbery is conducted using a patrol unit from a light workload beat. With written instructions detailing time, location, and suspects information, the patrolman dispatches himself on the assignment. The communications center then notifies those patrol units contiguous to the vacated beat that they should extend their patrol responsibilities to include this vacated territory. The deterrent vehicle remains highly mobile and is not disturbed by any calls to handle complaints.

West Haven. West Haven in its directed patrol operation uses floater cars which carry out written instructions detailing time and location for deterrent patrol to take place. These floater cars exist on all shifts and are used in a variety of different crime deterrent assignments.

Each town's unique approach shares the common need for well-defined communications procedures, written instructions, effective supervision, and a high degree of flexibility to adjust to changing crime patterns. Feedback from the officers in the field is a vital element in directed deterrent patrol. Upon completion of directed patrol assignments, the patrolman fills out

Figure 6.13 *Milford police officer feedback sheet (sample)*

Milford Police Department
Directed Deterrent Patrol

Date: _____   *Officer Badge #:* _____

Crime type: _____   *Officer's signature:* _____

Location: _____   _____

Findings	Comments
Stopped John Doe WM DOB/9/18/51 Stated waiting for friend to leave work	The assignment needs to be lengthened in time so that more attention can be given to rear area of commercial complex.
1974 Blue Ford Mustang CT71245 Parked near rear of Stop & Shop 2314 Hrs.	Suggest that patrol be extended to include Maplehill store grouping – potential targets for armed robbery at closing time.
1969 Green Van Econoline CT 66412 Idling near Cumberland Farms at 2145 Hours. Operator checked. Refer to memo attached.	I think that patrol instructions should include map of assignment area. It is difficult to know exactly where area covers first few nights.
Garden Center now closing at 2100 Hours.	Not being interrupted for calls is good – it allows me to continuously patrol the areas as a deterrent to criminals.

Attention Crime Prevention Unit:

Several convenience stores have signs in the windows which obstruct the officer's view of counter area. See reverse for list.

Door lock on rear of Albrights broken, easy access to building.

Officer's Signature

_____

Source: Reprinted by permission of the Connecticut Planning Committee on Criminal Administration.

a feedback sheet with crime intelligence information, memos to the crime prevention unit and most importantly his comments and suggestions for the improvement of the deterrent patrol operation. Planning team members review these suggestions and respond, often in written form, to each patrolman. A substantial increase in intraorganizational communication and cooperation is evident in many project departments.

Which method is best? The innovative nature of the project has engendered many diverse viewpoints among project participants of its structure and effect.

There exists a difference of opinion concerning the amount of discretion that should be left with a patrolman conducting his assigned directed deterrent patrol. The viewpoints can be arranged along a continuum, the extremes of which reflect the degree of self-determined action by field officers. While one department leaves almost no choice to the officer in the time, location, or strategies to be followed in the assignment, another department has decided that the field officers themselves should determine their own strategies, times, and locations for deterrent operations. All departments, however, agree that the core element of crime data assessment is a prerequisite to any effective crime deterrent patrol planning.

Effect.   The consideration of the effect of the deterrent strategies leads to a discussion among project participants of the displacement of crime. Is crime simply moved from one area or time period to another? Some feel that displacement may take place, but that it would not be a complete displacement, thus creating at least a partial reduction. Others feel that if displacement takes place it means that the strategies have had an effect on criminals and that expansion, not termination, of the operation would be appropriate. Still others feel that knowledge of displacement, facilitated by continuous crime data assessment, can be a valuable tool in reviewing and improving deterrent patrol strategies.

Directed Deterrent Patrol is a radical departure from traditional random patrol. Along with other innovative approaches to the patrol function, it must be tested and evaluated for its effect on the organizational structure of the police and its impact on crime.

Workload Analysis

The second major component of the project is an assessment of manpower resources needed in relation to police services workload.

Evaluation

Several levels of evaluation are necessary in order to assess the impact of the new system. Determining the effectiveness of any crime control measure is a difficult task due to the many interesting variables which can affect measurable results. While the reduction of crime may be attributable to a new patrol system, cautions must be raised, and other factors examined which may have contributed to the reduction. Such factors as seasonal differences (time of sunset and weather conditions), apprehension rates, changes in citizen reporting of crimes, and a host of other influences may combine to make less clear the effect of any one crime control effort.

Nevertheless, it is imperative that all attempts be made to gauge the effects of experimental programs. With these cautions in mind, a presentation of statistics gathered on a sample of directed deterrent patrols is offered below.

Future Directions

The project will continue to focus on improvements in manpower resource utilization. The remaining towns in the South Central region not now project participants will be integrated into the allocations, deployment, and patrol system improvement phase of the project. For the six towns which have progressed through this phase there will be a continued collaborative relationship to revise and refine new implemented systems and assist in the evaluation of new methods of patrol. In addition, assistance will be offered for the improvement of other manpower resource areas.

A. Supportive systems. Project plans for the future include efforts to develop and implement better supportive functions such as information flow, storage and retrieval systems, and dispatch-communications procedures. Consideration of the computerization of crime data collection, reporting, mapping, and patrol evaluation is already in progress.

B. Refined patrol systems. Other opportunities for improvements in patrol related operations exist including:

- The development and implementation of a crime deterrence reward system and the eventual examination and revision of present performance evaluation systems.
- Improvement of response sets (on-scene procedures) used by field officers for a variety of situations.
- Examination of alternatives in the handling of citizen calls for service (i.e., taking reports by phone instead of dispatching a patrol unit).
- Improvement of officer report writing skills with emphasis on information flow and utilization.
- Exploration of avenues toward increased participation by patrolmen in decision-making of the organization, toward a collaborative model of management-union relations.

Along with continued attention to patrol operations a second major phase of the project will be initiated in the next year. Concern about optimal

MILFORD

Directed Deterrent Patrol—Armed Robbery
Time: 7:30 p.m.–midnight
Area Z
Period: October 15–December 30

During this period of time a deterrent patrol was conducted in an extensive commercial area to reduce armed robbery. Normally, this season experiences an increase in robberies of stores but in this area only one robbery occurred during the deterrent patrol.

BRANFORD

Directed Deterrent Patrol—Traffic Accidents
Time: 4 p.m.–6 p.m.
Location: Main St.
Period: September 1–Current

Month	# of accidents Target Area	# of Accidents Town-Wide
June	16	84
July	10	91
August	16	88
September	8	77
October	5	74
November	3	82

HAMDEN

Directed Deterrent Patrol—Commercial Burglary
Time: 9 p.m.–midnight
Location: State Street
Period: August 18–September 15, 1975

Month	# of Incidents Target Area	# of Incidents Town-Wide
May	6	32
June	3	32
July	3	33
August 1–17	2	30
August 18–31	1	30
September	0	30
October	3	19

WEST HAVEN

Directed Deterrent Patrol—Residential Burglary
Time: 10:00 a.m.–4 p.m.
Location: Apartment Complex
Period: September 1-30; November 1-30

Month	# of accidents Target Area	# of Accidents Town-Wide
August	10	20
September	2	47
October	8	50
November	3	53

NORTH HAVEN

Directed Deterrent Patrol—Vandalism
Time: Various Evening Times
Location: Town-Wide
Period: October 15–November 15

Month	Year	# of Incidents
October	1974	152
November	1974	81
October	1975	109
November	1975	76

The number of patrols initiated in November 1975 was decreased after the Halloween season.

Source: Reprinted by permission of the Connecticut Planning Committee on Criminal Administration.

manpower resource utilization is important to both units of a police department's field services division; Patrol and Investigative services.

C. Investigative services. Opportunities for improvement in the structure, functions, and procedures of the Investigative services unit of small and medium size police departments will become another major component of this project. There are several areas upon which to focus our efforts, including case management procedures, investigative information systems, and investigation responsibilities and procedures.

Further, improvements in the cooperation between patrol and investigative units, including more open communications channels, and the consideration of the applicability of team policing will also occur in the future of this project.

Foremost in future actions will be our continued commitment to meaningful change in law enforcement and the development of communications with similar jurisdictions throughout the country which might benefit from the progress we have made in South Central Connecticut.

AGGRESSIVE PATROL

In the chapter on patrol and criminal investigation there is a discussion on the behavior of officers. The point of that discussion is that patrol administrators should try to cause all officers to behave the way the best officers behave. Past studies have dealt with attempts to measure only the effect of greater or lesser police presence on crime, as in the Kansas City patrol experiment (Kelling et al., 1974). However, no studies have made a significant effort to monitor what the police actually did. The San Diego field interrogation experiment, which analyzed the effect of street cops on crime and community attitudes, is closest.

> Two studies of police response time contain some evidence that aggressiveness can make a difference. Isaacs (1967), studying the Los Angeles police, and Clawson and Chang (1975), studying the Seattle police, came to similar conclusions: a greater proportion of patrol unit responses to citizen calls resulted in arrests as response time decreased. There are limits, of course, to how much the arrest productivity of police units can be raised by accelerating their response: once a certain minimum has been achieved (roughly 3 minutes), differences in response time cease to affect arrests.

Wilson and Boland state:[20]

> We believe that our studies, together with other research findings, are consistent with the view that police activity can reduce the rates of some serious property crimes, and at least offer a compelling case for experiment designed to test this conclusion and identify the process by which arrest rates can be increased. An active patrol strategy can reduce robbery rates according to *The Effect of the Police on Crime,* a study by James Q. Wilson and Barbara Boland.

In defining aggressive and passive patrol strategies, police may affect crime rates less by how many of them are on patrol than by what they do there. What they do includes many things in addition to and perhaps more important than making arrests. The continuing conflict of which approach is more effective, aggressive or passive patrol, has at last begun to be answered. The study concluded that cities where police departments employ an aggressive patrol strategy – i.e., making frequent street stops or issuing an above-average number of traffic tickets – generally have a higher arrest rate and lower crime rate for robberies than cities with a passive patrol strategy. Aggressive does not mean hostile, but rather that officers maximize the number of interventions in and observations of the community. An officer follows a passive strategy when he or she rarely stops motor vehicles to issue citations for moving violations or to check for stolen cars or wanted fugitives, rarely stops and questions suspicious persons, and does not employ decoy or stakeout procedures in areas with high crime rates. The opposite is the aggressive officer. The patrol strategy adopted by the department often affects the robbery rate just by changing the probability that an arrest will be made. If a criminal knows that the police are actively stopping suspicious persons and making field checks, or if he sees more police on patrol, he may not commit a robbery because of the perception that the chance of being caught is greater. This perception itself will often lower the crime rate.[21]

The administrator must be careful to evaluate the political and human ingredients of the community to determine any change designed to lower crime using this approach. One advantage for the professional manager is that careful planning can produce a patrol strategy that can be more productive.

CRIME PREVENTION AND PATROL

Crime is a community problem and must be viewed as such by citizens before significant crime reduction can be expected. Citizen participation in crime prevention means much more than cooperation with police; it includes citizens working with educational institutions, with all segments of the criminal justice system, and as individuals in their homes and neighborhoods. Collective security will not be achieved unless individuals are convinced that they must protect themselves and their neighborhoods from their homes.

Jane Jacobs was one of the first to call attention to the crime-preventive role of neighborhoods. Her vivid description of the uses of sidewalks begins with the dominant function of providing public safety:

> The first thing to understand is that the public peace – the sidewalk and the street peace – of cities is not kept primarily by the police,

necessary as police are. It is kept primarily by an intricate, almost unconscious network of voluntary controls and standards among the
people themselves, and enforced by the people themselves . . . . No
amount of police can enforce civilization where the normal, casual
enforcement of it has broken down.[22]

Others have also asserted the importance of safety in the neighborhood environment. As the sociologist Gerald Suttles puts it:

> The quest for a good community is, among other things, a quest for
> a neighborhood where one does not fear standing at arm's length
> from his neighbor, where one can divine the intent of someone head-
> ing down the sidewalk, or where one can share expressions of affect
> by the way adjacent residences dress up for mutual impression
> management.[23]
>
>   "The defended neighborhood," according to Suttles, "segregates
> people to avoid danger, insults, and the impairment to status
> claims."[24]

Yin suggests:

> Policymakers have traditionally seen community efforts only a sup-
> plementary resource for preventing crime. In contrast, this paper
> makes the following proposition: *Community efforts, far from being
> a supplementary resource, may actually be the essence of successful
> crime prevention activities.* To the extent that this is true, research
> on citizen crime prevention must begin with adequate operational
> definitions of these activities. Otherwise, few conclusions can be
> drawn concerning the most desirable community conditions or the
> most effective interventions. Thus, this paper is based on a second
> proposition: *Most research has failed to describe properly the actual
> activities involved in citizen prevention.*

Some writers and teachers of crime prevention feel that the police
and the criminal justice system provide the major alternative for crime
prevention. As part of this same viewpoint, private citizens are thought
to play only a limited role in crime prevention, even though they may
engage in any number of private activities (e.g., keeping private vehicles
locked when not in use, using door bolts, or installing new alarm systems),
in various group activities (e.g., watching a neighbor's property), or in assisting in law enforcement (e.g., reporting all crimes, assisting police investigations, or serving as witnesses in the prosecution of offenders).
    Yin continues:

> The suggestion of this paper, however, is that it is the criminal justice
> system that serves as the supplemental resource, and that effective

crime prevention must primarily be based on the informal social controls imposed by residents. Thus, the maintenance of public safety is seen as an integral function of the community, and effective crime prevention only occurs when this function is performed properly.[25]

Bayley indicates that, in a comparison between Japan and the United States, a major reason for less crime in Japan is the existence of neighborhood associations. Japan has one in nearly every neighborhood, and they promote public safety and crime prevention.[26] "The basic element of citizen crime prevention appears to be social interaction, in which residents retain an everyday familiarity with each other. One mechanism derives implicitly from normal or routine neighborhood behavior: The more that such behavior follows certain patterns and rituals, the easier it is to detect the presence of a stranger. One of the most important neighborhood functions is therefore the establishment of norms and a particular culture of normality."[27] A second mechanism for neighborhood defense is "to stimulate as much casual and public surviellance as possible."[28] Referring to Oscar Newman's research,[29] "defensible space," which is more than architectural planning, i.e., surveillance by residents, Yin's third mechanism states, "Citizen crime prevention need not be carried out in complete independence from the criminal justice system. In fact, the success of most activities depends on positive interaction with local law enforcement agencies."[30] Reppetto's study of residential crime concluded with the suggestion that the most fruitful course of future action would be the development of a crime prevention approach that would:

> ... blend the deterrent effects of the criminal justice system with citizens' anticrime efforts. ... It is possible, for example, that the "rapid response" techniques of the police could become a more meaningful deterrent to residential crime if environmental characteristics could be modified to maximize surveillance possibilities and encourage a sense of territorial concern among residents; citizens would take a few more precautions aimed at "slowing down" the prospective burglar so that his suspicious activities might attract the attention of neighbors; and observing neighbors might feel a "social commitment" sufficient to prompt them to summon the police.[31]

Citizen crime prevention is complex and in need of further research. Yin[32] has suggested the necessity for the operational definition of five sub-activities:

- Outreach efforts: The efforts made to recruit participants;
- Organizational form: The nature of the organization, whether formal or informal, that

	is responsible for administering the crime prevention activity;
• Relationship with the local police:	The nature of communication and cooperation between the citizen activity and the local police;
• Implementation process:	The ways in which specific activities are designed and initiated; and
• The activity itself:	The amount and nature of surveillance, preventative patrol by citizens, or other actions that actually constitute the crime prevention activity.

Yin's work is an excellent contribution to the literature on citizen crime prevention. To my way of thinking, he is saying, "Let's begin at the beginning."

Crime Prevention and Community Relations

Citizen patrol and escorts. New York City has developed a program to assist community organizations in helping in crime prevention. The organizations include block, neighborhood, civic, tenant, and business associations. These associations must contribute funds to be used for collective purposes in the crime prevention programs. Equipment purchased includes fences, whistles, flashlights, floodlights, cylinder locks, and portable radios. The radios are used in citizen patrol and escort programs for the neighborhood. The patrol and escort program is told to patrol in pairs, stay in assigned neighborhood areas, to report crimes in a specified way, and to consider themselves the eyes and ears of the police department. The goal of the program is to stimulate private investment in security improvement and to bring people together with a new spirit and understanding of community protection and closer relationships with police, which will provide togetherness in crime prevention.

Yin[33] lists nineteen different kinds of citizen crime prevention activities (Figure 6.14). There is a brief description of each activity, but all require some degree of formal organizational effort. This list includes a variety of voluntary efforts that may be sponsored by the police or a community organization or both. The purpose of the figure is to show the varied forms that citizen crime prevention can take, and to suggest that, just as with the problem of defining "block organization," each of these activities must be described in considerable detail before any transfer of the ideas to new sites or before any multi-site assessment can occur. The patrol administrator must view each program as a component of a total patrol strategy designed to reduce criminal activity.

Figure 6.14 *Different types of citizen crime prevention activities*

Program	Description
Block Security Programs	Attempt to improve residents' awareness and education concerning public safety, and may also assign surveillance or assistance responsibilities to specific individuals such as block mothers. These programs are very diverse and may include actual patrol activities.
Blockwatchers and Neighborhood Watch Programs	Attempt to improve citizen reporting of crimes and suspicious events in the neighborhood. Residents are sensitized to signs of criminal activity and are given specific names or numbers to call in case of emergencies.
Citizens Alert Programs	Attempt to improve citizens' education about public safety and ability to report crimes. Typical emphasis is on disseminating information about physical security for the home and giving citizens a specific name or number to call in case of emergencies.
Citizen Volunteer Programs	Attempt to reduce crime pressure in the community at large. Typical activities are aimed at: improving educational and employment opportunities for youths, providing recreation services, and providing counseling and rehabilitation services. Many programs cover courts and corrections activities and not just police-related activities.
Community Radio Watch	Attempts to improve citizen reporting of crime and other emergencies. Business firms or private citizens with vehicles having two-way radios are encouraged to report incidents to their dispatchers.

Program	Description
Community Service Officers	Attempt to improve communications between police and community. A neighborhood youth is trained by the police to perform community services. The services do not necessarily involve serious crime prevention responsibilities.
Escort Services	Attempt to reduce vulnerability to crime. Residents escort children to school or elderly persons when collecting and cashing checks. Escort service follows specific routine and time of operation.
Home Security Program	Attempt to reduce vulnerability to crime. Citizens are encouraged to install new and more effective security devices to protect their homes.
Improved Alarm Systems	Attempt to provide improved reporting of crimes in progress. In some cases, citizens carry special devices that transmit digital signals indicating need for help. In other cases, special alarms are installed in adjoining homes so that neighbors can help each other out.
Police-Community Councils	Attempt to increase informal contact between citizens and the police. Resident groups may be organized as an advisory body, meeting at intervals with the local police. The meetings increase communication in both directions, with residents having an opportunity to voice complaints and the police having an opportunity to explain regulations and other departmental changes.
Police-Community Relations Programs	Attempt to increase informal contact between citizens (mostly youths) and the police. Typical activities are: officers speak at school functions, officers and youths go on outings, and youths ride in police cars to get exposed to the officer's world.
Police Reserve Units	Attempt to reduce vulnerability to crime. Volunteers undergo extensive training and devote specific periods to police work. Volunteers may be considered part of an auxiliary police group, and the activities of such groups are fully controlled by the local police authority.

Program	Description
Property Identification	Attempt to reduce vulnerability to crime. Citizens are encouraged to mark property and to report · registration numbers to police so that property may be more easily traced if stolen.
Resident Patrols	Attempt to reduce vulnerability to crime. Residents actively monitor specific physical locations, either by patrolling or by observing for a given period of time. Locations may involve either streets and outdoor areas or hallways and corridors within housing projects.
Secret Witness Programs	Attempt to increase information from citizens about criminal activities. A community organization or newspaper may offer monetary rewards for information from anonymous callers regarding a particular crime or specific lawbreakers, including pushers or fences.
Security Guards	Attempt to reduce vulnerability to crime. Citizens hire guards to patrol specific areas, usually a residential block or a housing project. Guards may operate in isolation or may be part of a professional security service.
Street Lighting Programs	Attempt to reduce vulnerability to crime. Brighter street lights are installed in public areas.
Vigilante Groups	Attempt to enforce laws and administer own justice. Volunteers exist outside of the regular public safety network and carry out both surveillance and apprehension activities.
Youth Patrols	Attempt to reduce tensions in times of neighborhood disorders and to reduce crime vulnerability. Volunteers circulate within the community, especially during times of civil unrest, and attempt to reduce hostilities among residents and between residents and police.

Source: Robert K. Yin et al., *Patrolling the Neighborhood Beat: Residents and Residential Security*, R-1912-DOT (Santa Monica, Calif.: The Rand Corporation, 1976). Reprinted with permission. Also see "Partnerships for Neighborhood Crime Prevention," *Tactics for Neighborhood Crime Prevention* (1983), p. 59, U.S. Dept. of Justice, National Institute of Justice for a more extensive list.

NOTES

1. George L. Kelling, *Foot Patrol Evaluation* (Newark, N.J.: Safe and Clean Neighborhood Programs, Police Foundation, Governor Brandon Byrne of N.J., 1979). Major portion taken from the conclusion of the evaluation report with permission.
2. Chicago Police Department, *Training Bulletin* 13, no. 36 (September 1972).
3. "Crime Prevention," *Training Key* (Gaithersburg, Md.: International Association of Chiefs of Police, 1974).
4. Federal Bureau of Investigation, *Uniform Crime Reports, 1979* (Washington, D.C.: U.S. Government Printing Office, 1979), p. 309.
5. Edward H. Kaplan, "Evaluating the Effectiveness of One Officer versus Two Officer Patrol Units," *Journal of Criminal Justice* 7, no. 4 (New York: Pergamon Press, 1979): 325–355.
6. Raymond A. Walton, Jr., *Study of Twenty-Four-Hour Patrol* (Indianapolis: Indiana Police Department), 1974.
7. Ibid.
8. Federal Bureau of Law Enforcement, *Law Enforcement Bulletin* (Washington, D.C.: U.S. Government Printing Office, 1979): 300.
9. Federal Bureau of Investigation, *Uniform Crime Reports, 1979* (Washington, D.C.: U.S. Government Printing Office, 1979): 304
10. Charles B. Moorman and Rich Wemmer, "Learning Points from Murders of California Law Enforcement Officers," *Police Chief* (October 1979): 74. International Association of Chiefs of Police, Gaithersburg, Md.
11. Public Relations Department, Metropolitan Police Department, London, England, January 1972.
12. Robert L. O'Block, Stephan E. Doeran, and Nancy J. True, "The Benefits of Canine Squads," *Journal of Police Science and Administration* (1979): 155–160. International Association of Chiefs of Police, Gaithersburg, Md.
13. Mayor William J. Burns, "The Lakewood Story" (Hughes Tool Company). 1975
14. Sheriff Peter J. Pitchess, *The Sky-Knight Project Report* (Los Angeles: Los Angeles County Sheriff's Department, 1968).
15. Ibid., p. 96.
16. Aerial Patrol, Kansas City Metropolitan Police Department, Planning and Research Unit, 1967.
17. Michael D. Maltz, "Evaluation of Police Air Mobility Programs," *Police Chief* (April 1971): 34.
18. See the May 1972 issue of *Police Chief* for further details of this program.
19. This section on Innovative Patrol Operations is reprinted by permission of the Connecticut Planning Committee on Criminal Administration.
20. James Q. Wilson and Barbara Boland, *The Effect of Police on Crime* (Washington, D.C.: U.S. Department of Justice, Law Enforcement Assistance Administration, National Institute of Law Enforcement and Criminal Justice, 1979), p. 19.
21. *Justice Assistance News* 1, no. 4 (1980):1. U.S. Department of Justice, Washington, D.C.
22. Jane Jacobs, *The Death and Life of Communities* (Chicago: University of Chicago Press, 1972), p. 234.
23. Gerald Suttles, (NO COPY)
24. Ibid., p. 264.
25. Robert K. Yin, *What Is Citizen Crime Prevention, how Well Does It Work: Review of Criminal Justice Evaluation* (Washington, D.C.: U.S. Department of Justice, Law Enforcement Assistance Administration, National Institute of Law Enforcement and Criminal Justice, 1978), p. 197.

26. David H. Bayley, "Learning about Crime–The Japanese Experience," *The Public Interest* 44 (Summer 1967): 55–68.

27. Yin, op. cit., p. 110.

28. Ibid.

29. Oscar Newman, *Defensible Space: Crime Prevention through Urban Design* (New York: Macmillan, 1972).

30. Yin, op. cit., p. 111.

31. Thomas A. Reppetto, *Residential Crime* (Cambridge, Mass.: Ballinger, 1974), p. 87.

32. Yin, op. cit., p. 124.

33. Yin, op. cit., p. 113.

·7·

Special Operations

Special operations are those that require flexibility in the deployment of personnel and the application of new patrol techniques to resolve complex problems. Maximum use of personnel is achieved by analyzing specific incidents that recur in a similar manner and under similar circumstances. Offensive methods of patrol should follow the analyses.

Patrol commanders, patrol supervisors, and patrol officers assigned to be the front line of special operations should have additional training in adaptability, crisis intervention, conflict, and confrontation. The critical performance of a patrol field commander is to achieve the goal when commanding an operational situation. Confrontation tactics require excellent planning and an ability to understand the people involved and their goals. When a patrol commander resolves an explosive situation without loss of life or injury to the persons involved or to his men, he has succeeded in crisis confrontation. The ability to understand the issues (political, economic, etc.) and the people comes from experience and analysis of the means and needs that might be used to achieve goals. One difficulty in the analysis comes from the intellectual dishonesty of persons involved in the issue. Patrol commanders should always be aware that words are just that, even when used by persons who seem trustworthy, and so should be accepted objectively and with caution until credibility is developed.

Another difficulty in the special-operations techniques of patrol involves the application of responsibility, authority, and accountability. Inherent in the fact that flexibility and mobility are essential to the success of special operations is the fact that productivity must be measured by the totality of assignments, not by an isolated task. Patrol administrators must require excellence in performance of all the assignments. Since these assignments change more quickly than regular patrol operations, documentation of performance becomes quite complex. If, for example, special-operations forces are involved in saturation patrol to resolve a robbery or burglary problem and a school disruption or prison riot occurs, there is a movement of forces to the immediate school or prison problem. The particular problem may continue for days; therefore, continuity for evaluation purposes is lost. Special-operations forces (some departments may use the name "tactical," "task force," or "crime-control force") should be evaluated on the basis of their effect as it pertains to the assignment at hand and on their ability to move from one assignment to another maintaining swift superior responses and activity. This does not mean that personnel should not be held accountable for each assignment. When squads are assigned to a high-crime area, either prevention of the crime by decreasing crime incidents of the particular category or the arrest of perpetrators should be expected. Documentation of special-operations forces for accountability purposes is a must.

Commanders and officers of the special-operations forces should be highly skilled in tact and diplomacy and in specific crime analysis as it relates to categories of crime (robbery, burglary, auto theft, etc.). Some should have a knack for disguise, normal patrol, traffic, and investigative techniques. All need the ability to adjust to the changing situations. Special training is necessary in various concepts of special-operations tactics as well as specific types of operations.

PREVENTION-APPREHENSION/ PREVENTION-APPREHENSION THEORY, OR TWENTY-THREE-HOUR, FIFTY-NINE-MINUTE THEORY

The traditional theory of prevention by patrol and apprehension by detectives should be reviewed in today's police world because of the concepts of team policing and special-operations forces. Jealousy and mistrust between these two operating units must end and total teamwork become the byword of all police departments. Many departments use the policy of placing information transferral on official reports to decrease the possibility of patrol officers losing deserved credit in solving cases. This method documents the time and manner in which information received affected the solution of a particular case. Some patrol administrations meticulously analyze preliminary investigations to assure that full and complete information is passed on to detectives in order to avoid duplication and wasted energy, hoping that this effort will produce a reciprocal attitude on their part and set an atmopshere of cooperation.

The concept of apprehension/prevention or the twenty-three-hour, fifty-nine-minute theory, is based upon the following principles: (1) Saturation patrol can prevent crime and assist apprehension. (2) Professional criminals, or those criminals who take the time to plan, cannot be prevented from committing crime as can those who are mere opportunists. (3) Police coverage of a criminal target, say a liquor store, by placing a patrol officer in front of the store for twenty-three-hours and fifty-nine-minutes can prevent the store from being robbed during that time, but the minute the officer leaves the assignment, the professional criminal who plans will strike. (4) The cooperation of special-operation forces and the detective unit evolves from a goal of mutual benefit. Cooperation is illustrated in the zeroing in on the professional through the use of saturation patrol (both uniformed and plainclothes patrol), detective follow-up (including the technique of mobile and stationary stake-outs), and plainclothes officers in disguise (as street cleaners, truck drivers, door-to-door salesmen–decoy squads). (5) This mutual benefit comes from the fact that the arrest of the individual results in an increase in the clearance rate for detectives and prevention of any further crimes being committed by the professional, thereby causing a decrease in crime (no more multiple offenses). (6) This effort, even though performed flexibly and on a need basis, will enhance teamwork, since the total application is necessary in most cases. (7) Juvenile officers, who are intimately familiar with the workings of juvenile court and diversion techniques can improve upon the team effort when juveniles are arrested.

One method used by the author when an attack on crime involved the apprehension/prevention theory was an in-depth analysis of reports and an acting-out of simulated crimes (stopping before the commission of an offense) by disguised police officers. For example, the crime of dwelling burglary, committed in an area one-half mile square, was studied. Reports indicated method of entry and egress, articles taken, vehicles used, etc. Special-operations officers entered the area and used the same methods as the perpetrators, while observing patrolling officers' activities. This simulated exercise revealed many interesting deficiencies. Additional information and training were used to alleviate these problems. Inspection following these simulations and corrections found improved capability of officers in the areas of legal considerations, stop and frisk techniques, determination of probable cause and its development, patrol techniques and observation, effectiveness while on foot patrol, etc.

It is recommended that patrol administrators use these methods in their respective areas. The results will be surprising. One patrol supervisor actually had two of his officers (in disguise) walk by another officer while carrying a television set in order to determine the need for guidance and counseling in the area of probable cause and stop and frisk. This method should not be attempted without appropriate consideration of the safety of all concerned.

The goal of teamwork can be achieved with continued task force, team policing, and apprehension/prevention experiments if communication, planning, understanding, and a desire for success on the part of the leaders of each participating unit are shown preceding the application and implementation.

INDIVIDUAL OR TEAM CONCEPT

From the time an officer enters a police department he is trained to operate as an individual, making individual decisions and judgments about situations as each arises. Officers are also trained during the latter part of their recruit experience in crowd control and other team-related situations. For the most part, this training is necessary and should be continued. However, it is only *training*, and consequently can be realistic only to a certain point.

Officers working platoons or regular patrol usually function on an individual basis. They do not need the degree of adjustment required by special-operations officers to change from the individual to the team-member concept. The amount of training necessary for each group is determined by the size of the department and the number of occasions on which officers must change from acting as individuals to acting as team members.

Special-operations officers are usually members of a squad made up of a sergeant and twelve patrol officers. Again, the size of the department has an effect on the content of the squad. The smaller department may use a sergeant and ten patrol officers or a sergeant and five patrol officers.

The special-operations officer must understand the need to remain a part of the team when responding to situations requiring the team effort. For example, an assignment for a platoon of special-operations officers may be to saturate a given area of the community to combat robbery. Planning has taken place, and team assignment and rotation procedures are in effect. Officers are responsible for specific beats and are held accountable. Individual performance is being evaluated. Sometime during the evening an explosive situation occurs and the platoon must be reassembled to act as three squads in the team concept. Officers are now required to act as part of a four-man fire team or as part of an arrest team. It is important that they act not alone, but always as members of the team. The safety of all concerned is paramount, and maximum effectiveness during these conditions is based upon the unit-team effort. When an arrest is necessary, the team should execute it. There is less chance for resistance and less chance of anyone being injured when the team concept is used. Individual performance is discouraged, but obviously exceptions will be made when the saving of a life is involved.

Patrol commanders should insure that each supervisor and officer is aware of the differences between performing as an individual officer and as a team member. This is especially true when the commander has a situation in which he decides to make arrests. The procedure used in performing the arrests under team policing is most important, since the success of prosecution and possibly the outcome of the confrontation may depend on efficient operations. There have been many cases where officers have not been able to identify persons arrested by the team, resulting in dismissal of the case. Arrest teams should practice arrest procedures in a simulated fashion so that when the real thing arises, the goal is achieved.

Each person arrested should be matched up with a specific officer so that reliable testimony can be given as to the time, place, and specific offense. One way to do this is for the officer to have his photograph taken with the prisoner. Another method is to use flexicuffs (plastic handcuffs). Officers receive several sets prior to the incident. Each officer signs his name on the cuff, and a code is set up for specific violations. The list of violations (with matching code numbers) that are more likely to occur, such as disorderly conduct, assault, malicious destruction, looting, and arson, is disseminated throughout the force. When arrests are made, the officer adds the code, time, and location to the cuffs he uses. (Officers stationed on the mobile-detention vehicles can carry the pens to mark the cuffs or arrest teams can be provided with several pens.) When the prisoners are taken to a holding facility and photographed, the officer's name on the cuffs is then attached to the photograph of the person arrested, and the photograph and the cut flexicuff are filed under the name of the officer. When the officer arrives for a hearing, he merely asks for his file and is automatically matched with his prisoner. However, taking a photograph of the officer and prisoner together is the preferred procedure.

These situations can be very sensitive, and, if possible, teams of police photographers should be on hand to film the professional performance of the force.

POLICY ON DEADLY FORCE

In all likelihood, discussion concerning the formulation of policy on the use of deadly force by police officers will continue. There is no escape from this important feature of police administration. The author believes that a firearm policy must be written in order to provide guidelines for officers that, in some cases, may save their lives or the lives of innocent citizens. Police officers generally, but patrol officers specifically, have a very real need to be completely clear on when and where firearms may be used. A written policy will enhance the potential for using good judgment and making accurate decisions when an officer is faced with a situation where deadly force is an alternative. See Appendix A for an example of a written policy.

First, patrol administrators should be keenly aware of the impact that misuse of firearms may have on their ability to achieve the objective of maintaining community stability. More than once, riots have resulted from the belief by citizens that police have shot (and killed) unreasonably a member of the community. This is especially so if the victim is young. In some cases, the citizens do not wait for a ruling, administrative or otherwise, before they take to the streets under these conditions.

Second, there is a very distinct relationship between an enlightened firearms policy and its implementation and the patrol administrator's ability to achieve the objective of creating an internal esprit de corps. When a fellow officer becomes involved in a controversy over the use of firearms, morale problems become a very real probability.

Third, the legal ramifications, both in liability and politically explosive terms, can result in a continuing embarrassing situation.

The object of a written policy on the use of firearms includes safety of the officers, safety of the citizens, professional performance, and a sense of social and human responsibility. Urban law enforcement especially must use these professional police principles in order to resolve its most complex problems.

The following statement on firearms policy was issued by the President's Commission on Law Enforcement and Justice.[1]

> It is essential that all departments formulate written firearms policies which clearly limit their use to situations of strong and compelling need. A department should even place greater restrictions on their use than is legally required. Careful review of the comprehensive firearms use policies of several departments and discussions with police administrators indicate that these guidelines should control firearms use:
>
> 1. Deadly force should be restricted to the apprehension of perpetrators who, in the course of their crime, threatened the use of deadly force, or if the officer believes there is a substantial risk that the person whose arrest is sought will cause death or serious bodily harm if his apprehension is delayed. The use of firearms should be flatly prohibited in the apprehension of misdemeanants, since the value of human life far outweighs the gravity of a misdemeanor.
> 2. Deadly force should never be used on mere suspicion that a crime, no matter how serious, was committed or that the person being pursued committed the crime. An officer should either have witnessed the crime or should have sufficient information to know, as a virtual certainty, that the suspect committed an offense for which the use of deadly force is permissible.
> 3. Officers should not be permitted to fire at felony suspects when lesser force could be used; when the officer believes that the suspect can be apprehended reasonably soon thereafter without the use of deadly force; or when there is any substantial danger to innocent bystanders. Although the requirement of using lesser force, when possible, is a legal rule, the other limitations are based on sound public policy. To risk the life of innocent persons for the purpose of apprehending a felon cannot be justified.

4. Officers should never use warning shots for any purpose. Warning shots endanger the lives of bystanders, and in addition, may prompt a suspect to return the fire. Further, officers should never fire from a moving vehicle.
5. Officers should be allowed to use any necessary force, including deadly force, to protect themselves or other persons from death or serious injury. In such cases, it is immaterial whether the attacker has committed a serious felony, a misdemeanor, or any crime at all.
6. In order to enforce firearms use policies, department regulations should require a detailed written report on all discharges of firearms. All cases should be thoroughly investigated to determine whether the use of firearms was justified under the circumstances.

If all departments formulated firearms use policies which included the above principles and these policies were consistently enforced, many of the tragic incidents which had a direct bearing upon community relations could have been avoided.[2]

PRIMARY-SECONDARY MISSION CONCEPT

In most cases, the primary mission of the patrol force and the special-operations forces relates to crime. The patrol force is distributed according to workload studies, and special-operations forces supplement as needed at the times calls for service deluge the regular patrol (normally in the highest-crime areas of the community). The decision to move the special-operations forces from their primary mission to the secondary mission of crowd control or one of the many other tasks depends upon time, location, and manpower. If the primary mission of the special force on a given day is in the western part of the community and a youth-oriented performance is taking place in the downtown business district, clear instructions to the special forces about the time and method of transition are necessary. If the time of the shift is 1800 to 0200, and the exit for the performance is approximately 2300, the move from the primary mission should be made in such a manner that minimum time is lost from the primary mission but officers are at their assigned location for the secondary mission in time to fulfill their responsibility. Each officer should be used for maximum effectiveness. Careful review and assignment of tasks will allow for minimum waste of effort. The use of the primary-secondary mission concept in conjunction with the pyramid of forces allows the patrol administrator to obtain tremendous gains from the limited resources available.

PYRAMID OF FORCES

Webster's *New World Dictionary* supplies the following definition for the word "pyramid": to engage in a series of buying or selling operations during an upward or downward trend in the stock market, working on margins with the profits made in the transaction. The conscientious patrol administrator realizes he is involved in work where margin is important. Increased manpower is not easily obtained. The fluctuating market of crime, crowd control, and potential disorders (schools, campuses, prisons) must be met with the special tool of flexibility and deployment. The profit in the transaction of primary-secondary mission concept and pyramiding of forces is the ability to make ten men look like a hundred. This may be somewhat exaggerated, but it is intended to emphasize what this concept may bring about in terms of reduction of crime and meeting needs of the many tasks required of a special-operations force. For a patrol administrator to take the offensive in crime and still fulfill the other tasks, he must conduct intensive and timely research to identify those crimes most susceptible to the patrol techniques he intends to apply and then pinpoint the time and location of these particular crimes.

He must coordinate the concept of saturation patrol with the concepts of primary-secondary mission and pyramid of forces. This is not easy and requires intense desire on the part of the patrol chief and each special-operations commander, supervisor, and officer. The impact of this type of planning and dedication cannot be measured until implemented by each patrol administrator, and the specific impact differs in each department. Personnel should be assigned on the basis of need. Manpower distribution is a way of discovering the need of the regular patrol force. Special-operations forces are usually manned according to need, but the exact number required is difficult to determine, since there is no formula that can be equated to the flexibility necessary. Each police chief and patrol administrator must reach the decision on an individual departmental basis. One department in a large urban area may have a special-operations force of five hundred men while another department whose total complement is one hundred may have a special force of only five men and a supervisor. Whatever the number, it is possible to make the five look like fifty and the five hundred look like five thousand in the offensive against crime and other complex tasks.

All patrol administrators can relate to the following example, increasing or decreasing the principle and manpower according to the individual department. The special-operation force of city Y contains the following personnel: one lieutenant, five sergeants, and twenty-five officers. The span of control for the lieutenant is 1–5 and for each sergeant, also 1–5. There

Figure 7.1 *City Y. X = Location of robbery*

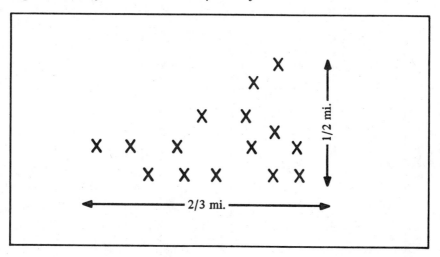

are five teams of special-operations forces. After an intensive review of crime reports on robbery, the information shown in Figure 7.1 was gleaned.

The attack on this problem will use the patrol method of foot, plain-clothes, car, etc. One important consideration to remember is aggressive patrol officers become bored if confined to a very small area (e.g., the size of a regular patrol beat in a high-crime area) with nothing but prevention of crime as a goal. Second, in order to facilitate saturation patrol and the illusion of patrolling with ten times the number of men, it is necessary to identify the location and time of crime to the half-hour time frame.

With the problem as stated for the special-operation commander possessing the five teams, the following procedure can be used. Divide the crime problem into four areas. Apply a code to each area (Green I–II, Red I–II, Blue I–II). Determine the time of the crime by area. For example, Green I robberies may be occurring between 1200 and 1400; therefore, saturation of the area and method of patrol would occur there for those hours. The number of teams used in the area will depend on what time the maximum number of robberies are occurring. From the time frame (Figure 7.2) we see that most are occurring between 1600 and 2000 hours. The other consideration involved is the fact that a tour of duty lasts eight hours normally.

With five teams available, crime occurring on a twelve-hour period, and the majority of crime occurring between 1600 and 2000 hours, the pyramid of forces has to be between those hours.

Information also shows that robberies are occurring in Red II, the majority between 2230 and 2330 hours. Additionally, the number of rob-

Figure 7.2

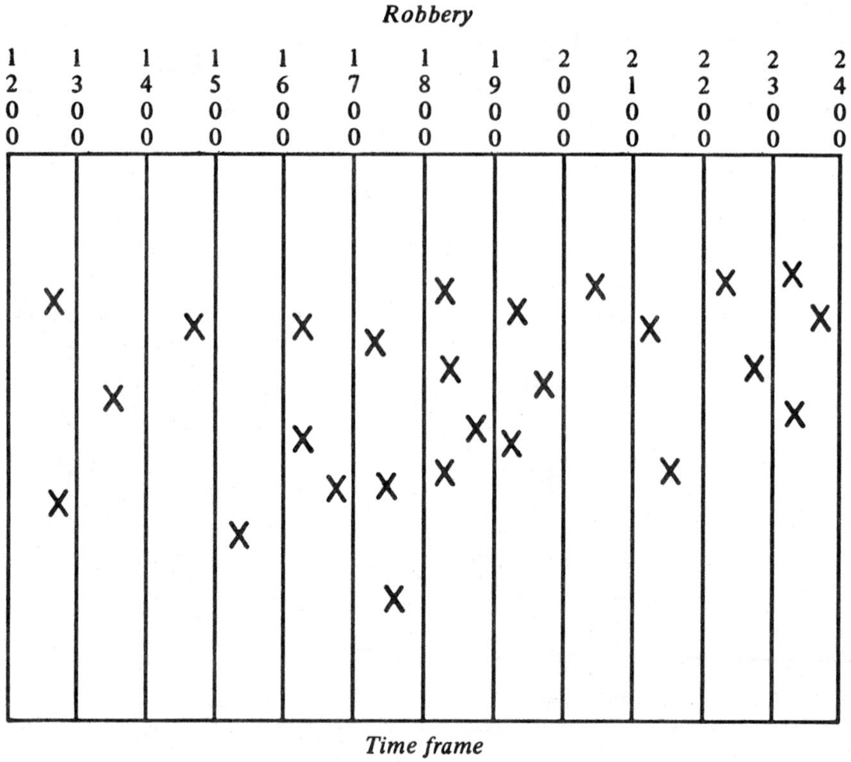

Robbery

Time frame

beries occurring in Red II are more than those occurring in Green I between 1200 and 1400 hours. To take the attack in this situation, teams A and B would begin their tour of duty at 1200 hours and saturate Green I. (Method of patrol is the decision of the operations force commander.) Since the major portion of the Red area crime is occurring after 1600 hours, part of the Green area crime is occurring after 1600 hours, and the major portion of all the robberies is occurring between 1600 and 2000 hours, teams C, D, and E would report to their tour of duty at 1600 hours. Therefore, all five teams would be on duty and pyramid the special-operation force between 1600 and 2000 hours.

The rotation of the teams between Green I and II and Red I and II would be determined by the time of occurrence of the robberies and their location. It is therefore possible for all five teams, at some period, to be saturating Green I and II or Red I and II, or any combination thereof.

The application of pyramid of forces will apply maximum manpower according to need by time and place. An additional component is the day of week. Patrol administrators should apply the same principle here, if crime is occurring by day of week in a proportion that requires the principle to be implemented. There should be no hesitation. Officers may be required to work from Tuesday through Saturday, if the information gleaned from the crime reports indicates that this deployment would produce maximum effectiveness.

Patrol administrators should be familiar with the *principle of mass* in mounting an attack on crime or fulfilling all other missions of this nature. This principle states that special-operations forces should be committed to a problem in sufficient strength (number) at the time crime is occurring and at the location crime is occurring. It will be apparent to the patrol commander that committing forces on a piecemeal basis will not solve the problem. This also applies to the mission of crowd control and disorder. It is the sine qua non of the effective special-operations forces. When applying this principle to crime, the usual information is necessary; i.e., time, place, MO, description, escape route, etc. Application to crowd

Figure 7.3

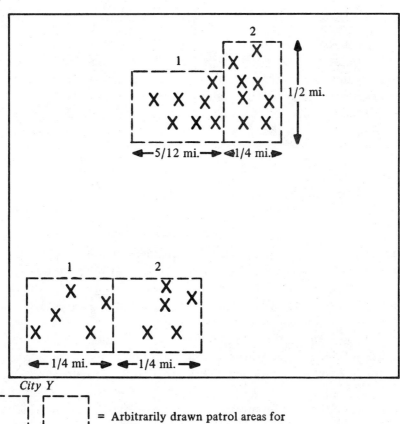

control and disorder will entail intelligence information about attitudes of crowd, size, location, potential leaders, etc.

Coordination is necessary to meet the other needs of the patrol force. Continuing our example, suppose there is a large group of young people attending a performance in the business area of the community. Information reveals the youths will exit from the performance at about 2230 hours. The secondary mission of the special-operations forces would be to supply manpower so that an orderly exit and removal from the area will take place, since A and B teams are now off duty. A decision would have to be made concerning the remaining three teams, C, D, and E. Should all teams leave the primary mission, or should two teams leave for the secondary mission and one team remain on the primary mission? Good planning will answer these questions and the principles involved can reduce any potential loss of efficiency. Another consideration is the potential for disorder at the youth performance. If intelligence indicates strongly that there will be trouble at the performance, then all five teams should be on duty at the time the performance ends. Decisions such as these are command decisions and the need for valid community feedback is important. It is again emphasized that good organizational relationships contribute to the effectiveness of the whole department.

The rotation of the teams from area to area should provide the illusion of omnipresence. The pyramid of forces and principle of mass should provide the coverage by time and place of crime control, and the primary-secondary mission procedure should emphasize the ability to be flexible in order to fulfill the many tasks assigned to the special-operations force.

STAKEOUTS

Traditionally speaking, stakeouts are usually implemented by putting an officer or officers in the rear of an establishment to wait for long periods of time for the perpetrator to attempt the next robbery. This is an excellent method at times and should continue to be used as appropriate, but limited manpower should stimulate patrol commanders to use different techniques and seek technological help.

Two stakeout methods that may provide an increase in effectiveness of the patrol function are the mobile and the mobile-stationary stakeouts. One uses a mobile technique and the other uses technology.

In the mobile technique, several teams of special-operations forces cover the many establishments requiring stakeouts. For example, if liquor establishments have been the target for holdup men and there are twenty-five liquor establishments in the community, the twenty-five would be divided up by time and location and the teams would stake these out at given times. Using the teams in the example above, a sergeant and five men, there would be six two-man units to cover the stakeouts. These stakeouts may be on the inside of the premises or on the outside and may be covert or overt. In the covert method, the officers are in an unmarked car and in plainclothes. With the overt method, the officers of the teams are well armed and make continuous and constant inspections of those establishments assigned to them for stakeout. The word usually spreads very quickly throughout a community that special-forces officers are inspecting the particular premises in the manner described. This inspection method can be used by the total department for any given target. For instance, one way to decrease bank robberies is to have officers in and out of all the banks in the community at different times. This obvious omnipresence and inspection will have a definite effect on bank robberies and usually are beneficial to the total community.

The second method uses technology. This is the electronic stakeout. Electronic equipment is placed in the rear of the establishment and hooked up to an alarm in the front of the store. When a holdup is occurring, the clerk simply activates the alarm and the location of the robbery is immediately known by the police. Special-operations officers in patrol cars are patrolling the area where the electronic stakeout has been installed, and regular patrol forces are also notified of the stakeout information. The examination of new technology is necessary if law enforcement is to continue the offensive on crime, and patrol administrators should be in the forefront in their quest for alternative methods.

MOBILE COMMAND POSTS

Most departments across the country have some type of mobile command post. One department has converted a trailer that even has an area large enough to hold conferences. Smaller departments have converted station wagons, vans, buses, or other vehicles that fit the needs of the specific department. Depending on the size of the vehicle, equipment can include wall maps and charts; telephones and intricate communications systems that allow contact with any agency that may be needed during times of emergency; lighting equipment, etc. An essential consideration whenever a mobile command post is used is complete cooperation and coordination with the normal communication center. Confusion and chaos will result if both attempt to issue instructions to field personnel. Written guidelines will help alleviate this problem.

Mobile command posts came into being for most police departments during the civil disorders of 1968. Federal troops and National Guard personnel mingled with civilian police and much talk of the CP (command post) was heard. Coordination between troops and police became complex because of the necessary increase in communication. Decentralization of control of police personnel was in order, and the mobile command post served as the headquarters for patrol field commanders. The mobile command post allowed the field commander to account for assigned personnel and deploy differing amounts of men according to each situation. At the same time, the staging area concept came into being.

The *staging area* is usually that part of the mobile command post where personnel are assembled, equipped as needed, and accounted for, and where equipment can be stored. There may be times when staging areas are part of the command post and other times when the two are separated. As circumstances change, so does the decision concerning the location.

The field commander responsible for the area in which a mobile command post has been installed should assign a special-operations supervisor the responsibility of the command post activities. This assignment is probably best done prior to any actual situation and expertise should be developed through simulated exercises. The operation of a mobile command post requires a minimum of a commander, assignment officer, logistics officer, and transportation officer.

The *assignment officer* maintains records of the number and identity of all personnel assigned to the particular post, maintains maps showing community areas involved in the situation and personnel assigned to these areas, structures zones of patrol using priorities to achieve maximum control, and coordinates the activities of all concerned.

The *logistics officer* receives, accounts for, and issues all personnel equipment, provides food and sanitary facilities, supervises accounting for all evidence and property recovered, and maintains liaison with central logistics.

The *transportation officer* controls parking and security of all vehicles, maintains records of vehicle assignment, supervises shift changing regarding vehicles, and provides prisoner transportation and security.

If there is a need to assign additional personnel to these officers, it should be done on a need basis. It is not necesary to provide these assignments in all cases. Mobile command posts may consist of only one police car as the situation demands. However, if the problem escalates, these responsibilities should be assigned.

The patrol administrator and his patrol commanders should review strategic areas throughout the community for potential command post locations. All hazards related to possible civil disorder will affect those selected locations. This review should be done in conjunction with determining related sites for staging areas. When the selection is completed, arrangements should be made so that once the mobile command post is set up, immediate telephone service and related communication are available. Cooperation of the local telephone company is necessary. Needless to say, without communication the procedure is ineffective.

RIOTS AND CROWD CONTROL

Nowhere in police work does the capability of a patrol administrator become more obvious than at the time of critical confrontations involving unlawful assembly and riot. Planning, coordinating, deploying personnel, organizing, and supporting are all part of leading the patrol force in its performance during these crisis situations.

Planning is the first step. Every department should possess a mobilization plan. It is recommended that the plan be written in stages in order to obtain maximum effectiveness of manpower and avoid any waste due to overdeployment.

Flexibility of forces and their ability to arrive at locations promptly is a key to controlling explosive situations. Most experienced patrol leaders agree that there is a direct relationship between resolving potential civil disorders and the ability to respond and handle situations promptly, intelligently, and with the appropriate number of personnel. A practical method for evaluating the ability of the special-operations force is to select a location with the potential for disturbance and request special-operation forces to respond. The simulation will keep the officers in training as well as indicate possible areas of improvement. The knowledge that the patrol commander and his officers are ready and capable should result in a strong esprit de corps.

Planning should also indicate the definition of each stage and its use, and a call-up system that allows all off-duty officers to report. Most departments use a pyramid call-up system. Each superior calls a given number of subordinates. For example, a sergeant with twelve officers reporting to him would call three key patrol officers and each of these three would contact four other patrol officers. A police department headquarters' command post must be established and responsibilities for its implementation and conduct during the emergency clearly defined. In conjunction with this, a procedure for field-command posts and accompanying operational guidelines should be established. Consideration must be given to the initiation of twelve-hour shifts, as well as time and shift schedule. When the twelve-hour periods begin, field commanders must be assigned and specific responsibilities for different areas of the community understood by each field commander. Additionally, locations of staging areas for officers to report to and locations of field-command posts should be identified, along with sensitive locations such as pawnshops, liquor warehouses, and gun dealers. In some situations the location of the staging area and the field-command post can be the same; for example, a shopping center, school playground, athletic field, downtown street, or public building.

Support planning or logistics includes: assignments of communications personnel and physical security for the police buildings, emergency arrest, booking and detention procedures, and property security (personal and evidence).

Assignments must be made to accomplish military liaisons in case National Guard or federal troops have to be called in. Personnel assigned on military liaisons should have a working knowledge of military terminology, in order to translate police and military terms, and the ability to coordinate maps between military and police indicating sensitive and explosive areas. (Civil defense liaisons are discussed in the section on natural disasters.)

Crowds occur at parades, athletic contests, and school dances and usually can be safely handled. At times, however, a crowd ignites into an unlawful assembly or riot. Political rallies or demonstrations attract crowds of different sizes. Each situation must be judged on its merits, but there are certain signs that may indicate the potential for disorder to patrol administrators. Several assassinations of police officers took place across the country after pamphlets saying "Kill the Pigs" were distributed among crowds. A certain type of atmosphere indicates oncoming disorder. Some other signs of potential disorders are outright hostility toward officers, unfounded accusations of police brutality, general threats of violence toward police, and an increase in the number of times officers need assistance in making what should be routine arrests. All of these signs should be analyzed for hidden intent.

The patrol field commander arriving at the scene of a disturbance must not forget his mission. Protection of life and property and the restoration of peace and tranquility are fundamental. The assessment made by the patrol field commander will guide the optional capability of the patrol force and department. The personnel and type of equipment necessary to accomplish the mission are determined by the field commander, who must communicate his judgment immediately so that these forces can be accumulated as quickly as possible. After this first act, the field commander may resort to whatever dialogue he thinks has a chance of quelling the situation without the use of force. The patrol field commander should always remain flexible and control as many alternatives as possible. This position allows the commander to reciprocate as needed.

If his assessment indicates the need to act, the field commander must never bluff. Before he makes a move, he should consider the consequences. If he attempts to disperse a crowd with too few officers, the end result may be looting and arson, with the men arresting people charged with disorderly conduct while the looters and arsonists escape. The disorder must not spread. Therefore, before the order to disperse is given (the use of a bullhorn is recommended because the commander can carry it with him), the leader should cover his flanks, make sure the teams are available to arrest, and cordon off the area to avoid the spread of destruction. Usually the first order to disperse will cause the onlookers who have no real interest to leave. After the second order, those who are interested, but not committed to the point of arrest, will leave. The momentum achieved and action taken at this point should result in the successful conclusion of the incident within the rule of law.

Smaller departments without adequate personnel to achieve disturbance control should formulate mutual aid pacts with adjacent jurisdictions.

A Sociological Analysis of Crowds

Sociologically, a crowd "is a temporary, largely unorganized group of persons in physical proximity to one another and mutually influencing each other to a significant extent."

The phrase "to a significant extent" is important to the definition. Twenty men watching the construction of a new building are not a crowd. They do not have much intercommunication, and they influence each other only nominally, if at all.

Police history is replete with examples where a little training and knowledge of human mass behavior would have prevented serious incidents, and in many instances loss of life would have been prevented.

Types of Crowds.   Basically, crowds may be divided into three subdivisions. The "sidewalk superintendents" gathered around a building under construction, although not a true crowd, may be classified as a *casual crowd* or a *physical crowd*.

The *expressive crowd* is usually a controlled crowd. Not all crowd behavior is spontaneous, this type of crowd requiring little policing and seldom becoming riotous.

The *acting crowd* is one that becomes organized around a particular purpose, its behavior directed toward the achievement of that objective. One example of an acting crowd is a *mob*. When a crowd becomes a mob, restraint and control are lost. Mobs are characteristically emotional and always irrational. Most members of a mob have a temporary common feeling with the other members of a mob. Certain principles apply themselves to mobs in general, and mobs, according to their intent, can usually be classified by type, and as having the following specific characteristics:

1. *An aggressive mob* riots and terrorizes, as in the case of race riots, lynchings, political riots, and prison riots.

2. *An escape mob* is in a state of fright, attempting to secure safety by flight. Panic creates an escape mob. In their panic, members of the escape mob have lost their power of reasoning and may go so far as to destroy each other unless controlled.

3. *An acquisitive mob* is motivated by a desire to acquire something. The mobs in food riots are acquisitive mobs. An acquisitive mob frequently results as the aftermath of an aggressive mob.

4. *An expressive mob* is a mob expressing fervor or revelry, such as following some religious activity, a sports event, or New Year's Eve celebration. An expressive mob is seldom of such proportions as to be capable of overpowering police forces.

Sociological Influences That Work in Favor of the Agitator. Why do peaceful people participate in mob actions? What is there about a large crowd or mob atmosphere that causes a person to react differently than he does in his normal day-to-day living? Factors contributing to abnormal behavior:

1. Novelty: When an individual is confronted by new and strange circumstances, the habits which he has formed may not be fully operative.

2. Anonymity: When an individual is with a mob, he may tend to lose self-identity, because his identity may merge with that of the mob.

3. Release from repressed emotions: In a mob, the prejudiced and unsatisfied desires of the individuals, which are normally held in restraint, are readily released.

4. Force a numbers:
   a. The size of a mob gives the individual a sense of power and a desire to use it.

5. Heightened suggestibility:
   a. A group will accept the idea of a dominant personality. Ideas spread without raising thought or objection on the part of the individuals.
   b. People in a mob action are not aware of the real causes of their difficulty, or at least are not convinced of them. Because of this lack of understanding they readily accept the ideas of a leader.

6. Emotional contagion:
   a. People are curious.
   b. People become emotionally stimulated by the actions of others even though they may not share the grievance from which the emotion orginated.

7. Conformity: The urge to do what others do is always very strong.

The mob is quick to sense fear, indecision, poor organization and training on the part of officers, and will take instantaneous advantage of it. The responsibilities placed on the officer, therefore, are important if he is to maintain the public tranquility and well-being.

Riot control is not dependent upon individual acts of heroism, but rather upon perfectly executed tactics and maneuvers of a group of officers dedicated to teamwork, mutual support, and a high degree of *esprit de corps*.[3]

Mob Psychology

The most important thing a patrol commander must remember in confronting a mob or in crowd control is to have enough manpower available to accomplish the mission with a minimum use of force. Police action should never be the catalyst to destruction and violence. Without sufficient manpower at the onset of the situation, it is more likely that extra forces will have to be used later, resulting in the escalation of events. Patrol supervisors should be advised to respond quickly to any incident where the potential for mob violence exists and to remove the originating cause. If arrest occurs, the prisoner(s) should be removed from the area as soon as possible. This procedure should be strictly enforced.

Most situations of this type are sensitive and the proper method to use after a crowd has gathered is not absolute. Many times the presence of a number of personnel on the scene is sufficient to quell any violent action. In other situations the best method may be to station the majority of officers in a reserve or standby position readily available in case of need. Undercover officers who are familiar with the area and the issues can identify the leaders of any large gathering and relate the mood and attitude. Intelligence information and experience will guide the action of the force in each situation. The enlightened patrol commander, however, will always maintain sufficient strength to meet any situation.

Other aspects of the situation to consider are:

1. Types of leaders involved; the best procedure to remove them and disperse crowd at the same time.
2. Obvious agitators and their positions in relationship to the crowd (center, periphery).
3. Mood of participants.
4. The point at which action would gain maximum benefit. This requires a judgment by the patrol commander. If he waits too long, the events may reach a point where it is too late to act; if he acts too soon, the results may be chaotic, with charges of violation of civil rights to peaceful assembly, etc.
5. Exit routes for participants if action is taken. Streets leading to business districts should be blocked and other streets open, so people can leave without being tempted to break windows, etc.
6. Use of the bullhorn or public address system to give the order to "move on." It may be necessary for more than one patrol com-

mander to do this, according to the size of the group. Coordination should be planned.

7. News coverage of the incident. Progressive police agencies realize the value of accurate news dissemination to the community. Charges of police brutality can more easily be challenged. Openness in police procedures enhances the professional image.

Demonstrations

This is the age of demonstrations. Whatever the size, adequate manpower must be assigned to insure peace. Manpower is a precious commodity, however, and should not be wasted at all. Planning for the small demonstrations should depend on intelligence information, intent and purpose of the demonstration, times indicated that the demonstration will take place, and identification of potential troublemakers. If at all possible, meet with the leaders of the demonstration to lay the ground rules under which the demonstration will take place. The meeting will decrease the possibility of misunderstanding and lessen the possibility of minor disagreements developing into real problems.

Deployment at the scene should be minimal, with reserve forces performing other tasks unless needed. The places where squads will form should be clearly understood by all so that response to the location is quick.

There is always the possibility of a large demonstration developing into a riot situation because of the lack of control alleged leaders of the demonstration hold over the many participants. What should the patrol administrator do to decrease this possibility? The first consideration is to determine if communication should be established before the demonstration. Past experience of policing demonstrations in which the present leaders were involved will determine the need for this step. If a meeting does take place, it should be cordial and candid. There should be no doubt in anyone's mind about the reaction of police to a given set of circumstances. These rules should be communicated politely but firmly, so that the whole episode begins with the police commander in a position of authority.

Intelligence personnel should provide confidential, reliable, and valuable information. This information has a direct bearing on the determination of manpower needed to provide coverage for the demonstration.

Personnel should be deployed in a manner that allows for response by a squad or a platoon or several platoons as the need requires. Patrol commanders should be briefed about the importance of communicating, at any given time, information about the demonstration concerning (1) fact, (2) rumor, (3) size, (4) location, (5) attitude of demonstrators, (6) attitude of leaders, and (7) possible intent of groups and demonstrators in totality. Support, as stated earlier, should include arrests, and booking and detention assistance. Mobile jails can be stationed at locations that offer the greatest potential for unlawful acts that would lead to an arrest.

The patrol commander should be prepared to respond swiftly with enough force to snuff out any demonstration that develops or may develop into a riot. Planning is essential, training is a must, and decisiveness on the part of the field commander should be inspiring. A well-disciplined patrol force with special-operations personnel using the team concept and the military formation of the squad wedge, diagonal, and line, should be able to move demonstrators in a professional manner. Additional help in this area is given by the officer whose personal appearance commands respect, who projects a cool, mature image, and who provides sensitivity where applicable and force when needed.

During demonstrations and riots, newsmen are all over the place seeking information. If at all possible, a public-information officer should be available. Orders instructing the force to refer all inquiries concerning the incident to the public-information officer should be disseminated. Updating information for the public-information officer by operational personnel also should be required.

Campus demonstrations. One of the major problems in responding to campus demonstrations is that the police officer is placed in the unenviable position of "bad guy." Patrol administrators should not allow indecisive school administrators to place the police in a position of "opposing force." Questions concerning the legal position of the police on campus should be answered. For example, when is someone trespassing? Who will act as a complainant? At what stage will the police be requested to take action? Will the police be expected to be baby sitters?

Remember, patrol commanders, administrative disagreements over rules, regulations, traditions, etc., between the administrators of the school and the students are just that: between the school administrators and the students. The police should not get involved. Naturally, overt acts of destruction should not be tolerated and arrest should be swiftly performed where appropriate.

The leaders of the patrol force assisting a school should meet with the campus security chiefs and school administrators to develop workable procedures. Careful analysis of the issues and possible answers and consequences are key aspects. The use of chemical agents as a primary tool is recommended for campus disorders. Because of the wide-open area of many schools, it will be necessary to have available the pepper-fogger and gas-grenade launching equipment. These tools will allow you to keep distance between the disruptive students and their goals, which will lessen the possibility of injury to anyone. As in any similar situation, action if taken should be swift and sure, always thinking about the consequences of each action and insuring that strength is available to complete the action.

SUMMARY CHECKLIST 1980[5]

Long-Term Prevention

Full employment; absence of discrimination. (Police can do very little to correct problems of unemployment, poverty, and discrimination. However, advocating elimination of these social causes of crime and disorder is in order.)

Short-Term Prevention

This category includes the prevention of those actions or attitudes by police that may contribute to disorders, as well as the development of programs that can strengthen resistance to disorders and at the same time build support for the police.

The police should review actions, attitudes, and practices which contribute to minority community tensions and grievances.

Several categories of police action have been identified as contributing causes for disorders:

Poor judgment or inappropriate response. Some incidents may be routine actions on the part of the police, but because of misjudged timing, over-reaction, or some other inappropriate response, they may become triggers for disorders—for example, allowing an arrestee to be exposed to public view for too long a period, or the continued presence of too many patrol cars at the scene following a routine call.

Actions and attitudes resulting from prejudice by police. The police executives at the conference recognized that blacks believe they are deliberately and disproportionately the victims of police prejudice against them. The complaints relating to manifestations of the prejudice tend to fall into the following groupings:

- The failure to provide the same quality of police service as that received by whites.
- Police misconduct and abuse—in general, those acts which are illegal or against departmental regulations.
- Police practice which may be legal but is viewed by the black community as harassment.
- The failure to establish a grievance procedure which would lead to correction of abuses.
- The failure to recruit representative numbers of minorities into the police department, and inequities in assignment and promotion of minorities.
- Absence of strict policy on the use of deadly force.
- Misperceptions of police misconduct and abuse must be counteracted.

- Building support in the community. The department should adopt a comprehensive police community relations program.
- The development of personal liaison with TV/radio, newspaper, and other media executives, and meeting with them periodically to discuss community and police problems.
- The publication of a newsletter.
- The creation of awareness and understanding of cultural differences in minority groups among police officers and their commanders.
- Dealing with Spanish language problems.
- The development of a police-community information system.
- Police interest in social and community problems.

Preparation for Control: Some Basic Considerations in Planning for the Control of Civil Disorders

A comprehensive plan for handling civil disorders should be created and continually updated.

Organization.   Control of civil disorders requires a more militaristic model of organization during the period of rioting.

Training.   Both supervisory and line personnel must be trained to operate as a disciplined, cohesive unit, under tight command and control. Officers must be trained in methods of control other than the use of deadly force.

Equipment.   Formal written agreements for emergency acquisition of equipment must be created.
Equipment must be periodically inspected and tested to ensure its ready use.

Some of the equipment necessary for controlling disorders is unique to these situations. Because such disturbances are relatively infrequent, this equipment can remain unused for long periods of time. This lack of use can lead to inattention or to deterioration from age. For example, tear gas canisters may deteriorate after a number of years.

To insure the ready availability of working equipment, the plan should specify the development of lists showing the kinds and amounts of equipment necessary. Periodically, supplies should be checked on the basis of this list, and updated as new types of disorder control equipment are developed. The list should at a minimum provide for the location, care, inspection, and numbers of the following:

1. Gas masks
2. Chemical agents
3. Protective vests
4. Firearms and ammunition
5. Helmets
6. Shields
7. Batons

8. Clothing for emergencies, including uniforms for detectives
9. Barricades for traffic control
10. Radios and batteries
11. Flashlights, batteries, and emergency power sources
12. Food service items

Mobilization.   An emergency mobilization plan to permit immediate response must be established and continually revised.

Coordination and mutual aid.   The relationship with the National Guard should be formalized and a general strategy developed.

It is imperative for police operational commanders to establish liaison with the local Guard commanders, and to prepare mutually acceptable written guidelines. This will lead to clear understanding of:

1. The role of the Guard
2. What are acceptable missions
3. Who will be in overall charge of the joint police-guard forces
4. Who will be the police liaison with the Guard and field units during the emergency
5. When the Guard will be notified in terms of mobilization and response
6. The logistics of coordination
7. Communications—Guard radios are usually limited to company level. The squad, which is the smallest unit normally assigned to a "mission," is unlikely to have communciations equipment. The police should try to provide radios, or access to them, by assigning a police officer to each squad.

An understanding must be established with the Governor's office regarding the Governor's policy on the use of the National Guard.
Coordination with other departments within the city and mutual aid pacts with law enforcement agencies of other jurisdictions must be formalized into written agreements, clearly delineating the responsibilities of each agency. Coordination of the response of the fire department must be established.

Communications.   The logistics of adequate radio communications within the police department and among the various agencies must be established in advance.

Decision-making procedures during a riot.   The comprehensive plan should spell out the decision-making process during a disorder.
A series of contingency plans should be developed for dealing with each escalating stage in a riot situation.

Rumor control.   The comprehensive plan shoud identify methods for handling rumor control and the persons who can assist in carrying it out. The media must be briefed as to the nature of a riot and provided with adequate and accurate information so as to minimize inflammatory reporting.

Containment procedures and de-escalation techniques. Control of the perimeters of the riot scene is imperative. Location and apprehension of snipers must be carried out as quickly as possible.

The key to controlling looting is through immediate application of manpower and early declaration of curfew. There should be immediate removal of individuals involved in potentially precipitating incidents.

Once a riot scene is under control, police presence should be maintained continuously for a matter of days, not hours. Efforts must be made to avoid inflammatory rhetoric by departmental personnel.

There should be a system for the identification of members of the community to operate as counter-rioters.

Mass arrest: Processing, transportation, and detention. Procedures must be established for processing mass arrests and transporting prisoners, and placing them in temporary detention facilities.

PREVENTION AND CONTROL OF URBAN DISORDERS: A STUDY[6]

The nation's police departments have a critical need to develop strategies for assessing the potential for urban disorders. The study is based largely on a review of the law enforcement response to the May 1980 riots in the Liberty City area of Miami and Dade County, Florida. In addition, police officers and executives outside Florida were interviewed and the literature on urban disorder was reviewed.

Disorder assessment is not widely viewed as a part of the disorder planning process. Police Departments need to learn how to carefully analyze neighborhood tensions. However, assessing the potential for disorder is not a one-time activity; it requires the establishment of new police functions which will involve police personnel at all levels of the organization, officers with special competencies and relationships, as well as neighborhood-based organizations.

Some cities have informally selected several types of indicators to help assess and analyze whether there is potential tension in an area to lead to an eruption, including: disturbance calls involving conflicts between groups, incidents in which the responding officer finds him/herself the target of abuse over what is considered routine police action, incidents of stoning of police or fire vehicles responding to calls for service, assaults between groups, assaults against police, citizen complaints of excessive force by police officers, changes in media coverage of police events or incidents, and lack of citizen willingness to assist police in routine matters.

The study lists problem areas cited by police commanders as contributing to the difficulty of mobilizing and responding to the rioting. Some of these problem areas are: lack of personnel on duty at the time of the first reports of the disorder, failure to update the Emergency Mobilization Plan of the Department of Public Safety to reflect reorganizations in the agency, confusion about the acceptable levels of use of lethal and non-lethal force, poor communications between command posts, both within and between departments, shortages of equipment, such as hand-held radios, gas masks, and rescue vans, absence of rumor control, lack of intelligence-gathering mechanisms or information systems which could have alerted police to the potential for disorder.

As a strategy to prevent disorders, the study suggested a creative intervention into community conflict, which involves a commitment by the police administrator to share power with the community for order maintenance and prioritization of police activities. Without the willingness to share power, police will find that communities will continue to force the police to assume total responsibility for dealing with all of the neighborhood's problems. The division between police and community will widen as the more stable members of a neighborhood will remain detached observers of the escalating state of community tension.

The patrol leader should acknowledge the very important role patrol officers play in the complex urban disorder problem. However, this study should be synthesized with other community facts and internal considerations, and result in a comprehensive strategy.

PRISON DISORDERS

Patrol administrators who anticipate future events will certainly develop a plan of action for fulfilling the department's obligation regarding prison disorders. The following section is presented in an effort to facilitate the patrol administrator's ability to fulfill that obligation.

> *Sample:* **Emergency response to prison, penitentiary, or jail facility** (in order to maintain continuity and understanding, jail, prison and penitentiary will be presented by the phrase "Prison Facility"). The plan should presume that riots and disruptions will occur in the future as they have in the past. Also, police personnel should have some general information as to the cause of prison riots just as they needed information concerning the causes and stages of civil disorder or riots in our cities. The ability to respond intelligently with sufficient service to quiet prison riots is determined in a similar manner as response to external disorder. In order to achieve the objective, planning and prompt response are key ingredients. At this point, information regarding why prisoners riot should be written:

General Information

Information obtained from official reports and news articles usually focuses on the following reasons as why prisoners riot: (1) overcrowding, (2) poor administration, (3) insufficient financial support, (4) political interference, (5) lack of professional leadership, (6) ineffective or nonexistent treatment programs, (7) disparities in sentencing, (8) poor and unjust parole policies, (9) enforced idleness of prisoners, (10) intractable prisoners.

In addition to these reasons, psychological viewpoints focus on aggressive and acting-out personalities in the prison population. Conditions mentioned in the sociological approach exist in most prisons, yet the majority have not experienced riots.

It is therefore tenuous when attempting to identify the cause of riots where official reports or statements after the riots are considered alone. It seems the reports written during the riot give a clear picture. As reported by Vernon Fox in *Federal Probation*, March 1971, pp. 9–14, "In decreasing order of validity and reliability the following material was used in making the report. (1) News stories during 20 serious riots since 1940 as reported in *The New York Times* during the action, (2) this writer's experience during the Michigan prison riot in 1952, (3) lengthy discussions with inmates involved in four prison riots, (4) conversations with prison personnel involved in seven prison riots, (5) literature concerning prison riots, (6) official reports and official statements after the riot, and (7) general literature on aggression, civil disturbance, and violence."

Causes must be divided into predisposing causes and precipitating causes. Just as in civil disobedience, there has to be a "readiness" to riot. Then, there has to be a "trigger." Too frequently, the predisposing causes have been used as causes for prison riots and the precipitating causes have been identified as causes for civil disorder. Neither is a cause in itself. The total social situation, with emphasis on the interaction or lack of it between dominant people and subjugated people, either in the prison or in the ghetto, must be evaluated to determine why people riot. It cannot be based simplistically on overcrowding, political interference, lack of treatment programs, or any other simple answer.

Riots are spontaneous—not planned—detonated by a spontaneous event. The inmates know who has the weapons and who has the force. The inmates know that no administration ever has to negotiate with them. Planned disturbances end in sit-down strikes, slowdowns, hunger strikes, and self-inflicted injury. The spontaneous event that detonates the riot may be almost anything from a fight in the yard that expands, someone heaving a tray in the dining hall, to a homosexual tricking a new officer to open his cell, as happened in the Michigan riot in 1952. Violent riots must happen spontaneously. Otherwise, they would not happen. There has to be pressure, though, that builds up the predisposition or readiness to riot and a spontaneous precipitating event to trigger or detonate the riot.

Riots tend to pattern in five stages, four during the riot and one afterward. First, there is a period of undirected violence like the exploding bomb. Second, inmate leaders tend to emerge and organize around them a group of ringleaders who determine inmate policy during the riot. Third, a period of interaction with prison authority, whether by negotiation or by force, assists in identifying the alternative available for the resolution of the riot. Fourth, the surrender of the inmates, whether by negotiation or by force, phases out the violent event. Fifth, and most important from the political viewpoint, the investigations and administrative changes restore order and confidence in the remaining power structure by making "constructive changes" to regain administrative control and to rectify the undesirable situation that produced the riot.

The first stage of riot is characterized by an event that triggered the unbridled violence. The first stage is disorganized among the prisoners and, too frequently, among the prison staff as well. It is at this point that custodial force could alter the course of the riot but, in most instances, custody is caught by surprise and without adequate preparation so that there is little or no custodial reaction other than containment. As a result, the riot pattern is permitted by default to move to the second stage. It is at this point the key ingredients of planning and prompt response with appropriate resources become essential.

The second stage is when inmate leaders emerge and the administrative forces become organized. Inmate leaders who emerge from this violence are people who remain emotionally detached sufficiently so that they lend stability to the inmate group. They don't "panic." They "keep their cool." As a result they attract around them lesser inmate leaders or "ringleaders" who similarly, do not panic but need to be dependent upon "the boss." In this manner, an inmate leader can gather around him probably two to six "lieutenants," each with some delegated authority, such as watching hostages, preparing demands, and maintaining discipline in the rest of the inmate group. Further, the inmate leader, like most political leaders, takes a "middle-of-the-road" position where he can moderate the extremes and maintain communication. In a prison riot, some inmates want to kill the hostages. Other inmates want to give up and surrender to the administration. The inmate leader controls these two extremes in a variety of ways and stabilizes the group into a position in the center.

The third stage is a period of interaction between inmates and prison officials. It has taken several forms, though they can be classified generally into (1) negotiation, and (2) force or threat of force. No administration has to negotiate with prisoners, but the chances for negotiation are greater when the prisoners hold hostages. The chances for force or threat are greater when the prisoners do not have hostages. In either case, the decision on the part of the inmates to surrender is subject to the general principles of group dynamics. When the inmate group is cohesive and their morale is good, the prisoners will maintain the riot situation, whether faced with force or negotiation. When the group cohesion begins to disintegrate by some inmates wanting to surrender, others wanting to retaliate, and the leadership wanting to maintain the status quo, the administration may manipulate it for an early surrender. This disintegration of group cohesion may be prompted by negotiation or by force or threat of force, depending upon the situation.

In case of negotiation, the group cohesion is diminished by the administration's demonstrated willingness to negotiate and by the personality of the official negotiators who convey a feeling of trust and confidence. The group can be disintegrated, also by gas, rifle fire, and artillery shelling, all of which have been used recently in American prison riots. The less destructive approach, of course, is to await disintegration of cohesion by periods of inaction that places strain to hold the group together on the leadership by fatigue and impatience. Faced with this situation the leadership frequently has to look for an honorable way out of a disintegrating situation.

The fourth stage, or surrender, may be the inmates' giving up after being gassed and shot at, or they may surrender in an orderly way, either after force or threat of force, or by negotiation. Political interference at the wrong time in the prison riot can affect the total situation in terms of negotiation, surrender, and subsequent investigations and administrative decisions.

The fifth stage, that of investigations, consolidation of the remaining power structure, personnel and policy changes followed by political fallout, is really the most important stage, since it sets policy for the prison and the system for years to come. Editorials and news commentators suggest solutions and interpretations. Administrators have to respond to pressures from interest groups. This is why "get-tough" policies become important after riots, even though they tend to intensify the problems.

Riots do not occur in prisons or correctional institutions with exceedingly high morale. Neither do they occur in prisons where the morale is so low that the prisoners endure penal oppression in a docile manner or break their own legs and cut they own heel tendons. Riots occur in prisons where inmates have medium to high morale and where some conflict appears in the staff, probably between treatment and custodial philosophies, and probably when the program is in a state of transition from one type of procedures and objectives to another.

Riots occur in prisons where there is a tenuous balance between controlling behavior and changing behavior. If there is a full commitment to either riots do not occur. The riot itself, results in a political decision to control behavior. Consequently, the behavior changing in treatment forces always loses in a riot, at least in the immediate future.

There is also a direct relationship between news coverage by the mass media and incidence of demonstrations, riots, and civil disturbances. This is one reason why riots tend to cluster in terms of time.

Guidelines for Action

Guidelines for action during the riot are important. The custodial staff is frequently untrained and the administration is just as frequently caught by surprise. Action during the riot has to be planned ahead of time and modified according to the situation.

During the first stage of a riot, the disorganized inmates could well be effectively faced with force. As a matter of fact, most riots appear to have been vulnerable to custodial force in the early stages because of disorganization on the side of the inmates. If disorganization occurs on both sides, however, then the riot cannot be contained early. Immediate custodial action could have altered the course of several riots. The lack of training, preparation, or even expectation of riot has resulted in disorganizations on both sides for hours.

During the second stage, after the inmates have organized and their leadership begins to emerge, there is the question as to whether force should be used. No prison administration ever needs to negotiate with rioting prisoners. The prisoners know this. If hostages are held, then negotiation becomes a real possibility, depending upon the other factors. If the inmates holding the hostages are young, reformatory-type people with short sentences and have not already demonstrated their capability to kill, if they are psychiatric patients who cannot organize into a team, or if their majority can see parole sometime in the future, then negotiation is not necessary.

The third stage of the riot is determined by the nature of the situation. If no hostages are held, or if the prisoners holding hostages are not hardcore intractables with nothing to lose, then force or threat of force is appropriate. If the hostages are considered to be in serious danger, the administration is placed in a real dilemma in determining action because lives have to be considered in relation to public and internal reaction and consequence. If waiting for fatigue to reduce the cohesion of the rebellious inmate group will accomplish the objective, then force is not necessary.

The fourth stage of the riot is the surrender. The regaining of custodial control is all that is needed. Any further action beyond the basic need has to be for public consumption or for the satisfaction of the prison administration.

The fifth stage of the riot is the aftermath where investigation, reinterpretations, and scapegoats are involved. There is not much the prison administration can do about this because the real power lies in the political structure. Free movement of newsmen and free access to information, both inmates and staff, is the only logical approach to take during this period. In this way, the administration can demonstrate that it is attempting to hide nothing, that it recognizes it has problems and is openly and honestly seeking the best solutions.

In summary, official reaction to riot is dependent upon the situation. As in judo, the reaction is determined by the action of the adversary. No negotiation is needed where no hostages are held or where they might be held by short-term prisoners not considered to be dangerous. Outwaiting might be an approach in doubtful situations, since an overshow of force is becoming decreasingly effective in American society and it invites unnecessary derision from some segments of the public.

Discretion rather than negotiation or force is at issue while handling a riot. A basic principle of police work or any other type of social control is a democratic society is to use the minimum amount of force and destruction needed to accomplish the objectives.

The correctional officer is the key to riot prevention, although a rough and harsh custodial lieutenant, captain, or deputy warden can use policies and behavior to neutralize the good work of a hundred officers. The entire custodial force has to be treatment-oriented, just as the entire treatment staff has to be aware of custodial problems, in order to emerge with an effective correctional program.

Readiness to riot results from the predisposing causes, such as bad food, oppressive custodial discipline, sadistic staff quick to write disciplinary charges against inmates, and general punitive attitude by administration and line personnel. The precipitating cause that "triggers" the riot is very seldom the real cause. A bomb is made by constructing a strong perimeter or casing and generating pressure inside. It blows at its weakest point, but it has to be detonated. The detonation is not the "cause of the explosion" although it "triggered" it.[4]

Policy

The next part of the plan should be a policy statement from the chief of police. The statement should concern the direction of the department prior to, during, and after the prison emergency.

Responsibility and Procedure (Usually the patrol administrator will be command at a prison riot.)

This area of the plan concerns itself with placing individual responsibilities and setting forth specific procedures responding to a prison emergency. If there is more than one prison facility location in the jurisdication of the department, a basic plan may be written with minor adjustments made for each facility. Considerations must be made regarding legal and jurisdictional responsibility.

The first step is to open up communication between the administrator of the prison and the police department. There should be a face-to-face meeting, which shall include the command staff of both agencies. Responsibility for action should be agreed upon at each step of the plan. At all times, the officer in command must be identifiable. If responsibility should include calling State Police officials or the National Guard, communication should follow with those organizations to insure a proper change of command if necessary and appropriate. This is similar to civil disorder and is most necessary. You cannot place too much emphasis on who is in command when confronted by a serious situation of this type. Once the question of responsibility at each step has been resolved, you can move on to the second step.

The second step should be to determine the authorized personnel from the prison facility who have authority to call for assistance. This avoids the problem of irresponsible reaction by lower-ranking prison authorities calling for assistance unnecessarily and causing the police to disrupt their organizations without due cause. By selecting only prison officials as authorized calling personnel, promptness, effectiveness, and coordination are enhanced. With the face-to-face meeting between the police commanders and their prison counterparts, formulation will take place and thus avoid unnecessary delay at the time of the incident.

Verification of the call for assistance is our next consideration and exchange of telephone information that can be used to validate verification enhances the operation. An exchange of pictures of the authorized officials of each agency is helpful. This information must be maintained and updated. A notification chart (Figure 7.4) and an alternate notification chart (Figure 7.5) depict the process. Circumstances existing at the time of the prison emergency will determine which planned emergency-response notification chart will be used.

As indicated by the chart, the notified member of the police who belongs to the authorized verification group will immediately verify the authenticity of the call for assistance by contacting one of the authorized prison officials. (Scheduling of command personnel leave and vacations will insure the contact of at least one member of the authorized verification groups.) This notification is done in most cases by private telephone. (In many cases where the author was the police verification, there was no delay in contacting an authorized prison official.)

As soon as verification is made, the notified member of the authorized verification group will be responsible for notifying the chief of police and the on-duty communication commander. If the notified member of the police group is other than the on-duty communication commander, that officer should then report to the office of operations where he should coordinate notification activities. If the notified officer has duties at the scene of the prison that would supersede the coordinating activities, he would then request a replacement for that responsibility and proceed to the location of the prison.

Figure 7.4 *Planned emergency-response notification chart for prison facility*

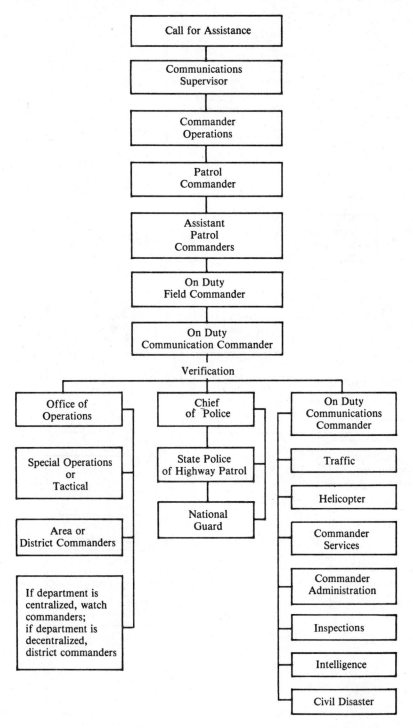

Figure 7.5 *Planned-emergency-response notification chart for prison facility*

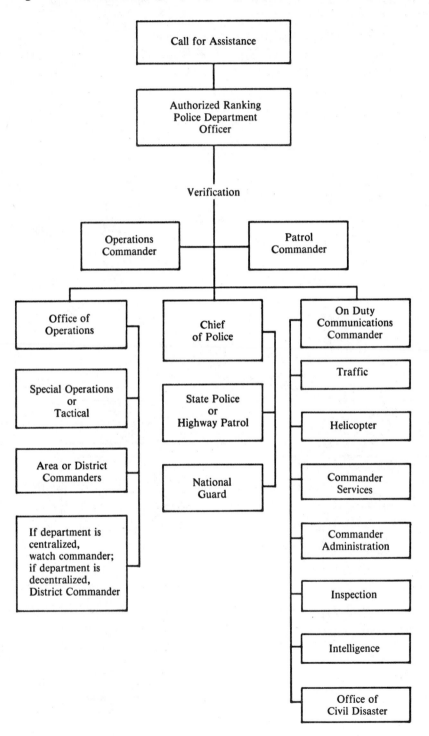

Those authorized ranking members of the police department who receive the call for assistance and verify, should then implement the planned emergency response by properly notifying indicated personnel. As shown in Figures 7.4 and 7.5, the completion of the notification process would be automatic, and officials can then carry out their respective responsibilities expeditiously.

Prison Visit

In order to resolve any delay that might take place on arriving at the prison, police commanders who may be responsibile for commanding the task force that would be assembled and respond to a prison riot should personally visit the facility. Together with the correctional officials, a tour should be taken where the many factors that need to be considered, especially if chemical agents may be used, can be discussed in depth. Some of the factors to consider would be (1) ventilation system, (2) location of potential weapons, (3) escape routes, (4) potential ingress and egress routes for police, (5) probable wind direction for a given area, (6) strength, (7) staging area inside the walls, (8) guard strength, and (9) prison population. These factors are not all-inclusive.

Communications

As in riot control, where many men are assembled, direction, coordination, and control become paramount when attempting to quell a prison riot. A decision must be made to clear all other personnel from a selected frequency that shall then be reserved for communications pertaining to the prison situation only. Communication discipline should be emphasized in any plan and subsequent orders evolving from that plan. The choice of what type of communciation should be used will depend on the location of the transmitting person, the equipment available, the degree of emergency, and the confidentiality of the message. The type of communication selected can be personal messenger, telephone, or portable radio.

Certain messages may have to be transmitted by radio because of their emergency, but for which confidentiality is preferred or required. In this case the use of a code is very helpful and decreases the possibility of citizen insecurity because of misunderstood or misrepresented transmissions that may be picked up by outside agitators, the news media, or the rioting prisoners themselves who may have a radio in their possession. Also, portions of the message taken out of context, or conjecture regarding the message itself, may be used for rumor and propaganda intentionally to try to incite others on the outside.

The following is a sample of a simple code and what information you might want to be included in code transmission:

P-1 – Police injured
P-2 – Prisoners have weapons (possible to mean only guns)
P-3 – Additional personnel necessary
P-4 – Additional equipment needed
P-5 – Rioters have taken hostage(s)

The assignment of the mobile-command vehicle to a strategic position near the prison is important. Located at this position should be a prepositioned telephone hookup, which would give immediate telephone communication with the communication center. At least one radio technician should be assigned to report to the operational mobile-command post to insure immediate repair of any breakdown in communication equipment. Other responsibilities of the communications unit would be (1) to activate a central command post, (2) to maintain a log book, (3) to provide adequate personnel to keep administrative telephone lines open and, (4) to insure appropriate repair equipment for an extended siege.

Traffic

The role of traffic officers during prison riots should be examined to insure maximum use. If the situation reaches a point where traffic officers must be put directly into battle, other help would probably be on the way. In most cases when the alert is sounded, traffic personnel should be assembled and given the responsibility for handling all vehicular and pedestrian traffic within the immediate area of the prison. The traffic officers should at this time be under the command of the field-force operational commander.

Helicopter

If the police department has a helicopter unit, the plan should cause the helicopter to take a position of advantage. Flexibility of operation is primary and easily attainable for this unit; therefore, this strength is what the Field Commander would utilize.

Inspection and Intelligence

The use of these units would be determined by many factors which are specific to each department. Possible uses are recording the event for after-action review and sensitivity to the perimeter of the facility regarding sympathizers who may create disruption to show support for inmates.

Public Information

Much has been learned from the civil disorders in the past. One thing is certain: the news media should be informed of events whenever possible. Having a public information office or the equal at the scene where information can be passed on in an enlightened manner helps the total operation. In this way, operational commanders are not being interfered with by groups of people, there is less potential for conjecture and rumor, rapport between the department and news personnel is maintained, and the whole operation runs smoother. The mobile press center should be identified for the news media, and they should be told that all information will be given from the press center.

Other Service Units

Other service units, such as property, should take a posture of providing appropriate logistical support for the operational forces. If the riot continues for an extended period, feeding of police personnel should be coordinated with other city agencies as appropriate. In some cases, this would be the office of civil disaster.

Support should be planned with any agency that might be able to supply needed services.

In addition to the information obtained during the prison riot, the following information should be maintained on a current level; (1) inmate population, correctional officer strength by shift; (2) strength at critical times, such as meal time, recreation time, and bed time; (3) civilian employees (this would be helpful in accounting for personnel re hostages); (4) inmate housing, dormitories, wings, block houses, diagnostic center, hospital; (5) clothing worn by inmates; (6) constant number for each location and fluctuating number of time of day and day of week as appropriate; (7) time of normal working for inmates (remember, the inmates who work in the kitchen would report to work earlier than the other inmates); (8) minimum, medium, and maximum security areas; (9) activity during evening hours, holidays, and weekends; (10) location and hours of workshops, such as the print shop, metal shop, wood shop, and laundry; (11) power house; and (12) storerooms and their contents.

As stated earlier, critical times for prison officials should be remembered by all police commanders. They should know that meal times create the greatest concentration of inmates, and historical data reveal that this is the time when most disorders take place. Another critical point is when the concentration of prisoners is at a high level and the assignment of correction officers is at a low level. Knowledge of the amount and quality of training possessed by the correctional officers regarding their ability to respond to such situations, and the volume and type of equipment possessed, will help police officers determine their optimum response. If possible, and the expertise is possessed by the police agency, arrangements can be made for training in such tactics as may be necessary to improve the ability of the prison officials to handle these situations. This training would benefit all concerned.

Operational Response

The planned emergency response notification chart would be implemented as indicated in Figures 7.4 and 7.5. At this point, all notified officers would be placed in one of four categories: (1) committed to the prison, (2) reserve status, (3) alert status, (4) function routinely. The change from one category to the next would come from orders given by the operational field commander.

The plan should then outline the number of personnel of each rank, depending on the size of the prison, inmate population, manpower available, and degree of seriousness of the situation. Whatever the case, if response is to be implemented, control, direction, and leadership exemplified by command personnel accompanied by supervisors and patrolmen in team or squad-concept will offer the best approach to prompt resolution of the problem. For example, squads of twelve patrolmen with a sergeant supervisor where the twelve men are broken into four-man fire teams are excellent to work with as a total team. Each fire team would have a unit leader, baton man, launcher man, and assistant launcher man. Each man would be equipped with appropriate fire-power which may or may not include minigrenades, CS grenades, baseball grenades, grenade launcher, launcher shells, triple chaser grenades, shotgun, etc. The team should be able to work as a unit and as close as possible to a total entity. Inspection of men should insure no loose equipment hanging from uniforms that might be taken by a rioting prisoner and used as a weapon against the officer. These precautions should be taken at the staging area, preselected for its advantage of the prison. The staging area should be large enough for congregation of personnel and have space available where proper information and instructions can be disseminated. If it is not close enough to walk to the prison, buses should be available to transport large numbers of men to the prison at one time. Armory support units should respond to the staging area in order to keep supplying the operational forces with proper equipment both in volume and complexity.

The operational commander will notify each group within the various categories in enough time so that smooth coordinated change from one category to the next takes place. This notification procedure will decrease the possibility of having confusion at the staging area. The change from routine function status to alert status to reserve status to committed status should be done on a timely basis and calls for planned decisive orders from the operational commander and his assistants.

Canine Teams

How canine teams will be used in prison riots should be considered ahead of time. They should be in the front ranks of committed personnel as soon as assessment of the situation takes place. The operational commander has at least three important decisions to make in determining which approach to use in quelling the disturbance. Should he use chemical agents, manpower in volume with canine teams in the lead, or should he shoot plastic bullets? All of these decisions (and there are more) will be determined by the situation as it exists in that instant. By developing options, the operational commander eases the tension and errors that might come from not knowing these options. We need only look around the country to find situations where alternate methods may have been the better solution.

When confronted by hundreds of inmates who are rioting in a prison, you will find them with headbands wrapped around their heads, towels around their faces, armed with everything from knives, guns, baseball bats, wooden poles, chairs, iron bed posts, and broken bottles. When the order is given to act, the moment of truth has arrived. The rioting prisoners may or may not obey. As the operational commander, your next move should be planned depending on the response to your order. If the order is disobeyed and action must be taken, the safety of police and correctional officers is the first consideration. Your action should accomplish the objective with minimum violence (including prisoners), remembering whatever the action, a decision must be made, and the consequence of the decision should be anticipated.

Under the conditions of a prison, canine teams in squads are one of the most effective weapons you can possess. In many instances, just the appearance of the canine teams will cause many of the rioting prisoners to have second thoughts about their actions, and may even be the reason for them giving up. If canine teams are used, they should be used in squads of 3, 4, 5, or 6 depending on the geography of the specific area. In smaller areas, one group of three teams could back up another group of three. If the area is open, one squad of six canine teams could back up another squad of six canine teams.

These fine animals can do the job if they are used properly. If it becomes necessary at some point during the riot to use chemical agents, the animals should be given consideration regarding their position to the chemical agents. The officers in charge of the canine team squads can easily be consulted prior to taking the specific action where chemical agents may be used. The use of this canine-team option can result in a very successful operation.

Identification of Inmates

Arrangements should be made to insure identification of inmates who might commit various violations during the riots, so prosecution can take place after the completion of the action. In most large disorders, the identification problem is one of the most difficult to solve no matter what procedure is used (taking pictures of officers with violators, using plastic handcuffs, etc.), and good planning will improve the percentage of rioters successfully prosecuted as a result of any committed violation.

Critique

In conclusion, the plan should end with a critique of the operation. Procedure should be outlined where constructive criticism is solicited. In this way improvements can be made in needed areas so that the next time the plan is implemented, a better product results.

BARRICADED PERSONS AND SNIPERS

The critical confrontation between police and barricaded persons or snipers is one of the most sensitive situations challenging the patrol administrator and the patrol force. Experience has shown that undisciplined firepower and confusion readily occur when police are dealing with reported snipers or armed persons barricaded in a home or building. The need for fire discipline, a calm and decisive leader, and a written procedure understood by all is essential. Add to this good weapons and training, and a successful conclusion to these explosive situations is readily achievable.

No two situations are exactly alike, but with planned operational procedures and special-operations teams, sometimes known as SWAT (*Special Weapons And Tactics*), patrol commanders can minimize the potential for loss of life and property. The primary officer responding to a call of a reported sniper or barricaded person should first determine the reliability of the report. If the report is true, he should call for assistance, evacuate innocent citizens, cordon off the area, and determine the exact location of the perpetrator if possible. When assistance arrives (and patrol supervision responsible for the areas should be prompt), assignments should be made in an effort to prevent escape, and a mobile command post set up. The SWAT team should respond to the location of the incident. During this period, the senior patrol officer on the scene should maintain strict fire discipline and begin to determine if possible:

1. identification of perpetrator;
2. identification of perpetrator's relative, friends, etc.;
3. if there are any witnesses to incident (if so, he should interview them for any pertinent information);
4. what weapons are possessed by the perpetrator;
5. if hostages are being held; and
6. the mental condition and probable intent of the perpetrator.

It is imperative to remember that fire discipline is essential. Revolvers are usually inadequate during these situations, and random firing may cause serious injury to innocent citizens and possibly a fellow officer. The detailed methodical approach by a trained SWAT team is the more enlightened course of action. If the area is cleared, there will be no target for the perpetrator. If there is no target, there will be no personal injury. The makeup of the SWAT team will depend upon the capabilities and training of the special-operations force personnel and the resources available to the department.

It should be presumed that all persons involved in these situations are dangerous, and extreme caution should be used. This is especially true where steps to develop a dialogue with the individual are taken. Developing a dialogue is preferable to the use of force. Another alternative, depending on the situation, is the use of chemical agents; therefore, gas masks should be considered along with bullet-proof vests.

The patrol commander in charge of this police action must demonstrate by example the qualities of leadership necessary to take firm command of the situation. Decisiveness, judgment, sensitivity, knowledge, and confidence should permeate the operation and cause all officers involved to respond similarly, resulting in a professional performance.

YOUTH-ORIENTED PERFORMANCES

Special-operations forces are usually the front-line officers in any explosive situation, and one of the special talents of these officers is to be able to relate to the young people of the country. Police agencies across the country are confronted with rock festivals and crowds of youths on the California and Florida coasts at vacation times. Urban police forces are expected to control the thousands of young people who exit from the amphitheaters of our cities in a high-pitched emotional state. All of these situations are sensitive, and tact, firmness, and good planning are necessary to reach a successful conclusion.

When force is necessary, enlightened leadership must dictate the proper procedure to prevent escalation to the point of riot. One preventive measure that has proven successful in the past is to request the promoters and performers of these youth-oriented activities to slow down the tempo at the end of each performance. Those persons who have cooperated in this area have generally found a more receptive government when applying for future performance dates. When the emotional state of the youths has been made more low-key by this procedure, they usually exit in an orderly manner. Tension is reduced, and opportunity for unruly conduct is lessened.

Cooperation and coordination between local police and special police officers (private security) hired for these events can help reduce the potential for disorder. Opening of some exits and closing of others or opening of all exits, as the case may be, will automatically route pedestrian traffic into areas that are less crowded and most convenient for the police agencies. The less time youths are milling around waiting for traffic to move, the less chance of an incident arising that may precipitate disorder.

Public transportation officials can be most helpful in supplying buses for immediate service in order to reduce the amount of time youths must stay in a crowded atmosphere outside the facility. Liaison between special-operations forces and public and private transportation officials can ensure a sufficient number of vehicles being ready.

Planning for these performances depends upon past experiences and information from law enforcement agencies confronted with similar situations. Special-operations forces should provide a sufficient number of personnel according to the estimate of the size of crowd, type of performance, and location of the performance. Provisions should be made for security of any nearby businesses. Some departments use K-9 teams for this type of security. Traffic personnel should be strategically placed to insure the best possible movement of traffic. Arrest teams and procedures for moving prisoners swiftly from the area should be available in case arrests become necessary. Weather predictions (wind speed and direction) should be reviewed to determine specific plans regarding the use of chemical agents and probable change in plans because of inclement weather.

One of the more important considerations is the acquisition of additional manpower if necessary, including the determination of the lead time. (How long will it take the manpower to arrive at the scene?) This information should be broken down into minutes. For example, would the special-operations force commander have ten men on the scene fifteen minutes after requested? How many would respond to the scene in twenty minutes? Thirty minutes?

The actions of youth groups are difficult to predict, and contingency plans must be completed in full.

DISASTER CONTROL

Whenever a disaster occurs, the patrol officer is usually first on the scene. Subsequently, special operation forces will be called upon to supply the expertise. Therefore, these forces should be prepared with the appropriate procedures and equipment to fulfill the police department's responsibility. The patrol administrator must plan for those disasters that are most prevalent in his specific community. Whenever it is impossible to cover all exigencies, the priority system can be implemented through analysis of potential disasters.

Professional approaches to disaster control require cooperation and coordination between many agencies. These agencies include all agencies of local government; the telephone, gas, and electric companies; American Red Cross; Salvation Army; National Guard; religious charities; and Civil Defense. The police department should draw on the expertise of all agencies in order to provide the most effective and efficient response. Simulated exercises that require all participants to take an active interest can provide the necessary communication between agencies for a "control emergency liaison communication center." All agencies practicing together will resolve the many minor problems beforehand and result in a smoothly operating disaster control procedure.

There are various types of major disasters, both natural and otherwise. Some natural disasters can be anticipated, e.g., because of weather and geography. The efforts of the police and other public and private agencies can help reduce the potential for loss of life and property. The patrol administrator should include in his list of anticipated disasters the following: airplane crashes, earthquakes, avalanches, tidal waves, hurricanes, building collapses, cyclones, blizzards, floods, dam collapses, explosions (internal and accidental), fires (hospital, school, hotel, nursing homes), mine cave-ins, railroads, ships, gas leaks, and forest fires. An awareness of what disasters may occur will help in meeting these tremendous challenges in an enlightened and constructive manner.

Proper disaster planning will produce a calm, efficient response and help greatly in reducing any hysteria on the part of citizens. In developing a plan for the patrol force, coordination with other agencies is of paramount importance. The special-operations personnel, however, will be called upon to supply primary control and must consider: (1) traffic control to, from, and within the disaster area; (2) identification of victims, living and dead; (3) removal and disposition of victims; (4) mobile command post; (5) security of area to reduce possible spread of disease where applicable; (6) provision for relatives of victims to proceed to receiving area to identify dead and unite with living (this temporary facility should contain a reception area and morgue area); (7) public information office; (8) after-action reports; and (9) evaluation of hazardous areas. Prompt identification of persons who have died as a result of a disaster is important because of relatives and the legal implications, such as those concerning estates, insurance claims, business enterprises, and remarriage of survivors. Special care should be taken to supervise the identification to avoid any possibility of destroying articles and other paraphernalia necessary for valid identification.

Command and control of a disaster situation are essential. The prompt action of the police department in communicating the nature and extent of the disaster and achieving the support of other agencies should result in minimizing loss of life and property.

LABOR RELATIONS

No one can predict when a labor strike will occur. Strikes involve most types of workers, private and public. Special-operations officers and supervisors should be well-acquainted with the legal aspects of labor relations. This most sensitive area requires patrol commanders to be ever alert for situations that will involve the department in a negative way. Fair and impartial treatment within the law is the order of the day.

What is an injunction? Who is required by law to enforce the injunction? What liaisons have been developed between the police department and the organization responsible for enforcing the injunction (if it is not the police department)? How much restraint will be used, if any? These questions should be answered before police involvement in a strike situation. Where there is the potential for violence, or when violence is imminent, action must be swift and professional.

All personnel of the special-operations forces should be trained in this sometimes volatile area. Labor problems have resulted in arson, assaults of a serious nature, and sometimes even murder. Any labor problem should be considered important and highly skilled officers in the field of human relations given first assignment to the problem. Many times, action taken at the height of emotional stress is unnecessary and lingering resentment may result from this demonstrated judgment. Patrol commanders capable of cool, calm, and objective decisions, but with the ability to decide immediately and, if necessary, to act, are preferred as supervisors at the scene of these sensitive situations.

DECOY OPERATIONS

The following is an application of the theory of Prevention-Apprehension/ Prevention-Apprehension. The material is reprinted by permission from a Law Enforcement Assistance Administration exemplary project carried out by New York City Police Department on street crime. This operation is one that integrates the patrol and investigative functions.

Violent street crime can be a source of constant fear to those who live and work in urban areas. There are different strategies for combatting this type of crime, and reasons for doing so, one being a demand for more police protection as the result of increased cost for police services. Recent studies done by the Police Foundation in Kansas City indicate that there may be a very real question concerning the impact of preventive patrol. The application of the findings of this study to a police department may be questionable; however, one thing lends itself to increased effectiveness and that is the development of alternative forms of policing to bridge the gap between visible police patrol and the investigation of reported crimes.

In the traditional sense, police in uniform are expected to be highly visible and deter crime by their omnipresence, while officers of the detective units are expected to investigate past crimes and apprehend perpetrators and measure their effectiveness through the resulting apprehension via clearance rates. It is very doubtful that increased uniform patrol, in the numbers necessary to combat the street crimes which exist in most urban areas today, is the most realistic and effective approach. In analyzing street crimes such as muggings and purse snatches, one draws a conclusion that they are so swiftly committed that many victims cannot identify their assailants even if they were later confronted by them in a one-to-one lineup.

One strategy that may have merit, and this will depend on experience, is a strategy of plainclothes surveillance decoy and response teams with the objective of apprehending perpetrators of street crimes during their commission. With the proper selection and training of patrolmen and supervisors utilizing a plainclothes surveillance decoy and response team strategy, it is possible to apprehend suspects in the act of committing particular crimes.

A decoy police officer disguised as a potential crime victim, taken from the profile of victims of a given area of previous crimes by category, is placed in the area where he/she is likely to be the victim. A backup team dressed to blend into the area is stationed nearby ready to come to the decoy's aid and effect an arrest. While decoy tactics are used in response to particular crime/victim patterns, blending techniques are used regularly to allow the officer to move freely on the street. The primary objective is to effect quality arrests (arrests which lead to convictions) with no increased danger to police or citizens.

The decoy section of the New York Police Department is under the command of a captain and incorporates the management philosophy of managing by objectives and participatory management provided through task force operations. This will be fulfilled by having periodic conferences with commanders, bulletins on tactics which are distributed to all precincts and anti-crime personnel, and analysis of precinct crime operations, methods, and tactics. It will be necessary for a crime analysis unit to provide the necessary planning information for deployment of these teams of officers. Crime information becomes an essential part of this type of strategy.

Personnel

As in any other area of policing the personnel of a decoy unit is its most important ingredient. Officers working in this type of strategy must, out of necessity, use their ingenuity and imagination because of the high-crime areas, the dangerous situations in which they are placed, and the minimum amount of supervision provided.

These officers spend their time and energy actively engaged in outwitting the street criminal in his own element—the street. They function exclusively in high-crime areas during hours of peak crime incidents. Their attention is focused on crimes of violence without the identification factor furnished to uniformed officers; therefore they place themselves in a disproportionate number of situations in which they have the potential for facing armed felons. This requires personal courage and a high degree of resourcefulness and tenacity.

Selection. Officers involved in this type of strategy should have the following qualifications:

1. Aggressiveness,
2. Motivation,
3. Curiosity,
4. Honesty,
5. Experience,
6. Productivity Orientation, and
7. "Street Smarts."

Since these officers must blend into the general street scene, they have to be able to act in such a way that they do not reveal themselves to potential felons or ordinary citizens. Experience is a very integral part of this selection process. Officers who would be working under these kinds of strategies should be investigated in the following areas: internal affairs, medical, complaints, personnel screening, and disciplinary records.

Interview. Officers assigned to this particular strategy should be interviewed by field supervisors. The supervisor should be made to state if he would want the applicant to work with him under these kinds of conditions. They must go into high-crime areas together and they deliberately expose themselves to criminal activity under unusual circumstances. They must depend upon one another for protection. The relationship between the members of the team is a very close one. Officers shoud be questioned about working with partners of the opposite sex, arrest activity, experience in this type of work, attitudes toward department policies, and firearms use. Officers should then be rated by these field supervisors with regard to their ability to work under trying conditions. Other qualities that should be looked for in the interview should be the following:

1. The willingness to accept responsibility;
2. The amount of maturity and stability;
3. A willingness to contribute to a team effort;
4. Initiative and resourcefulness;
5. Compliance with departmental policy and procedures and guidelines and directions of immediate supervisors; and
6. Job knowledge.

Conclusion. What appears to be important is that there is a big chance for minorities and females to be involved in this kind of an approach which would enhance the total participation of members of the police agency.

Training

The following areas are important for training officers who will be involved in plainclothes surveillance decoy response teams:

- Tactics and methods of plainclothes surveillance
- Tactics and methods of decoy policing
- Locations of areas—entrances, exits, street directions
- The various types of decoy roles
- Crime picture and modus operandi of criminals in assigned areas
- Police tactics and signals employed during a particular tour of duty
- Roll-call training where an atmosphere of open discussion permeates the training session
- The discussion of arrests, arrest procedures, critique of shooting incidents, and exchanging potentially successful decoy tactics and strategies

Supervision

Blending and decoy tactics reduce the effectiveness of ordinary supervisory practices. Consequently, ingenuity plays a large part in the performance of supervisory duties. These supervisors rely on participative management and team concepts to help achieve objectives in this work strategy. Participative management refers to a process in which officers are afforded an opportunity to have an input into decisions within areas where they are affected. Open discussion should be held on subjects ranging from human relations and racial problems to decoy tactics and deployment strategies. Input from officers should be analyzed and reviewed as feedback and used to develop other strategies which may have more value. This approach may not be quantifiable in terms of evaluation, but effect may be seen as a result of the increase in morale of unit members. The lack of morale may be measured. The reduction of isolation as far as decision making is concerned and the distance decision makers are from the realities of the working situation are observable and will show up in the team effectiveness.

The basis for this strategy is that it is similar to a football team where you have a quarterback who is the supervisor, and the runningbacks and line players, who make up the rest of the team and develop supportive relationships between one another. Supervisors are expected to motivate their men by vitally contributing to the development of common spirits of pride, devotion, and enthusiasm for police service in general and this particular aspect of patrol specifically.

Supervisors are charged with the responsibility of training, field supervision, arrest supervision, court review, report review, maintaining equipment for performance, crime analysis, and total administrative duties.

1. Supervisors are totally responsible for the deployment of personnel within their assigned area.
2. They re-deploy their personnel to cope with changing situations.
3. They determine the most effective manner of patrol to be utilized for a particular area at a particular time, such as foot-auto surveillance, taxi patrol, or fixed position observations.
4. They develop plans, discuss strategies, and implement tactics to cope with the ongoing situation.
5. They create disguises and encourage their use to blend the decoy tactics in the community and make them totally more effective.
6. They coordinate investigations with the regular follow-up detective responsibility.

Morale

This subtopic is included because it may not be defined positively but it can be defined when you find there is a lack of morale in the sense that you have a high degree of absenteeism and low productivity. There are certain reasons for high morale, some of which include:

1. The men are allowed to use their imagination and initiative in their work situation.
2. No artificial quotas are set or required of the men.
3. There is participation by officers in the decision-making process that affects their working conditions.
4. There are outstanding open lines of communication up and down the chain of command.
5. There are informal as well as formal exchanges and interaction among the men and between the men and their supervisors.
6. Positive supervision is the rule rather than the exception.
7. Staff units support and complement the field units rather than attempt to supervise them.

Good equipment and intelligent information is provided to support the operating personnel and there is sufficient recognition of the work that is produced by the unit. The motivation and commitment by the officers working this type of strategy is exemplified by role preparation for the decoy operation.

Crime Analysis

It is necessary to have crime analysis in conjunction with the street crime unit, especially those crimes that are part of the decoy operation, such as street robberies, burglaries, and auto theft. Priorities on certain types of crime should be based upon a detailed analysis of the situation within a given area. Spot maps and some type of pictorially depicted information along with detailed folders relating to the spot maps are useful.

A crime report and detailed informational crime patterns which include types of crime, time, location, description of perpetrators, and criminal modus operandi should be prepared. In addition, there should be displayed a statistical comparison of the area robbery complaints or whatever crime category is being analyzed to show one month's total versus those of the previous month or week, whichever is more appropriate.

Deployment

- The deployment of personnel in general will be based on the principle of need.
- Specific deployment tactics will be determined by the nature of the crimes being combatted.

For example, if a mugger has been preying upon nurses leaving the hospital and walking to the bus line or to their vehicles late at night, a female officer will be deployed as a nurse making repeated circuits from the hospital to the parking lot or whatever until the mugger attempts to victimize her. Or, in the case of taxi robberies, the point of origin of trips in which acts were committed can be traced to determine a possible single point of origin which can then be put under surveillance.

Patrol Preparation

The following guidelines should be used by memebers of the unit to properly prepare themselves for a tour of duty.

1. Prior to reporting for assignment, the officer should review the area of assignment and obtain the necessary equipment for the actual patrol strategy.
2. Equipment might include: walkie-talkies, binoculars, headbands, flashlights, helmets, and weapons.

Assignment

Officers should check the vehicle, if one is used, for gas, oil, spare tire, and all other equipment. Upon reporting to the area of assignment, officers should do the following:

1. Be sure that regular patrol officers are aware of the decoy operation and type of apparel. This is for the safety of the officer. This should be done in writing, so there is a log and no question about the information being distributed.
2. Latest crime patterns and analysis of criminal statistics should be reviewed by the officers.
3. A walkie-talkie on the frequency covering the assigned area should be available.

Assuming patrol in an assigned area:

1. A normal rate of speed should be used to patrol in the vehicle.
2. If it is necessary to observe on foot, park the car and use foot surveillance tactics.
3. Low volume on assigned walkie-talkies in the area by observer officers.
4. The use of a newspaper or hat is available for that type of approach.
5. Working this type of strategy, an officer should not respond to regular calls for service unless it is an emergency.

Identification of Officers

Some suggestions for identification:

- Headbands can be worn in certain positions or colors.
- Officers can wear armbands or maybe a hat with a certain color attached.
- Officers should be accessible, but out of sight.
- Officers should have ID cards available. There is a new three-part case which can be worn around the neck with a breakaway chain where a snap opens downward displaying the officer's ID card and his shield or badge. Officers can have different colors for each day and the colors can be interchangeable and be placed on reflectorized tabs.

Decoy Operations

Entrapment. The policy of this strategy is that there will be no tactics used that could be construed as entrapment, such as assuming a prone position, assuming the role of an intoxicated person, or flagrantly displaying U.S. currency or other items of value on the person of the decoy—for instance, having a $10 bill sticking out of the shirt pocket. These things may not be inherently illegal with regard to entrapment, but the rules should be instituted for the officer's safety so he can avoid allegations of entrapment which would hinder the successful prosecution, because quality arrest and quality prosecution are the essence of this strategy. Effective operations involve careful planning, adequate communication facilities, proper role playing, and an efficient backup team.

Decisions before decoy operations commence.

1. What type of decoy should be used?
2. Which decoy plan will most relate to the role and situation?
3. How shall the backup members dress to blend best into the area yet remain close enough to the decoy for safety precautions?
4. Role playing is the most important aspect of the decoy operation; are we prepared?

Where should the operation be instituted?

1. Where will the team have the advantage over the perpetrator?
2. Where will the place of attack look advantageous to the perpetrator?
3. Are suspects present in the area? This question can be answered affirmatively if suspects, among other things, are loitering in the specific area seemingly interested in certain types of people, such as females, act nervous or walk away when they see a patrol car, or instead of carrying on what looks like normal conversation they make discreet comments to each other and separate.

Suspects appear to be looking for victim—decoy operations should commence.

The following preliminary steps should be taken:

1. Each member of the team carefully observes and takes notes of the suspect's physical appearance and attire.
2. Does the suspect appear to be armed—a bulge under his coat or adjusting something inside his coat or his waistband? It is felt

that if the suspect is armed, the decoy operation is not used. The suspect is kept under surveillance and, as circumstances warrant, is stopped and frisked.

3. Other officers in the area are alerted if decoy operations commence.
4. If the need for additional personnel is felt, additional backup team or teams are requested.
5. Backup team members should know the planned route of the decoy.
6. Each member of the team is assigned an identification number for communication purposes. For example, number 1–the decoy, number 2–first backup, and number 3–second backup.
7. Each member has a transceiver or portable radio. The decoy usually has an earplug attached to allow constant communication without exposing the radio.
8. Number 2 is assigned on foot within view of the decoy, number 3 remains with the team's vehicle and avoids passing the decoy or suspects. He is continually apprised of the decoy's location by the number 2 man.
9. Each man, before assuming his position, has all necessary equipment, such as shopping bags, pizza boxes, tool boxes.
10. Signals are usually worked out so that each member can communicate basic messages such as change of direction or request to close in for an arrest without using the radios.
11. If the vehicles are left unattended for any reason, make sure that no police paraphernalia is exposed.
12. The route of the decoy allows for the direction of traffic so that officers assigned with the vehicle may close in where it is necessary.
13. Before the operation begins, a method to gain the suspect's attention should be decided upon by all members of the team.

Plainclothes Surveillance

Vehicle surveillance.

1. The speed should be consistent with traffic in the area.
2. Traffic laws should be obeyed unless absolutely necessary to maintain contact with the suspect.
3. Panic stops or other sudden movements of the vehicle should be avoided. They may attract attention.

Guidelines for following a suspected auto.

1. Thorough description of vehicle and occupants is written down.
2. Automobiles followed within one block's distance.
3. At night headlights are alternated between bright, dim, and full, but not while in range of subject's rearview mirror. Changes are made after subject has turned corner and before the tailing vehicle has made the turn.
4. Portable radios should be held below the dashboard while transmitting. If three men are assigned to a particular surveillance, the man in the rear should handle communication.
5. If survillance proceeds out of the assigned area, base stations should be notified so that the officer's location and direction of travel are given.

Guidelines on conducting surveillance from parked vehicles.

1. Do not maintain surveillance from the same location for extended periods.
2. In winter months, turn off the ignition.
3. Caution should be taken when lighting cigars or cigarettes at night.
4. The driver seat should be kept vacant. Observations should be made from the front passenger or rear seat and in a low position.
5. Rearview mirrors should be adjusted to permit street observation.
6. Vehicles should be parked between other vehicles rather than in an isolated position.
7. Care should be taken not to step on brakes inadvertently or alert suspects through the use of the lights.
8. Walkie-talkies should be kept on a low volume.
9. If it is necessary to move or change positions, traffic should be used to the advantage of the officer—for instance, using a passing bus or truck to travel behind while changing your surveillance location.

There is no specific rule to be followed as far as the distance you should maintain between you and the suspect under surveillance. Distance depends upon several factors, such as the number of persons on the street, the time of day or night, type of area, and number of suspects. If after an extended period, suspects do not make a move and there is a chance that the suspects may "make" the team if it remains in the area, planning will have allowed for another team to replace the first team. In this instance a thorough description of the suspects should be given to the replacement team.

Foot surveillance.

1. Insure that you have the proper equipment.
2. Avoid wearing conspicuous or flashy clothing.
3. Make sure that gun and handcuffs, if they are carried, are secured and not noticeable.
4. Make sure your walkie-talkie is on a low volume if the earplug is not being used.
5. Umbrella and raincoat should be available for inclement weather.
6. Playing a role is important. The personality the officer assumes should be properly portrayed.
7. Telephone booths, darkened doorways, bus stops, and empty lots are used as observation points.
8. Coins should be available for using telephones.
9. Eye contact with the suspect and frozen-face side glances should be avoided. All movements should appear as natural as possible.
10. Communication should be maintained with other members of the team.
11. Under certain lighting conditions, use should be made of store-glass reflections.
12. The officer should be ready for surprise communciation from a suspect, who may walk up and say to the officer, "Hey officer," and for no apparent reason start to run to see what your reaction to that would be. Officers should remain very calm. Surveillance should be rotated. In an automobile the lead surveillance should drop and be replaced by a second man if the lead man feels he is arousing suspicion.
13. Under crowded street conditions, the lead officer can maintain surveillance longer than in any less congested area.
14. When turning corners, the officer takes them as wide as possible to avoid a possible face-to-face confrontation.
15. If a female officer is assigned to the team, she walks with a lead to simulate a husband and wife shopping or a similar ploy.
16. Officers should always know where they are. As surveillance continues, officer should keep track of the streets he enters and the nearest cross streets. It may be necessary to take action in mid-block and he may require immediate assistance; therefore he should know exactly where he is.
17. If suspicions appear founded and the commission of a crime appears imminent, officer should not hesitate to call another backup team for assistance.

It should be remembered that each of these surveillance guidelines has variations, since no two situations are exactly the same. The effectiveness of efforts is proportionate to the ability to the individual officers. If one member of the team fails to carry out his assignment properly, the time and effort of his fellow officer may equal zero.

Experience has taught that there is a tendency among inexperienced officers using surveillance to become easily convinced that they have been made by the suspect. Rarely is there a sound basis for this belief. It arises merely from the inexperienced officer's self-consciousness. The suspect will make the officer only if his tactics are so poor as to make it obvious that he is not what he is purporting to be.

In conclusion, if the surveillance operation fails due to poor tactics, no only has the investment of time by the involved officers been wasted, but the subject under surveillance has been alerted and will become more devious in future attempts to violate the law.

ASSASSINATION OF POLICE OFFICERS

The potential for police officers to be assassinated still exists. It is believed that a federal judge was assassinated in Texas because he was too tough in the sentencing of narcotics peddlers. Regardless of whether these killings are intended assassinations or committed while in the act of attempting another crime, police officers have fallen. The majority of officers being killed will continue to be those involved in the area of arrests. The weapons most used will continue to be handguns. There is no way of predicting the exact situation, which might help prevent these horrible deeds. However, there are several points patrol commanders should keep in mind regarding the performance of the force during these critical and emotional times. An awareness of individuality, planning, timing, and use of simulation exercises may help resolve the possibility of escalation. Additionally, intelligence, quality of intelligence, emotional state of officers, and sensitivity on the part of patrol commanders regarding impulsive actions should be evaluated. Some officers want to be transferred from the critical area while others prefer to stay. Realizing the potential for several incidents to occur at the same time; increasing the number of officers in patrol cars; weapons used and backup units; changing the "procedure of response" to critical areas; using marked cars versus unmarked cars; and uniformed officers versus plainclothes officers; improving communication in critical areas; and upgrading backup tactics are all considerations for the leader in patrol relative to ambush and sneak attacks.

Among the factors that can be changed during normal times are physical shape of officers and firearms training. An officer in the eastern part of the United States who was the victim of an attempted assassination is alive today because of his excellent physical condition. Officers who are overweight may not be the best partners in critical situations. Training in double action and fast draw are extremely important since many shootings occur at close quarters. Firearms training at night is necessary if most shootings take place at night.

A deterrent to police killings is the realization on the part of the potential killer that all force will be brought to bear in the attempt to bring the perpetrator to justice. There may be outcries from the community regarding the number of personnel used to solve a police killing, but nothing should stop the effort since the killing of a police officer is an affront against the very heart of our country. When a police officer is attacked, a tremor is felt in almost every citizen of the community. The citizen is afraid. If a police officer is killed, how safe is an ordinary citizen? Another excellent tool that will aid in the deterrent attempt is a good liaison with federal agencies. Open communication and rapport with the Federal Bureau of Investigation, drug-abuse agencies, and intelligence units will improve a police department's chances of solving the crime.

Who is it that is most likely to attack police officers? Possibly the extremists of the radical organizations. Many times the organization is too soft for these individuals. Other times, the radical organization proscribes violence to a degree where the extremist member feels he must strike out; the organization then denounces the individual as not belonging any longer. Every attempt should be made to maintain communication with these radical groups. If at all possible, individual leaders should be identified and told of their responsibility regarding the organization and the actions of its members. Usually, leaders who know they may be held responsible for violence will not be so apt to preach what may cause others to commit violence.

NOTES

1. Also see "Model Firearms Use Policy," in Samuel G. Chapman, *Police Patrol Readings* (Springfield, Ill.: Charles C Thomas), 1972.
2. President's Commission on Law Enforcement and Administration of Justice, *Task Force Report: The Police* (Washington, D.C.: U.S. Government Printing Office), pp. 189, 190.
3. Paul F. Cromwell, Jr. and Robert L. Lewis, Jr., "Crowds, Mobs, and Riots: A Sociological Analysis," *Police* (September 1971). Reprinted by permission of Charles C Thomas.
4. George G. Killinger and Paul F. Cromwell, Jr., "Penology," in *The Evolution of Corrections in America* (St. Paul, Minn.: West Publishing, 1973), pp. 319–327. Reprinted by permission.
5. "Conference on Civil Disorders," (Washington, D.C.: Police Executive Research Forum, Police Foundation, 1980), pp. 7–20.
6. *Prevention and Control of Urban Disorders*, Law Enforcement Assistance Administration News Feature (Washington, D.C.: U.S. Department of Justice, 1980), pp. 1–4.

·8·

Patrol and Criminal Investigation

It is time for the leaders of professional police agencies to provide guidance to the patrol and detective managers so that through integration these operations become a coherent package. The standards of performance shall be measured in terms of the ability of the team to cooperate, resulting in the achievement of the goals and objectives of the agency.

To assist in this endeavor, an understanding of the following components is necessary: (1) evaluation, (2) the reporting system, and (3) system management.

WHAT DO YOU THINK: WHAT IS YOUR SOURCE OF AUTHORITY

> Crime cannot be measured directly. Its amount must be inferred from the frequency of some occurrence connected with it, for example, crimes brought to the attention of police; persons arrested; prosecutions; convictions and other dispositions, such as probation or commitment. Each of these may be used as an index of the amount of crime. In general, the sensitiveness of these indexes is in the order in which they are given above.
>
> *President Herbert Hoover's Research Committee on Social Trends, 1933*

- The success of criminal investigation has a direct impact on the amount of crime in a given community.
- As reported crime has increased, so have the number of detectives in police agencies in the United States.
- Proactive patrol strategies, reduced response time, and effective

437

preliminary investigation impact apprehension more than detective investigations do.

- A performance measure is invalid if it cannot be observed and recorded. (The measures chosen relate to objectives and if success or failure can be determined. In research, the measures are dictated by hypotheses.) Figure 8.1 shows police as a field of study and common measures connected with it.
- The quality of investigation suffers when the roles of patrol and detective are made interchangeable.

MYTHS AND REALITIES ABOUT CRIME[1]

Myth: Crime in the nation is rising by leaps and bounds.

Reality: The incidence of certain major crimes of violence and common theft is just about keeping pace with population growth.

Myth: Most crimes measured as taking place in the United States are of a violent nature.

Reality: Of the NCS-measured offenses, the vast majority are against property only and do not involve personal violence or threat.

Figure 8.1 *Common police field service study performance measures*

PATROL	
Type of Study	*Associated Measures*
Crime Prevention	UCR Index
	Local crime statistics
	Victimization rates (survey)
	Police visibility
	Probability of crime interception
	Citizen-perceived fear of crime
	Citizen-perceived level of safety
Police Response Time	Travel time (with/without dispatch time)
	Travel distance
	Apprehension probability
	Citizen satisfaction with response time
Patrol Productivity/ Manpower Allocation	Frequency of patrol passings
	Patrol officer workload
	Patrol officer safety (injuries)
	Crime/victimization rates
	Travel time
	Citizen complaints
	Officer complaints

Figure 8.1 (continued)

INVESTIGATION

Type of Study	*Associated Measures*
Crime Prevention	UCR Index Local crime statistics Victimization rates Citizen-perceived fear of crime Citizen -perceived level of safety
Investigator Productivity/ Personnel Allocation	Investigator caseload Investigator arrest rate Investigator clearance rate Investigator prosecution rate Investigator follow-up rate Citizen complaints Officer complaints Organizational structure Evidence collection.
Police Response Time	Travel time (with/without dispatch time) Travel distance Prioritization of calls Apprehension probability Citizen satisfaction with response rate

Source: Michael F. Cahn, Edward H. Kaplan, and John G. Peters, Jr., "Police Field Studies: A Review of Evaluation Research." in *How Well Does It Work,* Review of Criminal Justice Evaluation, 1978, U.S. Department of Justice, Law Enforcement Assistance Administration, National Institute of Law Enforcement and Criminal Justice, Washington, D.C. Reprinted with permission.

Myth: The larger the city, the greater the likelihood that its residents will be the victims of crime.

Reality: For certain crimes the residents of smaller cities have higher rates than those of our largest cities.

Myth: In general, residents of large cities believe their police are doing a poor job.

Reality: If the opinions of residents of numerous cities across the nation are indicative, the vast majority is satisfied with the performance of their police.

Myth: Most crime is reported to the police.

Reality: Slightly fewer than half of all offenses measured by the National Crime Survey are known to the police.

Myth: Blacks or Hispanics are less likely than the population as a whole to report personal crimes to the police.

Reality: By and large, the offenses experienced by members of those two minority groups are just about as apt to be reported as are crimes against victims in general.

Myth: The residents of our large cities regard crime as the most important neighborhood problem.

Reality: Judging from the opinions of many residents, environmental problems cause just about as much concern as crime.

Myth: Most residents of large cities think their neighborhoods are not safe.

Reality: Most individuals feel at least reasonably safe when out alone in their neighborhoods either in the daytime or at night.

Myth: Most residents of large cities have limited or changed their activities because of the fear of crime.

Reality: If the assessments of an estimated 21.1 million persons are indicative, slightly fewer than half of all big-city residents have personally altered their lifestyles because of crime.

Myth: Elderly persons make up the most heavily victimized age group in our society.

Reality: Rates of victimization are far higher for young individuals than for senior citizens.

Myth: Women are more likely than men to be the victims of crime.

Reality: For various personal crimes, men are victimized at higher rates than women. For personal robbery or assault, as well as for personal larceny without victim-offender contact, men have been victimized at appreciably higher rates than women.

Myth: A weapon is used by the offender in nearly all rapes, robberies, and assaults.

Reality: Weapons are used in far fewer than half of all those crimes.

Myth: A victim is more likely to be injured during an armed assault or robbery if the offender wields a firearm rather than a knife or other weapon.

Reality: The victim's likelihood of sustaining injury at the hands of an armed offender is lessened if the weapon is a firearm.

Myth: People often use force or weapons for self-defense from criminal attack.

Reality: Although victims defend themselves in a majority of rapes, robberies, or assaults, passive methods are more commonly used for protection.

Myth: More often than not, the victims of violent crimes other than homicide end up in the hospital.

Reality: Relatively few victims of rape, robbery, or assault get hospital care, either in an emergency room or as in-patients.

Myth: The typical personal robbery is carried out against a lone pedestrian by an armed offender operating alone.

Reality: Although the victim is usually alone and outdoors, the robber does not necessarily work alone or use a weapon.

Myth: Household burglars usually commit their crimes by breaking into the premises.

Reality: In a majority of completed residential burglaries committed throughout the United States, burglars gain entry into homes or apartments without resorting to force.

Myth: The victims of crime seldom know or recognize their offenders.

Reality: A substantial number of crimes are committed by persons known to their victims.

Myth: Aggravated assaults are more likely to result in physical injury if the attacker is a total stranger.

Reality: One's chances of being injured and ending up in a hospital are somewhat greater if the assailant is not a stranger.

Myth: The typical prison inmate is a "loner" with no family or friends and little social contact.

Reality: Perhaps because most had lived in a family situation prior to their arrest, prisoners are quite likely to maintain regular social contacts during incarceration.

Myth: People are usually under the influence of drugs when they commit a crime.

Reality: If the experience of those imprisoned for all types of offenses is indicative, the occurrence of most crime cannot be attributed to drug-induced aberrant behavior.

Myth: The typical person who commits a crime is either unemployed or on welfare.

Reality: Based on what is known about imprisoned criminals, most persons who engage in crime have jobs and very few are welfare-dependent.

Myth: Although blacks are overrepresented on death row across the nation, this overrepresentation is more pronounced in the South than in other regions.

Reality: Black overrepresentation on death row is less pronounced in the South than in the other regions.

1980 Update[2]

The National Crime Survey found that serious crime rates remained essentially unchanged between 1973 and 1979, but household larcenies and simple assaults were up.

The six-year trend showed that household larceny and simple assault increased 25 and 16.8 percent, respectively, while burglary decreased 8.3 percent.

The 1973–1979 rate changes in rape (up 13.7 percent), robbery (down 7.1 percent), aggravated assault (down 1.5 percent), personal larceny with contact (down 6.5 percent), personal larceny without contact (up 1.1 percent), and motor vehicle theft (down 8.2 percent) were too small to be significant. Statistical significance is related to the size of the sample and the magnitude of the change.

The National Crime Survey statistics are gathered through U.S. Bureau of Census interviews in 60,000 households in which persons twelve years of age and older are asked what crimes they were the victims of during the preceding six months.

The survey defines a "simple assault" as an attempted or completed attack without a weapon that results in minor injury at most.

The comparison of crime victim rates per 1,000 persons or households for 1973 and 1979 are:

	1973	1979
Rape	1.0	1.1
Robbery	6.7	6.3
Aggravated assault	10.1	9.9
Simple assault	14.8	17.3
Personal larceny without contact (purse snatching, pocket picking)	3.1	2.9
Personal larceny without contact	88.0	89.0
Household burglary	91.7	84.1
Household larceny	107.0	133.7
Motor vehicle theft	19.1	17.5

While every single criminal act is to be deplored, a notable finding in the National Crime Survey is the that violent crimes people most fear are not showing significant increases. In some cases they are declining.

Household larcenies, which have increased, are thefts or attempted thefts from a residence and its immediate vicinity. They do not involve either forcible or unlawful entry. If people would look after their valuables with more care and be alert to their neighbors' vulnerability, we believe that this type of crime would decline, too.

The estimated total number of burglaries throughout the nation rose from 6,458,700 in 1973 to 6,685,400 in 1979 (the rate per 1,000 households fell from 91.7 to 84.1 between those two years), whereas the number of household larcenies rose from 7,537,300 in 1973 to 10,630,100 in 1979.

I think that greater community crime prevention efforts are needed.

PATROL AND CRIMINAL INVESTIGATIONS STUDIES: A REVIEW

Hopefully, the cooperation and coordination of the professional leaders of patrol and criminal investigation can produce the organizational product as efficiently and effectively as possible. Herbert Isaacs addressed the issue of preventive patrol at the first Science and Technology Conference at the Illinois Institute of Technology in 1968. I must admit, at the time, I questioned his hypothesis wherein he questioned the merits of preventive patrol.

Another issue, which most practitioners at the time concluded was a "rapid response," would result in more on-scene arrests; however, for rapid response, there must be appropriate manpower allocation and distribution systems, based on workload analysis.

The Crime Control Team Experiment[3]

Beginning in July, 1968, an experiment involving an organizational restructuring of the police department was conducted for a one-year period in Syracuse, N.Y., a joint effort of General Electric's Syracuse Electronics Laboratory and the Syracuse Police Department. It utilized patrol strategies such as:

- the use of one-officer patrol cars;
- the use of time-*dependent* manpower allocation schemes; and
- the use of a mathematical model in an attempt to increase the detection probability of patrol.

The Crime Control Team Experiment was evaluated, and the results of the research included several interesting findings:

- The substitution of two one-officer units for one two-officer unit was shown to increase the apprehension capability of the patrol force.
- The use of systematic patrol procedures increased the crime interception rate to about six times the pre-experimental level.
- The new patrol strategies implemented were viewed favorably by citizens of the local community.

Although the Crime Control Team Experiment was not able to show conclusively that the program strategies reduced crime rates, it did demonstrate that organizational structures other than those normally associated with traditional police departments could effectively control crime in an urban area.

The Kansas City Preventive Patrol Experiment[4] (Also see Chapter 9)

The intent of the Police Foundation's Kansas City Preventive Patrol Experiment was to determine the effect of varying levels of preventive patrol on outcome measures such as the crime rate and citizen satisfaction with the police. Beginning in October, 1972, fifteen Kansas City police beats were divided into three groups of five beats. Each group of five beats was to receive one of the following three levels of patrol activity for a one-year period:

1. *Reactive Beats*—no preventive patrol was to be performed in these areas.
2. *Control Beats*—preventive patrol was to be carried out as usual.
3. *Proactive Beats*—two to three times the normal level of patrol was to be implemented.

The general finding of this study was that variations in the level of preventive patrol had no effect on the relevant outcome measures. Stated differently, the crime rates and levels of citizen satisfaction found in reactive, control, and proactive beats were not significantly different from each other at the end of the one-year experimental period.

This study causes one to think about the allocation of manpower for certain tasks. Traditional preventive patrol was in need of change and direction.

Police Response Time: Its Determinants and Effects[5]

The Kansas City Preventive Patrol Experiment generated large amounts of data useful for testing hypotheses other than those central to the relationship between patrol and crime. In particular, data on response time and related outcome measures such as arrest rates and citizen satisfaction were collected. A detailed analysis of these data was released by the Police Foundation, in 1976, in a study entitled *Police Response Time: Its Determinants and Effects.*

While the small samples involved in this study render its findings somewhat weak, three separate surveys indicated that there was no relationship between response time and arrest rates (contrary to the drift of the 1967 Science and Technology Task Force results). Similarly, when examining the impact of rapid police response on citizen satisfaction with the police, researchers found that citizen satisfaction with response time remained at a (high) constant level over a large range of response times, thus demonstrating that citizen satisfaction does not depend on rapid police response.

Instead, the researchers found that citizen satisfaction with the police depended upon the *difference* between observed and expected response times, a difference that was previously not given much thought. If the police were able to respond quicker than expected, the citizen involved was more likely to be satisfied than if the police responded slower than expected.[6]

Kansas City Response Time Analysis[7]

Another major study which examined the merits of rapid police response was also undertaken in Kansas City when, in 1973, LEAA awarded a grant to the Kansas City Police Department. Published in 1974, the report *Response Time Analysis* examined several hypotheses similar to those scrutinized by the Police Foundation's response time study just discussed. With respect to arrests, response time was shown to be inversely related to apprehension probability, but only marginally so. Also, surveys confirmed the earlier result that most of the population was satisfied with response time regardless of the actual response time involved, though the difference between observed and expected response time was again shown to be a determinant of citizen satisfaction with the police.

This study is important for another reason; it was the first study which attempted to determine the length of the delay associated with citizen's reporting of crimes to the police. This delay was shown at times to be larger than typical response times (including dispatch delays). Based on this finding and the results discussed earlier, it was concluded that the minimization of response time is not an empirically justifiable goal.[8]

The Worcester Crime Impact Program[9]

In March, 1974, Public Sytems Evaluation, Inc., undertook a six-month after-the-fact evaluation of the Worcester Crime Impact Program, whose main innovative feature was the use of some forty-one Police Service Aides. This study demonstrated that for many police calls, a trained civilian can handle the work required at a lower cost without compromising the quality of service provided. In fact, the fraction of calls handled by civilians can approach the fraction of calls handled by uniformed police officers.

> As part of the evaluation effort, researchers were interested in whether or not the response times of Police Service Aides were acceptable to the public. As in the two Kansas City studies discussed earlier, citizen satisfaction with response time was consistently high despite wide variations in response time. While this indicates that Worcester residents were happy with the attention they received, it also indicates that citizen satisfaction is not too dependent on response time.[10]

Patrol Staffing in San Diego: One- or Two-Officer Units[11]

When considering the allocation and deployment of police responses, a seemingly simple decision such as whether to staff a patrol unit with one or two officers can give rise to rather complex implications. Traditionally, many police departments have staffed their cars with two officers, primarily for reasons of safety. Those departments which have used one-officer patrol (such as the Crime Control Team in Syracuse) have usually exchanged two one-officer units for each two-officer unit.

> In October, 1975, the Police Foundation began an experiment in San Diego where only one one-officer unit was substituted for each two-officer unit. It was found that, in terms of response time, on-scene arrests, officer injuries, and other performance measures, one-officer units performed at a satisfactory level of efficiency and effectiveness. The cost implications of this drastic reduction in manpower are clear; if one wished to retain equal-cost staffing options, the potential for increased productivity through the use of one-officer patrol is very great. Thus, a simple switch in staffing policy may have significant implications toward patrol productivity.[12]

The St. Louis, Missouri AVM experiment,[13] and the Wilmington, Delaware Split-Force experiment are discussed elsewhere in the text.

NATIONAL ADVISORY COMMISSION ON CRIMINAL JUSTICE STANDARDS AND GOALS: STANDARD 9.7

Criminal Investigation

Every police agency immediately should direct patrol officers to conduct thorough preliminary investigations and should establish in writing priorities to insure that investigative efforts are spent in a manner that will best achieve organizational goals.

1. Every police agency should recognize that patrol officers are preliminary investigators and that they should conduct thorough preliminary investigations. However, investigative specialists should be assigned to very serious or complex preliminary investigations whan delay will not hamper the investigation.
2. Every police agency should establish only as many specialized criminal investigative units as needed, staffed only with the number of personnel necessary to conduct timely investigations that lead to organizational objectives. The thoroughness of preliminary investigations by patrol officers should be insured, to reduce followup investigative efforts.
3. Every police agency should establish investigative priorities according to the seriousness of the crime, how recently it was reported, the amount of readily available information about suspects, the availability of agency resources, and community attitudes.
4. Every police agency employing 75 or more personnel should assign full-time criminal investigators. Every agency with fewer than 75 personnel should assign criminal investigation specialists only where specific needs are present.

   a. Specialization within the criminls investigation unit should take place only when necessary to improve overall efficiency within the agency.
   b. Criminal investigation operations should be decentralized to the most effective command level. However, unusual cases or types of cases may be investigated by a centralized unit.

5. Every police agency should establish quality control procedures to insure that every reported crime receives the investigation it warrants. These procedures should include:

   a. A followup report of each open investigation every 10 days and command approval of every continuance of an investigation past 30 days;
   b. Constant inspection and review of individual, team, and unit criminal investigation reports and investigator activity summaries; and
   c. Individual, team and unit performance measures based at least on arrests and dispositions, crimes cleared, property recovered, and caseload.

6. Every police agency with 75 or more personnel should consider the use of a case preparation operation to insure that all evidence that may lead to the conviction or acquittal of defendants is systematically prepared and presented for review by the prosecuting authority. A technician should be employed to handle any or all of the functions listed, whenever an agency can improve the quality of case preparation at the same or reduced cost.

a. Policies and procedures should be developed in cooperation with representatives of the local prosecutorial and judicial systems, and should contain the information required by all three systems.

b. All police information on each case prepared for prosecution should be in a systematically prepared, written report that contains the following documentation; copies of the incident report, followup reports, identification and laboratory reports, and any other reports necessitated by the investigation.

c. Every case also should contain written documentation relating to all case disposition information and notification records.

d. The case preparation technician may: establish case files and insure their completeness; present case files to prosecutors; present subjects in custody for arraignment, or obtain a warrant and disseminate warrant information; represent the agency at all pretrial hearings; notify witnesses; document final dispositions of cases; and return the case report file to the originating unit for retention.

7. Every police agency should coordinate criminal investigations with all other agency operations. This coordination should be supported by:

a. Clearly defined procedures for the exchange of information between investigative specialists and between those specialists and uniformed patrol officers;

b. Systematic rotation of generalists into investigative specialties; and

c. Equitable publicity of the efforts of all agency elements.[14]

Municipal Detective Systems – a Quantitative Approach[15]

Folk's research in criminal investigation employed a computer simulation model which incorporated a "minimum service-time" criterion, "interrupt" matrices, and case priorities.

Folk reported:

1. that eyewitnesses were the most frequent and valuable sources of evidence;

2. that Boston detectives had caseloads too heavy to allow for detailed case-solving procedures;

3. that Boston district detectives were being assigned too many special details, thus reducing the investigative manpower;

4. that the supervisor's estimate of minimum investigation times was unrealistic;

5. that mug shots, eyewitnesses, or victim's friends and relatives can be helpful in the investigation of certain Section A crimes (classified by Folk as homicide, rape, robbery) and in less than 20 percent of Section B crimes (classified by Folk as burglary, larceny, auto theft, etc.);

6. that there was a correlation between case closing and seriousness of crime; and
7. that physical evidence was seldom found in Boston.

Folk acknowledges that his effort is a first-cut and by definition also parochial in nature. Despite these admitted short-comings, Folk's effort was, and still remains, one of the very few mathematically based investigative research efforts.[16]

The Investigative Function: Criminal Investigation in the United States[17]

While Folk was conducting his research in Boston, Richard Ward was preparing his doctoral dissertation (at the University of California at Berkeley) which was completed in 1971. Unlike Folk, who reviewed operations in only one police department, Ward expanded his research to include several. Comparing detective operations in the New York City and San Francisco Police Departments, he set out to determine:

1. if there were any differences in investigative effectiveness between these two departments, and
2. whether or not investigative effectiveness was dependent upon detective organization (generalist vs. specialist).

His sample for the latter comparison consisted of twenty-one police departments which employ one or the other style of organization. Ward, a former New York detective, found that upon examination of burglary and robbery clearance rates there were no significant differences between New York and San Francisco generalist and specialist detectives. However, in his comparison of the larger grouping of agencies, he concluded that "generalist or specialist detectives have no impact upon robbery arrests . . . but those departments using generalists had greater success in the burglary arrest category than those using burglary specialists."[18]

Like Folk, Ward also found detectives to be overburdened with cases, and a correlation between the seriousness of the crime and the likelihood of the case-closing. In addition, he cited a high physical evidence recovery rate and suggests that the processing limitations of the crime laboratory limit its value. Raising serious questions about the efficacy of arrest and clearance rates as a measure of detective productivity and efficiency, Ward cites a lack of uniform standards among police departments regarding these rates. Some departments clear a case based upon suspect-related information, others clear it upon arrest, and still others only upon conviction for the offense.

Because his work is frequently cited in the investigation literature, one must look beyond Ward's own caution to the reader and examine his methods carefully. (Ward cites many methodological problems which include: lack of adequate records, agency non-cooperation; lack of relevant data; absence of related studies; use of comparative systems approach; size of the police department; and the year of the study.) Under close scrutiny there appear to be some questions about the validity of his conclusions. However, the data needed to verify his computations are not available in text.[19]

Stanford Research Institute: Enhancement of the Investigative Function[20]

In 1973, Bernard Greenberg et al. of the Stanford Research Institute completed a major research effort and produced what is now known as the SRI solvability model. In essence, this model helps police officers identify those burglary cases which are most likely to be solved through further investigation.

Focusing upon the type of information obtained by the police officer after arriving at the scene, it was found that during the officer's preliminary investigation certain types of information about the crime itself (e.g., a vehicle license number) were found to be of greater value than a description of the stolen item.

Upon close examination, the SRI researchers were able to develop a burglary investigative checklist, which aided officers and police managers to decide which cases would most likely be solved. Under their system each piece of information is assigned a numerical value, based upon its importance. For example, usable fingerprints are assigned a higher value than a description of stolen property. After totaling the values assigned to all the information obtained at the crime scene, a case with a number exceeding a prescribed threshold is pursued; a case with a number below the threshold is not considered likely to be solved.

The results of the study have been adopted by many police departments in an effort to increase the productivity and efficiency of the investigative unit. In most cases the implementing departments have been successful in focusing greater attention upon the cases that have a higher probability of solution. Other researchers have replicated this study and further replications are currently underway to verify, refine, and add precision to the model.[21]

Rochester Criminal Investigation Study[22]

Bloch and Weidman evaluated the effectiveness of Coordinated Team Patrol (CTP) to make arrests and to clear cases.[23] The CTP was a variation of team policing which emphasized

> ... closer coordination between patrol and investigators. The study, using five months of data on burglary, robbery, and larceny offenses, attempted to delineate factors associated with quality arrests. An "early case closure" procedure was used to drop cases that had virtually no chance of being solved. This procedure was developed in a way similar to the development of the SRI model. To develop the early case closure procedure, a new preliminary report form was developed to isolate specific solvability factors which contribute to case clearance.
>
> The study found the CTP teams to be significantly more productive than the non-CTP personnel. The study found that the CTP organization was responsible for increased arrests, both on-scene and followup, and that the CTP teams were better at assembling information for followup investigations, leading to a greater likelihood for case clearance and subsequent prosecution. Utilizing the early case closure approach, the department was able to identify specific information elements critical to followup arrests. It was found that CTP teams: (1) were able to close more cases based on preliminary reports, (2) uncovered more new information during followup investigations, and (3) were able to close cases more quickly.
>
> Although, as witnessed by these studies, criminal investigations have received increased attention in recent years, there is an absence of research specifically directed at (1) the development of accurate measures of investigative productivity and (2) understanding the real contribution each component of the investigative system makes to case clearance and prosecution. A comprehensive, empirical examination of the total investigative function performed by all involved police personnel has yet to be undertaken. This is in large part due to the fact that there is no recognized approach for evaluating the total information input of police personnel.

Sunnyvale ICAM System[24]

The Investigative Control and Management System (ICAM) developed by the Sunnyvale (California) Department of Public Safety conceptualized the investigative process as a series of activities that generate information for apprehensive purposes. Emphasizing the value of information from a system perspective, ICAM models the flow of resources and information through the investigative process and then evaluates how the information relates to arrest. ICAM has specialized report forms as a means of "measuring, monitoring, and managing the productivity of the apprehension system." ICAM further considers the value of specific kinds of information as a means of determining the effectiveness of any particular police activity. For example, the system is capable of indicating the effectiveness of traffic stops toward the generation of information.

The ICAM system is the most complete system to date for monitoring the performance of the investigative process. Unfortunately, the system has been used only for internal management control and not for research into the investigative process.

Rand Analysis, the Criminal Investigation Process[25]

The Rand study dispelled many of the myths associated with detective activity. A review of the investigative function of twenty-five police departments and a questionnaire completed by 153 jurisdictions focused on four major areas: describing current investigative practices, measuring the contributions made by investigations to a case; gauging the effectiveness of techniques for gathering physical evidence; and assessing the impact of organizational styles on investigations. One aspect of the study required the development of an instrument to determine, from a prosecutor's viewpoint, the thoroughness of the information collected by the detective.

The scope of the Rand study was limited to police investigation of serious reported crime: homicide, rape, assault, robbery, burglary, and theft.

Major Findings

- On investigative effectiveness: Difference in investigative training, staffing, workload, and procedures appear to have no appreciable effect on crime, arrest, or clearance rates.
- The method by which police investigators are organized (i.e., team policing, specialists vs. generalists, patrolmen-investigators) cannot be related to variations in crime, arrest, and clearance rates.
- On the use of investigators' time: Substantially more than half of all serious reported crimes receive no more than superficial attention from investigators.
- Our data consistently reveal that an investigator's time is largely consumed in reviewing reports, documenting files, and attempting to locate and interview victims on cases that experience shows will not be solved. For cases that are solved (i.e, a suspect is identified), an investigator spends more time in post-clearance processing than he does in identifying the perpetrator.
- On how cases are solved: The single most important determinant of whether or not a case will be solved is the information the victim supplies to the immediately responding patrol officer. If infor-

mation that uniquely identifies the perpetrator is not presented at the time the crime is reported, the perpetrator, by and large, will not be subsequently identified.

- On how cases are solved: Of those cases that are ultimately cleared but in which the perpetrator is not identifiable at the time of the initial police incident report, almost all are cleared as a result of routine police procedures.
- On collecting physical evidence: Most police departments collect more physical evidence than can be productively processed. Our analysis shows that allocating more resources to increasing the processing capabilities of the department can lead to more identifications than some other investigative actions.
- On the use of physical evidence: Latent fingerprints rarely provide the only basis for identifying a suspect.
- On investigative thoroughness: In relatively few departments do investigators consistently and thoroughly document the key evidentiary facts that reasonably assure that the prosecutor can obtain a conviction on the most serious applicable charges.
- On investigative thoroughness: Police failure to document a case investigation thoroughly may have contributed to a higher case dismissal rate and a weakening of the prosecutor's plea bargaining position.
- On relations between victims and police: Crime victims in general strongly desire to be notified officially as to whether or not the police have "solved" their case, and what progress has been made toward convicting the suspect after his arrest.
- On investigative organization and procedure: Investigative strike forces have a significant potential to increase arrest rates for a few difficult target offenses, provided they remain concentrated on activities for which they are uniquely qualified; in practice, however, they are frequently diverted elsewhere.

Other Findings

- That in over one-half of cleared cases, the identification of the offender was supplied to the reporting officer by the victim (supporting a Task Force finding);
- That most cases receive cursory attention (if there are few leads, little follow-up will occur);
- That investigators choose cases using the strength of leads and seriousness of the crimes as selection criteria;
- That more evidence—especially latent fingerprints—was being collected than could be effectively used;

- That the structure in which police investigators are organized—specialist vs. generalist—had no correlation with crime, arrest, or clearance rates;
- That investigative strike forces possess the potential to increase arrest rates for a few target crimes; and
- That differences in investigative training, staffing, workload, and procedures have little effect on crime, arrest, or clearance rates.

Proposed Reforms

1. Reduce follow-up investigation on all cases except those involving the most serious offenses.
2. Assign generalist-investigators (who could handle the obvious leads in routine cases) to the local operations commander.
3. Establish a Major Offenders Unit to investigate serious crimes.
4. Assign serious-offense investigations to closely supervised teams, rather than to individual investigators.
5. Strengthen evidence-processing capabilities.
6. Increase the use of information processing systems in lieu of investigators.
7. Employ strike forces selectively and judiciously.
8. Place post-arrest (i.e., suspect in custody) investigations under the authority of the prosecutor.
9. Initiate programs designed to impress on the citizen the crucial role he or she plays in crime solution.

Glick and Riccio explain:

While the Rand study illuminated some of the ineffectiveness of the criminal investigator, it was not capable of exploring all dimensions of investigative work in the detail that is required to know fully about the productivity of detectives. Some of the limitations of the data collection were:

1. The lack of detail to the information collected about specific case facts
2. The prosecutor orientation of the information elements analyzed
3. The inability to attribute the collection of new (first-time) data to specific police units
4. The inability to determine how often the collection of specific information is duplicated during an investigation.

The first two reflect the fact that the information elements analyzed were based on the requirements for prosecution rather than on the police informational needs for case clearance. The third and fourth reflect the notion that to understand detective productivity fully, one must examine the total information generation process to determine who collects new information and who repeats or verifies information already gathered.

Gates and Knowles[26] question the validity of the study by challenging the methodology employed, the sufficiency of the data base, and the subsequent conclusion drawn by the author.

Cahn, Kaplan, and Peters[27] conclude: Comprehensive in scope, the Rand study had many outcomes.

One, in particular, was reduction in the "mythology" which hitherto had surrounded the detective. For example, the finding that in more than half of the cleared cases the identification of the offender was supplied to the police all but erases the image of the detective as a "super sleuth."

Sanders's[28] study revealed that information supplied to police about a crime is significant; in many cases, the important case rule was at work in that only cases deemed important by investigators were investigated; and the workable case rule applied in that where no leads appeared to exist, cases would not be pursued. Also, there was a correlation between case closing and seriousness of the crime; that little could be done with physical evidence because of processing limitation; that various specialized investigative units produce higher clearance rates on target crimes (e.g., homicide, burglary, robbery); and that certain types of investigation require unique methods of investigation (e.g., arson), hence specialized training is required.

James Q. Wilson,[29] in *Varieties of Police Behavior*, characterized police departments according to their operational modalities. The three styles were: watchman, emphasizing maintenance of public order; legalistic, which promotes the law enforcement role; and service, where police respond to the community as if it were the "market" and they the producers of a product which meets the demands of the community.

In Wilson's view, a police department's style will affect its procedures, hence oftentimes influencing its arrest or clearance rates. The notion of different styles of policing has important consequences for the involvement of patrol officers in the investigative process. It seems likely that in a legalistic police department arrests and clearance rates may be more important than in a watchman-style department. As Wilson notes, "a watchman-like department is interested in avoiding trouble and in minding its own business. . . . The pre-disposition to avoid involvement—to control (not eliminate) public disorder rather than to enforce the law—depends not on corrupt motives, but on the inclinations of the men recruited into police work and the norms of the organization to which they belong."[30]

The legalistic department, according to Wilson, ". . . tries to get the men to work harder, confident in some areas (for example, vice suppression) and hopeful in others (for example, preventive patrol, field interrogation, juvenile citations, traffic summons) that will achieve a desired objective."[31] As Wilson notes, in this style, there has been an attempt made by some police chiefs to erase the long-standing separation between the patrol forces and the detective force, so that men could be assigned from one area to another.

Patterns of Metropolitan Policing[32]

In 1977 Elinor Ostrom et al. released a study of the organization of metropolitan police departments in eighty Standard Metropolitan Statistical Areas (SMSA's) across the country. While most of their report does not impact greatly upon the investigative function, portions of it do support other investigation evaluative research studies. Closely related to Wilson's perception of a service-style of policing, Ostrom et al. view police departments in an industrial framework – a concept of producers (police) and consumers (users of police services).

The researchers noted, in general, that detectives were overworked; observed a high recovery rate of physical evidence that was seldom used due to the inability of crime labs to process it; perceived that investigators are assigned differently depending upon geographical areas, and that such assignments may impact upon productivity and cost-effectiveness (one- vs. two-man detective car); and that "more than 80 percent of the 'producers' of burglary investigation in the eighty SMSA's (Standard Metropolitan Statistical Areas) assign police generalists to investigate residential burglary."[33]

Cahn, Kaplan, and Peters[34] discuss their review of patrol and criminal investigation studies indicating three hypotheses were studied:

1. Hypotheses which postulate the merit of case-closing and -clearance methods;
2. Hypotheses which postulate the merit of the collection and use of evidence; and
3. Hypotheses which postulate the merit of alternative personnel allocation schemes and other productivity improvement schemes.

They go on to suggest ten substantive hypotheses which have been examined by only a few major studies but not enough to yield conclusive results. Most remain as "dangling hypotheses" yet to be tested.

- Increasing patrol intensity increases the number of crimes intercepted in progress.
- Response time is inversely related to citizen satisfaction.
- Response time is inversely related to apprehension probability.
- Response time is inversely related to the number of officers in patrol.
- Automatic Vehicle Monitoring reduces response time.
- Automatic Vehicle Monitoring increases officer safety.
- One-officer patrol is more efficient than two-officer patrol.
- One-officer patrol is characterized by a higher workload than two-officer patrol.
- Two-officer patrol is safer than one-officer patrol.
- "Specialized" patrol is more productive than "routine" patrol.

However, some authors make statements which seem to be fact, such as Reiss:[35] "There is no feasible way to solve most crimes except by securing the cooperation of citizens to link a person to the crime."

Greenwood et al.[36] say "Some characteristics of the crime itself, or of events surrounding the crime, that are beyond the control of investigators, determine whether it will be cleared in most instances." Skogan and Antunes, "We believe that the availability and reliability of information about incidents and offenders play a key role in determining the ability of the police to solve crimes and apprehend offenders."[37] Glick and Riccio[38] used the Case File Review Instrument in their study of the productivity of detectives and explained it thusly:

> The product of investigative activity is information. There are three aspects to the CFRI that relate to the police objective. First, the CFRI is a list of information bits that, if known, could potentially assist in case clearance and/or disposition. The instruments used in the Rand study, SRI's study, and the Rochester study, as well as the forms used in the ICAM and PROMIS systems, were reviewed during the development of the CFRI. The lists of information bits used in each of those studies were only slightly different from the one used in the CFRI, the major differences being due to informational needs. For example, the Rand study and the PROMIS system dealt only with information that was believed to be desirable by the prosecutors; and the SRI model was not concerned with analyzing the investigative productivity of different types of police officers.
>
> Information contained in the reports is divided into five specialized areas: description of the suspect, description of the crime scene, description of a person's actions at the scene, the results of laboratory tests, and the collection of physical evidence (see Figure 8.2). Each specialized area is broken down into a list of variables that are likely to be encountered.

Figure 8.2 *Case file review form*

CASE FILE REVIEW FORM—INVESTIGATIONS

Master No. _____   Date_____ Date_____ Date_____
Case File No. _____   Report _____ Report _____ Report _____
                          Charge_____ Charge_____ Charge_____
                          Unit _____ Unit _____ Unit _____

A. Info. describing Suspect

   1. Name *_____ *_____ *_____
   2. Nickname, Moniker *_____ *_____ *_____
   3. Residence *_____ *_____ *_____
   4. Possible location, hangout *_____ *_____ *_____
   5. Physical Characteristics *_____ *_____ *_____
   6. Clothing *_____ *_____ *_____
   7. Familiarity w/suspect *_____ *_____ *_____
   8. Reason for suspect
      behavior *_____ *_____ *_____
   9. Statements made by
      suspects *_____ *_____ *_____
  10. Means of Escape *_____ *_____ *_____
  11. Other, specify _____ *_____ *_____ *_____

B. Inf. describing scene

  12. Location *_____ *_____ *_____
  13. Date or Time *_____ *_____ *_____
  14. Type of crime *_____ *_____ *_____
  15. Physical characteristics of
      scene *_____ *_____ *_____
  16. Witnesses *_____ *_____ *_____
  17. Use of Force *_____ *_____ *_____
  18. Description of Weapon *_____ *_____ *_____
  19. Possession of illegal goods *_____ *_____ *_____
  20. Property damage *_____ *_____ *_____
  21. Injuries *_____ *_____ *_____
  22. Vehicle i.d. *_____ *_____ *_____
  23. Other, specify _____ *_____ *_____ *_____

C. Person's Actions at Scene

  24. Victim's Actions *_____ *_____ *_____
  25. Witness' Actions *_____ *_____ *_____
  26. Police Actions *_____ *_____ *_____
  27. Suspect's Actions *_____ *_____ *_____
  28. Other, specify _____ *_____ *_____ *_____

D. Lab Tests

  29. Specify _____ *_____ *_____ *_____
  30. Specify _____ *_____ *_____ *_____

E. Physical Evidence

  31. Fingerprints *_____ *_____ *_____
  32. Weapons, Ammunition *_____ *_____ *_____
  33. Crime Tools *_____ *_____ *_____

34. Narcotics	*	*	*
35. Stolen Property	*	*	*
36. Clothing	*	*	*
37. Blood	*	*	*
38. Vehicle	*	*	*
39. Other, specify _____	*	*	*

Source: Barry D. Glick and Lucius J. Riccio, "Productivity of Detectives: A Study of the Investigative Function of Police Juvenile Units," *Journal of Police Science and Administration,* 7, no. 2 (1979). International Association of Chiefs of Police, Gaithersburg, MD. Reprinted with permission.

Second, the CFRI distinguishes between information collected by patrol officers, detectives, juvenile officers, and any other type of officer including private security guards. It is designed to track the totality of information generated or collected by all involved police personnel. It recognizes that the roles of the patrol officer and detective are intertwined and dependent on each other for case completion. Use of the CFRI enables a police administrator to determine the relative contribution made by specific units and to adjust manpower allocations.

Space is provided on the CFRI so that each police report in a case file can be individually listed. In addition, the date, type of report, charge, and the unit completing the report are placed at the top of the column. The unit completing the report is identified through a roster of assignments for that time period.

Third, the CFRI has the added dimension of recognizing if information contained in a report is recorded for the first time or if it has been previously collected. Information is coded into one or a combination of three categories:

1. *New*—any information collected that has not been previously known to the police
2. *Repeat*—information collected that has previously been collected from the same source
3. *Verified*—information that confirms existing information. This type of information differs from *repeat* in that it is obtained from a different source.

New information represents the most desirable of the three since it provides facts that have been previously unknown. Verified information is the second most desirable since it allows corroboration of existing information. Repeat is the least desirable since it does not contribute anything new to the investigation.

This last dimension to the CFRI is perhaps its most important contribution to the study of investigative work, because it enables greater insight into the productivity of detectives and the relative performance of different types of investigative officers.

The development and use of the CFRI has provided a clearer way of viewing the investigative process and evaluating the relative contributions different police units make to case investigations while working in different organizational arrangements. Further work using the CFRI could lead to the development of better measures of detective performance and the identification of optimal organizational arrangements for conducting investigations.

This use of the CFRI has raised a number of important issues not covered by other studies of detectives. For example, very little is known about the relative value of new, repeat, and verified information. As stated earlier, it would seem reasonable to assume that new information is the most valuable. However, verified and repeat might be critical—first, in the mind of the investigator and, second, for case prosecution. The importance of each type of information could be estimated by using the CFRI to analyze a large sample of cases, some of which were cleared and prosecuted and some of which were not. The resulting information could assist in determining the best ways to organize department personnel to conduct investigations.

Also little is known about how a detective goes about trying to gather case facts. It might be true that to collect a small (but perhaps critical) amount of new information, a detective might have to collect a lot of repeat or verified information. (That is, to get new information a detective might have to interview witnesses that have already been interviewed by patrol and, in the process, obtain a lot of repeat information.) Research should be directed at learning what investigative activities lead to new or other valuable information. Also, little is known about how a detective uses verified or repeat information—whether that encourages detectives to pursue a case further and whether that information finds its way into official reports.

One final comment should be made about measuring detective productivity. It really is not completely fair to compare the investigative work of detectives with that of patrol. First, patrol probably collects most of the new information simply because they arrive at the crime scene first. If detectives arrived at the scene first, they would probably collect most of the new information themselves. Also, it is possible that if detectives did arrive first, they might collect more than patrol now collects. New information collected by detectives in follow-up investigations is probably more difficult to collect than information collected by patrol. Second, the additional information collected by detectives, which perhaps is small in comparison to patrol, might be critical.

These are all issues that need to be researched further.

Additionally, research and study of the patrol-criminal investigation integration for effect should continue.

SYSTEMS APPROACH TO MANAGING PATROL AND CRIMINAL INVESTIGATION

The introduction to the proposed reforms suggested by Peter W. Greenwood and Joan Petesilia appears to be an introduction to the systematic review of where we were and might be in criminal investigation. It is worth repeating:

> The above findings imply that traditional approaches to criminal investigation by police departments do not significantly affect the rate at which cases are solved. It appears, rather, that most cases are solved by the application of routine administrative procedures. If these implications are valid, then several policy changes are suggested. We set forth a number of such "reforms" whose rationale is consistent with our findings. We do not expect a police department to adopt them uncritically. Rather, it should first assure itself of the relevance of our work to its situation and then introduce the changes on an experimental basis, together with a careful evaluation program that enables their effects to be identified and assessed. If these experimental implementations have favorable outcomes in several departments, then the change(s) involved could be promoted for national adoption.[39]

The controversy caused by Rand was worth more than the findings, since it stimulated discussion and caused police managers to find out where they were and to review systematically their process to determine where they wanted to be and what changes would be necessary to get there. Therefore, we have the systems approach to managing patrol and criminal investigation.

The objectives of patrol and criminal investigation can be said to be at least similar in crime prevention, suppression, apprehension, and investigation. Some differences occur in the amount and type of investigation, and the techniques of prevention. However, as an organizational objective, their activities should be directed to the same end-product. The systematic approach to this end includes reporting and an analysis of each componant in order to bring about a synthesis of the total investigative process. Figure 8.3 provides one view of the systems approach to managing criminal investigation.

Figure 8.3 *Systems approach to MCI*

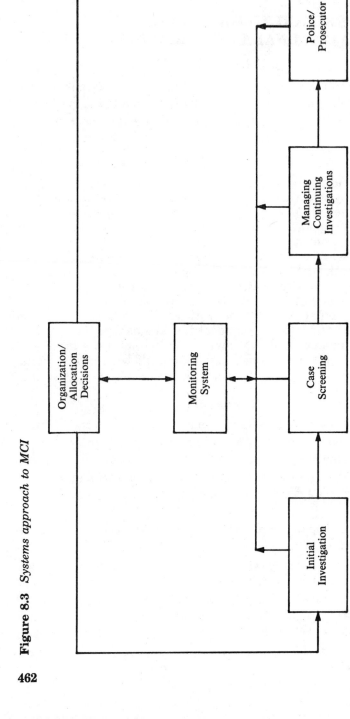

Source: University Research Corporation, *Managing Criminal Investigation* (Washington, D.C.: U.S. Department of Justice, Law Enforcement Assistance Administration, National Institute of Law Enforcement and Criminal Justice, 1977).

In achieving the total process, the first thing to be done is to deal with the role of the patrol officer. Commissions and studies have recommended the enhancement of the role of patrol officer. One way to do this is to determine the extent of investigative activity based on an analysis of the agency and personnel. One way to analyze is to review the models of Figure 8.4

The models should be viewed as flexible, with each agency fitting the individual (modified) model to the specifics of the organization. For example, an agency which is using the typical model should use an evolutionary process to reach the enhanced model because of the need for universal training and general sophistication of the personnel as you move from one stage to the next. The scope of the process includes organizational structure, policy, procedures, training, and management participation in the predetermined evolution criteria for measuring improved performance of the organization, unit, and individual.

REPORTS AND INFORMATION

In our review of studies, we can at least agree that the timely collection of sufficient, accurate information at the initial contact with victims and witnesses largely determines the ultimate outcome of the investigation. Information, to be effective, must be systematically collected, analyzed, and disseminated. To enhance its effectiveness, the potential for information overload (too much information in a complex form and incapable of assimulation by the users) must be reduced. One way to do this in the criminal investigative process is to develop the appropriate forms and identify the most valuable information. The people who use the information must be included in this planning process.

Based on the Rand analysis, "preliminary investigation," (see Chapter 5 on "Planning"), and personal observation, conflict between patrol and criminal investigation is stimulated by poor information in the initial report. Staff review of reports (departments using this concept organizationally place the review in a staff unit for what may be considered as independent evaluation, since it is not in the chain of command of the reporting officer) is designed to evaluate and insure good preliminary reports. One recent study[40] showed that if limited information from a witness or victim in burglary cases is gathered within at least one hour of the time of occurrence, the chances for a successful outcome of the case are increased 50 percent. Further, if suspect information in burglary cases is reported to the police within no more than eight hours after the burglary, the probability of successful case solution can be as high as 95 percent.

Figure 8.4 *Matrix of model roles of patrol officers in conducting criminal investigations*

Models	Patrol Responsibility	Case Referral Procedure	Consequences	Management Policies
A. Typical	• Prepare and complete basic report form.	• Refer all cases, including preliminary investigations, to detectives.	• Redundancy • Insufficient data collected • Low level of productivity • Low morale in patrol	
B. Better Information Collection	• Conduct a complete initial investigation and fill out revised initial investigation report for selected categories of crime.	• Refer the reports of the initial investigations for selected categories of crime to detectives for follow-up investigation. (In these types of cases, detectives do not conduct preliminary investigations.)	• Elimination of redundancy. • More complete data collected. • Productivity increased • Improved case load for detectives. • Better morale.	• Define crime categories to be investigated by patrol. • Define exceptions. • Design new initial investigation form. • Train patrol and detectives in use of new forms, • Train supervisors.

Role from the perspective of:

• The patrol responsibility

• The process by which patrol assists in referring cases for continued investigation.

• Some consequences of patrol activities on policies regarding investigation.

• Suggested organizational policy initiatives that can be taken by management.

C. Patrol Recommendation	• Conduct initial investigation and complete detailed investigation report. • Decide whether to call for forensic or evidence specialists.	• Supervisor reviews patrol recommendation. • Case screening criteria are used to close cases when initial investigation reveals lack of solvability factors. OR • Case screening criteria are used to refer to cases for follow-up investigation by detectives.	• Recommendation and screening, after initial investigation by patrol, focuses resources only on probably solvable cases. • Increases productivity. • Promotes interdependency between detectives and patrol.	• Establish policy and procedures for case screening. • Establish policy and procedures detailing the role of patrol and follow-up role of detectives. • Provide additional training for patrol and supervisors.
D. Limited Investigative Role of Patrol	• Investigate crimes in selected categories beyond initial investigation phase. • Patrol continues and completes investigation of certain categories of crime which do not require the service of detective specialists.	• Crime cases in selected categories are not referred. • Other cases are referred to detectives for follow-up investigation.	• Reduces detective workload. • Permits detective to increase speciality or to adopt new roles.	• Establish policy and procedures delineating investigative roles of patrol in selected categories of criminal investigation and of detectives in other categories of crime. • Provide additional training for patrol.

continued

Figure 8.4 *continued*

Role from the perspective of:

- The patron responsibility

- The process by which patrol assists in referring cases for continued investigation.

- Some consequences of patrol activities on policies regarding investigation.

- Suggested organizational policy initiatives that can be taken by management.

Models	Patrol Responsibility	Case Referral Procedure	Consequences	Management Policies
E. Enhanced Investigative Role of Patrol	• Investigate crimes in increased number of categories. • Closure can occur on scene after initial investigation.	• Refer only those cases which require high level of skill or which are of an exceptional nature.	• Maximal use of detectives by assigning them to follow up only those cases with high probability of solution and/or those which require specialized skills. • Maximal use of patrol resources in all investigations. • Improved relationships between public and police. • New roles and opportunities available for detectives.	• Establish policies detailing the differing authority and relationships between patrol and detectives. • Adopt case screening system which incorporates early, on-scene, case-closure criteria.

Source: National Evaluation Program, *Preventive Patrol.* National Institute of Law Enforcement and Criminal Justice, LEAA. (Washington, D.C.: U.S. Department of Justice, 1977). Reprinted with permission.

The Rochester, New York Police Department crime investigation report is an example of a form (Figure 8.5) designed to secure relevant, timely, accurate information from victims and witnesses. The structured questions on the form direct patrol officers to search for effective answers.

The form contains twelve essential questions which need direct answers (unless an immediate, on-scene arrest is made). These questions were developed by the agency after an analysis of cases previously cleared or solved by the agency which showed that twelve factors were dominant in successful clearance of crime cases. The use of background shading and different typeface for the twelve structured questions on the form highlights the importance of the solvability factors, so that they cannot be overlooked.

These 12 factors are:

1. Immediate availability of witnesses.
2. Naming of a suspect.
3. Information about suspect's location.
4. Information about suspect's description.
5. Information about suspect's identification.
6. Information about suspect's vehicular movement.
7. Information about traceable property.
8. Information about significant M.O.
9. Information about significant physical evidence.
10. Presence of evidence technician who indicates an *a priori* judgment that good physical evidence is present.
11. A judgment by the patrol officer that there is enough information available that, with a reasonable investment of investigative effort, the probability of case solution is high.
12. A judgment by the patrol officer that there is sufficient information available to conclude that anyone other than the suspect could not have committed the crime.

These dominant factors—termed "solvability factors"—are also logically based on the existing operational policies and practices in place in the agency. Other agencies with different capabilities and procedures might develop a slightly different list of solvability factors.

No numerical weights are attached to any of the twelve solvability-factor questions; each is judged to be as important as the other. If all factors are present—that is, all of the questions are answered positively—the inference is that the case is probably solvable by the follow-up investigative efforts of the detective unit. The agency's policy is that if at least one of the factors is present—that is, if one of the questions is answered positively—the case is transmitted to the supervisor for review and decision concerning assignment to the detective division.

Figure 8.5 *Rochester police department crime investigation report*
(Courtesy of Rochester, N.Y. Police Department)

1. OFFENSE OR CHARGE (INCLUDE DEGREE)
2. CLASSIFICATION OF OFFENSE (SUPERVISORY REVIEW)
3. C.R. NO. (ORIGINAL ONLY)

4. TIME OF OCCURRENCE — M----D----Y----T----
5. WHEN AND WHERE REPORTED — M D Y T
6. LOCATION OF OFFENSE (HOUSE NO. STREET NAME)

7. VICTIMS NAME (LAST, FIRST, MIDDLE) OR FIRM NAME IF BUSINESS
8. VICTIMS ADDRESS (HOUSE NUMBER, STREET NAME)
9. RESIDENCE PHONE — DAY / NIGHT

10. VICTIMS PLACE OF EMPLOY. OR SCHOOL NAME
11. BUSINESS PHONE — DAY / NIGHT
12. SEX / RACE / AGE — VICTIMS
13. PERSON REPORTING — SIGNATURE – DATE

IF ARREST IS MADE, NAME ARRESTEES IN NARRATIVE. PLACE THE NUMBER OF ARRESTEES IN BOX A. IF NONE PLACE AN X IN BOX A — 14.

INDICATE WITH PROPER CODE IN BOXES PROVIDED PERSONS RELATIONSHIP TO INVESTIGATION W-1 WITNESS #1, W-2 WITNESS #2, P-R REPORTING PERSON, P/K PERSON WITH KNOWLEDGE (INCLUDING REPORTING PERSONS NAME IF DIFFERENT FROM VICTIMS) IF CITIZEN INFORMATION FORM R.P.D. 1148 IS LEFT WITH ANY OF THESE PERSONS INDICATE BY CIRCLING PERSONS DESIGNATED.

APT.#	PERSON INTERVIEWED	INFORMATION PROVIDED - USE NARRATIVE IF NEEDED
ADDRESS CHECKED	PERSON INTERVIEWED	
ADDRESS CHECKED	PERSON INTERVIEWED	
ADDRESS CHECKED	PERSON INTERVIEWED	
ADDRESS CHECKED	PERSON INTERVIEWED	
ADDRESS CHECKED	PERSON INTERVIEWED	
ADDRESS CHECKED	PERSON INTERVIEWED	

16. WAS THERE A WITNESS TO THE CRIME? — IF NO PLACE AN X IN BOX B — 16.
17. CAN A SUSPECT BE NAMED? — IF NO PLACE AN X IN BOX C — 17.
SUSPECT #1 (NAME INCLUDE ANY A-K-A INFO) — SUSPECT #2 (NAME INCLUDE ANY A-K-A INFO) — SUSPECT #3 (NAME INCLUDE ANY A-K-A INFO)

18. CAN A SUSPECT BE LOCATED? — IF NO PLACE AN X IN BOX D — 18.
SUSPECT #1 MAY BE LOCATED AT — SUSPECT #2 MAY BE LOCATED AT — SUSPECT #3 MAY BE LOCATED AT

19. CAN A SUSPECT BE DESCRIBED? — IF NO PLACE AN X IN BOX E — 19.
SUSPECT #1 DESCRIPTION — SUSPECT #2 DESCRIPTION — SUSPECT #3 DESCRIPTION

DESCRIBE EACH SUSPECT - USING AGE, SEX, RACE, HEIGHT, WEIGHT, ANY IDENTIFYING SCARS, MARKS AND CLOTHING DESCRIPTION

20. CAN A SUSPECT BE IDENTIFIED? — IF NO PLACE AN X IN BOX F — 20.
21. IF SUSPECT INFORMATION HAS BEEN GIVEN OUT VIA RADIO COMM. PLACE AN X IN BOX 21.
USING APPROPRIATE CODE IN THE BOXES PROVIDED-INDICATE WHO CAN IDENTIFY SUSPECT

22. FILL IN LICENSE PLATE INFORMATION IF IT IS AVAILABLE.

MODEL/MAKE	YEAR	TYPE	COLOR TOP/BOTTOM	IDENTIFYING CHARACTERISTICS

23. CAN THE SUSPECT VEHICLE BE IDENTIFIED? — IF NO PLACE AN X IN BOX G — 23.

PAGE OF

468

J 24.

IF SUSPECT VEHICLE INFORMATION WAS GIVEN VIA RADIO COMMUNICATION PLACE AN X IN BOX 24.

IF THE STOLEN PROPERTY IS TRACEABLE INDICATE IN THE SPACE PROVIDED BELOW — IF NO PLACE AN X IN BOX H

26. DESCRIBE PROPERTY TAKEN/DAMAGED	27. WHERE PROPERTY WAS REMOVED FROM	28. PROPERTY IDENTIFICATION INFORMATION	29. PROP. VAL.	25.
			TOTAL VALUE	

30. WHERE HOSPITALIZED	31. ATTENDING PHYSICIAN	32. DATE/TIME PRONOUNCED	33. PRONOUNCING PHYSICIAN – WHERE	34. MEDICAL EXAMINER NOTIFIED NAME

35. IS THERE A SIGNIFICANT M. O. PRESENT? IF YES DESCRIBE IN NARRATIVE   IF NO PLACE AN X IN BOX I — 35.

36. PROPERTY INV. NO.	37. NATURE OF INJURY	38. POINT OF CRIME	39. TYPE OF WEAPON, INSTRUMENT OR FORCE USED

40. IS THERE SIGNIFICANT PHYSICAL EVIDENCE PRESENT? IF YES DESCRIBE IN NARRATIVE   IF NO PLACE AN X IN BOX J — 40.

41. TECH WORK DONE BY   HAS AN EVIDENCE TECHNICIAN BEEN CALLED?   IF NO PLACE AN X IN BOX K — 41.
IS EVIDENCE TECHNICIAN REPORT POSITIVE?   PLACE AN X IN BOX K

42. IS THERE A SIGNIFICANT REASON TO BELIEVE THAT THE CRIME MAY BE SOLVED WITH A
REASONABLE AMOUNT OF INVESTIGATIVE EFFORT?   IF NO PLACE AN X IN BOX L — 42.

43. WAS THERE A DEFINITE LIMITED OPPORTUNITY FOR ANYONE EXCEPT THE SUSPECT TO COMMIT THE CRIME? IF NO PLACE AN X IN BOX M — 43.

44. NARRATIVE: SUMMARIZE DETAILS OF CRIME INCLUDING A DESCRIPTION OF EVENTS; ANY ADDITIONAL INFORMATION WHICH IS AN EXTENSION OF ANY OF THE ABOVE BOXES; NAMES OF ARRESTED; NAMES OF OTHER OFFICERS OR UNITS ASSISTING.

ASSIST

ASSIST

ASSIST

ASSIST

ASSIST

45. IS ONE OR MORE OF THE SOLVABILITY FACTORS PRESENT IN THIS REPORT?	46.	REPORTING OFFICERS	ASSIGNED BEAT #	51.

☐ YES (FIELD FOLLOWUP)   ☐ NO (OFFICE REVIEW)

FIELD SUPERVISORS REVIEW
47 ☐ COMPLETE   ☐ CONCUR _____ RECOMMEND _____

C.I.D. / SECTION COMMAND REVIEW
48 ☐ CONCUR / RECOMMEND _____ REVIEWER _____

49. ☐ OPEN   ☐ ARREST   ☐ NO ARREST

50. STATUS FOR REVIEW CENTER
☐ UNFOUNDED
☐ NO PROSECUTION
☐ WARRANT ADVISED

469

Requiring the patrol officer to check those questions which have *not* been answered provides an outline of what yet has to be done when the investigator plans his next steps, so that nothing is overlooked in conducting the follow-up. Thus, the detective is provided clear guidance for beginning work and an outline or an "investigative map" for proceeding with the investigation.

No definitive evaluation has yet been done on the amount of time it takes to complete this form in comparison with other types of crime report forms. But indications are that the time differential is minimal, and, in fact, with continued use, the amount of time spent by patrol on the initital investigation may actually be less than it was before the form was designed.

Clearly, one of the more important tasks which any agency would have to complete before redesigning its own form would be to determine what "solvability factors" contribute most to successful case clearance in its own jurisdiction.[41]

Figures 8.5A and 8.5B show the updated forms of the Rochester, New York Police Department which now tie the original crime investigation report and the identified solvability factors to the investigative action report. The two reports complement each other and present a complete investigation reporting system.

The crime investigation report provides a method of recording the preliminary investigation and, in the event there are no solvability factors, is the total report of the incident. In the event there are no solvability factors that are identified, this report provides a linkage to the investigative action report, which then lists the other actions taken by an investigator to report what he has accomplished regarding the listed solvability factors or the work that he accomplished regarding additional solvability factors.

Integrating the report with the previous matrix and improved performance is essentially a management responsibility. However, the patrol officer continues to contribute in a meaningful way to the total process and at the same time increases his or her skills, knowledge, and ability in effective decision-making.

Moving toward the previous model E (enhanced), the officer became part of the case screening based on solvability. Implicit in this early case-suspension system is the responsibility of the department to notify the victim(s) of the status. The role of the patrol officer is one of support for the criminal investigator, since the better the patrol officer performs, the more time the investigator has to perform. If we assume that most crimes are committed by multiple offenders, then the quicker the investigator can arrest the multiple offender, the fewer burglaries he or she can commit, therefore reducing further burglaries (this also assures that the criminal justice system is working). It is therefore beneficial to both to provide complementary excellent performance in the respective roles.

CASE SCREENING

Case screening is a mechanism that will facilitate making a decision concerning the continuation of an investigation based upon the existence of sufficient solvability factors obtained at the initial investigation.[42] The objective is for the police manager(s) to control the expenditures of resources to improve productivity. Simply put, management, "Getting the most for the least," investment, and dividends. There may be exceptions, where the reality of the environment (pressure) or seriousness of the offense necessitates an all-out effort. The real question of continuing an investigation should be determined by each agency in some systematic manner based on relevant information.

The following is presented for comparative analysis since the Oakland, California Police Department does not use the system any longer due to personnel shortages.

Oakland, California[43]

In 1975, the Stanford Research Institute (SRI) developed a case follow-up decision model for the Oakland Police Department (OPD). This *"Felony Investigation Decision Model"* study by B. Greenberg et al. grew out of a 1973 SRI study in Alameda County, California, "Enhancement of the Investigative Function." In the first study, the authors developed a checklist of activities to guide patrol officers and detectives in the investigation of burglary cases. A case follow-up decision model was statistically derived through an examination of past cases. A set of weighted variables emerged that predicted case outcome with a high degree of certainty.

Figure 8.6 shows the burglary case disposition decision rule that was developed.

The 1975 study, also conducted in Oakland, California, resulted in the development of a robbery decision model that could be used to identify cases that had sufficient probability of clearance to warrant follow-up investigation. The SRI research team sought to minimize the police investigator's intuitive judgment on case handling by statistically analyzing factors that have significantly contributed in the past to case clearance. The study results suggested that "unless offender identification was made by the responding officer, case solution at the detective level was minimal."

Figure 8.5A *Rochester Police Department Crime Investigative Report*
(Courtesy of Rochester, N.Y. Police Department)

1. OFFENSE OR CHARGE (INCLUDE DEGREE & LAW SECTION NO.)   2. CLASSIFICATION OF OFFENSE (SUPERVISORY REVIEW)   3. CR #

4. TIME OF OCCURRENCE   M___D___Y___T___

5. WHEN REPORTED   M   D   Y   T
DISPATCHED   TO

6. LOCATION OF OFFENSE (HOUSE NO. STREET NAME)

7. VICTIMS NAME (LAST, FIRST, MIDDLE) OR FIRM NAME IF BUSINESS

8. VICTIMS ADDRESS (HOUSE NUMBER, STREET NAME)   9. RESIDENCE PHONE   DAY   NIGHT

10. VICTIMS PLACE OF EMPLOY, OR SCHOOL NAME   11. BUSINESS PHONE   DAY   NIGHT   12. VICTIM'S   SEX / RACE / AGE   13. REPORTING PERSONS SIGNATURE   DATE

14. WAS THERE A WITNESS TO THE CRIME?   IF NO PLACE AN X IN BOX A ➤   A.

15. INDICATE WITH PROPER CODE IN BOXES PROVIDED. PERSON'S RELATIONSHIP TO INVESTIGATION W-1 : WITNESS #1 : NI : NOT INTERVIEWED #2. R:REPORTING PERSON; PK : PERSON WITH KNOWLEDGE INCLUDING REPORTING PERSON'S NAME IF DIFFERENT FROM VICTIM'(S). IF CITIZEN INFORMATION FORM R.P.D. 1 148 IS LEFT WITH ANY OF THESE PERSON'S INDICATE BY CIRCLING PERSONS DESIGNATED

ADDRESS CHECKED	APT.#	PERSON INTERVIEWED	AGE	HOME ADDRESS	APT#		
						T E L	RES. ____ BUS.
						T E L	RES. ____ BUS.
						T E L	RES. ____ BUS.
						T E L	RES. ____ BUS.
						T E L	RES. ____ BUS.

16. CAN A SUSPECT BE NAMED?   IF NO PLACE AN X IN BOX B ➤   B.

SUSPECT #1 NAME (INCLUDE ANY A-K-A- INFO)   SUSPECT #2 (INCLUDE ANY A-K-A INFO)

17. CAN SUSPECT BE LOCATED?   IF NO PLACE AN X IN BOX C ➤   C.

SUSPECT #1 CAN BE LOCATED AT   SUSPECT #2 CAN BE LOCATED AT

18. CAN SUSPECT BE DESCRIBED?   IF NO PLACE AN X IN BOX D ➤   D.

SUSPECT #1 DESCRIPTION   SUSPECT #2 DESCRIPTION

DESCRIBE EACH SUSPECT USING AGE, SEX, RACE, HEIGHT, WEIGHT, ANY IDENTIFYING SCARS, MARKS & CLOTHING DESCRIPTION

ARRESTED   □ YES □ NO
ARRESTED   □ YES □ NO

19. CAN SUSPECT BE IDENTIFIED?   IF NO PLACE AN X IN BOX E ➤   E.

USING APPROPRIATE CODES IN THE BOXES PROVIDED, INDICATE WHO CAN IDENTIFY SUSPECT.

20. TIME SUSPECT INFORMATION BROADCAST   20.

21. REGISTRATION INFORMATION	YEAR	MAKE	MODEL & TYPE	COLOR TOP/BOTTOM	IDENTIFYING CHARACTERISTICS
STATE					

PAGE 1 OF ___

472

22. CAN SUSPECT VEHICLE BE IDENTIFIED? IF NO PLACE AN X IN BOX F ——→ F.

23. TIME SUSPECT VEHICLE INFORMATION BROADCAST. PLACE TIME IN BOX 23 ——→ 23.

24. IS STOLEN PROPERTY TRACEABLE? IF NO PLACE AN X IN BOX G ——→ G.

25. DESCRIBE PROPERTY STOLEN / DAMAGED | 26. REMOVED FROM | 27. PROPERTY IDENTIFICATION INFORMATION | 28. PROP. VALUE

			TOTAL VALUE

29. NATURE OF INJURY | 30. TYPE OF INSTRUMENT, WEAPON OR FORCE USED | H.

31. WHERE HOSPITALIZED | 32. ATTENDING PHYSICIAN | 33. PRONOUNCING PHYSICIAN/ WHERE | 34. DATE / TIME PRONOUNCED | 35. NAME OF MEDICAL EXAMINER

36. IS THERE A SIGNIFICANT M.O. PRESENT? IF YES, DESCRIBE IN NARRATIVE   IF NO PLACE AN X IN BOX H ——→ H.

37. IS THERE SIGNIFICANT PHYSICAL EVIDENCE PRESENT? IF YES, DESCRIBE IN NARRATIVE. IF NO PLACE AN X IN BOX I ——→ I.

38. HAS EVIDENCE TECH WORK BEEN PERFORMED? (By:_____) REQUESTED? IF NO PLACE AN X IN BOX J ——→ J.
TECH WORK PERFORMED / REQUESTED: ☐PHOTO ☐FINGERPRINT ☐COMPOSITE ☐OTHER

39. IS THERE REASON TO BELIEVE THAT THE PRELIMINARY INVESTIGATION CANNOT BE COMPLETED AT THIS TIME? IF NO PLACE AN X IN BOX K ——→ K.

40. CAN CRIME BE SOLVED WITH A REASONABLE AMOUNT OF INVESTIGATIVE EFFORT?   IF NO PLACE AN X IN BOX L ——→ L.

41. WAS THERE A DEFINITE LIMITED OPPORTUNITY FOR ANYONE EXCEPT THE SUSPECT TO COMMIT THE CRIME? IF NO PLACE AN X IN BOX M ——→ M.

42. POINT OF CRIME | 43. PREMISE DESCRIPTION | 44. PROP. INV. #

45. NARRATIVE SUMMARIZE DETAILS OF CRIME INCLUDING PROGRESSION OF EVENTS, NAMES OF OTHER OFFICERS OR UNITS ASSISTING.
FOR ANY ADDITIONAL INFORMATION WHICH IS AN EXTENSION OF ANY OF THE ABOVE BLOCKS, INDICATE BLOCK NUMBER AT LEFT.

BLOCK NO.

	ASSIST
	ASSIST
	ASSIST
	ASSIST

46. IS ONE OF THE SOLVABILITY FACTORS PRESENT IN THIS REPORT? | 47. REPORTING OFFICER(S) | ASSIGNED BEAT NO. | 51.
☐NO, OFFICE ☐YES, FIELD ☐YES, CLOSED

48. FIELD SUPERVISORY DECISION   REVIEWER | 50. CLOSED BY
☐OFFICE ☐FIELD ☐CLOSED | ☐ARREST ☐WARRANT ADVISED
                          ☐NO ARREST ☐UNFOUNDED
                          ☐NO PROSECUTION ☐JUVENILE DIVERSION

49. IF FIELD, INVESTIGATOR SHOULD
FOLLOW-UP SOLVABILITY FACTORS

473

Figure 8.5B *Rochester Police Department Investigative Action Report*
(Courtesy of Rochester, N.Y. Police Department)

1. VICTIM'S NAME (LAST, FIRST, MIDDLE) OR FIRM NAME IF BUSINESS	2. LOCATION OF OFFENSE (HOUSE NO.-STREET NAME)	SEC.	3. CR #

4. TIME OF OCCURRENCE			5. OFFENSE/CHARGE/INCIDENT (FROM ORIGINAL)	6. CLASSIFICATION OF INCIDENT (AFTER INVESTIGATION)
M	D	Y	T		

7. SOLVABILITY FACTORS FOR INVESTIGATION

FROM CRIME
INVESTIGATION REPORT

8. NARRATIVE: DO NOT REPEAT THE RESULTS OF THE PRELIMINARY INVESTIGATION. REPORT ALL ACTIONS TAKEN AND ALL DEVELOPMENTS IN THE CASE SINCE THE LAST REPORT. DESCRIBE AND RECORD THE VALUE OF RECOVERED PROPERTY. LIST THE NAME, RECORD NUMBER AND DESCRIPTION OF PERSONS ARRESTED. EXPLAIN CLASSIFICATION CHANGE. CLEARLY SHOW THE DISPOSITION OF RECOVERED PROPERTY.

BLOCK NO.

ADDED INFO ☐
FOLLOW-UP ☐

PAGE ___ OF ___

474

A police investigation/case report form containing the following fields:

9. PERSON(S) ARRESTED — ☐NO ☐YES NO. _____

10. ARE ALL SUSPECTS UNDER 18 YRS. OLD ☐YES ☐NO

11. PROPERTY RECOVERED ☐NO ☐YES $ _____

12. PROPERTY INVENTORY ☐NO ☐YES # _____

13. MULTIPLE CLEAR UP? ☐YES ☐NO — COMPANION ARREST # _____

14. WORKING CR # _____ ☐YES ☐NO #

15. TELETYPE ☐SENT ☐CANCELED #

16. ☐PROPERTY ☐SUSPECT — ADDITIONAL TECHWORK ☐COMPOSITE ☐SKETCH/DIAGRAM ☐FINGERPRINT ☐OTHER — PERFORMED BY _____

17. SOLVABILITY FACTORS
- ELIMINATED BY INVESTIGATION
- DEVELOPED BY INVESTIGATION
- REMAINING FOR INVESTIGATION

SUPERVISOR

18. INVESTIGATIVE STATUS
- CONTINUANCE OF ☐FIELD ☐OFFICE
- CHANGED TO ☐FIELD ☐OFFICE
- CLOSED BY ☐ARREST ☐WARRANT ADVISED ☐NO ARREST ☐UNFOUNDED ☐NO PROSECUTION ☐JUVENILE DIVERSION

ESTIMATED HOURS FOR COMPLETION _____

19. FURTHER INVESTIGATION TO BE CONDUCTED BY:
☐INVESTIGATOR _____ ☐C.I.D. UNIT _____
☐YOUTH OFFICER _____ ☐SOCIAL AGENCY _____
☐PLATOON _____ ☐SECTION _____ ☐OTHER _____

20. DATE SUBMITTED

21. REPORTING OFFICER(S)

21. BEAT

22. SUPERVISOR APPROVING

475

Figure 8.6 *Burglary case disposition decision rule*[44]

Information Element	Weighting Factor
Estimated time lapse between crime and the initial investigation:	
Less than 1 hour	5
1 to 12 hours	1
12 to 24 hours	0.3
More than 24 hours	0
Witness's report of offense	7
On-view report of offense	1
Usable fingerprints	7
Suspect information developed—description or name	9
Vehicle description	0.1
Other	0
TOTAL SCORE:	

Instructions

1. Circle the weighting factor for each information element that is present in the incident report.
2. Add the circled factors.
3. If the sum is less than or equal to 10, suspend the case; otherwise, follow up the case.

Figure 8.7 shows the dominant case-solution factors related to the victim's knowledge of the offender.

Case screening consists of the following components:

a. Accurate and complete collection of crime information by the patrol officer.
b. An on-scene determination of the sufficiency of crime information collected.
c. Permitting the patrol officer to make decisions concerning follow-up investigation.
d. Review of that decision by a supervisor.

Putting these components into effect will require an agency to:

a. Redefine the mission of the major divisions.
b. Redefine roles for patrol officers, supervisors, investigators, and managers in the case screening process.

Figure 8.7 *Robbery investigation decision model*[45]

Information Element	Weighting Factor
Suspect named	10*
Suspect known	10*
Suspect previously seen	10*
Evidence technician used	10
Places suspect frequently named	10*
Physical evidence	
Each item matched	6.1
Vehicle registration	
Query information available	1.5
Vehicle stolen	3.0
Useful information returned	4.5
Vehicle registered to suspect	6.0
Offender movement description	
On foot	0
Vehicle (not car)	0.6
Car	1.2
Car color given	1.8
Car description given	2.4
Car license given	3.0
Weapon used	1.6

*These values as calculated actually exceed the threshold of 10. The values provided here are conceptually simpler and make no difference in the classification of groups.

   c. Develop and use criminal collection forms that incorporate early closure information; and

   d. Provide training in the use of the new system to all affected personnel.[46]

Contact with many police administrators has revealed the following considerations: (1) careful planning and training to communicate to the appropriate government officials regarding the end product of the case screening approach; (2) analysis of other agency procedures and communicating to the community the process to increase understanding; (3) a program designed to show all citizens the cost-effectiveness of the procedure for tax purposes; (4) training of supervisors and officers on the "how-to" of explaining the procedure to the citizens; (5) an analysis of paper flow to insure the minimum amount of paper work; (6) an organizational training program designed to show all officers the value of cooperation; and (7) a total information system based on planning, system analysis, system design, appropriate implementation, monitoring, feedback, evaluation, modification and re-implementation.

At a recent conference on Standardized Crime Reporting, a major discussion on loss of personnel which affects productivity concluded "the fact is, only a systematic approach can tell you what detectives can and cannot do regarding the extent of criminal investigation." Consequently, a case management system which sets forth guidelines on follow-up, continuing investigation, inspection on time, summary reports for management, and performance standards and outcome measures, insures the review and analysis of the system.

The cooperative effort in the systematic approach may call for the use of police service aides, which can provide lower costs for calls of certain types and free officers for more serious calls and investigation and thereby free detectives for more complex investigations. Figure 8.8 shows the Worcester, Mass. approach. In some cases, the patrol function has been enhanced depending on training and quality of police aides.

Figure 8.8

SERVICE CALL ASSIGNMENTS FOR SWORN OFFICERS AND POLICE SERVICE AIDES IN WORCESTER, MASSACHUSETTS

	PSA ONLY	PO ONLY	AMBIGUOUS
Route Assignments			
Report to Headquarters, Precinct I, etc. . . .			X
Standby (Precautionaries)	X		
Assist, Meet, Pick Up Officer			X
Pick Up Papers, Etc.	X		
Escort Duty			X
Snow Complaints	X		
Guard/Transfer Prisoners		X	
Found/Recovered Property	X		
Notifications			X
Assist Citizen			X
Verification			
Alarms			
House Alarm		X	
ADT Alarm		X	
Car Alarms (Burglary)	X		
Fire Alarms	X		
Bonfire	X		
Car Fires	X		
Disturbances			
Vandalism			X
Disorderly Person		X	
Disorderly Gang		X	

Figure 8.8 (continued)

	PSA ONLY	PO ONLY	AMBIGUOUS
Fight		X	
Drunk		X	
Suspicious Person (Prowler)		X	
Suspicious Car (Occupied)		X	
Children Disturbing	X		
Discharging Firearms		X	
Noise Complaints			X
Rubbish Complaints	X		
Animal Complaints	X		
Domestic Trouble		X	
Noncriminal Investigations			
Open Door/Window/Lights on in Building		X	
Defective Streets/Walks/Wires	X		
Licenses/Permits			X
All Points Broadcast			
Stolen/Recovered Car	X		
Stolen/Received Car	X		
Wanted/Located Car		X	
Missing/Located Person	X		
Wanted Person/Suspect		X	
Missing/Located Patient			X
Escaped/Apprehended Prisoner		X	
Lost/Stolen/Recovered Plates	X		
Medical Cases			
Sick Person	X		
Injured Person	X		
Dead Person		X	
Overdose		X	
Investigations			
Homicide		X	
Rape		X	
Assault		X	
Armed Robbery		X	
Unarmed Robbery		X	
Larceny from Motor Vehicle		X	
Attempted Larceny from Motor Vehicle			X
Breaking and Entering Dwelling/Commercial		X	
Bomb Threat		X	
Bombing		X	
Narcotics Offenses		X	
Traffic Incidents			
Auto Accident with Property Damage	X		
Auto Accident with Personal Injury		X	
Auto Accident with Hit and Run		X	
Auto Obstructing			X
Traffic/Parking Violations		X	
Abandoned Car (Empty)	X		

Figure 8.8 (continued)

	PSA ONLY	PO ONLY	AMBIGUOUS
Crimes in Progress			
Rape............................		X	
Assault		X	
Armed/Unarmed Robbery		X	
Larceny		X	
Breaking and Entering Dwelling		X	

Source: National Evaluation Program, *Preventive Patrol* (Washington, D.C.: National Institute of Law Enforcement and Criminal Justice, LEAA, U.S. Department of Justice, 1977).

POLICE–PROSECUTOR RELATIONS

The Montgomery County, Maryland Police Department has completed the evaluation of a managing criminal investigation pilot program for their department. One of the components of the program was to improve police–prosecutor relations, thereby upgrading the quality of the department. Most police agencies experience some problems with prosecutors, but, like the Dallas, Texas police–prosecutor program, both can help the criminal justice system through cooperation. One premise of the program was that investigations completed simply for the purpose of making an arrest and/or clearing a case did not contribute to system effectiveness. Rather, cases lacking sufficient information to ensure prosecution only burdened the system. Increasing the quality of case preparation and investigation is a two-part cooperative effort between police and prosecutor. The objectives of the program are:

1. Increase the number of cases accepted for prosecution.
2. Increase the number of cases resulting in a conviction.
3. Increase the amount of police–prosecutor case contact on serious cases prior to judicial proceedings.
4. Increase the use of prosecutor feedback in case preparation.[46]

Insufficient evidence and information by the police and lack of witness participation are important barriers to effective prosecution and should be considered with the above objectives.

As an example, we will use the first objective of increasing the number of cases accepted for prosecution. Under this objective, there were five activities: (1) meetings between the Chief of Police and the State's Attorney (usually conducted monthly) for purposes of discussing MCI and related subjects; (2) prosecutor training programs for police in case elements necessary for prosecution; (3) use of an investigative checklist to be used by investigators for purposes of enhancing case quality; (4) establishment of a system for conducting post-arrest conferences to informally review case elements for felony investigation; and (5) development of a case feedback system to inform individual officers of prosecutor decisions and to iden-tify training needs.[47]

Each objective and activity had an evaluation component. This objec-tive evaluation concluded that there was no evaluation because no program changes were implemented and no change in prosecution rates actually occurred. Also, as an evaluation of the total program states: "The police prosecutor component of the managing criminal investigation program can be characterized as the least successful project element from the stand-point of achieving stated objectives."[48] The principal factor for lack of program accomplishment . . . "The lack of management direction and fol-low-through to achieved stated objectives."[49] Specifically lacking were the commitment to change systematically, and understanding of the change agent. Strategy concept in its totality again was identified as a major prob-lem for improving the criminal justice system. As a student of management, reading the literature highlights the need to be aware of organizational behavior and change. Finally, the report recommends that relatively easy-to-implement procedures be formulated to ensure feedback and communi-cation, including: (1) the continuation of meetings between the Chief of Police and the State Attorney, (2) formal adoption of informal case review, (3) use of structured checklist for investigators,[50] and (4) appropriate feed-back system (PROMIS, or one that is not too cumbersome).

The assignment of a legal advisor to a police agency certainly has its advantages, and not the least would be to have liaison with the prose-cutor on an attorney–attorney basis. Other advantages include: daily ad-vice to the Chief on policy matters, review of legally related materials (training), warrant assistance, immediate on-street assistance in riots, demonstrations, etc. The problems of police–prosecutor relations can be solved through intelligent analysis and cooperation. Learning from our critics is one way to start. The following critical comments are a result of a systematic survey of opinions and can be used to improve cooperation.[51]

Police Criticisms of Prosecutors

Wrong kind of people:

"Rookies"
"Transient"
"Bookworms in a field of action"
"Innocents in a bloody arena"
"Insecure, so often officious"
"Timid, so uncommunicative when legal advice is needed"
"Overenthusiastic, meddlers to the point of interference with police functions"

Suggested Remedies

"Encourage career develop-ment to keep the good ones"
"Screen applicants for cool heads"
"Supplement law degree with specialized prosecutor train-ing, including 'cadet' duty with police"

Wrong attitudes:

"Patronizing toward cops"
"Suspicious of police methods"
"Prima donnas; grandstanders for
political or lawyer publicity"

"Service on the street"
"Orientation in police
academy curriculum"
"Canons of ethics for
prosecutors"

Wrong methods:

"Inexperienced complaint deputies
at the screening desk"
"Superficial screening"
"Peremptory refusals"
"Slow filing"
"Poor liaison, or none, re:
Further investigation,
settings,
continuances,
dispositions,
plea negotiations, and
critiques"

"Assign the old pros and pay
them extra"
"Staff up"
"Written reasons, with system
for review"
"Systematize"
"Assign people to it from
both ends"
"Phone crew with stand-by
system"
"Agree on priorities with cri-
teria for mutual guidance"

Prosecutors' Criticisms of Police   ## Suggested Remedies

Wrong kind of people:

"Not smart enough"
"Not trained enough"
"Not retrained for advancement"
"Too cynical; even paranoid"
"Too tired; waiting for retirement"

"Improved recruiting, screening, training, and retraining"
"Awareness of need for
programs to restore positive
outlook and job satisfaction"

Wrong attitudes:

"Officious"
"Hard-nosed; hostile"
"Uncompromising in negotiations"
"Indiscreet in their associations"
"Dishonesty; the end justifies
means"

"Leadership toward:
friendliness,
cooperation,
accommodation,
discretion, and
integrity"

Wrong methods:

"Low standard recruiting"
"Shallow training"
"Poor training for advancement"
"Bureaucratic buck-passing,
'It's the DA's case now.'"
"Poor crime-scene preservation"
"Casual evidence-gathering:
quit at probable cause
omit an element
omit negative proof
superficial interviews"
"Incomplete reports and statements"
"Insufficient warrant affidavits"
"Concealing exculpatory facts"
"Manipulating testimony to fit need"

"Attract more and better"
"Improve the academy"
"Add management courses"
"Emphasize the common
objective"
"Train and monitor with a
system to catch and correct
mistakes"
"Perfect a format and monitor
its use"
"Teach practical ethics and
fundamentals of the
investigator's mission"

The standards of excellence necessary to collect and analyze data (evidence) accurately and to present it in a logical manner in order to result in the conviction of perpetrators are essential, demanding, and self-actualizing; therefore, part of the police profession.

MONITORING AND MEASURING: HOW ARE WE DOING?

No matter what the organizational structure, size of department, individual manager, etc., the determination of success or failure based on predetermined measures is a necessity for police agencies. The University Research Corporation defined monitoring as "A management information system which provides police administrators with the statistical data on investigative performance that they can use to make judgments about performance." The following terms are used:

1. *Investigative Outcomes:* The investigative product or result produced at the end of an investigation. Outcomes must be stated in quantifiable terms, such as number of arrests, case suspensions, cases continued, case clearances, prosecutions, and convictions.
2. *Investigative Activities:* The specific activities undertaken by criminal investigators and patrol officers. Examples include interrogations, crime scene searches, interviews, and surveillances. These activities must be stated in quantifiable terms.
3. *Productivity:* The number of investigative outcomes or activities per person hour or person day (such as number of clearances per case assigned for each investigator per day). The greater the ratio of outcome per period of time worked, the higher the productivity of the unit or the individual investigator.[52]

In-depth knowledge of the investigation process as a management tool increases the conceptual skills of the administrator. Management personnel should be aware of workload analysis, time management, UCR and information systems such as the Standardized Crime Reporting System, performance by unit (patrol-CID), percentage of on-scene and follow-up arrests, and comparison of appropriate performance indicators, to name a few. To be sure of knowing how you are doing, data is necessary and must relate to what has been identified as good performance and to what was communicated to the patrol/investigator in terms of what was expected performance. Some management literature identifies this aspect as critical because it is a psychological contract between the doer/supervisor/manager organization. I would suggest you never make a contract you can't keep. Breaking the contract usually results in frustration for the employee, and the results for the organization are negative, to say the least.

Standards should be based on the needs and concerns of the local agency. However, determination of the needs and the related following procedures should be the result of a systematic approach. Figure 8.9 can be used as a guide to begin the development of standards of performance. I prefer to begin by using only three measurements: i.e., exceeds standards, and why; meets standards, and why; and does not meet standards, and this written documentation proves it. After three have been used, there may be a need to increase the degree of proficiency by weighting one to ten. However, this should be done in phases because of the difficulty in measuring in degrees. The traits to measure a detective in one department have been identified as initiative, problem analysis, decisiveness, planning and organizing ability, judgment, and writing skills. Would you add speaking skills and interpersonal relations? What else? Creating good informants? Intelligence gathering?

In his study of precinct investigative units and detective specialty squads of the New York City Police Department, Hillen[53] used the Case Management System flow-chart depicted in Figure 8.9 to show the flow of a case through the unit. The MCI case processing methodology shown in figure 8.10 was used by the Montgomery County, Maryland Police Department in the evaluation process for managing criminal investigations.

Hillen concluded:

> Although there is no overwhelming evidence that the Case Management System has had an outstanding positive impact on the quality and management of criminal investigations, it is apparent that there has been some significant movement in this direction. It is also significant to note that the majority of police investigators who participated in this study believed that the Case Management System has contributed to the improvement of the investigative process.
>
> Based on the available findings and data in this study, it may be concluded that the Case Management System has had modest success in reaching its objectives. More importantly, the system appears likely to produce more effective investigative means for ultimate improvement in the quality of criminal investigations. Hence, it may reasonably be asked: Are quality improvements the product of sound procedures or experienced people? In this regard, activity improvements under the Case Management System require each case to receive an appropriate level of investigative effort based on its merits. Under the previous procedures, criminal cases were investigated in an unsystematic and, often untimely, fashion. Such a practice is likely to create public disrespect and contempt for the law and may cause indifference among investigators.
>
> The apparent key to the quality control aspect of the Case Management System rests on the conscientious effort and involvement

Figure 8.9 *Case management system flowchart*

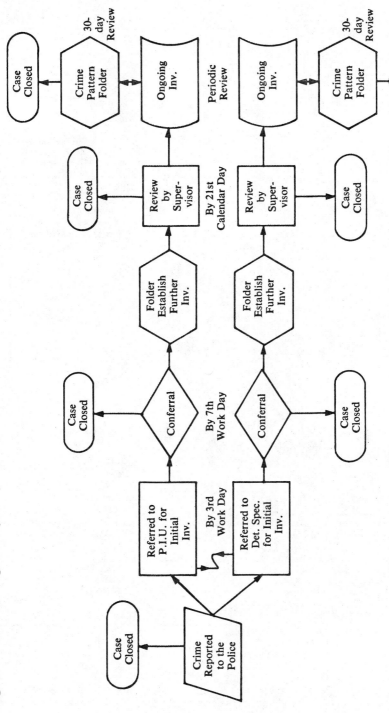

Source: Montgomery County Maryland Police Department, Evaluation Process for Managing Criminal Investigations

485

Figure 8.10 *MCI case processing methodology*

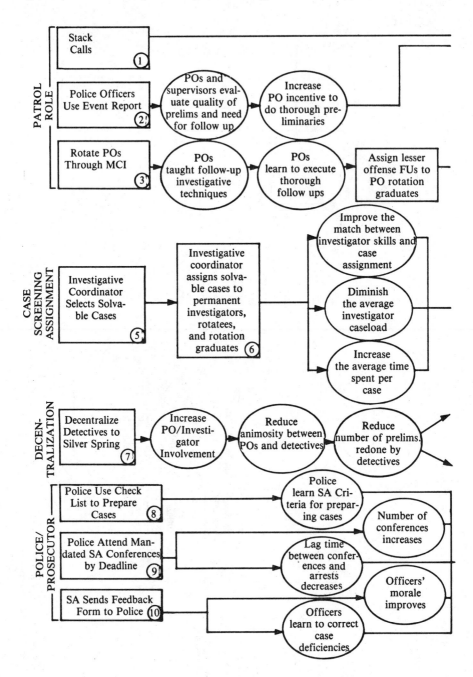

Source: Managing Criminal Investigations, Final Evaluation Report and Executive Summary, Department of Police, Montgomery County, Maryland, National Institute of Law Enforcement and Criminal Justice, Washington, D.C., 1979.

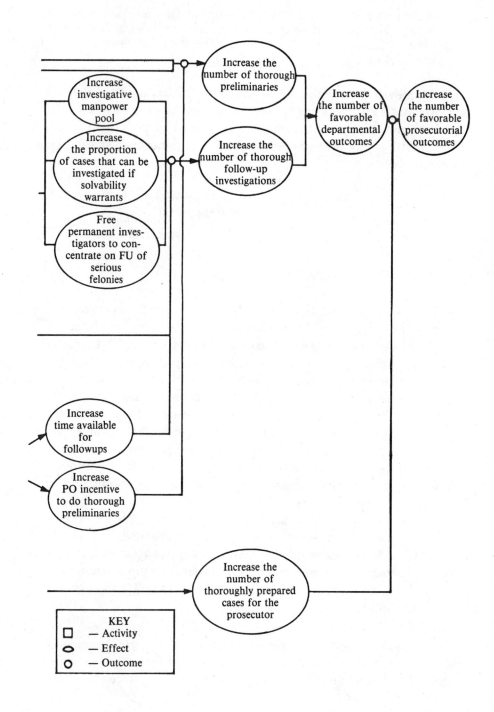

of the investigative supervisors. It is, after all, their leadership qualities and comprehensive application of the system's management procedures that will determine the degree of overall improvement in criminal case investigations.[54]

Whatever measures are to be used for organizational and individual performance, it is necessary to determine them in a systematic way. For example, one organizational measure suggested by the Urban Institute using existing statistics and designed to account for overall arrest productivity is:

$$\text{Apprehension \& Prosecution Productivity} = \frac{\text{The number of criminals apprehended and prosecuted}}{\text{The number of crimes}}$$

The formula has the following characteristics:

- It is proportional (the proportion depends upon the average number of criminals per crime) to the average rate that an individual will be caught as the result of committing one crime. (This is the best available measure of the deterrent effect of apprehension.)
- It counts arrested and prosecuted individuals and thereby avoids the necessity of making fine distinctions about the resulting number of "exceptional clearances" or "clearances by arrests" that might be permitted under FBI crime-classification guidelines. It also reduces the incentive for detectives to devote their time to investigations whose sole purpose is to increase the clearance rate by pinning more crimes on one individual without contributing to arrest productivity.
- It does not count the arrests not considered by the prosecutor or the judge at arraignment to be worthy of prosecution. It therefore counts only those cases where police procedures are well coordinated with the requirements of the local criminal justice system. These cases are the only ones in which criminals can be convicted and punished.

It should be noted that arrest productivity is more appropriate for measuring the performance of police units than for individual officers. Quite often arrest statistics do not give an accurate picture of an individual's contributions.[55]

The analysis of the measures of effectiveness to be used is an individual department decision. For example, Hastings[56] suggests the individual investigation performance analysis should include two kinds: (1) the comparison of the individual investigator's efforts at the lowest unit level and (2) the quality of final case preparation. In the former, the police administrator must be careful not to place primary emphasis on a comparison of number of arrests. To develop an effective evaluation system, a comprehensive analysis must be made of the total number of cases assigned to an individual investigator. A comparison must be made of cases eventually cleared by arrest with the total number of cases assigned, and of cases cleared by arrest in which the investigator developed solvability factors over and above those initially listed by the preliminary investigator.

In the latter, performance analysis involves the quality of final case preparation. For example, in those instances where the preliminary investigator has named a suspect or has described thoroughly the identity of a suspect, the assessment should determine whether the follow-up investigator obtained stolen property, obtained an admission, obtained the names of additional accomplices, or obtained additional witnesses and supporting affidavits. Factors such as these indicate the competence of an investigator who has enlarged the case beyond the preliminary investigation.

In addition, it is important to analyze how many additional cases were developed by the investigator from the original information. The importance of the multiple factors beyond the arrest itself as an indicator of performance is supported by studies which have indicated that, if a crime is not cleared at the original contact, or if evidence is not obtained at that time, the crime will probably never be solved.

Hastings[57] continues by addressing the organizational performance.

Organizational performance The second area of investigative effectiveness, organizational performance, is best evaluated through a monitoring system. Such a system effects periodic review of selected aspects of investigative performance by providing the administrator with data on both individual investigator performance (as previously described) and unit performance.

A system is needed for data collection to obtain the required input to the monitoring system. This requires crime and investigative follow-up reports which provide substantive input on the crime and the status of the investigation. There must be a structure for data analysis so that the data collected can be placed in a format responsive to management needs. A reporting mechanism needs to be developed that will present the results of the data analysis in a useful format: computer or hand tabulated reports are most common. There should be a system for data validation to ensure that the statistics reported are indeed an accurate representation of actual data, and evaluation criteria must be developed and tested. These criteria are the basis of value judgments the administrator makes about performance.

The measures which are selected for a monitoring system could include the following:

1. Number of offenses—citywide or in each district
2. Differences in offenses between present and past reporting periods
3. Number (and percentage) of cases closed after (a) preliminary investigation, and (b) follow-up investigation
4. Number of cases closed without follow-up investigation and comparison of resulting clearance rates for these cases and those receiving further investigation
5. Number of convictions versus arrests
6. Number of cases cleared by individual investigators versus number of cases assigned.

Numerous other measures can be identified. They should be based on the requirements that system users place on the monitoring system. Common requirements of the police chief, for example, may be personnel performance evaluation, resource allocation, case status, procedural effectiveness, and investigative outcome analysis. The monitoring system is the best method by which the police administrator can receive data on which these assessments can be based.

MANAGEMENT PHILOSOPHY

The traditional approach to management must also be analyzed when using a systems approach. This text supports managing to achieve results as long as the process is understood and there is planned implementation. The prescriptive package "Managing Criminal Investigation" explains management philosophy in two ways.

The traditional philosophy of managing police activities may be called: "seeing that certain tasks are performed properly." This attitude assumes that the police already know what to do and, to a great extent, the best ways to go about it. The role of the manager, then, is simply to solve problems which prevent performance of the tasks. For example, if the manager finds that he does not have enough evidence technicians to collect latent prints at all burglary scenes, he tries to get more technicians or sees that patrol officers are trained to lift prints. But the manager is unlikely to question, for instance, whether collecting prints for all burglaries is worthwhile. The task—to collect prints—is *given;* the manager sees that the prints are collected.

Under this approach, the manager has only one recourse if the results achieved are not satisfactory (if, for example, more and more burglaries remain unsolved): do more of the same. He may strive for greater efficiency or seek additional resources, but he remains bound by the traditional operating methods.

The philosophy of managing to achieve results, by contrast, starts with defining the desired results. It assumes that no one knows for sure what will work; even previously successful methods may not be best now. The manager's responsibility never stops. He carefully observes how well results are being achieved, modifies tasks to improve performance, and again observes the results.

There are several operational implications of the philosophy of managing to achieve objectives:

- The manager's objectives must be stated unambiguously, so that one can tell whether they are being achieved.
- There must be dependable means of measuring results achieved, and those means must be regularly used.
- The department must be willing to change tasks and methods to improve results.
- The department needs systematic procedures for changing task definitions so that adequate evidence is obtained about what works well and what doesn't.

For an objective to be a practical guide for action, it is necessary that:

- The personnel responsible for achieving the objective accept it as reasonable and desirable; and
- Everyone who must take action has a fairly clear idea of what steps he can take to bring about the desired results.

Thus, essential elements of this management approach are reaching agreement on objectives and obtaining broad participation in the management process.[58]

As you can see, the philosophy is based on the MBO approach and more recently the total "Policing By Objectives" concept. Evaluate to know where you are, plan to determine where you want to go, implement, monitor, and evaluate again to see if you got there, modify if necessary, continue to monitor to see how we are doing.

THE ENVIRONMENT AND OPEN SYSTEMS

The environment of the police agency consists of external influences including the criminal justice system, society, and government. This environment affects the ability of the administrator to define specific goals of apprehension, deterrence, prevention, community relations, education, decisions, recovery of stolen property, and cost-effectiveness. There must be a determination of which has first priority, and so forth. There are times when the goals may not be compatible with other agencies' and call for communication and coordination. Consequently, the goals may be difficult to translate into achievable objectives. The knowledge of planned changes, project management, and organizational behavior is helpful. Additionally, Munro has analyzed four basic characteristics of an open system which may help the administrator conceptualize the process of integrating patrol, criminal investigation, and the environment.

To begin with, social systems are interrelated and interdependent cycles of events. Unlike a mechanical system, a social system is dynamic and relatively fluid. The extent and activity of a social system may be observed by witnessing the events which characterize that system. These events are interrelated and interdependent, so that a change in one event, or one part of the system, produces a change of greater or lesser magnitude in all other parts of the system. This is a particularly useful method for examining criminal justice agencies in general and police services in particular. Frequently in the past such agencies have been assumed to be separate entities with an independent existence. However, by viewing police services as one subsystem within the criminal justice suprasystem (which would embrace such functional concerns as corrections, judiciary, probation and parole, in addition to policing) it becomes easier to judge the role of the police in the total system and the implications for the police of changes in other segments of the system.

A second characteristic of open systems is the importation of energy. Open systems do not run down, but rather bring in new energy from the environment to sustain further operation. In the police department the importation of energy includes recruits and money from the external environment. The major consequence of the importation of energy is, in the case of police departments, that virtually all of the members of the organization are in constant traffic with the external system. Interestingly enough it has usually been assumed that commerce with one's environment, except at the lowest operating level and then only when dealing with deviant clientele groups, was a threat to the department's integrity and a definite evil. Utilizing open-systems theory as the frame of reference, it quickly becomes obvious that far from being a deviant act, the intrusion of the environment, including the political subsystem, is an expected and normal occurrence. Obviously, this does not mean that the police will not experience threats to its integrity and challenges to its status. It does mean that rather than viewing these threats and challenges as illicit and deviant acts by nefarious politicians and reacting to these acts with disdain, scorn and/or outrage, the police administrator would be well advised to equip himself and the members of his department to handle, in a meaningful and problem-solving way, these necessary and inevitable contacts with the surrounding social systems.

The through-put is the third major characteristic of open systems. This is simply to say that the energy which is imported into the system is altered and used within that system. The budget which provides money for the operation of the police department is transformed into recruits, cars, fuel oil, electricity for the running of the organization and the production of the end product or output.

The output constitutes the fourth major characteristic of any open system. In the case of a police department the output is in terms of some services that are obvious and quantifiable, *i.e.,* traffic control or the number of doors checked by the patrolman on his beat. Other services are much more nebulous in character although they may have great social importance, for example the service rendered society called crime prevention and much that is meant by the phrase "law and order."

In summary an open system is one characterized by recurrent cycles of events, all of which are interrelated, and to some extent, interdependent. Furthermore the system imports energy from its environment and consequently does not run down. This energy is transformed into goods and/or services. It is well worth noting that a specific subsystem such as the police department may well be in commerce with a variety of other subsystems within the larger system. The police department, conceived of as a system, is itself composed of various subsystems some of which are known by conventional functional labels such as personnel, finance and patrol; other subsystems are known by process labels such as the authority system, the informal friendship system, etc. The use of system terminology appears at first glance to be needlessly adding to the already turgid waters of organizational theory. It may be seen that by focusing attention on the reality of social systems and their constituent subsystems, the administrator is helped in avoiding a simplistic view of complex organizational behavior.[59]

From Munro's analysis, it is clear why police agencies have to contend with the detective mystique. Television, newspapers, and most of the remaining media have presented the investigator as something other than what he or she really is and does. The implementation of an integrated patrol and criminal investigation in a systematic way must deal with people; i.e., status, ego, turf, emotionalism, and so on. Sometimes this is not easy, but that is why we need effective managers as leaders. Police leadership is difficult but fascinating. The accomplishment of coordinated, cooperative patrol and criminal investigation is productive for the community served. Present-day police managers are capable of producing this product. A systems approach can help.

A COORDINATED EFFORT, IS IT POSSIBLE? YES!

The systems approach so far has pertained to the patrol officer and the criminal investigator. The latter has been viewed in terms of individual productivity. However, for the administrator to view the system, he or she must also look to the productivity of the patrol officers in the interface area of criminal investigation. My purpose is to expose the patrol and criminal investigator leader to information worthy of examination and simple replication because of the potential productivity involved. All administrators would like to have all officers behave like the officers they think are best. This not being possible, the next best think is to identify the behavior of the best and try to train the others to behave this way. This information supports that approach.

We cannot learn all about a police officer's productivity from the data. The police perform many different functions, not only in the area of crime control, but in several other areas of public service as well. To produce a single measure of productivity that encompasses all these functions is beyond hope.

Even within the area of controlling crime, the measurement of an officer's performance is an awesome task. We really do not know how each of a particular officer's accomplishments contributes to the control of crime. Moreover, many of an officer's immediate accomplishments in this area are themselves not measurable. For example, suppose that an officer deals with a truant juvenile in a particularly creative and responsible way, so as to stimulate the eventual transformation of a borderline delinquent into a contributing member of society. The immediate police action in this instance—as well as the value that derives from it—will surely elude precise measurement.

Crime Control Measure for Officers

1. Number of Arrests
2. Types of Arrests
3. Conviction Rate
4. Number of Convictions
5. Consideration of Due Process for the above

The study was done for the Metropolitan Police Department, Washington, D.C. The purpose of this aspect was to examine differences in performance among officers and analyze the extent to which these differences are influenced by officer characteristics.

Among the 4,505 sworn officers who served on the force of the Metropolitan Police Department during 1974, 2,418 (54 percent of the force) made at least one arrest in that year. While many of the others may have been in positions to make arrests, we can assume that most were not. We obtain a sense of the value of taking the court perspective by noting that as many as 747 of the 2,418 officers–31 percent of all MPD officers who made arrests–made no arrests in 1974 that led to conviction.

Especially striking is the fact that over half of the 4,347 MPD arrests made in 1974 that ended in conviction were made by as few as 368 officers–15 percent of all the officers who made arrests, and 8 percent of the entire force. Eighty-four percent of all the convictions were produced by less than 1,000 officers (41 percent of all arresting officers and 22 percent of the force). And this phenomenon was not the result of a few officers making large numbers of arrests leading to convictions for victimless offenses. Over half of the 2,047 MPD arrests for felony offenses that led to conviction were made by a handful of 249 officers.

Nor do these prolific officers appear to have produced a large quantity of arrests at the expense of quality. The conviction rate for all the arrests made by the 368 officers who produced over half of all the MPD convictions was 36 percent–substantially higher than the conviction rate for the arrests made by all the other MPD officers who made arrests in 1974 (24 percent). This compatibility of quantity with quality of performance is further indicated in Figure 8.11. It is evident that the officers who produced the most convictions did not do so merely by making numerous arrests.

Among the officer characteristics in our data–length of service, sex, age, residence, and marital status–the characteristic we would expect to find most systematically related to productivity is length of service. In particular, it seems reasonable to expect that inexperienced officers would be less aware than their more senior colleagues of the procedures that are effective in causing arrests to end in conviction. The study confirmed this expectation.

Figure 8.11 *Conviction rates for MPD arresting officers, by number of convictions resulting from arrests made in 1974*

Number of Convictions	Number of Officers	Total Number of Convictions[a]	Total Number of Arrests	Conviction Rate
0	747	0	1,806	0%
1	679	679	2,588	26%
2	386	772	2,395	32%
3	231	693	2,022	34%
4	132	528	1,431	37%
5	98	490	1,352	36%
6 or more[b]	145	1,185	3,271	36%
Total	2,418	4,347	14,865	29%

Source: Prosecutor's Management Information System (PROMIS) and Metropolitan Police Department Personnel File, Metropolitan Police Department, Washington, DC.
[a]Product of column 1 times column 2.
[b]The mean number of convictions for these officers was 8.17.

Summary of Findings and Police Implications

We find substantial differences among the officers of the Metropolitan Police Department in their ability to produce arrests that lead to conviction. This is reflected in the fact that among the 2,418 officers who made arrests in 1974, as few as 368 officers produced over half of all arrests that led to conviction. The conviction rate for all the arrests made by these 368 officers, 36 percent, greatly surpassed that for the arrests made by the 2,050 other officers who made arrests (24 percent).

What is less evident are the reasons why some officers appear to be so much more productive than others. While some of the officers who tend to produce a larger number of arrests that lead to conviction may do so as a result of their assignment, the highly productive officers can be found in every major Washington assignment. Moreover, even if some assignments may present greater opportunities for the officer to make arrests, this does not ensure that the officer will necessarily produce more arrests that lead to conviction. Indeed, the conviction rate for the arrests made by the officers who made only one arrest in 1974 was higher than for the arrests made by the 111 officers who made at least 20 arrests each.

Nor is officer productivity closely tied to the officer's personal characteristics that are recorded in the data. While more experienced officers tend to produce more convictions and have higher conviction rates than officers with less time on the force, the other characteristics in the data—age, sex, residence, and marital status—are, at best, only mild predictors of an officer's ability to produce arrests that become convictions.

To the extent that we do find statistical relationships between an officer's personal characteristics and his or her performance, they appear to run counter to some conventional beliefs. For example, officers who reside in the community where they serve, in this case the District of Columbia, do not appear to perform at higher levels of productivity than officers whose ties to the community are non-residential. Indeed, nonresidents tend to produce more arrests that end in conviction than do other officers, and, they do not do so at the expense of their conviction rates. Nor does the performance of married officers appear to surpass that of single officers.

We find also that while policewomen are not involved as extensively in making arrests for crimes of violence and property as are policemen of similar experience levels, they do make such arrests, and they appear to do so with about equal competence as their male counterparts.

Implications

- Identify supercops such as the 368 noted above, and examine their procedures in making arrests and preparing for the prosecutor. This information is valuable for training.

- Identify those officers who have established a pattern of making arrests that do not end in conviction. These arrests should be examined for problems and corrective action taken.
- Acknowledge officers who produce convictable arrests.
- Provide incentives to make convictable arrests.[60]

The review of organization structure, allocation and distribution of personnel, role of patrol officer and investigator, case management, case closure, case supervision, relation with the other components of the system and the environment, organization atmosphere, management philosophy, organizational and individual performance analysis and measurement, and interpersonal relations (detective mystique, credit for patrol officers, etc.) in a systematic way may be difficult but not impossible. The alternative is, "We've always done it this way."

Summary: Integrated Criminal Apprehension Program

The ICAP attempts to produce the police product by providing a systematic approach to departmental cooperation. This type of foundation is then used to enhance a management philosophy of team building.

Because of myths such as the amount of time officers spend in crime-related activities and the detective mystique, police organizations must accept the challenge of effective performances. Developing and analyzing data and thinking through potential solutions to problems have to become a continuing managerial function. The first step is to to determine what it is the police organization should be held accountable for. Policing a free society effectively must be an overwhelming objective to achieve. To meet public expectations, fairness, courtesy, sensitivity, responsiveness, and cost-effectiveness are also appropriate objectives. However, another accountable objective should be managerial standards of excellence. It is essential that police administrators fulfill their managerial responsibilities by rejecting mediocrity. Therefore, in conjunction with ICAP, the realistic measuring of effectiveness and productivity should be provided. Needle presents this aspect as follows:

> Many police departments have not officially articulated their ultimate goals, however, and many have expressed their objectives in a fashion that is too unrealistic, too abstract, or too general for measurement. In those cases, goal statements must be refined and restated so as to be achievable, discrete, and concrete.
>
> As part of the research developing PPPM, a model structure of police objectives was prepared, specifically for measurement purposes. This structure begins with a general mission statement ("To promote

and maintain public security and order under law, and a sense of well-being in the community") and goes on to articulate 46 concrete, measurable, outcome objectives in 5 general and 19 more detailed areas.

1. Crime Prevention
    a. Part I, personal crimes
    b. Part I, property crimes
    c. Part II crimes (selected)
2. Crime Control
    a. Public reporting to police
    b. Case closure (solution)
    c. Case preparation and testimony
    d. Stolen property return
    e. Constitutional property
    f. Custody of prisoners
3. Conflict Resolution
    a. Inter-personal conflict
    b. Inter-group conflict
    c. Personal stress
4. General Service
    a. Traffic
    b. Miscellaneous services (to the public)
    c. Communication with the public
    d. Auxiliary services (to other agencies)
5. Police Administration
    a. Police integrity
    b. Community leadership
    c. Coordination with other agencies.

Within each subcategory are placed the basic and most specific goal statements for police service. For example, Objective 1.1.1 (reported, major, personal crimes) reads:

1.1.1 To minimize the number of those major, violent crimes against persons:
• homicide
• forcible rape
• robbery
• aggravated assault
that are preventable under the following circumstances:
• in public,
• in commercial or industrial establishments that are police hazards, or
• in situations where police assistance could be provided in time to prevent a crime or an escalation of the incident to a crime

as estimated from crimes reported to the police.[61]

Thus, as Needle points out, the ICAP programs, to be effective, must be accountable. To be effective and accountable, ICAP tries to achieve: (1) a sophisticated system of operation management; (Manpower Allocation and Distribution), (2) directed patrol and special operations, (3) the use of the total talent of patrol officers, and (4) cooperation and collaboration between and among units.

The decision model used by ICAP is depicted in Figure 8.12 and represents perhaps the most effective and basic management approach to police service delivery.

The need for systematic planning and analysis of information for input into the police decision-making process is clearly recognized. The approach is characterized by:

- Formal planning
- Decisions based on empirical information and structured methods
- Decision components measurable and subject to manipulation, based on feedback
- Operational identity of analytical capacity
- Prediction-oriented and active empirical perspective
- Consistency of direction despite staff change.[62]

ICAP provides decision-making information to assist the police managers in fulfilling the law enforcement, service, and order maintenance functions. This assistance is provided by crime, intelligence, and operations analysis using the functional flow process, i.e., data collection, collection analysis, dissemination, and feedback. The result of this systematic approach is information relative to:

- crime patterns and trend correlations
- personnel deployment (prevent, suppress)
- criminal investigation (arrest)

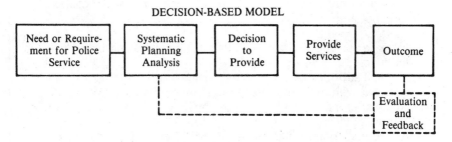

DECISION-BASED MODEL

Figure 8.12 *Service delivery based on formal decision model*

- managerial philosophy
  team policing
  team building (organization development)
  proactive-reactive directed patrol
  community participation
  use of strategic planning
  internalizing accepted management concepts
- target hardening (crime prevention)
- target criminals (career criminal program)
- potential challenges and opportunities for police performance
- the change process, change agent, change strategy approaches
- process and outcome measures
- culture and value analysis (department and citizenry)
- expected behavior (adequate policy, procedures, general orders)
- setting priorities
- effective communication and monitoring

Success in implementing change, including the ICAP program, depends partially on the process used. The unfreezing of the status quo through the provision of information, increased skills, and behavior modification followed by analysis, goal setting, training, and refreezing in the new model should assist the recipients of this program to accept and support it. However, the wrong approach to the change process can produce unnecessary resistance from mid-management and employee organizations, which can doom an otherwise admirable program. Attempts at team policing in several agencies were apparently unsuccessful because of poor change strategies. Hopefully, the evaluation component of ICAP will provide the necessary monitoring so administrators can make decisions to allow optimal opportunity for success.

PATROL AND CID STRIVE FOR BETTER RELATIONSHIP

The 10 proposed methods for C.I.D. personnel to enhance cooperation with Patrol are:

- Increase personal contacts with Patrol supervisors and beat officers in the field.
- Attend Patrol details at all district stations to become personally acquainted with more officers and exchange information.
- Notify arresting officers by memo of the results of their arrests including additional clearances resulting from the arrests.
- Assure that commendations are issued for exceptional assistance.
- Inform beat officers of wanted persons working or residing in their area.

- Provide information to Patrol supervisors and beat officers on suspect information and developing problems in their area.
- Utilize Patrol personnel in executing arrest warrants, waivers of search, and making on view arrests when possible.
- Offer all assistance possible to uniformed officers visiting C.I.D. offices.
- Assign an investigator to assist uniformed officers when they bring in prisoners. This enables the officers to complete their paperwork and return to service without undue delay.
- Reduce requests for Patrol elements to perform services that we can do.

Source: *The Dallas Police News,* Volume XXV., No. 23. Reprinted with permission.

NOTES

1. *Myths and Realities about Crime* (Washington, D.C.: U.S. Department of Justice, Law Enforcement Assistance Administration, National Criminal Justice Information and Statistics Service, 1980).
2. Ibid., 1980.
3. J. F. Elliott and Thomas J. Sardino, *"Crime Control Team: An Experiment in Municipal Police Department Management Operations"* (Springfield, Ill.: Charles C Thomas, 1971).
4. George L. Kelling et al., *The Kansas City Prevention Patrol Experiment: A Technical Report* (Washington, D.C.: Police Foundation, 1974).
5. Tony Pate et al., *Police Response Time: Its Determinants and Effects* (Washington, D.C.: Police Foundation, 1976).
6. Michael F. Cahn, Edward H. Kaplan, and John G. Peters, Jr., "Police Field Studies: A Review of Evaluation Research." in *How Well Does It Work, Review of Criminal Justice Evaluation* (Washington, D.C.: U.S. Department of Justice, Law Enforcement Assistance Administration, National Institute of Law Enforcement and Criminal Justice, 1978), pp. 218, 219.
7. Kansas City Police Department, *Response Time Analysis: Executive Summary: Volume I, Methodololgy; Volume II, Analysis* (Kansas City, Mo.: Washington, D.C., U.S. Department of Justice, Law Enforcement Assistance Administration, 1977).
8. Cahn, Kaplan, and Peters, op. cit., p. 219.
9. James M. Tein et al., *An Evaluation Report of the Worcester Crime Impact Program, Vols. I and II* (Cambridge, Mass.: Public Systems Evaluation, Inc., 1975).
10. Cahn, Kaplan, and Peters, op. cit., p. 220.
11. John E. Boydstun, Michael E. Sherry, and Nicholas P. Moelter, *Patrol Staffing in San Diego: One- or Two-Officer Units* (Washington, D.C.: Police Foundation, 1977).
12. Cahn, Kaplan, and Peters, op. cit., p. 221.
13. Richard C. Larson, Kent W. Colton, and Gilbert C. Larson, *Evaluation of a Police Implemented AVM System: Phase I with Recommendations for Other Cities* (Cambridge, Mass.: Public Systems Evaluation, Inc., 1977); Gilbert C. Larson and James W. Simon, *Evaluation of a Police AVM System: A Phase II City-Wide Implementation* (Cambridge, Mass.: Public Systems Evaluation, Inc., 1978).
14. National Advisory Commission on Criminal Justice Standards and Goals,

Report on Police (Washington, D.C.: Department of Justice, Law Enforcement
Assistance Administration, 1973), pp. 233, 234.

15. Joseph Frederick Folk, *Municipal Detective Systems: A Quantitative Approach*
    (Cambridge, Mass.: M.I.T. Press, 1971).
16. Cahn, Kaplan, and Peters, op. cit., p. 226.
17. Richard H. Ward, "The Investigative Function: Criminal Investigation in the
    United States." Dissertation, University of California at Berkeley, 1971.
18. Ibid., p. 231.
19. Cahn, Kaplan, and Peters, op. cit., p. 227.
20. Bernard Greenberg, Oliver S. Yu, and Karen I. Lang, *Enhancement of the In-
    vestigative Function, Volume I: Analysis and Conclusions, Final Report—Phase
    I* (Menlo Park, Calif.: Stanford Research Institute, 1973), Courtesy SRI
    International.
21. Cahn, Kaplan, and Peters, op. cit., p. 228.
22. Barry D. Glick and Lucius J. Riccio, "Productivity of Detectives: A Study of
    the Investigative Function of Police Juvenile Units," *Journal of Police Science
    and Administration* 7, no. 2 (1979). International Association of Chiefs of Police,
    Gaithersburg, Md.
23. Peter B. Bloch and Donald R. Weidman, *Managing Criminal Investigations*
    (Washington, D.C.: U.S. Department of Justice, Law Enforcement Assistance
    Administration, National Institute of Law Enforcement and Criminal Justice,
    1975).
24. Glick and Riccio, op. cit., p. 139.
25. Ibid., p. 140.
26. D. Gates and L. Knowles, "An Evaluation of the Rand Corporation's Analysis
    of the Criminal Investigation Process," *Police Chief* (July 1976): 20.
27. Cahn, Kaplan, and Peters, op. cit., p. 229.
28. William B. Sanders, *Detective Work: A Study of Criminal Behavior* (New York:
    The Free Press, 1977).
29. James Q. Wilson, *Varieties of Police Behavior* (Cambridge, Mass.: Harvard
    University Press, 1978).
30. Ibid., p. 148.
31. Ibid., p. 185.
32. Elinor Ostrom, Roger B. Parks, and Gordon P. Whitaker, *Patterns of
    Metropolitan Policing* (Cambridge, Mass.: Ballinger, 1978).
33. Ibid., p. 142.
34. Cahn, Kaplan, and Peters, op. cit., p. 232.
35. A. Reiss, *The Police and the Public* (New Haven, Conn.: Yale University Press,
    1971), p. 105.
36. Peter W. Greenwood, Jan M. Chaiken, and Joan Petersilio, *The Criminal In-
    vestigation Process, Vol. III: Observations and Analysis* (Santa Monica, Calif.:
    The Rand Corporation, 1975), p. 65.
37. Wesley G. Skogan and George E. Antunes, "Information, Apprehension and
    Deterrence: Exploring the Limits of Police Productivity," *Journal of Criminal
    Justice* 7, no. 3 (1979): 219.
38. Glick and Riccio, op. cit., pp. 142, 143, 154.
39. Greenwood et al., op. cit., p. ix.
40. Bernard Greenberg, *Felony Investigation Decision Model: An Analysis of In-
    vestigative Elements of Information* (Menlo Park, Calif.: Stanford Research In-
    stitute, 1975), pp. 42–43, courtesy SRI International.
41. University Research Corporation, *Managing Criminal Investigation,*
    (Washington, D.C.: United States Department of Justice, Office of Technology
    Transfer, National Institute of Law Enforcement and Criminal Justice, Law
    Enforcement Assistance Administration, 1977), p. 2.
42. B. Greenberg et al., *Enhancement of the Investigative Function,* Vol. IV (Menlo

Park, Calif.: Stanford Research Institute, 1972–73), p. 11, courtesy SRI International.
43. University Research Corporation, op. cit., p. 45.
44. Greenberg et al., op. cit.
45. B. Greenberg et al., "Felony Investigation Decision Model – An Analysis of Investigative Elements of Information," *Final Report* (Menlo Park, Calif.: Stanford Research Institute, 1975), p. xxv.
46. Robert I. MacFarlane, *Managing Criminal Investigation, Final Evaluation Report and Executive Summary* (Washington, D.C.: U.S. Department of Justice, National Institute of Law Enforcement Assistance Administration, 1979), p. 501.
47. Ibid., p. 5–9.
48. Ibid., p. 5–13.
49. Ibid., p. 5–14.
50. Greenwood, et al., op. cit., p. 11B.
51. University Research Corporation, op. cit., pp. 118–119.
52. Ibid., p. 120.
53. Brian F. Hillen, "New York City Police Department's Investigative Case Management System: An Impact Study," *Journal of Police Science and Administration* 7, no. 4 (1979): 402. International Association of Chiefs of Police, Gaithersburg, Md.
54. Ibid., p. 423.
55. Peter B. Bloch and Donald R. Weidman, *Managing Criminal Investigations* (Washington, D.C.: U.S. Department of Justice, Law Enforcement Assistance Administration, National Institute of Law Enforcement and Criminal Justice, 1975), p. 138.
56. Thomas F. Hastings, *Local Government Police Management* (Washington, D.C.: International City Management Association, 1977), pp. 229, 230.
57. Ibid., p. 231.
58. Bloch and Weidman, op. cit., p. 7–9.
59. Jim L. Munro, *Administrative Behavior and Police Organization* (Cincinnati: W. H. Anderson, 1974), pp. 63–64.
60. *What Happens after Arrest* (Washington, D.C.: Department of Justice, Law Enforcement Assistance Administration, Institute for Law and Social Research, 1977), pp. 47, 57.
61. J. A. Needle et al., "PPPM: A System for Measuring Police Performance," Final Report on NILECJ grant 76-NI-99-0119 (Sacramento, Calif.: American Justice Institute). As reported in Michael W. O'Neill, Jerome A. Needle, and Raymond T. Galvin, "Appraising the Performance of Police Agencies: The PPPM System," *Journal of Police Science and Administration* 8, no. 3 (1980): pp. 257, 258. International Association of Chiefs of Police, Gaithersburg, Md.
62. Integrated Criminal Apprehension Program, *Program Implementation Guide* (Washington, D.C.: U.S. Department of Justice, Law Enforcement Assistance Administration, 1978), pp. 22, 23.

•9•

Patrol and the Scientific Method

The beginning of this chapter addresses personnel research. Quality personnel are necessary to produce a standard of police excellence. The patrol function can be researched intimately, but the quality of patrol personnel will always be the bottom line.

POLICE WORK AS A PROFESSION

Police personnel administrators and others in police work like to view themselves as being part of a profession. One criterion of a profession is that its techniques are derived from a systematic body of knowledge that has been developed through research. The principles this body of knowledge embodies are the guideposts for performance in the profession. The knowledge is regularly subject to testing by the scientific method, and, when results require, it is revised. Research should be recognized as an integral part of all aspects of the practitioner's work.[1]

The Research Process

Research refers to the application of scientific methods of inquiry to discover answers to questions.[2] The research process has been defined as the . . .

> systematic study of problems for the purpose of extending knowledge which will lead to improved practices or confirmation of existing practices. Research involves the setting of hypotheses and their testing through organized, objective procedures. Research does not include the collection of data for management control or day-to-day decisions, the development of a specific pay plan for an organization, or a group

health or insurance plan, or the compilation of statistics on such subjects as employee turnover, absenteeism and employee attitudes for purely local use.[3]

Wilson and McLaren use a matrix with two dominant and opposite research titles, abstract and applied:

> Abstract refers to pure, basic, or nondirective research—to experimentation without knowing precisely what the final result or objective may be. It can also mean the invention of a new solution or concept to solve an existing problem. Its opposite, applied research, refers to the testing or evaluation of products or methods already in use, or to the application of a fully developed idea outside the police field to specific police use.[4]

Science is defined as the formulation of theory by the systematic, controlled, and empirical testing of relationships among phenomena with the purpose of explaining, understanding, predicating, and controlling these phenomena. Theory is the principal aim of science, not the betterment of mankind. However, explanation and understanding are also important. This is because of the definition and nature of theory.[5]

> A thory is a set of interrelated constructs (concepts), definitions, and propositions that present a systematic view of phenomenons by specifying relations *among variables* with the purpose of explaining and predicting the phenomenons.[6]

A good theory is one that produces hypotheses that predict the behavior or relationships of variables. There are at least four kinds of theories: (1) deductive and (2) inductive, both of which are logical and within the philosophical construct; (3) function, developed after experimentation and analysis of data; and (4) model.

A hypothesis is a statement of relationship between two variables; e.g., team policing improves performance. A variable is anything that changes. Four criteria must be maintained for a good experimental hypothesis:

1. Both variables must be operationally definable.
2. The hypothesis must be refutable (if it is so, why do it?).
3. It must be parsimonious (simplistic).
4. It must be testable.

A scientific law is a hypothesis that has been tested and verified innumerable times. A scientific law has the quality of knowing the relationship between variables whereas a hypothesis is a hypothetical statement of relationship between two variables. A scientific fact is simply a statement of the condition of a variable at any given point in time.

The patrol administrator must be able to synthesize professional judgment and scientific inquiry.

The Scientific Approach to Inquiry

The scientific approach and common sense differ in several ways. First, conceptual schemes and theoretical structures are used in a loose fashion on the street. The scientist, on the other hand, systematically building theoretical structures, tests each for internal consistency (validity) and subjects each to empirical tests. The scientist does not select evidence to test his hypothesis because it is consistent with his hypothesis. He is not satisfied with armchair exploration of relationship—he must test it in the laboratory and/or in the field.

Furthermore, the scientist systematically controls to rule out variables that are possible "causes" of the effects he is studying other than the variables that he has hypothesized to be the causes. The layman is not concerned with extraneous sources of influence and is content with his preconceptions and biases.

The final difference lies in the explanation of observed phenomena. The scientist rules out metaphysical explanations (e.g., it is *God's will,* it is *wrong* to be authoritarian). Science is not concerned with the metaphysical. Although the scientist would not necessarily rule out such statements or say they are not true, he would simply not be concerned with them as a scientist. Simply, science is concerned with things that can be observed and tested—measured. If questions do not contain observable and testable implications, they are not scientific questions.

For simplicity then, the scientific approach is a method of attaining knowledge with ultimate objectivity. Self-correction checks are built-in and are so concerned and used that they control and verify the scientist's activities and conclusions to the end of attaining dependable knowledge himself.[7]

There is only one scientific approach but individuals give numerous other reasons for the truth of hypotheses:

- tenacity—a statement is true because it has always been true.
- authority—a statement is true because O. W. Wilson said it is.
- a priori—the hypothesis is self-evident; "it just stands to reason."

If indiscriminately employed, these ideas may be errors in reasoning.

Kerlinger concisely summarizes the scientific approach to inquiry:

> First there is doubt, a barrier, an indeterminate situation crying out
> to be made determinate. The scientist experiences vague doubts, emo-
> tional disturbance, inchoate ideas. He struggles to formulate the prob-
> lem, even if inadequately. He studies the literature, scans his own
> experience and the experience of others. Often he simply has to wait
> for an inventive leap of the mind. Maybe it will occur; maybe not.
> With the problem formulated, with the basic question or questions
> properly asked, the rest is much easier. Then the hypothesis is con-
> structed, after which its empirical implications are deduced. In this
> process the original problem, and of course the original hypothesis,
> may be changed. It may be broadened or narrowed. It may even be
> abandoned. Last, but not finally, the relation expressed by the
> hypothesis is tested by observation and experimentation. On the basis
> of the research evidence, the hypothesis is accepted or rejected. This
> formation is then fed back to the original problem, and the problem
> is kept or altered as dictated by the evidence. Dewey pointed out that
> one phase of the process may be expanded and be of great importance,
> another may be skimped, and there may be fewer or more steps in-
> volved. Research is rarely an orderly business anyway. Indeed, it is
> much more disorderly than the above discussion may imply. Order
> and disorder, however, are not of primary importance. What is much
> more important is the controlled rationality of scientific research as
> a process of reflective inquiry, the interdependent nature of the parts
> of the process, and the paramount importance of the problem and its
> statement.[8]

The Need for Research

The Law Enforcement Assistance Administration adopted a project in 1966
with the following long-range goal:

> There is a need to devote systematic effort to stimulating more and
> better research. Among possible steps suggested to achieve this goal
> are the following:
>
> 1. Providing central clearinghouse facilities through LEAA with
>   respect to contemplated research, ongoing research, and the
>   publication of pertinent research findings.
> 2. Identifying needed research projects and developing research
>   designs for implementing such projects.
> 3. Providing financial grants to institutions and individuals for the
>   pursuit of promising research projects.
> 4. Maintaining close liaison with colleges and universities for the
>   purpose of suggesting needed research projects and maintaining
>   an awareness of ongoing research activities.
> 5. Giving recognition to persons making important research
>   contributions.[9]

THE CRITERIA OF POLICE EFFECTIVENESS

An acute need in police personnel administration is the development of criteria of police effectiveness. Criterion measures must take into account the situation and the environment in which the performance takes place. The reason for this is that police performance and its effectiveness rest on a situational—not only a task or positioned—base. Positional or task data that are divorced or isolated from the situation in which the person in the position will or does perform are useless.

An understanding of police effectiveness for personnel purposes requires answers to a number of questions about the skills and personal demands of a police job. The areas of research questions can be referred to as (1) the police person, (2) the police process, and (3) the police product.

The Police Person, the Police Process, and the Police Product

These three aspects of police effectiveness—person, process, and product—need to be studied situationally in relation to one another. It is through empirical research that the linkage can be discovered between (1) behavioral elements—the police person, (2) job or work behavior—the police process, and (3) desirable outputs—the police product.

Opinions, speculations, hunches, and expertise, no matter whose, will not suffice. Until research designs are developed that provide realistic descriptions of the phenomena with which police human resources management is concerned, prescriptions or predictions from existing practices are futile. This can be illustrated by reference to the following statements from a recent research report:

> Major open questions about police selection are whether the standards now in use, either individually or collectively, actually distinguish the candidates who will become successful policemen from those who will not, and whether the addition or substitution of new selection instruments can improve the predictive validity of the selection process. In addition, the question of whether the selection procedures discriminate against members of minority groups is being raised with increasing frequency.
>
> Although many studies have been undertaken in an attempt to answer these questions, they remain far from resolved, mainly for the following reasons:
>
> 1. No entirely satisfactory method has been developed to measure objectively the performance of police officers, once appointed; those performance measures which are in use tend to reflect the internal standards of police departments rather than the requirements of the community being served.

2. Within any given police department, there are a variety of functions to be performed, ranging from traffic control and patrol in low crime areas to undercover activities, crime investigation, operation of data processing systems, planning, and administration. Some persons who are able to perform certain of these functions extremely well may be unsuited for other tasks, and the selection process must provide adequate numbers of personnel in all categories.

3. If a substantial change in selection criteria is contemplated one would like to be able to estimate the expected change in performance levels. But it is rarely possible to find a sample of appointed officers who failed to meet existing standards, and the number of officers in a given department who might meet a set of higher standards is likely to be so small as to prohibit statistically significant findings.

4. Many researchers believe that the primary influences on an individual's performance as a police officer are encountered subsequent to appointment. These factors include the training process, socialization by fellow officers, the nature of the community in precincts of early assignments, and happenstances of acquaintance with officers who later rise to high command positions. If such later influences are in fact of major importance, then observed relationships between background characteristics and police performance measures can be artifacts of existing assignment procedures. For example, young recruits may be initially assigned on foot patrol in high crime areas more frequently than older recruits, and officers who perform well in high crime areas may later be eligible for appointment as plainclothes investigators. A comparison of age at appointment with ultimate assignment might then suggest that older officers do not become satisfactory plainclothes investigators, whereas the conclusion would actually be unwarranted from the data.

5. The findings of the studies themselves have in some cases been so ambiguous or negative as to preclude the possibility of drawing conclusions which are of practical use for improving selection or assignment procedures. Indeed, some of the findings are bizarre when viewed from the perspective of selection criteria. For example, Singer has remarked that a 1950 study of twenty-five New York police officers appears to show that one can identify successful police as persons who have low aspirations and are socially maladjusted.

6. The nature of police work differs substantially from one jurisdiction to another, so that findings in a given city are not necessarily applicable elsewhere.[10]

THE KANSAS CITY PREVENTIVE
PATROL EXPERIMENT

The quality of personnel was not considered in the Kansas City Preventive Patrol Study because they were not included in the hypothesis and because of other limitations. However, the study is important to anyone concerned with professionalism of patrol. The Kansas City Police Department and its personnel and the Police Foundation and its staff joined together to produce a milestone in the history of policing. This is exemplified by the following statement from the *summary report:*

> Some of these findings pose a direct challenge to traditionally-held beliefs. Some point to an acute need for further research. But many point to what those in the police field have long suspected—an extensive disparity between what we want the police to do, what we often believe they do, and what they can and should do.[11]

This statement also points up most emphatically the need for police administrators to develop a philosophy, goals, objectives, and direction for their respective agencies so that all police talent can be used to produce the product. Who are we? Where are we going? How do we intend to get there?

Davis and Knowles made the following conclusions, among others, in their critique of the Kansas City Experiment:[12]

> Continuing experimentation and dialogue are necessary for the advancement of professional law enforcement. Equally as strong as the professional responsibility is the responsibility of professional law enforcement administrators to carefully examine their use of resources and the effectiveness of their service delivery systems. For 150 years, police patrol operations rested on a number of untested assumptions. In 1930, Bruce Smith pointed out the need to test those elementary propositions underlying traditional patrol practices. To do so he called for a series of "controlled experiments." As professional police administrators, we should critically examine why, in the face of radically changing communities, such experimentation was not undertaken until proposed by a group of Kansas City, Missouri patrol officers in 1972.

> Continuing dialogue concerning the Preventive Patrol Experiment should broaden our understanding of patrol issues and problems. Hopefully, this will lead to the development of more effective patrol operations and will serve as a "springboard" for further research into the delivery of police services.[13]

> The most important fact about the truly objective, scientific testing of ideas and practices in policing is that so little of it has been done. That is one strong reason why so little is known even now in a proven way about the effects and effectiveness of what police do to control crime and to provide other services which people want. It is through such approaches that understanding and from understanding to true accountability to those the police serve, will eventually come.

> It takes courage, confidence, management skill, and an open, informed mind for police administrators to face successfully the hard

challenges of experimentation in large urban police agencies. FBI Director Clarence M. Kelley, then chief of police in Kansas City, had these qualities and had established the conditions to undertake and sustain rigorous scientific experimentation on a large scale not previously approached anywhere in policing.

As is always the case in large-scale social experimentation, not every aspect works perfectly. Although the Kansas City experiment is the best example of such research yet completed, there were difficulties and deficiencies which were alluded to in the *Summary Report* and fully reported along with the results in the 960-page *Technical Report*. Because of the careful design and multiple data sources of the experiment, these difficulties did not affect the results as reported in these two volumes.

As stated in the foreword to the summary, the Police Foundation welcomes the opportunity to assist police departments which seek answers to crucial questions about their use of resources and are willing to accept the burden and the challenge of joining in scientific research. The Foundation is interested, too, in objective data from serious experimentation and research by any police agency, however sponsored. The Foundation stands ready to help disseminate such scientifically derived knowledge to the worlds of police practices and research.[14]

How valid are the general conclusions based on experimental research in law enforcement practices of one jurisdiction when applied universally to other jurisdictions? Is there a yardstick for measuring the crime deterrent value of police patrol visibility? If experimental research on a limited basis indicates that high visibility preventive patrol has no significant impact on crime incidence, should all police departments curtail beat patrol in favor of response to called-for service? These questions and others must be considered in determining the validity of the Kansas City Preventive Patrol Study. The reader would find the following references helpful in answering such questions:

- Police Foundation, *The Kansas City Preventive Patrol Experiment: A Technical Report* (Washington, D.C.: Police Foundation, April 1975). 960 pp., $15.00. (Orders for the technical report should be accompanied by check or money order and addressed to: Communications Department, Police Foundation, 1909 K St., N.W., Washington, D.C. 20006.)
- George L. Kelling et al., *The Kansas City Preventive Patrol Experiment: A Summary Report* (Washington, D.C.: Police Foundation, October 1974), p. 4.
- The Davis and Knowles critique of the Kansas City Experiment in *Police Chief* (June 1975), pp. 32–38.

- Richard C. Larson, "What Happened to Patrol Operations in Kansas City"; Davis and Knowles, "A Review of the Kansas City Preventive Patrol Experiment"; and Tony Pate, George L. Kelling, and Charles Brown, "A Response to 'What Happened to Patrol Operations in Kansas City'," all of which appear in *Journal of Criminal Justice,* vol. 3 (New York: Paragon Press, 1975), pp. 267–320.

Conclusion

A review of the literature listed above provided the following conclusions:

1. Patrol administrators should look to research in their own departments before drawing any definite conclusions concerning preventive patrol (except for directed patrol, which is discussed later).
2. Patrol administrators can still prevent purse snatching (this crime is arbitrarily selected; the principles apply to crimes other than purse snatching if effective crime analysis is completed) if the time of occurrence, location, and other relevant information are learned by placing a uniformed officer at the specific location. Before doing so, a critical analysis of potential displacement should be completed.
3. A careful cost benefit analysis should occur before committing the agencies to in-depth research.
4. After the critical cost benefit analysis, professional judgment must be used to make the final decision since the investment in research may not result in the anticipated payoff.
5. Police agencies should consider hiring their own researchers, who can apply national research to local conditions. This may be done on a mutual aid basis, so that several agencies use the research capabilities of one individual. A request may be made to the regional crime commission for a staff researcher to be used by the several police agencies.
6. The quality of individual officer performance is critical.
7. About 60 percent (this will vary according to local or state conditions) of a police officer's time is typically noncommitted (available for calls); of this time, the *Summary Report* found, police officers spent approximately as much time on non–police-related activities as they did or do on police-related mobile patrol.
8. The *Report* also concluded that, in general, police officers are given neither a uniform definition of preventive patrol nor any effective methods of gauging its effect. While officers tend to be

ambivalent in their estimates of preventive patrol's effectiveness in deterring crime, many attach great importance to preventive patrol as a police function.

The Kansas City Preventive Patrol Study is important to police because it systematically recognizes the products of directed patrol. It thus in effect gives officers direction because it identifies objectives for them to achieve. In evaluating his own performance, an officer using directed patrol would be able to say, "I did a good job last year because the tasks and creative actions that I performed achieved the objectives my superior and I set." The officer's own objectives would have been congruent with those of the police department as a whole. His objectives would have been formal feeder objectives that assisted in achieving the objectives of the agency.

DIRECTED PATROL[15]

Directed Patrol is a program developed by officers of the Kansas City, Missouri Police Department's East Patrol Division. This division's complement of 154 officers serves the area bounded by Prospect on the west, the city limits on the east, and the area south of the Missiouri River to Brush Creek Boulevard. The program contains six major components designed to improve the delivery of police service and, at the same time, have an impact on the crimes of residence burglary and robbery. Program activities will be implemented in stages over the next twelve months in the East Patrol Division. Activities officers will perform are based on a comprehensive study of crime and call-for-service workload in the area. The major goals of the program are:

1. To control the level of occurrence of the crimes of residence burglary and robbery in designated communities; and
2. To establish and maintain a high level of community satisfaction with the delivery of police services throughout the East Patrol Division.

Program components include community education, crime prevention, case processing, tactical deployment, situational crime and workload analysis, and a new patrol deployment system. The latter two program components are designed to support the activities the officers will be performing in the other four components. Each of the program components contains specific activities which are described below.

Community Education

The community education component consists of four activities that officers will be engaged in. Essentially, they will provide citizens with timely and accurate information about crime in their community and will suggest specific actions citizens can take to reduce their chances of victimization and to assist the police in addressing problems in their community. Activities in this component include:

1. *Crime Information Distribution*—Flyers and brochures will be routinely distributed to residents and businesses by mail and by officers on patrol. This medium will contain information about neighborhood robbery and burglary trends and suggest ways to reduce chances for victimization.

2. *Community Meetings*—Patrol officers will be attending community meetings as requested to discuss neighborhood crime problems and encourage citizens to take specific actions to address crime problems.

3. *Crime Prevention Displays*—These displays will contain information about neighborhood crime problems, materials designed to inform citizens how to reduce the chances for victimization, and what departmental sponsored programs are open for their participation.

4. *Community Newspaper Articles*—Officers will write articles for publication in four area specific East Zone community newspapers. Articles will contain prevalent crime problem information, crime prevention tips, announcements of crime prevention displays, and answers to questions submitted by area residents.

Community Organization

The community organization component consists of three activities that officers will perform. It is designed to follow the community education component by providing specific programs citizens can participate in. These activities include:

1. *Operation Identification*—This activity is designed to use police supervised citizen volunteers who will engrave identification marks on property commonly taken in residence burglaries. This activity will be systematically implemented in specific geographic areas having incidences of residence burglary.

2. *Residential Security Surveys*—Patrol officers will perform residential security surveys for victims of residence burglary and at the request of citizens who want this service. Officers will suggest methods that citizens can use to strengthen the security of their homes.

3. *Community Block Watchers*—Community groups and residents in specific areas will be involved in crime observation during high incidence times for street robbery or residential burglary. They will be trained in the proper reporting of victimizations, suspicious activities, or unusual circumstances to the police. Patrol officers will recruit and train volunteers.

Tactical Deployment

The tactical deployment component consists of four activities to be initiated only in specific problem situations. These activities will be implemented *only* when crime analysis information indicates specific pattern information and the strategies are appropriate. These activities include:

1. *Safe Walkways*—This activity is designed to decrease street robberies of victim age groups of fourteen and under, and over fifty, by increasing patrol coverage at specified times and days on routes commonly traveled by people of these ages. The safe walkways will also have block watchers.

2. *Decoy Activity*—This program activity is designed to increase street robbery offender apprehensions by appropriately positioning officers in selected locations *when specific victimization patterns are evident.*

3. *Garage Sales and Swap Shop Activity*—This activity is designed to locate and recover stolen property where perpetual garage sales and swap shops can be identified.

4. *TAC II Alarms*—This program activity is designed to increase offender apprehensions by installing and monitoring TAC II alarms in selected high-risk locations.

Case Processing

The case processing component will improve the quality of preliminary investigations and increase the potential for identifying the perpetrators of armed robberies while reducing the time involved in identifying them. Activities officers will perform in this component include:

1. *Solvability Factors*–This activity will improve preliminary investigation quality when officers answer specific questions concerning the crime. Answers determine the potential for case solution and provide more structure on the conduct of the inquiry.
2. *Concealed Cameras*–This activity will aid in the identification and conviction of the commercial armed robbery offenders. Concealed cameras will be installed in selected business locations to obtain photographic evidence of perpetrators in the commission of the robbery.
3. *Identi-Kit*–This activity will enable victims and witnesses to assist the police in developing composite drawings of suspects. Trained officers will respond to crime scenes and develop composite pictures of suspects when feasible.
4. *Height Strips and Description Pads*–This activity will provide businesses with materials for recording a more accurate description of armed robbery offenders and encourage immediate reporting of robberies. Officers will contact businesses in the East Patrol Division and provide them with height strips, description pads, and phone stickers containing the police department Crime Alert number, and demonstrate how to use these materials.

Deployment System

To implement the above activities and maintain the ability to immediately respond to emergency situations, it was necessary to develop a deployment system whereby the department could manage its workload more effectively. Two methods were developed to allow more control over the workload and provide more efficient community service.

1. *Prioritization of Calls for Service*–Calls for service in the East Patrol Division will receive one of three classifications by Communications Unit personnel. Calls will be assigned a classification of immediate response, delayed response, and phone-in/walk-in calls based on an established set of criteria. The criteria are:

   1. Type of incident
   2. Is it in progress?
   3. Are the perpetrators present in the area?
   4. Is there danger to human life?
   5. Is evidence in danger of being destroyed?

A positive response to criteria two through five will require an immediate police response. Calls such as armed robberies, aggravated assaults, disturbances, and alarms will always receive an immediate response.

Calls that do not meet any of the above criteria, but the dispatcher believes that a police officer is needed at the scene, may be delayed up to forty minutes. Delayed calls will occur during peak activity hours when they are received. For example, when a call is received that can be delayed and there are only two cars in service in the area, it will be delayed up to forty minutes to allow a third car to return to service.

The final category is phone-in/walk-in. These are calls that do not require the presence of a police officer for any reason other than to take a report. Such calls will be referred to the station where clerks will take the report over the telephone or request the citizen to respond to the station to make the report. Examples of calls that will be handled in this manner include larcenies, loss, destruction of property, and auto thefts.

2. *Sector Flexibility*—This part of the deployment system will allow watch commanders and sector sergeants the flexibility to deploy resources according to need within the present sector boundaries.

Present beat boundaries will be maintained for reporting purposes and officers will be assigned to either Directed Patrol activities or to specific areas within the sector for responding to calls-for-service. Two aids have been developed to assist watch commanders and supervisors make deployment decisions.

The first aid is the SYMAP program. SYMAP is a computer program that will provide a pictorial display of calls-for-service demands within a sector. The second aid is the Manpower Utilization Forecast. This computer program provides projections of workloads within sectors on a daily and hourly basis. The program provides supervisors with the anticipated number of events and the number of man-hours expected to handle them.

Situational Analysis

This component is essentially a crime analysis model developed to provide detailed and timely crime information support to the program. Moreover, as the model continues to be refined, it will provide the entire department with relevant and timely crime information support.

Each of the major components described above is an intricate part of the Directed Patrol program. The program represents the department's most recent attempt to improve the quality of police services to the citizens of Kansas City, Missouri with existing resources. In order to determine the effectiveness of this approach to police patrol, an evaluation of the program has been developed. The evaluation will be concerned primarily with two areas:

1. *Process*–the degree to which activities are achieved–and why; and
2. *Product*–the extent to which the achievement of each objective results in its anticipated outcome.

The benefits to the police department from the program include: (1) the demonstration of an ability to control patrol workload enough to allow for directed activity; (2) testing a variety of patrol activities for their impact on citizen satisfaction and crime control; and (3) to further develop and refine a model crime analysis system.

PRODUCTIVITY IN PATROL

If an objective for the patrol administrator were to provide more man-hours of patrol for his community, then a subobjective could be to provide crisis intervention training for each patrol officer in an attempt to reduce arrests in situations in which a simple resolution of the problem is possible. The administrator must then direct the officer's effort during the time he is to produce this objective. The resultant productivity can be measured. The spin-off of this approach would be demonstrated reduction in persons entering the court room (criminal justice system), thereby giving the judge and prosecutor more time to deal with the more serious crimes, e.g., robbery, burglary, rape. This effort would thus also enhance the goal of "cooperating with the other components of the criminal justice system."

If the chief executive of the community were interested in productivity, then the social service agency responsibility for family counseling could provide follow-up assistance to families (when police get repeated calls reporting family trouble) in an effort to reduce family conflict. This would produce more police patrol time to be directed.

Police organizations are supposed to maintain order, provide service, and protect the community (law enforcement function). These responsibilities are performed in varying degrees by each department, based upon factors that differ from one community to the next. It is incumbent upon each police administrator to develop these measures of productivity which will indicate the level of performance of the police agency. In doing so, he should remember the forces (political, legal, etc.) that affect the performance.

Productivity[16]

Productivity means the return received for a given unit of input, or any activity that uses resources of one kind to produce a result of another kind. Productivity refers to the relationship between resources used and the results produced.[17]

Resources include manpower, captial, technology, machinery, land, energy, etc., anything that can be combined by the application of managerial intelligence into an end-product of some kind. Results of such efforts can be either goods or services.

Both resources and results can usually be described or summarized in monetary terms, as long as we remember that money is just a convenient means for expressing values and making comparisons. Thus, productivity improvement in manufacturing is the increase in output per man-hour expressed in constant dollar terms. But productivity could also be measured in terms of other scarce resources used in the production process, e.g., output per unit of energy.

What is the relationship of the concept of productivity to the concepts of effectiveness and efficiency? These terms often prove treacherous in public discussions, with debaters blithely sliding from one to the other and exploiting their favorable connotations without ever defining or distinguishing them. Here, because of the bearing the distinction has on the meaning of productivity, we want to distinguish the two terms with precision.

Effectiveness generally refers to achieving certain defined results or outcomes without regard to the cost of achieving them, whether these costs be calculated in terms of money and manpower or in some other way. A well-aimed sledgehammer will in fact kill flies, and can therefore be effective in that mission, although most people would use the analogy to describe a gross misallocation of resources. Or, if you are in fact ever confronted with an objective to be achieved at all costs or where cost is no object, then the standard by which your performance is being measured is an effectiveness standard.

Efficiency, on the other hand, refers to achieving any given result with the minimum expenditure of effort required to achieve that result. Efficiency is an extremely useful concept when the results obtained are within the range of desirable or acceptable results, but not otherwise. There is no virtue in having gone from New York to Indianapolis at the lowest possible cost if you were supposed to have gotten to Chicago.

Productivity is a combination of the effectiveness and efficiency concepts. Productivity asks both whether a desired result was achieved (the effectiveness question) and what resources were consumed to achieve it (the efficiency question). It is especially important to emphasize this combination of concepts when we talk about productivity improvement in services, where the output indicators are less likely to include a quality factor than they are in manufacturing.[18]

Ostrom defines efficiency in a police department by using an equation:

> The efficiency of any organization can be defined as a ratio between output and input factors. At the most general level, the efficiency (E) of a police department can be defined as the total separable benefits (SB) provided plus the total joint benefits (JB) provided minus the total joint costs (JC) produced divided by the amount of input resources (IR) utilized to produce these services. Using the abbreviations indicated, this general definition of efficiency can be summarized briefly in the following equation:

$$E = \frac{SB + (JB - JC)}{IR}$$

> If E is one or greater than one, the police agency is efficient. The larger the number, the more efficient the agency. If E is less than one, the agency is inefficient.[19]

Dealing with productivity in the public sector is difficult because of measurement. Quantity and quality of a service organization or the individual within that organization cannot be defined easily. However, the police leaders of this country cannot let difficulty stand as an obstacle. If the police do not define the criteria to measure productivity, then someone else will. The police administrator should also realize that defining what is expected for personnel and what will be produced for the community will assist him in: producing, defending his production where necessary, dealing with labor-management relations, and producing a cost-effective product comparable with the existing tax base. The other qualities he should possess or obtain are creativity, an understanding about who is most important in achieving objectives, and a management by objectives concept which values the patrol officer who performs and is closest to the problems. The police administrator should also be able to respond to the following: If department A lost 10 percent of its personnel due to budget constraints, and crime did not increase any more than it had in past years, then why do we need the number of personnel we presently have?

The Meaning of Output of a Police Agency[20]

The mission of police as stated here may be conceptualized as contributing to a general state of affairs which we call "the security of the community." The security of the community is composed of a large number of components including the following as a small sample:

1. The vulnerability of its citizens to various crimes of violence including homicide, assault, and rape.
2. The risk of property loss through theft or vandalism existing in the community.
3. The probability of being a victim from an accident on the highways of the community.
4. The extent of activities defined to be illegal existing in the community.

A perplexing problem in conceptualizing the output of a police department is that while its activities contribute to the security of the community, it is never the sole contributor to this state of affairs. The degree of security enjoyed by a community is created by individuals interacting with one another within a set of institutional arrangements. Institutional arrangements include among others: employment markets, product markets, housing markets, welfare programs, educational systems, community organizations, court systems, penal systems, and the police. All institutional arrangements are dependent, to some degree, upon the provision of police services. Thus, an employment, product or housing market cannot operate effectively if police services are not available to insure the exclusion of those unwilling to engage in quid pro quo relations. The general community organizations including welfare systems are as dependent upon the police to help enforce decisions as are the court and penal systems. A particular institutional arrangement may affect the general safety of the community in a positive or negative fashion. For example, an educational system coupled with an unemployment market that enables individuals to find productive opportunities for work will tend to increase the security of the community.

The police should not be blamed for crime. They cannot respond to a crime wave by doing nothing, but they must also be able to respond by referring the questions to the superintendent of schools, the judge, the correctional system, the welfare department, probation and parole, government, and the community. The police cannot be all things to all people.

Ostrom explains it this way:

The essential point of Figure 9.1 is the activity of a police department is only one of many factors affecting the general security of the community while all other factors might be a positive influence. The final result might be a relatively secure community in spite of the activities of the police. On the other hand, the police may be contributing in a positive manner to the security of the community while many other factors might be a negative influence. In this instance, the security of the community would be endangered regardless of how "productive" the police were. Thus, an analysis of the performance

Figure 9.1 *Factors affecting the security of the community*

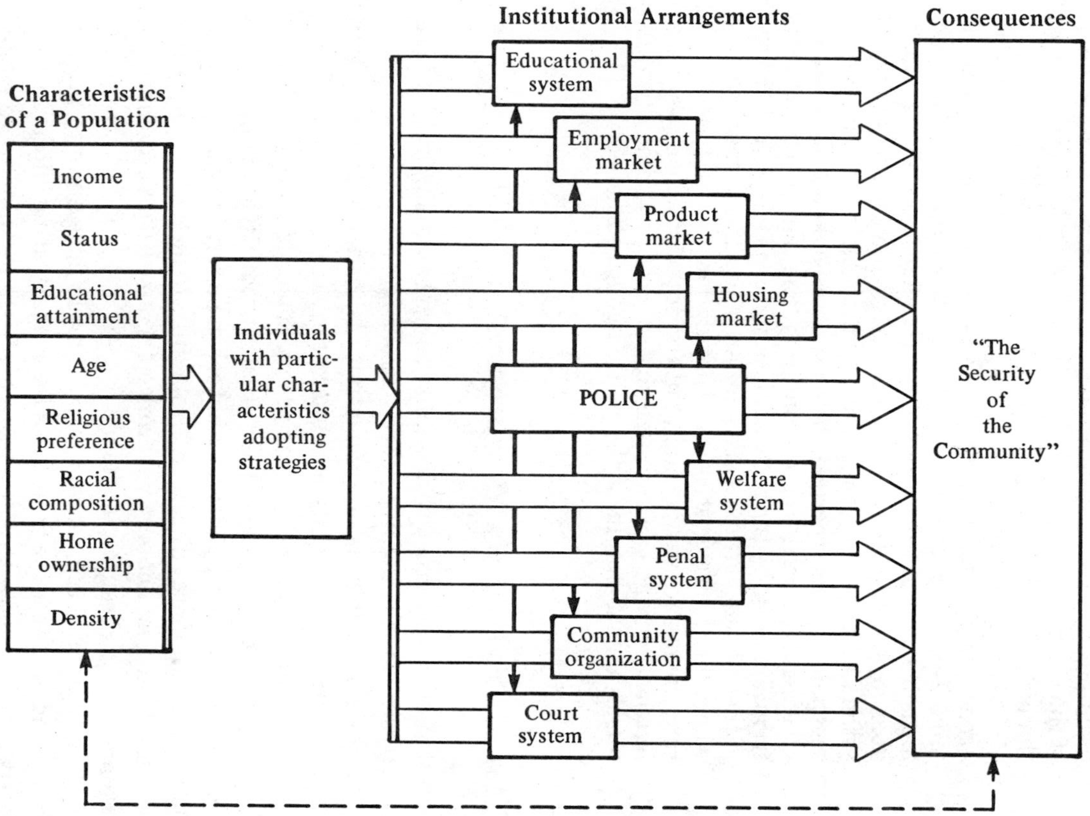

or output of a police department can never rely on an examination of the security of the community alone as an indication of output of the police.

Any analysis of the services performed, or the output of a police agency, must keep this complex interacting system of variables in mind. Because of this rich network of interacting variables, primitive measurement of the output of police agencies is all we will ever be able to achieve. The output of a particular police agency can be estimated only in a comparative sense. Since the characteristics of a population and the institutional arrangements other than police all affect the security of a community, one cannot determine the contribution made by the police unless one can isolate areas where most of these other variables are similar. Thus, if one can locate an area where the characteristics of the population and most institutional arrangements are very similar, but the organization of the police is different, then one can estimate the effect if any, that this difference makes on the output of the police agencies studied.[21]

Uses of Productivity Measurement

Productivity is concerned with quality as well as quantity. What is a quality arrest? What is quality police patrolling?

The new emphasis on productivity is instigating some totally new thinking on the part of city administrators and police officials as to how the police function should be carried out. Some old concepts of policing are being challenged in the search for greater productivity. Police officials are finding out that productivity does not mean merely "do what you have been doing, but do it more efficiently." Applying productivity to the police function is demanding not only new concepts, but also greatly more imaginative use of the resources at hand.

In matching the concept of policing by objectives to productivity, Heffner identifies some guidelines for concentrating efforts in setting objectives as it relates to doing more of the *same* thing more efficiently.

There is an old saying that the truly effective manager is the one who can tell the difference between doing the right things and doing things right. That is not to say that doing things right is not a desirable activity, but we must not confuse the relative importance of the two. Even if we only do them in an average way, we are better off doing the right things. If we concentrate our efforts on the right things and do them extremely well, we begin to multiply our effectiveness.

This concept is not a new one. In 1906, Vilfredo Pareto, an Italian economist, proposed an economic principle now known as "Pareto's Law," which stated that the distribution of wealth and income in a population was mathematically predictable. From Pareto's original work, which had nothing to do with management, other social scientists have been able to formulate a very useful principle for managers. More commonly called the Rule of 20/80, "Pareto's Law" says that for any given state of affairs or condition, 80 percent of that condition is a result of the influence of 20 percent of the possible influencing factors.

For example, very often 80 percent of the score in a baseball game is the result of 20 percent of the players. Also, many companies have found that 80 percent of their accidents are caused by 20 percent of their employees. The 20/80 Rule may not apply to all situations, but when it does seem to bear out, the manager interested in pinpointing his or her effectiveness will be well-advised to follow the steps outlined below.

Interestingly enough, the Rule of 20/80 can be applied to managing by objectives. If objectives are written properly, are well executed, controlled carefully, and measured accurately, we can still only expect results based on the appropriateness of the objective in the first place. We must learn to set objectives for the few critical factors that bring about the most important results.

Guidelines:

1. Carefully define the goals you expect to accomplish in your work.
2. List all the factors which will have an effect on each goal.
3. In each list of factors assign each factor a percentage weight relative to its effect on the overall goal. (You will usually find that if you have ten factors, two or three of them will be responsible for 70 to 80 percent of the results.)
4. Set your objectives for those vital few factors that influence the desired result more.

Be careful not to dismiss the trivial many as being totally unimportant. They account for 20 percent of your result and must be accounted for. However, they do not require the attention the critical few factors demand and often can be delegated or systematized.[22]

Former Secretary of Commerce Peter G. Peterson said in 1972 that productivity improvement without productivity measurement is not possible. At the time, Mr. Peterson was chairman of National Commission on Productivity. Mr. Peterson's statement may seem extreme to many; however, he was pointing to the difficulty of knowing whether any improvement has indeed been achieved and knowing where to direct one's attention if one does not have adequate productivity measurement. A number of general uses for productivity measurement can be identified:

1. By identifying current levels of productivity, measurement can indicate the existence of particular problems.

2. When productivity is measured over time, measurement can indicate the progress or lack of progress in improving productivity.
3. When collected by geographical areas within a jurisdiction, productivity data can help identify areas in particular need of attention.
4. Measurement can serve as a basis for evaluating specific activities. Measurement may indicate activities that need to be modified or personnel who need special attention, e.g., training.
5. Measurements of existing productivity can provide agencies with the information necessary to set productivity targets. Actual performance can subsequently be compared to the targets to indicate degree of accomplishment.
6. Performance incentives for both managerial and non-managerial employees might be established. Many communities have recently been trying out various aspects of management by objectives (MBO), program budgeting, and the like. The various productivity measurements would become inputs into such procedures. (The city of Orange, in a recent controversial experiment, has linked future salaries to selected reported crime reductions.) By utilizing a larger number of the productivity measurements presented later and not relying solely on such measurements as reported crime rates, it may well be that performance incentives could be placed in a reasonably comprehensive perspective and maintain public credibility.
7. Measurement of data can be used for in-depth productivity studies on ways to improve specific aspects of productivity.
8. Productivity measurement information can be a major way to account for government operations to the public. Accountability is becoming of growing concern and refers not only to the legal use of funds but also to the broader question of what is actually being accomplished by government operations.

Any productivity improvement program will need a productivity measurement component, both to help guide where productivity improvement is needed as well as to evaluate how successful the improvements have been.

While productivity measurement thus has many uses, it should be recognized that it is not an end in itself. By itself, productivity measurement will not tell a government what is wrong or what should be done to improve the situation. It exists to help guide government in its productivity improvement efforts.[23]

Whose Productivity Should Be Measured?

This is a basic question which must be considered in police productivity measurement. The following levels of concern can be distinguished.

1. The productivity of the individual police officer (or individual police employee, civilian or sworn).
2. The productivity of police units, such as shifts, police districts, neighborhood policing teams, or precincts.
3. The productivity of particular kinds of units, such as motorized police, foot patrols, investigative units, special tactical strike forces, canine corps, etc.
4. The productivity of the police department as a whole.
5. The productivity of the crime control system, including both police activities and private activities to reduce crime.
6. The productivity of the total community criminal justice system, including the police, the courts, the prosecutor's office, corrections and social service agencies, and private sector crime prevention activities (such as use of locks, watch dogs, etc.).

In one way, or another, a community is concerned with the productivity of each of these. However, each interest group in a community—citizens, city council, mayor or city or county manager, police chief, police division heads, police employees and their association—will have different priorities. The choice of viewpoint(s) desired by a local government will affect the set of productivity measurements that is needed. Some of the different perspectives are as follows:

- Measurements of the proportion of police time spent on "nonproductive" activities are likely to be of considerably more interest and use to police department managers and employees than to citizens, who are likely to be considerably more concerned about crime rates in their neighborhoods.
- City or county officials are likely to be most interested in the productivity of the crime control system, or the total criminal justice system (although in the latter case their interest will be tempered by their lack of responsibility for the courts, prosecution, and where controlled by a different level of government, the correctional system).
- For higher local government management levels and the council and public it probably is most important to be concerned with, on

one hand, the combined effectiveness of the police operations, and secondarily, of groups or teams of police.

- For internal management purposes (i.e., internal to the police agency), periodic examination of the productivity of individual employees may be appropriate – in the same way that annual performance appraisals are provided but with more output-oriented measurements.

A special note of caution seems appropriate for attempts to measure the productivity of individual police employees. The measurement of individual police officer performance is discussed later. Many if not most of the important products of police services such as deterrence of crimes and successful apprehensions of offenders are generally due to the combined activities of a number of persons in the police department. For example, for a successful apprehension there may be field work by the policemen at the scene of the incident, subsequent investigation by a police investigator, often supported by numerous crime lab operations such as fingerprinting and weapon analysis techniques, and perhaps crime analysis, communications, and data processing units.[24]

MEASURING PRODUCTIVITY IN POLICE PATROL

The following material is taken from the National Commission on Productivity, *Opportunities for Improving Productivity in Police Services*. The three objectives as stated are not all-inclusive but should be viewed as a great assistance to the patrol administrator of our country. Policing by objectives, the ability to implement change, innovation, and productivity should present a real challenge to patrol leaders. More work needs to be done, but the foundation has been laid and is presented so that the structure of patrol productivity can be built in a cooperative effort between the scientist and police practitioner.

The Advisory Group that prepared the report chose the following three objectives of police patrol for consideration:

- deterrence of crime;
- apprehension of criminal offenders; and
- satisfaction of public demands for noncrime services.[25]

These three objectives are closely related. Apprehension of criminal offenders, an end in itself, also has some effect – to what extent is uncertain – in deterring crime. Deterrence of crime, of course, reduces the need for apprehension. And better noncrime services enhance the image and public support of the police department, thereby strengthening crime deterrence and apprehension efforts.

To meet these objectives, the patrol force carries out a variety of activities, any one of which may contribute simultaneously to one, two, or all three of the objectives.[26] The activities include observation; response to calls for service; enforcement of the law; investigation; maintaining order; and various administrative and postarrest activities (e.g., report writing, court duty). Since any one activity may contribute to all three objectives, and since the objectives themselves are interrelated, the measurement and analysis of the patrol force can be a complex undertaking.

In an attempt to cope with this complexity in a practical way, the Advisory Group has identified three problem areas which begin to sort out the easier patrol problems from the more difficult ones. These areas are:

- Making a greater proportion of the existing patrol division (up to a reasonable limit) available for street assignment;
- Increasing the real patrol time of those who are given street assignments; and
- Utilizing patrol time to best advantage (i.e., to achieve the greatest impact in accomplishing patrol objectives).

It is important that the relationship among these three areas be clearly understood: The first two—the easier ones—are *preparatory* to increasing patrol productivity, a mobilization of resources with which to do the job. The maximum number of personnel is made available, and then the time of those people is unfettered by relieving them of useless or marginally useful activities. Thus, the pool of real manpower available to do the job is increased without any additions to the patrol force.

Neither step one nor two alone, however, will guarantee increased productivity. The payoff comes in using that manpower to the greatest advantage. That is the concern of the third problem area where the more difficult questions arise and the activities of the patrol force are related directly to patrol objectives.[27]

This chapter discusses, first, measurement; and, second, actual means of improvement, in each of these three problem areas. Many of the measures suggested are not "productivity measures" as some strict definitions may hold. But taken together they do suggest a set of quantitative measures that should prove helpful to police departments in assessing the performance of their patrol force.

MEASURING PATROL ACTIVITY

In order to determine the type of data now collected and used for patrol evaluation, and to assess the range of performance among departments for specific activities (use of patrol time, response time, misdemeanor vs. felony arrests, etc.), the Advisory Group surveyed several police departments throughout the United States. The results of the survey show that:

- many police departments keep statistics needed to compute productivity measures that are adaptable for widespread use; and
- the range of performance for a variety of measures (allowing for probable differences in definition) suggests a potential for productivity improvement in most departments.

Other, more specific, results of the survey are quoted, where appropriate, throughout the report.[28]

Making More Patrolmen Available for Street Assignment

Assigning more of the patrol force to street work and increasing their effective time on patrol are important steps toward expanding the use of the existing resources of the patrol force. Although these efforts may not insure better performance, they are important to maximizing useful patrol time, and to minimizing or even eliminating the need for increasing the overall size of the force.

At any given time, only a small percentage of a patrol force is on the street. In great part this is due to the need to provide seven-days-a-week, twenty-four-hour coverage; at least five men must be on the roster in order to fill any one patrol position around the clock. However, not all of the positions themselves are given to street assignments. Many are assigned to police headquarters, precinct stations, and other facilities in jobs that may not contribute directly to the crime-control and service-delivery objectives of the patrol function and that may not require the skills of a sworn officer.

A simple measure to help determine the ability of management to make manpower available for patrol is:

$$\frac{\text{Patrolmen Assigned to Street Patrol Work}^{29}}{\text{Total Patrolmen}}$$

The percentage of the patrol force assigned to patrol appears to vary considerably among departments, indicating that there may be opportunity for improvement. Figure 9.2 presents percentages of the patrol force with street patrol assignments reported by six of the police departments that

Figure 9.2 *Percentage of patrol force with street assignments for six departments, 1972.* (Letters used to designate departments do not necessarily correspond to letter designations in subsequent figures.)

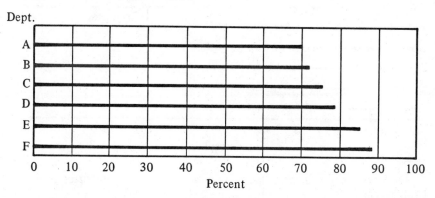

responded to this question in the Advisory Group's survey. At least two departments were able to maintain almost 90 percent of the patrol division on patrol duty.

It is impossible and unwise, of course, to put the entire patrol force out on the street. Some experienced patrolmen are needed for supervisory and other essential assignments at the station. The range of values for this measure, as shown in Figure 9.2 however, does indicate a potential in some departments for increasing the proportion of men on the street without adding any more sworn personnel.

Increasing the Real Patrol Time of Those Assigned

Once personnel are assigned to patrol duties, their time should be devoted to activities that may potentially meet patrol objectives. A simple measure to indicate the extent to which patrol time out in the field is being committed to patrol activites is:

$$\frac{\text{Man-Hours of Patrol Time Spent on Activities Contributing to Patrol Objectives[30]}}{\text{Total Patrol Man-Hours}}$$

Time can be "lost" by performing nonpatrol tasks during duty hours. Examples are filling out unnecessary forms, servicing vehicles, running errands, and spending unnecessarily long hours waiting for court appearances. An analysis of the percentage of time spent performing such activities would be a preliminary step in diagnosing how patrol man-hours are really used.

Figure 9.3 *Percentage of time spent on activities contributing to patrol objectives for five police departments, 1972*

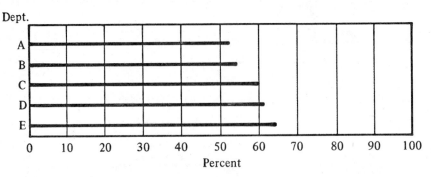

The percentages of time spent by a patrol force on activities germane to their function (that is, random patrol, directed patrol, and responding to crime-related and noncrime calls for service) are shown in Figure 9.3. It is, of course, unlikely that close to 100 percent of time would be spent directly on patrol-related activities. Some time must be allocated to meal breaks, vehicle servicing, clerical tasks, court appearances, and the like. But the statistics indicate room for some improvement in several of the departments surveyed.

Given the rapidly rising costs of sworn personnel, even a small increase in the percentage of time spent on patrol activities can lead to a significant savings and, potentially, to increased effectiveness. Breaking down these statistics into portions of time spent on specific kinds of activity shows significant ranges in time allocations to different activities performed on a normal tour of duty. (See Table 9.1.) The spread of time allocations is no doubt due to differing styles of operation and differing responsibilities of the police in their communities. But these ranges also suggest that some patrolmen may be spending too much time on non-patrol activities.

Maximizing the Impact of Patrol

So much for the relatively easy problems that focus on increasing the availability of existing resources. The more difficult problem is how to increase the effectiveness of those available resources. This requires relating patrol activities more directly to the three patrol objectives selected for consideration by the Advisory Group: crime deterrence, apprehension, and noncrime service.

Deterrence of crime.[31] A principal objective of most police departments is to deter crime. The patrol force bears an important responsibility in this

Table 9.1 *Ranges in the Percentage of Time Allocated to Different Patrol Activities,*
1972 Survey Data

Activity	Range (%)		Time Allocation Should Be*
	Low	High	
Random and other preventive patrol	16	36	High**
Crime-related calls for service	6	38	High
Noncrime calls for service	2	30	High
Training (on duty)	0	20	Medium
Report writing	2	6	Low
Arrestee processing	4	10	Low
"On duty" time in court	2	8	Low
Meal breaks	2	16	Low
Other	5	36	Low

*This column is included as a guide to help interpret the ranges in the table.
**Assuming a variety of patrol strategies and methods of deployment.

effort. Through its "preparedness" to respond to calls for service and its patrol activities, apprehensions, and investigations, the patrol force is expected to reduce the amount of crime actually committed by impressing would-be criminals with its ability to detect, to respond, to apprehend, and to marshal the support of the community.[32]

There are no altogether satisfactory measures of the success or failure of a patrol force's efforts to deter crime. Whereas apprehension, for example, can be measured directly from the number of arrests made, the number of crimes not committed—except for those few stopped in the act—is impossible to measure directly and can only be inferred. In fact, no persuasive relationship between overall patrol activities and crime deterrence has been established, as yet.

In the absence of a direct measure of deterrence three types of substitutes might be used:

- Existing reported crime indices used with discretion.
- Victimization surveys.
- Quantitative measurement of activities which professional judgment suggests contribute to deterrence.

For all its problems, reported crime is still one of the few measures that police managers have to provide some check—however general and unreliable—on their activities. Used judiciously, for specific types of crime, in specific districts, over specific periods of time, and with specific knowledge of what other factors (such as employment or age of population) may be affecting the result, reported crime can be a useful tool in evaluating the effects of patrol activities in deterring crime. There is hope that victimization studies will provide more reliable information; perhaps such information will permit a more accurate relationship to be established between the amounts of actual and reported crime, thereby increasing the usefulness of reported crime data.

This discussion[33] focuses on the third method of assessing crime deterrence: the more precise measurement of patrol activities which are thought to contribute to deterrence.

Among the patrol activities thought to contribute directly to deterrence are apprehension and the ability to respond quickly to calls for assistance. Theoretically, a high likelihood of arrest undermines the confidence of would-be criminals and deters them from future crime. The extent to which this assumption is valid remains open to question. In any case, apprehension is considered to be an appropriate objective of the patrol force in and of itself, and is treated as such in the following section.

The remainder of this discussion will address the question of how to measure response time.

Assessing patrol response time. Rapid response time may contribute to deterrence in at least three ways. First, there may be some deterrent effect in the knowledge that police can respond quickly to crimes in progress, although no indisputable correlation has been so established. Second, there is evidence that suggests that below certain time levels quicker response to crimes in progress does result in higher apprehension rates;[34] higher apprehension rates, in turn, may have some deterrent effect, although with qualifications as mentioned above. Third, rapid response probably does or could increase citizen confidence in the police, which in turn could encourage greater citizen involvement in the observation, reporting, and prevention of crime; such public involvement may, in turn, have some effect in deterring crime.

In short, there is no definitive relationship between response time and deterrence, but professional judgment and logic do suggest that the two are related in a strong enough manner to make more rapid response important. Moreover, response time is an important factor in achieving other police objectives, especially apprehension, which in turn contribute to increased deterrence.

Given these assumptions, we can turn our attention to the measurement of response time, bearing in mind that more rapid response is not an end in itself but a means of achieving patrol objectives.

Several factors must be considered in establishing a measure for response time. In the first place, different kinds of calls require different speeds of response. Nonemergency calls, for example, need not be answered as quickly as reports of crimes in progress. Some crime calls, in turn, may warrant a quicker response time than others, depending upon community priorities. Clearly, there are trade-offs in using existing men and equipment to respond to different kinds of calls. A low *average* response time for *all* calls, emergency and nonemergency, may mean sacrificing a quicker response capability for emergency calls. A decision to focus on emergency crime-related calls by deferring or "stacking" nonemergency calls may lengthen the overall average response time but significantly speed up responses to crimes in progress.

The desired response time to emergency calls must also be based upon some knowledge of the relationship between quicker responses and higher rates of apprehension. If reducing response time from fourteen to ten minutes produces little or no apparent increase in apprehensions or prevention of crime, its value is doubtful, except insofar as it may increase citizen confidence. Reductions from five to inside three minutes, on the other hand, may prove to produce significantly higher apprehension rates.

Still another important factor to be considered is the cost of reducing response time by given increments. If response time is already low, shaving off additional seconds may require heavy additional inputs of men and equipment or shifts of resources from other activities. The desired response time cannot be established on the basis of the projected result alone, but must also include consideration of the cost in new resources or men and equipment diverted from other activities.

The Advisory Group attempted to consider all of these factors in developing possible measures for patrol response time. No one measure adequately accounts for all of these factors, and consequently at least two measures should be used in concert with the kind of knowledge and judgment discussed above. Those two measures are:

$$\frac{\text{Number of Calls of a Given Type Responded to in Under "X" Minutes}}{\text{Total Calls of That Type}}$$

and

$$\frac{\text{Number of Calls Responded to in Under "X" Minutes}}{\text{Resources Devoted to the Response Function}}$$

"Resources devoted to the response function" is used in the denominator instead of patrol man-hours because of the potential for introducing capital-intensive technologies for improving the efficiency of response activities. Resources include patrol force salaries and benefits (still the major component) as well as the cost of computer-assisted dispatching systems and the salaries of nonsworn dispatchers.

"X" minutes is used in the numerator to indicate that different response times are appropriate for different types of calls. The value of "X" would depend on whether the call was an emergency or nonemergency call, or whether the call was about a crime-in-progress, suspicious activity, or previously committed crime. Additional breakouts by type of crime may also prove helpful. A report of a bank robbery, for example, may require a more rapid response than a larceny in progress. In each case, the department must determine for itself what is a desirable response time ("X") for a particular kind of call, based upon the considerations noted above.

To the extent that the measures reveal inefficient resource use, it would help, in diagnosing the problem, to divide response time into three segments:

- Dispatching delay
- Queue delay
- Travel delay

Dispatching delay is the time from receipt of a call to the time the dispatcher is ready to assign a unit. The queue delay is the time a dispatcher must wait before a unit is available for dispatch, and thus is calculated as zero if a car is available. Travel delay covers the time from dispatch of a unit to its arrival at the scene of an incident. To the extent that these components of response time can be recorded separately, they can be quite helpful in diagnosing the cause of an inefficient activity.

If a police manager is using his resources in the most effective manner, however, but response time still has not been reduced to an "acceptable" level, then the only available alternative is to seek an increase in resources that will be sufficient to enable him to obtain the desired response time. This assumes that emergency calls are being given priority, that nonemergency and service calls are being "stacked," that maintenance of patrols cars is managed in a way that keeps the maximum number available for responding to calls, and that shifts and positioning of cars place them where they are most likely to be requird at the times of greatest need. When a police manager can show that all these things are being managed with maximum efficiency, but the response time still is not meeting his and the community's needs, then he can present a justified request for the resources that are needed.

Table 9.2 displays the range of response times obtained in the survey of departments. It demonstrates that at least some departments are able to furnish the kinds of response-time statistics useful in troubleshooting the causes of poor productivity. Of course, the data cannot point directly

Table 9.2 *Response Time Component Delays, 1972 Survey Data*

Response Time Component	Category	Range (Minutes)	
		High	Low
Dispatch Delay	Emergency	3	1
	Nonemergency	10	2
Queue Delay	Emergency	1.5	0
	Nonemergency	10	0
Travel Delay	Emergency	5	3
	Nonemergency	14	3

to inefficiencies in the use of deployment of patrol resources, but they may assist in searching them out. Unfortunately, the survey did not yield sufficient data on the extent of patrol resources devoted to the response function, although most departments have the data available to do this. Consequently, ranges in the response productivity measure cannot be presented.

No matter how quickly a department can respond to a call for service, productivity is sacrificed if the quality of the response is not up to par.[35] Thus, a further indication of this quality is a necessary adjunct to the principal response measure, and in some cases can be provided by a follow-up recipient-of-service survey.

Most of the departments responding to the Advisory Group's survey indicated that they are already carrying out some such form of survey. Telephone surveys could reveal what percentage of recipients were satisfied with the service. Questions asked should cover the effectiveness of the officers in performing the particular service as well as their courtesy and general helpfulness at the time. Criteria could be developed for these surveys which differentiate between satisfactory and unsatisfactory police reponses to calls for service, and only a sample of recipients need be surveyed to obtain valid results. This information can be useful in uncovering persistent problems (or new ones) which may require some retraining of patrol officers.

Since one of the benefits of lowering response times is the opportunity to make more quality arrests by arriving at the scene of a crime in progress or by intercepting a fleeing suspect, departments might use the following measure of response effectiveness in leading to arrests:

Arrests Surviving the First Judicial Screening[36] Resulting
From a Response to a Crime Call

Crime-Related Calls for Service

Again, this measure should be applied to appropriate categories of arrest (felony, etc.) and be calculated separately for each major type of call.

Suspicious activity and past-crime calls may not result in many arrests, but they are important for maintaining public confidence in the police and a feeling of security. As noted above, rapid responses to calls, especially to crimes in progress, can result in a higher rate of apprehension.[37]

Apprehension of criminal offenders.   Traditionally, number of arrests has been used as an output measure of apprehension. Occasionally, other outputs, such as clearances and convictions, also are used. Although these may be useful "workload" measures for some police activities, as measures of output or results for productivity measurement, the Advisory Group found them subject to the following qualifications:

- Arrests themselves may be too easily subject to inflation; e.g., by making arrests of dubious merit (or increasing arrests for minor public nuisance offenses).
- Clearances (i.e., crimes for which police identify an offender, have sufficient evidence to charge him, and actually take him into custody) may be unsuitable because crime frequently cannot be attributed accurately to offenders. This figure can be adjusted according to particular department incentives—for example, over-attribution —if it becomes important to keep clearance rates high. In addition, clearance rates are not due solely to patrol activities, but also reflect investigative and prosecutorial activity.
- Although convictions reflect the quality as well as the quantity of patrol work, conviction rates usually are subject to many forces outside the control of the police (actions of courts, prosecutors, etc.).

Because of these difficulties, the use of arrests *surviving the first judicial screening* is a more appropriate "output." Although the process of judicial screening differs from one jurisdiction to another, thereby making interjurisdictional comparisons difficult, it usually involves an appearance before a judge or magistrate to assess whether or not a case has enough substance to merit a trial (probable cause). Survival of the screening process implies some measure of quality which arrests by themselves do not reflect (although some prosecutors and judges refuse to accept certain charges for various reasons).[38] Furthermore, the survival of arrests past the first judicial screening is less susceptible than convictions to forces outside police control. A poorly prosecuted case, for instance, can mean that an otherwise "valid" arrest will not result in conviction.

A suggested measure for apprehension productivity, then, is:

$$\frac{\text{Arrests Resulting From Patrol Surviving the First Judicial Screening}}{\text{Total Patrol Man-Years}}$$

Because patrol is a labor-intensive activity (80 to 90 percent of the costs of deploying a patrol force are salaries and benefits), patrol man-years is probably a more appropriate measure of resources than dollar costs.[39]

According to this measure, patrol productivity, in terms of the apprehension objective, would increase:

- if the number of arrests surviving first judicial screening per patrol man-year increased (e.g., through change in methods, deployment, etc.); or
- if the number of arrests per patrol man-year remained the same but the effective patrol time (number of patrol man-years actually employed in patrol activities) of the existing patrol force increased sufficiently to permit fewer sworn officers to be assigned to the patrol force.

To illustrate briefly, consider a patrol division having 500 sworn personnel which only manages to maintain 50 positions in the field round-the-clock. If each position accounts for, say 30 quality arrests per year, the above productivity measure computes to $(50 \times 30)/500 = 3$ quality arrests per man-year. If the department fielded more than 50 round-the-clock positions from its force of 500 (it is generally recognized that 5 men are required for every round-the-clock street position), then any number of additional quality arrests made as a result would increase patrol productivity so long as patrol strength remained at 500. An extra 10 fielded positions also averaging 30 quality arrests per year would yield an overall result of $(60 \times 30)/500 = 3.6$ quality arrests per man-year. If an extra 18 positions were fielded with a lower overall arrest rate of 25, patrol productivity would still be increased from 3 to 3.4 quality arrests per man-year.

In addition to the productivity measure suggested above, police departments can develop other, more detailed, measures to provide useful information. Among the most important of these is an apprehension productivity measure for each major arrest category. For example:

$$\frac{\text{Felony Arrests Resulting From Patrol Activities Surviving First Judicial Screening}}{\text{Total Patrol Man-Years}}$$

This measure can be modified for consideration of different kinds of arrests, including:[40]

- Felonies.
- Misdemeanors that involve a particular victim.
- Consensual crime misdemeanors as determined by local jurisdiction.
- Other violations.

Different types of arrests have different values, which can in turn vary from community to community. An armed robbery arrest and an arrest for public drunkenness clearly are not equivalent. Arrest totals may be inflated by legitimate arrests for petty and often so-called "victimless" crimes, which do not reflect police goals for more serious crimes.

Moreover, using the measure to calculate separately one arrest productivity measure for each of these categories may tell managers where their arrest emphases lie, and will allow them to assess whether or not the results are in accord with their particular priorities.

For example, the ratio of felony to misdemeanor arrests in Long Beach, California, is 0.22, while in nearby Compton the ratio is 0.77. For drug offenses, the ratios for the same two cities are even more extreme— 0.66 in Long Beach and 114.3 in Compton. As the study reporting these statistics explains:

> They (the range of these ratios) . . . cannot be accounted for by differences in crime patterns; they flow mainly from differences in police arrest policies.[41]

Schemes that give weights to different types of arrest and that compute a combined arrest index are generally undesirable because the weights often must be arbitrarily chosen and are therefore unrelated to public concerns about certain crimes.

A variant of the preceding measure can be applied when evaluating the success of a specific, directed patrol strategy—for example, the concentration of uniformed or plainclothes preventive patrols in areas with particular crime problems. The measure would read:

$$\frac{\text{Arrests (Resulting From a Directed Patrol Strategy)}}{\text{That Survive the First Judicial Screening}}{\text{Total Directed Patrol Man-Years}}$$

This measure could be adjusted, as above, by specifying the type of arrest to evaluate the impact of the strategy on a particular crime category.

It is important to remember that the amount of crime in a jurisdiction may bias apprehension productivity data. Because different crime rates represent different opportunities for making arrests, it is often easier for a patrol force to make more arrests in the presence of a higher crime rate. By close examination of the productivity improvements, those due merely to an increase in the crime rate could be distinguished from those due to better use of the patrol force. The clearance rate also may be of some use as an adjunct because it reflects to some extent how well a department is matching apprehensions to crimes that actually occur.

A second important source of information for police managers is the ultimate disposition of arrests, which provides an additional check on the quality of apprehensions and postarrest activities. Even though judicial screening, used in the original arrest productivity measure, imposes some quality standard for arrests, such screening occasionally can be perfunctory. Two additional measures of the quality of arrests are:

$$\frac{\text{Convictions}}{\text{All Arrests Made by Patrol Force}}$$

$$\frac{\text{Convictions}}{\substack{\text{Arrests Resulting From Patrol That} \\ \text{Survive the First Judicial Screening}}}$$

These measures also may be calculated separately for each arrest category to provide more detailed information. Although these two measures are determined by factors beyond police control, they do reflect somewhat the quality of police discretion in making arrests and the effectiveness of postarrest activities (e.g., preparation for testimony).

Thus, police managers may determine—by breaking down the apprehension productivity measure according to crime category and comparing the results to crime statistics—what relative importance the department places, implicitly or explicitly, on various types of crimes. Police managers can evaluate, further, the quality of police arrests by examining the portion of all arrests surviving first judicial screening made in a given crime category and resulting in conviction of the offender.

Responses to an Advisory Group survey question on the number of felonies and misdemeanors surviving first judicial screening per patrol man-year showed a wide variation among police departments.[42] Whereas one department reported a combined number or felony and misdemeanor arrests surviving judicial screening of 61.5 per man-year, another reported only 9 per man-year.[43]

Figure 9.4 shows not only a range of arrests per patrol man-year among seven police departments, but also reflects the relative emphasis placed by these departments on felony vs. misdemeanor arrests. The department which reported the highest number of arrests surviving judicial screening also reported over 80 percent of these as misdemeanors.

Four other departments, though with lower overall arrest productivity levels, also reported a much higher percentage of misdemeanor arrests than felony arrests. Two departments reported more felony than misdemeanor arrests.

Figure 9.5 shows the number of felony and misdemeanor arrests surviving first judicial screening for the portion of the patrol force actually

Figure 9.4 *Felony and misdemeanor arrests surviving the first judicial screening (resulting from patrol) per patrol man-year, 1972 data for seven police departments*

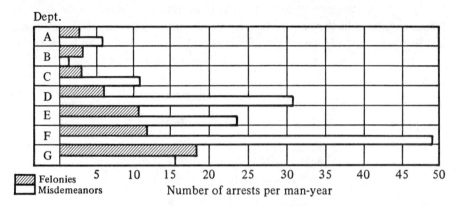

engaged solely in patrol activities (for the four departments that could provide such information). Although arrest rates are higher for all four departments because the patrol force resource base is lower, those departments that have the largest percentage of the patrol force on the street and expend the largest percentage of time in patrol activities have the highest number of arrests per patrol man-year.

Provision of noncrime services.   Services provided by the patrol force that do not relate to incidents of crime or suspicious activities make up the large majority of calls for service, often 70 percent or more. Despite their predominance in the patrol workload, police departments put the most emphasis on crime-control activities and stress crime control in their training programs. Many departments are actively turning some of their noncrime responsibilities over to other city agencies or performing them with

Figure 9.5 *Felony and misdemeanor arrests surviving the first judicial screening (resulting from patrol) per man-year actually spent on patrol, 1972 data for four police departments*

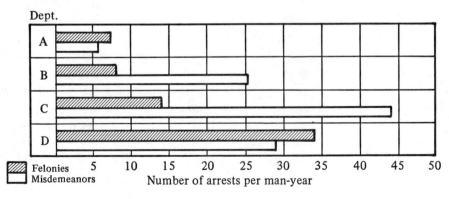

nonsworn personnel. These steps, they argue, are essential to release police resources to be directed at growing crime problems.

Some government managers argue, on the other hand, that the police are well suited to respond to a variety of noncrime situations and that it would be expensive and unproductive to establish a separate agency to perform those tasks. In the end, the mix of services that the police do provide is a function of local objectives and priorities. Whatever the mix, it is certain that the public will continue to expect the police to provide a twenty-four-hour response capability for a variety of emergency and nonemergency needs. Even if some of these needs are met by nonsworn personnel, they still remain the concern of police managers. To the extent that police continue to provide noncrime services, with both sworn and nonsworn personnel, these services should be provided as efficiently and effectively as possible.

The measures presented in this section apply to both emergency and nonemergency services and are probably applicable to any department regardless of its mix of services. A department's service mix may include emergency responses such as ambulance runs, calls to assist ambulance crews, rescue runs, and deployment at the scene of disasters. Nonemergency calls may include quieting a noisy party or a barking dog, helping a resident who is locked out of his house or a motorist whose car has broken down, or "adjudicating a dispute" between two neighbors or between a landlord and a tenant. In providing noncrime services, a patrol force's productivity may be determined by the following measure:

$$\frac{\text{Number of Noncrime Calls for Service Satisfactorily Responded To}}{\text{Man-Hours Devoted to Noncrime Service Calls}}$$

Here the number of calls includes both emergency and nonemergency situations. The quality of the response should be sufficient to satisfy the recipient of the service. Therefore, supplementary information provided by a followup survey should be used in conjunction with this measure.

Calculating the measure separately for emergency and nonemergency noncrime calls may be useful, but not as useful from a management point of view as the calculating separately of measures for major categories of noncrime service calls. This more detailed kind of information is likely to indicate where action can be taken to improve noncrime service productivity.

For example, the effectiveness of the force in responding to medical emergencies (accidents, impending births, etc.) could be assessed by a measure of this type:

$$\frac{\text{Medical Emergency Calls That Emergency Room Personnel}}{\text{Total Medical Emergencies}}$$
$$\text{Evaluate as Having Received Appropriate First Aid}$$

An evaluation procedure can be developed to provide data for this measure in cooperation with emergency room staffs at local hospitals. A sample, rather than an evaluation of every case, may be sufficient for determining effectiveness in this area. Too low a value for this measure may indicate inadequate first-aid training or equipment.

Another measure may be developed for calls regarding noisy disturbances in the community:

$$\frac{\text{Noisy Disturbance Calls for Which No Further Attention Is Required (For the Remainder of the Patrol Tour)}}{\text{Total Noisy Disturbance Calls}}$$

Too low a value of this measure may indicate a lack of respect for the police in the community or a lack of tact on the part of officers handling such incidents. A low value may also indicate a need for additional training of some officers and/or a better community relations program.

Regardless of the service mix provided by a particular department, these measures may be helpful to the police manager in diagnosing a productivity problem in the patrol force's provision of noncrime services.

Several of the departments responding to the data survey were able to provide data on numbers of calls for noncrime services and the man-hours devoted to answering those calls during 1972. Figure 9.6 presents the ratios of noncrime calls for service to man-hours spent in answering such calls.

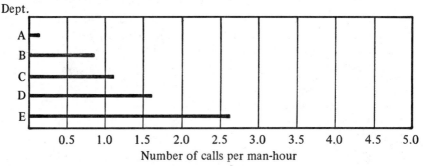

Figure 9.6 *Number of noncrime calls for service per man-hour spent answering those calls, 1972 data for five police departments*

Some of the reasons for the wide range of these statistics may merely be such factors as larger patrol sectors and the longer travel times they imply. Other factors, however, may be excessive service times or excessive amounts of paperwork associated with each incident.

Police departments can be more productive in meeting noncrime service objectives if they carefully analyze what is required to provide these services. For example, is a sworn officer always needed? Can a report be taken by phone? How much time is really needed for this type of call? By answering such questions, police managers can apply the necessary resources and accomplish noncrime service objectives more productively.

LIMITS OF PRODUCTIVITY: ARE WE DOING THE WRONG THING BETTER?

England has gone to consolidation, so that the smallest department is approximately 600 personnel. The Jacksonville, Florida Police Department and the Duval County, Florida Sheriff's Department consolidated in 1968. Nashville-Davidson County, Tennessee, Lexington, Kentucky, and Las Vegas, Nevada have all been involved in consolidation of police services. Will all of these or any of these bring improved productivity, i.e., same product—less cost, same or improved product—same cost (less cost)?

Parks reports the following on the Jacksonville-Duval County, Florida consolidation after his review of "Consolidation of Police Services Case Study: Jacksonville, Florida (Falls Church, VA., Koepsell-Girard and Associates, Inc., 1973):

> The major shortcoming from the perspective of this review is that they do not tell whether consolidation led to more or less effective police service in Jacksonville, or whether services have been provided more or less efficiently following consolidation. Still, they represent a mountain of information in comparison with that found bearing on other large-scale consolidations.[44]

Other problems of productivity and the determination of success or failure are brought out in an evaluation of the Allegheny Regional Narcotics Task Force, where the authors noted:

> Evaluation efforts are uniformly limited by (1) the unavailability of baseline data, (2) the lack of or a poorly organized record system, (3) the absence of a management information system related to goals and objectives and their measurable criteria; (4) a sub-conscious, if not conscious, opposition of project managers to evaluation—partly due

to a fear of being measured by often limited and not especially relevant quantitative data, and, lastly, (5) limitations in the funding allocated to evaluation.[45]

Parks continues,

This literature review is embarrassing in its brevity, yet reflects an interesting phenomenon. In spite of many recommendations for structural changes in the organizational and interorganizational arrangements for policing in America, there is no evidence based on careful evaluations of organizational changes that can be brought to bear on this issue.[46]

The National Sheriffs' Association found in a literature review of contract law enforcement and police consolidation:

In larger measure, the reported assessments of the efficacy or the utility of a particular program were found to be anecdotal or impressionistic evaluations with few data of valid measurement criteria or other information upon which sound evaluative judgements could be made.[47]

Skoler concluded:

. . . it can be fairly said that the nation is being urged to proceed with major structural reform based on professional perceptions of deficiencies and problems that need to be addressed rather than research-validated data on the new solutions proposed.[48]

Ostrom says

It is possible for reformers operating with such a dearth of empirical evidence on the effects of their reforms to be very righteous, yet, simultaneously, dead wrong with respect to the presumed consequences of adopting their recommendations.[49]

Any public organizational rearrangement necessarily involves power and politics. Professional perception, gut-reaction, and self-serving measures of effectiveness for the politician generally negate careful evaluation-planning, evaluation-implementation, evaluation-evaluation without even considering the cost of evaluation. You see, what should be done is to evaluate, to find out the nature and state of affairs, and then plan the action. After implementation, evaluate the process to determine if you have produced. Then evaluate the outcome based on predetermined objectives formulated in the beginning.

Politicians (maybe because of the nature of democracy) must state what they will do, and sometimes use professional management statements like "the objectives of my administration are 1, 2, 3, 4, 5." However, for the same reason, police chiefs do not return government money half way through a program (admit defeat or, since we have the money, spend it), even though they realize the objectives cannot be achieved and outcome measures are not around (baseline data and comparable data for measuring the difference) to show the success or failure of programs. Campbell states it this way: "In the present political climate, reformers and administrators achieve their precarious permission to innovate by over-promising the certain efficacy of their new programs. This traps them so that they cannot afford to risk learning that the programs were not effective."[50]

Parks concludes:

In spite of substantial rhetoric on the perceived need to restructure American police organization, and a number of organizational reforms along the lines recommended, no information deriving from evaluation research could be found with respect to the effectiveness or efficiency of the reforms. None of the consolidations of police agencies, officers, or both, or smaller efforts jointly to produce particular services has been subjected to any effective evaluation. It is clear that advocates of major structural changes in American policing base their arguments on tenets of good government and public administration theory rather than empirically grounded research findings. At the same time findings from comparative studies of existing police organization cause one seriously to question the efficacy of the reform recommendations.[51]

CONCLUSION

The difficulty of defining productivity, relating the definition to standards of performance, and then distinguishing which officer or sergeant or lieutenant or captain produced more than another, and to what degree, is obvious. However, to at least attempt to begin at the beginning, let's review some interesting findings on street patrol as it relates to organizational size, structure, and productivity.

The Workshop in Political Theory and Policy Analysis conducted a Police Services Study[52] in which they examined the impact of the size of police departments on the organization of police service activities. Two interesting findings from the study of eighty metropolitan areas concern the relationship between police department size and

1. patrol deployment (proportion of an agency's officers assigned to patrol), and
2. patrol density (ratio of citizens to patrol officers on the street).

One finding was that the larger the local police agency that produces patrol service, the lower the proportion of the agency's officers assigned to patrol duties (patrol deployment). This relationship is found among all types of local patrol agencies (Table 9.3). There are various reasons for this relationship. One is that larger departments tend to assign more officers to specific non-patrol direct-service duties, such as traffic control or criminal investigation. Larger departments are also more likely to produce their own auxiliary services and to assign officers to these non-patrol duties. Training of recruits, radio communications, and adult pre-trial detention are auxiliary services produced more often in larger departments than in smaller ones.

For municipal patrol agencies, variations in proportion of departmental sworn personnel actually deployed for street duty (patrol density) have a direct bearing on the ratio of citizens to patrol officers (Table 9.4). A patrol officer in the median municipal department of five to ten sworn officers serves slightly fewer than 2,400 citizens, while a patrol officer in the median department with more than 150 full-time sworn officers serves more than 4,200 citizens. One should remember when considering these figures that the larger departments generally tend to have more sworn officers per 1,000 residents than do the smaller. But the larger departments have not translated this relative personnel advantage into an on-street presence as well as do the small- to medium-sized agencies.

The finding that smaller municipal departments usually deploy more officers per thousand citizens suggests that consolidation of patrol agencies might increase rather than decrease costs. If the larger, consolidated departments followed the pattern seen here, more officers would need to be employed to maintain the ratio of citizens to officers on patrol which existed prior to consolidation of the small agencies. Conversely, if the department failed to employ additional officers, the ratio of citizens to officers on patrol would increase for consolidated departments.

We need to question and search for realistic answers in the existing real world. Our conclusion: "Let's keep on trying by working smarter."

In summary, productivity for patrol administrators must be viewed in conjunction with the scientific method. The patrol administrator should be constantly aware of the purpose of the scientific method—e.g., to provide sufficiently precise information to enable patrol administrators to: evaluate the patrol force performance; identify and diagnose problem areas; design solutions; stimulate constructive thinking; and provide a means for

Table 9.3 *Deployment of Sworn Officers for Patrol Duty in Local Patrol Agencies*

Type of Agency and Number of Full-Time Sworn Officers	Percent of Full-Time Sworn Officers Assigned To Patrol Duty	Ratio of Officers on the Street (10 pm) to Number Assigned to Patrol Duty	Ratio of Officers on the Street (10 pm) to Number of Full-Time Sworn
	Median	Median	Median
Municipal Police Departments	83	.28	.22
1 to 4 Full-Time Off	100	.50	.50
5 to 10 Full-Time Off	100	.29	.25
11 to 20 Full-Time Off	73	.27	.20
21 to 50 Full-Time Off	68	.24	.16
51 to 150 Full-Time Off	63	.22	.14
Over 150 Full-Time Off	56	.21	.12
County Police and Sheriffs	52	.29	.15
1 to 4 Full-Time Off	100	.33	.33
5 to 10 Full-Time Off	80	.33	.25
11 to 20 Full-Time Off	56	.33	.18
21 to 50 Full-Time Off	56	.29	.13
51 to 150 Full-Time Off	45	.26	.11
Over 150 Full-Time Off	44	.22	.10
Other Local Patrol Agencies	100	.29	.25
1 to 4 Full-Time Off	100	.50	.50
5 to 10 Full-Time Off	100	.25	.25
11 to 20 Full-Time Off	93	.33	.25
21 to 50 Full-Time Off	82	.24	.19
51 to 150 Full-Time Off	66	.17	.13
Over 150 Full-Time Off	—	—	—

Table 9.4 *Patrol Deployment and Density: Municipal Police Departments*

Number of Full-Time Sworn Officers in Municipal Police Departments:	On-Street Patrol Force (10 pm)	
	Number of Officers on the Street Median	Number of Inhabitants per Officer on the Street Median
Municipal Police Departments:		
Part-Time Only	1	1,107
1 to 4 Full-Time Off	1	1,623
5 to 10 Full-Time Off	2	2,383
11 to 20 Full-Time Off	3	2,877
21 to 50 Full-Time Off	5	3,244
51 to 150 Full-Time Off	13	3,985
Over 150 Full-Time Off	30	4,256

linking one activity to another or one part of the management process to another. In other words, to "relate resources to output."

In dealing with measurements, the patrol administrator should be aware that measurement is not a substitute for sound professional judgment. It should assist in making decisions, not dictate the decisions. Measurement should not provoke negative activity; i.e., measuring a patrol unit solely on the basis of arrests without considering the validity of the arrests; nor should it result in meaningless and costly activity (Pareta's Law). Rather, it should provide the patrol administrator with information that accurately assesses performance quantitatively and qualitatively. The measuring of public sector organization is divided into two fundamental types: the measure of results (output) and the measure of resources (input). The patrol administrator should deal with results achieved compared with results intended and consider how much it costs to achieve a given objective.

It is essential that the measurement of individual or unit activity always be understood in the context of department goals, objectives, and performance. Instruction should be given to the leaders of patrol and detectives to integrate the diverse operations of each into a coherent package.[53]

NOTES

1. Nesta M. Gallas and William H. T. Smith, "What It Takes to Make Professionals in the Public Service," in *Public Service Professional Associations and the Public Interest,* Monograph 15 (Philadelphia: The American Academy of Political and Social Science, February 1973).

2. Jacques Barzun and Henry F. Graff, *The Modern Researcher,* rev. ed. (New York: Harcourt, Brace and World, 1970); Paul E. Lazarsfield and Morris Rosenberg, eds., *The Language of Social Research* (New York: The Free Press, 1955); Robert Habenstein, *Pathways to Data* (Chicago: Aldine, 1970); and Clare Selltix et al., *Research Methods in Social Relations,* rev. ed. (New York: Holt, Rinehart and Winston, 1962).

3. Cecil E. Goode, *Personnel Research Frontiers* (Chicago: International Personnel Management Association, 1958), p. 2.

4. O. W. Wilson and Roy C. McLaren, *Police Administration* (New York: McGraw-Hill, 1972), p. 173.

5. R. Paul McCauley, "Scientific Inquiry for Police Administrators," lecture presented at the Southern Police Institute, University of Louisville, Louisville, Ky., 1977.

6. Fred N. Kerlinger, *Foundations of Behavioral Research,* 2d ed. (New York: Holt, Rinehart and Winston, 1973), p. 2.

7. Ibid., p. 6.

8. Ibid., p. 14.

9. Committee on Long-Range Goals of the Public Personnel Association, *Long-Range Goals of the Public Personnel Association* (Chicago: Public Personnel Association, 1966), p. 3.

10. Bernard Cohen and Jan M. Chaiken, *Police Background Characteristics and Performance,* report prepared for the National Institute of Law Enforcement and Criminal Justice (New York: New York City Rand Institute, August 1972), p. 3.

11. George Kelling et al., *The Kansas City Preventive Patrol Experiment: A Technical Report* (Washington, D.C.: Police Foundation, 1974), p. 4.

12. Reprinted by permission from the June 1975 issue of *Police Chief.*

13. Joseph D. McNamara, "The Kansas City Preventive Patrol Experiment," *Police Chief* (June 1975), p. 30.

14. Patrick Murphy, *Police Chief* (June 1975), p. 30.

15. George J. Sullivan, *Directed Patrol* (Kansas City: Kansas City Police Department, Operations Resource Unit, 1976), p. 1. Reprinted by permission.

16. The following four sections are reprinted from: National Commission on Productivity, *Opportunities for Improving Productivity in Police Services* (Washington, D.C.: U.S. Government Printing Office, 1973).

17. *Readings on Productivity in Policing* (Washington, D.C.: Police Foundation, 1975), p. 2.

18. Ibid., p. 3.

19. Elinor Ostrom, *Workshop in Political Theory and Policy Analysis* (Bloomington: Indiana University, 1972).

20. Ibid., p. 7.

21. Elinor Ostrom et al., "Community Organization and the Provision of Police Services," *Sage Professional Papers in Administrative and Policy Studies* (Beverly Hills, Calif.: Sage Publishers, 1973).

22. Landon Heffner, *Policing by Objectives,* vol. 1 (Hartford, Conn.: Social Development Corporation, 1976), p. 2.

23. Harry P. Hatry, *Readings on Productivity in Policing* (Washington, D.C.: Police Foundations, 1975), pp. 86–87.

24. Ibid., pp. 90–91.

25. Two other important objectives should also be mentioned. The first is the recovery of stolen property, which is relatively easily measured either by the value of stolen goods or units of stolen items recovered. The second objective is to provide the community with a sense of security and a feeling of confidence in its police force, a more difficult objective to measure. The public's attitudes toward crime and the police nevertheless can be assessed through a variety of means,

including opinion surveys. And while the Advisory Group did not have the time to examine this question, its importance should not go unrecognized.

26. This material is reprinted from National Commission on Productivity, *Opportunities for Improving Productivity.*

27. Clearly, discretion must be used in determining the division of labor within any police department or patrol division. Some sworn officers will always be needed for other than street assignment, and some of their time may be required for what are considered to be non-patrol-related activities. The Advisory Group's approach focuses on the situation found in many departments across the country: within the patrol division, too many sworn officers are performing jobs they should not be performing, and of those officers with street assignments, too much time is spent on activities unrelated to patrol objectives. Improvement in these two areas could, in most departments, contribute significantly toward making more people available for the real role of the patrol force, regardless of how departments wish to define that role. This does not necessarily mean that additional men should be assigned to traditional patrol activities, as will be discussed further in this chapter.

28. The survey was conducted by distribution of three questionnaires (one each on Patrol, Crime Prevention, and Human Resources) to the following eleven law-enforcement departments and agencies: Police Departments of Boston, Massachusetts; Charlottesville, North Carolina; Cincinnati, Ohio; Kansas City, Missouri; Miami Beach, Florida; New York, New York; Oakland, California; and Washington, D.C.; the Los Angeles (California) Sheriff's Department; the Michigan State Police; and the St. Petersburg (Florida) Department of Public Safety.

This sample was not intended to be statistically valid on a nationwide basis. It was considered, sufficient, however, for the limited objectives of the survey, which were:

- To check whether data required for use in measures being developed are normally available.
- To test whether the measures are feasible when actual data are applied to them.
- To obtain some idea of the ranges (or disparities) existing so that the potential for improvement could be assessed.

Time available for conducting the survey did not permit a pretesting of the questionnaires, which would have enabled the Advisory Group's staff to refine definitions of the terminology used. Therefore, not all respondents provided comparable data in response to all questions. For that reason, the survey results, as depicted in figures and tables throughout this report, provide approximate data for those departments (eight in some cases, only four in others, etc.) whose responses seemed to reflect a common understanding of the categories of data solicited.

It should be noted in particular that, to preserve the anonymity of respondents, identifications of departments is by letters only; moreover, Department "A" in Figure 9.2 does not necessarily correspond with Department "A" in Figure 9.3, etc.

29. This measure does not, of course, indicate whether the patrol officers thus assigned are accomplishing anything useful. It is an indication of the department's success in making sworn officers available for more directly patrol-related activity.

30. As noted for the previous measure, this measure does not indicate whether the time made available is put to good use. It does measure success in making more time available which can be turned to good use.

31. This section deals with the crime deterrence activities generally associated with the work of patrol.

32. Richard C. Larson, *Urban Police Patrol Analysis* (Cambridge, Mass.: M.I.T. Press, 1972), p. 32.

33. For a thorough discussion on this subject, see Franklin E. Zimring, *Perspectives on Deterrence,* prepared for the National Institute of Mental Health Center for Studies of Crime and Delinquency, Public Health Service (Washington, D.C.: U.S. Government Printing Office, January 1971).

34. See Appendix B, "A Study of Communications, Crimes, and Arrests in a Metropolitan Police Department," in Herbert H. Isaacs, *Task Force Report: Science and Technology,* President's Commission on Law Enforcement and Administration of Justice (Washington, D.C.: U.S. Government Printing Office, 1967).

35. The arrival of an officer at the scene of an incident assumes a certain "quality" factor – i.e., a police officer is on the scene. That has some intrinsic value, but more discriminating information is needed to determine what the officer does when he or she gets there, i.e., the "quality" of the response.

36. See the following section on "Apprehension of Criminal Offenders" for explanation of this language.

37. Herbert H. Isaacs, "A Study of Communications."

38. In Los Angeles County, District Attorney rejection rates in cases involving possession of dangerous drugs vary from 26 percent for the Whittier Police Department to 69 percent for the Long Beach Police Department. For robbery, the rejection rates vary from 6 percent in Compton to 53 percent for the Los Angeles Sheriff's Department. A major reason cited in the report from which figures are taken, though by no means the sole one, for these rejection rates is that police departments vary greatly in their own screening of felony cases. See Peter W. Greenwood et al., *Prosecution of Adult Felony Defendants in Los Angeles County: A Policy Perspective,* Report R-1127-DOJ (Santa Monica, Calif.: Rand Corporation, March 1973), p. ix.

39. "Total Patrol Man-Years" refers to all sworn officers in the patrol division whether or not they are assigned to street work. Note that, instead of years, such other units of time as months, days, or hours can be used, depending upon which makes more sense to the user.

40. Individual police departments should develop and use crime categories which reflect as accurately as possible the true mix of arrests in the community and which provide them with the specific information that they require.

41. Greenwood et al., *Prosecution,* pp. viii, ix. It should be mentioned that the report does not make clear whether these arrest ratios are for arrests that survive the first judicial screening. The ranges indicated, however, would not change very much if the data were qualified by judicial screening.

42. The man-years include those expended by members of the patrol force in supervisory, clerical, and other non-patrol assignments to give a clear picture of the total resources expended.

43. Although these data have not been adjusted for definitional differences among departments, differences in the definition of misdemeanor and felony alone could not account entirely for the range in performance.

44. Roger B. Parks, "Police Reorganization, A Review of Its Evaluation," in *How Well Does It Work? Review of Criminal Justice Evaluation, 1978* (Washington, D.C.: U.S. Department of Justice, Law Enforcement Assistance Administration, National Institute of Law Enforcement and Criminal Justice, 1979), p. 243.

45. William Kornfeld and John D. Riordan, *Evaluation Study of Allegheny Regional Narcotic Task Force* (Chicago: IIT Research Institute, 1974).

46. Parks, op. cit., p. 243.

47. Robert R. Delahunt, Richard D. Engler, and Susan B. Petinga, "An Evaluation Study in the Area of Contract Law Enforcement: A Review of the Literature" (Washington, D.C.: National Sheriffs' Association, n.d.), p. 197.
48. Daniel L. Skoler, *Organizing the Non-System* (Lexington, Mass.: Lexington Books, 1977), p. 80.
49. *Urban Affairs Quarterly* 10:464–486.
50. Donald T. Campbell, "Considering the Case against Experimental Evaluations of Social Innovations," *Administrative Science Quarterly* (March 1970), p. 111.
51. Parks, op. cit., pp. 252–253.
52. Elinor Ostrom, Workshop in Political Theory and Policy Analysis, *Workshop Report, On-Street Patrol: Interesting Findings* (Bloomington, Ind., 1976), pp. 1–3.
53. National Commission on Productivity, *Improving Opportunities for Productivity in Police Services,* (Washington, D.C.: U.S. Government Printing Office, 1973)

·10·

Patrol Personnel Distribution

The patrol force *is* the police department. To the extent the patrol force fails to achieve the police goal, specialized units within the police agency are necessary. Therefore, patrol administrators must manage personnel as if they were in business with a profit motive. Deployment of each officer should be done in a manner that optimizes cost-effectiveness. The introduction of profit orientation into patrol distribution will be welcomed by leaders of the community and exhilarate overburdened taxpayers.

For the patrol force to succeed, studies on patrol personnel distribution and equalization of workload should be carried out. How much time should an officer spend on preventive patrol? What effect does the arrest rate have on crime? To what extent should an officer inspect police hazards on his or her beat? What is an acceptable response time to a call for service: two minutes? three minutes? What size should the patrol force be to achieve its goal? What should the task priorities be for each patrol officer during a tour of duty? What should be the workload of each patrol officer in order to have an equitable distribution?

There are no exact or easy answers. However, the citizens of any community have a right to the highest level of service the police department is capable of producing. Budget restrictions, personnel competence, volume of traffic service, calls for service, and criminal activity weigh heavily on the department's ability to provide service. Thus the patrol force should be distributed according to a proportional need, geographically and temporally. To accomplish this, an analysis of statistical data is necessary.

To develop a data base that has a high degree of accuracy, a valid reporting system is essential. In order to determine the distribution of personnel, all factors contributing to the deployment must be documented. Police departments that arbitrarily distribute their patrol force by assigning equal numbers of personnel to each of three shifts (watches) are not providing the community with the highest possible level of service. Three by-products of the patrol personnel distribution studies for patrol deployment are: (1) the fact that administrators are able to give an equal workload to each patrol officer; (2) accountability by both officers and supervisors for total police service, because leaders assign officers to regular beats; and (3) directed patrol.

Chapter 2 discussed the mission of law enforcement as related to goals and priorities. In order to achieve the goals and priorities, a formula for personnel distribution must be developed that is concomitant with the priorities. For example, if a community wants the patrol force to respond to all calls for service within one minute, a formula devised to distribute personnel in a manner capable of doing this is possible. But it must be understood that, to the extent the formula favors one priority, the other tasks will suffer. In this case, the ability to reduce crime through preventive patrol and the inspection of police hazards by officers will be decreased.

In the management by objectives approach to patrol administration, the objectives of patrol personnel distribution are to place the patrol officer in the right place at the right time to prevent crime; to develop a systematic approach to determine as accurately as possible the place and time; to use a businesslike approach (i.e., viewing investment of each officer and the dividend expected as a management concept; assigning officers to a beat of the size and configuration that equalizes workload and allows response to calls for service at an acceptable level of proficiency); to provide the officers time to inspect police hazards; to improve community support and cooperation; and to decrease the chance of calls for police service to back up.

While there are several approaches to the personnel distribution problem, all have the common denominator of workload by time of day, day of week, shift or watch, month, and reporting areas or census tract. The other factor of workload, classes of events, has been weighted according to expenditures of patrol time; for example, the amount of time necessary to investigate a simple larceny as opposed to a bank robbery. Using the proportionate-need distribution, the weight for the bank robbery would be more than the weight for the simple larceny or a simple assault. These weightings are not perfect, but until an improved system is developed, the assignment of weights according to classes of events is the best available.

COLLECTION AND ANALYSIS OF DATA

Before any workload studies can be accomplished, accurate data must be collected. In order to collect the data, a reporting system that insures the recording of every call for police service must be instituted. This can be done by using a radio-complaint card. Personnel of the communication center initiate the complaint card and record a complaint number, date of occurrence, location of the incident by address, time officer dispatched, time of officer arrival at scene, time of return to service, and type of incident. (In a computer-assisted dispatching system, each call is recorded in the computer and is retrieved via the computer process.) The complaint card is then sent to the records section, where the report written by the patrol officer is used to verify the validity of the incident and a reporting area number is placed on the complaint card. The complaint card is then filed and used for workload studies. Usually the first workload study is attempted after the first year of data collection.

Reporting Areas

A *reporting area* is a certain section of the city, the size of which is determined by an estimated amount of police work. One method used to devise a reporting area is to allocate two reporting areas to each 1,000 population. Another method is to align the reporting areas with census tracts in order to develop data relative to population measurements and socioeconomic factors. The method selected should be that which provides data compatible with the objectives of the police department. The method described here is designed primarily for providing distribution according to crime needs (preventive patrol), calls for service, and inspections or back-up calls.

The first step is to place a large map of the community on the wall. Experienced patrol commanders then outline on the map, using different colors or shadings, areas of high, medium, and low crime. This is used to design reporting areas related by size to density of crime. If experience has shown a high level of crime in the downtown area, reporting areas there should be made smaller. In outlying areas of the community where crime is low, reporting areas should be made larger. Patrol commanders should be advised that the reporting areas will be grouped together in order to create a patrol beat. Therefore, the boundaries of these reporting areas should follow actual boundaries, such as railroad tracks, main arteries, freeways, rivers, and bridges. The reporting area boundaries should be numbered. They will not change. Some reporting areas may consist of five or six city blocks in a straight line. This type of reporting area design usually occurs in the downtown area of the community.

This procedure is used prior to any accumulation of data. Once the data has been accumulated, the following procedure is used.

Sampling

The original map outlines each reporting area. Since these reporting areas will not change, but analysis of the workload necessitates writing figures and making adjustments, clear acetate should be placed over the map. In this way, workload may be overlaid onto the reporting areas and beat size and configuration may be adjusted without ruining the original map.

A sampling of 20 to 25 percent of the complaint cards (source documents) is then taken. The sampling should be spread over a twelve-month period, using equal numbers of each day of the week. For example, if the total number of calls for service for the department in the ac-cumulated data for the year was 100,000, then 20,000 to 25,000 complaints or incidents would be analyzed.

The analysis would first categorize each incident according to:

- Part I crimes (index crimes)
- Part I arrests
- All other offenses
- All other arrests
- Traffic accidents
- Miscellaneous calls for service

Weightings

Weights are assigned to the specific incidents based on the amount of time necessary for the patrol officer to properly handle the incident at the preliminary investigative stage and on the seriousness of the event. A modification of the basic weighting for each individual police department can be meaningful. Most weighting systems have allocated a lesser weight to accidents than to Part I crimes; however, a close analysis may show that the weight of accidents should be increased from two to three or possibly four. The following procedure is based on the author's experience in distributing patrol personnel.

Type of Incident	Weight	Type of Incident	Weight
Part I crimes		*Part II crimes*	
Murder	4	Arrests	2
Rape	4	Traffic accidents	2
Robbery	4	Miscellaneous calls	1
Burglary	4	for service	
Aggravated assault	4		
Larceny over $50	4		
Auto theft	4		

In the case of traffic accidents, it is recommended that in-depth analysis be given in order to insure the most accurate weights. The list of incidents and weights is easily understood. For example, it would take twice as long to investigate a rape or robbery as it would to make an arrest, or it would take four times as long to investigate a burglary as it would to properly handle a call such as a sanitation complaint, parking violation, or loud party.

Analysis

The next step is to determine the month of the year, hour of the day, day of the week, type of incident, and location (reporting area) of each incident. This means analyzing each of the 20,000 to 25,000 sampled incidents. This information is gleaned from the source document (complaint card). The most expeditious manner in which to do this is by using a computer. For example, code each list of information from the complaint card, key punch, and enter into the computer. The program of the computer would do the actual work and a printout would be received showing:

1. the number of incidents multiplied by the weight in each reporting area by shift (watch);
2. workload by day of week;
3. totals by time of day in hours; and
4. "within-shift" variations in workload.

Within-shift variations means the optimum arrangements of working hours by shift, or what shift- (watch-) hour arrangement would cause the least internal variation of workload. The shift hours selected should be those that have least variation in that the difference in workload between hourly peaks and valleys regarding activity is minimized. This method will allow for the assignment of officers by shift, thus reducing the possibility of having too many or too few officers on duty at any given time.

Shift-change decision. When determining the basic shifts under which the patrol force will operate, the patrol administrator should not base his decision on the within-shift variation alone. Personnel problems may arise if the selected shifts are unacceptable to the majority of personnel. Before he announces the new shift schedule, he should analyze the potential consequences. For example, if the present shifts are changed at 0800, 1600, and 2400 and the study reveals (as Figure 10.1 does) that the optimum change-of-shift time should be one hour later, the difference in variance may be so minor that what might be gained in efficiency would be lost in personnel/organization conflict. However, if the existing shift change took place at 0300, 1100, and 1900 or at 0700, 1500, and 2300, the change should be made to the 0100, 0900, and 1700 because of the greater difference in variance.

Patrol administrators should not recommend decisions for the sake of efficiency alone. The production-oriented leader must keep in mind who is doing the producing. People-oriented leaders will consider the patrol officer and balance decisions between people and production. The long-range result will usually be maximum benefits.

ASSIGNMENT-AVAILABILITY FACTOR

The potential personnel for one year in a patrol force is eight hours a day by each patrol officer. Each patrol officer is assigned a beat, and the beat is manned for each tour of duty. However, in reality, no officer will man her or his beat each day because of several factors. To determine the

Figure 10.1 *The least variance as indicated by the chart is when the shifts begin at 0100, 0900, and 1700. By changing shifts at this time, there is least variance from the* average *hourly workload.*

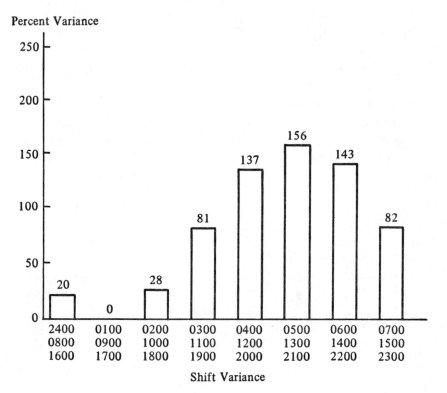

number of officers necessary to man each beat at all times, it is necessary to find out in hours what is potentially available and what is actually available due to the loss of officers' time because of these several factors.

The potential available hours for each officer are simply 365 days a year of eight-hour tours of duty, 2,920 (365 × 8) hours. The factors to be considered are vacations, regular days off, medical leave, training, holidays, military leave, court time, overtime, officers suspended from duty, and any other loss of time that may have a significant effect on the availability factor. Special details, officers acting as supervisors, and riot duty in other jurisdictions for extended periods should be considered under a miscellaneous category. Table 10.1 shows the calculations for one officer.

Each factor in Table 10.1 should be computed on an individual department basis. Several of the factors will probably be different for many departments. For example, the answer to the question mark beside "line-of-duty injury," "overtime," and "disciplinary suspension" depends on the department. Also, these ingredients may be so small they would not be significant. The vacation factor may differ, but two weeks or ten days is usual. Two days off each week is the typical regular time off. Medical leave should be based on the average time and, hopefully, this will amount to approximately seven or eight days a year. The training factor may be different; however, most progressive departments can only afford forty hours per year for each officer.

Table 10.1

Potential Hours Available		2,920
Vacation (10 days × 8 hours)	80	
Regular days off (102 days × 8)	816	
Medical leave (7 days × 8)	56	
Training (in-service) (5 days × 8)	40	
Holidays (10 days × 8)	80	
Line of duty injury (?)	?	
Military leave (1 week × 8)	56	
Court time (4 days × 8)	32	
Overtime (?)	?	
Suspensions, discipline?	?	
	1,160	
		−1,160
Remainder		1,760

$$\text{Assignment-Availability Factor} = \frac{2,920}{1,760} = 1.6$$

Table 10.1 shows the assignment availability factor to be 1.6. This simply means that 1.6 officers must be allocated to each shift in order to have a man or woman actually on duty at all times.

In order to give the student a more realistic picture of an assignment availability factor, a patrol force of one hundred officers is used as an example in Table 10.2. Department X had one hundred officers available for patrol duty during the past year. (Personnel-distribution studies should be completed once each year.) Therefore, the number of potential man-days for the coming year in Department X would be 100×365, or 36,500 mandays. Using the same figures as in Table 10.1, the computation in Table 10.2 would be made for Department X to determine the assignment availability factor.

BEAT REQUIREMENTS PER SHIFT

Formula in personnel distribution studies refers to the amount of time the patrol administrator wants each officer to apply to the selected tasks. Some departments separate the tasks of the personnel on a shift into two distinct activities: one, responding to calls for service, and the other, carrying out repressive or preventive patrol. The disadvantage of this method of distribution is that some officers may become bored and others may become mere report takers. Highly trained officers should not have to take reports of serious incidents without the opportunity to continue with the

Table 10.2 *Department X 100-Personnel Patrol Force*

Potential Personnel-Days Available		36,500
Vacation (10 days × 100)	1,000	
Regular days off (102 × 100)	10,200	
Medical leave (7 days × 100)	700	
Training (in-service) (5 days × 100)	500	
Holidays (10 days × 100)	1,000	
Line of duty (?)		
Military leave (7 days × 100)	700	
Court time (4 days × 100)	400	
Overtime (?)		
Suspension, discipline (?)		
	14,500	
		−14,500
Remainder		22,000

$$\text{Assignment-Availability Factor} = \frac{36,500}{22,000} = 1.6$$

investigation to some extent. Experiments in this type of patrol assignment (separate tasks) should continue until proper evaluation can be made concerning the total patrol effectiveness.

Highly sophisticated computerized systems of manpower allocation and distribution are experimenting with forecasting assignments of patrol beats by the hour. A potential pitfall of this method is the loss of familiarity by officers who presently have permanent beat assignments. However, formulas that assign various percentages of time with a tour of duty to different tasks may develop basic designs that could assist patrol forces across the country.

Another aspect of this split approach to patrol (calls for service and preventive patrol) is that it cannot develop the generalist police officer. Modifications can be made and have been made in the split approach to compensate for this, but results are not yet complete regarding the total effect.

The formula in most basic personnel distribution studies is to assign one-third of an officer's time for responding and handling calls for service, one-third of the time for preventive patrol, and one-third for citizen's calls to be grouped (queuing), as opposed to being equitably spaced throughout a tour of duty. (This one-third is sometimes referred to as "all other activities"; it may also be set aside for administrative duties.)

To determine the average time required to respond to a call for service and complete a preliminary investigation, time studies should be conducted. If it is not practical to do this, a department can use the standard average time factor of forty-five minutes. The number of beats is then determined by considering (1) forty-five minutes as the average for each call for service, (2) repressive patrol time, and (3) time necessary to reduce potential for cases to occur in groups.

Special Assignments

Other factors to consider in determining the number of beats are:

1. Areas that have such high density/volume of crime and need so much service that an arbitrary decision is made in designating the beat. These beats are often in the downtown business areas. They have workloads distinctly out of proportion to their size.
2. Areas that are isolated (parks, lakes, etc.). Assignment of officers must be based on the distinct nature of the geographical area.
3. Areas that are unique in terms of diversity, size, and hazard potential. A good example of this type of area is the garment area

of New York. Citizens walk these streets with unprotected valuable property and an arbitrary assignment may be necessary.

Each patrol administrator in conjunction with his patrol commander can evaluate those areas of the community necessitating special assignment. Additionally, depending upon the procedure used to transport prisoners, a wagon driver and partner may have to be assigned. Some vehicles used to transport prisoners require only one officer. These vehicles can be locked from the outside so a partner is not necessary. Another procedure requires the officer effecting the arrest to ride behind the wagon to the place of detention or holdover. Patrol administrators should review alternative procedures and select the one compatible with conditions in the community. In some cases, radio cars are equipped with screens and other equipment so that they can be used to transport prisoners, thus reducing the need for special wagons.

The same type of decision should be made concerning assignment of station-house personnel. Desk sergeants or officers necessary for booking and turnkeys for searching prisoners and detention procedures (these officers may also be used for fingerprinting and photography procedures) are assigned according to the need of the department. Civilian personnel and female officers are also available for assignment to desk duties.

Normal Requirements

Again considering Department X, which has one hundred patrol officers available for patrol duty, the following calculation can be made using a sample number of incidents for the shifts 0100, 0900, 1700 hours (2,100 sample incidents for Shift 1, 0100 to 0900; 3,400 sample incidents for the 0900 to 1700 shift; and 4,700 sample incidents for the 1700 to 0100 shift.) The calculation is as follows:

SHIFT I 0100–0900

Number of incidents sampled (20% of total)	2,100
Converted to 100%	10,500 per yr.
Multiplied by .75 hours (45 minutes)	7,875 hours
Multiplied by 3 (This adds the repressive patrol time and time to reduce potential for cases to occur in groups. This is also known as "buffer time.")	23,625 hours

Divided by the number of hours necessary to provide personnel for one patrol
beat on one shift for one year (8 × 365 =
2,920 hours) = 8.09 or   8 beats

SHIFT II 0900–1700

Number of incidents sampled (20% of
total)   3,400
    Converted to 100%   17,000 per yr.
    Multiplied by .75 hours (45 minutes)   12,750 hours
    Multiplied by 3 (buffer time)   38,250 hours
    Divided by the number of hours neces-
sary to provide personnel for one patrol
beat on one shift for one year (8 × 365 =
2.920 hours) = 13.09 =   13 beats

SHIFT III 1700–0100

Number of incidents sampled (20% of
total)   4,700
    Converted to 100%   23,500 per yr.
    Multiplied by .75 hours (45 minutes)   17,625 hours
    Multiplied by 3 (buffer time)   52,875 hours
    Divided by the number of hours neces-
sary to provide personnel for one patrol
beat on one shift for one year (8 × 365 =
2,920 hours) = 18.1 =   18 beats

These figures do not take into account the possibility that days of the week may have large differences in workload. If this is the case, the same format would be used for those days with large volumes of workload, and assignments of beats would be made accordingly. Crime hazards are considered, since any incidents occurring as a result of crime hazards manifest themselves in the total call for service statistics. Areas of high density and high-hazard locations as opposed to large residential areas and low-hazards conditions will be proportionately covered by patrol because of the workload study of the previous year.

ONE- OR TWO-OFFICER BEATS

The next personnel decision to be made is the number of beats that need one-officer coverage and the number needing two-officer coverage. Most departments do not have enough personnel to assign two officers to each beat, but in most communities there are some beats that should have two officers assigned. Therefore, patrol administrators must make enlightened decisions based on personnel and budgetary restrictions concerning which beats should be one-officer and which should be two. When one-officer beats are used, the team procedure between the dispatcher and the one-officer car is essential.

The decision should be made after the following elements of each area are considered:

1. safety of the officer – some beats are isolated by natural barriers that preclude assisting officers from responding as back-up units in a reasonable amount of time;
2. number of times arrests are made and resistance is offered by the arrestee;
3. number of incidents in which multiple arrests are made;
4. number of arrests where violence is involved – knife, gun, assaults;
5. volume of calls for service;
6. available access to area, density of population, street design, etc.;
7. atmosphere of community (Does the area contain radical elements who have demonstrated dislike of police officers? Have threats emanated from the area causing belief that officers may be seriously injured?) Under certain conditions, it may be necessary to assign three-officer cars or two-officer cars to an area. These conditions do not usually exist over an extended period of time; however, it is a very serious consideration; and
8. the number of multiple dwellings on the beat. In high-crime hostile areas, officers should not be required to be alone on upper floors. (Patrol officers should be consulted.)

Once the decision has been made regarding general areas in which a two-officer car should be assigned and the exact number of two-officer cars, a participatory management approach is helpful. This means allowing officers and supervisors assigned to the selected areas to be involved in making the choice concerning the specific two-officer beats.

TOTAL CALCULATION OF PATROL PERSONNEL

After determining the number of one- and two-officer cars necessary for each shift, the total number of officers necessary to man each shift can be ascertained. The assignment availability factor will also be considered. If the same figures used in determining the number of beats for each shift are also used in this format, the following calculations would be made. An assumption can be made concerning the number of two-officer cars on each shift: that it is necessary to have two two-officer beats assigned to Shift

I, three two-officer beats assigned to Shift II, and five two-officer beats assigned to Shift III.

> *SHIFT I*–8 beats (2 two-officer beats and 6 one-officer beats)
> The eight beats require 4 officers to man the two-officer beats and six officers to man the remaining one-officer beats, for a total necessary strength of ten officers. Allowing for the assignment availability factor of 1.6, it would be necessary to assign a total of sixteen officers to Shift I.

> *SHIFT II*–13 beats (3 two-officer beats and 10 one-officer beats)
> The 13 beats require 6 officers to man the two-officer beats and 10 officers to man the one-officer beats, for a total strength of 16 officers. Allowing for the assignment availability factor of 1.6, it would be necessary to assign a total of 25.6, or 26 officers to Shift II.

> *Shift III*–18 beats (5 two-officer beats and 13 one-officer beats)
> The 18 beats require 10 officers to man the two-officer beats and 13 officers to man the one-officer beats, for a total strength of 23 officers. Allowing for the assignment availability factor of 1.6, it would be necessary to assign 36.8, or 37 officers to Shift III.

Patrol Force
Shift I   = 16
Shift II = 26
Shift III = 37
Total   = 79 officers

BEAT SIZE, DESIGN, AND EQUALIZATION OF WORKLOAD SUPERVISION

In order to make each officer's workload equal and to ensure that all workloads together perform the total police mission, average workloads must be determined. This is done by shift. The first step is to total the workload for each shift by adding the weights of all the reporting areas. Then the total is divided by the number of beats for that particular shift.

For example, using the number of beats by shift in the previous illustration, the following method would be used:

> *SHIFT I*–8 beats: If the total workload for Shift I calculated by adding the weights of the reporting area runs 8,000, then each beat should have a workload of 1,000.

> *SHIFT II*–13 beats: If the total workload were 13,000, then each beat would have a workload of 1,000.

> *SHIFT III*–18 beats: If the total workload were 18,000, then each beat would have a workload of 1,000.

The figures used are for explanatory purposes only; usually the workload would not be in rounded figures. The point is, that if each beat is designed to have a workload of 1,000 in each example, the officer workload will be equal. To achieve the size and design of the beat, simply add a number of reporting areas together until 1,000 is reached. In most cases, exact workload equalization is impossible. The totals in this case would probably be 990, 1,005, 1,010, 1,020, 980, etc. This is because in high-crime areas, the difference of one city block will change the workload drastically while the same change in a low-crime area will affect the workload only minimally.

Other factors to be considered in the design/workload relationship are neighborhood makeup, accessibility, a desire to have beat boundaries meet at high-crime locations, and uniqueness of geography. Because population in the downtown areas of cities changes so drastically because of people coming in to work there during the day, special attention to this factor is necessary.

Another consideration is the size of the beats in low-population areas (suburbs). If the beat is too large, even though statistical analysis indicates low workload, an officer cannot patrol it properly. It may take half an hour to travel from one end to the other, reducing the officer's effectiveness.

In contrast to the large beat is the very small beat. Extremely high-crime areas may have workloads reaching the average contained in one reporting area. In this case, the beat size is the same size as the reporting area and may be of a design one block by two blocks. If the decision is to leave the beat at this size, it should probably be a walking, bicycle, or motor-scooter beat. An alternative would be to raise the workload slightly to reduce officer boredom, creating a larger beat and providing an automobile for the officer.

One beat that the author is familiar with contained 286 business establishments. Officers were required to patrol the beat on a priority basis. Businesses having alarm systems were inspected differently from those not possessing this security. This type of beat points out the real need for crime prevention through physical security. One goal of the officer on this beat was to stimulate the use of improved physical security.

Beat size, design, and workload equalization are important considerations, especially to the officers who are required to patrol them. Naturally, the workload study is done from statistical analysis on a scientific basis. However, if at all possible, patrol officers and patrol supervisors should be consulted on beat size and design. Their in-depth knowledge of the area will supply information unavailable from statistics alone. This total approach by the patrol administrator will pay dividends for the department through employee motivation.

Supervision

Span of control and unity of command are necessary principles of organization. Officers should report to one, and only one, supervisor. A supervisor should have a given number of officers working as part of his or her team. What is the optimum span of control? Who should lead the team when the supervisor is not there? Our example indicated eight beats on Shift I. Should one, two or three sergeants be assigned to the shift for supervisory purposes? A process similar to that for determining beat size and design is necessary. If sectors (supervisory areas of responsibility) are too large, supervisors will see officers only once during a tour of duty. If sectors are too small and the workload not sufficient, manpower is wasted.

Each department should consider the following in the assignment of supervisors:

1. level of sophistication of supervisory personnel;
2. level of sophistication of subordinate personnel;
3. geographical obstacles (community may be divided by natural boundary);
4. physical restrictions;
5. each supervisor's willingness to delegate authority;
6. the possibility of the patrol administrator's overestimation of his ability or underestimation of the ability of subordinates;
7. amount of support resources, communications, vehicles, etc.; and
8. responsibilities—regarding the number, complexity, and priority of tasks (this relates to the objectives of the department, and the order or priority in which the different goals have been placed).

The number of supervisors necessary in the patrol force of evolving police agencies should be flexible and allocated on an individual department basis. As team-policing and horizontal-growth concepts are used more, the new patrol officer may require less supervision. The decision concerning the number of supervisors should be made in accordance with existing conditions.

When each decision is being made, however, the assignment availability factor is important. Shift III required 18 beats. How many sergeants are necessary to supervise that number of beats and officers? There are a total of 37 officers assigned to the shift. Should the shift be divided into 3 sectors with 6 beats in each sector? Should the number of sectors be 4 with the beats assigned 5, 5, 5, and 3 respectively? All ingredients considered in the personnel distribution process must be weighed. However, if the 18 beats are divided, for example, into 3 sectors, 3 supervisors must be assigned. If the same assignment availability factor of 1.6 is used, 4.8, or 5, supervisors must be assigned to Shift III. Each supervisor would then have a given number of two-officer and one-officer beats within his or her sector. Sector I, Shift III could contain 2 two-officer beats and 4 one-officer beats; Sector II, Shift III could contain 2 two-officer beats and 4 one-officer beats; while Sector III, Shift III would contain 1 two-officer beat and 5 one-officer beats. The assignment is shown in Table 10.3

Another technique requires the supervisor to select an officer of his team to replace the supervisor when he is off duty. Advantages of this method are: (1) training of officer in the knowledge of supervisory responsibility; (2) understanding and awareness by officer of supervisory problems; (3) motivation of subordinates to learn and develop themselves as individuals in job context and expand their education into other disciplines; (4) immediate feedback to the supervisor, resulting in his improved performance; (5) available leader in times of emergency, riot, crowd disturbance, serious investigations such as homicide, and injury to supervisor; and (6) budget savings because fewer supervisors are needed. Disadvantages of this approach are: (1) fewer supervisory positions exist, which may reduce incentive of officers; (2) possible conflict between officers selected to replace supervisor and the other officers, since the individual selected is working in a supervisory capacity one day and an officer capacity the next; (3) potential jealousy between officers selected and those not selected; and (4) possible charges of favoritism by the supervisors. Consequently, if this method of distribution is used in patrol supervision, it is essential that written policy be disseminated to the force clearly outlining the procedure.

Table 10.3 *Shift III*

Sector I		Sector II		Sector III	
	Officers		Officers		Officers
2 two-man beats	4	2 two-man beats	4	1 two-man beat	2
4 one-man beats	4	4 one-man beats	4	5 one-man beats	5
	8		8		7
Assignment availability	1.6	Assignment availability	1.6	Assignment availability	1.6
	12.8(13)		12.8(13)		11.2(12)

Total Assigned Patrol Officers to Shift III = 37.

ALTERNATIVE ALLOCATION AND DISTRIBUTION METHODS

So far in this chapter we have discussed the traditional method of patrol force allocation and distribution. The following information is presented so that there may be a choice in the selection of a patrol personnel allocation and distribution method. The selection should be made on the basis of philosophy, goals, and objectives of the individual agency.

In recent years a number of advances have been made in police command and control operations through the application of computers. These advances include computer-aided dispatching, mobile digital communications and message switching, and automatic vehicle location systems. These innovations have made possible the reporting and analysis of crime patterns on a near-real-time basis, better anticipation of incidents, and reduced response time to calls for service. Computer techniques can also help agencies to improve the allocation of their forces by analyzing the effects of different allocation strategies.

The computer serves to analyze how well patrol forces are being distributed to meet various workloads in different places and at different times. It also permits the evaluation of different allocation strategies with respect to certain measurable factors such as workload and response time. Where it is not feasible for an agency to acquire and operate these computer-based analysis tools, a knowledge of the available techniques and programs will be useful as a basis of soliciting assistance and interfacing with consultants and organizations specializing in field operations analysis. With modern performance-oriented techniques it is possible for the planner to specify some level of performance (such as minimum delay in responding to calls for service, a given patrol frequency, or a maximum permissible imbalance among workloads of different units or precincts) and have the computer program calculate the patrol force allocation that best satisfies the performance requirement.

When does the police planner need to establish or reexamine his or her force allocations? Probably the most useful indication is an evident imbalance in the workloads of different units, beats, tours, or precincts. Excessive response times to calls for service, delays in answering calls, inadequate preventive patrol hours, major changes in patrol beat boundaries, and rapid growth of crime rates in certain areas all indicate the need for changes in force allocations. The factors affecting patrol performance are numerous and have complex interactions that can vary under different circumstances; such situations are difficult to handle by simple formulas, but are easily analyzed by computer-based patrol force allocation techniques. These can optimize force allocations to improve key performance factors and can resolve workload imbalances as well.

Efficiency of patrol force allocation is especially of interest because it has the potential of alleviating the cost pressures felt by police departments everywhere. Typically, 80 to 90 percent of the police department's budget is taken up by salaries and payroll-related expenses such as fringe benefits. Therefore, even a small percentage increase in the efficiency of personnel utilization can yield a large dollar saving, or can at least minimize the cost of attaining a given level of service.

Dollar savings are not the only reason for considering patrol force allocation analysis. Some other effects of improving allocations are not measurable in dollar terms, but are still important. Among these are shortened response time, better equalization of work loads, and improved officer morale.

The discussion of patrol force allocation studies is organized around the four sequential steps in such a study:

1. Predicting rates of calls for service.
2. Determining how many patrol units are needed.
3. Designing patrol sectors or beats.
4. Analyzing different dispatching strategies.

Predicting Rates of Calls for Service

Predictions of rates of calls for service are necessarily based on the department's previous experience with calls, and it is essential to have a good base of statistics indicating the pattern of calls for given hours of the day, days of the week, and seasons of the year. These statistics should also show a breakdown of calls by type, since each type tends to have its own pattern. The data should include the length of time required to service calls. For a department with a computer-aided dispatch system, the required statistics are readily generated from the computerized logs of incidents.

Most police departments have adequate records of calls for service over an extended period, with breakdowns by type of incident, location, and time and date. These are readily averaged, and it would seem to be a simple matter to extrapolate any trends (growing population, changing neighborhood, changing crime patterns) to derive estimates for future workloads on patrol units. These estimates must necessarily be expressed in terms of averages, however. If they are to be used as a basis for determining the numbers of patrol units needed and how best to allocate them in space and time, however, averages alone are somewhat misleading because of peak loads caused by the random rate of calls for service. Patrol strengths must be set to handle these peak rates.

Calls for service are random in nature. A month or a week, or even a day, may be average but any particular ten-minute period is very unlikely to be average. If calls average ten per hour over the course of one day they will average one every six minutes, but any police department knows that during the busy hours there will probably be two to five times as many calls; and that during a busy hour, some ten-minute periods will have twice the average number of calls.

Ideally, a police department would like to have a patrol unit available to handle every call for service with no waiting, even during peak load periods. Practically, this would mean having too many units most of the time because short-term peak loads are brief and come at unpredictable intervals. What is done in most cases is to try to have enough units to handle all but the highest peaks—those that occur only a small fraction of the time. Stated the other way, the department can define a level of service in terms of having calls answered without delay 85 percent of the time, or some other percentage that appears practical. Another standard can be to define a desired maximum delay time for calls that have to be placed in queue. This too has to be stated in terms of percent, however; for example, "85 percent of delayed calls should remain in queue no longer than three minutes."

Given the complete statistics of calls for service in the past, a computer program incorporating the standard equations for statistical probability can determine the probabilities of given peak loads. These are given in terms of means and deviations, or confidence limits. Confidence limits are expressed in such terms as: "The pattern of calls for service in the past indicates that if I provide twenty patrol units during the second tour, 90 percent of all calls will be assigned to patrol units without delay and 98 percent will be dispatched with a delay of no longer than ten minutes." If the command and control system makes use of a (formal or informal) priority structure, the computer can readily incorporate this into its calculations and indicate the probability of no delay or of a specified delay for dispatches in each priority category.

The calculations of probabilities and confidence limits are complex and tedious to do by hand, but are carried out quickly by computers. The necessary computation routines are standard modules available to any computer user and do not have to be programmed by each new user.

Determining How Many Patrol Units Are Needed

Once the workload in terms of calls for service has been established, it is possible to estimate how many patrol units will be required to meet that workload. The two essentially equivalent techniques developed some decades ago—hazard formulas and workload formulas—are reasonably straightforward, although the calculations can become tedious without a computer, and are widely used today. Their main drawbacks are that they can easily lead to strategies having the opposite of the desired effect, and the planner cannot tell in advance what impact the reallocations will have on patrol force performance measures such as workload balance, patrol frequency, and delays in responses to calls for service.

Another difficulty with the hazard formula is that the weights assigned to different factors (which are necessarily arbitrary) can bring about a situation in which assigning more weight to a given factor can result in assigning fewer units to a precinct with more of that factor. The workload formula has the drawback that it can at best equalize the workload of different precincts, without regard to any of the other measures such as response time, queuing delays, travel times, or others. It can also have the perverse effect of indicating a need for more units in an area that already has a disproportionately large share (if an area has more units, it is likely to have more arrests and more reports of crimes, which would lead to assigning still more units at the expense of other areas where crimes may be going unreported and arrests are few because there are too few patrol units).

There are now better methods, based on computer simulations, that can be used to determine how many patrol units are needed to meet specified performance standards or how a fixed number should be allocated to different areas on the basis of best overall performance. The recently developed allocation-by-performance methods are significantly better than the early hazard formulas because they give the planner a much better indication of changes in performance that he or she can expect as a result of reallocations.

We have already seen that the number of patrol units on duty cannot be derived by simply multiplying the average number of calls per hour times the average service time per call to find the total number of patrol-unit hours to be provided per hour. This would be satisfactory if calls for service could be scheduled, but in fact they arrive at random intervals, and the laws of statistics tell us that a certain percent of the time the rate will be half again as high as the average, another (smaller) percent of the time double the average, and so on. All random events such as the roll of dice, the drawing of cards, accidents, and calls for service follow the same laws of probability.

The number of patrol units needed, therefore, has to be stated in terms of probabilities: there should be enough units in a given geographical area so that calls for service can be assigned to an available patrol unit without delay a certain percent of the time, or with not more than a specified delay a certain percent of the time.

There are existing computer models that can be used to determine required numbers of units in accordance with specified performance measures.[1] The most recent of these is PCAM (Patrol Car Allocation Model), developed by New York City–The Rand Institute. It incorporates most of the features of previous programs, but does not estimate call rates and service times itself.

PCAM calculates performance measures according to the principles of statistical probability. For each geographical area, the user provides the following input information:

- Call rates and service times by hour of the day and day of the week and by up to three priority levels.
- Area to be served, in square miles.
- Street miles in the area.
- Response speed and patrol speed of patrol units.
- Crime rates.
- Data indicating what fraction of a patrol unit's time is spent, on the average, on activities other than patrol or responding to calls for service.

From this data, PCAM will estimate all of the following performance measures if the total number of units on duty is known:

- Average number of units available (i.e., the number not responding to calls for service or not available because of other activities).
- Frequency of preventive patrol.
- Average travel time to incidents.
- Probability that a call will be delayed in queue.
- Average waiting time in queue for calls of each priority level.
- Average total response time.

PCAM can be used in either a batch mode (the program, with its input data, is run through the computer, which prints out the results) or in an interactive mode (the user sits at a console with a display screen, calls up the program, and enters the input data in response to requests for it displayed on the screen; the output parameters are then displayed on the screen). It operates by having the user specify some allocation of units to geographical areas and telling him the effect this allocation will have on the performance measures listed in the output. It can also determine the minimum number of units needed to meet any standard of performance specified in terms of these measures.

Designing Patrol Sectors or Beats

Previously established sector boundaries can easily be moved if there is reason to think that such changes would result in improvement such as:

- More equal workload balance among patrol units.
- Better response time average for the precinct or for a given sector.
- Fewer dispatches of patrol units outside their beats.
- Improved administration through consolidation (or splitting) of beats or precincts.

Extensive work has been done on the development of computer models that can be used to analyze different beat or sector designs to determine how these different designs would affect certain selected performance measures.[2] The performance measures most likely to be affected by redesign of patrol unit beats are the workload balance among patrol units, response time, and fraction of dispatches that take a patrol unit out of its home beat mentioned above, as well as average travel time for all the beats in a precinct taken together. Another factor that can be influenced by beat design, but which is not usually taken as a measure of performance, is reasonably equal access to police service in the different parts of a precinct. Response times to some areas should not consistently be significantly longer or shorter than the average for the precinct as a whole.

The work that has been done on patrol beat design has brought out some general relationships that appear to be consistent and that are useful starting points for any exercise in beat design. These can be stated as useful rules of thumb, and are summarized in the following paragraphs.

Beat area and in-beat travel time.   In general, it has been shown that the travel time average within any area, including a beat, is proportional to the square foot of the area; thus a sector twice as big as another will have travel times only 1.4 times as great. What this means in practical terms is that travel times are unlikely to vary appreciably among beats as long as they are roughly similar in area. It also means that there is a built-in conflict between workload balance and travel times in cases where some sectors have a high population density and others have a low population density. If beats are designed so as to equalize workloads, those in low-population-density areas will be much larger and have longer travel times. If they are designed to have roughly equal areas in order to make travel times equal, the high-population-density beats will have a much higher workload than the low-density beats.

Beat shape.   Within the constraints of existing barriers, the beat designer will want to provide good police accessibility to every point in the beat for the assigned patrol unit and, to the extent possible, for units from other beats. This usually dictates a fairly "compact" shape, in which the long dimension is not more than twice the wide dimension. Other considerations, such as one-way streets or major arteries, may lead to exceptions to this rule of thumb. If a planner is concerned with the worst possible situation, he or she will want to determine the longest possible travel time within the beat and use that as an element in his or her best design.

Travel speeds. Travel speeds may differ in different directions; a clear case is that of Manhattan in New York, where travel in the north-south direction is much faster than in the east-west (crosstown) direction. In such cases the beats may be designed longer in the faster direction of travel in order to equalize travel times in the various directions within the beat.

Fraction of out-of-beat dispatches. Both experience and computer models indicate that dispatches in which the patrol unit assigned is not the one in whose beat the incident is located become an increasing fraction as the workload of the precinct increases. A rule of thumb is that the fraction of out-of-beat dispatches is very nearly the same as the "busy time" fraction of the patrol units. That is, under light load conditions the patrol units may be busy answering calls for service only 15 percent of the time, and about 15 percent of the dispatches will require a unit to leave its beat because the "normal" patrol unit is already busy on a call for service. When the load increases to 50 percent busy time, 50 percent of the dispatches will take a unit out of its beat. When the system is saturated to the point where significant numbers of calls are held in queue, the fraction of out-of-beat dispatches drops to slightly less than the workload or busy time fraction.

Patrol unit workload versus beat workload. Since patrol units spend a considerable amount of their time answering calls outside of their beats, the workload of a patrol unit is not necessarily the same as the workload of its beat. The actual relationships are quite complicated, and can best be handled in a computer model, but in the design of patrol beats it should not be assumed that, for example, "If beat A generates twice the workload of beat B, then patrol unit A works twice as hard as patrol unit B." And a design that equalizes beat workloads will not necessarily equalize patrol unit workloads.

The burden of central location. A patrol unit in a beat that is centrally located in its precinct will be a frequent candidate for out-of-beat dispatches because it will be the nearest unit in more than half of the dispatches to the ring of beats surrounding it (if the assigned unit is not available). On the other hand, a patrol unit in a beat on the outer perimeter of the precinct will seldom be a good choice for out-of-beat dispatches. This is called the "burden of central location." About all the beat designer can do is to design his or her centrally located beats with a less-than-average call for service volume and outlying beats with higher-than-average call for service volume. This, however, will create another problem: the higher the workload of outlying beats, the longer the average travel times for patrol units dispatched to those beats from others.

Analyzing Different Dispatch Strategies

Once the rates of calls for service have been predicted, the number of patrol units per precinct determined, and the boundaries of individual beats defined, it is possible to put all these results together into a computer simulation of the complete precinct patrol force. For maximum usefulness, such a simulation should include the command and control center operations such as receipt of calls by complaint board operators, messages between dispatchers and patrol units, and the dispatching operation itself. In this way it is possible to evaluate not only the effects of different dispatching strategies, but also the loading on the radio channels and the queuing delays at all points in the system from complaint board operators to dispatcher and patrol unit (which may experience a delay in gaining access to the radio channel).

The performance measurement that is affected by all the links in the command and control chain is response time, as measured from the receipt of a call at the complaint board to the arrival of a unit at the scene of the incident. Figure 10.2 shows graphically all the elements that enter into police response time; these can be affected by call rate, number of complaint board operators, number of dispatchers, dispatching procedures (which are usually accelerated by computer-aided dispatch), communication channel availability, patrol unit availability, and travel time.

Construction of a simulation, whether of the complete command and control system or only of the portions necessary for patrol force allocation studies, is not difficult with the special simulation languages (such as GPSS) that are widely available.

Some elements of dispatching strategy that can be evaluated with such a simulation as to their effects on specific quantitative performance measures are:

- Number of patrol units dispatched to various types of incidents.
- Selection of a patrol unit for dispatch, primarily on the basis of geographical considerations.

Figure 10.2 *Police emergency response system: timed sequence of activities*

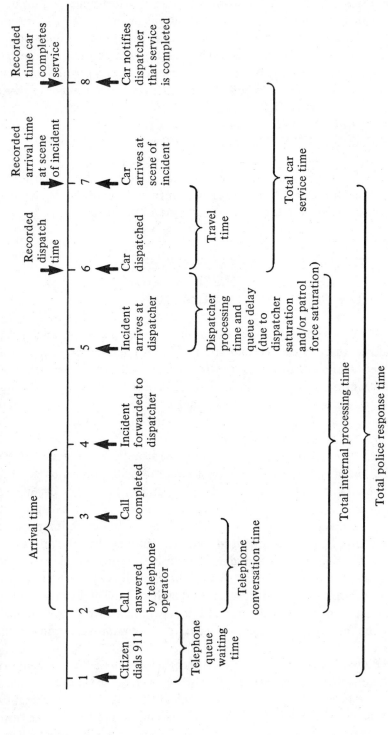

- Priority structure – how many levels of priority are required, the rules for dispatching calls of different priority, and the response times to be expected for each priority level during busy periods.
- Queuing policy, determining when a given call will be placed in a queue (when the individual dispatcher's units are all busy, when all units are busy, when all but some specified number of reserve units are busy, when the call is of a lower priority, etc.).
- Dynamic changes in the calls for service rates.
- Communications channel limitations.

Simulation techniques offer much greater insight into the the physical operation of patrol fleets, and are easier for the planner to understand and work with, than the more complex analytical methods.

DEVELOPING NEW METHODS FOR PATROL PERSONNEL DISTRIBUTION THROUGH TOTAL PARTICIPATION

In order for any police department to develop the proper strength of the patrol force, there must be total participation by police officers at all levels, as well as technological assistance. The most effective policies, tactics, and distributions according to time and location of patrol forces will be found through continued experimentation and research. As each new method is developed, an exact evaluation must be made to determine the value for broad use by all police departments.

It is obvious to any patrol administrator that the most effective distribution of the patrol force is not equal distribution on three shifts. Proportionate need is the basis for distribution by time of day, day of week, and location. A system of weighting and calls for service has been presented in which each department modifies the procedure to match its individual needs. Emphasis must be given to good reporting so that the appropriate data are collected, analyzed, and used accurately. The total plan must consider the assignment availability factor, the possibility of overlapping shifts where necessary, and the formulas for distribution. The formula selected should be based on the objectives of the department, which should be decided upon mutually by the chief executive, the community, and the chief of police.

All methods of patrol resource allocation and distribution emphasize the fundamental need for accurate reporting of crime so that data collected can be used to reveal information of past conditions as well as predict future conditions on which the allocation and distribution of manpower can be based. The prediction method is preferred by some researchers to the hazard and weighted workload methods because they feel that these two methods do not take into account interaction among factors; they do not focus upon any single factor; they do not reflect meaningful measures of effectiveness to operational policy; and they are based upon past events.

Phoenix, Arizona, uses three constructive innovations. Patrol personnel distribution is based on (1) predicted calls rather than calls actually experienced in the past; (2) elapsed time rather than just volume of calls; and (3) allocation simultaneously by day, shift, and district rather than by district alone. Preventive aspects of patrol are not addressed, but preliminary reports from Kansas City, Missouri question the value of preventive patrol.

St. Louis, Missouri uses a method in which demand for police service is predicted by hour and geographical area. A technique is then used to estimate the number of patrol cars needed to immediately answer, without dispatching delay, 85 percent of the predicted incoming calls for service in each geographical area by day and four-hour time periods. The remainder of the patrol force is assigned to preventive patrol. This method is limited in that role criterion used in the technique to determine the required number of response cars (i.e., the split of the patrol force into response and preventive patrol units) does not take into account the fraction of calls that cannot be answered immediately by a response car. Requirements for preventive patrol are not explicitly considered when assigning cars, nor is the question of the relative value of a car on response and on preventive assignments addressed.

Experiments such as those conducted in Kansas City, St. Louis, and Phoenix should continue at a greater rate. There is a very real need to know if the methods of patrol deployment now being used are the most effective. New criteria upon which evaluation of patrol distribution can be based are being developed. Reported crime versus unreported crime, victimization rates, victimization probability, and simulation of patrol operations by a computer (now in progress at the Massachusetts Institute of Technology) are only part of a group of terms now being used in determining patrol deployment.

In a report prepared for the Department of Housing and Urban Development by the Rand Corporation in 1971, authors Sorrel Wildhorn and James S. Kakalik recommended that research and experimentation be undertaken:

> (1) to identify the relationship between police preventive patrol activity and crime prevention, deterrence, and on-scene criminal apprehension; (2) to identify the quantitative and qualitative relationships between speed and type of police response, on the one hand, and crime rate, deterrence of crime, probability of on-scene apprehension, availability of witnesses, and the public's satisfaction with police

patrol services on the other hand; (3) to predict crime and the volume of calls for police services, so that police can be recruited and deployed based on more accurate knowledge of the need for police service in each geographic area and time period; (4) that improved methods for deploying patrol manpower be tested experimentally, modified if indicated by test results, and implemented.[3]

The authors are engineers and scientists in operations research, applying their talents to police problems. This type of total participation is necessary to deploy our patrol forces at the right place and time to attain maximum effectiveness.

Police commanders who distribute the personnel of the patrol force in proportion to need have a ready answer to groups who exert pressure for special assignment of officers to specific areas. Proper distribution within an open police agency allows patrol leaders to present deployment practices to all citizens of the community honestly and professionally. Demands for increased patrol coverage in areas that do not show the need can be responded to with accurate data and pictorial displays. When citizens are allowed to examine police deployment practices and professional procedures are obvious, their confidence in the department is enhanced, their fear of crime in the community is lessened, and their support is more likely to be forthcoming. Patrol administrators who use the personnel distribution process effectively, make all patrol personnel aware of its goals, and allow participation in the decisions, increase their ability to accomplish the leadership responsibility: "stimulate motivation of the patrol force to achieve the objective."

> The success of a patrol deployment system depends directly upon the support afforded by all personnel involved in the program. The active participation and willing cooperation of all personnel are greatly enhanced if representatives of all levels within the agency are included in the planning and implementation of the system.
>
> Procedures for the implementation and ongoing operation of the system should be established and distributed in the form of agency directives from the police chief executive. These directives should provide procedural guidelines and detailed information on the need for an adequate and accurate deployment data base, the purpose of proportional need distribution of patrol personnel, and the objectives and goals of the deployment system.
>
> Procedures should include periodic deployment-system evaluation based on timely information derived from an analysis of current patrol deployment data. Personnel allocations to geographic divisions or precincts in decentralized agencies should be evaluated and appropriately revised at least yearly. Shift, day of week, beat configurations, and personnel complements should be evaluated and appropriately revised at least quarterly.

Appropriate training programs should be established for all personnel involved in the system. The training should be tailored to the needs of personnel responsible for the various facets of the system, including the reporting, collection, and analysis of deployment data, and the use, evaluation, and revision of the deployment system.

Provisions to insure the adequacy of deployment data and to facilitate the use of the data in allocating personnel should include the development of new forms and source documents, or the revision of existing reports, to accommodate the required information. Data source documents should be subject to supervisory review and approval to enhance the accuracy of the data base.[4]

THE WILMINGTON SPLIT-FORCE EXPERIMENT[5]

Yet another approach to the utilization of police resources was tested in Wilmington, Delaware. The concept of split force, which involves separating the preventive patrol and call-for-service response functions of the patrol force, was first tried in St. Louis in 1966 and in Chicago in 1971. An LEAA-funded test of the split-force approach was conducted in Wilmington in 1975.

The results of this study showed that split-force patrol does increase the efficiency of the patrol force in both the call-for-service response function and the preventive patrol function. This improvement was achieved without decreased effectiveness on the part of the patrol force. Thus, this program was able to demonstrate the feasibility of split-force patrol as a cost-effective alternative to traditional patrol strategies.

Another interesting result from this study was in the area of response time, where it was *again* found that response time had no effect on citizen satisfaction. In addition to this, a limited number of citizens were formally informed that a response delay would occur, and 45 percent of these citizens responded that they "couldn't care less." Hence, the Wilmington study supports the contention that police response time is *not* an important factor contributing to citizen satisfaction with the police.

As of 1981, the Wilmington, Delaware Police Department has abandoned the split-force or structured concept. They have returned to the traditional method and resolve the crime officer assignment of split force by moving regular shift officers into especially troubled crime areas.

NOTES

1. Jan M. Chaiken and Peter Dormont, *Patrol Car Allocation Model*, R. 1786/1 (*Executive Summary*), R-1786/2 (*User's Manual*), R.1786/3 (*Program Description*) (Santa Monica, Calif.: The Rand Corporation, 1975).

2. Richard C. Larson, *Hypercube Queuing Model*, R-1688/2-HUD, (*User's Manual*) (The Rand Corporation, 1975); Jan M. Chaiken, *Hypercube Queuing Model*, R-1688/1-HUD (*Exeuctive Summary*) (Santa Monica, Calif.: The Rand Corporation, 1975).
3. James S. Kakalik and Sorrel Wildhorn, *Aids to Decisionmaking in Patrol*, a report prepared for the Department of Housing and Urban Development, Rand Corporation. An overview of study findings by the authors was reported in *Police* (February 1972): 41–44.
4. National Advisory Commission on Criminal Justice Standards and Goals, *Report on Police* (Washington, D.C.: U.S. Government Printing Office, 1972), p. 204.
5. James M. Tien, James W. Simon, and Richard C. Larson, *An Alternative Approach to Police Patrol; The Wilmington Split-Force Experiment* (Cambridge, Mass.: Public Systems Evaluation, Inc., 1977).

Change and the Patrol Administrator

New horizons for patrol and patrol leaders require a liberal education as part of the cultural endowment necessary to manage change and conflict. Whatever the horizons, people are the prime ingredient, and flexibility and adaptability the prime attributes. The patrol officer must be flexible in performance. The organization needs flexibility to allow performance by all employees. The patrol leader must deal with change, change strategy or techniques, change models, change implementation, resistance to change, and change agents. Most likely, the patrol officer will be a change agent. Questions concerning, for instance, the extent to which women in patrol will affect the complexity of tasks or personnel distribution or the assignment of women in patrol to handle the calls for service will surface. Additionally, the interaction between the patrol force and the community calls for understanding, mutual awareness, and careful analysis of change strategy. Relationships between patrol leaders and employee organizations, and between patrol leaders and leaders of other units within the police departments, must be positive so that conflict does not disrupt goal achievement.

The urban patrol leader must continue to improve his or her ability to relate to confrontations, because the situations that require police intervention will not change: domestic problems, assaults, homicides, robberies. These incidents will always need effective and understanding response. Decision-making will be the center of administration, and operational police ability, judgment, and discretion highlighted in the daily execution of the patrol force.

The good patrol administrator will realize the importance of personnel with those qualities that enable them to be good police officers. Education is an asset but not a panacea. Once hired, personnel possessing the right qualities should be trained to perform professionally those tasks assigned to the patrol force. If tasks are presented realistically and officers are required to resolve the tasks using simulated exercises, excellent performance can result. After six months in the field, officers should return to the police academy to evaluate what was taught, the procedures presented, and the difference between the academy and the field.

As a manager of conflict, the patrol administrator has to be a problem solver. The ability to influence people is synonymous with power in many respects, and a real attribute to any individual who must resolve conflict. In the management by objectives approach to patrol administration, knowledge of traditional organization and how to make it flexible in order to achieve goals is essential. The patrol administrator who develops his ability to think is like a sponge in his thirst for knowledge, reading and retaining everything available that is written about patrol. He will use his talent to see the forest rather than the trees. The criminal justice arena needs coordination and cooperation from all participants. This expanding role of the patrol leader should save the chief of police as much work as possible so that he may use his time in resolving problems and doing those things (usually external) that no one else has the position or authority to do. The patrol function has been elevated to the position it deserves in a police department. Now enlightened, planning patrol leaders must produce the positive change and superior performance expected by the citizens of our country.

CHANGE

Patrol administrators must develop an ability to control the rate and direction of change in our society as it applies to the patrol force. Knowledge of current issues, politics, special interest groups, legal questions, and employee organization relationships should enhance this ability. For example, the national unions are highlighting the humanistic aspect of employer and employee relations. The principle of considering workers as the individuals they are, rather than as machines or numbers, has been the central issue of many negotiations. The idea of control of one's own destiny is taking its place as a real part of the negotiating process. Management is being required to consider the human side of the worker in planning and implementing work organization and production. Self-actualization is becoming a reality. For example, auto workers, instead of placing a siren into position every ten seconds, now participate in building a total part of a particular car so that they can see actual results from their efforts.

Team policing has evolved into the generalist/specialist concept with a change in tasks for each member. The approach of using the total talent of each participant in producing the police function is increasingly important in police departments around the country. The management by objectives approach to patrol administration allows the personnel responsible for achieving the goals to participate in setting the goals. This has become a reality in more and more police departments. When management takes this initiative in sharing power, there is a greater possibility of controlling the rate and direction of change for the organization.

The patrol administrator cannot look upon change as a series of one-time events, but rather as a continuing part of the crisis-oriented nature of the job. Consequently, he/she must be trained to meet each crisis with effective decisions based upon accumulated knowledge. This knowledge should consist of a broad background in political science, history, sociology, philosophy, psychology, mathematics, planning, management, urban studies, labor relations, social psychology, law, and experience. It should also include being flexible, being able to adapt to changing situations with the appropriate decisive response. The patrol administrator must know how to evaluate situations and programs for their effectiveness. This directly relates to goal setting and changing goals after evaluation. Cooperation between patrol leaders and the academic and scientific community is necessary in order to determine the meaning of crime prevention and apprehension, as well as to understand how different patrol techniques affect these goals. There should never be change just for the sake of change, but willingness to change as appropriate is essential to avoid management failure.

Change must be related to the individual organization. Patrol administrators within each department should reflect on the part they must play in the change in attitude, values, behavior, policies, and structure of the total police organization. Change should be tailor-made for the individual department. Patrol must be able to work with the resources available in order to achieve the goals assigned to it. The ability to communicate will continue to be an important factor for the patrol leader because of the need to disseminate information. Patrol officers will continue to use discretion, but management responsibility will be to provide information in sufficient amounts so that decisions made at the level of execution will be improved as a result of accurate, timely information.

History is full of examples of external forces causing police agencies to change. These changes (especially court decisions) have been largely for the better. One of the qualities for the police administrator mentioned in the American Bar Association's "Standards Relating to the Urban Police Function" is "sensitivity to policing in a democratic society." The President's Commission on Law Enforcement and Administration of Justice, through its report *The Police,* has had a profound effect on law enforcement and the total criminal justice system. As a result of this report, the

Omnibus Crime Control Bill, or the Safe Streets Act of 1968, has caused a great move forward in the administration of criminal justice. These examples indicate that law enforcement has been the target, rather than the initiator, of change.

One realistic method of having a voice in change decisions is to be the initiator of change. In order to become an initiator of change, it will be necessary for law enforcement to become more sophisticated as an entity in its relationship to other institutions and agencies within and without the criminal justice system. It will also be necessary to teach the formal planning process to all members of patrol to enhance the total participation in and understanding of organizational goals and assist in paralleling goals of the individual and the organization. Then, the entire patrol force will be working together to achieve the objective. As the first step of planning is recognition of need, so the first step in change must be to recognize the need to develop the patrol force in a manner that makes it capable of change. This awareness regarding change capability and implementation includes a sense of timing. The patrol administrator should plan the implementation of the planning process into all levels of the patrol force so that an organized, coordinated effort will result.

Whisenand and Ferguson express this quite clearly: "Planning is the process by which the police department adapts its resources to changing environmental forces and achives its goals. It is a highly dynamic function and must be carried out effectively so as to provide a solid foundation for the remaining managerial activities."[1] This is reinforced by Blumenthal: "The planning function in the police organization can be considered as an integrated decision system which established the framework for the activities of the organization."[2] Whisenand and Ferguson go on to say, "It is the responsibility of management planning to plan an integrated planning system that will enhance organizational performance. In other words, planning for planning."[3] Planning must not be done in a vacuum.

Types of Change

Timothy Costello, in his analysis of change in municipal government, lists the following categories of change:

1. *Planned change.* Structural reorganization is undertaken with assistance of outside consultants; operating units are regrouped and integrated according to a carefully devised plan.
2. *Confluence of forces.* A variety of interest groups and forces within the community combine to bring situations to a head and move things in the direction of change. An example is the combination of forces that brought about school decentralization.

3. *Event-dominated change.* Changes that are unplanned and unanticipated occur through a sequence of events. Each event is linked to past and future events in a chain-like fashion with the outcome being a result of the various events leading up to it.
4. *Accidental innovation.* A significant amount of innovation and change comes about by accident. Methods developed to deal with one problem are found useful for dealing with others, and new ideas arise unexpectedly.
5. *External intervention.* Outside groups such as legislative bodies or administrative agencies impose change upon the organization externally through funds, regulations, etc. In a similar fashion, interest groups, professional or scientific experts, and others intervene from the outside with formally or informally imposed change.[4]

Only the first type of change, planned change, comes about largely because of prior analysis and problem solving by managers. Planned change as described by Costello may be reactive to problems or conditions, and it may well be imposed through the use of authority. There may be some elements of planned efforts in the second and third categories (confluence of forces and event-dominated change), but these and the last two (accidental innovation and external intervention) call for significant reactive responses on the part of the organization and require adaptation to— rather than development of—change.

CHANGE STRATEGY

In the management by objectives approach to patrol administration, it will be necessary to innovate, because of the fact that additional resources, particularly manpower, cannot be counted on. Additionally, the hard-earned tax dollar should be spent efficiently and economically; therefore, all needs for additional resources should be justified in depth. This will cause broad exploration about what procedures are presently used and what alternate procedures may be used to accomplish the same goals with existing resources. Most police departments have some form of research and development unit. (The author recommends that this unit include the formal change agent of the department.) *Research* is the detailed process by which new knowledge may be gained and precipitate change. *Development* is the next stage of implementation. *Innovation* is a part of development in which a new device or idea is introduced to a number of people. It is only at the stage of development and innovation that most operating managers become involved with changing situations.[5]

In developing a change strategy, the patrol administrator first must consider the personnel of the patrol force. The degree of sophistication, status of recruit and in-service training, extent of formal education, executive development programs, existing atmosphere regarding participatory management concepts, and conditions of the personnel after completion will affect this aspect of the strategy.

Second, the police agency as a whole and the change itself must be evaluated before the strategy may be implemented.

Third, the change should begin at the point where a problem has been identified so that positive results from the change will be obvious. For example, if the leader wishes to change the method of officer reporting—that is, to change from having the officer drive to the police facility to write his report to having him write his report in the field so that he does not leave his patrol area—then he or she should identify a situation in which an apprehension could have been made if the officer had been on his patrol beat, not in the police facility. Additionally, the leader can emphasize that the procedure is obviously more economical, that routine contact with the supervisor will enhance training, and errors in report writing will be corrected immediately, decreasing the potential of the officer staying behind after shift change to correct the report.

Fourth, the patrol leader should include the formal and informal organization and the personnel who will be affected by the change in the diagnosis, data collecting, formulating, goal setting and total planning of the change. Using the example above, the better approach to change would be to use a pilot district, shift, or sector so that an evaluation of the change could be made. Making a total change rather than a limited one may cause confusion and result in a negative attitude about the change. Potential for success of the selected area is important. If success is attained in the pilot area, then the results can be used to show the potential for total change. Then, each stage of implementation can be refined, making it easier to conclude each subsequent stage successfully.

CHANGE MODELS

Numerous specific change models are pertinent to law enforcement. Each model deals with some aspect of the process of change. The following review will help the patrol administrator in analyzing the approaches to change.

1 Modification Model for Dealing with Changes in Knowledge and Information

For managers of organizations to become professional, they must learn to use and modify the knowledge of others. But the knowledge has to be applied in the manager's world rather than in the scientific or academic world.[6]

The orientation of the manager is toward action, and his or her payoff comes in results and problem solving. This model views knowledge and the scientific world in a way that does not require polarization. The manager is not forced to have his head in the clouds or his hands in the grease. He modifies the one world to fit the other.[7]

2 Planned Change Models

There is concentration on the deliberate and collaborative idea of planned change.[8] For change to be deliberate, there must be an effort by some party or parties called *change agents* to affect the client system. The client system is usually the person or unit in need of and desiring the change.[9]

The Lippitt-Watson-Westley model focuses on the relationships between a change agent and client system and postulates the following stages:

1. The development of a need for change
2. The establishment of a change relationship
3. The clarification or diagnosis of the client system's problems
4. The examination of alternative routes and goals; establishing goals and intentions of action
5. The transformation of intentions into actual change efforts
6. The generalization and stabilization of change
7. Achieving a terminal relationship[10]

Similarly, the National Training Laboratories postulates a model of planned change that has eight phases:

1. Diagnosis of the problem of the client system
2. Assessment of the motivation and capacity of the client system to change itself
3. Assessment of the motivation and resources of the change agent
4. Establishing and maintaining a working relationship with the client system
5. Choosing the appropriate role
6. Selecting appropriate change objectives and targets
7. Provide support and encouragement for change behavior
8. Termination (or new continuity) of helping relationships[11]

Buchanan puts forth a nine-step process model of planned change:

1. Clarify or develop the client's motivation to change
2. Assess the change agent's potential helpfulness

3. Establish effective relations between the change agent and the client system
4. Clarify or diagnose the client system's problems
5. Establish instrumental objectives for change
6. Formulate plans for change
7. Carry out plans for change
8. Generalize and stabilize changes
9. Institutionalize planned development or self-renewal[12]

No matter how it is expressed, the first step in planning is the recognition of need for change. For example, if the housing authority of a community can be shown that architectural design can help reduce crime, the need for change will be obvious. In *Defensible Space,* Oscar Newman states that "an architect, armed with some understanding of the structure of criminal encounter, can simply avoid providing the space which supports it."[13]

Arnold Judson, in *A Manager's Guide to Making Changes,* discusses another planned change model: how people are affected and respond to changes and why their resistance is primarily based upon attitudes.[14]

Judson's approach is very close to the formal planning process, except for the inclusion of a communication stage that is a key aspect in change. The innovator or change agent must understand the value of the ability to communicate and that attitudes are directly affected by the communicative ability.

Social psychologist Kurt Lewin suggests an analysis model for change. He argues that in any change situation, the pressures for and against the change may be viewed as a field of opposing forces. One set of forces moves the situation in the direction of the anticipated change. These forces are called driving forces. The opposite set of forces tending to restrain or repress the situation from moving in the direction of the anticipated changes are called restraining forces. (See Figure 11.1.) These two sets of forces working against each other tend to create a dynamic equilibrium called a *quasi-stationary equilibrium,* that is, "a balance that can be distributed at any moment by altering either the driving or restraining forces which keep a situation as it is."[15]

The use of force field analysis can be illustrated as follows: A person has been told that he is overweight and should go on a diet. There are several driving and restraining forces maintaining the situation as is. The imbalance must be created so that change can take place in the direction desired. Some possible driving forces at work may be: advice of physician, the fact that he would feel less tired, and improved personal appearance. Some possible restraining forces might be: giving up a favorite dessert, altered clothing, and lack of personal discipline.

Another example is the problem of getting patrol and detectives to collaborate more effectively. Some driving forces toward more effective collaboration might be:

Figure 11.1 *Force field analysis by driving and restraining forces*

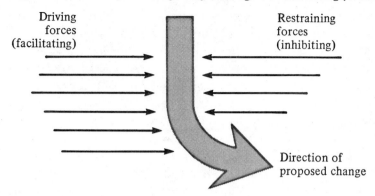

1. Directors of the two departments have expressed desire for better collaboration.
2. Projects get slowed down when these departments do not collaborate well.
3. Chief executive of organization has requested better collaboration among units.
4. Awareness of the problem exists on the part of both groups.

Some of the restraining forces might be:

1. There is a long history of rivalry between the two departments.
2. Professional jealousy exists among some employees of the two departments.
3. Units are physically separated from each other.
4. Top management tends to look for one or the other department to blame when something goes wrong, causing buck-passing.
5. There are few organization provisions for departmental collaboration, i.e., no joint committees, no personnel to act as links between units, etc.
6. People in the organization lack skill in teamwork across units.

By analyzing and documenting a given change problem the manager can look quickly at what seem to be the major forces operating in the situation. It is often useful to check these perceptions against those of others who also have familiarity with the situation. After determining the forces it may also be useful to attach weights or values to the forces on both sides—that is, to decide which ones are strongest and most important. It is then possible to discuss ways of either increasing the strength or number of the forces for change or decreasing the number or strength of the resisting forces.

In the example above, it may well be that the long history of rivalry and professional jealousy will not be overcome to any extent by the administrative orders of the heads of the units. It may be necessary to take other measures. Alternatives might include a training workshop involving members of both departments, in which the feelings of rivalry and jealousy are addressed directly and explored and, hopefully, overcome; or a process of temporarily exchanging members across the two units so that each can gain understanding of the problems and dilemmas of the other unit.

It may be more effective to reduce the resisting forces than to attempt to increase the driving forces. This strategy, of course, runs counter to the usual approach. That is, we often try to overcome resistance by invoking more rules, administrative orders, and persuasive techniques instead of attempting to understand and deal with the causes. Simply increasing the strength of the driving forces seems sometimes to increase the amount of tension in the system and also to bring about the addition of still further restraining forces.

A study of these models will prepare the patrol administrator, no matter which model or combination of models he or she chooses. Simplistic attitudes toward change, assumptions that the problems of crime are caused by police inefficiency, or the idea that one type of police deployment is best for all departments are unsupportable. The enlightened management of change, coupled with flexibility of action and evaluations of change, will determine future ideas in patrol concepts and operations.

IMPLEMENTING CHANGE: THE CHANGE AGENT

The time has arrived for the patrol administrator to take his or her proper place in law enforcement. Opportunities abound for enlightened patrol leaders to experiment with new patrol approaches to achieve the objective. In order to implement change, the change agent must understand the meaning of power and be able to identify the decision-makers of government and his or her department: in other words, to identify those individuals who have the authority to make things happen internally and externally. It is difficult to induce change without some person taking the situation in hand, confronting it, and then acting as a catalyst to initiate the change. It is proposed that the patrol administrators of our country seriously consider being change agents. The willingness to change with the new demands of the position of patrol administrator will enhance the individual departments.

The patrol administrator cannot be alone in his or her role of change agent. He or she should select enlightened patrol leaders of his command to participate in being change agents. He/she should ask leaders of other units of the department to join in forming a task force to solve complex problems and generate cooperative ideas in developing procedures that would enhance the total ability of the department to achieve goals. This group could pave the way for participatory management concepts that would permeate the entire department. In some cases the patrol administrator and his contemporaries may be too busy. An alternate course of action could be to allow middle management to form the task force. The assignment of one middle manager from each unit to act as change agent for the respective units could produce a task force of change agents with a goal of total development of the department. This type of approach would direct change at three levels: (1) the individual, (2) the group, and (3) the department or system, whichever is appropriate.

Another approach at implementing change involves the research and planning unit of a department. With the emphasis on participatory management and the evolvement of the consideration of personnel in a department as individuals, the humanistic view, career development, and career-path concepts are primary considerations. Change agents and career development officers should be identified as a part of the research and planning units of police departments (see Figure 11.2).

One of the primary responsibilities of the change agent unit would be to determine the capability of the department to change. This is obviously a prerequisite to initiating change. Most police departments' awareness of the need for change and capability to plan and manage change is limited. Considerations involved in determining a department's capability to change are: need for change, individual conditions, and resolution of conflict over proposed change and its implementation. Premature, prompt, or unnecessarily delayed acceptance of change does not preclude consideration of other changes.

The change agents must also determine where change is desirable and necessary; accurately define problems; assess and utilize resources within and without the department; and innovate, adopt, or adapt solutions in an effective, efficient, and further change-inducing manner. One method that could help improve the change agents' impact on change in

Figure 11.2 *Research and development organization (including change agent and career development sections)*

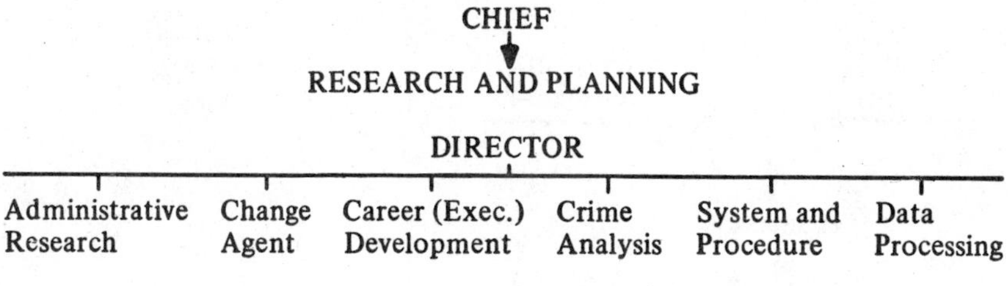

CHIEF

⬇

RESEARCH AND PLANNING

DIRECTOR

Administrative Research	Change Agent	Career (Exec.) Development	Crime Analysis	System and Procedure	Data Processing

the department would be to have them act as an animate suggestion box. The usual procedure for offering suggestions and new ideas is to have individuals write out their suggestions and put them in a suggestion box. The proposed method would identify the personnel who are acting as change agents to the department and replace the suggestion box procedure with a telephone call. This simplified procedure would of itself stimulate participation and elicit freedom of expression at all levels.

Change decision will cause conflict between competing interests, and these conflicts should be resolved before the final decisions or changes are made. Personnel should have a voice in change decisions before they are made. It is imperative that consultation take place with the people who will be affected by the change. The change agent, when implementing change, therefore should first and foremost communicate with the recipients of the change.

Niehoff emphasizes this communication by the innovator (change agent) and response to change by people with a diagram (see Figure 11.3). He discusses various aspects of communication:

- *Formal.* The transmission of information by means of formal group meetings, usually neighborhood councils and sometimes in classroom situations.
- *Personal.* The transmission of information by means of face-to-face interaction between the change agent and the recipients, usually in paired or small-group situations.
- *Audio-visual.* Methods of transmitting information regarding innovations by means of audio-visual devices such as printed materials, pictures, charts, loudspeakers, radio, television, and other mechanical aids that have been developed for influencing public opinion.
- *Demonstration.* The techniques of showing in a pragmatic fashion the advantage of a new idea or technique as a means of convincing the recipient to adopt it.

Figure 11.3

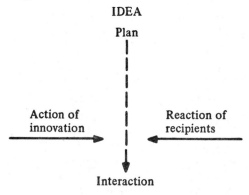

IDEA

Plan

Action of innovation

Reaction of recipients

Interaction

- *Feedback.* The response to the innovator regarding the proposed new practice.[16]

The goal of this communication is to bring about a willingness to accept the intended change. The five methods proposed by Niehoff should be used in combination to suit the need. Voluntary compliance can be accomplished if the change is understood and improvement of the organization and its members are the goals.

Obstacles to Change

If the patrol administrator is to implement change successfully, he or she must be aware of the many obstacles that he or she will confront. These will come from a variety of areas. Consideration should be given to the following:

1. *Political factors.* These involve conflict over goals and methodology. Political factors influencing change include: dependence, authority, power, city manager, city council, legislature, and employee organizations.
2. *Rate of change.* The rate of change must be controlled. Change may be good or bad; it is wrong to assume that all change is good. Change for the sake of change is wasteful. The suggested change may sometimes have to be slowed, for no other reason than to think out the situation more clearly. In some cases, a certain amount of change has to take place before its merits are clear enough so that a decision to continue or not can be made.
3. *The criminal justice system.* Change can be hindered simply because the intended change may be good for police, but bad for prosecution or corrections. Each change must be reflected upon with the total system in mind.
4. *Community organization.* The patrol administrator as well as the chief of police knows full well the power that can be wielded by community organizations. Texts on police administration instruct the potential chief how to use community power to initiate change. By the same token, a failure on the part of the patrol leader to include the community in planning and implementing change can result in a negative response and a failure of the intended change. For example, a patrol administrator may wish to patrol an area of high-incidence purse-snatch with a K-9 team on foot. If the residents of the community are not considered and informed, any unfortunate incident (such as a dog bite) may cause

a negative reaction from the community, which may then organize and force the discontinuance of the patrol. The patrol technique may be resulting in a decrease in purse snatching, but because the issue has changed all further potential improvement is lost.

5. *Crisis factor.* Patrol administration may begin to implement a change that primary evaluations indicate has the potential of excellent success, and then resources must be diverted because of riots, athletic contests, etc. Maintaining a constant application of resources to the change becomes difficult. Planning for such obstacles is most important.

6. *Financial support.* Even though the power may lie in different points depending on the situation, money is always necessary in implementing change and without it there is no change to any extent. This obstacle may be overcome, but it takes the highest administrative ability and personal diplomacy.

7. *Credibility.* Mutual trust must be developed between the line and staff members of the change team. Whenever change is implemented, a sincere reciprocal projection of support from both line and staff is necessary. Understanding the role of line and staff and the potential for conflict is important. Ways of alleviating the conflict can be developed so change implementation can be achieved.

8. *Acceptance of failure.* Every attempt at change has a certain amount of risk involved. Change agents should not delude themselves or others into thinking every change will result in success or is a "can't miss." Awareness of potential failure allows for realistic approaches, reexamination of methods, and self-renewal. Also, if the possibility of failure is accepted, failure will not preclude attempts at future changes.

9. *Decisiveness.* Risk is inherent in change. If effective change is to take place, the faint of heart or insecure should not be in an important position of change implementation. Indecision may well be considered negativism by many and cause the intended change to fail.

Leadership for Change

The effective change agent cannot forget that important trait of leadership, setting examples. If the patrol administrator is to be a change agent, he must be willing to change and to take steps to demonstrate his ability to do so. His ability to change should be shown to all both internally and externally. The initiation of participatory management programs would

Figure 11.4 *Change encounter*

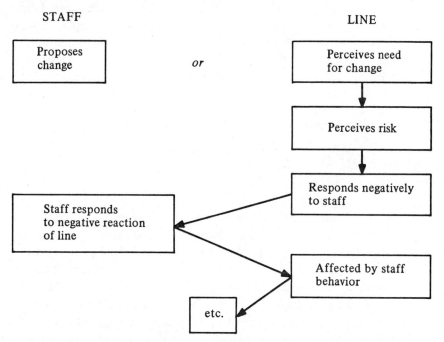

Source: From: Chauncey F. Bell and Donald B. Manson, "Mythology and the Management of Change" (Monograph presented at the Fourth Symposium, Science and Technology, 1972).

be an excellent method of demonstrating his ability to change (see Chapter 5, on the Patrol Planning Council). This team method of participatory management has by-products both for the patrol administrator as a change agent and for the implementation of change itself:

1. Voice for the personnel affected by change;
2. Broad input, which enhances the chance of success;
3. Improved validity and accuracy of information;
4. Improved communication process;
5. Expeditious feedback necessary for change in objectives (this self-renewal may or may not be necessary; however, the feedback is imperative);
6. Improved efficiency of the patrol force and the total police department. Relationships with other units are more compatible because of increased confidence and self-actualization of the members of patrol; and
7. A better understanding of the goals of the patrol force and expected performance by each member.

Patrol commanders everywhere are being cast as important figures in police departments. Seminars and workshops on patrol are being presented in many parts of the country in which leaders in patrol exchange ideas and techniques. A revolution is taking place in patrol, which should lead to improved strategies for management by objectives and achievement of goals. The untapped talent of the emerging patrol commander will be used, not to the detriment of anyone, but for the betterment of everyone in our country.

CHANGE: FROM THE BOTTOM TO THE TOP OF THE HIERARCHY

"How can I bring about change; I am only an officer (or sergeant)?" This question is asked many times. One thing is certain—attending a supervisory, management, or executive law enforcement school and returning with a know-it-all attitude is definitely not the best approach. Those officers who wish to be innovative and bring about change should first study power and authority in the organization. Power and authority come from the person and the hierarchical position. The big question to be resolved is, Why should the person in power change the status quo? What benefits will that person derive from the change? Will it make that person look better or work harder; will it possibly enhance the individual? These issues must be clearly thought out before the person at the bottom of the ladder begins to attempt change. Remember, if you truly want change, and the change is a good idea and will improve the organization if implemented, do not think you will always get the credit. If you are looking for credit you may be disappointed. Take a professional view: change to improve the profession is good no matter who gets the credit. Perseverance, smart work, and good interpersonal relations will bring the rewards and self-actualization for the professionally intended change by a professional police officer.

The change process from the bottom will be most successful if the scientific method is used. Therefore, the skills, knowledge, and abilities of the change officer should include: (1) the planning process (chapter on planning); (2) how to do a complete staff study; (3) the ability to communicate; (4) the ability to use flowcharts and other training aids; (5) understanding power and authority; (6) use of a systematic approach (input, output, process and outcome measures, costs, time, alternatives, solutions); (7) identifying the best strategy for approaching the individuals needed to assist in the change; (8) knowing how to accept a small but successful change rather than biting off too much, since a small success can lead to larger successes; (9) remaining in the adult ego state; (10) understanding the structure of your organization (organization chart, operational chart, and the difference); and (11) understanding the difference between conflict, collaboration, and cooperation to insure the use of these aspects of the change strategy.

The change process can be made easier by the sincere commitment demonstrated by the officer attempting change. In possessing the integrated knowledge of managing by objectives, planning, and change, a change officer will develop a persistent attitude which will assist in handling failure. Failure is only one stage in a complete change process; there will be another ballgame. By showing respect for other people and their thoughts, by being able to cope with frustration, by knowing how to collect and analyze accurate relevant data and how to present your case, and by being persistent, the officer at the bottom has a chance to bring about change. If the officer begins, but meets obstacles, reverts to the child ego state, becomes frustrated and disappointed, and does not persevere, then there probably is less chance that he or she will bring about change. It is difficult but not impossible for the professional police officer. Remember, do not suggest change only to have your supervisor ask why and you answer, "because." Do your homework! Explain why.

MAJOR ISSUES OF CHANGE

It would be naive to believe that any police leader has the power or the resources to control the rate and direction of change completely. However, by understanding the processes of change and its components, it is possible to make sure that change does not control the leader. In order to do this, it is suggested the leader learn about the dozen issues involved in change:

1. Realistic approaches to change through knowledge about restrictions on himself and his organization and methods to remove those restrictions as necessary.
2. Goals and priorities set for his department through equal partnership by himself, the chief executive, and the community. These goals and priorities must also be realistic.
3. Reactions to failure and criticism.
4. The process of lateral entry and the consequences this process may bring.
5. Pressure groups within the department and the community (goals, tactics, and techniques).
6. Presenting an open police agency. The leader must allow citizens to participate in policy and procedures. He can disseminate information about crime and its effect in totality and can cause citizens to come to the department and view patrol allocation,

deployment, and distribution. These honest and open methods should stimulate community support and cause the patrol force and the department to become an extension of the community. This extension can be very positive if the patrol leader communicates the goals and strategy of the force effectively. For example, "Let us show you how we are using our patrol force to protect you. We use a priority approach, and with help from the citizens we can do a more effective job." A high-crime area could be pointed out and an explanation given on how it was reduced: citizens agreed to report for work within a given hour and police were specifically assigned to the area for that hour. Result: citizen participation in crime prevention. Change? It sure is, and a good one. There will be no great impact on crime without citizen participation.

7. Career paths—the identification of individuals who have the potential to be leaders and the design of a plan to develop known human resources. This change can make possible in the future police departments in which the total command structure is qualified as administrators. There will be a collegiality of command. Each command officer of future police agencies will have enough responsibility, authority, and accountability to self-actualize. Additionally, the interchange of department heads and deputies of governmental agencies can produce a total effort against crime. Does the sanitation department have an effect on crime? Does the health department? Does the department of public works? Do the officials of each ever converse with one another? If so, has crime and the impact each agency can have upon it ever been the topic of discussion? Efficiency and economy in government can be improved if middle and upper management are allowed to exchange positions along with the knowledge they possess.

8. The fact that it is the nature of law enforcement to be involved in change and crises. Society changes. Society is people. People are the clients of police. Therefore, change is the client of police. This fact should cry out to police departments asking for change from the rigid structure to the fluid-flexible organization that: cuts red tape; allows for freedom of expression and thought; teaches that some issues cannot be answered by yes or no, right or wrong, good or bad; provides information to all personnel in direct proportion to their decision-making needs (if patrol officers are going to use discretion and alternatives, they need the information that will make the decisions effective and efficient); and accentuates the individuality of members of the department.

9. Other departments throughout the country and their approach to change and organizational development. New concepts are emerging with regard to structure and personnel. Equipment is not the only thing that needs to be changed in the police agencies of our country. The Kansas City, Missouri Police Department is experimenting with proactive, reactive patrol, peer-group management, and change in organizational form to provide the necessary services. One form is called ARGUS (Area Responsibility Giving Unified Service). The Dayton, Ohio Police Department has been experimenting with a centralized-decentralized organization mode.

10. Ways of improving communications. One has been mentioned (Patrol Planning Council). Other methods of improving the communication process are the team-policing concept; hiring communication experts to fromulate programs to increase open communication; better equipment (closed-circuit television, audiovisual tape); shortening the chain of command; career development; and well-defined and planned departmental conferences.

11. The amount of personal attention the leader must commit to the implementation of change and its follow-up evaluation in order to make the change meaningful.

12. The climate of the organization with regard to change. What are the attitudes of the men and women about change? Do they like the status quo? Are they proud of the department, or do they think the department is not progressive and rates lower than others of the same size and population? Has change come easily in the past, or has resistance been large and organized? Can participation of the persons involved in the change improve chances of success? Many questions need to be answered by the patrol administrator/change agent before he or she implements change if success is to be achieved.

All of the dozen are important, but number twelve should be considered first. The diagnosis of the personnel attitude toward change is essential, because the results will determine the approach and procedure for the change. Those persons selected to be change agents must be aware of the existing conditions and attitudes toward change. For example, if the department were found to have a negative attitude toward change, the change agents would have to be leaders who were respected, had credibility, and an ability to communicate. There would have to be a selling job done in order to create an atmosphere in which the change could take place. If the wrong person is selected for change agent, the program is doomed to failure before it even starts.

RESISTANCE TO CHANGE

The folklore of management holds that employees are naturally negative toward change – any change – and may generally be expected to resist it. Thus the manager, according to this myth, must use persuasion, coercion, and patience to overcome resistance. But, in reality, this is not always the case.

Research evidence about employee attitudes toward change indicates that, under some circumstances, some proportion of the employees in a given situation will resist certain kinds of change introduced in certain ways. Under other circumstances there will be no resistance. In other words, employee response to change depends on a variety of factors, including: (1) the characteristics of the employee; (2) the climate or general feelings in the organization in which the change is taking place; (3) the nature and extent of the change; and (4) the methodology used to implement the change. Fortunately, enough is known about resistance factors to provide some assistance to the manager who must grapple with change situations. Some of these resistance factors involve:

Threat to job, wages, and security. It is sometimes assumed that the major threat involved in change, especially technological or structural change, is economic. Since workers are often thought of as primarily economic creatures it is natural to assume that economic concerns are the major source of fears of change. However, although economic factors may be important in some situations, it would be a mistake to assume that they are always at the bottom of resistance to change.

Coping with new situations. Fear of being unable to adapt to new situations may account for resistance to change. It has been found that workers who are felt to be most competent (by themselves and others) and who have positive past experiences with change are likely to be least resistant. Fear of failing may stem from a variety of real or imagined problems.

Status. Changes may be perceived by employees as threats to their status. They may fear that they will be unable to adapt to the new way of doing things and will be seen by others as inferior. Or the initiation of a change may be taken as a signal that the individual has been performing his job inadequately. Or, as is sometimes the case, changes that bring about switches in job titles, chains of command, or scope of responsibility are resisted because employees experience them as threats to their present levels of influence or standing.

Social relationships. For many employees the establishment of social relationships is extremely important. Changes that break up cohesive groupings, prevent friends from talking or getting together, isolate individuals, or create new conflicts or competition are likely to be resisted.

Importance of changed aspects. Some aspects of work are extremely important and central to one's job and to one's conception of oneself. Other aspects are relatively unimportant and, if changed, are less likely to be resisted. The important aspects may include such factors as freedom to operate as a "professional" in one's chosen field, amount of authority (number of people supervised), latitude in decision-making, and access to positions at higher levels in the organization.

Employee trust and confidence in the organization. If, in the employee's views, the organization has a record of demonstrated concern for its workers and has protected them in past changes, there probably will be less resistance. In organizational climates in which the trust level is low and the past history of change has been unpleasant, there is likely to be resistance regardless of programs undertaken to overcome it.

Uncertainty. Most managers are aware that employees react negatively to uncertainty. When upcoming changes are suspected, the rumor mill goes into high gear and the air is filled with talk of dire possibilities. Fear of the unknown is probably greatest in organizations that have a history of unannounced, unpleasant changes.

Reactions against authority and manipulation. Some employees resist change because they respond negatively to any attempt by persons in higher positions of authority to influence or determine their behavior. Thus, it is not the change measures themselves that cause the resistance; it is the fact that they are being imposed by management.

Generalized resistance to change. It is probably true that some individuals are generally less ready than others for change of any kind. They may be individuals who, because of past experience with a number of the above factors, just do not want to have things changed. It should be noted, however, that this group does not usually constitute a majority of employees, as has been sometimes assumed.[17]

There are three other general reasons for resistance to change in patrol. First, the patrol force has received only lip service regarding its position in police departments. Statements indicating that patrol is the backbone of the department have been just that. Patrol has been the first step in the career of an officer who has used it as a stepping-stone to a specialized position, usually in the criminal investigation or detective unit. Laymen look upon the plainclothes police officer as having more capability. The news and electronic media have displayed the patrol officer as someone used merely to handle the routine police service, who steps aside for the detective when he or she arrives upon the scene of an incident. In some cities the business community will not even give a preliminary report of a burglary to a patrol officer, but want the detective to respond. It matters not why or who is to blame for this view of the patrol officer; what really matters in today's American society is that it change.

Even though there are situations where patrol officers will, out of necessity, continue to direct traffic, guard prisoners or witnesses, and so forth, enlightened patrol leaders must insure the presentation of an accurate picture of the patrol officer. The concern of citizens over increasing crime, riots, civil and campus disorders, and the involvement of citizens in crime prevention and community relations show that the process has begun to change the image and importance of the present-day patrol officer. Team policing concepts are just the beginning of patrol experiments that should result in concrete facts concerning the impact patrol has on the administration of criminal justice. Enlightened police leaders are using manpower distribution studies to deploy patrol personnel in a manner that solicits creativity and innovation in patrol strategies.

Second, there has been a lack of initiative on the part of young police officers, rising through the ranks, to accept the very real challenges of the patrol function. This lack of initiative has been assisted by neglect on the part of police chiefs to assign the appropriate personnel to patrol positions. Consequently, the change agents in the police field have not been the patrol leaders. However, this is also changing now.

Many progressive law enforcement agencies require field command as a prerequisite for promotion to a higher echelon of the police department. This is as it should be. The increase in the number of innovative commanders will produce an organizational climate conducive to developing change agents. Concurrent with this will be the increasing importance of the training effort within police departments. There will be more in-house executive development programs with upper-level courses, such as the process of innovation and the management of change. Limited resources in manpower and support services will make the innovator the most important manager because of the ability to produce an improved police agency with existing resources.

The third basic reason for resistance to change in patrol has been the lack of any volume of body of knowledge in the patrol function. Questions such as: How do we measure preventive patrol? What effect does saturation patrol have on a specific crime in a specific area? Is it better to have officers work permanent shifts or rotating shifts? What is the crime displacement factor? and What effect, if any, will employee organizations have on a department's ability to affect crime rates? need to be answered. Additionally, the influence of health, sanitation, employment, type of population, and economic factors on crime should be included in any research if realistic solutions to the total problem are to be reached. The symposiums on Law Enforcement Science and Technology have had a profound effect in the area of research for police. LEAA and the Police Foundation are welcome participants in our country's battle for a safe and secure society.

Attitude and Behavior

There is no such thing as an inherent human quality to resist change. People resist change for several reasons. If a patrol officer views a sergeant with respect and credibility, that sergeant will have very little difficulty presenting new ideas and concepts to the officer. This pattern usually occurs throughout the several levels of authority. Patrol leaders who have this attitude usually are aware of the necessity of mutual confidence, respect, trust, loyalty, empathy, and people-oriented management. The needs and desires of the recipients of change are considered. All this results in a lessening of resistance to innovation. The feeling of belonging, that someone cares for the officer and his or her opinion, results in a positive attitude toward the change agent. His attitude of concern permeates the department, and the involvement of subordinates in the planning and the decision-making processes confirms it.

Participation in the change process takes time, but confrontation will result if orders for change are given as they have been in the past. The confrontation may not be face to face or physical, but will be seen in the mental attitude of the recipient officers. Rules, regulations, manuals of procedure, and general orders are all necessary in a police department, but "Obey the order or suffer the consequences" is not the best approach. Alternate approaches designed to implement change in specific situations will reduce attitude and behavior resistance. The prime example of this activity is the difference between departments that developed grievance procedures in anticipation of employee organization and those departments that did not and now have conflict. Sharing power and participation in decision-making will result in police leaders successfully achieving the goals of law enforcement. An unwillingness to accept change (or to change on the part of police leaders) will result in having the power taken away, which will affect the opportunity for success in achieving goals.

A change in the attitude and behavior of management is necessary if change in the attitude and behavior of the recipients of change (subordinates) is to take place. If management in the patrol force projects an attitude of, "I only have five years until I retire so don't make waves," or, "I don't need any education and training. I've been doing it this way for twenty years and it works, so why should I change? I've been around for twenty years and you young men who have been around only five or ten think you have it all," mediocrity will continue. In order to be objective, two viewpoints of these comments should be taken. One is that the leader may indeed have twenty years experience, but more than likely it is one year, twenty times. The other is that there are young men and women who do not plan their strategy for change and attack the power instead of trying to persuade. Naturally, when the attack on the leader's position of power is made, the power is threatened and resistance and confrontation result. Young patrol leaders should be willing to practice patience and the art of compromise. Remember, patrol administrators, do not be afraid to innovate and create, but do not burn your bridges behind you. Once you have projected an attitude of scorn or condescension, you may have produced an opponent who will resist any change you suggest or attempt to implement. The statement "If I can take one step forward even though I may have to back up three, it is still progress" is not without validity. If a patrol administrator can develop an attitude of "reducing the crime of robbery by one each month on each beat," the result at the end of the year will be surprising. This approach is also realistic and easily grasped, and officers can relate to it rather well. Sometimes change must be very basic and pragmatic in order for it to work. The basic change of attitude is essential for reducing resistance to change. "Turning officers off with a bad attitude" implies that they are working only *for* the leader, not *with* him. Contemporary patrol leadership requires that officers be led as individuals, not as machines or beats or numbers.

VOLUNTARY ACCEPTANCE OF CHANGE

The willingness to change can be developed only if effective communication, understanding of interpersonal relationships, and integration of theory and practice are introduced and totally assimilated by the recipients. The patrol leader must not be afraid to face any subordinate or group of subordinates and allow open and honest discussion of the particular change. The cliché "If two people always agree, one is unnecessary" should be carried to the level of execution throughout the patrol force. Whenever a presentation of change is communicated by a patrol commander, he should have present all levels of authority between himself and those to whom he is making the presentation; e.g., if a captain were communicating an intended change, asking for participation in planning, to patrol officers he should have the lieutenants and sergeants present (if this is the rank structure).

This concept is close to that of a problem-solving or brainstorming session with everyone participating. In many cases the time it takes to carry out this approach is minimal and the dividends are tremendous. However, a reminder to patrol leaders before using this approach: Do your homework. Plan for anticipated questions and appropriate responses. Do not make the presentation until it is as complete as possible. Select the proper time—timing can make the difference between successful change and failure. After the presentation, stimulate reaction and project the relationship between change and failure. Be objective and honest by stating both advantages and disadvantages. Maintain a position of flexibility (if voluntary acceptance would be attainable by modifying your position, be prepared to make the decision weighing alternatives). Explain incidents and intermediate and long-range expectations, and offer as much support as you may possess for your position of leadership.

Many times, the response may be to give it a try. The patrol leader finds himself in an advantageous position because he can now win the battle. He must pay personal attention to the trial, and follow-up and evaluation become necessary. Additional presentations of status, success, and failure are required, and self-renewal should cause increased positive response to the change. The resistance to change caused by forced acceptance has been overcome. Voluntary acceptance becomes synonymous with broad support for the change. Once that has been accomplished, there should be smooth sailing. There is an art to the process of change, implementing change, and overcoming resistance to change, and patrol administrators should study that art.

CHANGE AND CONFLICT

More and more it has been recognized that conflict is a central part of police work, especially patrol, because of the numerous contacts between citizens and police. However, for the patrol leader conflict takes on new meanings. He must self-analyze, diagnose, and understand the difference between his own value systems and those of others, as well as be aware of his particular modes of behavior and leadership styles, in order to determine which style to use for a given set of circumstances. The diagnosis should consider the factors involved in the conflict; i.e., he or she should be sure of proper identification of problems and accuracy of information.

There can be some very real conflicts over methodology. Usually, the goals of the organization can be agreed upon quite easily. However, the choice of method used to reach these goals involves sensitive issues. The patrol leader has to know (after self-analysis) where to intervene in the differences of his or her subordinates so that the differences do not become open disruptions.

The willingness to change on the part of all concerned is an asset in the lessening of conflict, and knowledge is directly related to the willingness, especially at the command level. Conflict is related to the perceptions of each individual: each sees a different picture—values, experience, intelligence, education, and perception play a part in his or her position. The patrol administrator must know the when, where, how, and why of intervention in order to resolve conflict. One basic point is to always keep conflict eyeball to eyeball. Whatever the conflict, it is not necessary to push an opponent into the corner, so to speak, over an issue. When whatever is valued by the individual is attained, the conflict should end.

Time can be a very effective tool in resolving conflict. What looks like an impossible issue one evening may diminish into nothing by the next morning. Patrol leaders should realize the value of time.

The ability to identify issues and the participants in issues may result in preventing conflict. When the patrol leader analyzes the problem and realizes the conflicting parties are outside the police department, noninvolvement may be the best answer. Liberal educational backgrounds are most helpful in resolving change/conflict situations.

MANAGING CONFLICT: A PHILOSOPHICAL ANALYSIS

Obviously, conflict management is an important part of patrol managers' responsibility. Their perception of the adjudication of conflicting demands is supported by Katz and Kahn.[18]

Robbins differentiates three philosophies that reflect managerial attitudes toward conflict: traditional, behavioral, and interactionist. The first two are descriptive because they represent predominant views espoused in the management literature. The third is normative, which Robbins supports.[19]

The traditionalists believe conflict should be eliminated because it is destructive. The behaviorists' view is described as accepting conflict, since complex organizations by their nature have built-in conflict. These complex organizations disagree in methods, units compete for recognition and prestige to increase boundaries, and all compete for power. As Bennis points out,

> We do not believe that the elimination of conflict is invariable or even typically the desirable goal in wise management of conflict as many who identify consensus with agreement tend to do. Conflicts stem basically from differences among persons and groups. Elimination of conflict would mean the elimination of such differences. The goal of conflict management is, for us, better conceived as the acceptance and enhancement of differences among persons and groups.[20]

The third philosophy is the positive approach. The interactionist philosophy differs from the behavioral in that it

1. recognizes the absolute necessity of conflict,
2. explicitly encourages opposition,

3. defines conflict management to include stimulation as well as resolution methods, and
4. considers the management of conflict as a major responsibility of all administrators.[21]

Robbins continues to support his position by suggesting that external factors in society are dynamic in nature, and those organizations that do not adapt will not survive. The Hegelian dialectic recognizes that all change develops from conflict, or through the clash of opposites, and the interaction in the clash produces a new situation. Thus, change develops from dissatisfaction, desire for improvement, and creative development of alternatives, and is inspired in the interactionist philosophy.

> Managing conflict is the nucleus of successful administration. An organization and its administrators must be primarily concerned with survival, which can only result from adaptive change. Because change is an output of conflict, an understanding of conflict should be a significant part of the study of administration and organizations.
>
> The conflict management process is not executed easily. Planning and evaluating conflict intensity makes administration one of the most difficult professions. Each administrator is responsible for creating an environment that supports conflict and allows for appreciation of differences. Further, he needs to understand that conflict management is not merely conflict resolution, but stimulation as well.[22]

There are several approaches to change, which at the same time cause conflict. We can change the structure of an organization to bring about change (team policing, decentralization); or we can change people to bring about change (higher eductation, training programs); or we can use technology (automatic vehicle-locator or monitoring system, walkie-talkie, computer-assisted dispatching). In all these changes we must communicate so that the proper message is received. Therefore, the ability to effectively communicate is essential to managing conflict and change. An analysis of the leaders of change—i.e., style of leadership, self-esteem, and stress levels—is important when selecting the proper approach.

Figure 11.5 *Conflict-survival model*

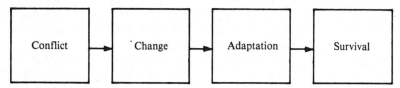

If we attempt to implement change, and we select the people approach, then we have to deal with (1) insuring that proper information about the change can be transmitted to the recipient of the change, (2) providing the skill development necessary, and (3) identifying changes in behavior and attitudes required so that the relationship to change can be examined. The collection and analysis of relevant data would have to be included and related to the overall goal of the change, and proper implementation procedures would have to be planned for appropriately.

Whatever approach patrol managers select for change in their organizations, they should be aware of how they impact other peoples' attitudes and behavior, provide a climate for open communication (listen), encourage the scientific generalist approach (use data if possible and integrate with professional knowledge), develop conflict strategies, solicit and reward creativity, enhance self-actualization in others by self-actualizing themselves, use the leadership principle of supportive relationships, and totally develop interpersonal and group skills.

DIRECTION FOR THE POLICE AGENCY

John E. Angell and Fontaine Hagedorn suggest the following changes to allow municipal police agencies to operate as an effective part of government.[23]

> In order to organize a system capable of changing municipal police agencies to operate as an effective part of city government to support city-wide governmental objectives, several problems must be considered. These include the excessive independence of police departments from superior governmental officials, the difficulty of utilizing criminal justice research and local consultant studies, the high failure rate of police changes, the lack of coordinated planning among criminal justice agencies, and the lack of coordinated planning between police and other municipal agencies.
>
> The lack of coordinated planning among criminal justice agencies prevents the systematic operation of the criminal justice system. It allows each component to maintain its own view of the system. Police, public defender, courts, probation and corrections at times display open contempt for the actions and purposes of one another. Each develops programs to satisfy its own biases and needs with no concern about the effect on the others.
>
> In order to deal with implementation problems and make changes beneficial to the entire city, the police change components (planning, training, inspections) must be part of a city-wide system for change. (See Figure 11.6.) The city system must be organized to include planning, implementation, and feedback components.
>
> The police planning component should be established within the city planning unit. (Although this arrangement has been used in

Figure 11.6

Commonly Existing Organization

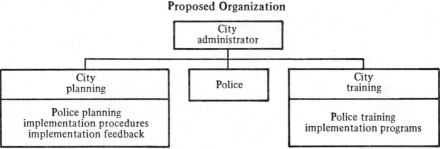

Proposed Organization

Source: From John E. Angell and Fontaine Hagedorn, "A Municipal System for Improving Local Police," *Journal of Police Science and Administration* 4, no. 2 (1976): 220.

small cities, Seattle, Washington, is the first major city to experiment with its use.) Civilian planners from the police planning unit should be transferred to the city planning unit. In most instances, sworn officers can be returned to operational units. Since the workload of police planning units consists largely of answering correspondence, a correspondence unit can be established in the office of the police chief to replace the planning unit. Significant research projects needed by the chief would be referred to the city planning unit. Supervision of police planning by the city unit will ensure that police planning complements planning for other criminal justice and city agencies. It is a concept which needs detailed review, especially in this era of productivity.

DIRECTION FOR PATROL

Accreditation: Critical to the Future of Law Enforcement[24]

For years, people have been looking to the Uniform Crime Reports to evaluate the quality of police operations. Police managers have been called on every time the crime rate goes up to explain rising crime rates without standard measurements for planning or defending their operations. Although the UCRs are very important, they are not an appropriate way to evaluate the quality and effectiveness of police work.

Over the past twelve years there have been three major national initiatives to develop recommendations for upgrading the American police service: the President's Commission on Law Enforcement and Administration of Justice (1967); the National Advisory Commission on Criminal Justice Standards and Goals (1973); and the American Bar Association's Advisory Committee on the Police Function (1973).

The findings of these groups provide a valuable source for the current accreditation effort. They identified the need for improvements, set out recommendations and standards, and established timetables for achieving the standards. However, there has been no major push in the ensuing years to modernize these standards in accord with swiftly changing police practices and societal needs or develop a certifying or accrediting process—an important addition to the current effort. And there has been no endeavor to provide police an incentive for implementing standards.

This new effort—being conducted jointly under a $1.5 million LEAA grant by the International Association of Chiefs of Police (IACP), National Organization of Black Law Enforcement Executives (NOBLE), National Sheriffs' Association (NSA), and Police Executives Research Forum (PERF)—will establish an independent accreditation process which aims to increase the effectiveness and efficiency of local law enforcement agencies in the delivery of police services; increase confidence of citizens in the effectiveness of the police, thereby providing community support for law enforcement agencies; increase confidence of individual police officers in the effectiveness of their own agencies; and standardize administrative and operational procedures among agencies to increase understanding and cooperation between police and other law enforcement agencies, and between the police and the courts, the prosecutors, and correctional agencies. All of this should serve to increase the effectiveness of the entire criminal justice system.

These aspects of the current accreditation effort—cooperation and coordination of the four agencies—distinguish it from previous initiatives. The standards are being developed by organizations that know law enforcement operations. They will not be promulgated by the federal bureaucracy, but will be formulated by law enforcement practitioners and outside citizen evaluators.

Each association will research and develop standards pertaining to various law enforcement functions and roles:

NOBLE will look at all areas of police jurisdiction, including sheriffs, independent county police, and state police organizations—focusing on the development of advancement, recruitment, and selection policies.

The NSA will direct its efforts exclusively toward the nation's sheriffs' departments.

PERF will focus on municipal police departments in communities serving a population between 100,000 and 500,000.

The IACP will develop standards in all jurisdictions for those topical areas not covered by other groups and exclusively in areas such as community resources, employee relations, support services, and internal discipline. The IACP also will provide coordination and administrative services for the program.

The Commission on Accreditation for Law Enforcement Agencies—composed of eleven officials from the enforcement community and ten representatives from government and the private sector—will review the standards and solicit views from local and state government officials, various community representatives, and public interest groups throughout the standards development stage to assure an acceptable nationwide accreditation process.

The aim of the Commission to establish an accreditation process which is accepted by the police, the public, and all components of the criminal justice system. To do this, the standards and guidelines must accurately measure the nature and manner in which an individual law enforcement agency is able to provide direct access to the public. To have lasting effectiveness, a uniform, systematic approach is needed with a built-in process for continual revision of the standards. The standards must provide the flexibility to accommodate changing conditions and the differences in individual jurisdictions.

The success of the entire accreditation process will depend upon the quality of the standards which are developed. They must be based on the knowledge and experience acquired over the years, and involve the most up-to-date and sophisticated thinking in the field. Most importantly, the standards must provide stimulation and challenge; they must move enforcement toward what ought to be.

It's an exciting, perhaps revolutionary program with limitless potential for the law enforcement community.

Law enforcement, like the citizens that it serves, is dynamic and ever changing. We must be prepared to meet the challenge of change in order to endure.

THE PATROL ADMINISTRATOR AND THE MICROCOMPUTER (THE FUTURE)

Change is usually brought about by using three approaches: people, structural, or technological. The people change deals with the concept of synergistics, which considers the whole of the organization to be more than the sum of its parts because of the competency of the people. The structural change deals with the changing of the organizational charts, or using matrix management or project management, or making the organization look like a football or circle. In this case, the structural change forces people to modify objectives and direct resources. The third change is the technology change. We have seen command and control, computer-assist dispatch, minicomputers, automatic fleet locator systems, (FLAIR–fleet locating and information reporting) and 911. One of the most important technology changes for the patrol manager is the ability to use the microcomputer as a management tool.

The objective of the following information is to emphasize the importance of the microcomputer as a management tool, rather than to present an in-depth discussion of the microcomputer.

The patrol administrator should familiarize him/herself with the relevant microcomputer terms. Some of these are: CPU (central processing unit), CRT (cathode ray tube display), disk drive, diskette, floppy disk, hard disk, monochrome monitor, color graphics monitor, printer, capacity and speed, internal/external memory, operating system, language, spreadsheets, word processing, management control, database systems, K, storage, modem, hardware/software, commands, sides, density, application software, user, etc. For a source, see American National Standards Institute, *American National Directory for Information Processing Systems*, X3/TR-1-82, American National Standards Institute, New York, 1982 (FIPS PUB 11-2).

There are at least six types of applications software for the microcomputer user: (1) word processing, for creating, editing and printing documents; (2) data management, for organizing, storing, and retrieving data (*Database II*); *Lotus 1-2-3* and *Symphony* are software packages which can work well for patrol managers to do correlation, measuring, validation, scheduling; (3) spreadsheets which can be used to perform calculations and forecasting; (4) graphics which can be used to present data graphs and prepare diagrams and illustrations, i.e., pie charts, histograms, and P-charts using standard deviations; (5) communications, which can be used to transfer data to and from other systems; and (6) other specialized software, such as accounting or statistical analysis.

The essence of the microcomputer for patrol is to increase the productivity of patrol managers. Paperwork has been the bane of patrol supervisors'/managers' existence. The use of microcomputers and systems design and development can reduce this obstacle to effectiveness by providing timely, accurate data with a minimum of effort. The manipulation of relevant data (which officers, sergeants, lieutenants produce more and why) can provide for increased effectiveness, cooperation, reliability, and credibility.

Some of the factors to consider in the microcomputer concept are: cost (hardware, software, installation, training, supplies, maintenance and communication), risks (potential liability, improper specification, vendor competence, user competence, hardware reliability, software problems, lack of standardization resulting in isolated use and waste and inability to network and communicate, loss of control over programs and data, security of data, and conflict with central processing).

It would be important for the patrol administrator to analyze the concept systematically so proper policy can be written in order to direct the use of microcomputers in the policy agency. All personnel in the organization should be working toward the same goals.

NOTES

1. Paul Whisenand and Fred Ferguson, *The Managing of Police Organizations* (Englewood Cliffs, N.J.: Prentice-Hall, 1973).
2. Sherman C. Blumenthal, *Management Information Systems: A Framework for Planning and Developing* (Englewood Cliffs, N.J.: Prentice-Hall, 1969).
3. Whisenand and Ferguson, op. cit., p. 95.
4. Timothy Costello, "The Change Process in Municipal Government," in G. Brown and T. P. Murphy, eds., *Emerging Patterns in Urban Administration* (Lexington, Mass.: D. C. Heath, 1970), pp. 18–22.
5. Joseph T. Massie, *Essentials of Management* (Englewood Cliffs, N.J.: Prentice-Hall, 1971), p. 232.
6. Charles E. Summer, Jr., "The Managerial Mind," *Harvard Business Review* (January/February 1959): 69–78.
7. Massie, op. cit., p. 237.
8. Warren G. Bennis, Kenneth D. Benne, and Robert Chin, eds., *The Planning of Change* (New York: Holt, Rinehart and Winston, 1961).
9. Massie, op. cit., p. 239.
10. Ronald Lippit, Jeanne Watson, and Bruce Westley, *The Dynamics of Planned Change* (New York: Harcourt, Brace and World, 1958), pp. 131–143.
11. Twentieth Annual Laboratories in Human Relations Training, *Reading Book* (Washington, D.C.: National Training Laboratories, 1966).
12. Paul C. Buchanan, "Crucial Issues in Organizational Development," in Goodwin Watson, ed., *Change in School Systems* (Washington, D.C.: Cooperative Project for Educational Development, National Training Laboratories, National Education Association, 1967).
13. Oscar Newman, *Defensible Space* (New York: Macmillan, 1972).
14. Arnold Judson, *A Manager's Guide to Making Changes* (New York: John Wiley & Sons, 1966).
15. Bennis, Benne, and Chin, op. cit. p. 34.
16. Arthur H. Niehoff, "The Process of Innovation," in A. H. Niehoff, ed., *A Casebook of Social Change* (Chicago: Aldine, 1966).
17. For a review of some of the research behind the above generalizations, see: W. A. Faunce, E. Hardin, and E. H. Jacobson, "Automation and the Employee," *Annals of the American Academy of Political and Social Science* 340 (March 1962): 60–68; E. Hardin, W. B. Eddy, and S. E. Deutsch, *Economic and Social Implications of Automation: An Annotated Bibliography* (East Lansing: Michigan State University Labor and Industrial Center, 1961); E. Hardin, J.

M. Shepard, and M. S. Spier, *Economic and Social Implications of Automation: Abstracts of Recent Literature* (East Lansing: Michigan State University, School of Labor and Industrial Relations, 1966).

18. Daniel Katz and Robert L Kahn, *The Social Psychology of Organizations* (New York: John Wiley and Sons, 1966).
19. Stephen D. Robbins, *Managing Organizational Conflict, A Nontraditional Approach* (Englewood Cliffs, N.J.: Prentice-Hall, 1974), p. 12.
20. Warren G. Bennis, Kenneth D. Benne, and Robert Chin, eds., *The Planning of Change*, 2d ed. (New York: Holt, Rinehart and Winston, 1969), p. 152.
21. Robbins, op. cit., p. 13.
22. Ibid., p. 20.
23. John E. Angell and Fontaine Hagedorn, "A Municipal System for Improving Local Police," *Journal of Police Science and Administration* 4, no. 2 (1976): 220.
24. Homer F. Broome, *Justice News Assistance* 1, no. 6 (August 1980). Office of Justice Assistance, Research and Statistics, Bureau of Justice Statistics, LEAA and National Institute of Justice, Washington, D.C.

Appendix A

Training Bulletin
Houston Police Department

SUBJECT: USE OF FIREARMS

Introduction

The Houston Police Department (HPD) recently has revised its policy governing the use of firearms. The policy and rules which accompany it are designed to guide Houston Police Officers in the exercise of their authority to use their weapons. The use of firearms is of such great importance that the policy and rules require more than normal discussion. The purpose of this training bulletin, therefore, is to instruct officers about the Department's guidelines for using firearms.

The policy and rules were finalized only after extensive research and internal discussion. Analysis was done of the prior HPD policy, prior incidents of officer-involved shootings, the policies of other major city police departments and the many volumes of research on this issue. Discussions were held among Command Staff, with representatives of the the employee organizations and other officers. Detailed video interviews were conducted with officers from various ranks, assignments and shifts in order to solicit their views and concerns.

There is no question that police officers' authority to use firearms to protect themselves and the public carries with it serious responsibility. It is necessary, therefore, that the Department provide appropriate guidance to its officers in order to ensure that the authority to use firearms is exercised in a manner consistent with the Department's basic duty to protect human life. Consequently, the Department has developed a concise statement of its policy regarding the use of firearms which is consistent with the policy followed since 1979. The new policy goes further than the prior HPD policy insofar as it includes a more detailed set of rules designed to guide officers in the decision to discharge their firearms.

The Values

The values which form the basis of the Department's policy and rules regarding the use of firearms are as follows:

- Human life is valuable and must be protected.

- Police officers have been given the unique power to use firearms in order to fulfill the responsibility entrusted to them by the citizens to protect human life.

- Therefore, officers must use utmost prudence and restraint in the exercise of their authority to use firearms. They should discharge their firearms only when doing so represents the only effective means to fulfill their responsibility to stop a person who poses an imminent threat of death or serious bodily harm to the officers or others.

These beliefs reflect the Department's strong commitment to ensuring for the safety of both its officers and the citizens of the city.

The Policy

The Houston Police Department's policy regarding the use of firearms sets forth the general values which must guide officers' actions. The policy is as follows:

- The use of firearms is never to be considered routine, is permissible only in defense of life, and then only when all other means have been exhausted.

The Department's policy is based on a belief that its primary duty is to protect life. Police officers, therefore, are to use firearms only to protect their lives or the lives of others. Since the use of firearms has the potential to endanger life, it should occur only when there is no other alternative. This means that officers are to use their firearms only when failure to do so would result in death or serious bodily injury to themselves or others.

In situations where officers consider using firearms, they must carefully determine whether it is probable that someone will be killed or injured as a direct result of the observed actions of the suspect. Only when officers have substantial reason to believe that there is an immediate potential for serious bodily injury to self or another can they use their firearms.

The Department, valuing the lives of both officers and citizens, believes that the use of firearms must be treated as an unusual occurrence. In addition, available alternative means of resolving the dilemma should be used whenever they will not endanger the officers. Indeed, as the policy states, the use of firearms is never to be considered routine, but rather should be viewed as a last resort action.

Situations which require an individual police officer to use a firearm are generally rare occurrences. Day after day, police officers resolve potentially dangerous situations without resorting to the use of their firearms. Officers deescalate situations by using a variety of methods ranging from persuasion, application of psychology, and use of back-up personnel. Indeed, it is quite clear that a vast majority of our officers now execute their duties in a manner which is consistent with the department's policy and rules. By following the Department's policy, officers can avoid or minimize their criminal and civil liabilities.

The Rules

To provide guidance to officers in carrying out this policy, the Department has outlined several very important rules prescribing when firearms may and may not be used. Each of the rules is derived from the Department's policy and is consistent with the under-lying values. Again, these rules direct officers to be prudent and to use restraint in the exercise of their authority to use firearms in order to protect life.

The rules were developed to guide police officers in their determination of the most effective means of resolving issues of officer and/or citizen safety. The key to all of the rules is:

- Do not shoot unless your life or someone else's is in immediate danger.

Rule 1 represents the core statement of the key point made above about officers' use of firearms. It states simply that officers can shoot only to protect themselves or another person from imminent death or serious injury. In observing this rule, officers are well advised to remember the following:

- Always use the minimum force necessary to accomplish your mission; e.g., protect life, effect an arrest, restrain an escaping suspect.

- Do everything possible to deescalate situations so that you do not have to resort to the use of firearms.

It is important to remember that the premature use of firearms can escalate a situation and, thereby, unnecessarily increase the danger to fellow officers and others. Officers, therefore, should consider using alternative force methods, such as the baton, taser or nets. Whenever appropriate and prudent, officers should delay action and request specially trained persons or tactical units.

It is important to recognize that the Department can provide a variety of resources to diffuse or resolve dangerous or potentially dangerous situations with the minimal level of force. No one police officer stands alone in the responsibility to protect life, but rather each officer must look to all members of the department to work together to accomplish our joint mission.

Rule 2 directs police officers to exercise the utmost care in discharging their firearms so as to avoid endangering innocent persons. In every situation:

- Consider the possibility that the projectiles you discharge will hit innocent persons.

Rule 3 prohibits officers from shooting to threaten or to subdue a person whose actions do not present a direct life-threatening danger to the officer or other persons.

There are situations where suspects either have committed or are about to commit offenses involving the destruction of property and/or serious injury to themselves. It is important that such persons be taken into custody as quickly as possible. However, remember that:

- If the suspects' actions do not pose a threat of imminent death or serious bodily injury to persons other than themselves, do not discharge your firearms to achieve an arrest.

- Shoot only to protect life and never to protect property.

- You cannot protect a person's life by shooting the person even though they have placed themselves in peril.

Rule 4 directs police officers not to shoot fleeing suspects who do not pose an immediate threat of death or serious bodily injury. The key in this rule is the word "immediate". A suspect can be reasonably characterized as "dangerous", but at the time of an attempted escape, not pose an "immediate" threat. Be careful to:

- Assess the immediate danger posed by the suspect's actions rather than characterize the person as dangerous.

Of course, if a suspect is attempting to escape, officers should use all appropriate methods available to prevent that escape. However, it is not appropriate to shoot in this situation. Again, remember:

- Do not shoot unless your life or someone else's is in immediate danger.

Rule 5 prohibits officers from shooting at a moving vehicle unless it is absolutely necessary to do so to protect the lives of the officers or others.

Officers confronting an on-coming vehicle stand a better chance of avoiding injury if they follow instinct and move away from the path of the vehicle. Time taken to unholster, aim and attempt to stop an oncoming vehicle may place the officer in greater danger than simply jumping aside. The probability of disabling a vehicle with gunshots is low because a revolver is not intended for nor is it ordinarily effective in disabling a vehicle. Moreover, if the operator is disabled, officers and innocent bystanders then are faced with the danger created by an unguided moving vehicle.

The key to this rule, is:

- Follow human instinct and get out of the way of vehicles rather than shoot at them.

Rule 6 allows an on-scene supervisors to authorize the discharge of firearms to disable a vehicle, but only when they determine that the vehicle's continued operation is a direct threat to life. In those instances when authorization is given, the authorizing supervisor is responsible for the actions taken. Again, both supervisors and police officers should remember the key to the Department's use of firearms policy:

- Do not shoot except to protect human life from imminent danger.

Rule 7 clearly prohibits officers from firing warning shots. The dense population of a urban area such as Houston makes warning shots dangerous to innocent bystanders. Therefore, officers are directed:

- Never fire warning shots.

Rule 8 prohibits police officers from drawing or otherwise displaying their firearms without probable cause to believe there is a threat to the officers' life or safety.

Drawing or displaying a firearm can limit officers' alternatives in controlling situations, as well as create unnecessary anxiety on the part of citizens and result in unwarranted or accidental discharges. Officers' decisions to draw or display firearms should be based on specific aspects of the tactical situation. Something in the situation should indicate a substantial risk that the situation will escalate to the point where the officers will have to use their firearms to protect life. Officers should be guided by the following:

- Do not draw or display your firearm unless you have probable cause to believe that you will have to discharge it in order to protect life.

In summary, the Department has developed a sound and concise policy a d set of rules to guide its officers in exercising their authority to use firearms to protect life. The responsibility to learn and to follow the guidelines provided lies with each and every officer. Also, officers should realize that their judgments and actions will be assessed against the standard of this policy and these rules.

Index